QUICKER
BETTER
CHEAPER?

Managing Performance in American Government

Edited by Dall W. Forsythe

The
Rockefeller
Institute
Press

Rockefeller Institute Press, Albany, New York 12203-1003
© 2001 by the Rockefeller Institute Press
All rights reserved. First edition 2001
Printed in the United States of America

The Rockefeller Institute Press
The Nelson A. Rockefeller Institute of Government
411 State Street
Albany, New York 12203-1003

Library of Congress Cataloguing-in-Publication Data

Quicker better cheaper? : managing performance in American government / edited by
Dall Forsythe.
    p. cm.
  Includes bibliographical references and index.
  ISBN 0-914341-85-5 -- ISBN 0-914341-86-3 (pbk.)
    1. Administrative agencies--United States--Management. 2. Government
productivity--United States. I. Forsythe, Dall W., 1943-

JK421 .Q53 2001
352.3'75'0973--dc21

                                                                2001031828

       ISBN: 0-914341-85-5 (hardcover)
                0-914341-86-3 (paperback)

Table of Contents

iii

Table of Contents

Preface

Dall W. Forsythe

In 1998, two of America's top experts in public management agreed that government's use of performance management deserved a searching and critical review. Those experts were Richard P. Nathan, director of the Nelson A. Rockefeller Institute of Government, and Paul Light, then a program director at The Pew Charitable Trusts. This book is one of the products of their agreement.

As the bibliography in this volume demonstrates, the literature on performance management and measurement in the public sector is extensive. Most of the authors writing in this field advocate increased use of performance management systems, and see them as indispensable tools for improving management and accountability in government. Light and Nathan, however, were concerned that too little attention had been given to the problems of "managing for results," as performance management is sometimes known. As detailed in the cases and analyses in this volume, performance management initiatives in government face difficulties in implementation in the best of circumstances. At their worst, they create incentives for unexpected or even undesirable behavior by agency managers and front-line personnel.

To look more deeply into the problems and possibilities of performance management systems, The Pew Charitable Trusts and the Rockefeller Institute brought together a group of experts in public policy and management to discuss these issues. An effort was made to include critics as well as enthusiasts. In addition to Nathan and Light, members of the Task Force included:

❀ Walter Broadnax, dean of the School of Public Affairs at American University in Washington.

❀ Patricia Ingraham, professor at the Maxwell School at Syracuse University, and director of the Government Performance Project.

❀ Donald Kettl, professor at the University of Wisconsin and director of the LaFallotte Institute.

❀ Allen Schick, professor at the University of Maryland and senior fellow at the Brookings Institution.

As the Task Force was being assembled, the editor of this volume joined the Rockefeller Institute as a senior fellow, and was added to the Task Force and assigned responsibility as project director for its activities.

Members of the Task Force met twice to discuss performance management, once in Albany at the Rockefeller Institute, and the second time in Washington at American University. In these meetings, the Task Force members were joined by performance management experts in government, including Jonathan Breul of the U.S. Office of Management and Budget and J. Christopher Mihm of the U.S. General Accounting Office. Also invited were many of the authors of cases and essays included in this volume.

On behalf of the Task Force, the editor also interviewed performance management experts on Congressional staffs and in nongovernmental organizations specializing in this area. An early product of this work was a monograph on the status of the Government Performance and Results Act (GPRA) (Forsythe 2000). Presentations on performance management and GPRA were also made at a conference organized by the Council on Excellence in Government and several professional organizations. The *Public Administration Times* published a summary of the monograph. Finally, Forsythe and Nathan published an article in a collection edited by Mark Abramson to provide background for the incoming Bush administration (Forsythe and Nathan 2001).

While the work of the Task Force was under way, its members and other authors were preparing case studies and analytic essays for this volume. The question mark in the title is intended to remind the reader that the efficacy of performance management in American government is a question for discussion, not a settled issue. With that in mind, considerable care was taken to encourage dissenting voices on the topic, and case studies explored problems in performance management — JTPA and Empowerment Zones, for instance — as well as success stories. The logic of this point and counterpoint is developed in detail in Richard Nathan's introduction to the volume. The volume concludes with a chapter essay by the editor exploring the practical pitfalls and possibilities of performance management, using experience from state and local governments to outline the hurdles faced as the federal government continues to implement GPRA. The aim of these chapters — and the book as a whole — is to give the reader a richer understanding of when and how top managers succeed or fail in their efforts to use performance management systems to improve the functioning of government.

The editor would like to acknowledge many debts accumulated during work on this volume. This book could not have been completed without the generous support of The Pew Charitable Trusts, and Elaine Casey and Michael Delli Carpini provided encouragement and helpful advice as well as funding. While the Task Force members contributed critical intellectual guidance and the authors' contributions are obvious, several other people also provided knowledge and advice that shaped the final product in important ways. In addition to Jonathan Breul and Chris Mihm, Paul Posner of the GAO and Barry White of the Council on Excellence in Government were indispensable advisors. While most of the chapters in this volume are original, special thanks are also due to authors — Harry Hatry, Beryl Radin, and Virginia Thomas — who gave permission to reprint several important essays, and to their publishers.

Richard Nathan conceived this project, and provided invaluable advice at every single stage, from inception to final editing. His contributions are so extensive that a less generous colleague would have insisted on — and deserved — billing as a co-editor. As a consulting editor, Sandra Hackman applied her formidable skills to every original essay in the volume, challenging authors to clarify their thinking as well as their writing. Like Nathan, she did much of the editor's work, and deserves more credit than this acknowledgement. Ellen Blake's assistance as a project manager provided momentum to keep the book moving forward, and Rose Sullivan stepped in to help when Ellen moved on to another assignment. Michael Cooper, the director of publications at the Rockefeller Institute, expertly guided the project through its final production stages. Francine Spinelli painstakingly produced the bibliography. I am indebted to all of these people. Without their assistance, this volume would never have been completed.

I

Introduction

1

Introduction

Richard P. Nathan

One of the frustrating things about edited books is that they typically attempt, but fail, to instill cohesion into the work of academic experts who have a strong tendency to go their own way. This edited volume on performance management and budgeting in government, compiled by Dall Forsythe, takes a different approach. Forsythe deliberately selected authors who both offer a range of experience with the contemporary performance movement at different levels of government and present different voices on this subject. As a result, what comes through in this compendium is a strong point-counterpoint theme. The yin and yang of the performance movement in government is what the reader should take away.

This is what the Rockefeller Institute sought to achieve when we initiated this project three years ago. In his foreword to this book, Dall Forsythe discusses the tasks he pursued for the project, including the wide dissemination of a white paper issued in February 2000: *Performance Management Comes to Washington: A Status Report on the Government Performance and Results Act*. The report was the first product of the Rockefeller Institute's project on performance management and measurement, supported by The Pew Charitable Trusts.

Although we instigated the project particularly to take a close look at the budget reforms embodied in the 1993 Government Performance and Results Act, we have also stretched the canvas more broadly to consider state and local budget reforms of the same genre. These reforms emphasize outputs rather than inputs. They are often referred to in governmental shorthand as focused on "results." The results focus launched by the 1993 GPRA produced "little GPRAs" among state and local governments, as often occurs with new managerial reforms in American federalism.

Dall Forsythe and I have had more than a dozen conversations about how to view this new period of budget and management reform. It is interesting that, although our ideas are similar, our roles have reversed. I began as highly skeptical, while Forsythe was more of an enthusiast for GPRA and the performance management and budgeting movement generally. However, Forsythe's ideas metamorphosed into a viewpoint, presented in the final chapter of this book, that highlights problems entailed in fulfilling the goals of GPRA. On the other hand, I became increasingly impressed with the way the idea underlying "results management" and "results budgeting" has permeated the thinking and conversations in and around governments, reflected in subtle ways in the questions policymakers and public managers ask and the kinds of conversations they have. The simple idea is appealing, namely to focus attention on the outcomes of government programs. That is, what happens to people as a result of government programs (i.e., the *outputs* and *outcomes* of governmental action), not the *inputs* of government programs, is what really counts. This idea has become more than a slogan. It has become a way of viewing decisions and issues across the governmental landscape.

It is not possible to measure this subtle internalization effect. Moreover, it may be too much to expect that it could ever be formularized in the ways the elaborate GPRA law stipulates. Still, I can imagine that deep down in the innards of public management, gnarled hands experienced in the game of government knew all along that the real goal of GPRA was to change the way people think. Indeed, it can be argued that this, more than anything, is the purpose of the perennial reform exercises intended to introduce greater rationality and intellectual rigor in the give-and-take of what is (and always will be) an intrinsically pluralistic and yeasty American political process.

In sum, the 1993 Results Act is not a whole new ballgame. Although it has distinctive features, it must be seen as one in a long line of efforts to introduce greater rationality into government decisionmaking generally, and particularly into the budgetary process.

Past Federal Budget Reforms

Performance Budgeting. In 1949, the Hoover Commission, appointed by President Truman, issued a report calling for "performance budgeting." The commission recommended "that the whole budgetary concept of the Federal Government should be refashioned by the adoption of a budget based upon functions, activities, and projects."[1] According to political scientist Frederick C. Mosher: "The central idea of the performance budget...is that the budget process be focused upon program functions — that is, accomplishments to be achieved, work to be done."[2] The budget process had traditionally emphasized developing a reliable system of expenditure accounts. Like GPRA, the rhetoric of the reform was to shift the focus from inputs (items of expense, number of federal employees) to outputs (activities, accomplishments, and their related costs). Costs and appropriations were to be related to productivity or services rendered. For example, the U.S. Postal Service, according to this theory, would calculate the personnel required for the coming budget year by identifying the number of letters that could be processed by one employee and by estimating the number of letters to be processed.[3] Five years later, the second Hoover Commission, established in 1953, picked up this same theme. Its report observed that federal budgeting inadequately linked programs with costs "and suggested that budget activities and organization patterns be made consistent and accounts established to reflect this pattern; and, that budget classifications, organization, and accounting structures should be synchronized."[4]

Planning-Programming-Budgeting (PPB). A decade after the report of the second Hoover Commission, Lyndon Johnson announced his much-hyped "Planning-Programming-Budgeting

System" (PPB), which was grounded in systems analysis — the process of defining objectives and designing alternative systems to achieve them. PPB was developed under Secretary of Defense Robert McNamara, who had previously been president of Ford Motor Co. President Johnson was so impressed with McNamara's application of this approach to the U.S. Department of Defense that in 1965 he ordered PPB to be used right away across-the-board in every federal agency. According to the *Bulletin* issued by the Budget Bureau,[5] the objective of PPB was "to improve the basis for major program decisions in the operating agencies and in the Executive Office of the President. This requires clear statements of alternatives and of the reasons for decisions. Program objectives are to be identified and the alternative methods of meeting them are to be subjected to systematic comparison." The system had three basic elements. First, *program memoranda* (PMs) compared the cost and effectiveness of major alternative programs and provided documentation for strategic decisions recommended for the budget year. Second, *special analytic studies* (SASs) provided analytical groundwork for the decisions reflected in the PMs. And third, *program and financial plans* (PFPs) provided multi-year summaries of the outputs, costs, and financing needs of agency programs over a five-year period.[6]

Management by Objectives (MBO). Management by Objectives was Richard Nixon's brand of budget reform, based on the idea of setting objectives for agencies in terms of the work they were expected to accomplish. More flexible than PPB, it allowed agency managers to choose how to achieve their goals. But MBO also required periodic reports on progress toward planned objectives. In an April 18, 1973, memorandum to federal agencies, President Nixon said: "I am now asking each department and agency head to seek a sharper focus on the *results* which the various activities under his or her direction are aimed at achieving.... This conscious emphasis on setting goals and then achieving results will substantially enhance federal program performance." The director of the Office of Management and Budget, in a follow-up memo to department heads, explained the purposes of the new initiative as being better communication, faster identification of problems, and greater accountability of managers to supervisors. Included in the president's memorandum was a request to each agency for its proposal of 10 to 15 most important "presidential objectives" to be accomplished in the coming year, with the goal being the identification of 100 presidential objectives governmentwide. MBO did not make an explicit connection to the budget process during its first year. And then in the second year, efforts to tie the initiative to the priority-setting processes of the federal budget were overwhelmed by Watergate-related events that led to Nixon's resignation.

Zero-Base Budgeting (ZBB). Jimmy Carter had the most radical concept for budget reform. His approach, called Zero-Base Budgeting, constituted a rejection of incremental decision making.[7] ZBB required each agency to justify its entire budget submission each year (i.e., "from ground zero"). In a memorandum dated February 14, 1977, President Carter directed all agency heads to apply ZBB in preparing the fiscal year 1979 budget. "A zero-base budgeting system permits a detailed analysis and justification of budget requests by an evaluation of the importance of each operation performed.... By working together under a zero-base budgeting system, we can reduce costs and make the Federal Government more efficient and effective." ZBB included three basic elements. First was identification of "decision units" — the programs or organizational units for which budgets are prepared. Second was preparation of "decision packages" — brief justification documents that included the information necessary for managers to make judgements on program or activity levels and resource requirements. And third was ranking of decision packages in decreasing order of priority by program managers and agency officials. Like its predecessors, ZBB was oversold and largely disappeared.

However, all four budget reforms invariably left a mark. In particular, the introduction of PPB in 1965 resulted in the creation of policy-analysis staffs in almost all federal agencies and in many counterpart state and local government agencies. In so doing, it has had the most lasting and important institutional effect on governmental decisionmaking at all levels — national, state, and local.

Leaders of the GPRA Movement

Unlike its predecessor reforms, the Government Performance and Results Act of 1993 — "the newest sliced bread" of budget reform focused on results — was a congressional rather than a presidential initiative. Also distinctively, it allowed for a much longer gestation period than its predecessors. Like earlier reforms, GPRA affected state and local as well as national practices.

Four chapters in this book were written by people who are among the strongest advocates of GPRA. These authors include Virginia Thomas, who had a major hand as a congressional staffer in writing the 1993 GPRA law; Harry Hatry, who is one of the most well-known advocates of performance management and budgeting; Patricia Ingraham and Donald Moynihan, who focus on performance management and budgeting by state governments; and Katherine G. Willoughby and Julia E. Melkers, who consider performance budgeting at both the state and local levels.

Virginia Thomas describes the mission and the potential that proponents envisioned for the 1993 law:

> *The act's power lies in its focus on measuring the effectiveness of all existing federal programs and providing Congress with that information in order to determine whether the agencies are achieving the intended results.*

> *Americans will benefit from such a bottom-up review of existing programs. Although the federal government should use every dollar it truly needs, the current approach is to pile new laws, regulations, and federal spending priorities on old ones without regard to effectiveness or mission overlap. As a result, the size, cost, inefficiency, and scope of the federal government continue to grow relentlessly.*

Patricia Ingraham heads the Alan K. Campbell Public Affairs Institute at the Maxwell School of Syracuse University, which works to stimulate and assist states, federal agencies, and local governments in "managing for results" (MFR). Ingraham and Moynihan in their chapter in this volume are upbeat about the effects the results movement can have on the states:

> *State governments are using these tools, and gaining proficiency in their use. While legislative intent and rhetoric may be more*

ambitious than practice, elements of MFR are common enough in government to shed the "novelty" tag. Members of the public service have moved beyond the basic questions: "What is strategic planning?" and "What is benchmarking?" to the questions so important to success: "How do these tools fit with each other?" and "How can I make them work?" Committing to the strategic significance of MFR – and integrating it into the everyday processes of governance – provides one way to answer such questions and to ensure improved performance for the future.

Katherine G. Willoughby and Julia E. Melkers report on mixed results from a survey of staff members of state budget agencies and legislative committees. A majority (61 percent) of the respondents said they believed budget reforms related to results had not directly affected appropriations, and an even larger portion of respondents (81 percent) noted that lack of legislative interest is a problem. However, 85 percent said they viewed such reform as "better than doing nothing" and a worthy purpose to pursue over time.

Taken together, these authors provide a useful and nuanced portrait of the aspirations of the performance management movement. If readers combine these ideas with the case studies by other authors in this volume, they can obtain a balanced picture of the pluses and minuses of the performance management movement.

Experience with GPRA

Two chapters in this book deal with experience under the Government Performance and Results Act from the perspective of the national government. The first, by Chris Mihm, who heads the General Accounting Office group responsible for overseeing execution of the law, presents a status report on its implementation. Under GPRA, all federal agencies were required to report on their actual performance by March 31, 2000. These reports, and the transition to the Bush presidency, mark critical junctures for the initiative. Mihm's chapter reflects the book's duality theme. He cites GAO reports that say fiscal year 2001 performance plans show "continuous improvement," and singles out several federal agencies for commendation, but he also notes that "much additional work is needed."

Although the fiscal year 2000 performance plans indicate that the federal government continues to make progress in showing that crosscutting efforts are being coordinated to ensure effective and efficient program delivery, agencies still need to complete the more challenging task of establishing complementary performance goals, mutually reinforcing strategies, and common performance measures, as appropriate.

He points to the challenge of GPRA for intergovernmental programs that depend on states and localities to provide "timely and reliable results-oriented performance information." Citing the Department of Health and Human Services' need for state and local data, Mihm says that "time lags in obtaining these data from the states make it difficult to provide a comprehensive summary of agency performance."

The account of performance management in the Social Security Administration presented by Walter Broadnax (who had a major hand in it) and Kevin Conway is a story of process budgeting, as opposed to budgeting for outcomes (the effects of governmental activities on people). These authors bring out a key theme of this volume: the public agency that calls the tune has to be the one that pays the piper. The Social Security Administration calls its tune for its operations: the agency (not another governmental level or outside organization) is directly responsible for paying Social Security benefits accurately, on time, and in a user-friendly way.

But even for Social Security, the GPRA system of measuring agency performance has its limitations in that it is process rather than outcome oriented. In my view, this is as it should be — at least for this program. Systematically measuring the effects of the Social Security Administration on the lives of recipients (the aged, disabled, and poor) is a much tougher and more elusive task. The authors claim success for the Social Security Administration's implementation of GPRA, though ironically, it does not fully illustrate the use of outcomes to assess governmental effectiveness.

Some Views of Skeptics

Allen Schick says he has heard it all before: "Efforts to budget on the basis of performance almost always fail." Referring to claims of success stories for the Government Performance and Results Act, Schick adds, "After four decades of being fed such stories, the writer is convinced that most are exaggerations and the few genuine successes are outliers." Somewhat ironically, Schick then turns around and advances his own brand of budget reform — one focused on measuring the cost of activities as opposed to outputs.

Activity-centered measurement is at the leading edge of management reform. Activity-based costing (ABC), developed by Robert Kaplan, who produced the balanced scorecard, is a widely applied cost allocation and analysis system which has infiltrated public sector financial management. The basic idea of ABC is that activities drive costs; hence to control costs they must be charged to the activities generating them. This approach enables managers to measure the costs that would be incurred or avoided if a firm undertook or terminated a particular activity. Cost measurement is a critical, oft-neglected prerequisite for using performance measures.

In a case study of the Job Training Partnership Act (JTPA), Gerald Marschke takes an economist's point of view. He says evidence "shows that performance measures backed by financial incentives are no cure-all for inefficiency and mismanagement in the public sector." Relying on the principal-agent model in economics, Marschke concludes that this approach works better in the private sector because the incentives can be much stronger.

While we cannot rule out that performance incentives in the Job Training Partnership Act have increased that program's efficiency, it is apparent from the effects of recent reforms that the U.S. Department of Labor has had difficulty designing incentives. The evidence suggests that the measures used so far are misaligned and distortionary, making the JTPA incentive system subject to "the folly of rewarding A while hoping for B."

Federal Grants-in-Aid

My colleagues at the Rockefeller Institute of Government, James Fossett, Thomas Gais, and Frank Thompson, contribute a well-told story of performance management for the nation's largest federal grant-in-aid program, Medicaid. The U.S. government fulfills most of its domestic purposes by providing grants-in-aid to state and local governments, and sometimes to private (mostly nonprofit) organizations. The success of these intergovernmental and interorganizational relationships is an essential subject for assessments of public management reforms. In the Medicaid case, the difficulty of providing incentives for performance, and the diversity of policy goals in federal law, are greatly compounded by the layered lines of responsibility under American federalism. The authors of this chapter offer the following generalization:

> *Proclaiming the virtues of mission-driven federalism is, of course, one thing and success in implementing it quite another. Intergovernmental arrangements complicate virtually all aspects of performance management — agreement on key goals, the development of indicators, the timely collection of pertinent and valid performance data, the interpretation of these data, the implementation of an incentive system (e.g., rewards for strong performers), and more.*

In my opinion, the intergovernmental arena is where GPRA is weakest — i.e., in implementing such grant-in-aid programs. Several chapters in this volume address this challenge in managing for results. Kate Boyer and Catherine Lawrence of the Rockefeller Institute, with Miriam Wilson, describe performance management as applied to the welfare reform act President Clinton signed in 1996. Although the 1996 law contains numerous requirements to assess its results, echoing GPRA — that is, focusing on outcomes — the authors show that this is extraordinarily hard to do because the 1996 act devolved so many responsibilities to states and localities, both for making policy and for administering human services. Still, although federal oversight has been restrained, Boyer, Lawrence, and Wilson believe that state governments are in a good position to highlight performance goals in their management of work-focused cash assistance and related human services for poor families.

David Wright tackles an even more complex intergovernmental case study in his chapter: the start-up period for the federal program establishing empowerment zones and enterprise communities, which foster neighborhood social and economic development. The effort to monitor "benchmarks" from Washington came up against the great complexity of urban programs, generally leading more to disappointment than to managerial innovation. Wright credits the U.S. Department of Housing and Urban Development for its flexible approach — having aid recipients set and monitor performance against their own benchmarks. However, he found the oversight necessary to ensure the success of these local-area benchmarks lacking.

Beryl Radin, who also deals with intergovernmental programs, focuses on what she calls "pathways that can be taken to join the federal government's concern about performance with sensitivity to the needs of third parties." Radin reviews six important areas of managerial activity. These include federal experience with performance partnerships in the environmental field, performance bonuses under the 1996 national welfare reform law, negotiated performance measures for maternal and children's services, the use of performance standards in employment and training programs, the application of program standards in educational testing, and waivers that allow state and local governments to disregard certain federal requirements if they evaluate such special efforts and the efforts are "cost neutral." Radin's conclusion is one I agree with wholeheartedly: she urges a *disaggregation approach* to performance management. "The process of defining performance measures seems to work when it is devised in the context of specific programs, sensitive to the unique qualities surrounding those initiatives."

I would like to add to Radin's observations that within state governments, performance measures often work better at the functional-area and agency levels than they do at the level of the governor's office or the central budget process. Agency-level performance measures often can be more discrete and can be more widely and effectively used at that level than centrally in the management of states and large local governments.

State and Local Practices

Two cases in this volume highlight personal experience with efforts by state and local governments to manage for results. Robert Bradley recounts his personal experiences as budget director in Florida in establishing and administering a performance management and budgeting system. This case again reflects the book's point-counterpoint theme:

> *In the final analysis, the extended implementation has diffused the intellectual coherence of the initiative. ... The continuing debate over agency flexibility and control was not worked to resolution. The process of rewarding agencies was not formalized. Incentives and disincentives have not been deployed to good effect. Legislative aspirations to make performance central to allocation decisions have been largely deflected in the face of persistent technical problems.*
>
> *Implementation of Performance-Based Program Budgeting (PB²) continues. Its full potential has yet to be realized.*

Dennis C. Smith and William J. Bratton describe the widely cited effort in New York City to apply performance management to the police department. Here, too, the key point is that the agency that is predominantly responsible for results should be held responsible for achieving them. The record of New York City for performance management under Mayor Rudolph Giuliani in these terms is an admirable one. Giuliani applied performance management techniques in many fields, including health and welfare as well as policing.

Joseph Burke, director of the Rockefeller Institute's Higher Education Program, describes efforts by states to set measurable goals for public institutions of higher education and to reward individual institutions for fulfilling them. Burke has been a strong advocate and leading innovator in developing such approaches. Although a number of states have adopted these reforms, they tend to be small, involving no more than 5-6 percent of state aid to campuses as a bonus for achieving performance goals.

A Possible Synthesis

Ann Blalock and Burt Barnow suggest a synthesis of approaches to performance assessment and budgeting. They call for integrating evaluation studies by academic experts — which seek to assess hard-to-measure policy outcomes — with performance management and budgetary systems:

> *Our recommendation is that competent evaluation research, or applied social science research, must be coordinated with or integrated within performance management systems if precise, valid, reliable information about social programs is to be made available to decisionmakers.*

Blalock and Barnow point out that the evaluation movement was developed in the "crucible of academia" while the performance management movement has its roots in administrative bureaucracies. They believe, and I agree, that greater coordination between these two movements would yield important benefits:

> *We recommend that the major direction for the future is to coordinate evaluation research with performance management systems more fully, moving toward full integration of evaluations within performance management. Such integration will require that performance management systems treat evaluators not as aliens from outer space, who land only periodically to study and give advice, but as part of an interdisciplinary team. It will require that evaluators become more sensitized to managers' needs, to have ongoing information for tracking outcomes, and to express the benefits of their professional roots with greater humility.*

All things considered, the obstacles entailed in improving management in government can never be fully surmounted.

However, the strong signaling of management and budget reforms like GPRA sets a tone stressing the importance of productivity and program effectiveness in government. This is a good thing. Dall Forsythe and I hope that the ideas advanced, and the experiences described in this book bring needed realism to the hard job of pursuing management reform in the dynamic, complex, and always and inherently political environment of American government.

Endnotes

1   U.S. Commission on Organization of the Executive Branch of the Government, *Budgeting and Accounting* (Washington, DC, 1949), 8.

2   Frederick C. Mosher, *Program Budgeting: Theory and Practice, with particular reference to the U.S. Department of the Army* (Chicago, Public Administration Service, 1954), 79.

3   Allen Schick, "The Roads to PPB: The Stages of Budget Reform," *Public Administration Review* 26 (December 1966): 252-253.

4   U.S. General Accounting Office, *Performance Budgeting: Past Initiatives Offer Insights for GPRA Implementation,* GAO/AIMD-97-46 (Washington, DC, March 1997), 33.

5   The Budget Bureau was established by the Budget Accounting Act of 1921 as a formal budgeting mechanism to be controlled by the executive branch.

6   U.S. Bureau of Budget Bulletin No. 68-9, April 12, 1968, in *Government Budgeting: Theory, Process, Politics*, Albert C. Hyde and Jay M. Shafritz, eds. (Oak Park, Moore, 1978), 129-130.

7   Aaron Wildavsky, *Budgeting: A Comparative Theory of the Budgetary Processes* (Boston, Little Brown, 1975).

2

What Types of Performance Information Should Be Tracked?

Harry P. Hatry

The central function of any performance measurement process is to provide regular, valid data on indicators of performance outcomes. But performance measurement should not be limited to data on outcome indicators.[1] It should also include information that helps managers measure the incoming workload and gain insight into causes of the outcomes.

No two people will categorize every single element in a data set in exactly the same way. Gray areas inevitably exist because it is not always clear where a particular piece of information falls. In addition, for some performance information, the category may depend on the perspective of the agency. For example, to the state agency that develops an educational reform strategic plan, the completion of that plan is an output. However, to the U.S. Department of Education that encourages such plans, their completion by states is an intermediate outcome, as discussed later.

Box 1 presents the categories of performance information I discuss in this chapter. Data on the amount of resources expended for particular programs (inputs) are different from internal information

Reprinted with permission from Harry P. Hatry, *Performance Management: Getting Results*, Washington, D.C.: Urban Institute Press, 1999.

Box 1
Categories of Information Used
in Performance Measurement Systems

❀ Inputs*

❀ Process (Workload or Activities)

❀ Outputs*

❀ Outcomes*

- Intermediate Outcomes
- End Outcomes

❀ Efficiency and Productivity*

❀ Workload Characteristics

❀ Explanatory Information

❀ Impacts

* These are the categories usually labeled performance indicators in performance measurement systems.

---

that indicates the amount of activity a program is undertaking (process). These data, in turn, are quite different from the products and services a program has completed (outputs), which should be distinguished from results-bases information (outcomes). These distinctions are important in order to avoid misleading those who use the information.

Each of these categories is discussed briefly in turn. Box 2 provides summary definitions of key performance measurement terms.

Categories of Performance Information

Inputs

Input information is the amount of resources actually used, usually expressed as the amount of funds or the number of employee-years, or both.

Box 2
Performance Measurement Definitions

❀ **Inputs**: Resources (i.e., expenditures or employee time) used to produce outputs and outcomes.

❀ **Outputs:** Products and services delivered. Output refers to the completed products of internal activity: the amount of work done within the organization or by its contractors (such as number of miles of road repaired or number of calls answered).

❀ **Intermediate Outcomes**: An outcome that is expected to lead to a desired end but is not an end in itself (such as service response time, which is of concern to the customer making a call but does not tell anything directly about the success of the call). A service may have multiple intermediate outcomes.

❀ **End Outcomes**: The end result that is sought (such as the community having clean streets or reduced incidence of crimes or fires). A service may have more than one end outcome.

❀ **Efficiency, or Unit-Cost Ratio**: The relationship between the amount of input (usually dollars or employee-years) and the amount of output or outcome of an activity or program. If the indicator uses outputs and not outcomes, a jurisdiction that lowers unit cost may achieve a measured increase in efficiency at the expense of the outcome of the service.

❀ **Performance Indicator**: A specific numerical measurement for each aspect of performance (e.g., output or outcome) under consideration.

Source: Adapted from *Comparative Performance Measurement: FY 1996 Data Report* (Washington, D.C.: International City/County Management Association, 1997), 1-4.

This category, when related to figures on the amount of output or outcome (see further below), produces indicators of efficiency or productivity. *For performance measurement purposes, the amounts that were actually used, not the amounts budgeted, are the relevant numbers.* An occasional practice has been to call the *workload* that comes in the agency an input. I do *not include* workload data in this category, because the amount of incoming work is quite different from the amount of cost or staff time expended.

Process (Workload or Activities)

This category includes the amount of work that comes into a program or is in process but not yet completed. For some agencies, such as human service agencies, the workload is usually expressed in terms of the number of customers that come in for service (individual clients, households, or businesses). For others, the number of customers is not appropriate. Road maintenance programs, for example, might express their workload as number of lane-miles of road needing repair.

Amounts of work are not considered performance indicators because they do not indicate how much product is produced by the program. Workload information is very important to program managers when tracking the flow of work into and through their programs, however. (For example, the amount of work pending from the previous reporting period plus the amount of new work coming in indicates the workload on the program during the current reporting period.)

While amounts of work by themselves are not outputs or outcomes, workload data can be used to produce outcome data. In some programs, the amount of work not completed at the end of a reporting period can be considered a proxy for delays of service to customers (an intermediate outcome). Examples include the size of the backlog of eligibility determinations for loan applications and the size of customer waiting lists. However, more direct, and probably better, indicators of delays and backlogs would be: (a) a direct indicator of the extent of delays, such as the percent of cases in which the time elapsed between the request for a service and when the service was provided exceeded X days, where X is a service standard established by the program; and (b) the percent of customers who reported excessive waiting times to obtain service.

Outputs

Output information indicates the amount of products and services delivered (completed) during the reporting period. Reporting of output information is standard in agencies throughout the world. Keeping track of the amount of output accomplished is good management. Common examples of outputs include number of miles of roads paved, number of reports issued, number of training programs held, and number of students served by the program. However, outputs do not by themselves tell anything about the *results* achieved, although they are expected to lead to desired outcomes. (Program personnel should ask what results are expected from each output. Those results should be included under the next category, *outcomes*.)

As defined here, *outputs are things that the program's personnel have done*, not changes to the outside or changes that outside organizations have made.

Outcomes

In some contexts the word *output* refers to any product of work, whether the product is a program's completed physical product or the outcomes (results) of that work. *The field of performance measurement of public services makes a sharp distinction between outputs and outcomes.*

Outcomes are the events, occurrences, or changes in conditions, behavior, or attitudes that indicate progress toward achievement of the mission and objectives of the program. Thus, outcomes are linked to the program's (and its agency's) overall mission — its reason for existing.[2]

Outcomes are not what the program itself did but the consequences of what the program did. An excellent example illustrating the difference between outcome and output comes from the state of Texas:

*The number of patients treated and discharged from a state men-
tal hospital* (output *indicator) is not the same as the percentage
of discharged patients who are capable of living independently*
(outcome *indicator).*[3]

Outcomes may be something the program wants to maximize,
such as evidence of increased learning by students, or to minimize, such
as crime rates. Some outcomes are financial. For example, for public assistance programs, reducing the amount of incorrect payments
(whether overpayments or underpayments) is likely to be an appropriate outcome. Another example, recovering owed child support payments from absent parents, is an appropriate outcome of child support
offices. In such cases, outcomes can be expressed in monetary terms.

Outcomes include side effects, whether intended or not and
whether beneficial or detrimental. If the program recognizes in advance that such side effects can occur, it should design the performance measurement process to regularly measure them.

As long as they are important and can be tracked, outcomes
should be included in the performance measurement system, even
if they are not explicitly identified in the program's mission and objective statements. Formal program mission and objective statements seldom include all the outcomes that an agency needs to
track. It is not the function of such statements to itemize all the outcomes that the program should seek, just the central, most vital
ones. For example, complaints against police officers should be
tracked as well as crime clearance rates, even if the mission statement of the police agency does not include statements about providing law enforcement in a fair and honest manner.

It is important to distinguish *intermediate* outcomes from *end*
outcomes. This will help programs differentiate between the ends
ultimately desired from a program and interim accomplishments,
which are expected to lead to those end results (but may or may
not). The following discussion highlights the difference with definitions and examples.

Intermediate outcomes. These are outcomes expected to lead to
the ends desired but are not themselves ends.

A Compliance Perspective Can Be at Odds With an End-Outcome-Based Focus

The U.S. General Accounting Office noted in June 1998 that the federal Head Start program provides a number of performance standards that are actually program regulations defining local government activities, *not outcomes.* Grantees must adhere to these regulations in operating their programs. The GAO report goes on to say: "HHS ensures local government quality by monitoring and enforcing compliance with these regulations." But monitoring for compliance provides incentives for compliance; *it may or may not produce effective services.* To the extent that such a compliance perspective continues to be the primary program emphasis, the real intent of managing-by-results and outcome-based performance measurement will be heavily diluted. The GAO report identifies this limitation and notes the HHS "in the next few years" intends to provide information on real program outcomes — such as the gains made by participating children and their families in vocabulary, literacy, and social skills and the extent to which families have become economically and socially self-sufficient.

Source: U.S. General Accounting Office, *Head Start: Challenges in Monitoring Program Quality and Demonstrating Results* (Washington, D.C., June 1998).

Examples of intermediate outcomes:

* People completing employment training programs where program participation is *voluntary.* This reveals how successful the program has been in getting customers not only to participate in, but also to complete, the sponsored training sessions. However, completion is only one step toward the ultimate end of improving the condition of those persons completing the program.

* Citizens doing more exercising or switching to a better diet, as recommended in an agency-sponsored health program (perhaps as measured by surveying clients 12 months after they complete the agency's program).

Such changed behavior is expected to lead the participants to better health, but since this is uncertain, it is an intermediate outcome.

❀ A state or local agency completing the development of a comprehensive plan of action encouraged and supported by a federal program (where acceptance of the assistance is voluntary). For the federal government, the fact that states or local governments actually completed a reasonable plan can be considered to be an initial step toward improving services, although it says nothing about the end outcome of service improvement.[4]

For most agencies and products, whether something is an output or an intermediate outcome is clear, but there are exceptions. One example is the number of arrests for a law enforcement program. Many persons believe that arrests are an output because they are actions taken by agency employees. On the other hand, arrests involve citizens outside the agency, the persons arrested, and their families. In that sense, they might be better counted as intermediate outcomes. And they usually indicate that the process of bringing guilty persons to justice has begun.

Other examples include qualities of how well a service is provided to customers, such as response time to requests for service.

Service quality characteristics: A special type of intermediate outcome. As used here, quality indicates *how well a service was delivered, based on characteristics important to customers.* It does not tell what results occurred *after* the service was delivered. Since such characteristics are important to program customers, even though the characteristics do not represent final results, they can be considered intermediate outcomes an agency should track. Box 3 lists quality characteristics that might be considered by an agency when developing a list of outcomes to track for a program.

Some persons label quality characteristics (such as response times to requests for services) as outputs because they are characteristics of the outputs. However, if a characteristic is expected to be important to customers, it is better to consider it as an intermediate outcome, not an output. Because quality characteristics usually are important to customers, they are better labeled as outcomes to help ensure that they are given proper attention by agencies.

For some customers and under some circumstances, one or more of these quality characteristics might be extremely important — and can even be considered end outcomes. For example, it is vital for low-income families that assistance checks (whether Social Security or any public assistance payment) arrive on time and be accurate. Otherwise, these families will be unable to pay their bills and may be evicted or go hungry.

End outcomes. These are the desired results of the program — conditions of importance to program customers and citizens more generally. End outcomes might, for example, be aspects of health, safety, educational achievement, employment and earnings, or decent homes, such as:

Box 3
Typical Service Quality Characteristics to Track

❀ Timeliness with which the service is provided.

❀ Accessibility and convenience of the service.

  ● Convenience of location.

  ● Convenience of hours of operation.

  ● Staff availability when the customer needs the service (whether by phone or in person).

❀ Accuracy of the assistance, such as in processing customer requests for service.

❀ Courteousness with which the service is delivered.

❀ Adequacy of information disseminated to potential users about what the service is and how to obtain it.

❀ Condition and safety of agency facilities used by customers.

❀ Customer satisfaction with a particular characteristic of the delivery of the service.

❋ Reduced incidence of specific diseases.

❋ Improved student test scores.

❋ Lower crime rates.

❋ Less violence in schools.[5]

❋ Reduced number of households living in substandard housing.

❋ Increased real household earnings.

❋ Reduced household dependency on welfare.

For some programs, customer satisfaction with the *results* of a service can be considered as an end outcome. For example, satisfaction ratings of customers' experiences with parks, recreational activities, libraries, and cultural programs, or children's satisfaction ratings of the homes in which they are placed by child welfare agencies are likely to be considered by many citizens as end outcomes — even though those programs have aims that go beyond satisfaction, such as a library's mission to increase public access to information.

Many programs produce *both short-term and long-term end outcomes*. Education is a classic example. Educational programs produce early improvements in student learning, but they also help students obtain employment, and higher salaries, later on. Employment, ability to support a family, and reductions in welfare dependency are long-term outcomes of education programs. Information on long-term end outcomes such as posteducation employment and earnings, however, will not be available early enough to guide program personnel on the success of most of their current activities. Short-term end outcomes need to be tracked to encourage ongoing program improvement. Short-term outcomes related to learning and dropout rates, for example, are outcomes of key concern to education managers, staff, and parents — and can be considered end outcomes for this reason.

Box 4 summarizes a number of other issues related to the relationship between intermediate and end outcomes.

Box 4
Other Issues Related to the Relationship
Between Intermediate and End Outcomes

Intermediate outcomes, by definition, occur before — and are expected to help lead to — the end outcomes. *Thus, intermediate outcomes are important to program managers and usually provide more timely information than end outcomes.* For example, customers complete employment counseling programs (intermediate outcome), which is expected to occur after completion of the program. For long-term end outcomes for which data may not be available for many years (such as reduction in adverse health effects due to smoking and achieving rewarding careers), the program can usefully focus on short-term ends (such as reducing smoking and improved learning and skills). Much evidence exists that both reduced smoking and improved learning and skills directly affect the long-term end outcomes and intermediate outcomes.

Early occurrence of an outcome does not necessarily mean that it is not an end outcome. For example, family counseling programs hope to produce more stable and happier families in the short run as well as in the long run. Some treatment actions produce quick ends (purification of drinking water), while others require many years before water quality improves significantly (clean-up of rivers).

Another important advantage of including intermediate outcomes is that programs *almost always have more influence over intermediate outcomes than they do over end outcomes.*

For example, many federal programs (such as education, health and human services, housing and community development, and employment programs) provide assistance to states, local agencies, and/or nongovernmental organizations rather than directly to citizens. Changes sought by the federal programs and made by these other organizations can be considered intermediate outcomes. The federal programs have more direct influence on these outcomes than on the end outcomes, which are also affected by many other factors (such as family circumstances and motivation). The same is true of state programs that work through local governments, and of local government programs that work through the business or private/nonprofit community.

Intermediate outcomes usually are related to the particular way that the service is delivered by the program, whereas end outcomes typically do not vary with the delivery approach. For example, a government attempting to improve the quality of rivers and lakes can use many ways to achieve this, such as providing funding for wastewater treatment, providing technical assistance to certain classes of businesses, and encouraging lower levels of government to pass stricter laws and ordinances. Each such approach would have its own intermediate outcomes. However, regardless of the approach, end outcomes, such as the quality of rivers and lakes, apply.

Efficiency and Productivity

The ratio of the amount of input to the amount of output (or outcome) is labeled *efficiency*. Flipping this, the ratio of the amount of output (or outcome) to the amount of input is labeled *productivity*. These are equivalent numbers.

Efficiency and productivity have traditionally related costs to outputs (labeled *technical efficiency* by economists). However, to the extent that the performance measurement system provides data on *outcomes* (sometimes called *allocative efficiency* by economists), it provides a much truer picture of efficiency and productivity. This is because focusing on output-to-input ratios carries with it the temptation for managers to increase output at the expense of results and service quality.

Examples of outcome-based productivity indicators:

❁ Number of persons gaining employment after completing an agency's training program per dollar of program cost (or per program employee-hour).

❁ Number of customers who reported that the service received had been of significant help to them per dollar cost of that service (or per employee-hour).

Flip these ratios over and they become efficiency indicators.

For example, if 160 customers reported being significantly helped, and the program cost $96,000:

❁ Efficiency = $96,000 / 160 = $600 per customer helped.

❁ Productivity = 160 / $96,000 = 1.67 customers helped per $1,000.

Efficiency and productivity ratios can be calculated for any *output* indicator. For *outcome* indicators to be incorporated into these ratios, however, the outcomes need to be expressed as something to be maximized. Let us take crime as an example. "Cost per reported crime," though easy to calculate, makes no sense as an efficiency indicator (although it does make sense in the context of measuring the total costs of crime to a community). The output to be maximized here is *crimes prevented*. "Cost per crime prevented" would be a highly desirable indicator. Unfortunately, valid data on crimes prevented by a program are virtually never available on a regular basis. (Estimation of number of crimes prevented, if it is to yield reliable information, requires ad hoc studies that are usually quite costly, and even then the estimates are likely to be highly uncertain. This measurement problem applies to most prevention programs.)

Efficiency ratios using outputs are common. Thus far, however, efficiency ratios using outcomes are rare. This is partly because few outcome data have been developed in the past by public or private agencies. With the growth of more outcome-based performance measurement systems at all levels of government and in the private, nonprofit sector, more use of outcome-based efficiency ratios is becoming possible.

Characteristics of the Workload

If agencies are to make full use of their performance data, information on the amount of work coming into a program (sometimes called *demand*) and key characteristics of that work (such as those relating to its difficulty) needs to be collected and linked to outcome information. Thus a program that processes applications wants information on the complexity of the incoming workload. A program working with business customers wants information as to each business's industry classification, size, and location. A road maintenance program needs to be concerned with the amount and type of traffic and soil conditions for specific road segments. A hospital needs information on the severity of illness of its patients to help it interpret changes in outcomes of patients.

Similarly, programs that use a variety of service delivery approaches need to have information on the particular approach used to produce particular outputs and outcomes. The number and types of assistance provided to customers with similar problems may vary. Programs may use private contractors for some of their work and their own employees for other, similar work. Programs need to know which work was done using which service approach and then link the outcomes to each approach.

Explanatory Information

Programs should be encouraged to provide explanatory information (qualitative or quantitative) to help readers of their performance report properly interpret the data — especially for outcomes that were poor or much better than expected. In some instances, this will be information about internal factors (e.g., the program unexpectedly lost funds or key personnel during the reporting period). In other cases, the explanations will identify external factors over which the program had little or no control (e.g., a major change in economic conditions or highly unusual weather conditions).

Impacts

A number of analysts have begun to use the term *impact* to refer to data that estimate the extent to which the program actually *caused* particular outcomes.[6] For example, an indicator of impact would be labeled something like the following: Number of expectant teenage mothers who, *because of the program*, had healthy babies. (Without the program, they would have lost their babies or had babies with substantial health problems.)

However, *the outcome data likely to be obtainable from ongoing performance measurement systems will seldom, if ever, reveal the extent to which the program has caused the outcome.* Other factors — over which the program has only partial control — will inevitably be present. For example, some participants may stop unhealthy habits because of pressure from family and/or a health care professional, not because of the program. In-depth studies, such as formal program evaluations, may at times be able to estimate the program's impact on some outcomes reasonably well. When available, those data should also be included in the program's performance report.

Because of the time and cost required to obtain impact data, such information is likely to be available only infrequently on any given program (or group of programs).

Output or Outcome? Indicators That Are Particularly Difficult to Categorize

Many service attributes are easy to classify, but some are not. Here are some typical attributes that have caused healthy debates.

Customer Participation

The number of customers participating in a program is an ambiguous indicator because it depends on the particular situation in which it is used.

❀ If attendance is mandatory, the number of participating would be, at best, output information.

❀ For programs in which participation is voluntary, and which include activities aimed at attracting customers (such as employment training program and professional development activities), participation can be categorized as an intermediate outcome because it depends on the program's ability to attract participants. Similarly, the program's ability to retain participants until the activities are completed is another intermediate outcome. Completion is more important than participation, because it indicates that the activity has been sufficiently attractive for customers to have stuck with it until the training program's end.

❀ For public programs such as parks, recreational facilities, libraries, and public transit, and for private programs such as those of boys' and girls' clubs (all activities in which participation is voluntary), the number of participants can be considered an intermediate outcome. (Examples of outputs are the number of programs or classes held, number of bus miles, and amount of reading materials purchased.) A good case can also be made that participation is an end outcome of such programs if enjoyment of the activity is hoped to be a major product of such programs.

Customer Satisfaction

A guiding principle in the search for outcomes, as stressed earlier, is to identify elements of direct concern and value to the public and to direct customers. Since customer satisfaction and similar service attributes, such as courteousness and accessibility, fit this description, they are categorized here as outcomes.[7] Elected officials and donors certainly treat them as outcomes.

What kind of outcome are these? They are usually *intermediate* outcomes because they cannot take the place of measuring the actual condition of customers after receiving the service. For example, customer satisfaction with the employment and training services they receive is not ultimately as important as whether these customers find employment. (But is not *satisfaction with their jobs* also a major value to these customers?)

For certain services — recreational activities, libraries, and marital counseling, for example — customer satisfaction can be an end outcome. Even here, though, satisfaction is seldom the only outcome sought. In virtually all cases where customer satisfaction is important, other outcomes must also be included to obtain a comprehensive picture of a service's performance.

Response Times for Service Request

Some people label response time as an output and others label it as an intermediate outcome. Because response time is usually of direct concern to customers, I include it in the intermediate outcome category. By the same logic, the level of satisfaction customers have with the response times to their requests is also an intermediate outcome.

Relationship Among Types of Performance Information

Diagramming the continuum of relevant factors for measuring performance using a logic model (outcome-sequence chart) is a highly useful way to summarize the flow across the information categories just discussed. Box 5, based on material developed by United Way of America, displays such a system.

A consistent set of definitions categorizing various types of performance information – to be used across all programs – is the cornerstone of any performance measurement system. All too often, confusion among programs within an agency occurs due to unclear, inconsistent use of terms.

Definitions – or labels – perform the crucial function of enabling users of performance information to distinguish reliably among categories of data that have different implications and different uses. Numerous labels have been used over the years to

---

Box 5
Logic Model (Outcome Sequence Chart)
for Human Services Program

INPUTS	ACTIVITIES	OUTPUTS	OUTCOMES
Resources	**Services**	**Products**	**Intermediate**
● money	● shelters	● classes taught	● new knowledge
● staff	● training		
● volunteers	● education	● counseling sessions conducted	● increased skills
● facilities	● counseling		
● equipment and supplies	● mentoring	● educational materials distributed	● changed attitudes or values
		● hours of service delivered	↕
			● modified behavior
		● participants served	↕
			● improved condition
			● altered status

Source: Adapted from *Measuring Program Outcomes: A Practical Approach* (Alexandria, VA: United Way of America, 1996). Reprinted by permission.

---

categorize performance information. Which particular set of labels an agency or program chooses is not the primary issue. The primary issue is to be able to determine which items should be regularly tracked. Appropriate labels help with that.

Endnotes

1   The words *indicator* and *measure* are essentially interchangeable, but *indicator* seems preferable. The word *measure* is ambiguous because it can also mean either an action taken to improve a situation or the act of measuring.

2   The word *effectiveness* has been used by some governments in place of *outcomes*. However, *effectiveness* implies more a casual linkage than usually warranted by the data, so the word *outcome* seems preferable and is more often used (such as in the federal Government Performance and Results Act of 1993).

3   Texas Governor's Office of Budget and Planning, Legislative Budget Board, *Instructions for Preparing and Submitting Agency Strategic Plans: Fiscal Years 1999-2003*, Austin, January 1998, p.39.

4   From the perspective of an individual state or local government, completion of its own plan is an output.

5   Some may prefer to consider this an intermediate outcome needed to achieve improved learning.

6   Some agencies have used the word *impact* to refer to social outcomes, as distinguished from outcomes to individuals. Such social outcomes are better considered as broad end outcomes.

7   Some analysts view them as outputs, which demeans their importance. Fortunately, even these analysts often agree that these service characteristics should be measured and tracked.

II

Performance Management and the Federal Government: Skeptics and Enthusiasts

Skeptics

3

Getting Performance
Measures to Measure Up

Allen Schick

In 1938, when the public administration movement was at its
apogee in the United States, the executive director of the International City Managers' Association and a future Nobel laure-
ate in economics teamed up to propose methods for measuring
government performance. In *Measuring Municipal Activities*, Clarence Ridley and Herbert Simon devised a measurement scheme
based on the proposition that "the *result* of an effort or performance
indicates the effect of that effort or performance in accomplishing its
objective."[1] They further argued that efficiency should "be measured in its relation to several factors: expenditure, effort, and performance."[2] Ridley and Simon constructed measures for all major
municipal services including education, health, public works, police, fire, and libraries. They proposed, for example, that measurement in education should go beyond performance tests of student
progress to include delinquency and truancy rates as well as the cultural level of the community.

As prescient as their work may appear to a 21st century performance measurer, it was far from the first word on the subject. During the previous several decades, scientific managers in search of
numeric standards, municipal reformers on the prowl for efficiency,
and budgeters seeking rational methods for allocating public

money flooded the public administration literature with new schemes for measuring and improving government work. In fact, Ridley and Simon were the culmination of the first measurement movement, not its genesis.

From the vantage point of the new millennium, we have come a long way since Ridley and Simon. Public-sector managers and analysts have developed sophisticated measures such as police response time which were not conceived in their day. They have econometric models and discounting techniques, benchmarks and targets, and so on. The vast contemporary literature on performance measurement has added considerably to our methodological stockpile.

But has performance measurement really advanced much beyond the codified wisdom of the 1930s? If it has, why did performance guru Donald Kettl quip, "Measuring government performance is like the weather. Everyone talks about it. . . . But there is no consensus on how to do it"?[3] As will be evident shortly, I do not agree with Kettl's diagnosis, but something is amiss when there are endless arguments as to whether a particular measure is an output or an outcome, whether something is an intermediate outcome or an end outcome, whether measurement should assess benefits or only effectiveness, and so on. Surely, there is something amiss when, after decades of patient explanation, just about every treatment of this subject has to present a set of basic definitions, as if words such as inputs and outputs are so obtuse as to defy ordinary understanding.

These interminable arguments often make it appear as if performance measurement were an end in itself, as if measuring performance has no utility other than to generate measures. A related problem is that, if performance measures really were used, they would likely be misused because targets skew behavior by emphasizing some aims and leaving others out. In many situations emphasis on measurement leads to misbehavior, such as forged results or reckless actions to meet the targets. The fact that performance records are not audited in the same manner as financial statements opens the door to mischief and abuse.

What's more, the reported numbers are only the visible tips of the performance iceberg; key assumptions and models are buried well below the water line, beyond the vision of critical observers. Such was the case during the 1990s when the U.S. Health Care Financing Administration (HCFA) published mortality scores for the thousands of hospitals serving Medicare patients. These scores — which received considerable media attention because they claimed that patients were more likely to die in some hospitals than in others — habitually showed much higher mortality scores in city hospitals serving poor people than in suburban hospitals stocked with more affluent patients. HCFA claimed that the scores were normalized to take account of the age, gender, race, and medical condition of patients, as well as other critical variables. Yet HCFA stopped issuing the scores when it turned out that the models on which they were based were biased. As popular features of contemporary performance measurement, published scores and rankings may seem to be quite simple, but the numerical exercises and assumptions underlying them are often complex and questionable. Scorecards are constructed by assigning weights to a number of variables, computing the value of each variable, and combining the values into a single number. Ranking takes the process a step further by comparing the scores of different "performers." Journalists like rankings because they make communicating the results easy. Headlines announce that local schools are fifth or fiftieth, but little, if anything, is said about the variables that go into the score, or about the weight assigned to each variable. When performance measurement becomes a beauty contest through scorecards and rankings, what the process gains in popularity it surrenders in rigor and soundness.

Yet performance measurement cannot be brushed aside as a misleading fad, for politicians of all stripes embrace it. In the homestretch of the 2000 presidential campaign, Vice-President Al Gore noted that while he and George Bush disagreed on many educational policies, "we both are in favor of having new accountability on schools, new performance measurements."[4] With consensus spilling over party lines, who can be against holding public schools and educators accountable for results? Who can oppose compiling data on what government programs are accomplishing, and on whether they are meeting expectations? Performance measurement is the handmaiden of government reinvention — an essential element of the new accountability demanded of public officials. At the federal level, the concept is enshrined in the Government Performance and Results Act of 1993 (GPRA), as well as in dozens of other laws that pay homage to the cult of measurement; in the states, it is powerfully reflected in legislated demands for better schools as well as improvements in other program areas.

But how can one measure performance if, in Kettl's words, "there is no consensus on how to do it"? How can we measure performance if there is no agreement on what we are measuring? In my view, there is a problem, but not the one noted by Kettl. The problem is not in how we measure performance but in how we use the results. Too much attention has been paid to the former, not enough to the latter. With some notable exceptions, governments that measure performance rarely use the results in managing their programs. They do not base civil service salaries on performance, nor do they hold employees accountable for results or allocate resources on the basis of actual or promised performance. Efforts to budget on the basis of performance almost always fail, as occurred with performance budgeting in the 1950s, program budgeting and planning-programming-budgeting systems in the 1960s, and zero-based budgeting and management by objectives in the 1970s. The 1990s version, performance-based budgeting, is too new to permit a reliable assessment, but one should not be surprised if it fares little better than its once-acclaimed predecessors.

Many of the claims that performance measures have improved public policy or management are anecdotal. The "success stories" industry operates at full throttle when an innovation is fresh and politicians and bureaucrats alike scan their portfolios to label ordinary programs as amazing successes. After four decades of being fed such stories, this writer is convinced that most are exaggerations and the few genuine successes are outliers. Rather than representing the reality of government in action, the anecdotes are carefully selected to make things appear better than they are. Even supposedly systematic evidence of success tends to be flawed and misleading. Genevieve Knezo of the Congressional Research Service found that twice as many laws enacted in the 105th Congress (1997-98) had provisions pertaining to performance as those enacted by the previous Congress. Moreover, she concludes, the 105th Congress sharply increased the number of times performance measures and other GPRA-related matters were mentioned in committee reports.[5] Her data, however, prove only that buzzwords buzz around — that once a term gains popularity, smart people make sure to use it. The more talk there is about performance measurement, the more it filters into laws and legislative reports. But verbiage should never be mistaken for usage. If one wants evidence of GPRA's true impact, the place best to look is in appropriations legislation, which still doles out most of the money the old-fashioned way, on the basis of incremental norms and political influence.

The great mistake of the performance measurement industry is the notion that an organization can be transformed by measuring its performance. This is the logic of GPRA, which prescribes performance measurement in a sequence of steps that leads to strategic and performance plans, then to performance reports, and finally to pilot tests of performance budgeting linking results to funding (or some definition of self-budgeting). This optimism is not justified, for organizations — public and private alike — can assimilate or deflect data on performance without making significant changes in their behavior. Performance information can affect behavior only if it is used, and it is used only when there are opportunities and incentives to do so.

I believe that organizations must be transformed to use data on results. If this argument is valid, organizational change has to precede, not follow, performance measurement. This is the sequence used in Britain's Next Steps initiative. First, the government established new agencies by separating service delivery from the policymaking functions of ministries. Then it set performance targets. More than 100 agencies were created, and each was given operating independence and a charter (called a framework document) that spelled out its responsibilities and the manner in which it is to be held accountable. Each negotiates annual performance targets with the parent ministry to which it is responsible, and each compares results to these targets. The Next Steps reforms are generally regarded as among the most effective innovations in British public management. Although the Conservative Party initiated them, the Labour Party continued and deepened them when it came to power in 1997.

Next Steps has succeeded because newly independent agencies and newly empowered managers could put performance measures to good use. If the government reversed the sequence, performance measures would have made little difference.

The true test of performance measurement is in its use as the means by which organizations are managed and resources are spent. The next section identifies various channels for incorporating performance data into managerial decisions and actions. The process begins with the simple act of measurement, moves through various means of presenting the information, and ends with performance budgeting.

By examining each of these aspects, this chapter will present a scenario for effectively using performance measures that encompasses reports, benchmarks, and audits employed to promote and assess changes and measure the cost of activities and services. I believe the practice of performance measurement would be much further advanced if American governments followed this logical sequence.

Using Performance Information

A number of parties have a legitimate interest in the fruits of performance measurement, including service providers, policymakers, clients or customers, and policy analysts. To satisfy their interests, it is essential that these parties have input into the assumptions underlying measures and timely access to the results. Good measures that are locked away (as was the common practice not long ago with respect to measures of school and hospital performance) do little good. Table 1 lists various opportunities for governments to communicate performance information. The list begins with simple measurement and concludes with performance budgeting. It thus progresses from the easiest step to the hardest, at least when the allocation of resources is at stake. Other observers might create different lists — for example, a human resource manager might emphasize pay-for-performance schemes — but the important aspect is not the entries but the notion of a hierarchy of uses, with each use building on preceding applications.[6]

Table I	
Using Performance Information	
Use	*Purpose*
Performance Measurement	*Provides* basis for specifying expected performance and assessing managers and results.
Performance Targets	*Notifies* managers of results they are expected to achieve and establishes basis for appraising performance.
Performance Reports	*Compares* actual and targeted performance, and provides scorecards to enable citizen/customers to judge the services they receive.
Performance Audits	*Assesses* independently the reliability and relevance of performance reports.
Performance Benchmarks	*Sets* performance targets in reference to results achieved by best producers.
Performance Contracts	*Creates* a formal agreement between the government and providers on output and price.
Performance Budgets	*Allocates* resources on the basis of expected performance: each increment of resources linked to a specified increment in results.

Targets. As I have already argued, measurement does not accomplish much unless it leads to productive use of data on performance. One such use is the specification of targets that notify managers of the results expected of them and sets a baseline for assessing their performance. Two characteristics of targets distinguish them from other performance measures: they are specified in advance, and they are few in number. Targets furnish information for assessing results; their main purpose is to influence performance by measuring it. By informing politicians and/or managers what is expected of them, the supposition is that they will behave differently than if they were not so notified.

The potency of targets in swaying political or managerial behavior comes from singling out particular aspects of performance for special attention. Targeting everything is equivalent to targeting nothing. Britain's Next Steps initiative has been singularly effective in using targets. The government publishes annual targets for each of the approximately 150 Next Steps agencies along with a comparison of targets and results from the previous year.

The school accountability movement in the United States also makes extensive use of targets, but these usually are in the form of norms or standards. I am wary of normative standards such as graduation rates, which often have political ends and a weak empirical basis. Normative targets were used in the Soviet Union and other planned economics with damaging results because they distorted incentives and led to the misallocation of resources. Because targets are few in number, it is important that the right ones be selected. If educational targets single out reading scores, school administrators and teachers are likely to assign more classroom time to this activity and less to others. There is no way to entirely eliminate this side effect, but performance measurers should be careful to obtain wanted effects, not unwanted ones.

Performance Reports. These reports take performance measures a big step forward by comparing targeted and actual performance. Rather than analyzing whatever data are available, performance reports focus on precisely the dimensions previously targeted. GPRA intends federal agencies to report on performance just that way.

However performance reports are effective only if they have an audience — if the results garner attention. The public and media tend to be more vigilant in democratic countries than in authoritarian regimes, affluent recipients are more likely to use information on the quality of services they receive than poor ones, and services that are directly delivered to citizens, such as health and education, are likely to evoke more interest than those for which the connection is less direct. Obviously, if school performance scores are sealed, as was the case in many American communities until the 1980s, they are unlikely to generate support for improving education.

The scorecards and rankings discussed earlier are forms of performance reports. As evidenced by the popularity of the college rankings published by *US News and World Report* and the countless rankings published by interest groups to promote their cause, these performance reports are here to stay. Gresham's Law is at work in the performance business: *simplistic reports drive out complex ones.* So scorecards gain an audience, but they tend to be simplistic.

Performance Audits. The more performance data are used, the greater the incentive to manipulate the findings by selecting and weighting variables in ways that yield the wanted results. To counter this tendency, some governments have sought to broaden the audits of reports from the financial side of the ledger to encompass substantive results as well. The Government Accounting Standards Board (GASB) invested considerable effort in the 1990s in devising service and effort measures, and audit agencies in Canada and Sweden have explored the feasibility of reviewing agency statements on performance.[7]

Performance auditing has branched off in two directions. One parallels financial auditing in that the auditor's role is limited to determining whether the performance statements are a fair and accurate account of results. An alternative approach is for the auditors to devise reporting standards to which agencies must conform. Although auditing is likely to become a more prominent feature in performance measurement, much work remains to be done in defining the role of auditors and the division of responsibility between them and reporting agencies. The early experience in Sweden, where the National Audit Office (NAO) maintains a staff of almost 100 performance auditors, is not encouraging. According to NAO, "The audit cannot give the same guarantee of reliability for a performance audit as for the other parts of the annual report. It is important to diminish the 'gap in expectations' between what the audit can actually guarantee and what the parties interested in the audit expect."[8] Thus far, this gap has been narrowed more by diminishing expectations about what auditing can do than about what performance measures promise.

Performance Benchmarks. Benchmarking is one of the many managerial practices that has migrated over the past decade from business firms to governmental organizations. At its core, benchmarking aims to boost performance by stimulating managers to match results achieved in comparable or best-performing organizations. Benchmarking can therefore be combined with the three previously mentioned uses — targets, reports, and audits. The practice differs from standards in that its targets are descriptive rather than normative and act as incentives, not as prescriptions. Benchmarking also differs from performance rankings, which usually are based on composite scores and layers of assumptions. Benchmarks tend to be unidimensional and focus on only one aspect of performance such as cost, productivity, or customer satisfaction.

This focus grounds benchmarking on a sounder empirical basis; it does not use hidden or questionable assumptions to smooth out differences among the entities being ranked. Benchmarking makes no assumptions as to why costs or effects are higher in one entity than in another; it simply notes the differences and thereby impels managers to investigate the causes of the differences and to take appropriate action.

The problem, however, is that the conditions that account for performance are not unidimensional. Many factors may account for why one organization is more efficient than the other. These factors may include location, age of equipment or the workforce, and cultural features, the quality of the managers, internal controls, and production methods. Firms cannot ignore these "drivers" of cost differences because markets penalize inefficient producers. To remain competitive, a firm must strive to meet benchmark costs. In the public sector, however, the differences can be explained away. In business, benchmarking is an impetus for improvement; in government, it often is an impetus for excuses.

Performance Contracts. Contracts convert targets into formal agreements between the government and its agencies (or external providers) on the amounts they will spend and how much they will produce. Such contracts can be in the form of performance agreements, such as those negotiated between President Clinton and department heads in the early years of the reinventing government movement, or in the form of memoranda of understanding spelling out expectations for a certain period. Performance contracts can also extend downward in public bureaucracies, negotiated between senior managers and their subordinates.

Unfortunately, these contracts usually cannot establish legally enforceable claims. As one of the contracting parties, the government has little recourse if internal suppliers fail to perform according to the terms of the contract. Such contracts would not be significantly more effective if government were reorganized to establish internal markets by separating service producers from policymakers. Internal markets are not real markets, and internal contracts are not real contracts.

But even if they do not enforce claims, contracts may be useful in establishing expectations of performance and forging relationships between government and service providers based on their outputs. The term "relational contracting" is sometimes used in new institutional economics to describe these expectations.[9] Do they make a difference in results? There is little evidence on the impact of such contracts in the public sector.

Performance contracts often are coupled with two other changes in public management. One is to broaden the discretion of managers in using resources and fulfilling their responsibilities. The other is to introduce new means of accountability into government. The former is a precondition for contracting; the latter seeks to compensate for the inherent weakness of performance contracts. Obviously, contracts cannot be written if one or another party lacks the freedom to implement its terms. Thus, liberating managers from *ex ante* controls is a necessary step in enabling them to contract for their performance, but it may not be sufficient. Similarly, new accountability regimes such as performance audits may be needed to enforce contractual demands, but they may not suffice to get managers to perform better.

Performance Budgeting. The last entry on the list, performance budgeting, represents the fullest use of performance measures and is, therefore, the hardest to implement. Performance budgeting comes in two versions: the weak version merely specifies the results expected but does not explicitly link them to spending levels, the strong version expressly relates increments in resources to increments in performance.

Organizations as Performers

In measuring performance, many thousands of managers and analysts have been schooled in the differences between inputs and outputs, and in terms such as benefits, results, outcomes, and effectiveness. They have been indoctrinated in the notion that what should be measured are not the inputs or processes used to get results, but the results themselves. Yet one of the most popular contemporary innovations in performance measurement openly violates this creed. The "balanced scorecard" approach views outputs as only one of four sets of related performance measures. The other three pertain to internal processes and practices, staff quality and morale, and customer needs and satisfaction.[10] The four sets of measures are balanced in the sense that managers pay attention to all of them, not just one. Yet it is possible to attach numerical scores to each of the four variables (and to subsets within each), the main gain comes from recognizing that organizations and internal processes also matter.

This approach was designed for firms in the early 1990s in response to the growing perception that financial results were an inadequate measure of the full range of factors determining future capacity. As explained by Robert Kaplan and David Norton, the architects of the scorecard, it represents a *balance*

> *between external measures for shareholders and customers and internal measures of critical business processes, innovation, and learning and growth. The measures are balanced between the outcome measures — the results from past efforts — and the measures that drive future performance. And the scorecard is balanced between objective, easily quantifiable outcome measures and subjective, somewhat judgmental, performance drivers of the outcome measures.[11]*

What is this alien approach doing in the contained world of performance measures, and why has it rapidly gained application in American governments? To pioneers of performance measures, such as Harry Hatry, the balanced scorecard is retrograde. He worries that the balanced scorecard could confuse public managers who have been told singular focus on outcomes is the final step in the evolution of measurement systems. "There has been considerable effort and progress made on performance measurement; a reasonably common language has evolved around it, along with a growing recognition of a basic hierarchy of performance indicators." The balanced scorecard, Hatry fears, "implies that all these areas are of equal value. But we've been trying to get public officials to focus on outcomes . . . there's a danger of a return to an over-emphasis on internal process."[12]

The balanced scorecard will turn out to be just another "flavor of the month" in the never-ending parade of management reforms, aggressively promoted by entrepreneurs who make a fast buck out of the latest fad, and then thrown onto the scrap pile of failed reforms. My sense, however, is that balanced scorecards tell us a few things about the state of the art in performance measurement. One is that scorecards are popular, as noted. But more importantly, they indicate that conventional measures are inadequate to cover the full gamut of factors that produce outputs and outcomes. Perhaps for the wrong reasons, the balanced scorecard looks at the right places to assess performance. It assesses the quality and capacity of the organizations that generate outputs.

The conventional output-focused measurement literature begs fundamental questions: Where do results come from? Who produces the outputs and outcomes that are at the center of the measurer's universe? What has to be done to obtain the desired performance, and who has to do it? Performance is not manna that falls from heaven; organizations have to be structured, mobilized, and funded to carry out the activities that generate results. This simple truth often is ignored in performance measurement. If it were followed, measurement would be one of the final steps in the GPRA process, not the first. There would be more emphasis on transforming organizations and less on measuring results. In fact, performance measurement has ample warning from the failure of past reforms that organizations matter. Each of the budget reforms mentioned above failed for its own reasons, but all shared a common defect. They assumed that budgeting could be oriented to performance, even if the organizations that make and implement budgets are not driven to perform.

The balanced scorecard, by contrast, seeks to assess organizational capacity. This is hard work, as I learned firsthand in the mid-1990s when the New Zealand government invited me to assess its public-sector reforms.[13] One element of the New Zealand model was to distinguish the government's role as the purchaser of output from state agencies from its role as the owner of these agencies. The government's purchase interest is short-term; it focuses on the outputs produced during the current or next fiscal year. The government's ownership interest is long-term; it concerns the capacity of public agencies to respond to future needs and demands. Various methods have been devised to gauge the purchaser interest, such as output budgets, purchase agreements, and performance reports, but the government lacks comparable instruments for evaluating its ownership interest. This is where the balanced scorecard may fit in. It calls attention to organizational capacity and connects performance to the entities delivering the services. Even if the balanced scorecard does not have lingering success, it should drive home the message that processes matter, as do staff training and morale, internal controls, customer interests.

Performance as Change

Most performance measures are snapshots; they display the volume of outputs produced during a particular period, or outcomes at a particular moment in time. These snapshots produce useful data, but they do not reveal all that is important about performance. From the standpoint of policymakers, service providers, and citizens, the key performance question should be: what will be different as a consequence of government action? In each area of public activity, this question can be disaggregated into specific performance measures. For example, in education: How many more children will reach the 60th percentile on standardized tests because of smaller class sizes? How many more will go on to college because of additional guidance counselors? How many more disabled students will be mainstreamed because of a boost in special education services? Especially from the vantage point of the budget, where the key policy issue is how much more or less shall be provided than in the previous year(s), performance indicators shall be framed in terms of the output and outcome changes ensuing from the budget.

The notion of change is embedded in the concept of effectiveness. To be effective is to make a difference, to produce a result that would not happen absent the action. Somehow, however, effectiveness seems to have fallen out of favor in the performance industry, and most output and outcome measures are cast in absolute terms— not in reference to a previous (or "default") condition.

It is feasible to incorporate change into routine measures of performance. One approach would be to construct a services baseline that parallels the spending baseline that is widely used in preparing and analyzing budgets. The spending baseline represents the expenditures projected to occur in the next or future years if current policy were continued without change. The baseline is adjusted periodically for changes in economic conditions, program workload, and estimation errors. By definition, once these adjustments have been made, any variance from the baseline is the result of policy change. The money value of such changes is measured as the size of the variance. A similar baseline would estimate the types and volume of services that would be provided if current policy were continued without change. Where relevant, it should be possible to build qualitative indicators into this baseline. Many questions would have to be resolved in constructing a baseline, but they are not inherently more difficult than in baselining expenditures. Both types of baselines rely on assumptions, estimation rules, procedures for updating the projections, and so on. Just as government estimates the cost of program initiatives, it would estimate the service impacts of policy changes.

If a service baseline were constructed, performance targets could be cast in terms of projected changes. For example, proposals to reorganize the police department or to appropriate more money for it would be assessed in terms of estimated changes in response times, arrest rates, and other measures. Such change-oriented data would sharpen understanding of the implications of proposed or implemented policy changes, and would provide a firmer basis for evaluating government programs. Evaluation would then determine whether the expected changes have materialized, whether policy innovations had the intended impacts, and whether the method for estimating service changes should be altered.

Some analysts may argue that baselining services in the manner suggested here would further entrench incrementalism in the allocation of public resources. That is, rather than focusing on the aggregate outputs or outcomes, policymakers would consider incremental changes to the baseline. This may be so, but structuring policy choice in incremental terms is logical because policymakers almost always behave in this manner. I will argue in the final section that the most fruitful path for performance budgeting is likely to be one that recognizes the hold of incrementalism on budget decisions.

Moreover, absolute performance measures can be displayed alongside those derived from baseline estimates. In the case of school reform, it should be possible to measure both the graduation rate and changes in the rate owing to policy changes. Those who use performance information would be free to draw on the measures they deem to be most appropriate. They would also be free to devise additional measures that suit the particular use they have in mind.

Activities as Drivers of Performance

If performance refers to change, which changes should be measured? The confident answer, from the conventional point of view, is outputs and outcomes — the goods and services produced by governments and the social conditions affected by or influencing public policy. But in line with my argument that organizations are the performers, let me suggest a supplemental approach, one that may either coexist with conventional measures or replace them. Government should measure performance in terms of the activities carried out by its agencies. Activities are not often referred to as indicators of performance, though other measures, such as workload and services, convey some of the same meaning. In some settings, outputs also may refer to activities.

Activity-centered measurement is at the leading edge of management reform. Activity-based costing (ABC), developed by Robert Kaplan, who produced the balanced scorecard, is a widely applied cost allocation and analysis system which has infiltrated public-sector financial management.[14] The basic idea of ABC is that activities drive costs; hence to control costs, they must be charged to the activities generating them.[15] This approach enables managers to measure the costs that would be incurred or avoided if a firm undertook or terminated a particular activity. Cost measurement is a critical, oft-neglected prerequisite for using performance measures.

Firms measure activities because these are the things they do to produce goods and services. Activities drive their costs and outputs, and the efficiency with which activities are conducted determines the efficiency of the firm. To change what a firm spends money on or what it produces, it must change what it does. But does the same logic hold for government? Does it make sense to assess costs and performance in terms of work rather than results? Arguably, government does not perform its activities for their own sake but to provide services (outputs) and improve social conditions (outcomes). Governments don't run schools just to give courses in reading or science, but to develop students who are competent in those subjects. Taken too literally, activity-centered performance would measure the number of classes taught but not whether students graduate or can function effectively in the job market or the supermarket. True enough, but this is why activity measures should supplement regular performance measures. By themselves, activity measures do not provide much of the information policymakers need to design and implement effective programs. But activity measures provide essential information for budgetary decisions and program managers. For example, inasmuch as the teaching of reading skills still is organized around classroom activities, budget makers and educators need data on the number and types of classes, class size, the number of remedial and advanced reading courses, and other measures of school activity. These measures strongly influence how public money is spent and educational services are delivered.

The further one moves from budget and operational decisions to analysis and evaluation, the more one needs broader measures of performance oriented to effectiveness and outcomes. But in allocating resources, activities are an indispensable yardstick for decisions. I sense that if measurers had emphasized activities, performance budgeting would be more advanced than it is. There would be less wrangling over definitions and more attention to allocations. Managers would have a clearer understanding of what is being measured and what they are expected to do.

Cost as a Measure of Performance

Performance budgeting failed half a century ago for many reasons, but one of the most prominent facts was the inadequacy of government cost-accounting and allocation systems. The lack of data on the costs of particular services made it exceedingly difficult to link resources and results. Government agencies were given bundles of money with little awareness as to how the volume or quality of services would vary if more or less funding were provided.[16]

Fifty years later, cost accounting still is underdeveloped in the public sector. There are few university courses or textbooks in government cost accounting, and few governments allocate budget resources among cost centers, or distinguish between fixed and variable or average and marginal costs. These cost measures are essential for successfully implementing performance budgeting.

Cost accounting figured prominently in the efficiency movement of the 1920s and 1930s. As early as 1925, the Municipal Finance Officers Association published a handbook on government cost accounting, and followed this up with a number of articles showcasing the use of cost-measurement techniques in local governments.[17] Considerable work was done on identifying standard costs for government activities such as road and building maintenance.

The launch of performance budgeting in the 1950s renewed interest in cost measures, but Congress on this front was meager. Congress passed legislation requiring federal agencies to prepare cost-based budgets, but as has often happened with administrative reforms, this prescription was largely ignored.[18] Various efforts were made to apply cost accounting and analysis in performance budgeting, but none of these efforts advanced to full implementation. New York State conducted the most interesting such experiment using cost accounting to construct performance budgets in a number of hospitals. The state did so by dividing the institution's budget into a number of cost centers. As in business, a cost center was defined as an operating unit that performs a major activity; it generates costs, and is the responsibility of a designated person. The next step was to separate variable and fixed costs, after which variable unit costs were computed. These calculations allowed funders to build a budget for the institution by multiplying the number of work units by variable costs, and adding fixed costs.[19] The cost-accounting experiment was technically successful, but it withered away for lack of interest.

Interest in cost accounting and measurement was revived by a number of developments in the 1990s including the Chief Financial Officers Act of 1990, the work of the Federal Accounting Standards Advisory Board, and the requirement that federal agencies prepare audited financial statements.[20] Current federal policy codified in Statement of Federal Financial Accounting Standards Number 4, *Managerial Cost Accounting Concepts and Standards for the Federal Government*, requires each entity to account for the costs of outputs and the total net cost of operations. The statement gives agencies leeway in using costing methodologies, such as activity-based costing, but it does require that the cost-accounting system be capable of accumulating costs in defined cost centers that are associated with defined performance measures.[21]

I am not aware of any study of the extent to which federal agencies comply with these standards. It would not be surprising if many are not yet in full compliance, as the promulgation of standards has invested cost accounting with significantly more prominence than the last time performance budgeting was tried.

Performance Budgeting

Although performance budgeting is the most advanced use of performance measurement in allocating financial resources, policymakers hold alternative conceptions of what performance budgeting entails. A liberal definition would include any system that relates budget resources to the services or products produced by government. By this standard, a government would maintain a satisfactory performance budgeting system if it classified expenditures by services or outputs. A more stringent standard would require it to link each increment in budget resources to an increment in outputs or outcomes. Although this standard is a much more demanding standard, the payoff would likely be far greater because it would enable governments to decide budget increments based on actual or expected volume or quality of performance.

Can governments successfully implement this version of performance budgeting? One must be mindful of the failure of earlier drives in the 1950s. I believe the fate of performance budgeting will depend on two factors: the quality of public management, and the quality of public measurement. The first is beyond the scope of this chapter but requires brief explanation; the second is what this paper is all about.

Earlier performance budgeting, like other previous budget innovations, assumed that budgeting drives management; if the budget is oriented to performance, managers will drive their organizations to perform. This reasoning led government to single out budgeting for reform without bothering to change other managerial behavior or incentives. But this approach was congenitally flawed, for it failed to recognize that budgeting is shaped by the managerial context within which resources are allocated and services provided. If managerial conditions discourage attention to results, efforts to introduce performance budgeting will fail. Budgeting cannot be reformed in isolation from the managerial systems and practices in which it is embedded. Only if government entities are managed on the basis of results will they be able to allocate resources on this basis.

The second precondition is that government have data to link resources and results. If the government is informed on the type of data called for here — the performance and capabilities of its organizational units, proposed or budgeted changes in the volume or quality of operations, the types and volumes of activities, and the variable and marginal costs of activities — it should be able to install a performance budget that makes sense to politicians, program managers, and citizens.

Such a performance budgeting system would hew closely to the more demanding version. Rather than linking total performance to total resources, it would relate increments in results to increments in cost. The driving question in resource allocation would be: "How much more or less activity could be undertaken if more or less resources were provided?" This methodology is somewhat similar to that introduced by zero-based budgeting (ZBB) in the 1970s. Because of its misleading label and rigid methods (decision packages and rankings), ZBB was misunderstood, and few governments implementing it recognized that what ZBB actually did was to divide budget requests and decisions into incrementally differentiated packages.[22] In ZBB, each decision package above the base or minimum level represents increments in funding and work (or results).

Budgeting by performance increments is not a new idea. Verne Lewis, who sought to institutionalize marginal analysis into resource decisions, proposed it in a 1952 article.[23] But it is an idea that has never been broadly tried. To budgetary rationalists, it would be a step backward — far short of the comprehensive budget review they have forever been seeking. To me, however, it would give performance budgeting a fighting chance to make it this time.

Endnotes

1   Clarence E. Ridley and Herbert A. Simon, *Measuring Municipal Activities: A Survey of Suggested Criteria for Appraising Administration.* (Chicago: The International City Managers' Association, 1943), p. 2. The first edition of this book, published in 1938, was drawn from monthly articles serialized in *Public Management,* the ICMA magazine.

2   Ibid, p.3.

3   Quoted in David Osborne and Peter Plastrik, *The Reinventor's Fieldbook* (San Francisco: Jossey-Bass, 2000), p. 249.

4   Reported on CNN.com, October 10, 2000.

5   Genevieve J. Knezo and Virginia A. McMurtry, "Performance Measure Provisions in the 105th Congress: Analysis of a Selected Compilation," Congressional Research Service, January 7, 1999.

6   See Robert D. Behn, "Why Measure Performance? Different Purposes Require Different Measures," paper presented at the Fall Conference of the Association of Public Policy and Management, November 2000.

7   In the United States, the Governmental Accounting Standards Board has explored the feasibility of prescribing reporting standards for service efforts and accomplishments. See Harry P. Hatry and others, *Service Efforts and Accomplishments Reporting: Its Time Has Come* (Norwalk, Conn: Governmental Accounting Standards Board, 1990).

8   Quoted in Organization for Economic Cooperation and Development, *Modern Budgeting* (Paris: author, 1997), p. 112.

9   See Oliver E. Williamson, "Transaction-Cost Economics: "The Governance of Contractual Relations," *Journal of Law and Economics*, vol. XXII (October 1979).

10   Robert Kaplan and David Norton, *The Balanced Scorecard: Translating Strategy Into Action* (Boston: Harvard Business School Press, 1996).

11   Ibid, p. 10.

12   Quoted in Jonathan Walters, "Buzz over Balance," *Governing* (May 2000) p. 60.

13   Allen Schick, *The Spirit of Reform* (Wellington: The State Services Commission, 1996).

14   See Robert Kaplan and Robin Cooper, *Cost and Effect: Using Integrated Cost System to Drive Profitability and Performance* (Boston: Harvard Business School Press, 1998).

15   The application of activity based costing in government is described in Government Finance Officers Association, *Activity-Based Costing and Management: Issues and Practices in Local Government* (Chicago: author, 1997)

16   The fate of performance budgeting is discussed in Allen Schick, *Budget Innovation in the States* (Washington: The Brookings Institution, 1971).

17   See Carl W. Tiller, *Governmental Cost Accounting* (Chicago: Municipal Finance Officers' Association, 1925); and Fred B. Wilson, "Municipal Cost Accounting: A Preliminary Report of the Committee on Cost Accounting," *Municipal Finance*, vol. 12 (May 1940), pp. 26-41.

18   Public Law 84-863 (1956), Stat. 782.

19   See Daniel Klepak, "Performance Budgeting for Hospitals and Institutions." *Municipal Finance* (1954), pp. 17-24.

20   See Chief Financial Officers Act of 1990, P.L. 101-576, the Government Management Reform Act of 1994, P.L. 103-356, and the Federal Financial Management Improvement Act of 1996, P.L. 104-208.

21   Joint Financial Management Improvement Program, *Managerial Cost Accounting System Requirements*, February 1998.

22   See United States Congress, Senate Committee on Government Operations, *Compendium of Materials on Zero-Base Budgeting in the States*, Committee Print, January 1977.

23   Verne Lewis, "Toward a Theory of Budgeting," *Public Administration Review,* vol. xii (1952), pp. 42-54.

4

The Economics of Performance Incentives in Government with Evidence from a Federal Job Training Program

Gerald Marschke

Many analysts of the public sector see government ineffi-ciency as a management problem and advocate remedies from the private sector. Some analysts maintain that for many government bureaus a set of quantifiable objectives can be identified and linked to explicit performance measures backed by cash incentives (for example, Gore, 1993, Chapter 2). Cash-backed performance measures communicate to bureaucrats a clear objec-tive and act to commit the government to reward them for progress toward this objective. Advocates of such systems argue that shifting the focus towards objectives through performance measures and away from bureaucratic inputs through procedural rules and regu-lations encourages bureaucrats to use their initiative and creativity to manage public resources more efficiently.

We can use the principal-agent model — a rationale for perfor-mance-based incentives inside organizations — to understand how incentives might be constructed for government agencies, and for troubleshooting incentives that are in place. While the theory is not detailed enough to generate an incentive policy for any particular government program, it provides a way to characterize bureaucratic effectiveness and a short list of features of the agency, worker, and mission that policymakers should consider before designing performance incentives.

This chapter attempts to meet two goals. The first is to lay out the principle-agent model and recent advances in the theory that focus on aspects of public sector organizations that are important in the design of performance measures.[1] This discussion shows that when bureaucratic output is difficult to evaluate — as it is in many government agencies — performance incentives should be used sparingly or not at all. I also use the theory to analyze the experiences with performance incentives created under the Job Training Partnership Act (JTPA) of 1982, one of the first large-scale experiments with performance incentives in a federal bureaucracy.[2] The JTPA experience shows that bureaucrats do respond to financially backed performance incentives, but that bureaucratic response is often dysfunctional, and that government incentive designers have difficulty constructing appropriate incentives.

The Principal-Agent Model

The principal-agent model provides an analytic framework for understanding the agency relationship, in which one party, the principal, contracts with another party, the agent, for the performance of some task or tasks. The principal may wish to delegate the task rather than perform it herself because the agent possesses specialized knowledge or skills, or because of the complexity or scale of the principal's enterprise. Agency relationships are ubiquitous: patient-doctor, student-teacher, client-lawyer, stockholder-CEO.

The fundamental agency problem is that the principal, after engaging the agent, cannot be assured that the agent will perform the task contracted upon according to the principal's wishes. The agent has his own preferences, which deviate from the principal's. The agent's ability to hide his efforts from the principal allows him to pursue his own objectives. Nevertheless, by appropriately designing the contract, the principal can structure the agent's incentives to limit such opportunistic behavior by the agent — called *moral hazard* in the economics literature.

Anecdotal examples of moral hazard in agency relationships abound. In a recent, much-publicized case, several states sued Sears Auto Centers for charging customers for unneeded or unperformed repairs. Sears settled these cases for approximately $20 million. Sears' investigation of the overcharging revealed the cause to be the company's compensation system, which paid sales people commissions based on store revenues, and bonuses for meeting sales quotas for services and products. Sears eventually removed these incentives.

While Sears' sales staff apparently cheated their customers, agents committing moral hazard — or "shirking," for short — are not always venal or lazy, in spite of the term's connotations. Take, for example, Medicaid, the federal-state program that provides health insurance to low-income and disabled persons. Medicaid is an instrument of the voters/legislators (the principal) for providing medical services to the disadvantaged. Through Medicaid, the voters/legislators delegate this task to doctors (the agents). Consider the doctor who lies about a patient's diagnosis to induce the state Medicaid administrators to pay for a needed test or treatment. This behavior, while laudable at some level, nevertheless may be contrary to the interests of the voters/taxpayers. It is moral hazard because if it were observed, the principal could always identify and punish it. Moral hazard — whether it originates from purely selfish behavior or not — is the subject of this chapter.

As in the private sector, agency relationships are common in the public sector. Government is a multi-tiered, hierarchical organization. Agency relationships exist between the voter and the legislator, Congress and the federal agencies, managers and workers within an agency, the agency's clients and its caseworkers, and so on. The simple agency model provides a framework for thinking about the moral hazard problem and shows how contracts can be used to reduce moral hazard.

The Simple Agency Model

I first assume a very simple world that contains a single principal and a single agent.[3] The principal cares only about a single well-defined objective. For example, the principal might be the owner of a firm, and the agent a worker, and the objective her profit. I assume that the agent is risk averse. In the economics literature, this means that he always prefers to receive a dollar with certainty, rather than to receive a payoff whose average or expected value is a dollar, but is sometimes more and sometimes less. The agent cares only about his earnings, and also about the effort he exerts, which he finds costly.

The basic model is usually presented with a risk-neutral principal — one who cares only about the expected value of her payoff and is indifferent to the level of risk she must bear. The principal's risk preferences are assumed different from the agent's because the model is frequently used in contexts where the principal is the stockholder and the agent a worker in a firm. The firm's stockholders may have a comparative advantage in risk management because they can more easily spread their wealth among different assets (diversify their portfolio), while workers may have most of their wealth tied up in their (non-diversifiable) human capital, limiting their ability to manage their risk.[4] Rather than explicitly modeling this constraint, economists simply assume that the principal is risk-neutral. These attitudes toward risk are probably reasonable assumptions when the principal is the owner of a firm and the agent a worker. They are less defensible in other contexts. (I return to this point below.)

The principal contracts with the agent to perform a single task. I assume that the principal cannot observe the agent's effort, and cannot precisely infer it from measures of organizational performance such as share price, in the case of publicly traded firms. But holding everything else equal, the more effort the agent exerts the more the principal benefits. I assume effort is costly to the agent. In addition to assuming that the agent is risk-averse, I assume that the agent cares about his net earnings. That is, holding constant the risk he bears, he is interested in making his monetary compensation, less the cost of his effort, as large as possible.

The assumptions that the principal cannot detect (and therefore punish) shirking, and that effort is costly to the agent, ensure that the agent will shirk in the model. Knowing this, the principal will be much less likely to contract with the agent in the first place. Moral hazard imposes costs on the contracting parties. These costs mean that some exchanges between the principal and agent that would otherwise benefit both parties will not take place. It is therefore in the interest of both parties to find ways to limit moral hazard.

The source of the moral hazard problem is that the parties cannot contract on the agent's effort because the principal cannot observe it. Suppose, however, the agent's effort yields a random variable, or performance measure, which, I assume, both the principal and third parties are able to observe.[5] The value of the measure rises with the agent's effort. While the performance measure partly reflects the agent's effort, however, it is also affected by external factors that are not observable to the principal. These external factors introduce noise into the measure of effort. The smaller the noise introduced by the external factors the more closely the performance measure reflects effort. If the noise introduced is sufficiently small, the performance measure can be used as a stand-in for effort in an explicit contract that links the agent's pay to the performance measure.

For example, a board of shareholders might base part of a CEO's compensation on the net earnings of the firm. The firm's net earnings in a year are a function of the CEO's effort and the quality of his decisionmaking. Basing a CEO's compensation on net earnings therefore provides him with a greater incentive to work hard and to make wise decisions with the firm's resources.

The next question is how to use the performance measure in an incentive contract to reduce shirking. One of the simplest such contracts the principal can offer is a linear contract: the agent receives a salary independent of the agent's effort and performance, plus a sum that varies with performance. The variable part is a piece rate — a fixed amount of compensation per unit of performance — times measured performance. Let us call the piece rate *the intensity of incentives*. The higher the incentive intensity, the greater is the fraction of the agent's compensation that stems from performance and the stronger the incentive to exert effort.

Conventional wisdom holds that in private sector workplaces, more often than not, some portion of each worker's pay is explicitly based on performance. In the public sector, on the other hand, conventional wisdom holds that a worker's compensation is usually invariant to performance.[6] The issue is how government principals can best choose the salary level and particularly the incentive intensity to improve the performance of government agencies.

The more intense the incentives, the greater is the role played by factors outside the agent's control. That is, the riskiness of the agent's compensation increases with the incentive intensity. While a firm's net earnings reflect CEO effort, for example, also they are a function of factors outside of his control, such as the business cycle, energy prices, and acts of nature. Therefore, net earnings are an imperfect proxy of effort. As far as the manager is concerned, net earnings are risky. Why should the principal care about the riskiness of the agent's compensation? The principal must care because the agent has alternatives to entering into a contract with the principal. The principal must offer a level of compensation and risk that appear to the agent at least as attractive as his next best alternative. Therefore, the greater the risk the principal makes the agent bear, the greater must be the salary level to compensate. On the one hand, a high incentive intensity provides incentives for the agent to work harder and thus increases the benefit to the principal. On the other hand, a high incentive intensity leads to a higher wage bill and higher costs. The principal therefore chooses the salary level and incentive intensity by considering the effect of incentives on his willingness to supply effort, and by ensuring that the package is attractive enough to lure him away from his next best alternative.

According to this simple model four factors determine the incentive intensity that optimally balances incentives and the costs of risk-bearing: the added benefits created by additional effort, the risk-aversion of the agent, the noisiness of the performance measure, and the sensitivity of the agent's supply of effort to an increase in the incentive intensity. These factors suggest several important implications for designing effective performance measures and contracts.[7]

Implication 1: The sensitivity of an agent's compensation to performance should be higher the more beneficial is an increase in effort. Raising the incentive intensity is costly to the organization because it increases the risk the agent bears and therefore the compensation necessary to retain him. Thus, raising the incentive intensity makes sense only if the added effort is consequential to the value of the organization.

Implication 2: The sensitivity of an agent's compensation to performance should be lower the higher the agent's risk aversion. Where the principal is a firm's owner and the agent the firm's single worker, the performance measure amounts to the value of the firm. Choosing the incentive intensity is equivalent to choosing a rule for sharing the risky profits generated through the agent's exertion. The sharing rule balances the benefits of incentives against the costs of risk bearing. The smaller the incentive intensity the more the compensation scheme behaves as an insurance contract, insulating the worker from fluctuations in the firm's value. But the smaller the incentive intensity the more the agent will shirk. The insurance feature of the incentive contract is of value only to risk averse agents. Therefore the lower the agent's risk aversion, the stronger the principal can afford to make the incentives.[8]

The assumption that the principal is risk neutral and the agent risk averse makes sense when the principal is a large firm and the agent is a worker. The firm's stockholders can more easily use the capital market to diversify away the risk in the firm's net earnings. In the public sector, the goal of the organization is not profit but policy, and the principal is not the owner of a firm but a public sector manager or politician. The public sector principal cannot easily diversify away the risk of managerial or policy failures by purchasing assets whose risk will offset policy risk.[9] In other words, it is now costly for the principal to bear risk. Under the optimal contract the agent bears more of the risk when the principal is herself risk averse than when she is risk neutral. This is an argument for the greater use of performance pay in the public sector than in the private sector, *everything else being equal.*

Implication 3: The sensitivity of an agent's compensation to performance should be lower the noisier the performance outcome. The less informative the performance outcome is about effort, the less the principal should rely on it as a signal of effort. Consider, for example, that a general sometimes is awarded a promotion upon winning a battlefield victory. A battlefield outcome is a useful measure of a general's efforts because the decisions a general makes about how troops are deployed in the field can be decisive. However, whether the army wins the battle is a much noisier indicator of the effort exerted by a particular private. In this example, Implication 1 is also relevant. The battlefield outcome should be given little weight in evaluating a private because rarely do the actions of a single private affect that outcome.

Implication 4: Incentives should be more intense the more responsive is the agent's effort to an increase in the intensity of incentives. In many government bureaucracies, workers are bound by procedural rules and regulations and have little discretion. The general principle here is that incentives should be placed on agents who are able to respond to them. In organizational environments where agents have wide discretion over how they perform their work, agents often respond to performance incentives with innovative ways of generating value for the organization. Imposing performance incentives on agents who have little discretion needlessly subjects them to increased earnings risk.

Implication 5: Linear performance incentives may be superior to nonlinear ones because they put constant pressure on agents to exert effort. A nonlinear scheme, where the agent receives a bonus for exceeding a performance threshold, creates little incentive late in the period when the agent's performance late in the period is either far in excess or far short of the threshold.

I have laid out the principal-agent model assuming a linear contract: the payoff of a one-unit increase in performance is constant. Under nonlinear schemes, performance is aggregated over, say, a quarter or a year. The agent receives a high award when performance exceeds some threshold, and a low one otherwise. Bonus schemes are of this form. For example, a salesperson might win a trip to the Bahamas only if his annual sales exceed 100 units.

Under certain conditions linear contracts outperform nonlinear ones. An agent who in the middle of a period finds himself well above or well below the standard has little incentive to exert effort (Courty and Marschke, 2000, find evidence of such responses to nonlinear incentive schemes in JTPA; see below). Linear schemes outperform nonlinear ones because they apply uniform pressure on the agent to perform that is independent of past performance or the height of the standard.[10]

Implication 6 (in the case of multiple agents): In addition to agents' efforts, performance outcomes are affected by external events, some of which affect all agents equally. When the principal suspects that the error in performance measurement caused by these common events is potentially large, she should base an agent's compensation on his performance relative to the performance of other agents (relative performance evaluation).

In the private sector, firms often pay a worker incentive pay based not on his absolute performance but on his performance relative to other workers in the firm, or even to workers outside the firm who are performing in an identical or similar role. Firms sometimes run tournaments, wherein only top-performing workers receive performance-based awards, for example. In the public sector, the principal often supervises multiple agents performing similar tasks who may be separated geographically or by the types of clients they serve. For example, the postmaster general's office supervises thousands of local post offices, each providing the same kinds of services but to different populations of clients. A pay-for-performance scheme might be constructed in which a post office manager's pay is linked to his performance on some measure relative to the performance of other offices' managers.

It is better to base the agent's pay at least partly on relative performance when the performance of an agent's peers allows the principal to better distinguish the agent's effort from external, random factors. Suppose, for example, two umbrella vendors employed by the same firm are working opposite sides of a busy street corner.

The number of umbrellas each sells is a function of the effort he exerts, but also a function of external, random factors. Some of these external factors are idiosyncratic, such as the vendor's health. Others are shared, such as the weather. Should the firm's owner use as her measure the number of umbrellas he sells alone, or in combination with how many he sells in excess of the amount sold by the other vendor? In making this decision, the principal should be guided by how using relative performance changes the noise in the performance measure. The principal should use relative performance when the noise introduced by the common random component (weather) is large relative to the idiosyncratic noise (health). Relative performance evaluation works by differencing out a common external factor that affects all agents' performance equally (weather, in the umbrella example). This reduces the risk the agent faces, and allows the principal to raise the incentive intensity.

While relative performance evaluation among agents within an organization may lead to a more precise estimate of agent effort, it may also promote counterproductive behavior. Pitting agents against each other can reduce their incentive to cooperate and increase their incentive to sabotage one another's performance. These behaviors would militate against the use of relative performance evaluation where the gains from cooperation are great, even though it would produce a more precise estimate of agent effort.

Implication 7 (contracting over multiple periods): The principal can reduce the noise in the agent's performance measure by basing pay on the difference between current performance and past performance, as past performance contains information about the agent's capabilities.

If the principal is able to observe the agent over several years, she can use past performance to learn about the size of the random component. A given level of performance is more likely to represent extraordinary effort if it is greater than past levels of performance. The principal sets her expectation on the basis of an agent's performance during an initial assessment period. Where the agent is a shirt-maker, for example, the owner of the firm might base her expectations on the number of shirts produced during the average week of the assessment period. In a simple compensation scheme, the shirt-maker receives a bonus whenever his output exceeds the average output during the assessment period.

Implication 8 (ratchet effect): If the agent anticipates that his current performance will be used to set standards for future performance, he has an incentive to withhold effort. This reduces both the output in the assessment period and its information content for setting expectations of the agent's capabilities.[11]

Using past performance to gauge how much effort the agent is putting forth can increase the effectiveness of performance incentives, but also create an incentive for the agent to withhold effort, as exceptional performance in the assessment period will raise the bar and lower his compensation in subsequent periods, everything else being equal. This is the so-called *ratchet* problem.

One way to make use of the information contained in past performance while avoiding the ratchet problem is to rotate workers through tasks. By setting the standard for an agent based on the performance of the agent who occupied the position in the previous period, the perverse incentives that lead to the ratchet problem are eliminated.[12]

Researchers have investigated whether real world, mostly private sector, principals and agents write contracts that take into account agency concerns.[13] They have found that agents respond powerfully to performance incentives (see, for example, Lazear, 2000, and Paarsch and Schearer, 1996), but that explicit, financially backed performance incentives are relatively rare. While for some job titles such as CEO performance-based bonuses and stock options are an important part of compensation, a salary or an hourly wage constitutes the compensation of most employees in firms. Even when performance incentives are used, their incentive intensity is often low (see Baker, Jensen, and Murphy, 1988: Jensen and Murphy, 1990: and Medoff and Abraham, 1980.) In the model outlined above, because effort is costly, performance-based compensation is necessary to elicit the optimal level of effort. Taking the simple agency model at face value, the scarcity of incentives and the absence of risk in labor contracts seem peculiar. One possible explanation for the scarcity of explicit incentives in contracts is the complexity of tasks assigned to agents — that is, they are not single-dimensional, as the simple agency model treats them.

Multitasking

In most jobs, workers perform multiple tasks. For example, a university professor teaches, conducts research, and helps with the administrative chores of running his academic department. In government agencies, both the tasks and the objectives are multidimensional. Wilson (1989) argues that each government agency has a primary goal (or a small number of primary goals). For example, a police department's primary goal is to maintain law and order. Over time, however, a government agency becomes saddled with more and more ancillary goals. These goals may be outcome-oriented, but often their focus is *how* the agency conducts its activities. For example, whom the agency hires and how equitably the agency dispenses its services (if the agency provides services to citizens) often become as important as the primary goal. This is in contrast to shareholder-principals in the private sector, whose interests are reducible to a single dimension, such as profit or share value, which remain the firm's focus over time.

Relaxing the assumption that tasks or goals are one-dimensional changes the simple agency model's implications. Suppose the agent performs two activities, *task 1* and *task 2* — which are both useful to the principal. (The results from the two-task case generalize to cases of more than two tasks.[14]) Once again, the principal cannot observe the efforts devoted to these two tasks, but suppose each task generates a separate performance measure that she can observe. These measures are, as before, imperfect indices of effort because they also reflect external, random forces. To keep things simple, suppose that efforts are the minutes spent on the activity, and that the number of minutes in the agent's day is fixed. If these are the only two activities to which the agent can devote effort, then increasing the effort devoted to one activity must come at the expense of effort devoted to the other.

We can see the implications of multiple tasks or goals for constructing incentives by examining the agent's compensation. With two tasks, the agent's linear contract contains a salary component, as it did with one measure. We add to that two components that are sensitive to performance: one component whose payoff is proportional to performance measure 1 plus one component whose payoff is proportional to performance measure 2. If the agent's payoff for task 1 is greater than his payoff for task 2, he will devote no effort to task 2. Only when the incentive intensity is the same for both measures will the agent devote effort to each task.

In the real world, agents are not likely to be indifferent at the margin between time spent on one activity versus another. The agent may, for example, find effort spent on task 1 less taxing than effort spent on task 2, in which case the principal would have to set the payoff for task 2 higher than the payoff for task 1 to induce the agent to allocate time to both activities. Likewise, if the agent *enjoys* task 1, the principal may have to penalize him for time spent on task 1 (a negative payoff for performance measure 1). The model's primary implication can be stated as follows.

Implication 9: If the principal wants the agent to devote effort to each of several tasks or goals, then each task or goal must earn the agent the same marginal return to effort. Otherwise, the agent will devote effort only to the task or goal that has the highest return to effort.

This principle has two important implications. The first and more important for this chapter is the following: the presence of productive activities for which effort cannot be measured, even imprecisely, is an argument for setting the weights on measurable performance to zero. That is, the optimal compensation package in the presence of unmeasurable tasks is one that pays the agent only a fixed salary.

Second, we now see one of the ways in which incentive design is complementary to the design of other features of the organization. In a multitasking environment where some tasks produce measurable outcomes and others do not, the principal may be able to use incentives by reorganizing work (Holmstrom and Milgrom, 1991). If one group of agents performs only measurable tasks and another group performs unmeasurable tasks, the principal can exploit the motivating power of incentives, at least for some workers.

Note that the assumption driving *Implication 9* is that efforts devoted to the multitude of tasks are substitutes. Sometimes, however, efforts toward alternative tasks are complementary. To illustrate: in addition to crime prevention, the racial and ethnic makeup of police forces has become a social objective, made explicit by federal and state incentives to local departments to increase minority hiring and promotion rates. Such incentives placed on new objectives need not lower a police department's crime-fighting effectiveness. In fact, a police department may be in a better position to meet its traditional goal if the marginal minority officer is also the most qualified. In terms of the model, if efforts devoted to each of the tasks are complementary, the principal will elicit increases in *both* task 1 and task 2 efforts by raising *either* the incentive intensity of task 1 or the incentive intensity of task 2. That is, the incentive intensities of the two measures do not have to be equivalent to ensure that the agent devotes effort to both activities.

Baker (1999) presents a formulation of the multitasking model that clarifies how incentive pay may lead the agent to take actions that raise or lower organizational value. The simple agency model emphasizes the trade-off between the benefits of insuring the agent against risk and of providing incentives to motivate effort. Baker's formulation of the multitasking model emphasizes the tension between motivating the agent to supply effort and motivating the agent to supply effort to the "right" kinds of tasks, undoubtedly a more important trade-off in real world incentive contracts.

In Baker's formulation, the quality of the performance measures available to the organization takes center stage. Performance measures can sometimes be tied very closely to firm value, as when firms base performance evaluation (especially for managers) on accounting profits or on stocks or stock options. However, in nonprofits and public sector organizations direct measures of organizational value rarely exist. Performance measures in the public sector will thus be indirectly related to organizational value. Still, some activities may move the performance measure and the value of the organization in the same direction. These activities, in Baker's terminology, are "aligned." Other activities move the performance measure and the value of the organization in opposite directions. Baker calls these activities "distortionary."

Implication 10: The sensitivity of an agent's compensation to performance should be smaller the more misaligned or distortionary the performance measure with respect to the value of the organization. A performance measure is misaligned if it does not induce agents to undertake the activities that raise organizational value. A performance measure is distortionary if it induces agents to undertake activities that reduce organizational value.

Take, for example, a salesperson working in a car dealership. Suppose that return customers account for a large portion of the dealership's profit. In this case, both sales-related and service-related activities after the sale promote firm value. Commissions motivate the sales person to work hard selling cars, but may also encourage him to devote too little time to customer service, discouraging return visits and cutting into the long-run value of the firm. A salesperson who devoted time to customer service would increase the firm's value, but at the expense of his commissions. The fundamental problem with this incentive scheme is that activities that promote large commissions are not the same activities that increase the long-term value of the firm.

The challenge for the designer of incentives is finding performance measures that are aligned with the value of the organization. Baker's model shows that there is no easy way to find such measures. The following implication of the model constitutes a warning to policymakers searching for effective performance measures for a government agency.

Implication 11: In the optimal compensation scheme, the sensitivity of an agent's compensation to performance is independent of the correlation between the performance measure and the organization's value.

Baker shows that in general the optimal incentive weight is independent of the sign and magnitude of the correlation between the measure and organizational value. This correlation is uninformative because it is driven by the correlation between external factors that affect the performance measure and those that affect the organization's value. What matters is not the correlation between the measure and organization's value, but the correlation between the effects of agent actions on outcomes and on the organization's value. The performance measure and the organization's objective can be positively correlated — yet the principal may place no weight on it if she anticipates that it will lead the agent to take the wrong actions. Similarly, one can imagine situations where the performance measure and organizational objectives are *negatively* correlated — that is, when the measure is high, the value of the organization is low, and vice versa — yet the principal places on the measure a *positive* weight. Baker illustrates the point this way:

> Consider the following personal example. The neatness of my office is negatively correlated with my level of activity and productivity: when I am busy, my office is a mess, when I am not, my office is neat. But having a neat office clearly increases my productivity. Thus, a savvy incentive contract designer might give me incentives to keep a neat office, even though the performance measure is negatively correlated with productivity. (p. 9, footnote 10).

A related implication of the model is that the correlation of a seemingly promising performance measure with the value of the organization will often degrade as soon as the measure is compensated. Before the principal compensates the measure, workers do not focus on it. Once the principal compensates the measure, however, it becomes the workers' objective. The new incentive causes workers to take actions that raise the performance measure, without regard to their effect on the organization's value. If these actions do not also raise the organization's value, the correlation between the performance measure and organizational value may fall.

Consider again the Sears Auto Center case. Before Sears implemented the incentive scheme, Auto Center profits may have been positively correlated with the number of repair jobs. This statistical relationship may have prompted Sears officials to use the number of repairs as a performance measure. Once Sears began paying managers bonuses for meeting service quotas, however, those service quotas became the managers' objective. It was not long before the managers had found easy ways to boost sales volume that did not also result in higher store profits. By charging customers for unneeded and unperformed repairs, store staff uncoupled the performance measure from the store's long-term profits. Their response to the incentives drove up the value of the performance measures while eventually driving down profits. Thus, repairs and long-term profits were positively correlated so long as Sears did not base pay on the number of repairs performed.

Finally, note that what matters in the selection of performance measures, according to the principal-agent model, is not whether the measure is an "output" (e.g., number of enrollees a job training center placed in employment) or an "input" (e.g., the number of hours a case worker works), but how risky the measure is and how aligned it is with the organization's objectives. Theoretically, any piece of data generated by the agent is a candidate for use as a performance measure.

Performance Incentives and the Job Training Partnership Act

The Job Training Partnership Act (JTPA) created one of the largest federal employment and training programs serving the economically disadvantaged.[15] JTPA is distinguished from its predecessor training programs and from most other federal bureaucracies by its highly decentralized administrative structure and its set of financially backed performance incentives.

Some 640 JTPA training regions exist across the U.S. Congress allocates an annual JTPA appropriation to the states based on their shares of the national JTPA-eligible and unemployed populations and their unemployment rates. Each state distributes its allocation among its job training regions by a formula similar to the state allocation formula. Within each substate region, a single administrative agency manages the region's budgetary appropriation. This agency will be referred to as a training center or agency.

Congress, the Department of Labor, and state and local authorities share in designing and enforcing the program's rules and incentive policies, and hence in the allocation of resources under JTPA.[16] While these entities have different motivations, in this chapter they constitute the *principal* in the JTPA organization; the training centers constitute the *agents*. The act delegates to the managers and case workers of the training center the business of enrolling, training, and finding employment for the program's clients. Training centers enjoy unusual (for government bureaucrats) discretion over how they perform their tasks.

JTPA is not an entitlement: the program funds job training for only about 1 to 3 percent of the eligible population each year. Because many more persons meet the income test of eligibility than the program can accommodate, training centers decide whom to enroll. After accepting an applicant, training staff members orient him or her to services that may include vocational classroom training to become, for example, nursing assistants, office managers, computer programmers, or security guards, on-the-job training, basic or remedial education, and job search assistance, which can include resume writing and interviewing workshops as well as employment referrals. Because federal rules do not limit the length, kind, or expense of training activities,[17] the choice of such activities allows centers again to exert their preferences.

Performance Incentives

To motivate training centers to serve the program's goals rather than their private goals,[18] the act makes a portion of their budgets contingent on objective measures of performance. Each state pays out budgetary awards to successful training agencies from a fund equal to 6 percent of their annual appropriation. Some training centers have seen substantial incentive awards. For example, in 1986, the most successful training center won the equivalent of almost 60 percent of its budget. Awards this high are unusual, however. In the median training center that year, the award equaled 7 percent of the budget.[19]

Even though the act requires training centers to use award money to provide additional training, it places fewer restrictions on the use of award monies than on budgetary monies. For example, training centers may spend a larger fraction of their award on staff compensation. Courty and Marschke (forthcoming) argue that while these financial awards are often significant, career concerns, the desire for professional recognition, and political motivations also make training center bureaucrats covet the award.

In contrast to the simple principal-agent model above, the agent is an agency and the budgetary award is a function of the collective effort of all bureaucrats in the agency. Unlike individual incentives, group incentives are subject to the classic free-riding problem. By increasing his effort, any single bureaucrat in the center raises not only his own award but also raises the award to all others. Under group incentives, because he does not enjoy the full benefit of his effort, he may exert too little effort. Ultimately, whether budget-based awards mute incentives and the significance of the free-riding problem must be resolved empirically.

The Department of Labor must find proxies for the effort and activities of training centers that are aligned with the objectives of JTPA's stakeholders. These measures would likely be imperfect for the same reason that share price is an imperfect indicator of managerial effort, yet they could still improve the performance of the JTPA program. With varying degrees of success, DOL has tried several alternatives.

Multiple goals. What are the goals or objectives of JTPA's stakeholders? For the purposes of the following discussion, let us take as the stakeholders the nation's citizens, as represented by the legislators that brought the act into existence. A reading of the act turns up several potential goals of these legislators. The act directs training centers to establish programs that help the economically disadvantaged and others "facing serious barriers to employment" to develop skills that will enable them to obtain employment and increase their earnings, reduce welfare dependency among the eligible population, provide job training services equitably among the eligible population, and "contribute to occupational development, upward mobility, development of new careers, and overcoming sex-stereotyping in occupations traditional for the other sex." These goals or tasks may be substitutes in the sense of the multitask agency model above. For example, because not all eligibles may benefit from training, a strategy of offering training services widely and equitably may sometimes be inconsistent with producing the greatest gains in skill development and earnings. The act does not offer any guidance as to how to resolve conflicts among different objectives. It directs DOL to set performance measures only for the program's first goal — return on human capital investment (JTPA, Section 106(a)).[20]

For the time being, let us assume that human capital investment is the program's sole objective. This translates at the training center level to maximizing the amount of human capital value-added, net of training expenses. How might we measure human capital value-added? While an enrollee's human capital stock is not directly observable, any increase in human capital stock should be reflected in labor market earnings. Thus, a measure of the impact of job training on a single enrollee's human capital is the sum of her earnings from the beginning of her training into the future, minus the sum of earnings over the same period had she *not* experienced training.[21] The total impact of job training over the course of a fiscal year, say, would be the sum of earnings impacts of the year's individual enrollees minus their cost of training.[22]

The chief difficulty is that while the costs and earnings of program enrollees may be measurable, their earnings had they not received training — the counterfactual — are not directly measurable. DOL's response to this problem is to use earnings and employment levels measured at or shortly after the conclusion of their training — very different from measures of *changes* in enrollees' earnings ability and employability. A measure of training cost is included only in the first decade of JTPA.[23] Evidence on the consequences of the misalignment of JTPA's performance measures with its goal is explored below.

Nonlinear awards. One can imagine several ways to use performance measures to reward training centers. A training center could receive a lump sum bonus for each enrollee who finds employment after training, for example. The JTPA incentive system differs from this simple piece rate in two ways. First, the JTPA award is a nonlinear function of the performance measures. Simply by meeting the numerical standards corresponding to a set of performance measures, agencies win a substantial monetary award. Second, performance outcomes are computed as the *average* outcome over all enrollees terminated (that is, officially removed from the program's rolls) over the course of the year. For example, until 1992 an important performance measure in JTPA was the employment rate at termination. For fiscal year 1990, a training agency's employment rate at termination was computed as the fraction of enrollees who were employed on the dates of their termination. If the training center's year-end employment rate at termination exceeded the standard for that measure, the training center in a typical state would win an award. While the award's construction varies slightly from state to state, typically the more standards the training center exceeds, the greater its award. In addition, the awards have been independent from year to year. The slate is wiped clean at the beginning of the each year, and performance measurement begins anew.

Relative performance evaluation. DOL sets performance standards for a particular training center on the basis of the performance of other training centers in the system. For example, in constructing the employment rate standard, DOL initially sets the standard at the 25th percentile of performance among all training centers nationwide over the previous two years. While a training center's standards are based on past performance, there is no ratchet problem, because the standards are based on the past performance of over 600 training centers. Thus, no single center can appreciably lower its future standards by suppressing performance.

Because training centers operate in widely different circumstances, simple comparisons among them are not always meaningful. To address this, DOL adjusts the standards by the characteristics of the labor market in which the training center operates, and by the characteristics of the training center's enrollee population. The adjustment model uses multivariate regression techniques and data on the recent performance of JTPA training centers to estimate the relationship between characteristics of the training center and the training center's performance.[24] These estimated relationships are then used to adjust each training center's performance standards. The purpose of adjusting the standards for the characteristics of persons enrolled is to limit the incentives for agencies to choose enrollees based on their projected scores on performance measures — that is, to *cream skim.* Adjusting the standard by the characteristics of the local labor market levels the playing field, so training centers operating in labor markets where job openings are scarce face standards that reflect the relative difficulty of placing enrollees in jobs. The adjustment scheme turns the training center's performance standard into an estimate of what an average training center in a similar labor market with a similar population of enrollees has produced in the past. The performance standard adjustment methodology recognizes the value of drawing from available information on the bureaucrat's environment to enhance the precision with which effort is measured.

The Effects of JTPA's Performance Incentives

The goal of JTPA is to exert long-run impacts in employment and earnings, but DOL's measures reflect employment and earnings levels at or shortly after the end of training. Still, numerous studies have attempted to test the validity of JTPA's performance measures by correlating them with earnings/employment gains (and sometimes the reduction in welfare recipiency) at the individual enrollee level. The correlation studies use a variety of techniques to estimate the earnings and employment counterfactual. Some use the employment histories of a comparison group composed of persons who are observationally similar to the enrollees but who do not take training. However, these comparison groups are probably different in motivation and other unobserved ways that would bias earning impact estimates. Others use estimates generated from several social experiments used to evaluate the effectiveness of selected government training programs, during which persons who apply and are accepted into a training program are randomized into a treatment and control group. Because the control and treatment groups start out virtually identical, any difference in their earnings or employment experiences can arguably be attributed to the training. These estimates are still imperfect, as the experimental subjects are followed for only a few years following random assignment, and control and treatment groups become dissimilar because members of the treatment group drop out. (Readers interested in the issues of estimating treatment effects can refer to an extensive literature; see Ashenfelter, 1978: Lalonde, 1986; Heckman and Robb, 1985; and Heckman, Lalonde, and Smith, 1999; among others.[25])

Several studies using data from various government job training programs that do not operate under a JTPA-style incentive system correlate earnings impacts and performance outcomes at the level of the enrollee. The Friedlander (1988) and Zornitsky, et al. (1988) studies report that enrollees who are likely to produce high scores on JTPA-style performance measures are also likely to generate high earnings and employment impacts. Gay and Borus (1980), however, found that the correlation of the employment measure and earnings impacts was sometimes negative.

Heckman and Smith (1995) estimated earnings impacts from data produced by the DOL-commissioned National JTPA Study (NJS). The NJS was an experimental study of the effectiveness of JTPA involving 16 training centers in 16 states and conducted between 1987 and 1989. During the study, persons who were accepted to the program were designated at random to a treatment group and a control group. Persons in the treatment group were offered the opportunity to enroll in JTPA and receive services. Persons in the control group were embargoed from JTPA for eighteen months.[26] The study found at most a weak, positive relationship between the short-run employment-outcome based performance measures and net earnings impacts — estimated earnings impacts minus the costs of training. For some measures, in fact, performance negatively correlated with net earnings impacts. Barnow (2000) found weak correlations using the same data whether he considered performance measures or net performance — defined as the performance measure minus the performance standard. (By subtracting the standard from the measure, he more closely simulates the actual incentive faced by the JTPA training center.)

To conclude, only the studies of programs where performance is uncompensated show statistically significant correlation between JTPA-style performance measures and impacts. The two JTPA studies show little or no statistical correlation. Indeed, these studies show that the correlation sometimes has the wrong sign. The contrast in results between JTPA and the other programs is consistent with *Implication 11*. While the techniques and data are different, finding that the strongest correlations are in the non-JTPA programs suggests that when performance measures are compensated, bureaucrats respond by finding the least-cost strategies of boosting

these performance measures. As the next section reveals, these results provide indirect evidence that JTPA performance measures
are misaligned.

Why JTPA Performance Measures Do Not Create the Right Incentives

Training center staff choose which applicants to enroll, how to
train the enrolled, and when to terminate them. Each of these
choices has consequences for the training center's performance
score and award, but also for the benefits enrollees take away from
training.

Enrollment. Cream skimming — the use of the training center's
considerable discretion to select enrollees on the basis of their expected effect on performance outcomes — is the core concern of
most of the analyses of JTPA's incentive system. As noted above,
this system judges training centers on the basis of post-program employment and earnings levels, whereas the objective of training is
skill development. Such performance outcomes induce training
centers to choose persons with high permanent levels of labor market success at the expense of persons who would most benefit from
training.

The incentive system's critics also note the absence of performance measures that reward the act's non-earnings and employment goals. The principal omitted goal is the equitable provision of
services. Persons who are the most attractive to award-maximizing
training centers, may not be "worst-off" of eligible enrollees —
those with the least pre-training earnings, labor market experience,
and education.

Both of these concerns can be framed in terms of the
multitasking model. The first concern is about whether the incentives lead training centers to make the enrollment choices that maximize enrollment impacts — that is, whether the performance
measure and the objective are aligned. The second concern is about
whether by setting the marginal return on the equitable provision of

services to zero, the JTPA incentive system leads training centers to neglect equity in their enrollment and training decisions.

The evidence that training centers choose enrollees based on their expected effects on performance outcomes is, at best, mixed. Anderson, Burkhauser, and Raymond (1993) examined the enrollment patterns of training centers in Tennessee for evidence that JTPA bureaucrats prefer persons who are likely to score high on a single JTPA performance measure — the employment rate at termination. They find that some of the personal characteristics that predict high post-training employment rates are positively correlated with the likelihood of enrollment. Nevertheless, it is impossible to tell from their study whether this relationship represents bureaucratic screening behavior, the applicant's decision whether to enroll, or a combination of the two. They do not consider performance measures other than the employment rate.

Cragg (1997) studied the effects of the variation in the construction of awards across states on enrollment and other decisions. The act requires only that each state governor implement an incentive scheme that rewards training centers that exceed their performance standards. The act also requires that the governor reorganize any training center that fails its performance standards two consecutive years. (The reorganization may include replacing the training center's management.) The remaining particulars of the award's construction are up to the state governor.

Cragg contrasted the characteristics of a sample of about 200 JTPA enrollees distributed across the fifty states to a sample of JTPA eligibles. He obtained both samples from the National Longitudinal Survey on Youth (NLSY) data set. He hypothesized that in states where the award was more attractive and challenging to obtain, training centers would pursue high-aptitude eligibles more aggressively. He used labor market experience as a measure of applicants' aptitude. He considered four aspects of the state's incentive policies: whether the state has a formal procedure for training agencies to appeal a low award, the number of standards agencies must meet to win an award, the number of standards agencies must meet to avoid sanctions, and the size of agencies' potential awards. He found that only one of these has a statistically significant effect on the training center's enrollment rule. He found that an absence of an appeals procedure coincides with a preference for enrollees with more labor market experience. The absence of an appeals procedure means that the training center could not apply to have a low award overturned for having experienced an unusually difficult year. This is evidence of an incentive effect, Cragg argues, because training center staff realize that whether they win an award will be determined solely by whether they attain their performance standards. Because the eligible person's decision to enroll is not likely to be influenced by whether the state he or she resides in allows appeals, Cragg argues this is evidence of cream skimming and not a depiction of the applicant's decision.

Heckman and Smith (1995) investigated the cream-skimming issue using data from four of the sixteen NJS training centers. At these training centers, Heckman and Smith could identify who among the accepted eventually enrolled in the program. They found the transition from acceptance to enrollment was non-random: blacks, persons with less than a high school education, persons from poorer families, and those without recent employment experience are less likely to enroll conditional on application and acceptance. Their evidence suggests that applicants who would be anticipated to produce low performance measures are less likely to enroll. Their evidence also suggests a selection process that some would consider inequitable: blacks and the least educated and experienced are less likely than others in the applicant pool to enroll. Nevertheless, as was the case with Anderson et al. and as the authors acknowledge, some or all of the evidence may be due to self-selection on the part of applicants.

Heckman, Smith, and Taber (1996) studied the determinants of the enrollment decision at a single Texas training center, again using the NJS data. For this training center, they had data not only on which persons were accepted into the program but also on who applied. The authors found that applicants with the lowest prospects for employment after training were more likely to be accepted in the program. They also found that the applicants with the greatest expected earnings gain were neither more nor less likely to be accepted. They argued that whether the applicant reaches the acceptance stage mostly reflects the preferences of training center bureaucrats, not the preferences of applicants.

Thus, the evidence as to whether training center bureaucrats express a preference for eligible persons who are most likely to produce high measures of performance is mixed. The best evidence that such cream skimming occurs comes from Cragg and Heckman and Smith. Likewise, the evidence that training center bureaucrats discriminate against the most disadvantaged among the eligible is inconclusive. Finally, while the literature offers some evidence that training centers are enrolling persons more likely to produce high levels of performance measures, studies offer no evidence that training centers are enrolling persons who are more likely to produce high earnings impacts (value-added).

Training selection. Researchers have also investigated the effects of JTPA performance incentives on centers' training choices. While training choice has received less attention than the cream- skimming issue, its study is motivated by similar concerns — that existing incentives encourage training centers to emphasize "quick fixes" that have no long-term impact on enrollee skills.

Marschke (2000) studied the effects of two performance measure reforms on the training strategies of JTPA training centers. In the early 1990s, DOL moved away from termination-based measures toward performance measured three months *after* termination. DOL also eliminated measures that rewarded training agencies that kept the average cost of training an enrollee low. Both reforms occurred in response to a growing perception that the training centers were relying heavily on job-placement-oriented services at the expense of more intensive kinds of training. Many policymakers also felt that the typical JTPA training spell was too short to be effective (average enrollment in the first decade of JTPA lasted only about five months).

Marschke found that these performance reforms produced mixed results. The switch to performance measurement three months after training ends appeared to encourage agencies to offer the kinds of intensive training that raise the long-term earnings abilities of JTPA enrollees, but the impacts from this reform were offset by the elimination of the cost measure. Apparently the cost measure had been discouraging training agencies from offering classroom vocational training because it is one of the more expensive kinds of training. After the cost measure was removed, training agencies offered more classroom vocational training, but earnings impacts fell because classroom vocational training produces the smallest earnings impacts of the main kinds of training offered.[27]

In the context of the principal-agent model, rewarding the employment rate at termination measure, for example, was leading the center to prescribe training activities that increased the training center's employment rate but reduced the earnings ability of JTPA enrollees. The employment rate at termination measure and earnings impacts are misaligned. The cost measure, on the other hand, was leading training centers to prescribe training that increased both earnings impacts and the training center's award. The cost measure appears to be aligned.

Performance accounting. Using data from the NJS, Courty and Marschke (2000) document how agencies delayed terminating unemployed enrollees, even after their training concluded, because unemployed enrollees who were terminated counted against the training agencies in the first decade of JTPA. Thus, an agency usually arrived at the end of the fiscal year with an inventory of idle, unemployed enrollees on its books. At the end of the year, the training agency would then decide which fiscal year to terminate the unemployed enrollees. If the center found itself either comfortably above or hopelessly below its standard, it could enhance its odds of winning an award in the next fiscal year without jeopardizing its award in the current year by terminating most or all of its inventory. If the training center found itself above but close to the standard, it could increase its award in the present year by postponing termination until the following year. Courty and Marschke found that by timing performance measurement in this way training agencies boosted their performance, and their awards, without providing higher-quality services, or providing services more efficiently. In addition, the authors found that this kind of gaming behavior consumed program resources.

Other features of these measures suggest other avenues for gaming. Because the measures are based on averages instead of aggregate outcomes, they may encourage training centers to enroll too few enrollees. Training centers may enroll too few enrollees and thus allow a higher level of per capita spending. This makes it easier to beat the minimum per capita measure of performance necessary to receive an award (Barnow, 1992; 2000). Enrolling a smaller-than-efficient population may also be an optimal strategy in areas where able applicants are scarce. Rather than enroll less-able enrollees who lower per capita scores, training centers may prefer to leave some of their budget unspent. While these responses seem possible, to my knowledge researchers have not investigated them.

Can Performance Incentives Help in the Public Sector?

For the designers of incentives in government, agency models show how the type of performance measures and the shape of the award function (whether the compensation scheme is linear or nonlinear, for example) matter. Noisy performance measures should receive little weight in compensation schemes. Noisy performance measures can sometimes be made more effective when the performance of similar workers can be compared. Where bureaucrats are expected to perform multiple tasks and some tasks are unmeasurable, performance incentives should be kept to a minimum, as they increase worker effort but at the cost of neglecting some tasks. Sometimes, however, tasks can be grouped into jobs by their measurability. In that case, the principal can exploit the power of incentives by using performance pay for workers who perform the measurable tasks.

Another implication of the model is that performance measures that are misaligned with the objectives of the organization cause wasteful or dysfunctional behavior. We see this in JTPA. First, we find this indirectly, as the correlation of JTPA's performance measures with the earnings and employment impacts deteriorates after the performance measures become incentivized. Second, we find this directly, as case workers use their discretion over when enrollees are released to game their performance awards.

What does the history of JTPA's performance incentives suggest generally about the promise of incentives for making government more efficient? First, government bureaucrats are indeed motivated by financially backed performance incentives, even when the award is not in the form of salary increases or bonuses. This offers the hope that, if the incentives are properly designed, bureaucrats can be motivated to work more efficiently. Second, incentive designers may have difficulty finding measures of performance that reflect the true productivity of bureaucrats. While we cannot rule out that performance incentives in JTPA have increased that program's efficiency, it is apparent from the effects of recent reforms that DOL has had difficulty designing incentives.[28] The evidence suggests that the measures used so far are misaligned and distortionary, making the JTPA incentive system subject to "the folly of rewarding A while hoping for B."[29]

In any case, evidence from the empirical side of the economics incentive literature clearly shows that performance measures backed by financial incentives are no cure-all for inefficiency and mismanagement in the public sector. The private sector would appear to present an environment more conducive to the use of performance incentives, as organizational objectives would seem less complicated, more stable, and more clearly defined. Better measures of performance are also available in firms, which would seem to possess fewer competing principals and objectives. In firms, workers possess more discretion over how they conduct their jobs. The principal-agent model implies that incentives have a better chance of success under these circumstances. Even so, compensation schemes that place a significant weight on output-driven measures of performance are rare; workers are more often paid a fixed salary or an hourly wage than a piece rate or other kind of performance-based compensation. If performance-based compensation is relatively uncommon in the private sector, then public-sector opportunities to successfully apply such compensation are also likely to be uncommon.

Endnotes

1   This chapter samples only a portion of the (economic) theoretical literature on organizations. Readers interested in a more thorough survey of the literature should see, for example, Milgrom and Roberts (1992) or Brickley, Smith, and Zimmerman (1997).

2   In the economics literature, Dixit (1999) and Burgess and Metcalfe (1999b) survey selected topics in the incentives literature that bear upon issues of governance in the public sector, and also review some of the empirical evidence on performance incentives in government.

3   A precise mathematical derivation of the model can be found in, for example, Milgrom and Roberts.

4   Moreover, persons selecting into occupations by their ability to tolerate risk implies that the owners of firms will be less risk-averse than firms' workers.

5   The assumption that third parties can observe the performance measure makes contracts written on it enforceable through the courts.

6   See Burgess and Metcalfe (1999a) for some evidence that performance pay is indeed more often seen in the private sector compared to the public sector in the U.K.

7   The implications that follow would hold to a greater or lesser extent under more realistic sets of assumptions. With more general assumptions, however, the implications are richer. Indeed, the model has been extended in a number of interesting ways, which for reasons of space, I do not treat here. One could assume, for example, that workers would work even in the absence of performance pay. Workers would work because "work is its own reward," or perhaps because they know the labor market will eventually learn about their productivity and reward it with higher future pay (economist call these motivations "career concerns"). One could assume the availability of alternatives to explicit incentive pay, such as the ability to monitor agents. Monitoring activities are activities with the objective of verifying that a certain task has been performed. Allowing principals in our model to combine monitoring and incentive pay makes incentive pay more effective by reducing the error with which effort is measured. In many work environments, it is impossible to fully specify the nature of the task required of the worker in an explicit contract. In such environments, subjective performance evaluation by a worker's supervisor allows for a more nuanced and balanced appraisal of the worker's effort. Such evaluation — based on judgment and more qualitative and flexible than explicit performance incentives — can be used to determine workers' bonuses, raises, and promotions. Subjective evaluation is itself imperfect, because it is based on measures that outside parties cannot verify. Consequently, supervisors may distort their evaluations for private gain, or workers may attempt to influence their supervisor's evaluations. See Brickley et al., Milgrom and Roberts, and the references cited therein for fuller discussions of these extensions.

8   In the extreme case, if the agent like the principal is risk neutral, it is easily shown that under the optimal contract the agent receives the full benefit of each unit of effort. In the firm-worker example, this is tantamount to selling the firm to the worker. In the public sector case, this suggests privatization (Dixit).

9   A point made by Dixit, p. 5.

10   See Holmstrom and Milgrom (1987) for a formal statement of this result.

11 See Milgrom and Roberts for a mathematical explanation of the ratchet effect.

12 Another way to set standards and avoid the ratchet problem is by conducting a time-and-motion study.

13 Excellent surveys of this work can be found in Prendergast (1999) and Gibbons (1998).

14 For formal statements of the multitasking model see Holmstrom and Milgrom (1991) and Baker (1992).

15 In 2000, a new program created under the Workforce Investment Act (WIA) of 1998 supplanted JTPA. While many organizational details of WIA remain to be worked out, the change appears to be an evolutionary one. WIA retains the decentralized nature and the performance incentives of JTPA. Innovations include some streamlining of services and a role for vouchers, giving WIA enrollees new discretion over what sorts of training they receive and from whom they receive it.

16 For a discussion of how these entities share authority in JTPA, see Heinrich, Marschke, and Smith in *Performance Standards in a Government Bureaucracy: Analytic Essays on the JTPA Performance Standards Systems*, Heckman, ed. (book will appear in 2002).

17 The one significant exception: agencies were not allowed to subsidize a client's on-the-job training for more than 6 months at a time.

18 Westat, Inc (1985) and Walker et al. (1984; 1985) document some of the non-training objectives of training centers and the influence of area politics on training decisions.

19 These figures are based on data collected by SRI International and Berkeley Planning Associates, described in Dickinson et al. (1988). The JTPA funds are allocated among three purposes: 78 percent of a state's allocation is set aside for training services (and allocated to training centers), 6 percent is set aside for the incentive system, and the remaining 16 percent is retained by the state for administrative and other expenses. Thus, the award money distributed is 7.1 percent of the budget for training services (6/(78+6)), if one assumes that all award funds are eventually disbursed to the training centers. The actual figure has typically been a little less than 7.1 percent because states use some of the award fund to administer the incentive system.

20 States are allowed to implement additional performance measures of their own construction, and many do. Some state-defined measures are designed to meet the other objectives enumerated in the act.

21 These earning streams would be appropriately discounted.

22 A weighting scheme could be used if the legislators were not indifferent about who among the enrollees gained. For example, a weighting scheme could attribute a higher weight to impacts enjoyed by the most disadvantaged.

23 Most other measures that could be used to capture the long-term gains or impacts have drawbacks. One possible measure is the difference between earnings before and after training. However, research shows that persons who apply for programs experience a rebound in their earnings, even if they do not receive any training (Heckman and Smith, 1995). Another way to improve the types of measures JTPA has used is to lengthen the period over which employment outcomes are measured. Lengthy tracking periods are expensive, however.

24 See Barnow (2000) for a description and analysis of these techniques.

25 The data and methodological requirements for constructing reliable estimates of earnings and employment impacts make these analyses impractical as a measure of performance for every-day award or managerial purposes. For example, in the late 1980s, an experimental evaluation of JTPA involving only 16 of the then 620 training centers took seven years to complete and, according to one estimate, cost over $21 million (Smith, 1995).

26 See Doolittle and Traeger (1990) for a description of the implementation of the NJS. See Orr et al. (1994) for a detailed description of the results of the NJS.

27 This finding is consistent with the results of the NJS, which found that compared with job search assistance and on-the-job training, vocational classroom training produced the weakest earnings and employment gains (see Orr et al.). Vocational classroom training is also the most time intensive and costly (on average) of the three major kinds of training.

28 While the evidence suggests that performance measures based on employment levels are imperfect, we cannot on the basis of the evidence claim that performance incentives do not increase the efficiency of job training under JTPA. We cannot claim this because we cannot compare the behavior of JTPA bureaucrats in the present incentivized environment to the behavior of JTPA bureaucrats in an unincentivized environment, because that environment has never existed. If we could observe the counterfactual, we might find that the incentives produce beneficial effects that more than balance out, for example, the gaming responses.

29 This is the often-cited title of a paper by Steven Kerr (1975).

References

Anderson, Kathryn, Richard Burkhauser, and J. Raymond. 1993. "The Effect of Creaming on Placement Rates under the Job Training Partnership Act." *Industrial and Labor Relation Review* 46, 4: 613-624.

Ashenfelter, O. 1978. "Estimating the Effect of Training Programs on Earnings." *Review of Economics and Statistics* 60: 47-57.

Baker, George P., Michael C. Jensen, and Kevin J. Murphy. 1988. "Compensation and Incentives: Practice vs. Theory." *Journal of Finance* 43: 593-615.

Baker, G. P. 1992. "Incentive Contracts and Performance Measurement." *Journal of Political Economy* 100, 3: 598-614.

Baker, G. P. 1999. "Distortion and Risk in Optimal Incentive Contracts." Unpublished manuscript, Harvard Business School.

Barnow, B. 1992. "The Effect of Performance Standards on State and Local Programs." In Charles Manski and Irwin Garfinkel, eds., *Evaluating Welfare and Training Programs*, Cambridge, MA: Harvard University Press, pp. 277-309.

Barnow, B. 2000. "Exploring the Relationship Between Performance Management and Program Management and Program Impact: A Case Study of the Job Training Partnership Act." *Journal of Policy Analysis and Management* 19, 1: 118-141.

Brickley, J., C. Smith, and J. Zimmerman. 1997. *Managerial Economics and Organizational Architecture.* Chicago, IL: Irwin.

Burgess, S., and P. Metcalfe. 1999a. "The Use of Incentive Schemes in the Public and Private Sectors: Evidence from British Establishments." Centre for Market and Public Organisation, Working Paper No. 99/015.

Burgess, S., and P. Metcalfe. 1999b. "Incentives in Organisations: A Selective Overview of the Literature with Application to the Public Sector." Centre for Market and Public Organisation, Working Paper No. 00/16.

Courty, P., and G. Marschke. Forthcoming. "The JTPA Incentive System: Program Years 1987-1989." In James Heckman, ed., *Performance Standards in a Government Bureaucracy.* Kalamazoo, MI: W.E. Upjohn Institute for Employment Research.

Courty, P. and G. Marschke. 2000. "An Empirical Investigation of Gaming Responses to Explicit Performance Incentives." Unpublished manuscript. Albany: State University of New York.

Cragg, M. 1997. "Performance Incentives in the Public Sector: Evidence from the Job Training Partnership Act." *Journal of Law, Economics and Organizations* 13, 1: 147-168.

Dickinson, Katherine P., Richard W. West, et al. 1988. "Evaluation of the Effects of JTPA Performance Standards on Clients, Services, and Costs." National Commission for Employment Policy, Research Report No. 88-16, September, Washington, DC.

Dixit, A. 1999. "Incentives and Organizations in the Public Sector: An Interpretative Review." Unpublished manuscript. Princeton University, December.

Doolittle, F., and L. Traeger. 1990. *Implementing the National JTPA Study.* New York: Manpower Demonstration Research Corp.

Friedlander, D. 1988. *Subgroup Impacts and Performance Indicators for Selected Welfare Employment Programs.* New York: Manpower Demonstration Research Corp.

Gay, R. and M. Borus. 1980. "Validating Performance Indicators for Employment and Training Programs." *Journal of Human Resources* 15, 1: 29-48.

Gibbons, R. 1998. "Incentives and Careers in Organizations." *Journal of Economic Perspectives,* Fall.

Gore, A. 1993. *From Red Tape to Results: Creating a Government That Works Better and Costs Less.* Office of the Vice President, Washington, DC.

Heckman, J., C. Heinrich, and J. Smith. 1999. "Understanding Incentives in Public Organizations." Unpublished manuscript. University of Chicago.

Heckman, J., R. LaLonde, and J. Smith. 1999. "The Economics and Econometrics of Active Labor Market Programs." In O. Ashenfelter and D. Card, eds., *Handbook of Labor Economics,* Vol. 3. New York: Elsevier North-Holland.

Heckman, J., and R. Robb. 1985. "Alternative Methods for Evaluating the Impact of Interventions." In J. Heckman and B. Singer, eds., *Longitudinal Analysis of Labor Market Data.* Cambridge, UK: Cambridge University Press.

Heckman, J., and J. Smith. 1995. "The Performance of Performance Standards: The Effects of JTPA Performance Standards on Efficiency, Equity, and Participant Outcomes." Unpublished manuscript. University of Chicago.

Heckman, J., J. Smith, and C. Taber. 1996. "What Do Bureaucrats Do? The Effects of Performance Standards and Bureaucratic Preferences on Acceptance in the JTPA Program." In Gary Libecap, ed. *Advances in the Study of Entrepreneurship, Innovation, and Growth,* Vol. 7. Greenwich, CT: JAI Press, 191-217.

Heinrich, C., G. Marschke, and J. Smith. Forthcoming. "The JTPA Program: Basic Information on its Design and Implementation." In James Heckman, ed., *Performance Standards in a Government Bureaucracy.* Kalamazoo, MI: W.E. Upjohn Institute for Employment Research.

Holmstrom, B. and Milgrom, P. 1987. "Aggregation and Linearity in the Provision of Intertemporal Incentives." *Econometrica,* 55, 2: 303-328.

Holmstrom, B. and P. Milgrom. 1991. "Multitask Principal-Agent Analyses: Incentive Contracts, Asset Ownership, and Job Design." *Journal of Law, Economics, and Organization* 7, 0: 24-52.

Jensen, M. C., and K. J. Murphy. 1990. "Performance Pay and Top-Management Incentives." *Journal of Political Economy* 98, 2: 225-64.

Kerr, S. 1975. "On the Folly of Rewarding A While Hoping for B." *Academy of Management Journal* 18, 4: 769-783.

Lalonde, R. 1986. "Evaluating the Econometric Evaluations of Training Programs and Experimental Data." *American Economic Review* 76, 4: 604-620.

Lazear, E. P. 2000. "Performance Pay and Productivity." *American Economic Review* 90, 5: 1346-1361.

Marschke, G. 2000. "Performance Incentives and Bureaucratic Behavior: Evidence from a Federal Bureaucracy." Unpublished manuscript. Albany: State University of New York.

Medoff, J., and K. Abraham. 1980. "Experience, Performance, and Earnings." *Quarterly Journal of Economics* 95, 4: 703-736.

Milgrom, P. and J. Roberts. 1992. *Economics, Organization, and Management.* Englewood Cliffs, NJ: Prentice Hall.

Orr, L. L., et al. 1994. *The National JTPA Study: Impacts, Benefits, and Costs of Title II-A.* Bethesda, MD: Abt Associates.

Paarsch, H. and B. Shearer. 1996. "Fixed Wages, Piece Rates, and Incentive Effects." Unpublished manuscript. University of Laval.

Prendergast, C. 1999. "The Provision of Incentives in Firms." *Journal of Economic Literature* 37, 1.

Smith, J. 1995. "A Note on Estimating the Relative Costs of Experimental and Non-Experimental Evaluations Using Cost Data from the National JTPA Study." Unpublished manuscript. University of Chicago.

Walker, Gary, et al. 1984. *An Independent Sector Assessment of the Job Training Partnership Act — Phase I: The Initial Transition.* Chapel Hill, New York, Syracuse: MDC, Inc., Grinker, Walker and Associates, Syracuse Research Corporation, March.

Walker, Gary, Hilary Feldstein, and Katherine Solow. 1985. *An Independent Sector Assessment of the Job Training Partnership Act — Phase II: Initial Implementation.* New York: Grinker, Walker and Associates, January.

Westat, Inc. 1985. *Implementation of the Job Training Partnership Act: Final Report.* Washington, DC: Report to the U.S. Department of Labor.

Wilson, J. Q. 1989. *Bureaucracy: What Government Agencies Do and Why They Do It.* New York: Basic Books.

Zornitsky, J., M. Rubin, S. Bell, and W. Martin. 1988. "Establishing a Performance Management System for Targeted Welfare Programs." Washington DC: National Commission for Employment Policy, Research Report 88-14.

Enthusiasts

5

Implementing GPRA: Progress and Challenges

J. Christopher Mihm

The federal government is now moving to a more difficult but more important phase in implementing the Government Performance and Results Act of 1993 (GPRA). Federal agencies have issued performance reports for fiscal years 1999 and 2000, showing the degree they met their goals and developed actions, plans, and schedules to address unmet goals. The issuance of these reports, in addition to agencies' updated strategic plans, annual performance plans, and the governmentwide performance plans, completes two full planning and reporting cycles under GPRA. The federal government is thus at a key juncture in examining the status of GPRA and the use of results-oriented performance information as a routine part of agencies' day-to-day management and congressional and executive branch decisionmaking.

Such an examination is important to ensure that GPRA planning and reporting do not become merely an annual paperwork exercise unrelated to the real work of agencies and the Congress. GPRA should be a foundation for congressional oversight, helping

The material presented here is drawn in large part directly from published U.S. General Accounting Office (GAO) reports and testimonies. Nevertheless, the material has been sufficiently updated so that the issues and opinions expressed should not necessarily be considered those of the GAO.

the Congress to maximize the performance and ensure the accountability of the federal government for the benefit of the American people. GPRA should also provide a management framework for agencies to set goals, measure progress toward those goals, deploy strategies and resources — such as human capital — to achieve them, and, ultimately, use performance information to make the programmatic decisions necessary to improve performance. However, much work remains before GPRA is effectively implemented across the government, including transforming agencies' organizational cultures to improve decisionmaking and strengthen performance and accountability.

As the country moves further into the 21st century, it becomes increasingly important for the Congress and executive agencies to face two overriding questions:

❀ What is the proper role for the federal government?

❀ How should the federal government do business?

GPRA serves as a bridge between these two questions by linking results that the federal government seeks to achieve to the program approaches and resources that are necessary to achieve those results. The performance information produced by GPRA's planning and reporting infrastructure can help build a government that is better equipped to deliver economical, efficient, and effective programs that can help address the challenges facing the federal government.[1] Among the major challenges are:

❀ Instilling a results orientation.

❀ Ensuring that daily operations contribute to results.

❀ Coordinating crosscutting programs.

❀ Understanding the performance consequences of budget decisions.

❀ Building the capacity to gather and use performance information.

Instilling a Results Orientation

The cornerstone of federal efforts to fulfill current and emerging public demands is to develop a clear sense of the results an agency wants to achieve, as opposed to the products and services (outputs) it produces and the processes it uses to produce them. Adopting a results orientation requires a cultural transformation for many agencies, as it entails new ways of thinking and doing business. This transformation is not an easy one and requires investments of time and resources as well as sustained leadership commitment and attention.

Based on the results of GAO's governmentwide survey in 2000 of managers at 28 federal agencies,[2] many agencies face significant challenges in instilling a results orientation throughout the agency. For example, at 26 agencies, fewer than half of the managers perceived, to at least a great extent, that employees received positive recognition for helping the agency accomplish its strategic goals. At 22 agencies, at least half of the managers reported that they were held accountable for the results of their programs to at least a great extent; however, at only 1 agency did more than half of the managers report that they had the decision making authority they needed to help the agency accomplish its strategic goals to a comparable extent.

Additionally, in 2000, significantly more managers overall (84 percent) reported having performance measures for the programs they were involved with, compared to the 76 percent who reported that in 1997, when GAO first surveyed federal managers regarding governmentwide implementation of GPRA. However, at no more than 7 of the 28 agencies did 50 percent or more of the managers respond that they used performance information to a great or very great extent for any of the key management activities GAO asked about.[3]

Strong support and sustained commitment by top leadership is essential if GPRA is to fulfill its potential. In responding to GAO's 2000 governmentwide survey of federal managers, only 53 percent of federal managers reported, to a great or very great extent, that their agencies' top leadership demonstrated strong commitment to achieving results.[4]

To build leaders' commitment and help ensure that managing for results becomes the standard way of doing business, some agencies are using performance agreements to define accountability for specific goals, monitor progress, and evaluate results. Performance agreements ensure that day-to-day activities are targeted squarely at achieving results, and that the proper mix of program strategies and budget and human capital resources are in place to meet organizational goals.

The Congress has recognized the role that performance agreements can play in holding organizations and executives accountable for results. For example, in 1998, the Congress chartered the Office of Student Financial Assistance as a performance-based organization and required it to implement performance agreements.

GAO has identified five common emerging benefits from the use of results-oriented performance agreements.[5] Such agreements:

❀ Strengthen alignment of results-oriented goals with daily operations.

❀ Foster collaboration across organizational boundaries.

❀ Enhance opportunities to discuss and routinely use performance information to make program improvements.

❀ Provide a results-oriented basis for individual accountability.

❀ Maintain continuity of program goals during leadership transitions.

Ensuring that Daily Operations Contribute to Results

GPRA is showing itself to be an important tool in helping the Congress and the executive branch understand how the agencies' daily activities contribute to results that benefit the American people. Such understandings are by no means easy or straightforward, especially since virtually all the results that agencies hope to achieve must be accomplished through the coordinated efforts of several players. The challenge for each agency is to understand how it can best influence the desired results. Agencies that do not have a clear understanding of the ways in which what they do now contributes to results are hard pressed to determine how to improve performance. Specifying clearly in performance plans how strategies will achieve results also enables the Congress and managers to determine the right mix of strategies and to maximize performance while limiting costs.

The Department of Transportation's performance report for fiscal year 1999 shows how knowledge of the factors that affect results is key to designing improvement strategies. Transportation did not achieve its fiscal year 1999 goal concerning recreational boating fatalities. In its 1999 performance report, Transportation notes that most recreational boating fatalities are the result of accidents involving factors under the operator's control, and that boaters tend not to wear life jackets, although doing so would vastly improve their chances of surviving accidents. To achieve this goal, Transportation's strategy now includes boater education and research on life jackets to promote greater use.

GPRA, with its explicit focus on program results, can serve as a tool for examining the programmatic implications of an agency's strategic human capital management challenges. Attention to strategic human capital management is important because building agency employees' skills, knowledge, and individual performance must be a cornerstone of any serious effort to maximize the performance and ensure the accountability of the federal government. However, GAO reported in April 2001 that, overall, agencies' fiscal year 2001 performance plans reflected different levels of attention to strategic human capital issues.[6] When viewed collectively, GAO found that there is a need to increase the breadth, depth, and specificity of many related human capital goals and strategies and to better link them to the agencies' strategic and programmatic planning. Very few of the agencies' plans addressed:

❀ Succession planning to ensure reasonable continuity of leadership.

- ❀ Performance agreements to align leaders' performance expectations with the agency's mission and goals.

- ❀ Competitive compensation systems to help the agency attract, motivate, retain, and reward the people it needs.

- ❀ Workforce deployment to support the agency's goals and strategies.

- ❀ Performance management systems, including pay and other meaningful incentives, to link performance to results.

- ❀ Alignment of performance expectations with competencies to steer the workforce towards effectively pursuing the agency's goals and strategies.

- ❀ Employee and labor relations grounded in a mutual effort on the strategies to achieve the agency's goals and to resolve problems and conflicts fairly and effectively.

In a recent report, GAO concluded that a substantial portion of the federal workforce will become eligible to retire or will retire over the next 5 years, and that workforce planning is critical for assuring that agencies have sufficient and appropriate staff considering these expected increases in retirements.[7] Actions taken by the administration indicate growing interest in working with agencies to ensure that agencies have the human capital capabilities needed to achieve their strategic goals and accomplish their missions. For example, the administration requested agencies to submit workforce analyses to address areas such as the skills of the workforce necessary to accomplish the agency's goals and objectives and the expected skill imbalances due to retirements over the next 5 years.

Coordinating Crosscutting Programs

Virtually all of the results that the federal government strives to achieve require the concerted and coordinated efforts of two or more agencies. Crosscutting program areas that are not effectively coordinated waste scarce resources, confuse and frustrate taxpayers and program beneficiaries, and limit overall program effectiveness.[8]

GAO's work in over 40 program areas has repeatedly shown that mission fragmentation and program overlap are widespread and that crosscutting federal efforts are not well coordinated. For example, GAO reported on 50 programs administered by 8 federal agencies that serve the homeless: 23 programs operated by 4 agencies provide housing services and 26 programs administered by 6 agencies offer food and nutrition services.[9]

GPRA offers a structured and governmentwide means for rationalizing these crosscutting efforts. The strategic, annual, and governmentwide performance planning processes under GPRA provide opportunities for agencies to work together to ensure that agency goals for crosscutting programs complement those of other agencies; program strategies are mutually reinforcing; and, as appropriate, common performance measures are used. If GPRA is effectively implemented, both the governmentwide performance plan and agencies' annual performance plans and performance reports should provide the Congress with new information on agencies and programs addressing similar results. Once these programs are identified, the Congress can then consider the associated policy, management, and performance implications of crosscutting programs as part of its oversight of the executive branch.

Understanding the Performance Consequences of Budget Decisions

A key GPRA objective is to help the Congress and executive agencies develop a clearer understanding of what is being achieved in relation to what is being spent. Linking planned performance with budget requests and financial reports is an essential step in building a culture of performance management. Toward this end, GPRA requires that annual performance plans link performance goals to the program activities in agencies' budget requests.[10] Such an alignment infuses performance concerns into budgetary deliberations, prompting agencies to reassess their performance goals and strategies and to more clearly understand the cost of performance.

GAO has found that agencies are making progress in developing useful links between their annual budget requests and performance plans, observing that performance planning cycles for fiscal years 1999 and 2000 produced useful experiments in "connecting resources to results."[11] Collectively, the actions by many agencies could be seen as a baseline from which to assess future progress. Consistent with other aspects of GPRA implementation, the fiscal year 2001 performance plans showed continued improvement in this area as well.

Agencies have developed a variety of approaches and techniques to show the relationship between budgetary resources and performance goals, thereby making performance plans more relevant for budget decisionmaking. For example, the Environmental Protection Agency and the Nuclear Regulatory Commission revised their budgets' program activity structures to reflect their plans' strategic goals and supporting performance goals. The Internal Revenue Service and the Federal Bureau of Investigation fully integrated their performance plans with their budget requests producing a single submission. And several administrations within the Department of Health and Human Services and the Department of Housing and Urban Development developed summary crosswalks that consolidated or aggregated funding from separate budget accounts and program activities and related this information to strategic objectives or discrete performance goals.

Building the Capacity to Gather and Use Performance Information

Agencies need reliable information during their planning efforts to set realistic goals and later, as programs are being implemented, to gauge their progress toward achieving those goals. Over the past several years, GAO has identified limitations in agencies' ability to produce credible information on program performance and cost, as well as approaches to improving these data.[12] The limitations are substantial and long-standing, and they will not be quickly or easily resolved. GAO has found in its assessments of performance plans that agencies had limited confidence in the credibility of their performance information. This limited confidence is one of the single greatest weaknesses in GPRA implementation.

One challenge confronting agencies in obtaining timely and reliable results-oriented performance information is their dependence on state and local agencies to provide data. The federal government provides services in many areas through the state and local level, thus both program management and accountability responsibilities often rest with the state and local governments.[13] In an intergovernmental environment, agencies are challenged to collect accurate, timely, and consistent national performance data.

To address this challenge, GAO has noted that agencies can use their GPRA planning and reporting documents to discuss how they will compensate for unavailable or low-quality data. For example, earlier this spring, the Environmental Protection Agency identified, in its fiscal year 2000 performance report, data limitations in its Safe Drinking Water Information System. The agency reported that these limitations were due to recurring reports of discrepancies between national and state databases, as well as specific misidentifications reported by individual utilities. Discussing data credibility in performance reports can provide important contextual information to the Congress. Members of Congress can use such discussions to raise questions about problems in collecting results-oriented performance information and the trade-offs in cost and quality associated with various data collection strategies.

Strengthening GPRA

In the four years since federal agencies began implementing GPRA, the act has produced new and valuable information on the plans, goals, and strategies of federal agencies. As the Congress expected in crafting the legislation, each successive cycle of annual performance planning has seen improvements over prior years' efforts. Congressional and executive branch decisionmakers are using the information to an even greater extent, and the issuance of agencies' annual performance reports each March represents a substantive stage in implementing GPRA. These reports give decisionmakers the opportunity to assess federal agencies' actual performance for a specific fiscal year and to consider the steps needed to improve performance and reduce costs in the future.

GPRA clearly has the potential to help the Congress and the executive branch ensure that the federal government provides the results that the American people expect and deserve. The planning and reporting efforts under GPRA to date are generating new and important information that had not been available in the past — information that congressional and executive branch decision makers can use to help assess what government should do in the 21st century and how it should do it. However, more needs to be done before GPRA's potential benefit is realized.

Endnotes

1   *Managing for Results: Opportunities for Continued Improvements in Agencies' Performance Plans* (GAO/GGD/AIMD-99-215, July 20, 1999); and *Managing for Results: An Agenda to Improve the Usefulness of Agencies' Annual Performance Plans* (GAO/GGD/AIMD-98-228, Sept. 8, 1998).

2   These 28 agencies include the 24 agencies covered by the Chief Financial Officers Act of 1990 with an additional break-out of four selected agencies from the departments—the Federal Aviation Administration at the Department of Transportation, the Forest Service at the Department of Agriculture, the Health Care Financing Administration at the Department of Health and Human Services, and the Internal Revenue Service at the Department of Treasury. For additional details on the governmentwide surveys, see *Managing for Results: Federal Managers' Views on Key Management Issues Vary Widely Across Agencies* (GAO-01-592, May 25, 2001); *Managing for Results: Federal Managers' Views Show Need for Ensuring Top Leadership Skills* (GAO-01-127, Oct. 20, 2000); and *The Government Performance and Results Act: 1997 Governmentwide Implementation Will Be Uneven* (GAO/GGD-97-109, June 2, 1997).

3   GAO asked about five key management activities including setting program priorities, allocating resources, adopting new program approaches or changing work processes, coordinating program efforts with other organizations, and setting individual job expectations.

4   GAO-01-127, Oct. 20, 2000.

5   *Managing for Results: Emerging Benefits From Selected Agencies' Use of Performance Agreements* (GAO-01-115, Oct. 30, 2000).

6   *Managing for Results: Human Capital Management Discussions in Fiscal Year 2001 Performance Plans* (GAO-01-236, Apr. 24, 2001).

7   *Federal Employee Retirements: Expected Increase Over the Next 5 Years Illustrates Need for Workforce Planning* (GAO-01-509, Apr. 27, 2001).

8   *Managing for Results: Using the Results Act to Address Mission Fragmentation and Program Overlap* (GAO/AIMD-97-146, Aug. 29, 1997).

9   *Managing for Results: Barriers to Interagency Coordination* (GAO/GGD-00-106, Mar. 29, 2000).

10 Subject to clearance by the Office of Management and Budget and generally resulting from negotiations between agencies and appropriations subcommittees, program activities are intended to provide a meaningful representation of the operations financed by a specific budget account.

11 *Performance Budgeting: Fiscal Year 2000 Progress in Linking Plans With Budgets* (GAO/AIMD-99-239R, July 30, 1999); and *Performance Budgeting: Initial Experiences Under the Results Act in Linking Plans With Budgets* (GAO/AIMD/GGD-99-67, Apr. 12, 1999).

12 *Managing for Results: Challenges Agencies Face in Producing Credible Performance Information* (GAO/GGD-00-52, Feb. 4, 2000); and *Performance Plans: Selected Approaches for Verification and Validation of Agency Performance Information* (GAO/GGD-99-139, July 30, 1999).

13 *Managing for Results: Challenges Agencies Face in Producing Credible Performance Information* (GAO/GGD-00-52, Feb. 4, 2000); and *Performance Plans: Selected Approaches for Verification and Validation of Agency Performance Information* (GAO/GGD-99-139, July 30, 1999).

6

Restoring Government Integrity Through Performance, Results, and Accountability

Virginia L. Thomas

Opinion polls consistently show low levels of public trust and confidence in the federal government. These low expectations of federal performance reflect the widespread belief that Washington is wasting a high proportion of the tax dollars Americans pay each year. In 1998, a survey conducted by the Washington-based Pew Research Center found that 64 percent of Americans view the government — with a burgeoning budget of $1.8 trillion — as "inefficient and wasteful," while only 48 percent believe that it is "run for the benefit of all people."[1] It is understandable that taxpayers expect the federal government to use their money wisely, minimizing waste, inefficiency, and mismanagement. Yet Washington seems to have set its course on automatic pilot. It continues to create new programs and new spending without regard for how well current programs are doing. Few federal agencies consistently document what their programs are accomplishing to provide Congress and the American public with credible and objective evaluations of their performance.

The author wishes to thank Margaret E. Mehan, a Research Assistant in Government Studies, and Richard S. Dunn in Government Relations at The Heritage Foundation, for their able assistance with this paper. Reprinted by permission of The Heritage Foundation.

The 103rd Congress sought to correct this problem when it passed — and President Bill Clinton signed — the Government Performance and Results Act in 1993. This law has become the centerpiece of a new effort in Congress and in the Bush Administration to make federal program management, decisionmaking, and accountability even more performance-based. Efforts to truly "reinvent" the way Washington works will require a nonpartisan framework for implementing common sense government reforms. Congress and the Administration will need credible performance information, objective program evaluations, and other sound reviews of existing federal programs before they can make the sorts of changes that are needed to improve federal performance and regain the confidence of the American people.

Why Performance Measures Are Important

The Government Performance and Results Act (P.L. 103-62) was signed into law on August 3, 1993. It requires federal agencies to establish clear goals that matter to taxpayers and to report annually on their progress in meeting those goals. The bill's passage meant that, for the first time, federal agencies would have to prepare multi-year strategic plans, annual performance plans with outcome measures (rather than process-oriented measures) of existing programs, and annual performance reports for Congress.

The act's power lies in its focus on measuring the effectiveness of all existing federal programs and providing Congress with that information in order to determine whether the agencies are achieving the intended results. As Senator Ted Stevens (R-AK) explained at a hearing in June 1997:

> *If properly implemented, the Results Act will assist Congress in identifying and eliminating duplicative or ineffective programs. We intend to monitor compliance with the Results Act at every step of the way to ensure that agencies are providing us with the information necessary to do our job, spending the taxpayers' money more wisely.*[2]

Americans will benefit from such a bottom-up review of existing programs. Although the federal government should use every dollar it truly needs, the current approach is to pile new laws, regulations, and federal spending priorities on old ones without regard to effectiveness or mission overlap. As a result, the size, cost, inefficiency, and scope of the federal government continues to grow relentlessly.

For example, the growing federal entitlements consume approximately 52.7 percent of the federal budget today, compared with 26.1 percent in 1962. Although all federal spending has increased, the percentage of funding for the discretionary portions of the budget has decreased: While 67.5 percent of the budget was spent on discretionary accounts in 1962, the latest figures show discretionary spending consuming less than 34 percent — a significant squeeze that is redistributing Washington's escalating resources. Meanwhile, interest on the national debt during this same time period has increased from 6.4 percent to 13.5 percent ($220 trillion in 1999).[3]

Having access to reliable performance information is the first step in any effort to reform the government by eliminating costly waste, duplication, and error. Programs that do not work or that are redundant should be terminated, streamlined, or consolidated, and programs that could be run more efficiently by the private sector should be privatized.

The Results Act's effectiveness will depend on the willingness of Congress to engage agency officials in regular dialogue, to ask results-oriented questions at meetings or hearings, and to include the information on performance they gain from these interactions in their decisions about reauthorization, appropriations, and oversight. But even with the requirements of the Results Act, Congress may still need to demand that federal agencies provide credible, accurate, and objective information on their performance. If need be, it should seek assistance from agency inspectors general (IGs), the U.S. General Accounting Office (GAO), the Congressional Research Service (CRS), other external auditors, and its own investigators.

Congress's Increasing Focus on Performance

Congress has begun to use the performance information already provided by agencies since the Results Act was enacted in its decisions on funding, oversight, and reauthorization. However, this has occurred largely outside of media scrutiny and represents the beginning of a quiet but fundamental change in the way Washington works.

For example:

- A December 1998 CRS report showed an increased use of performance measures, particularly by appropriators during the 104th and 105th Congresses. During the 105th Congress, the CRS found 45 public laws and 78 reports accompanying bills that referenced performance measures or the Results Act. This compared with 14 public laws and 27 reports during the 104th Congress.[4]

- In June 2000, the Senate Appropriations Committee published a *Special Report on the Results Act* that presented the findings of an evaluation of major agency compliance with the act and implications for the appropriations process.

- On March 10, 1999, Representative Dan Burton (R-IN), chairman of the House Government Oversight Committee, and Representative C. W. "Bill" Young (R-FL), chairman of the House Appropriations Committee, wrote to the 24 agencies covered by the Chief Financial Officers Act, threatening to cut their funds if they did not improve agency performance, particularly on major management problems.[5]

- On March 31, 2000, Senator Fred Thompson (R-TN), chairman of the Senate Governmental Affairs Committee, asked the GAO, the CRS, and the agency inspectors general to review key policy objectives of the same 24 federal agencies to assess their performance with results that matter to the American people. For the first time in the Results Act's history, this comprehensive request will focus agencies and Congress on the government's *policies* rather than on technical compliance or process-oriented goals.[6]

❋ Since 1997, to assist in its efforts to hold federal agencies accountable, Congress has asked the GAO to produce over 200 reports, testimony, or products related to the Results Act.

Excessive Program Overlap

Assessing the federal government's performance results has been made difficult by the sheer complexity of the federal government. As the box on the next page shows, duplication and fragmentation abound among federal agencies and programs, at great cost to the taxpayer.

As the GAO reports show, dozens of programs in various agencies may be directed at the same problem. As former Comptroller General Charles Bowsher stated in testimony before the Senate Governmental Affairs Committee in 1995:

> *The case for reorganizing the federal government is an easy one to make. Many departments and agencies were created in a different time and in response to problems very different from today's. Many have accumulated responsibilities beyond their original purposes. As new challenges arose or new needs were identified, new programs and responsibilities were added to departments and agencies with insufficient regard to their effects on the overall delivery of services to the public.[7]*

David Walker, the current Comptroller General, reiterated the problems of duplication and fragmentation in recent testimony before the Senate Budget Committee:

> *Virtually all of the results that the federal government strives to achieve require the concerted and coordinated efforts of two or more federal agencies. Yet our work has repeatedly shown that mission fragmentation and program overlap are widespread and that crosscutting federal program efforts are not well*

GAO Reports Show Extensive Program Duplication and Overlap

Education: 788 federal education programs in 40 agencies cost $100 billion annual (GAO/T-HEHS-98-46). There are over 90 early childhood education programs in 11 agencies and 20 offices (GAO/HEHS-95-4FS).

Troubled Youth: 117 federal programs for at-risk youth in 15 agencies cost $4.4 billion annually (GAO/T-HEHS-98-38).

Economic Development: Little coordination exists among 342 economic development programs managed by 13 agencies (GAO/RCED-96-103).

Food Safety: The Food and Drug Administration and 11 other federal agencies administer over 35 different laws to oversee food safety (GAO/RCED-98-224).

Water: 17 programs in eight federal agencies administer rural water and wastewater programs (GAO/RCED-95-85FS).

Job Training: 163 programs administered by 15 different federal agencies cost about $20 billion annually (GAO/HEHS-95-85FS).

Terrorism: More than 40 federal agencies are involved in combating terrorism, spending $6.5 billion on unclassified activities in 1998 (GAO/T-NSIAD-98-164).

Drug Prevention: 70 federal programs in 57 different departments and offices fight the "war on drugs" at a cost of $16 billion a year (GAO/T-GGD-97-97).

Research: 17 federal departments and agencies operate 515 research and development laboratories (GAO/RCED/NSIAD-96-78R).

Statistics Gathering: 70 federal agencies collect statistics at a cost of $1.2 billion a year (GAO/T-GGD-97-78).

Exports: 10 agencies are involved with export promotion at a cost of $1.9 billion a year (GAO/NSIAD-00-119).

Services to the Homeless: 50 federal programs administered by eight federal agencies provide services to homeless people; 16 of these programs spend $1.2 billion per year (GAO/RCED-99-49).

*coordinated. In program area after program area, we have found
that unfocused and uncoordinated crosscutting programs waste
scarce resources, confuse and frustrate taxpayers and program
beneficiaries, and limit overall program effectiveness.*[8]

Walker cited a number of familiar examples, such as the 13 different federal agencies that administer over 35 different food safety laws and the eight agencies that administer 17 different programs dealing with rural water and wastewater systems.[9] Other examples noted by the GAO include 50 programs for the homeless administered by eight agencies[10] and hundreds of programs aimed at low-income urban communities. Regarding the urban programs, the GAO reported in 1995 that:

*The federal government assists distressed urban communities
and their residents through a complex system involving at least
12 federal departments and agencies. Together, these agencies
administer hundreds of programs in the areas of housing, economic development, and social services. For example, we reported that there are at least 154 employment and training
assistance programs, 59 programs that could be used for preventing substance abuse, and over 90 early childhood development programs. Considered individually, many of these
categorical programs make sense. But together, they often work
against the purposes for which they were established, according
to the National Performance Review report.*[11]

Persistent Program Obsolescence

In addition to the problem of overlapping missions, many federal agencies and programs have become obsolete, are demonstrably ineffective, or otherwise are of dubious value to the public. In connection with its testimony before the Senate Budget Committee in November 1999, the GAO submitted a list of 61 such programs.[12] Some examples are listed in the box on the next page.

As the GAO indicates, these federal services are representative of many other problems, including:

Government Performance Challenges[1]

Federal Services that Could Be Better Provided by the Private Sector:

The Power Marketing Administration, which cost $1.5 billion to operate between 1992 and 1996, provide only a small percentage of the total power consumed within a state; the program should be reassessed in light of the restructured and increasingly competitive electricity industry.

The Market Access Program subsidizes the promotion of U.S. agricultural products in overseas markets.

The Rural Utilities Service (RUS) electricity loan program has had significant financial problems. Since 1994, the RUS has written off debt of more than $2 billion, and it is now writing off an additional $3 billion.

Cargo preference laws increased the federal government's transportation costs by an estimated $578 million per year between 1989 and 1993, and continue to affect those costs today.

Federal Subsidies that Are Not Needed or Poorly Targeted:

Under the Community Development Block Grant formula, Greenwich, Connecticut, received five times more funding per person in poverty in 1995 that Camden, New Jersey, even though per capita income in Greenwich is six times greater than in Camden.

The National Flood Insurance Program has lost about $2 billion from 36 percent of its claims, which are repetitive loss properties.

The tax treatment of health insurance, amounting to $70 billion in exemptions in 1999, means that workers have little incentive to economize on consuming health insurance.

The Mining Law of 1872 allows holders of economically minable claims on federal land to obtain all the rights and interests by patenting claims for $2.50 or $5.00 an acre, well below market value.

The Medicare+Choice program was created with a forecasting error that continues to cost millions in excess payments to health plans participating in Medicare. The Health Care Financing Administration (HCFA) cannot fix this situation without a statutory change.

1.   U.S. General Accounting Office, *Budget Issues: Effective Oversight and Budget Discipline Are Essential — Even in a Time of Surplus*, GAO/T-AIMD-00-73, February 1, 2000, pp. 4-15.

Federal Facilities that Are Outmoded or Ineffective:

The Department of Defense spent 58 percent of its budget in 1998 on infrastructure requirements such as the upkeep of unnecessary and excess buildings.

Veterans' health care delivery locations could be consolidated to achieve a savings of at least $132 million.

The Department of State has no system in place for "rightsizing" posts as overseas missions change.

The Department of Energy's science budgets are spent increasingly on maintenance of obsolete and inappropriate infrastructure rather than on innovative research and development.

❀ Programs or services that could better be provided by the private sector;

❀ Outdated services or poorly designed federal subsidies;

❀ Federal facilities that are outmoded or ineffective; or

❀ Major federal investments that are not cost-effective.

Unnecessary Pork-Barrel Spending

Another common source of government waste is the pork-barrel programs and projects that spend taxpayer dollars to benefit a few special interests or small groups of people. Citizens Against Government Waste (CAGW) estimates that the appropriation bills enacted for FY 2000 contained over $17.7 billion in pork-barrel spending, a 47 percent increase over FY 1999. Since 1991, CAGW has identified a total of $100 billion in such federal spending, some examples of which are listed the box on the next page.[13]

Waste, Fraud, and Mismanagement

For all the criticism it receives, pork-barrel spending represents the legal use of taxpayer funds that have been duly appropriated for the purposes stated. But millions of federal tax dollars are lost because

Examples of Federal Pork-Barrel Spending in FY 2000[1]

Shrimp Aquaculture Research: $3.3 million for a program in Arizona, Hawaii, Massachusetts, Mississippi, and South Carolina that U.S. Department of Agriculture officials estimated would be completed in 1987. Since 1985, $45 million has been appropriated for this research.

Franklin Delano Roosevelt Memorial: An addition $3 million to expand the Roosevelt Memorial even though the House reminded the National Park Service that private fundraising efforts fell short of projections and that the expansion should not be done at taxpayer expense.

Columbus Port-of-Entry Realignment: $1 million appropriated even though the New Mexico Secretary of Transportation tried to reject this funding because the state would be liable for 25 percent of the cost of an unnecessary project.

Rural Health, Safety, and Security Institute at Mississippi Valley State University: A $2.5 million earmark added to the Labor/Health and Human Services/Education appropriations bill.

Los Angeles County Museum of Natural History: A $1 million earmark for a "Discovering the Tiniest Giants" exhibit on the newly discovered dinosaur eggs from Argentina.

Cayuga County Regional Application Center (for upstate New York): A $10 million project for Earth Science included in the Veterans Affairs/Housing and Urban Development appropriations bill.

Denali Commission: $27 million for federal economic development aid to Alaska, which already receives $636 per capita in federal aid. The national average is $25.92 per capita.

---

1. Citizens against Government Waste, *2000 Congressional Pig Book Summary*, March 2000, pp. 3, 11, 16, 25, 28, 30, 34, 40, 44, and 51.

Table 1
Waste Found by the Senate Governmental Affairs Committee

	GAO or Agency Inspector General (IG) Report	Waste in Millions of Dollars
Agriculture	Food Stamp Program overpayments for FY 1998 (GAO/AIMD-00-10)	$1,425
	Improper research expenditures (IG letter, 11/29/99)	$6.5
Commerce	National Technical Information Service, cumulative losses FY 1995-1998 (IG letter, 12/13/99)	$4.8
	Amount the National Oceanic and Atmospheric Administration spends annually on in-house aircraft above comparable private-sector costs (IG letter, 12/13/99)	$1.9
Defense	$11 billion in unneeded inventory; the U.S. Navy wrote off $3 billion of inventory as lost in transit (GAO/T-NSIAD-99-83)	$14,000
	New inventory ordered in excess of current needs (GAO/T-NSIAD-99-83)	$1,500
	Potential annual fraud and abuse in TRICARE, the military health care program (GAO/HEHS-99-142)	$500
	Between FY 1994 and FY 1998, $984 million erroneously paid to contractors that they voluntarily repaid (GAO/AIMD-00-10)	$984
Education	In FY 1997, more than $3.3 billion was paid to make good the Department's guarantee on defaulted student loans (GAO/OCG-99-5)	$3,300
	Estimated Pell Grant overpayment in 1995. 1996 caused by underreporting of income (IG report can: 11-50001, 1/97)	$177
Energy	In 1980-1996, 31 major systems acquisition projects were terminated after expenditures of over $10 billion (GAO/OCG-99-6)	$10,000
Health and Human Services	Estimate of Medicare fee-for-service overpayments for FY 1998 (IG letter, 12/7/99)	$12,600
	Improper Medicare payments in 1998 for rehabilitation services (IG letter, 12/7/99)	$1,000

Table 1 (Continued)
Waste Found by the Senate Governmental Affairs Committee

	GAO or Agency Inspector General (IG) Report	Waste in Millions of Dollars
Housing and Urban Development	Erroneous rent subsidy payments estimated to be $857 million in FY 1998, or about 5 percent of all payments (IG report 99-FO-177-0003)	$857
	Revenues lost as a result of changes in irrigation assistance repayment policies (IG letter, 12/1/99)	$1,200
	Amount by which fluid mineral royalties may have been underpaid (IG letter, 12/1/99)	$43
Interior	Losses indentified in various IG reviews based on fees that agency failed to collect or misused (IG letter, 12/1/99)	$25.8
	Losses on land exchanges that did not comply with applicable requirements (IG letter, 12/1/99)	$18.2
NASA	Cumulative cost overruns on the international Space Station (IG letter, 12/1/99)	$708
Office of Personnel Management	Cost of 1 percent premium surcharge paid to carriers (so far) to cover costs resulting from enrollment discrepencies in the Federal Employees Health Benefits Program (FEHBP). Figure represents the government's share; plan subscribers have paid another $11.9 million (IG letters of 12/1/99 and 1/7/00)	$30.5
	Estimated annual losses to fraud, waste, and abuse in the FEHBP (IG letter, 12/1/99)	$1,800
	Cost of defaulted guaranteed loans for which the guarantee should not have been honored (IG letter, 12/2/99)	$16.2
Small Business Administration	Cost of additional questionable guaranteed loans (IG letter, 12/2/99)	$3.7
	Value of Section 7(a) loans under criminal investigation which may have been procured by fraud (IG letter, 12/2/99)	$84
	Estimated loss to the government from loans procured by false certifications (IG letter, 12/2/99)	$27

Table 1 (Continued)
Waste Found by the Senate Governmental Affairs Committee

	GAO or Agency Inspector General (IG) Report	Waste in Millions of Dollars
Social Security Administration	$2.5 billion in gross receivables reported for Supplemental Security Income (SSI) overpayments. Includes $1.65 billion in new overpayments for FY 1998, out of total payments of $27 billion (GAO/AIMD-00-10)	$2,500
	Reported Old Age and Survivors Insurance overpayments for FY 1998 (GAO/AIMD-00-10)	$1,154
	Reported Disability Insurance overpayments for FY 1998 (GAO/AIMD-00-10)	$941
Treasury	Revenues that Customs and Alcohol, Tobacco and Firearms (ATF) agents failed to collect (IG letter, 12/13/99)	$651.6
Internal Revenue Service	Unpaid taxes supported by taxpayer agreements or court rulings (GAO/HR-99-1)	$90,000
	Estimated annual Earned Income Tax Credit (EITC) overpayments (IG letter, 12/1/99)	$8,000
	Estimated annual benefit overpayments from failure to deduct disability compensations from military reserve pay (IG letter, 12/10/99)	$8
	Estimated erroneous benefit payments to prisoners and deceased persons (IG letter, 12/10/99)	$103.9
Veterans Affairs	Estimated savings that could be realized from improved debt management (IG letter, 12/10/99)	$260
	Estimated future savings that could be realized by better oversight of Federal Employees Compensation Act claims (IG letter, 12/10/99)	$247

Quicker, Better, Cheaper?
Managing Performance in American Government

Table 1 (Continued)
Waste Found by the Senate Governmental Affairs Committee

	GAO or Agency Inspector General (IG) Report	Waste in Millions of Dollars
	At the close of FY 1998, delinquent non-tax debt totaled $60 billion. This is an $8.1 billion increase from FY 1996 (OMB Federal Financial Management Status Report and Five-Year Plan, June 1999)	$60,000
Multiple Agencies	According to Congressional Budget Office cost estimates, a series of GAO recommendations to improve the economy and efficiency of various government operations would save $6.5 billion in annual budget authority (GAO/OCG-99-26)	$6,500
	Estimated annual savings that could be realized by consolidating most federal in-house aircraft operations (Commerce IG letter, 12/13/99)	$92
Total Indentified Waste		**$221,284**

Source: Press release, Senate Governmental Affairs Committee, "Thompson Details $220 Billion in Government Waste," January 24, 2000; available at www.senate.gov/~gov_affairs/012400_press.htm.

of fraud and abuse and erroneous benefit payments to individuals who do not qualify for them.

Last November, Senator Fred Thompson identified $19.1 billion in improper payments to ineligible beneficiaries from large federal social programs. As Table 1 shows, his committee documented over $220 billion of wasteful federal spending, including $984 million in defense overpayments to contractors who voluntarily returned the funds over a five-year period.[14]

In 1990, the GAO began to compile a "high-risk list" of federal programs and activities that were most vulnerable to fraud, waste, abuse, and mismanagement. This high-risk list started with 14 problem areas and has been expanded with every update issued by the GAO. The current list, released in 1999, includes 26 federal agency problem areas.[15] (See Table 2.) Although new areas are added regularly, few qualify for removal. In fact, only one high-risk area has been removed since 1995. Ten of the 14 original high-risk areas in 1990 remain on the list, despite the attention the list has brought to those areas.

A similar pattern is found in the reports of agency inspectors general. In each of the past three years, the IGs of major federal agencies reported to Congress the most serious performance problems they faced. Like the GAO high-risk areas, the problems identified by the IGs remain much the same year after year.[16]

The GAO and IG reports point to several recurring root causes of these problems,[17] including the fact that most federal agencies suffer from one or more core weaknesses that would undermine the ability of any organization, whether public or private, to succeed. These weaknesses include:

❀ Pervasive financial management deficiencies;

❀ Inability to use information technology effectively; and

❀ Inability to hire, retain, and effectively manage an adequate workforce with the skills needed to carry out the agency mission.

Quicker, Better, Cheaper?
Managing Performance in American Government

Table 2

Activities and Programs Identified by GAO As "High Risk" and Year Designated

Reducing Inordinate Program Management Risks

Asset Forfeiture Programs	1990
Defense Infrastructure Management	1997
Department of Housing and Urban Development Programs	1994
Farm Loan Programs	1990
IRS Tax Filing Fraud	1995
Medicare	1990
Student Financial Aid Programs	1990
Supplemental Security Income	1997
The 2000 Census	1997

Managing Large Procurement Operations More Efficiently

DOD Inventory Management	1990
DOD Weapon Systems Acquisition	1990
DOD Contract Management	1992
Department of Energy Contract Management	1990
NASA Contract Management	1990
Superfund Contract Management	1990

Table 2 (Continued)
Activities and Programs Identified by GAO As "High Risk" and Year Designated

Ensuring that Major Technology Investments Improve Services

Air Traffic Control Modernization	1995
DOD Systems Development and Modernization Efforts	1995
National Weather Service Modernization	1995
Tax System Modernization	1995

Providing Basic Financial Accountability

DOD Financial Management	1995
Federal Aviation Administration Financial Management	1999
Forest Service Financial Management	1999
IRS Financial Management	1995
IRS Receivables	1990

Resolving Serious Information Security Weaknesses

Government Wide Year 2000 Computer Risks*	1997

Note: * No longer on the list.
Source: U.S. General Accounting Office, *Congressional Oversight: Opportunities to Address Risks, Reduce Costs, and Improve Performance*, GAO/
T-AIMD-00-96, February 2000.

129

Challenges to Implementing Reforms

Although the federal government's watchdog agencies — the GAO, Office of Management and Budget (OMB), Congressional Budget Office (CBO), and agency IGs — continue to highlight poor agency performance in their reports, and although agency Results Act reports repeatedly have exposed waste, ineffectiveness, and inefficiency, neither the Administration nor Congress has demonstrated the will to improve performance by demanding reform.

The Clinton Administration

Despite six years in office since signing the Results Act, President Clinton failed to tackle the core performance problems of the agencies under his control. Even the White House Office of Management and Budget seemingly abdicated its management responsibilities, failing to meet such specific legal obligations under the Results Act as establishing statutory pilot programs.

The stated objectives of the National Partnership for Reinvention (NPR) — a project to "reinvent government" espoused by Vice President Al Gore — were laudable. However, specific NPR projects at best merely tinker at the margins of the government's most serious performance challenges. The GAO has been unable to verify the claimed cost savings or programmatic reform from this initial effort.[18]

Little direct correlation existed between NPR projects and the "high-risk" or other mission-critical problems highlighted by the GAO and agency IGs. Indeed, the NPR's efforts often were counterproductive. Efforts to "downsize" the federal workforce, for example, occurred randomly rather than strategically, with no effort to make a distinction between essential and unnecessary employees. The indiscriminate downsizing that followed actually exacerbated many of the core performance problems within each agency.

While the direct federal payroll was reduced under the Clinton Administration, most of the cuts have come from the Department of

Figure 1
The Shadow Federal Government

One study found that in 1996, the "Shadow Government" Included 4.25 Million People Who Were Directly Employed by the Federal Government and 12.7 Million People who Performed the Work and Set the Policy of the Federal Government

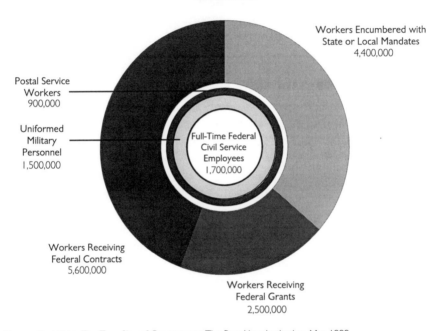

Workers Encumbered with
State or Local Mandates
4,400,000

Postal Service
Workers
900,000

Uniformed
Military
Personnel
1,500,000

Full-Time Federal
Civil Service
Employees
1,700,000

Workers Receiving
Federal Contracts
5,600,000

Workers Receiving
Federal Grants
2,500,000

Source: Paul Light, *The True Size of Government*, The Brookings Institution, May 1999.

Defense budget and have more to do with the end of the Cold War than with the NPR. Also, many former federal jobs migrated to a "shadow" federal workforce consisting of contractors, state and local employees, and private-sector employees who spend valuable time carrying out the federal mandates (see Figure 1). For example, the Department of Education may show a 6 percent reduction in federal civil servants, but it experienced at the same time a 129 percent increase in the number of contract workers.[19] Considering all those working to carry out federal mandates, the number of people employed by the "shadow" federal government is actually much larger than the number on the federal government's direct payroll.

Congress

With the exception of admirable attempts by two members of the House and Senate — Senator Fred Thompson, former Republican chairman of the Governmental Affairs Committee; and Representative Steve Horn (R-CA), chairman of the Government Management, Information, and Technology Subcommittee of the House Committee on Government Reform — to use their committees' jurisdiction to expose waste and mismanagement, Congress has shown limited leadership in this regard.

To date, Congress has done a relatively poor job of forcing agencies to improve their efficiency and cut waste. One reason for this mediocre performance is that the annual appropriations process itself is inefficient and consumes huge amounts of time and effort.[20] It is virtually impossible for Congress to enact the 13 regular appropriations bills by the start of each new fiscal year.

Consequently, the usual finale to the appropriations cycle is a massive omnibus bill pulled together at the end of each session after intensive 11th-hour negotiations. These negotiations typically involve very few participants and take place out of the public eye. Most Members of Congress have only the vaguest idea of what they are voting on when they approve the omnibus bill. Following its enactment, it can often take weeks to sort out what is included in the spending bills. This end-of-session process is so intensive and exhausting that mistakes are inevitable and the participants are left feeling like victims.

One reason for the breakdown in the appropriations process is the increasing burden of substantive legislative provisions that can be enacted only as part of "must pass" spending bills. This problem stems from the inability of Congress to enact authorizing legislation for many spending programs during the regular course of business.

The Congressional Budget Office recently reported that Congress had enacted about $121 billion in FY 2000 spending for programs whose authorization had already expired.[21] This included about $8.2 billion in funding for foreign aid programs that were last authorized in 1987 and $4.4 billion for Department of Energy programs last authorized in 1984. The CBO report does not take into account funding for programs that never were authorized. Appropriating funds for unauthorized programs violates both House and Senate rules, yet these rules are routinely waived as a way to garner necessary votes to pass critical legislation. Controversial reauthorization efforts are not likely to be passed if slim margins exist between the two parties.

Adding to the difficulties Congress encounters in passing legislation is the fact that it rarely conducts meaningful oversight of existing programs and activities to determine which ones are working and which are not. Currently, most oversight activity focuses on alleged scandals or consists of quick expositions of isolated problems with no follow-up. As Senator George Voinovich (R-OH) recently observed:

> [F]rom career bureaucrats to Cabinet Secretaries, nearly everyone in the Executive branch knows that when they're asked to come up to the Hill for an oversight hearing, once it's over, it's over — rarely do they have to worry about any follow-up hearings because Congress just doesn't have the time.[22]

It should be noted that some congressional committees provide valuable feedback to agencies on their performance information, and this feedback has encouraged an improved policy debate between Capitol Hill and the agencies. These committees include the Senate's Governmental Affairs and Appropriations Committees and the House's Education and Workforce, Science, Transportation, and Veterans Affairs Committees.

Congress as a whole, however, tends to focus on *passing legislation* to effect permanent change in the government. Legislating is what Members of Congress do, and what their staff and the press focus on. Overseeing existing laws and programs, on the other hand, takes specialized knowledge about such programs, agency budgets, personnel, media, and even the U.S. General Accounting Office. Different skills — such as the tenacity to find the truth, the ability to work with the press, or the commitment to protect witnesses who risk their livelihoods and reputations to tell the truth

— are needed if the oversight function is to convey a compelling case for change.

What Washington Must Do

There is much that can be done to improve the federal government in tangible, nonpartisan ways that transcend policy stalemates and bridge the political divides in Washington. An agenda along these lines should start from and build on basic common sense principles that address concerns upon which most people can agree, regardless of their political leanings.

Any new orientation for government, however, must rest on a foundation of objective and credible performance data that enable Congress, the President, and the American public to see what is being accomplished with the tax dollars collected. Yet, in a significant warning to Congress and the agency offices of inspectors general, the GAO recently said that 20 of 24 major agencies are incapable of providing credible performance data on the objectives they are trying to achieve.[23]

Moreover, the information they do provide is often misleading. For example, the Legal Services Corporation (LSC) reports to Congress each year the number of cases in which federal dollars provided legal assistance to the poor. This figure is used to support its request for sustained or additional funds. However, in 1999, evidence of widespread over-reporting of case figures by the LSC was disclosed. Based on case reports submitted by 269 LSC grantees across the country, the LSC reported that 471,600 cases remained open at the end of 1997, while 1,461,013 cases had been closed during the year. The 1997 program had received funding totaling $511.8 million from Congress and non-LSC sources. Based on the reported closed case count, the average cost per case for the entire 1997 program was $350.

After months of denying a problem and under pressure from Congress, the media, and the GAO, the LSC reported in September 1999 that in 1998 it closed only 1.1 million cases — about 360,000 fewer than it reported closed in 1997. This is the lowest recorded and reported closed case-count total in the history of the agency. The lower number translates into a $465 average cost per case, which is the highest cost of federal aid to the poor in the history of the program.[24]

Such a difference is important in evaluating the agency's effectiveness. If Congress receives incomplete or inaccurate information about an agency's performance, its subsequent decision will not correct the problem; the inefficiency will continue, and public cynicism will likely increase.

Good information, on the other hand, can result in tangible improvements in the way government delivers its services. For example:

❀ Using the Veterans Health Administration (VHA) database, veterans' hospitals began to compare their own performance with other hospitals. Based on the various success rates for cardiac surgeries, the VHA made changes in how it conducted diagnostic testing to handle post-operative procedures. According to the GAO, the VHA found that the performance data showed that cardiac teams had lowered their mortality rates between 1988 and 1996 by an average of 13 percent.[25]

❀ When towing industry data for 1982 through 1991 showed that 62 percent of marine casualties were due to human error, the U.S. Coast Guard realigned its marine safety program away from inspections (outputs) and toward efforts to reduce casualties (outcomes). This joint effort between the Coast Guard and the shipping and towing industry, which began in 1994, brought about a decline in the fatality rate — from 91 per 100,000 employees in 1991 to 27 per 100,000 employees in 1995. The program not only improved the Coast Guard's effectiveness, but did so with fewer people and at a lower cost.[26]

Congress and the Administration must continue to assess — systematically and continuously — what federal agencies and programs are in fact accomplishing with their tax dollars. Funding should be linked to actions that lead to positive performance results. To do this, a number of steps must be taken by both branches of government.

The Administration

To improve management of government, the Bush Administration should:

❀ **Manage for results by focusing agency performance and accountability requirements on key outcomes.** Selecting appropriate measurements of performance, obtaining credible data, and using those data to make decisions are activities that should occur with greater regularity within the federal government. Some agencies are driving over 900 measures through their systems to comply with the Results Act. The law would work better if fewer, more manageable numbers of measures were used on priority programs.

❀ **Link funding to performance results by attaching consequences to good and bad performance.** The Administration, the OMB, and the agencies must tie funding of specific programs to performance in their budget formulations. Agencies and programs that pursue and achieve important results should be rewarded in financial and non-financial ways, including public recognition. Those that do not achieve good results should be fixed or eliminated.

❀ **Link related program actions to performance results.** More needs to be done to coordinate and rationalize the myriad overlapping or duplicative programs that now exist. New interagency coordination teams should share valuable performance measures and data, using the same performance measures to determine which programs are working and which are not. It is particularly important that Administration proposals for new or revised programs identify the intended results and point out how the programs relate to similar existing programs.

❀ **Subject administrative regulations to the same performance scrutiny and accountability that apply to programs and activities.** Regulations should incorporate specific outcome-oriented performance goals and measures to the extent possible.

❀ **Resolve mission-critical management problems that could undermine the capacity of agencies to achieve results.** Many of the recurring performance problems stem from a lack of sustained commitment to resolve them. Experience demonstrates that an effective way to focus accountability on problems is for agency heads to adopt specific and measurable performance goals to address those problems.

❀ **Suggest legislation to promote pay-for-performance in the federal civil service.** Innovations are needed in the federal pay system that transform the inflexible pay and bonus systems into a more merit-based system with incentives that reward managers for achieving program outcomes. Incentive bonus programs need to be flexible enough to reward top performers and innovations in the federal government.

❀ **Require agency heads to form performance-based organizations (PBOs).** These PBO units have a competitively hired chief operating officer who commits to annual performance agreements and agrees to tie a share of his or her pay to the organization's performance. (Nine agencies are already structured this way.) The chief operating officers have broad latitude to design reward systems and management processes that meet their agency's needs. Pay adjustments are based on performance. Bonuses are available for superior individual or group accomplishments, documented productivity gains, or sustained superior performance.

❀ **Expand performance-based contracting.** Performance-based contracting should be the rule rather than
the exception in the federal government. Federal contractors should be held to a higher standard for achieving results; payment should be withheld until contract
performance is met. Awarding contracts for noble purposes but without follow-up that ensures that quality
service has been delivered should end. Stricter contracts
and better monitoring to assure accountability are necessary; otherwise, the people who should benefit from
the program will suffer.

Congress

To increase its oversight of existing programs and laws, Congress
should:

❀ **Conduct comprehensive, systematic reviews of the
stated goals of agencies within committee jurisdictions.** Regular bipartisan and systematic oversight of
what the federal agencies are accomplishing and how
performance could be improved should be conducted
by each House and Senate committee. Agency performance plans and reports submitted according to the Results Act should be used in this effort because they can
promote more informed policy discussions and debates. Too often, Congress considers its job done once
programs are enacted by law. Before passing authorizing or reauthorizing legislation, committees should be
able to fully appreciate what past federal allocations
have accomplished. Committee members should monitor the rulemaking and enforcement stages of the laws
they pass by holding more hearings, having more briefings, commissioning better GAO studies, or working
with the agency IGs. The information gained should be
used to identify whether the private sector or the state
or local government is in a better position than the federal government to accomplish the stated goal.

❀ **Enact authorizing legislation for spending programs.** Congress regularly ignores its own rules and approves hundreds of billions of dollars in unauthorized spending each year. Congress should enforce its rules that prohibit the consideration of appropriations for unauthorized programs. If the votes to authorize a program through the normal legislative process are not certain, the program should not be funded.

❀ **Incorporate specific performance goals and measures in authorizing legislation.** Congress should adopt rules prohibiting the consideration of significant program authorization or reauthorization legislation unless that legislation incorporates specific performance goals and measures. Congress should insist that the Administration address these issues as well when it submits a new budget or program proposals.

❀ **Incorporate regular program evaluations into key spending priorities.** Congress has been reluctant and often even negligent in demanding sound studies of program effectiveness from agencies. These evaluations should consume an increasing portion of the GAO's workload or should be contracted out to independent accountability professionals.

❀ **Enact appropriations bills on a timely basis that provide funding based on proven performance.** Congress should start enforcing the "regular order" through which decisions on individual appropriations bills are openly and knowingly made. It should also practice "truth in budgeting" by abandoning accounting gimmicks that often make a mockery of the appropriations process.

❀ **Consider adopting a biennial budget.** Sentiment is growing that the only way to effect fundamental reform of the appropriations process is by moving to a biennial budget cycle. A biennial process would have the added benefit of freeing more time for Congress to improve oversight of the federal bureaucracy. Regardless of the budget process timeline, Congress and the executive branch must have the will to make the funding decisions in a more timely and appropriate way.

Conclusion

Washington largely ignores the day-to-day functioning of the massive federal bureaucracy, but its blinders are exacting a toll on federal agency performance, as well as on the public's perception of and trust in the government.

If Congress and the Administration continue to seek Results Act reports from federal agencies and ensure, with help from the offices of inspectors general and the GAO, that the performance information they provide is credible and objective, the American public will be better able to identify which techniques of lawmaking — regulations, tax incentives, subsidies, grants, partnerships, or education campaigns — are most effective. Ineffective efforts could be fixed or eliminated.

Yet performance-based data will be useless unless Congress brings this information alive in oversight hearings, floor debates, or changes in authorizing or spending legislation. A results-oriented approach that adheres to the principles of accountability and performance results could lead to a smaller, smarter, more commonsense federal government that is truly worthy of Americans' trust as well as their hard-earned tax dollars.

Endnotes

1   Pew Research Center for the People and the Press, "Deconstructing Distrust: How Americans View Government," March 10, 1998; available at www.people-press.org/trustrpt.htm.

2   Statement of Senator Ted Stevens, Chairman of the Senate Appropriations Committee, at a joint hearing with the Senate Governmental Affairs Committee on *Implementation of the Results Act*, S. Hrng. 105-198, June 24, 1997, p. 2.

3   See *Historical Tables: Budget of the United States Government, Fiscal Year 2001*, pp. 110-111, 119.

4   Genevieve J. Knezo and Virginia McMurtry, "Performance Measure Provisions in the 105th Congress: Analysis of a Selected Compilation," Congressional Research

Service, December 1998, p. 3; available at www.freedom.gov/results/crs/getsresults-sum.asp.

5 March 10, 1999; referenced at www.house.gov/reform/press/99.03.10.a.htm.

6 March 31, 2000; referenced at www.senate.gov/~gov_affairs/040400_walker_letter.pdf.

7 U.S. General Accounting Office, *Government Reorganization: Issues and Principles*, GAO/T-GGD/AIMD-95-166, May 17, 1995, pp. 2-3.

8 U.S. General Accounting Office, *Budget Issues: Effective Oversight and Budget Discipline Are Essential — Even in a Time of Surplus*, GAO/T-AIMD-00-73, February 1, 2000, p. 11.

9 *Ibid.*, pp. 11-12.

10 U.S. General Accounting Office, *Homelessness: Coordination and Evaluation of Programs Are Essential*, GAO/RCED-99-49, February 26, 1999, p. 2.

11 U.S. General Accounting Office, *Community Development: Challenges Face Comprehensive Approaches to Address Needs of Distressed Neighborhoods*, GAO/RCED-95-262, August 3, 1995, p. 4.

12 U.S. General Accounting Office, *Potential Candidates for Congressional Oversight*, GAO/OCG-00-3R, November 1, 1999.

13 Citizens against Government Waste, *2000 Congressional Pig Book Summary*, March 2000, pp. 1.

14 Press release, Senate Governmental Affairs Committee, "Thompson Details $220 Billion in Government Waste," January 24, 2000; available at www.senate.gov/~gov_affairs/012400_htm.

15 U.S. General Accounting Office, *High-Risk Series: An Update*, GAO/HR-99-1, January 1999.

16 The one notable exception most recently was the Year 2000 (Y2K) computer conversion problem.

17 U.S. General Accounting Office, *Major Management Challenges and Program Risks: A Government-Wide Perspective*, GAO/OCG-99-1, January 1999.

18 U.S. General Accounting Office, testimony of Christopher Mihm before the Senate Governmental Affairs Subcommittee on Government Management, Restructuring and the District of Columbia, *Management Reform: Continuing Attention Is Needed to Improve Government Performance*, GAO/T-GGD-00-128, May 4, 2000, and *NPR's Savings: Claimed Agency Savings Cannot All Be Attributed to NPR*, GAO/GGD-99-120, July 1999.

19 See generally, Paul C. Light, *The True Size of Government* (Washington, D.C.: Brookings Institution Press, 1999).

20 For example, at least half of all Senate roll-call votes for each year since 1991 have been related to the annual budget. In 1996, 73 percent of all roll-call votes were budget-related. *See Senate Report No. 106-12 on S. 92*, Committee on Governmental Affairs, U.S. Senate, 106th Congress, 2nd Session, 1999, pp. 6-7.

21 Congressional Budget Office, *Unauthorized Appropriations and Expiring Authorizations*, January 7, 2000.

22 *Congressional Record*, February 2, 2000, p. S291.

23 U.S. General Accounting Office, *Managing for Results: Challenges Agencies Face in Producing Credible Performance Information*, GAO/GGD-00-52, February 2000, p. 6.

24 For more information, see Virginia L. Thomas and Ryan Rogers, "Time to Hold the Legal Services Corporation Accountable," Heritage Foundation Backgrounder No. 1312, July 22, 1999; available at www.heritage.org/library/backgrounder/ bg1312.html.

25 U.S. General Accounting Office, *Executive Guide: Effectively Implementing the Government Performance and Results Act*, GAO/GGD-96-118, June 1996, pp. 32-33.

26 *Ibid.*, pp. 36-37.

7

The Social Security Administration and Performance Management

Walter D. Broadnax and Kevin J. Conway

The Government Performance and Results Act (GPRA) is the most recent in a long series of initiatives designed to improve management in federal agencies. This chapter examines one agency, the Social Security Administration (SSA), and its experience implementing the tenets of performance management. SSA was selected as the focus of our study for several reasons. First, the agency is one of the most well known and easily recognized agencies at the federal level, and its influence is felt by virtually every American. Second, SSA has historically been committed to customer service and continuously sought better ways to serve its beneficiaries. And third, SSA has a long tradition of management reform. If the goal is a successful performance management initiative, SSA should have a better-than-average chance of fulfilling that goal.

We base our information on interviews with over 45 individuals,[1] including SSA employees at all levels of the agency, House and Senate Committee staffers, and the General Accounting Office (GAO).[2] We have supplemented that information with SSA publications and written correspondence, committee reports and testimony, GAO documents, and data from nongovernmental sources.

Taken together, this information yields a dynamic story showing how SSA has managed to successfully implement GPRA and performance management initiatives.

SSA's success, we argue, is a result of several related factors. First, the agency is led by a commissioner who has embraced performance management and sought to ingrain its tenets into the very fabric of the organization. Second, SSA cooperates closely with the relevant congressional committees and the GAO. This shared commitment has improved the delivery of benefits and helped the agency overcome and avoid many obstacles. Third, the agency has made a concerted effort to push its vision of performance management down and throughout the organization — a real challenge given its size and structure. Fourth, SSA has built accountability measures into virtually all facets of its strategic and performance plans. More importantly, accountability is incorporated into the daily management of programs. Finally, SSA's history of management reforms has taught the agency that no management tool is ever perfect and the agency continually looks for ways to improve its performance. We hope that other organizations will be able to extract from the SSA experience a useful guide in their own quest to improve performance.

The Social Security Administration

The Social Security Act of 1935 and its subsequent amendments created the Social Security Administration (SSA) and established the basic framework for a national "safety net" for elderly Americans, disabled workers and their dependents, as well as the poor aged, blind, or disabled. SSA administers three major entitlement programs that together deliver cash benefits to about 50 million beneficiaries every month — roughly one in every five Americans.[3]

To shoulder this responsibility, SSA relies on a national infrastructure headquartered in Baltimore, MD. That office is supplemented by 10 regional offices across the country, 7 processing centers, 1,343 field offices, 1 data operations center, 36 teleservice centers, 132 hearings offices, and 65,000 employees. SSA also depends on 54 Disability Determination Services (DDS) located in all

50 states plus the District of Columbia, Guam, and Puerto Rico.[4] This organizational structure is meant to provide both swift and accurate service to the public. The structure has been enhanced by SSA's 800-number telephone service, which served 58.8 million customers in FY1999 alone.[5]

The key feature of the Social Security Act is Old Age Survivors' Insurance (OASI). This program, funded through payroll taxes[6], covers more than 90 percent of all workers. The only large group it does not cover is federal employees, who have their own retirement system. Under OASI, an insured worker is eligible for monthly cash benefits upon retirement[7] and eligible dependents and survivors also receive benefits. The amount received is determined by two basic factors: age at entitlement, and the amount earned during the insured's working years.[8] In 1999, 91 percent of people 65 or over were receiving OASI benefits.

SSA also administers the Disability Insurance (DI) program, which was added by amendment in 1956. The DI program, funded through payroll taxes, provides benefits to disabled workers and their eligible dependents. As of 1999, three of four working Americans age 21 through 64 are covered under DI and can count on benefits if they become disabled. Together, OASI and DI are popularly known to most Americans as Social Security since they provide comprehensive protection against loss of earnings owing to retirement, disability, and death.

The third program is the Supplemental Security Income (SSI) program.[9] SSI, added by amendment in 1974, is a means-tested program funded through general revenues that pays monthly cash benefits to aged, blind, or disabled people with limited income and resources. SSI uses the same definitions of disability and blindness as the DI program, but unlike OASI and DI, eligibility for SSI does not require a work history.[10]

The growth of all three programs has been dramatic, as reflected in Table 1. In 1940, only 222,488 people received monthly Social Security benefits; that number grew to 44.6 million people by 1999. The SSI program has seen similar growth, nearly doubling since its inception in 1974. The large number of beneficiaries for these programs translates into enormous sums of money that SSA disburses each month. Table 2 compares the growth of OASI/DI and SSI program expenditures. In 1999 alone, OASI/DI programs paid beneficiaries $385.8 billion while the SSI program disbursed $30.1 billion.

Table 1: Number of Social Security Administration Beneficiaries Over the Years			
Old Age Survivors' Insurance/ Disability Insurance		*Supplemental Security Income*	
1937	53,236*	1974	3,996,064
1938	213,670*	1975	4,314,275
1939	174,839*	1980	4,142,017
1940	222,488	1985	4,138,021
1950	3,477,243	1990	4,817,127
1960	14,844,589	1995	6,514,134
1970	26,228,629	1996	6,613,718
1980	35,584,955	1997	6,494,985
1990	39,832,125	1998	6,566,069
1995	43,387,259	1999	6,556,634
1996	43,736,836		
1997	43,971,086		
1998	44,245,731		
1999	44,595,624		

Source: OASI/DI and SSI data for 1937 through 1999 as listed in "Social Security: A Brief History," SSA 2000a as of November 27, 2000.
* Recipients of one-time lump-sum payments.

These programs differ in the level of administrative complexity, however — and thus influences how SSA manages them. Because OASI deals with retirement benefits based on a known work history, the program is relatively uncomplicated to administer once an applicant's eligibility is confirmed. The DI and SSI programs tend to be much more complex because of the inherent difficulties of determining what constitutes a disability, as well as the sensitive nature of monitoring a claimant's disability. For example, each program defines "disability" as a physical or mental condition that is permanent or can be expected to last for a continuous period of not less than 12 months and prevents the claimant from working. Yet because of advances in medical science and workplace adaptability, what was a disability yesterday may not be a disability tomorrow. SSI is further complicated by the fact that even slight changes in a recipient's monthly income can require the program to reestimate benefit levels. And while SSA monitors financial status and claimants are required to report income changes, delays in adjustment are likely.

Table 2: Social Security Administration Payments Over the Years			
Old Age Survivors' Insurance/Disability Insurance		*Supplemental Security Income*	
1937	$1,278,000	1974	$5,096,813,000
1938	$10,478,000	1975	$5,716,072,000
1939	$13,896,000	1980	$7,714,640,000
1940	$35,000,000	1985	$10,749,938,000
1950	$961,000,000	1990	$16,132,959,000
1960	$11,245,000,000	1995	$27,037,280,000
1970	$31,863,000,000	1996	$28,252,474,000
1980	$120,511,000,000	1997	$28,370,568,000
1990	$247,796,000,000	1998	$29,408,208,000
1995	$322,553,000,000	1999	$30,106,032,000
1996	$347,088,000,000		
1997	$361,970,000,000		
1998	$374,990,000,000		
1999	$385,768,000,000		
Source: OASI/DI and SSI data for 1937 through 1999 as listed in "Social Security: A Brief History," SSA 2000a as of November 27, 2000.			

Such complexity prompted SSA to engage in intense strategic planning exercises long before passage of GPRA. This vast experience, along with the agency's willingness to constantly evolve, is one of the major management lessons of SSA's successful implementation of GPRA. SSA officials recognize that "at this point in managing for results, performance measurement has to be described as an imperfect place, at best. But I think it is always going to be that way. To the extent GPRA survives, you are going to see more and more evolution." In both philosophy and deed, SSA has positioned itself to make improvements at each step of the process and find better ways of doing the public's business.

SSA published its first long-range strategic plan in 1988 and a significantly revised version, entitled "Framework for the Future," three years later. The latter laid out agency goals and objectives and established five strategic priorities. Under a unified planning system created in 1992, SSA linked strategic, tactical, and budget planning processes. And in 1995, the agency published its first annual "business plan," which describes overall business strategy for the coming fiscal year, presents targets for agency performance indicators, and describes key initiatives as well as tactical plans for implementing them. So while strategic planning and developing measurable goals were foreign to many agencies, they are a part of SSA's culture. Still, even SSA has had to confront hurdles in implementing performance management.

GPRA, SSA, and the
Power of the 800-Number

GPRA distinguishes between types of measures, focusing particularly on outputs and outcomes. Outputs are completed activities (process and/or workload measures) that can be described in quantitative or qualitative terms and reflect products or services produced by a program and delivered to customers. Outcomes are the results impact of a program activity compared with its intended purpose. GPRA looks to push performance measures toward outcomes by asking: what difference does it all make?

Measuring outcomes is somewhat difficult at SSA because so much of what the agency does is process-oriented. While SSA has always been adept at measuring outputs like time and productivity rates, for example, agency officials admit that "SSA doesn't have much experience or comfort level with this type of orientation." The decentralized nature of various processing tasks further reinforces the tendency toward measuring outputs. For example, it is relatively easy to provide 1,343 field offices with reports on timeliness and efficiency, but it becomes significantly more difficult and expensive to produce data on outcomes such as work accuracy for each of those offices.

GAO has criticized SSA for its inability to differentiate between outputs and outcomes. One particular criticism has concerned the agency's effort to speed up eligibility determination and move claimants onto disability rolls. While this effort is important to the well-being of eligible individuals and their families, GAO has noted that SSA fails to put an equal degree of emphasis on helping claimants return to work and moving them off disability rolls.[11] Hill staffers concur: "Moving people off the disability rolls is an outcome that SSA could probably do more with trying to transition people from disability to work status." Simply put, SSA is quite competent in processing disability claims, but has more difficulty assisting claimants in their efforts to return to a working life.

In essence, then, GPRA forces SSA to measure the more difficult tasks. But it also forces SSA, like other agencies, to ask whether established measures actually improve customer service. SSA's most visible performance measure — 800-number access — offers a prime example of how the agency dealt with these challenges. The evolution of the 800-number system, both pre- and post-GPRA, underscores the tensions that can arise when an agency specifies an imperfect target indicator, diverts substantial resources towards attaining it, and then struggles to improve upon that imperfect measure.

SSA's national toll-free 800-number represents one of the world's largest telephone networks. Initiated in October 1988 to improve customer service, SSA now has 3,900 teleservice representatives (TSRs) answering phones from 36 teleservice centers (TSCs), supplemented by a "spike" cadre of 3,200 employees — employees from other areas of SSA who assist TSRs during peak demand.[12] Through direct person-to-person contact and automated options, callers may use the 800-number to implement a wide range of transactions.

Demand for the 800-number service has grown dramatically.[13] In its first full year of operation (1989) over 39 million calls were placed.[14] That number peaked at 121.4 million in 1995, but fell sharply as improved technology allowed more callers to get through on their first attempt. In 1999, the number of calls placed stood at 78.7 million.[15] More meaningful, however, is the number of calls *actually handled* by TSRs or the automated service.[16] This number has risen steadily from 42.8 million in 1995 to 58.8 million in 1999.[17] The 58.8 million calls — 23 percent of which were handled by the automated system — represent approximately 236,000 calls each workday.[18]

Responding to the increased interest, SSA in 1994 sought to provide access to the 800-number, without a busy signal, within 5 minutes of the caller's first try. This was a dramatic shift in SSA's priorities from the previous target of providing access within 24 *hours* of the caller's first try.[19] SSA then applied percentage goals to the new access rate — 85 percent in 1996 and 95 percent in 1997. In the first years of GPRA, 95/5 access (95 percent of callers in 5 minutes) has been a cornerstone indicator in achieving SSA's second strategic objective — world-class service.

SSA's performance has matched its increasingly aggressive goal. While only 74 percent of callers reached SSA within the first 5 minutes in 1995, that rate rose to 83 percent in 1996 — falling just short of the established goal by 2 percent. SSA exceeded the 95/5 goal in 1997 with a 96.2 percent access rate and met it in each of the following two years, with a 95.3 and 95.8 rate in 1998 and 1999, respectively.[20]

The 95/5 access rate is more than a mere percentage: quick access affects how people perceive the agency. A recent survey conducted by SSA's Office of Finance, Assessment and Management showed that 84 percent of callers rated their overall service as "good," "very good," or "excellent," while 78 percent of callers gave similar marks for access. And the ratings follow a pattern based on access: customer satisfaction reaches "92 percent for service overall and 94 percent for access for callers who get through right away. Satisfaction falls to 73 percent and 58 percent, respectively, when callers experience both a busy signal/message and time waiting on hold."[21]

Unfortunately, success in achieving 95/5 access and high customer satisfaction rates has come at a price. Because TSC resources have not expanded commensurately with growing demand, SSA has had to look elsewhere for resources. The agency has managed to handle the higher volume while maintaining access rates largely by training and diverting employees from other offices — primarily from the Program Service Center (PSC) — to answer calls during peak periods.[22] Yet demand is consistently so high that all PSC spikes rarely dedicate their entire workday to their primary assignments. Of the 251 workdays in 2000, for example, the annual workplan for SSA's Philadelphia Region Processing Center Operations (PCO) require spikes for all but 33 days.[23] Nationwide in 1999, spikes handled 24.6 percent of 800-number network calls.

Transferring these resources has adversely affected pending workloads. PSC employees are "back-end" operators responsible for post-entitlement actions that fall out of the automated process. Their tasks include processing difficult and complex claims, mailing out complex notices, and managing debt collection activities. Their work often affects the payments existing beneficiaries receive each month. But answering 800-number calls has become such a major workload for PSCs that their traditional duties have suffered. Before the demanding access targets took effect, PSCs ended fiscal years with about 2 weeks of pending work. But at the end of 1996, when the target was 85 percent, these centers finished the year with 3.5 weeks of pending work despite 840,000 hours of overtime.[24]

And pending workloads represent more than simple paper files. "Each pending is an actual person whose account needs to be reviewed. That pending relates to a definite, existing beneficiary." The GAO has reported that "delays in processing these workloads can affect SSA payments to beneficiaries and have caused additional inquiries to the 800 number by affected customers."[25] While SSA does not track the extent to which people call the 800-number owing to delays in processing transactions, our interviews with many SSA employees corroborate this contention. TSRs, their managers, and regional officials alike have made the connection that PSC backlogs create more 800-number inquiries, prompting more frequent use of spikes — leading to even more PSC delays.

In view of this unintended result, the broader question becomes whether the 95/5 access goal is justifiable. In late 1999, Commissioner Kenneth Apfel implemented several short-term initiatives to sustain the access rate goal and mitigate the impact of spiking on PSC pending workloads.[26] In essence, he realized that changes were necessary but was not yet ready to back down from the aggressive access goal. However, across-the-board budget cuts for FY2000 prompted SSA to make the difficult decision to reduce the access goal to 92 percent of callers in 5 minutes (92/5) because PSC backlogs would have grown to unacceptable levels.

But more than a mere question of resources, many SSA managers at the local, regional, and national level believe the 800-number access target raises the question of priorities. While all agree an access standard is a necessary component of performance management, many SSA officials believe the 95/5 goal — and now the 92/5 goal — may be doing more harm than good. They argue that a caller to the 800-number *may or may not* be a beneficiary that needs a question answered, yet *every* pending file represents an existing beneficiary whose benefit adjustment is delayed. The choice, then, is between achieving a visible, easily monitored target and reducing pending workloads so that actual beneficiaries receive the attention required to correct their benefits.

Although 800-number access is an output measure based on traditional concepts of performance management, some congressional committee staffers also question whether this indicator is the type emphasized by GPRA. Some suggest updating the target to reflect the "three-ring or fifteen-second standard" of private-sector telemarketing firms, while others argue that SSA should not focus so much on how quickly employees answer a call but on whether they provide correct answers. Nonetheless, because access has an impact on outcomes — the public's perception of SSA's competence — the 800-number is soundly rooted in GPRA's philosophy.

While some may view such debate as a sign of planning problems, we argue the opposite. The philosophy of GPRA and performance management allows for — and even encourages — continuous discussions about how best to achieve certain goals and objectives. GPRA itself underscores the changing nature of politics and practices and demands that agencies constantly reevaluate their priorities. The debate within and around SSA regarding 800-number access is one meaningful example of how the agency is taking the philosophy of GPRA to heart by engaging in discussions that reevaluate the way they conduct business. And members of Congress appreciate this effort. A Senate Committee remarked that "SSA is an agency that cares about selecting appropriate measures . . . and, that interest and commitment comes from the top of the agency. That helps a lot — you don't necessarily get that from all agencies."

SSA's Strategic Plan

Towards the end of GPRA's pilot phase, GAO reported that SSA was a frontrunner among federal agencies in developing a performance management framework.[27] In 1999, SSA received the highest marks for government management among federal agencies in a survey conducted by the Maxwell School at Syracuse University and *Government Executive* magazine.[28] The survey evaluated 15 federal agencies on five critical management areas[29] and awarded SSA the only overall "A" grade. Later that year, SSA was one of only two federal agencies to receive the Association of Government Accountants' Certificate of Excellence in Accountability Reporting for its *Accountability Report for Fiscal Year 1998*.

In meeting the first requirement of GPRA, SSA's framework for measuring performance is set forth in the agency strategic plan "Keeping the Promise," released in September 1997. Codifying the SSA's mission was a rather simple task because the agency "has always had a strong sense of mission." Some argue, in fact, that SSA's success is due primarily to its specific mission because "Social Security faces fewer challenges than other agencies. It's a discrete, holistic agency compared to a lot of departments and other agencies." While it is true that the mission of SSA lends itself well to the use of GPRA in measuring certain performance indicators, we argue that the agency's history of strategic planning and the other lessons we highlight are the reasons for the agency's success.

Although SSA is responsible for over 50 million beneficiaries each month, its mission statement is quite brief: *"To promote the economic security of the nation's people through compassionate and vigilant leadership in shaping and managing America's social security programs."*[30] Five strategic goals, listed in Table 3, flow directly from that mission statement, and a set of objectives flows from each of those strategic goals. Executive sponsors, who answer directly to the commissioner, are accountable for achieving each of these strategic objectives.

Table 3: Social Security Administration's Five Strategic Goals	
Strategic Goal	*Definition*
Responsive Programs	To promote valued, strong, and responsive social security programs and conduct effective policy development, research, and program evaluation.
World-Class Service	To deliver customer-responsive world class service.
Best-in-Business Program Management	To make SSA program management the best in business, with zero tolerance for fraud and abuse.
Valued Employees	To be an employer that values and invests in each employee.
Public Understanding	To strengthen public understanding of the social security programs.

Source: Listed in the Social Security Administration's *Annual Performance Plan for Fiscal Year 2001.*

Given the public nature of GPRA, some within SSA were initially uneasy about publishing such specific objectives and measures, preferring to describe even the agency's vision in "softer" words. But these pockets of nervousness and hesitancy quickly dissipated. In fact, the agency now "takes pride in the fact that it has made outside commitments and will meet them if it's at all possible."

The agency used an inclusive process to devise its mission, goals, and objectives. The driving force behind the plan was a committee of 42 senior executives drawn from all of SSA's components. This committee first reviewed information received from stakeholders collected over the previous four years to identify recurring priorities and preferences. The agency then conducted focus groups with employees and briefed unions and management associations early in the process. Throughout the process of developing the plan, the agency consulted with the Office of Management and Budget, Congress, and GAO.[31] SSA is now updating its strategic plan, initiating that process in June 1999 with a stakeholders' meeting attended by representatives from management, unions, and state agencies, as well as an expanded strategic planning committee. Thus, SSA has made sure that employees at every level were involved in developing the agency vision. As one executive put it, "While the emphasis and the seriousness of the effort is being directed from the top . . . the process belongs to all."

The committee submitted its original findings and recommendations to SSA's Office of Strategic Management (OSM) to formalize into a comprehensive document. OSM then began a practice that has improved implementation of performance management at each stage. Specifically, SSA established a cooperative, pro-active partnership with Congress and its committees. To a degree, the positive relationship emanates from the fact that there are risks on both sides and each would fare better by working together. The committees have not looked to publically chastise SSA for failings — or in the words of one House Committee staffer "the relationship between the committees and SSA is not a 'gotcha' game." Of course, it took time for each side to realize the need to work together and develop this level of cooperation. "Initially, there was some resistance to working closely together, but that has changed over time. This building of trust on both sides seems to have enabled SSA to improve."

Throughout the entire GPRA process, SSA has also consulted with the General Accounting Office. GAO has provided the agency with guidelines for meeting GPRA requirements, evaluated SSA submission for both weaknesses and strong points, suggested areas for improvement as well as means for making those improvements, and established a framework for Congress to make its own independent judgements.

A draft copy of the strategic plan was shared with congressional committees and provided briefings to staff of the House Ways and Means Committee and Senate Finance Committee.[32] Under congressional assessment, that draft ranked first among all agencies.[33] Leaders on the House Ways and Means Committee applauded the agency, stating that "SSA's long-term experience in strategic planning has enabled the agency's draft plan to meet and, in certain circumstances, exceed the basic requirements set forth in the Results Act.[34]

After the draft submission, the Ways and Means Subcommittee on Social Security took an active role in improving the plan. In addition to discussions with OSM, the Subcommittee held panel discussions that brought together former and current SSA officials, representatives from the Congressional Research Service, the Congressional Budget Office, GAO, and SSA employee and management groups.[35] The feedback from these stakeholders bolstered the strategic plan, especially its discussion of policy development, research, and program evaluation. These efforts paid off: SSA's official strategic plan ranked third among all agency plans under congressional assessment.

Annual Performance Plans

Annual performance plans (APPs) support the goals set forth in the agency strategic plan and serve as a link to SSA budgets. SSA has published three APPs, steadily providing more details on areas most important to agency beneficiaries. In evaluating the agency on its APPs, it is important to look both at the APPs separately and as an evolving process.

Early in the development of the 1999 APP, SSA officials decided to issue the plan within the agency's budget submittal and assigned responsibility to the Office of Finance, Policy and Operations (OFPO). OFPO took a minimalist approach to the APP because it felt it had received little guidance from either the law or any oversight entity. That meant that OFPO's "interpretation of what [SSA was] trying to create would be extremely simple, stating in the fewest possible terms what the agency was going to try to accomplish."

The 1999 APP thus consisted largely of a list of 67 performance indicators and target levels for the fiscal year and totaled only 18 pages in length. While indicators were nestled under the agency's five strategic goals, the quality and clarity of those measures varied widely.[36] For instance, ten of the performance goals set forth "N/A" as the goal for FY1999. The APP also failed to provide baseline data from previous years, "making it difficult to determine whether the targeted performance [was] reasonable."[37]

Not surprisingly, the 1999 APP was widely regarded as a failed effort. Based on a scoring system devised by GAO and published by Majority Leader Dick Armey's (R-TX) office, SSA ranked twenty-third out of 24 agencies. Observers were shocked that SSA "took a real step backwards in the quality of their initial performance plan." Critics said that the plan lacked a systematic and strategic orientation, instead pulling information from various sources haphazardly. GAO wrote that the APP provided only a partial picture of SSA's intended performance, failed to detail how the strategies and resources would lead to results, and lacked verification and validation of information on performance.[38]

In responding to this failure, the agency found that cooperation with congressional committees could quickly and effectively create an understanding of what exactly an acceptable APP should contain. The House Ways and Means Subcommittee on Social Security, working with SSA to improve the APP, held several in-depth investigative meetings. The subcommittee then put together a systematic report highlighting each aspect of the APP that SSA needed to address. Framing the critique in a spirit of cooperation, the committee also provided possible remedies. Ultimately, this cooperation increased the chance that SSA would improve its service while spending taxpayers' dollars wisely — an objective of both SSA and the subcommittee.

Another management lesson also emerged: stable and assertive leadership provides a critical sense of direction. Without it, strategic planning is little more than a futile exercise. In fact, various committees and GAO had cited a lack of focus at the highest levels within SSA as one reason for the APP's poor showing. During the development of the 1999 APP, SSA was led by an acting commissioner and awaiting confirmation of its first commissioner as an independent agency. Interim leadership, while not deliberately destructive, often leaves an organization uncertain as to its strategic direction.[39]

When Commissioner Apfel was sworn in on September 29, 1997, he immediately exerted his influence. According to Director of Strategic Management Carolyn Shearin-Jones:

> *Commissioner Apfel made it absolutely clear, from the time he first arrived, that planning was a priority for him; that he believed in the concepts of GPRA; and, that it was the right thing to do. And he practices what he preaches . . . Whenever we talk about any kind of project or any kind of initiative, the first sentences out of his mouth are almost always: "How are we going to measure this? What are the quantifiables? What are the indicators?"*

By embracing the principles of performance management, Commissioner Apfel energized SSA to meet the challenges GPRA presented as well as adapt to changing environments. Instead of trying to please oversight entities, the commissioner instructed planners to start from scratch and focus their efforts on writing a plan that would help SSA manage for results and improve its services. According to Shearin-Jones, the commissioner made "GPRA a living breathing thing inside the organization."

With criticisms in hand and a new, permanent commissioner in place, SSA was much better prepared to produce a quality APP. Realizing that the document did not "fall within the organizational bailiwick" of OFPO, the commissioner assigned responsibility for the 2000 and future APPs to the Office of Strategic Management (OSM). OFPO, nonetheless, remains an integral part of APP's development because that office collects the required data.

Where the 1999 APP took a minimalist approach, the 2000 APP was a stand-alone document fully incorporating the 1997 strategic plan. With over 130 pages of detail, the second APP turned weaknesses into strengths[40] and was singled out as the most improved performance plan among federal agencies. The Subcommittee on Social Security wrote:

> *SSA's attention to strategies and resources for achieving intended performance, relating budgetary resources to performance goals, and recognizing crosscutting agencies and*

organizations, have culminated in a strong, stand alone presentation of the agency's intended performance for the year.[41]

Although greatly improved, the 2000 APP still had its faults. At this point, the Senate Governmental Affairs Committee began to work closely with SSA. The committee responded to the 2000 APP by issuing a letter pointing out "persistent management problems."[42] As an example, one of SSA's top management problems was SSI fraud, abuse, and overpayments which cost taxpayers over a billion dollars a year. Committee staffers argue that while "SSA has a goal of zero-tolerance for fraud, [it] seems to cry out for specific outcome-oriented indicators for reducing SSI fraud and other areas of overpayment." SSA responded to these inquiries with a 45-page letter, and followed up with an in-depth meeting with committee staff detailing how the agency planned to face management challenges.

Besides addressing planned performance and incorporating resolutions to management challenges, the 2001 APP revised certain goals and indicators in the 2000 APP. GPRA allows revisions when congressional action and/or updated program information materially affects goals and indicators.[43] And because plans are created up to 18 months in advance, significant revisions are often necessary. According to Shearin-Jones, "It's hard to imagine that in a twelve-month period you wouldn't have to provide additional clarification about how things have changed and what you are doing to accommodate those shifts in emphasis as well as outright changes in direction." The revised 2000 APP changed one performance objective, altered three performance indicators, corrected the definition of three indicators, and adjusted ten performance targets (reduced three and increased seven).[44]

Annual Performance Reports

GPRA's third requirement is for agencies to report on their actual performance in the previous fiscal year. Here again SSA's history has served it well. According to GAO, "SSA was among the first federal agencies to produce an accountability report" providing a comprehensive picture of the agency's performance.[45] The existing

Accountability Report was a natural place to include the GPRA annual performance report (APR). Combining the two and creating the new document occurred smoothly because "the groundwork had been laid many years in advance."

The Office of Financial Policy and Operations (OFPO) is responsible for creating the APR, but its role is subtle because it depends on information gathered from every SSA component. Rather than producing the APR, OFPO "collects the information from the responsible components and assembles the report." More than an annual report, the process of assembling the APR begins when the agency establishes the goals, objectives, and indicators for the coming year. The needed data are gathered throughout the year in monthly *Commissioner's Tracking Reports* and at quarterly management meetings. These reports and meetings are structured around GPRA's strategic goals, objectives, and indicators and serve three critical functions.

First, they provide managers with time-sensitive data that allow them to assess and improve program performance. Commissioner Apfel and his executive staff review the monthly tracking reports to determine SSA's overall performance, examine the progress of each performance indicator every month, ask pointed questions of responsible managers and elicit explanations as to why goals are not being met, and decide on plans of action based on that information. The quarterly management meetings bring together about 80 to 90 managers from across the country, including each of the 10 regional commissioners, and perform similar functions but within a larger forum.

Second, the tracking reports, quarterly management meetings, and the APR ingrain an important source of accountability because managers are repeatedly "called on the carpet" if they are not meeting their goals. In each case, "executives are often literally put on the spot" to answer for their performance. More importantly, "because they know they are going to be held accountable, they stay on top of these items." Serious accountability structures have been integral to SSA's success.

And third, the tracking reports and quarterly meetings are essential facets of SSA's attempts to keep the tenets of GPRA on the mind of its managers. Simply put, top management places so much emphasis on the monthly reports, meetings, and the APR that managers cannot escape thinking about performance management on a daily basis. Congressional staffers hail the quarterly management meetings specifically as "an example of the fact that the agency as a whole is paying the right amount of attention to performance management" and its requirement for successful implementation.

The agency assembles the actual APR by compiling all the performance data gathered in the tracking reports and quarterly management meetings and devising meaningful narratives for each indicator. The first part is a simple and straightforward mathematical task. The narratives are more complex, however. OFPO writes to each deputy commissioner outlining his or her areas of responsibility and instructing them on "writing-up" explanations of performance. These must be "concise, understandable, plain English" discussions that shed light on successes and failures and describe corrective action being taken to improve performance. After receiving responses, OFPO sets out to make them speak in "one voice."

As in any large organization, responses on these components vary. Yet according to the director of the Office of Program Accounting Operations, variations are largely "dependent upon the goal itself." For example, when an automated system provides indicator results, there is no doubt about performance levels. Thus, explanations are straightforward. On the other hand, some indicators are not so easily measured, and in fact may have been changed over the year to a more useful measure. In these cases, explanations must not only explain performance but also the reasoning behind any changes.

SSA has included an APR within its *Accountability Report* for the last two years. The 1998 APR, which appeared a year ahead of the mandated GPRA schedule, addressed the progress of 57 performance indicators through a ten-page report.[46] Performance was mixed: where information was available, our calculations show that SSA achieved about 60 percent of the goals it had set for FY1998. Because the 1998 APR was not a requirement, neither Congress nor

GAO provided feedback, although SSA did receive the Certificate of Excellence for the *1998 Accountability Report* of which the APR was a substantial part.

The 1999 APR was a 23-page document released ahead of every other agency in November 1999.[47] Instead of waiting for every bit of information, SSA "weighed the benefits of having the information available to the user early for 93 percent of the indicators. We don't think there is much to be gained by delaying the issuance of the report to firm up those numbers."[48] Getting the information out to the public quickly allows those who wish to evaluate SSA performance to do so when the data are most relevant.

The 1999 APR reviews the 59 performance indicators set forth in SSA's 1999 APP, categorized under its five strategic goals. In addition to showing actual data and goals for FY1999, the report includes performance data for the three previous fiscal years.[49] Performance results for 1999 were similar to those in 1998: the agency met 60 percent of the goals set forth in the 1999 APP.[50] More telling is the fact that the agency met or surpassed 1998 performance levels on 73 percent of the numerical indicators, indicating a favorable trend in performance. The APR also provided concise explanations if goals were not met, and included information on what actions the agency was taking to meet targets in the future.

Assessing Performance Management at SSA

No matter how detailed and well written, strategic plans are meaningless if they are not accepted by managers or fail to improve performance. An interesting question to begin with in examining how managers at all levels view GPRA and performance management is: would SSA have implemented performance management initiatives had GPRA not been enacted? The answer seems to be that while such initiatives might not have been implemented to the same degree, performance management would undoubtedly exist at SSA today with or without GPRA.

SSA's history of strategic planning suggests that the agency was already moving in that direction. But the installment of

Kenneth Apfel as commissioner also guaranteed a strong role for performance management. Commissioner Apfel's mantra, often cited by agency officials, is that "SSA would be focused on performance with or without GPRA. SSA would be focused on results because it is the right thing to do." One senior executive noted that "GPRA has been the driver only in the case of refocusing on outcomes. There was another trump card. And that is the commissioner and the framework he has established."

While some make the point that an effective leader is "someone whose followers do the right things,"[51] others argue that a leader "creates a sense of purpose and of direction, who analyzes and anticipates and inspires his or her people."[52] Commissioner Apfel has done both by nurturing performance management so it would be accepted and allowed to flourish. In short, employees buy into GPRA in large part because of the commissioner. This is explained by an executive intimately involved in assembling the APR:

You see that there is an Annual Performance Report; and it is all filled out; and it was done in November. If the Commissioner didn't believe that it was important, you would never have it finished. The fact you get this done, you get it done quickly, and you have viable reporting, speaks volumes for agency leadership.

Regarding GPRA itself, managers express approval with the structure linking priorities, goals, and plans to operational activities. The business-like approach ensures that daily actions contribute to SSA's mission, and that the agency anticipates and deals with problems. The process itself has formalized what SSA does and "provides a concrete base for both decisions and expectations." And this has had a domino effect: the refinement of goals at the national level has forced regions to refine their goals, and in turn, forced local offices to refine their goals. In the words of several SSA officials, GPRA provides a "common understanding of what is expected of the organization . . . and it lets you know that we are all in it together." In short, it "is a tremendous energizer for people in an organization to have a common understanding of what it is you are trying to accomplish."

Managers also extol the fact that most of the goals and indicators have evolved through management and employee input. Strategic planning activities at each stage incorporate the results of employee surveys and discussion/focus groups. Through these and more informal avenues, SSA elicits responses and opinions on goals, including what does and what does not work. This has created a real sense of ownership and fosters a strong "commitment towards working toward those goals." And even where people disagree, resolving this disagreement comes second to meeting as many of the commitments as possible.

GPRA has also encouraged managers to have discussions that would never have occurred in the past. While meeting targets remain a priority and a hot topic, more discussions center around whether the targets themselves are actually in the best interest of customers. And when they fail to benefit customers, managers feel empowered to suggest alternate targets, goals, and objectives.

A major obstacle to implementing GPRA is the need to spread its message throughout the agency so that every employee understands its tenets. For an agency as large and as decentralized as SSA, the challenge is particularly difficult. But managers are pleased with SSA's diligence in driving the philosophy of GPRA down in the agency. According to the director of strategic management, one of the most important things SSA does is "inculcating the idea of outcome orientation throughout the agency." Besides relying on the commissioner's tracking reports and quarterly management meetings to spread performance management throughout the agency, SSA pursues many other avenues to promote awareness and responsiveness at every level.

At the national level, senior executives — including the director of strategic management — travel across the country to discuss with employees SSA's mission, goals, and objectives. SSA also frequently updates managers and employees on performance management initiatives through agency newsletters and bulletins, e-mail and Internet sites, and interactive videos and teleconferencing. Every GPRA report is available in hard copy and on SSA's Intranet and Internet web sites. In fact, interested employees can check on the status of each indicator at any time during the year and follow up with a contact person to gain answers to any questions.

SSA has also taken advantage of its decentralized network to drive GPRA down the organization. Most basic is the fact that agency goals and objectives are posted in every office. Many regional offices have also created their own strategic plans tying the values and principles of each region to the national plan. For instance, the Philadelphia region has developed a strategic plan asserting that the region is "committed to quality and creativity in public service." Developed in the late 1980s, with updates in 1992 and 1998, the plan ensures that "regional strategic goals and objectives reflect the ideas and concerns of employees and align with the direction set for all of SSA through the Agency Strategic Plan."[53]

And like their national counterparts, executives from regional offices get out into the field. As one regional commissioner puts it: "You don't change culture through memos." By meeting directly with field office managers, this intra-agency communication fosters strong commitment at every level to achieve the agency's goals and objectives, and disseminates the philosophy of GPRA throughout the agency. While not every claims representative may be fully versed in the tenets of GPRA or be able to recite the agency's strategic goals, he or she knows that his or her duties have an impact on the agency's mission.

Another benefit of GPRA, though not yet fully realized, is that it provides SSA with a better way to operate within a restricted budget framework and climate. Managers are especially excited about the chance to link performance with budget allocations. The commissioner reasons "if you can articulate performance in credible, quantifiable, measurable terms, it becomes a baseline for making the case for resources where we really need them." Hill staffers agree: "The performance measures are a way for the SSA to identify where additional funding is necessary and that puts pressure on the committees." Managers, unfortunately, widely believe that Congress is standing in the way of this particular principle. Some are unsure whether Congress will ever fully embrace the tenets of GPRA. Put simply, they fear that if GPRA does not move "seriously into the appropriations and authorizing arenas then it is just going to gradually go away."

The November 1999 budget negotiations, which resulted in an across-the-board budget cut, is a case in point. This non-performance-related cut demoralized managers and employees who had devoted their energies to meeting agency goals and objectives. Because most believed that SSA was spread too thin in attempting to meet FY1999 goals and objectives, managers and employees alike felt a tremendous sense of pride in having achieved or exceeded so many of the goals in that year. Yet managers were dumbfounded by being "rewarded" with a budget cut. "It was as though when SSA stepped up to the plate and achieved the level of success that was required of it, the rules were suddenly changed."

Yet even in these circumstances GPRA's tools are quite useful. "From an agency planning perspective, it's just going back to the drawing board and saying for $200 million less, what is it that we can accomplish?" In such cases, the commissioner must ultimately make hard decisions, but the GPRA reports provide an outline of obligations and suggest where cuts can be made. GPRA specifically empowers SSA to reduce targets or otherwise alter goals to meet new budget levels — even though such reductions may be distasteful to some in Congress — as long as the agency provides the necessary information supporting such decisions.

Lastly, managers are pleased that accountability is ingrained in the GPRA process. Experience has taught SSA that accountability is vitally important in any endeavor. One executive stated that:

The most important part of having any kind of action plan, goals, or objectives is the actual assignment of responsibility to an individual. By doing that, somebody actually sits up the entire year and thinks "How am I going to achieve this goal?" The assignment of a particular person really drives the process.

Executive sponsors, commissioner's tracking reports, and quarterly management meetings are all elements of this overall accountability structure.

But there are other levels of accountability as well. One individual is held accountable for actually achieving the targets set by each indicator. Each deputy commissioner chooses this person, usually based on his or her position within the agency — an analyst, manager, office director, or team leader depending on the component. SSA has "tried to make it the most knowledgeable person so that if you called them, you can actually find out something about the particular item." Perhaps the most important aspect of the assignment of accountability is that it is made explicitly clear in the beginning of the Fiscal Year. This avoids all confusion as to who is responsible for what goal.

Day-to-day accountability reaches field office managers, as they are accountable for the office's performance on established measures. In claims offices, managers have transformed these measures into 21 service-level indicators that are constantly monitored to ensure that SSA is progressing as planned. Unfortunately, accountability does not extend to front-line employees — thereby failing to exert a positive effect on individual performance.[54]

The reason stems from past agreements with employee unions that prohibit managers from sharing individual-level performance information with the employee, so they cannot meaningfully reward success, curtail mistakes, and improve performance. Further, SSA's annual evaluations are based on a pass/fail system where "99.9 percent of employees are deemed to be satisfactory." This leads to questions of fairness, since the system treats employees of varying abilities equally. In effect, the evaluations very often reward mediocrity, erode motivation, and fail to promote success. One "protected" employee wondered, "Why should anyone push themselves above and beyond when their efforts go unrewarded?"

Even given the lack of true street-level accountability, GPRA and performance management have become institutionalized throughout SSA because managers have a sense of ownership regarding their goals and objectives, and they are comfortable with the agency's attempts to build accountability into almost every facet of its operations. In their words, GPRA is the "genie out of the bottle" and there is no turning back from an approach that has significantly improved the delivery of services to SSA beneficiaries. And with the dramatic growth in SSA workloads expected over the next decade, the performance management process gives the agency a way to effectively meet the inevitable challenges.

Management Lessons

The story we have told regarding SSA's success in implementing GPRA and its performance management tenets is dynamic. While SSA was already on the path of implementing performance management prior to GPRA, the law spurred additional efforts. As GPRA intended, the strategic plan, annual performance plan, and annual performance report are directly related — and each iteration of one document helps to improve future versions of all. While SSA has made some mistakes, the agency has also made substantive improvements in managing for results. SSA provides a worthy example of how to implement performance management initiatives not because the agency has achieved some level of perfection, but because it has fulfilled both the letter and the spirit of GPRA.

Five specific, yet interrelated management lessons emerge from our case study. Together they provide a guide as to why the Social Security Administration has had success in implementing GPRA:

1. *The importance of leadership from the top:* Without stable and assertive leadership, performance management is a futile exercise. At SSA, Commissioner Kenneth Apfel provided a renewed sense of direction with his enthusiastic acceptance of the tenets of GPRA. By believing that performance management was the "right thing to do," and, more importantly, acting upon that belief, the commissioner ingrained those tenets into the very fabric of the agency. In turn, SSA employees were convinced of the worthiness of the initiatives and fully embraced GPRA. Future leaders must continue along the path of enthusiastic support for GPRA and performance management.

2. *The importance of developing strategic partnerships:* The relationship between SSA, Congress, and GAO

provides an impressive model for implementing performance management initiatives. Other agencies would benefit from similar interactions with important stakeholders. While positive relationships do not occur overnight nor will they always be free of tension, the improvements in agency performance and greater appreciation from Congress make the efforts worthwhile.

3. *The importance of driving performance management "down the agency":* Given the size and structure of SSA, ensuring that the overall mission and tenets of GPRA infiltrate every level of the organization is a daunting task. Nevertheless, SSA has made a concerted effort to do just that. While the task is incomplete and perhaps always will be, the agency is already benefitting from the energizing fact that SSA employees have a common understanding of what exactly the agency is trying to accomplish.

4. *The importance of meaningful accountability structures:* The "teeth" behind performance management is individual responsibility for achieving particular indicators, objectives, and goals. Without accountability, there is no way to ensure that daily tasks will focus on achieving the agency's overall mission. From senior executive sponsors to field office managers, SSA employees are "called on the carpet" to explain both their successes and failures. This is done to ensure that problems are quickly identified, successes are noted, and actions are taken to improve service to beneficiaries.

5. *The importance of a "continuous search for improvement":* The philosophy of GPRA encourages an ongoing search for better ways to provide services and manage programs. SSA managers have embraced the view that no measure is ever perfect and feel empowered by their ability to offer new ideas and perspectives. Rooted in SSA's history of reform, this

"continuous search" keeps focused on its pursuit of excellence. While excellence may never be attained, the search ensures sustained progress.

While these lessons learned are not meant to suggest that there is a "one best way" to implement performance management initiatives, at the same time, agencies at every level of government would do well to take note of them and their importance to achieving success within a very large and complex enterprise. They would undoubtedly be helpful to organizations beginning to implement performance management avoid some major obstacles, while also enabling more established agencies to improve existing programs. Managing and improving performance is truly a journey and not a destination.

Endnotes

1   Special thanks to Monisha Dandridge for her research assistance. We also want to extend our appreciation to all of the interviewees who patiently answered our questions and offered wonderful insights. We must explicitly acknowledge Mark Nadel, Carolyn Shearin-Jones, and Carl Rabun at Social Security for both their interviews and their efforts in coordinating all meetings with SSA officials. Thanks also to Regional Commissioners Larry Massanari (Philadelphia) and Carmen Keller (Seattle) and their staffs for their warm hospitality; the evaluators at the General Accounting Office; and the House Ways and Means Subcommittee on Social Security, the House Appropriations Subcommittee on Labor, Health and Human Services, and Education, and the Senate Governmental Affairs Committee.

2   To maintain the anonymity of all interviewees, we have omitted identifying references. As such, all quotes without a reference or citation are drawn from our interviews.

3   Social Security Administration, Office of Financial Policy and Operations, Accountability Report for Fiscal Year 1999 (SSA Pub. No. 31-231, 1999a).

4   Ibid.

5   Ibid.

6   Payroll taxes are paid by workers, their employers, and self-employed people. The first Federal Insurance Contributions Act (FICA) taxes were collected in January 1937.

7   Congress recently eliminated the "retirement test" upon attainment of full retirement age. That means that a person may receive full benefits and continue to have earnings at that age. The test, however, still applies to persons who receive Social Security retirement benefits and are between age 62 and full retirement age.

8   Retirement benefits are based on a formula that gives more credit to workers with low levels of earnings.

9   SSA also provides a significant degree of support to the following programs: Black Lung Program, Medicare, Medicaid, Railroad Retirement, Food Stamps, and various state and local programs.

10 Social Security Administration, *Accountability Report for Fiscal Year 1999*.

11 General Accounting Office, *Major Management Challenges and Program Risks* (GAO/OCG-99-1, January 1999).

12 Social Security Administration, *Short-Term Initiatives to Improve National 800-Number and Program Service Center Service to the Public* (November 1999c).

13 In the discussion of the 800-number, years represent fiscal years.

14 Callahan, John J. Office of the Commissioner, Social Security Administration, "Letter to Ms. Jane L. Ross, Director, Income Security Issues, U.S. General Accounting Office," (April 23, 1997).

15 Social Security Administration, *Accountability Report for Fiscal Year 1999*.

16 The difference between calls placed and calls handled is a technical, but important one: calls placed measures simply the number of times people dial up the 800-number, while calls handled is the number of calls that get through the system and are actually handled by a TSR or the automated system.

17 Social Security Administration, *Accountability Report for Fiscal Year 1999*.

18 Social Security Administration, *Short Term Initiatives*, 4.

19 General Accounting Office, *Social Security Administration: More Cost-Effective Approaches Exist to Further Improve 800-Number* (GAO/HEHS-97-79, June 11, 1997a).

20 Social Security Administration, *Accountability Report for Fiscal Year 1999*, 62.

21 Social Security Administration, Office of Finance, Assessment and Management, Office of Quality Assurance and Performance Assessment, *800 Number Customer Survey for February 1999*. (July 1999), 7.

22 Call volumes are generally higher on Mondays or the day following a holiday, the first week of the month, and the first three months of the calendar year. Workdays are categorized as one of four levels that determine spike involvement: Level 1 days require 80 percent of spikes on telephone duty; Level 2 days require 40 percent; Level 3 days do not require any spikes; and, Level 4 days require 20 percent.

23 Social Security Administration, Philadelphia Region, *Philadelphia Region FY2000 Workplans* (October 1999d), Section 8: 4.

24 General Accounting Office, *More Cost-Effective Approaches*, 22.

25 Ibid., 22-23.

26 Social Security Administration, *Short-Term Initiatives*.

27 General Accounting Office, Social Security Administration: *Effective Leadership Needed to Meet Daunting Challenges* (GAO/HEHS-96-196, September 12, 1996), 3.

28 Laurent, Anne, "Stacking Up: The Government Performance Project Rates Management at 15 Federal Agencies," *Government Executive*, February 1999, 31 (2).

29 The five areas include financial management, human resource management, information technology management, capital management, and managing for results.

30 Social Security Administration, Office of Strategic Management, *Keeping the Promise: Strategic Plan 1997-2002* (SSA Pub. No. 01-001).

31 Ibid.

32 Ibid.

33 Armey, Richard K, Majority Leader of the U.S. House of Representatives, "The Results Act: Setting a New Course" (www.freedom.gov, 2000).

34 Bunning, Jim, Barbara Kennelly and John Edward Porter, Subcommittee on Social Security of the Ways and Means Committee, "Letter to the Honorable John C. Callahan, Acting Commissioner of SSA" (September 11, 1997).

35 Ibid.

36 Social Security Administration, "Annual Performance Plan for Fiscal Year 1999," in *Social Security Administration FY1999 Budget* (1998b), 145-162.

37 General Accounting Office, *SSA's FY1999 Performance Plan* (GAO/HEHS-98-178R, June 9, 1998), 8.

38 Ibid.

39 Farquhar, Katherine, "Leadership in Limbo: Organization Dynamics During Interim Administrations." *Public Administration Review,* 1991, 51 (3): 202-210.

40 Social Security Administration, *Performance Plan for Fiscal Year 2000* (SSA Pub. No. 22-001, February 1999b).

41 Shaw, E. Clay, Jr., and Robert T. Matsui, Subcommittee on Social Security of the Ways and Means Committee, "Letter to the Honorable Kenneth S. Apfel, Commissioner of Social Security" (May 11, 1999).

42 Thompson, Fred, Chairman of the United States Senate Committee on Governmental Affairs, "Letter to the Honorable Kenneth S. Apfel" (August 17, 1999).

43 Social Security Administration, Office of Strategic Management, *Performance Plan for Fiscal Year 2001, Revised Final Performance Plan for Fiscal Year 2000* (SSA Pub. No. 22-001, 2000).

44 Ibid., 3.

45 General Accounting Office, *Social Security Administration: Significant Challenges Await New Commissioner* (GAO/HEHS-97-53, February 20, 1997b).

46 Social Security Administration, Office of Financial Policy and Operations, *Accountability Report for Fiscal Year 1998* (SSA Pub. No. 31-231, 1998a).

47 Social Security Administration, *Accountability Report for Fiscal Year 1999.*

48 Only 4 of the 59 indicators listed in the 1999 Performance Report were incomplete.

49 Social Security Administration, *Accountability Report for Fiscal Year 1999,* 56.

50 Ibid., 3.

51 Drucker, Peter, "Foreword," in *The Leader of the Future: New Visions, Strategies and Practices for the Next Era.* Frances Hesselbein, Marshall Goldsmith, and Richard Beckhard, Eds., (San Francisco, CA: Jossey-Bass Publishers, 1996).

52 Bichard, Michael, "Developing Structures, Processes and Leaders for the Future," *Public Administration Review,* 1996, 18: 327-333.

53 Social Security Administration, Philadelphia Region Strategic Planning Team, *Regional Strategic Plan: Committed to Quality and Creativity in Public Service* (1998c), 3.

54 Locke, E. A., D. B. Feren, V. M. McCaleb, and A. T. Denny, "The Relative Effectiveness of Four Methods of Motivating Employee Performance," in *Changes in Working Life,* K. D. Duncan, M. M. Gruenberg, and D. Wallis, Eds. (New York, NY: Wiley, 1980), 363-388.

References

Armey, Richard K. Majority Leader of the U.S. House of Representatives. 2000. "The Results Act: Setting a New Course."

Bichard, Michael. 1998. "Developing Structures, Processes and Leaders for the Future." *Public Administration and Development.* 18: 327-333.

Bunning, Jim, Barbara Kennelly and John Edward Porter. 1997. "Letter to The Honorable John C. Callahan, Acting Commissioner of SSA." Subcommittee on Social Security of the Ways and Means Committee. September 11.

Callahan, John J. 1997. "Letter to Ms. Jane L. Ross, Director, Income Security Issues, U.S. General Accounting Office." Office of the Commissioner, Social Security Administration. April 23.

Drucker, Peter. 1996. "Foreword." In Frances Hesselbein, Marshall Goldsmith and Richard Beckhard, Eds. *The Leader of the Future: New Visions, Strategies and Practices for the Next Era.* San Francisco, CA: Jossey-Bass Publishers.

Farquhar, Katherine. 1991. "Leadership in Limbo: Organization Dynamics During Interim Administrations." *Public Administration Review.* 51 (3): 202-210.

General Accounting Office. 1996. *Social Security Administration: Effective Leadership Needed to Meet Daunting Challenges.* GAO/HEHS-96-196. September 12.

General Accounting Office. 1997a. *Social Security Administration: More Cost-Effective Approaches Exist to Further Improve 800-Number.* GAO/HEHS-97-79. June 11.

General Accounting Office. 1997b. *Social Security Administration: Significant Challenges Await New Commissioner.* GAO/HEHS-97-53. February 20

General Accounting Office. 1998. *SSA's FY 1999 Performance Plan.* GAO/HEHS-98-178R. June 9.

General Accounting Office. 1999a. *Major Management Challenges and Program Risks.* GAO/OCG-99-1. January.

Laurent, Anne. 1999. "Stacking Up: The Government Performance Project Rates Management at 15 Federal Agencies." *Government Executive.* 31:2 (February).

Locke, E.A. D.B. Feren, V. M. McCaleb, and A. T. Denny. "The Relative Effectiveness of Four Methods of Motivating Employee Performance." In K.D. Duncan, M.M. Gruenberg, and D. Wallis, Eds. *Changes in Working Life.* New York, NY: Wiley: 363-388.

Shaw, E. Clay, Jr., and Robert T. Matsui. 1999. "Letter to The Honorable Kenneth S. Apfel, Commissioner of Social Security." Subcommittee on Social Security of the Ways and Means Committee. May 11.

Social Security Administration. 1998b. "Annual Performance Plan for Fiscal Year 1999." In *Social Security Administration FY1999 Budget.* 145-162.

Social Security Administration. 1999b. *Performance Plan for Fiscal Year 2000.* SSA Pub. No. 22-001. February.

Social Security Administration. 1999c. Short-Term Initiatives to Improve National 800-Number and Program Service Center Service to the Public. November.

Social Security Administration. 2000a. "Social Security — A Brief History." www.ssa.gov/history/history6.html.

Social Security Administration, Office of Finance, Assessment and Management, Office of Quality Assurance and Performance Assessment. 1999. "800 Number Customer Survey For February 1999." July.

Social Security Administration, Office of Financial Policy and Operations. 1998a. *Accountability Report for Fiscal Year 1998.* SSA Pub. No. 31-231.

Social Security Administration, Office of Financial Policy and Operations. 1999a. *Accountability Report for Fiscal Year 1999.* SSA Pub. No. 31-231.

Social Security Administration, Office of Strategic Management. 1997. *Keeping the Promise: Strategic Plan 1997-2002.* SSA Pub. No. 01-001.

Social Security Administration, Office of Strategic Management. 2000b. *Performance Plan for Fiscal Year 2001. Revised Final Performance Plan for Fiscal Year 2000.* SSA Pub. No. 22-001.

Social Security Administration, Philadelphia Region. 1999d. "Philadelphia Region FY2000 Workplans." October 20.

Social Security Administration, Philadelphia Region Strategic Planning Team. 1998c. "Regional Strategic Plan: Committed to Quality and Creativity in Public Service."

Thompson, Fred. 1999. "Letter to the Honorable Kenneth S. Apfel." United States Senate, Committee on Governmental Affairs. August 17.

Performance Management and the Federalism Challenge

8

Performance Management: Does It Matter in the New World of Welfare?

L. Kate Boyer
Catherine Lawrence
with Miriam Wilson

The Government Performance and Results Act of 1993 (GRPA) continues efforts of "good government" initiatives to improve performance and accountability in government. Among other things, GPRA seeks to have program management shift from a focus on processes to a focus on goals and outcomes. Echoing this emphasis on performance and accountability, federal legislation passed in 1996 made historic changes to America's welfare system, a government program widely criticized as poorly designed and serving neither the interests of the public at large nor citizens receiving aid. The Personal Responsibility and Work Opportunity Reconciliation Act of 1996 (PRA) sought, in President Clinton's well known phrase, to "end welfare as we know it" by repealing the sixty-year-old entitlement program for cash assistance (Aid to Families with Dependent Children, or AFDC) and replacing it with a block grant program characterized by sanctions and lifetime limits on aid (Temporary Assistance for Needy Families, or

The authors graciously acknowledge the assistance of Dr. Richard Nathan and Dr. Thomas Gais in developing the thoughts and themes of this chapter.

TANF). Prior to 1996, welfare management and federal evaluation of state performance focused on fulfilling administrative requirements.[1] Reflecting the purposes of GPRA, the Personal Responsibility Act added program goals to welfare at the same time that the legislation gave states more flexibility in program administration.[2]

This chapter analyzes the basic assumptions of GPRA by telling the story of how states have responded to the goal orientation incorporated in PRA, expressed through measurement of state performance. We base our analysis on research conducted by the Nelson A. Rockefeller Institute of Government's State Capacity Study, a field study of state and local changes to management and administrative structures under welfare reform. This research provides valuable lessons for understanding how and under what conditions the principles underlying GPRA may play out, at least in the area of cash programs and services to poor families.

While PRA has achieved partial success in adding a goal orientation to welfare, this success is dependent on the political consensus surrounding given goals, and their attendant performance measures. States have yet to include broad outcome goals suggested by PRA. This may be due to the flexibility that TANF allows states in determining their own measures of success, in spite of federal requirements for states to meet certain performance goals. Some of the more fully realized instances of performance management, meanwhile, offer insights into the on-the-ground realities of welfare management in state and county government.

This chapter has four parts. First, we describe the federal performance measures. We then consider which of the measures states have responded to, which they have not, and why. In part three we consider some of the more elaborate cases of performance management in TANF through a look at Wisconsin, Ohio, and Florida, three states in the State Capacity sample that have tried to develop their own systems for performance management. Finally, we consider the implications for welfare and performance management alike as the implementation of PRA continues.

Three Federal Measures

The Personal Responsibility Act not only ended an entitlement-driven welfare program, but also changed the focus of welfare management and federal-state relationships. Under AFDC, federal regulations governed welfare processes: the types of agencies that could administer welfare programs, the notification of applicants and recipients, how quickly states had to process applications, and other administrative procedures.[3] The PRA eliminated these procedural regulations in favor of giving states greater flexibility in how they administer and structure their programs. In return, PRA and the rules promulgated by the U.S. Department of Health and Human Services (HHS) have specified performance measures by which to judge states' performance and success in meeting the goals of PRA. These measures, which are backed by financial penalties or rewards and mandate the collection of data on individuals and families served by the states, are as follows:

1. The work participation rates of a state's welfare caseload, mitigated by a state's caseload reduction;

2. A bonus to states which show high performance in meeting PRA goals as defined each year[4], and;

3. A bonus to states that have the greatest reduction in nonmarital births without any increase in the state abortion rate.

Chief among these performance measures is the requirement that states engage historically high proportions of adult heads of household in at least 30 hours per week of some combination of eight "work activities." The work participation rate — the percentage of all households who are subject to the work requirements and meeting them — began at 25 percent in fiscal year 1997 for single-parent households and has increased by 5 percentage points each subsequent year. The required rate will reach a maximum level of 50 percent in fiscal year 2002. For two-parent households, the participation rate began at 75 percent and increased to 90 percent in 1999. Work participation expectations under the earlier JOBS program in AFDC were considerably lower, rising to 11 percent of the caseload for single-parent families at the highest level.[5]

TANF allows states some flexibility in achieving these work participation rates by giving them credit for reducing their caseloads. Caseload reduction credits are based on percentage changes in caseloads since fiscal year 1995, when case levels reached a historic high in many states.[6] This credit has given states more flexibility in fashioning program goals: they can either engage those on cash assistance rolls in work activities, they can get people off the rolls altogether (and presumably into unsubsidized jobs, though that is not part of the requirement), or they can do both. If states fail to achieve these target participation rates even after factoring in caseload reduction credits, the federal government may reduce the next year's TANF grant by 5 percent. If the state still fails to achieve its targets, the penalty increases, rising up to a maximum penalty of 21 percent.[7]

In contrast to possible penalties related to workforce participation rates, the high performance bonus in the Personal Responsibility Act rewards states that are the most successful in achieving federal program goals, as defined annually. Competition for the bonus money is voluntary on the part of the states. A total of $1 billion is available for distribution from fiscal year 1999 through 2003; in 1999, the U. S. Department of Health and Human Services awarded a total of $200 million to 27 states for their performance in 1998. The awards were based on criteria developed by the Administration for Children and Families in consultation with the National Governors Association and the American Public Human Services Association. The criteria included: the job entry rates for TANF participants and their success in the workforce (based on job retention and gains in earnings), as well as each state's improvement from the previous fiscal year on both measures. The size of each bonus is tied to state grants; the award may not exceed five percent of the state's yearly TANF block grant. Thus, bonus amounts range widely, from $0.5 million for South Dakota to $45.5 million for California in 1999.

The Personal Responsibility Act seeks to reduce welfare dependence not only by boosting the workforce attachment of participants, but also by promoting marriage, encouraging the formation and maintenance of two-parent families, and reducing out-of-wedlock pregnancies. The performance measure for PRA's family formation goals is the "illegitimacy bonus" to states with the sharpest decline in out-of-wedlock births. The "illegitimacy ratio" calculates births to unmarried women as a percentage of births to all women in the state. The states with the greatest decrease in nonmarital birth ratios are selected based on annual data gathered by the U.S. Department of Health and Human Services and notified that they are potentially eligible for the bonus. Those top five states may then choose to participate in the bonus contest by submitting their abortion rates and related information for the corresponding years; states do not qualify for the bonus if they show an increase in their abortion rates. The winning states then share the $100 million equally. Selected states may use the bonus money as they please as long as they spend it on broadly defined welfare-related purposes.

A more subtle performance incentive in TANF lies in the 60-month time limit for individual receipt of "assistance," which generally means recurring cash grants. The TANF program does not prohibit states from assisting families beyond the 60-month limit; they can support those families with non-cash assistance such as child care and vouchers for basic goods like clothing and housing. They can also continue to assist families with their own money, which can count as maintenance-of-effort funding. States therefore have a financial incentive to get families off cash assistance quickly, particularly where long-term dependency seems a possibility. Otherwise, states may face public pressure to spend their own money for families who have "timed out." In this way, federal time limits strengthen incentives to minimize caseloads and move families off cash assistance.

The Effects of Welfare Performance Goals on State Behavior

What did states do in light of new federal measures of their success? The performance goals in the federal law did not elicit equally strong responses among different states. The Rockefeller Institute's field research at both the state and local levels reveals that overall, the performance targets with the farthest-reaching effects are work participation and caseload reduction. In contrast, attention to family formation and workforce success has been uneven.

Work Participation and Caseload Reduction

States vary a great deal in how they are faring with respect to federal workforce participation requirements, although to date most states are meeting the goals (See Figure 1). In the scatter-plot, each dot represents a state's performance on caseload reduction credits for single-adult households from 1995 to 1999, and work participation rates in 1999. Nineteen states fell below the horizontal line (labeled A) that, at 35 percent, represents the 1999 requirement for the work participation rate. However, the caseload reduction credit allows states to meet the work participation rate by cutting caseloads: in effect, it means that states meet these performance requirements if they are above the diagonal line labeled B. None of the states fell below this level in fiscal year 1999. However, in each of the following three years, this line will move farther and farther out, until it coincides with line C in fiscal year 2002. States now below that line will be subject to financial penalties unless their performance improves.[8]

This comparison illustrates several points regarding TANF work participation goals. First, states show a wide spread with respect to their performance on the work participation/caseload reduction measure. Four states stand out as exceptionally high performers — these are the outlier states in the upper left-hand corner of the plot. Two of those states, Wisconsin and Oregon, are nationally known for their welfare reform efforts and have considerable experience in implementing the reforms, while the other two, Wyoming and Montana, are small states and likely face less severe program implementation challenges. The other states meet the minimum performance requirements, but by a much smaller margin. States in the lower left-hand side of Figure 1 have relatively low work participation rates and fairly high caseload reduction credits. By contrast, there are many states on the right-hand side of the figure that show relatively high work participation rates and relatively low caseload reductions. Of course, many states fall in the middle of the figure.

This variation seems to reflect a basic divide among state TANF programs — one roughly related to state policies and reflected in state implementation. Figure 1 demonstrates this by distinguishing between states that fall above or below the median level of monthly benefits for a family of three with no earnings. States that provide higher-than-average monthly benefits are indicated as circles, while those that offer below-average benefits are shown as solid dots. The figure shows that states providing higher levels of cash assistance tend to perform better on work participation rates and do not reduce caseloads as much as other states, while states that offer below-average levels of cash benefits tend to have lower work participation rates and show higher than average caseload reductions.

The relationship between welfare benefit levels and different patterns of program performance is not surprising. In states with low levels of cash benefits — mostly those in the south and the western mountain regions — nearly any caregiver who moves into a full-time job is no longer able to qualify her family for cash assistance. This is less often the case in states with high benefit levels. Thus, equal success in moving caregivers from unemployment to full-time (or even near full-time) employment will produce larger declines in caseloads in low-benefit states. States with high benefits, on the other hand, have an easier time increasing their work participation rates. Welfare rolls in high-benefit states are therefore less likely to be dominated by families with multiple barriers to employment because families can increase their earnings without losing their eligibility.

Somewhat less obvious is the importance of this relationship in structuring states' approaches to welfare reform. There seems to be a significant relationship not only between cash benefit levels and actual state performance but also between both of these factors and the basic operational goals of state welfare programs. A fundamental division seems to occur between states that stress work participation and work placement — with caseload reduction being an important but subsidiary goal — and those that stress work but also emphasize caseload reduction as a primary goal.[9]

Figure 1
Work Participation Rates and Caseload Reduction Credits
Under TANF, FY 1999

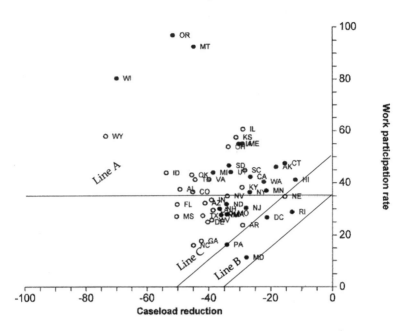

Source: U.S. Department of Health and Human Services. *Temporary Assistance for Needy Families (TANF) Program: Third Annual Report to Congress.* Administration for Children and Families, Office of Planning, Research and Evaluation, August 2000.

Legend
O State with higher-than-average benefit levels.
● State with lower-than-average benefit levels.
Horizontal A: The TANF caseload work participation rate of 35 percent, the required rate for 1999.
Diagonal B: Combined work participation/caseload reduction performance line for fiscal year 1999.
Diagonal C: Combined work participation/caseload reduction performance line for fiscal year 2002.

In short, state welfare programs have undergone substantial changes to include a focus on work. While the work participation goal has been expressed in distinct ways among state welfare programs, it has penetrated the state welfare systems with little exception. These changes are clear, even if it is not possible to separate the precise effects of the federal performance measures themselves from other factors in bringing about this change.

186

The High Performance Bonus

Caseload reductions and work participation numbers have captured news headlines. However, state activities go beyond such efforts. The high performance bonus in the PRA complements work participation targets by rewarding state performance on several specific work-related measures. For FY 1999 and FY 2000, these measures were job entry and success in the workforce — defined as job retention and earnings gain. State efforts are not equal in these two areas, however. Our research to date shows that states did focus on job entry activities in early efforts to implement TANF. However, job-entry activities outweigh efforts to increase workforce success, although more recent data show some states are beginning to focus on the latter as well.

Information we collected in late 1997 on thirty state and local plans for TANF intake processes shows that most include specific programs that provide upfront support for an applicant to find a job. Of the thirty plans, twenty-five include an assessment of employability and an assisted job search within the application process. This assistance with job attachment generally occurs later in the application process; in most locales it is a third or fourth or even last step, occurring following program orientations and assessments for other services. In contrast, fourteen (a little less than half of the sites) include a period of unassisted search for unsubsidized work. This period of independent job search is often the first step in the application process, prior to and often as a requirement of the more supported job search programs. Thus, while some states do require that TANF applicants try a job search on their own, most states in our sample encourage attachment to the workforce not only through mandates but also through services such as assessments and job search assistance.

That states are focusing on job entry is not surprising, as such activities overlap with work participation activities. States are less consistent in their "workforce success" efforts — helping TANF participants boost their earnings and keep their jobs. Programs that focus specifically on job retention did not appear strongly in our 1998 findings, although since then, some states have expanded these efforts. For example, seven states in our study (Florida, New

Jersey, Tennessee, Texas, Washington, West Virginia, and Wisconsin) now offer post-employment services. Many of these are relatively new programs — some as recent as 2000 — and are thus in early stages of implementation.

Other services may indirectly improve job retention, and several of these have been recent targets for increased spending. Child care programs are particularly popular; all states in our sample have substantially increased spending in this area. Transportation funding is also a frequently offered support service, in the form of vouchers for public transportation, driver education courses, and grants for emergency car repairs.

Efforts to increase the earnings of program participants are thin. To date, only three states in our sample report the use of a state earned income tax credit — a program that would make earnings more "powerful." Nor have wage subsidies been widely used. Five states — Florida, Kansas, New York, Wisconsin, and West Virginia — provide wage subsidies to employers, but it is not clear how this supports earnings gains for program participants.

The "Illegitimacy Bonus"

In addition to the work-related goals for TANF participants, the PRA includes a goal related to a state's population as a whole: the reduction of nonmarital pregnancies for all women. The related performance measure is connected to a bonus of $100 million to a maximum of five states that show the greatest decrease in their "illegitimacy ratio" while at the same time showing a stable or declining abortion rate.

In 1999, the first year the bonus was awarded, 12 states showed a decrease in their ratio of nonmarital births to all births across the state. The bonus of $20 million each went to Alabama, California, the District of Columbia, Massachusetts, and Michigan. The second year only 6 states showed a decrease in nonmarital births. The top 5 were Alabama, Arizona, the District of Columbia, Illinois, and Michigan.

While the bonus winners all show a decline in their nonmarital births, these states have rather different overall rates of nonmarital pregnancy. For example, although Washington, DC showed some of the greatest declines (-3.7 percent in the first year and -4.1 in the second), it also has the furthest to go: nonmarital births make up close to 65 percent of all births in the District. Fellow 1999 bonus recipient Massachusetts, in contrast, is well below the national average of 32 percent; its nonmarital birth rate for the 1999 bonus was 25.8 percent — a drop of 1.5 percent in two years. Still, the rate in Massachusetts was above that of many other states. The states with national lows for nonmarital pregnancy — Utah at 16.4 percent, Idaho at 21.0 percent, and New Hampshire at 23.6 percent — all showed increases in their nonmarital birth rates of 2 percentage points or less.

Although most states expressed interest in the bonus funds, they do not seem to be dedicating considerable resources towards reducing nonmarital pregnancy, especially compared to TANF's work-related goals.[10] This lack of activity may stem in part from the fact that states are currently engaged in several related prevention efforts, such as Title XX abstinence programs for teens, Title X family planning programs for adult women, and HIV prevention efforts in many communities. The PRA's goal of preventing nonmarital pregnancies is only one of many attempts to address pregnancy prevention across several populations.

The paucity of pregnancy prevention data in our field study may be because this activity is intermittent and localized. Unlike welfare cash assistance programs, most states in the study's sample have a decentralized system for pregnancy prevention policymaking and service delivery. For example, in both New York and New Jersey as many as five distinct entities play an important role in making policy decisions for pregnancy prevention.[11] State researchers also found a high degree of devolution in this area; state and local governments across the sample share responsibility for making and implementing decisions, as well as delivering actual services. Decentralization may inhibit implementation of a systematic statewide effort to reduce nonmarital births, but encourage local program efforts.

The 1996 federal welfare legislation includes all nonmarital births in its reduction goal; most states, however, have focused new efforts primarily on reducing births to adolescent females. Programs that address the issue among adults and men do exist, but they are in the minority. This is interesting in light of the fact that births to teens account for less than one-third of all nonmarital births. Furthermore, of all teen births, close to 25 percent are to married teens.[12] Teen birth rates have also declined recently and may account for even fewer nonmarital births. Thus, state programs reflect not the federal goals, but their own pregnancy prevention objectives.

The limited inclusion of nonmarital birth goals in state activity is also reflected in the performance measures states themselves are using. Only two states in the sample have established a measure connected to county performance in reducing nonmarital pregnancies. In Arizona, the EMPOWER program maintains eight performance measures, including the rate of additional births to adult recipient mothers and to teen recipient mothers. Ohio divides a small pot of incentive money ($1 million) among the best performing counties in reducing out-of-wedlock births. Florida initiated performance indicators for local WAGES coalitions for reducing teen pregnancy and nonmarital births, but these measures were never implemented.[13]

State Elaboration of Performance Management

In view of states' greater fiscal flexibility and decisionmaking power over program design, their responses to federal performance measures are only part of the story. Some states have used federal measures as a point of departure for more elaborate systems of program management. This section examines some of the more comprehensive efforts to measure program success, with special consideration of Ohio, Wisconsin, and Florida, three states where performance management has been taken farthest. To understand how different levels of administration are linked on questions of performance measurement, we also examine two counties in Ohio, where performance measures are determined jointly by counties and the state.

These cases reveal the nuances, potential results, and complications which can arise from the use of performance management in social programs characterized by devolution and flexibility. We find a high degree of variation in how states define program success, as well as variation in the institutional structures responsible for pursuing performance management. Even in states with more fully developed systems of performance management, evaluating the degree to which welfare systems are achieving their goals remains challenging.

State Variability in Defining Success for Counties

In spite of the importance of federal performance standards in shaping state measures, we also find states tailoring their management systems to reflect state-specific programming. Data collected on seventeen of the states included in the State Capacity Study reveal a total of 26 different measures, only one of which is required by the federal government (workforce participation rates). Taken together these measures fall into five substantive areas: client employment and wages, client participation in TANF programs, provision of work-support services, measures pertaining to family formation, and measures relating directly to program administration.

The measures that receive the most attention generally relate to employment, reflecting the strong emphasis on work under TANF. Nine of the seventeen states measured county rates of job retention and four measured earnings gains, both of which are used to calculate the high performance bonus. Six states measured earnings at job placement, also relating to employment but not required for the high performance bonus. Five states measured clients' full engagement in appropriate activities, while four more measured error rates in reporting information, reflecting the continuation of attention to processes found under AFDC.

Whereas states are relying on county-level performance measures to track work participation and wages, we do not see the same degree of institutional attention given to monitoring work-support programs. Only two states, Kansas and West Virginia, measure county-level performance on food-stamp take-up rates, and only three, Kansas, Florida, and Wisconsin, use measures relating to health insurance benefits. Measures of child support, prenatal care, child protective services, and drug and alcohol programs are used in only one or two states each. In the words of one Florida administrator, state initiatives to use work-support services to evaluate TANF program performance are still in an "embryonic" stage.[14]

A Cascade of Interpretation

In Wisconsin, federal performance measures serve as the basis for state measures, though past experience and state-specific program goals were also taken into consideration in their drafting. Beginning in January 2000, Wisconsin implemented six mandatory goals for local-level TANF contracts running through December 2001. These are: employment placement rate, average wage rate, job retention rate, availability of employer health insurance benefits, levels of engagement in appropriate activities, and level of engagement in basic educational activities (See Table 1). Wisconsin also offers two optional "bonus" measures: one for the use of faith-based contracts and another if fifty percent of the TANF caseload attains job skills. Low performing local service providers in Wisconsin are subject to sanctions in the form of contract cancellation or a "failure to serve" penalty, which carries with it a $5,000 fine. In an interesting reversal of strictly top-down performance management, the "failure to serve" penalty can be levied by a client as well as by the state.

Wisconsin's system for measuring performance is remarkably quantified and relatively complex. There are three possible levels of achievement for each mandatory measure, one mandatory level and two bonus levels. Each reflects different levels of achievement, and triggers a different bonus amount. In addition, service providers may also "use" performance in the optional bonus measures to "upgrade" one first bonus level to a second bonus level in the mandatory measures. Given the higher levels of attention paid to the more quantified performance measures, it will be interesting to see if Wisconsin's system achieves equivalent success.

Table 1 Performance Measures in Wisconsin, Florida and Ohio			
Performance Measure	*Wisconsin*	*Florida*	*Ohio**
Caseload Reduction		Case closures Recidivism	Caseload reduction
Work Engagement	Engagement in appropriate activities	Work participation rates	Family work participation rate
Educational Engagement	Basic educational activities		
Job Placement	Employment placement rate Average wage-rate	Earnings at placement	
Jobs, Post-placement	Job retention rate Availability of employer health insurance benefits	Employment retention, Earnings gain	
Family Formation			Reduction of out-of-wedlock births
Administrative costs			Administrative savings
* Measures serve as a baseline for state-county agreements			

Performance measures in Florida also echo federal performance standards and measures for the high performance bonus, which Florida received in 1998. As of the Fall of 2000, Florida used six measures to manage and evaluate performance in TANF contracts: work participation rates, case closures, recidivism, earnings at placement, employment retention, and earnings gain (see Table 1).[15] Florida is also moving toward a bonus system. As a result of Act 2050, passed in the summer of 2000, ten percent of the amount of TANF contracts in Florida is to be awarded to high-performing vendors. In an interesting expression of second-order devolution, criteria for the high-performance bonus will be determined not by the state, but by the twenty-four regional offices instituted under Florida's welfare administration. (Work And Gain Economic Self Sufficiency or WAGES).[16] Although local service providers administer TANF contracts, vendor payments pass through these regional offices, as will bonuses.[17] At this time, no system of penalties has been established.

Ohio presents another variation on second-order devolution. In this state, mandatory performance levels are determined jointly by each of the 88 counties and the state. These standards are formalized into partnership agreements, which are used to evaluate the performance of individual counties.[18] Partnership agreements are intended to identify county goals and objectives and outline specific strategies that the county will employ to achieve its results.[19] Baseline measures include work participation rates, out-of-wedlock birth rates, and participation in workforce development activities, but essentially counties are given freedom to create programs that meet local needs. Ohio also allocates bonus money to counties with the largest increases in work participation rates and those with the greatest reduction in out-of-wedlock pregnancies (see Table 1).[20]

In theory, the state passes down federal sanctions to counties that do not meet their own standards on a proportional basis.[21] However, there is no history of the state sharing any sanction with county governments, and the political nature of county governance in Ohio makes this unlikely to happen.

Ohio also rewards counties for controlling administrative expenses. Unlike in the past, when counties had to return unspent administrative funds to the state's general revenue fund at the end of the fiscal year, counties are now allowed to retain 50 percent of the savings in administrative costs up to a maximum of $15 million. It is hoped that this bonus program will encourage county innovation. The state has also recently created a $300 million fund (Prevention, Retention, and Contingency — Development Reserve) from surplus TANF funds to encourage counties to develop creative programs to help individuals meet their goals. To receive these funds, counties submit contract proposals to the state for programs that will help them serve their clients in innovative and creative ways. The state hopes that incentive programs like these will allow counties enough flexibility to develop new programs.

The Role of Administrative Structures

The course of performance management is shaped by each state's administrative structure. Salient differences among states include the number of administrative levels involved in TANF administration, the degree of competition between local offices, and the degree to which a state outsources social service provision to the private sector. Wisconsin offers an example of a highly privatized system. County agencies compete against both nonprofit providers and private companies for TANF contracts. In Ohio, administrative relations between local-level service providers and the state have been modeled on a service-retail business model.[22]

Following the success of Wendy's, a fast-food chain based in that state, Ohio has conceptualized local-level TANF service providers as franchises, with the state acting as the headquarters. Each of Ohio's 88 counties is assigned to one of 10 geographically based regions, and each region has an account manager who serves as the "coach" or liaison between the state and counties. In an effort to expand the resources available for clients, counties are also encouraged to incorporate community organizations into their overall welfare reform strategy. As a result, the number of county contracts with nongovernmental agencies has significantly increased. In Florida, legislation spurred by welfare reform led to the merging of several related departments and the creation of 24 regional boards responsible for administering social services. As in Ohio, local boards are encouraged to develop public-private partnerships. In Florida, welfare services are provided by vendors, constituting a separate administrative level below local boards.

In addition to relying increasingly on private-sector service providers, states are using performance-based contracts. In Wisconsin, counties that attain basic levels in all six mandatory measures are given the "right of first selection" for TANF contracts, before nongovernmental providers can submit bids. Within Wisconsin's system of welfare provision, the contract itself can be seen as a bonus. As of yet the state has not cancelled any contracts due to low performance, but administrators report that threats to do so have proven effective in getting local providers to comply.[23] With providers having already survived one round of competition to win the right of first selection in the first place, it is not surprising that sanctions are used only as a last resort.

Ohio, which has replicated the federal-state TANF funding structure by giving welfare-specific funds to county offices as a block-grant, presents a somewhat different picture. In contrast to Wisconsin, contract granting in Ohio is triggered by the successful negotiation of performance measures, determined jointly by county and state, with input from community organizations. Partnership agreements between the Ohio Department of Job and Family Services and each of the 88 counties are now complete, the process having taken three years.[24] The state monitors county performance primarily through two computerized systems, the Client Registry Information System — Enhanced (CRIS-E) and the Family and Children's Services Information System (FACSIS).[25] These data systems are used by each caseworker to record information on every client served by the human service system. The state provides monthly feedback to each county through reports generated by the systems.

To supplement the partnership agreements, Ohio's Office of Research, Assessment, and Accountability produces reports comparing counties' performance in ten different areas: food stamp payment accuracy, families facing cutoff, caseload reduction, work participation rate, family participation rate, Early Start enrollment, Healthy Start participation, paternity establishment, child support orders, foster child placement, and finalized adoption. Though not used to determine awards or sanctions, this document serves as a "report card" by which each county can compare its performance against that of the other 87 counties.

Performance Management in
TANF at the Local Level

Thus far we have examined states' responses to performance management from the federal level, and, in turn, how states have sought to manage performance at the county level. To complete our analysis of administrative change, we consider how performance management works at the local level. A brief look at performance management in two Ohio counties — Cuyahoga County, which includes Cleveland, and Hamilton County, which includes Cincinnati — tells a somewhat different story. Our research illustrates much flexibility and variation in the degree to which counties are managing for performance in vendor contracts.

Counties in Ohio vary in their sophistication and use of outside contracts. Cuyahoga County is the state's most populous county and has the largest welfare caseload. Data from this county suggest that over the past four years, as the characteristics of welfare "stayers" have changed, vendor contracting has changed in response. Prior to welfare reform, vendor contracts followed a three-stage fixed payment schedule based on success with clients. Vendors received approximately one-third of contract payment upon client placement, the second third upon client remaining in the job for 30 days, and the final third after 90 days. Over the past few years, counties have been encouraged to "manage to performance" in vendor contracting, just as the characteristics of welfare caseloads were also changing dramatically. The first clients to successfully transition from welfare to work have been those with the highest levels of job readiness, unhindered by significant barriers to employment such as physical or mental illness, or the primary responsibility for caring for a child (or children) with severe physical or mental illness.[26]

As the TANF client base has changed, so has the job of providing services. This has important implications for performance management. County officials felt that if changes in the contract process did not reflect the difficulty of the task, providers would go out of business or bids on county contracts would decrease. Some counties may not be managing for performance at all but rather simply trying to keep service providers from pulling out. Cuyahoga County has modified vendor contracts twice since the passage of welfare reform, both times to release more money earlier.[27] The most recent round of contracts allows vendors to obtain approximately half their fee upon referral to cover costs of skill assessment, skill development, and job search assistance. When the client enters the job market, the vendor receives an additional 30 percent payment to assist with job placement and follow-up for 30 days. The final 20 percent payment can be requisitioned after the client records 90 days of job experience.

Hamilton County offers a different story. This county developed a strong network of community service providers early in the welfare reform process, and has drawn on this network in contracting for services. As in Cuyahoga County, nongovernmental service providers are paid in installments after they meet specific benchmarks. Vendors receive only $500 upon client referral and additional amounts after meeting contracted goals (for example, after the client has been employed for three and then six months). Some contracts provide for additional payments to vendors if clients achieve interim goals such as making and keeping mental health appointments.

If vendors meet contract goals in a cost effective way they realize a bonus; if they do not meet agreed goals, they must repay fees. The county also monitors service quality and customer satisfaction. Hamilton County also uses performance management for internal assessment and allocating employee salary bonuses. Employee and management teams agree on eight performance objectives. The union negotiates regular pay increases for employees, but twice a year employees who meet or exceed preset objectives are given bonuses.

Patterns, Themes, and Implications

At this juncture, states are in the midst of a steep learning curve regarding performance management. State and local welfare systems have added a new emphasis on achieving performance goals, specifically, work participation rates and caseload reductions, which are central measures of performance in the Personal Responsibility Act. States have sought to meet these goals by front-loading work requirements, moving people into job search activities as quickly as possible, enforcing work requirements with sanctions, assigning new responsibilities to workforce development agencies, and, in some cases, providing work-support services at much higher levels than before.

In contrast, family formation goals have not received as much attention in the new welfare systems, and we find few measures or programs pertaining to marriage and out-of-wedlock pregnancies. Likewise, the more elaborate high performance bonus measures have not received the same emphasis as work participation rates and caseload reductions. A few states, such as Wisconsin, Ohio, and Florida, are beginning to move in this direction, but they are exceptions rather than the rule. Even these states have only just begun to implement more comprehensive systems of program measurement.

What lessons does this story have for those who care about the Government Performance and Results Act as well as the effectiveness of performance management? Performance management has made an impact on welfare administration and service provision, but it has not done so uniformly. Measures that have been implemented by states differ from those that have not in several ways: by the characteristics of the measures themselves, by the political context in which they were selected, and by the process through which they came to be goals. Requisite factors for performance measures to receive widespread attention by the states can be summarized as measures that reflect goals with broad political support and are closely tied to program functioning.

Measures That Reflect Goals with Broad Political Support

In order to implement a goal-oriented strategy, there must first be agreement on the goals. One clear difference between work goals and family formation goals is the degree of consensus around each one. There has long been public agreement that able-bodied adults should work, and now that the majority of women with children, even young children, are participating in the paid economy, this consensus applies to women who are welfare recipients as well.[28] Nathan and Gais found both broad and high-level political support for the work goals of PRA in states' legislative debates over their welfare reforms.[29] This political agreement was strengthened through federal-state interactions that took place in the early and mid-1990s.

The 1996 federal law largely ratified initiatives that states began to develop in the early 1990s under AFDC waivers. These activities included such policy ideas as family caps, work requirements, and time limits. Through state-level experimentation under waivers, the federal government already knew what states wanted to do and could act accordingly in developing the 1996 legislation. In turn, as each state designed its own program to comply with the PRA, it expressed its own interpretations of the federal law and its goals. This interactive process involved governors, legislators, and welfare commissioners, thereby strengthening political signals to welfare bureaucracies that the new work-related goals were important. The development of the law also increased states' sense of ownership of the programs and responsibility for their success.

In contrast, family formation goals were not included in this state-to-federal ratification, but rather added by federal initiative. While some states did include family formation features such as family caps, this was not widespread under waivers. The top-down nature of including marriage and nonmarital birth reduction goals did not inspire the same degree of state action. Far from reflecting political consensus, these goals have the potential for divisiveness; in one state, pregnancy prevention goals, which were formed over a three-year period by a statewide task force, provoked such controversy that they have not been implemented.

Political contexts are not static. As implementation efforts mature and if state economies remain sufficiently stable, states may include more family formation activity in their welfare planning. Although we are still collecting this data, the most recent information from the field shows some activity where earlier there was none, and several states show increases in spending on pregnancy prevention in FY 2000.

Measures Closely Tied to Program Functioning

The program measures with greatest implementation success are those over which program personnel have control, at least theoretically, on a day-to-day basis. In contrast to out-of-wedlock birth rates, program managers have a measure of control over caseloads and work participation activities. States and counties not only control program and eligibility rules but also design the administrative processes that communicate expectations to participants and collect information on their activities. The nonmarital birth ratio, on the other hand, measures a social trend rather than a specific program effort. The PRA's illegitimacy goal applies to all births in the population, not just births to families on welfare or at risk of being there, and it does not break out teen births from births to adult women. This measure goes well beyond the boundaries, and control, of the welfare system. A hypothetical argument illustrates: if births to married couples are declining, the nonmarital birth rate will increase even if the actual number of these births is stable, or if it is declining at a rate less than the decline of marital births. In other words, the bonus could reward states simply because the birth rate of married couples happens to grow.

Measures relating to illegitimacy are further complicated by the difficulty of gauging successful effort; measuring the *prevention* of an event is an elusive task. In some sense, prevention programs have no bottom line for total effort or cost — theoretically, more effort and funding only makes them better. The states that won the bonuses, interestingly, did not necessarily spend the most on preventing pregnancy among one population of unmarried women of childbearing age: teens.[30]

Lack of activity around this measure is understandable; the motivation for states to dedicate resources to decreasing nonmarital births is small because success is uncertain. States may be interested, but they may also recognize how difficult it is to influence fertility and marriage trends through a welfare program. There is furthermore little agreement in the research community on the best way to reduce unplanned pregnancies. Efforts to prevent nonmarital births, especially among teens, may be a popular program choice while states have surplus funds, it may even be a good long-term investment of state and local resources, but it is a risky investment for winning federal bonus money.

Issues in State Implementation of Performance Management

Underlying commonalities in which measures receive attention and which do not, we find variation in how program management operates on the ground. The three states considered here differ in how performance management has been implemented, as well as the degree to which it has been implemented. Their experiences raise additional questions regarding the administration of performance management in TANF across different regions within a state. Local history and political and administrative cultures may differ greatly from county to county within a state, and one might reasonably ask how these disparities influence the implementation of performance measures between local areas. On a related note, how are intra-county population differences accounted for in regard to performance measures? For example, where performance is measured by change in the TANF population, might figures for sparsely populated counties be skewed? A common challenge in program implementation is that of data reporting and tracking. Performance management requires transmitting data among different administrative levels; the degree to which these principles can be implemented depends on the efficacy of the information management system. States have had to enhance their information management systems to meet these needs, as well as address issues of human error in data reporting.

Research from the State Capacity Study also suggests differences in how performance management is viewed between state and local administrative levels. In several cases, local-level administrators reported that performance management seemed more useful for state-level administrators in tracking the performance of local offices than it was for local offices in improving their performance. In Wisconsin and Ohio, local offices report cynicism regarding the likelihood of receiving bonuses given an overall reduction of TANF funds.[31]

The application of performance management principles to TANF administration also reflects widely divergent management approaches. One way to think of these differences is in terms of the degree to which they echo management practices in the business world. Wisconsin has gone a considerable distance toward re-fitting its social service administration to a model of "free-market" competition. In contrast, Ohio's state and local programs are conceptualized as one "company" working cooperatively toward the same goal, with counties conceptualized as franchises. If bonuses are conceived of as profit, it is not surprising that Wisconsin has established the most comprehensive system for their allocation. If this is so, then performance management may not function so much as a means to change management culture, but rather as a means of amplifying it.

Conclusion

Research from the State Capacity Study provides a critique of GPRA's underlying assumptions. Yes, performance management is possible — it is even possible to transform a welfare system that focused almost exclusively on processes into one that puts much greater emphasis on certain goals. But this transformation has occurred under a particular set of political and administrative circumstances. The focus on reducing welfare dependency reflects not just political agreement on the goal but also its link to measures that program personnel can actually affect. These characteristics apply to caseload reduction and workforce participation, but not to saving marriages or preventing single parent families, which engender political divisiveness and are at best only weakly connected to specific programs. Yet GPRA strives to implement performance management in a wide range of agencies and programs, regardless of political context. Rather than wholesale attempts to direct agencies toward performance management, it may make more sense to implement measurable goals more selectively, depending on political constraints.

Performance management occurs during an era of widespread downward shifts in decisionmaking power in American federalism. This context of devolution offers the potential for state-level policymakers to take more control, and responsibility, for program outcomes. In such an environment, states also face substantive and challenging issues regarding what performance management ultimately accomplishes and whom these practices serve. For example, work participation rates, while politically popular and attractive in their neatly quantifiable results, do not tell us if poor families are actually achieving financial independence, or what states are doing to help welfare leavers survive in low-wage, no-benefit jobs. The adoption of measures that would provide a more comprehensive picture — such as tracking the degree to which Medicaid, food stamps, and child care are reaching eligible populations — has been slower and less widespread.[32] Such broader assessments call for the expansion of not only measures but also the population that is measured. An inclusive look would collect information from people on welfare, on the working poor, and on those who have disappeared from the system. Some states are moving in this direction, but the speed and vigor with which states choose to attend to these indicators remains an open question.

Endnotes

1 Mary Jo Bane & David Ellwood discuss this in their 1994 book *Welfare Realities: From Rhetoric to Reform.* Cambridge, MA: Harvard University Press.

2 Richard P. Nathan and Thomas L. Gais, *Implementing the Personal Responsibility Act of 1996: A First Look* (Albany: Rockefeller Institute of Government, 1999).

3 Ibid.

4 The law's four goals are: to provide assistance to needy families so that children may be cared for in their own homes or in the homes of relatives; to end the dependence of needy parents on government benefits by promoting job preparation, work, and marriage; to reduce the incidence of out-of-wedlock pregnancies, and to encourage the formation and maintenance of two-parent families. (P.L. 104-193, Title I, Sec. 401(a)).

5 Jan Hagen and Irene Lurie, *Implementing JOBS: Progress and Promise* (Albany: Rockefeller Institute of Government, 1994).

6 Caseload changes must result from reasons other than changes in eligibility rules.

7 U.S. Ways and Means Committee, *1998 Green Book,* p. 499.

8 For further detail on individual state rates, see the U.S Department of Health and Human Services, *Temporary Assistance for Needy Families (TANF) Program: Third Annual Report to Congress.* Administration for Children and Families, Office of Planning, Research and Evaluation. August 2000.

9 Nathan and Gais, *Implementing the Personal Responsibility Act of 1996.*

10 Cathy Johnson, Catherine Lawrence, and Paola Gentry, *Moving in Many Directions: State Policies, Pregnancy Prevention and Welfare Reform.* Paper presented at the Association for Public Policy Analysis and Management Annual Meeting, Washington, DC: November 4-6, 1999.

11 Field reports from New York and New Jersey indicate that state agencies, local offices of state agencies, local governments, statewide nonprofit organizations, local

nonprofit organizations, and private entities are involved in decision-making for pregnancy prevention.

12 For this and other demographic information, see the U.S. Department of Health and Human Services 1995 Report to Congress on out-of-wedlock childbearing (Washington, DC: U.S. Government Printing Office).

13 Interview with Robert E. Crew, July 14, 2000.

14 Interview with Jenny Lee Robins, June 26, 2000.

15 Robert E. Crew and Belinda Creel Davis, "Florida Welfare Reform: Cash Assistance as the Least Desirable Resource for Poor Families." In *Managing Welfare Reform in Five States: The Challenge of Devolution*, edited by Sarah F. Liebschutz (Albany: Rockefeller Institute Press, 1999).

16 WAGES Boards are the local units that administer welfare in Florida.

17 Jenny Lee Robins interview, June 26, 2000.

18 Partnership agreements were phased in over a two-year period in three waves. Once a county had developed an agreement with the state, it would receive its funds in a block grant rather than in 8 separate funding streams. This meant that counties would have increased flexibility in their spending, particularly for administrative expenses. The state selected counties based on the county's ability to include community groups into its plan and overall readiness for the increased responsibility.

19 The first community plans were to be submitted by each of the 88 counties by October 1997.

20 The state set the participation rate for counties at 5 percent above the federal participation levels in order to insure that Ohio would meet its mandated federal level for workforce participation.

21 The state currently has an appeal pending on a federal sanction. State officials interviewed felt that the state will be found in compliance. Federal inspectors are expected to make a ruling after visiting the state during November 2001.

22 Charles F. Adams and Miriam S. Wilson, "Welfare Reform Meets the Devolution Revolution in Ohio," In *Learning From Leaders: Welfare Reform Politics and Policy in Five Midwestern States*, edited by Carol S. Weissert (Albany: Rockefeller Institute Press, 2000): pp. 25-50.

23 Interview with Jude Morse, August 8, 2000.

24 The Ohio Department of Human Services merged with the Bureau of Employment Services in July 2000, creating a new department called the Department of Job and Family Services.

25 CRIS-E was developed in 1989 to allow caseworkers to register applications for public assistance, determine eligibility, and generate benefits.

26 Clients with multiple barriers to employment account for an increasingly high percentage of welfare stayers. Sandra Danziger et al., "Barriers to Employment of Welfare Recipients," Ann Arbor, MI: Poverty Research and Training Center, July 1999. http: //www.ssw.umich.edu/poverty/wesappam.pdf.

27 In an intermediary contract round, vendors were paid 20 percent per month for the first 2-3 months of the contract, with the remainder distributed at placement, 90 days after placement, and 180 days after placement.

28 See Hugh Heclo, "Values Underpinning Poverty Programs for Children," in *The Future of Children* 7, 2: 141-148, 1997.

29 Nathan and Gais, *Implementing the Personal Responsibility Act of 1996*.

30 General Accounting Office, "Teen Pregnancy: State and Federal Efforts to Implement Prevention Programs and Measure Their Effectiveness," Letter Report, GAO/HEHS-99-4, November 11, 1998.

31 Interview with Jude Morse, August 8, 2000.

32 Of the states reviewed in the State Capacity Study, Kansas was the only one to report measurement on these topics as part of their performance management of TANF.

9

Federalism and Performance Management: Health Insurance, Food Stamps, and the Take-Up Challenge

James Fossett, Thomas Gais, and Frank J. Thompson

The Government Performance and Results Act of 1993 (GPRA) paid scant attention to federalism — a fundamental feature of the American political system that profoundly shapes program implementation. But although GPRA slighted the propensity of the national government to rely on states and localities to administer its programs, the Clinton administration did take notice. The administration's reinvention initiative, the National Performance Review, envisioned a performance-driven model of intergovernmental management, with the national government as a strong player. As two top staff members from the White House Domestic Council observed soon after the Clinton administration took office: "In return for federal support, the federal government should craft and enforce rigorous performance standards that measure state and local progress toward national goals — standards that replace bureaucratic micro-management of inputs and processes" (Galston and Tibbetts 1994: 24). At least some state officials reacted warmly to the promise of intergovernmental arrangements focused on the bottom line, with some seeing it as the handmaiden of devolution. A Virginia administrator told a congressional committee in 1996 (U.S. House Committee on Government Reform 1996: 44):

> *Performance measures at the Federal Level may be used to support the turning back of responsibilities to States. As Congress is looking to transfer more programs to the States, State governments are looking for more flexibility in administering the programs. Performance measures can be used to maintain accountability in these programs, even as strict mandates are being rolled back.*

Proclaiming the virtues of mission-driven federalism is, of course, one thing, and success in implementing it quite another. Intergovernmental arrangements complicate virtually all aspects of performance management — agreement on key goals, the development of indicators, the timely collection of pertinent and valid performance data, the interpretation of these data, the implementation of an incentive system (e.g., rewards for strong performers), and more. Analysts note that principal-agent issues commonly surface under federalism as states pursue goals that conflict with those preferred or even mandated by national officials (e.g., Barnow 2000: 121). But as "sovereign governments" in the constitutional structure of the United States, state officials object to being thought of as agents of federal principals. Recognizing this power reality, the National Performance Review (1995: 35-37) emphasized to federal officials that in dealing with the states they should "negotiate, not dictate" and strive for performance partnerships. By the end of the decade, the federal government had made modest headway in forging these partnerships.

This chapter explores a particular kind of effort at performance management in the intergovernmental context — one rooted in attempts at *informal* leadership by federal officials. Specifically, it focuses on an initiative by top federal actors to elevate the significance of a particular performance measure — enhanced take-up in safety-net programs aimed at meeting the nutritional and health insurance needs of low-income families.

We use the term "informal" in a special sense. The national government's efforts to foster performance management become more formal to the degree that policymakers etch pertinent requirements into statutes or the code of federal regulations. As Boyer and associates document elsewhere in this volume, the welfare reform act of 1996 contained several provisions setting specific performance targets for states, with bonuses attached for meeting these targets and penalties imposed for missing them. However, the statutes and regulations for the programs we examine in this chapter — food stamps, Medicaid, and the State Children's Health Insurance Program (CHIP) — feature few such provisions. But they do represent cases where the president and other top federal officials strove to send strong signals to the states and others to prioritize efforts to boost enrollments and participation rates in these programs. The cases thereby cast some light on the potential and limits of informal federal leadership in elevating the importance of a performance indicator for states and localities.

The federal initiative to foster enrollments for food stamps, Medicaid, and CHIP can appropriately be seen as an important companion to the Personal Responsibility and Work Opportunity Reconciliation Act of 1996 (hereafter referred to as the Personal Responsibility Act). The new welfare law established Temporary Assistance to Needy Families (or TANF), which emphasized putting the needy to work, time limits on the receipt of benefits, and caseload reduction. The work-first philosophy of TANF has substantially penetrated welfare bureaucracies, but the elements associated with it have not so much dislodged the program in place prior to 1996 — Aid to Families with Dependent Children, or AFDC — as they have augmented its procedures, activities, and goals. Although states have used the discretion TANF provides to pursue multiple goals, they have generally followed one of two main avenues. One stresses the importance of work and reducing caseloads; the other places a premium on employment and work-related activities but not, per se, on shrinking TANF rolls (Gais et al. 2000). Whatever the emphasis, most states experienced sharp declines in caseloads during the late 1990s.

As federal and state policymakers moved to this policy of "tough love" with respect to cash assistance, however, they shied away from shredding other parts of the safety net. In fact, they went out of their way to delink cash assistance from eligibility for health insurance provided by Medicaid and CHIP and, to a lesser degree, food stamps. Hence, low-income working families who were no longer receiving welfare payments or had never received them became an increasingly salient target for non-cash benefits. By the late 1990s, top federal officials had adopted a proactive stance toward enhancing enrollments in these programs. In doing so, many of these officials at least implicitly paid homage not only to enrollment data but to a somewhat more complex performance indicator — take-up rates (also called participation rates). This rate refers to the percentage of individuals in a given territory who meet the formal criteria to participate in a safety-net program, such as with respect to income and assets, who actually are enrolled for benefits. In the case of health insurance for children, achieving a high take-up rate became an objective that the president personally endorsed and repeatedly emphasized. The federal commitment to higher participation rates was less dramatic in the case of food stamps, but by the end of the decade national officials and advocacy groups had begun to express concern about the importance of this performance measure.

In attempting to elevate the salience of enrollment goals for health insurance and food stamps, federal officials faced many challenges. Lacking a clear statutory foundation for their exercise, their success depended all the more heavily on the power of persuasion — on convincing states that take-up was an objective worth emphasizing. Federal prospects also revolved around the degree to which willing states acquired the capacity to design and implement strategies and systems that would in fact facilitate robust participation rates. National officials therefore faced pressing questions of how to provide technical assistance and, more generally, to build state and local capacity. In seeking to bolster state commitment and capacity with respect to take-up, these officials faced the distinct possibility that spillover from welfare reform would complicate their task.

Dissonant spillover arises when implementing agents working in the same general policy sphere (e.g., providing various safety-net benefits to low-income people) are expected to pursue conflicting objectives, depending on the particular program and benefit involved. This prospect loomed especially large in the case of TANF programs that emphasize caseload reduction and diverting people from signing up for cash assistance through such tactics as lump sum payments or job search requirements. As of 1998, 31 states had endorsed some form of diversion activity (Maloy et al. 1998). In this context, local welfare offices face conflicting imperatives to build barriers to enrollment on one front (cash assistance) while encouraging take-up on others (Medicaid and food stamps). The administrative difficulties involved in implementing these conflicting goals may well be substantial. Of course, not all states and localities emphasize diversion and caseload reduction for TANF, but even in these instances dissonant program spillover may well leave its mark. The culture of the TANF program, like that of its predecessor, AFDC, has not stressed vigorous marketing or other forms of outreach. Nor has it valued efforts to make eligibility intake and redetermination processes user friendly for low-income individuals. To the degree, therefore, that those involved in administering cash assistance also play a role in operating food stamps and health insurance, barriers to take-up rooted in inertia and organizational culture may well be formidable.

The next two sections of this chapter more fully describe enrollment challenges in health insurance and food stamps. We then examine the implications of these cases for a more general understanding of centrally driven efforts to foster performance management within the context of American federalism. In doing so we consider steps that might enhance participation rates in these safety-net programs, that would incline states to become more committed to take-up objectives, that might enlarge the capacity of states to spur enrollments, and that would improve prospects for more transparent performance measurement in this sphere. A concluding section assays the potential and limits of an informal performance approach, and considers whether alternatives to either informal or formal performance management might also galvanize take up.

Health Insurance: Promises Expand

During the 1990s, the federal government sent an array of signals that it wanted states to increase the enrollment of low-income children and their mothers in Medicaid and related health insurance programs. Established in 1965, Medicaid is a jointly funded federal-state entitlement program to provide health insurance. Nondisabled mothers and children typically comprise about two-thirds of Medicaid enrollees while accounting for one-third of the program's costs. Medicaid eligibility among this group had long been linked to the receipt of AFDC, although states could choose to cover those not on cash assistance through several methods. Over the last 15 years, Congress expanded coverage for pregnant women and children to income levels well above AFDC income limits and gave states the option of increasing coverage even further. Of particular note, mandates approved in 1989 and 1990 required states participating in Medicaid to insure pregnant women and children under age six in families with income up to 133 percent of poverty. The mandates also stipulated that states gradually extend Medicaid coverage to all uninsured children under 19 from poor families by 2002.

The Personal Responsibility Act fueled this delinkage of Medicaid from cash assistance by instituting several provisions to preserve and even expand access to Medicaid for women and children who were citizens. (Legally admitted resident aliens fared less well.) The new law froze the basic standards for Medicaid eligibility for children, pregnant women, and adult caretakers of children that had existed as of July 16, 1996. It retained both mandatory and optional eligibility expansions for pregnant women and children, and extended the life of the transitional Medicaid assistance program (often called TMA) through 2001. TMA preserves Medicaid eligibility for certain families who would otherwise lose this benefit as a result of gaining employment or greater income. Families moving from welfare to work can stay on Medicaid for an additional six months regardless of how much income they earn; after that, families earning less than 185 percent of poverty (after deductions for child care expenses) can be eligible for another six months. The Personal Responsibility Act also gave states the option, under Section 1931, to simplify Medicaid eligibility determination significantly and extend Medicaid benefits to new groups of people. It authorized $500 million that states could use in a variety of ways to maintain Medicaid coverage for families no longer receiving welfare payments.

Further impetus to expand health insurance enrollment emerged the year after welfare reform with the establishment of CHIP as part of the Balanced Budget Act of 1997. CHIP offered states the opportunity to expand insurance coverage for children beyond Medicaid income levels under a more generous federal match than they received from Medicaid. While the statute contained several requirements intended to assure that states did not reduce Medicaid income limits or enroll Medicaid-eligible children in CHIP to receive the higher match, it also gave states considerable flexibility in setting eligibility levels and designing the program. States could use CHIP funds to expand Medicaid programs, establish new separate programs, or combine these two approaches. States could employ certain asset and earnings disregards to enlarge the number of eligible children.

Although states vary considerably in their willingness to provide health insurance, CHIP has unquestionably fueled an expansion in the number of children eligible for this safety-net benefit. Six states established the upper limit on CHIP eligibility at 300 percent of poverty or higher (New Jersey set the pace at 350 percent). The upper limits in another 22 states met or exceeded 200 percent of poverty. Of the 10 most populous states, only 3 set CHIP eligibility below 200 percent of poverty — Illinois at 133 percent, Ohio at 150 percent, and New York at 192 percent (U.S. Health Care Financing Administration 2000a).

Signals from the Federal Government

Unlike TANF, where greater enrollments (let alone participation rates) tend to be suspect, federal officials have launched an almost unprecedented effort to minimize dissonant spillover from welfare to Medicaid and CHIP. In doing so, these officials could not rely on statutory-based performance targets and incentives for meeting them. Medicaid law (Title XIX of the Social Security Act) contains no major provisions of this nature. The CHIP legislation does call for states to submit plans that establish performance goals and measures as well as strategic objectives aimed at reducing the number of uninsured. But the law does not establish the federal government as a significant player in specifying precise standards for enrollment or in pinpointing targets for reducing the number or proportion of uninsured. Nor does the CHIP law explicitly tie state performance to federal rewards or penalties.

This absence of a firm statutory basis for performance management aimed at boosting take-up did not deter President Clinton, who repeatedly and publicly promoted enrollment in Medicaid and CHIP. The president directed eight federal departments to work together and outline their plans for helping enroll children in these two programs, and these agencies eventually proposed over 150 action steps (U.S. Department of Health and Human Services 1998). The White House and the Health Care Financing Administration (HCFA) also paid particular attention to building collaborative relationships with public interest groups, such as the National Governors Association and the American Public Human Services Association, and to soliciting media support for public service ads. Private foundations agreed to help as well. The Robert Wood Johnson Foundation, for example, pledged at least $47 million to fund community coalitions to conduct innovative outreach initiatives to enroll children in Medicaid and CHIP, and to galvanize state efforts to simplify and improve eligibility processes and computer systems. Senior administration officials publicized ongoing enrollment problems and state success stories, encouraging continued media attention to take-up (Thompson and Gais 2000).

These public initiatives have been reinforced by a steady stream of missives from HCFA to state Medicaid and CHIP officials. Many of these reminded and instructed states that their efforts to reduce welfare caseloads should not spill over into the health sphere, provided advice and examples of how to maximize coverage, and promised lenient treatment in the quality-control process for mistakes. In the spring of 1999, for example, HCFA joined with the Administration for Children and Families of the Department of Health and Human Services to issue a 28-page "Guide to Expanding Health Coverage in the Post-Welfare Reform World" (U.S. Department of Health and Human Services 1999). As a former Medicaid official observed, this document, which provided "a how-to guide describing how to extend eligibility to the maximum limits of the law," reflected a "major change in stance" from HCFA's historic behavior (Moore 1999). More recently, HCFA issued a "Dear Medicaid

Director" letter requiring states to identify and reinstate individuals and families who had been improperly terminated from Medicaid as part of their separation from TANF (U.S. Health Care Financing Administration 2000b).

Finally, HCFA officials have occasionally relied on admonition and the threat of sanctions to break down barriers to enrolling children in Medicaid and CHIP. When, for instance, New York City officials pursued an aggressive TANF diversion strategy that also erected barriers to enrollment for food stamps and Medicaid, HCFA administrators complained to state officials in Albany that they were not doing enough to monitor practices in New York City. In May 1999, HCFA administrators in the New York regional office announced that they would require officials in New York State to document their efforts to comply with federal enrollment requirements. In early August of that year, President Clinton announced that he was instructing HCFA to "conduct comprehensive on-site reviews of Medicaid enrollment and eligibility processes" in all states to determine levels of compliance with federal laws and to offer recommendations for improvement" (Pear 1999: 1, 27; see also Hernandez 1999).

Enrollment Erodes

It is premature to judge whether this informal yet persistent effort by the president, senior administrative officials, and private partners to elevate take-up as a driving objective for Medicaid and CHIP will bear fruit. Clearly, however, the approach has not proven to be an elixir. Data limitations preclude a definitive tracking of enrollment trends and take-up rates for nondisabled children and adult caretakers during the 1990s, but three central conclusions emerge from available evidence.

First, after rising throughout the first half of the decade, total Medicaid enrollment of children and nondisabled adults declined from 1995 through at least 1998, although it may have increased since then. While precise estimates vary, most analysts have concluded that Medicaid enrollments declined by 5 to 7 percent between 1995 and 1997, with adult enrollment falling by about 11 percent and that of children by roughly 3 percent (U.S. General Accounting Office 1999; Ku and Bruen 1999). At least 38 states, including the 10 most populous ones, saw Medicaid enrollments drop. More recent data, while fragmentary and not entirely comparable, suggest that this decline continued through 1998 (Holahan and Kim, 2000). Enrollment reports from 21 states suggest that aggregate Medicaid enrollment in these states increased slightly (1.4 percent) between 1998 and 1999, but remained below 1997 levels (Ellis and Smith 2000). Nor does it appear that gains in CHIP participation offset these losses. At the close of 1999, states had enrolled some 2 million children in CHIP. However, one preliminary analysis of the 12 states with the most uninsured children found that, under combined Medicaid and CHIP enrollments, a 2 percent decline had still occurred (Pulos 1999).

Second, program participation rates have in all probability fallen. While some of the decline in Medicaid enrollment is due to improved economic conditions that have reduced the number of persons with lower incomes (Holahan and Kim 2000), expansions in eligibility have likely added more people to the target population than economic growth has removed. States have historically done better at covering cash assistance clients under Medicaid than non-cash families, and the large reductions in cash assistance caseloads may well have produced at least a short-run decline in Medicaid enrollment. Sophisticated (albeit far from definitive) estimates suggest that as of the late 1990s, the Medicaid take-up rate for children who also qualified for cash assistance was nearly 80 percent. The Medicaid participation rate for children from families not on welfare, in contrast, was less than 60 percent, and the CHIP rate hovered at about 50 percent. By one recent calculation, half to two-thirds of uninsured children under 19 meet the income criteria for Medicaid or CHIP (Selden et al. 1998; 1999; U.S. Department of Health and Human Services 1999a; Almeida and Kenney 2000). Estimates of participation rates for nondisabled parents (primarily mothers) also point to the magnitude of the challenge. A significant percentage of adults who leave welfare do not receive the transitional Medicaid assistance to which the law entitles them. One recent estimate concludes that over 60 percent of the drop in Medicaid caseloads through 1998 was due to a decline in the probability of coverage among those qualified rather than improved economic conditions (Holahan and Kim 2000).

Third, states vary widely in the direction and magnitude of recent Medicaid enrollment trends. From 1995 to 1997, for example, changes in Medicaid enrollments varied from an increase of 26 percent in Delaware to a decline of 19 percent in Wisconsin (U.S. General Accounting Office 1999). More recent data from 21 states from 1997 to 1999 range from increases of more than 25 percent in Massachusetts, Oklahoma, and Arkansas to declines of 8 to 10 percent in Texas and Wisconsin (Ellis and Smith 2000).

While some of these disparities in state caseload trends are almost certainly the result of differences in economic growth and job opportunities, more may well be due to differences in state "performance" in developing the management systems and mechanisms to ensure that Medicaid eligibles become enrolled and remain covered. Worries that Medicaid caseloads may be too low are novel concerns in many states, as are experiences in designing and implementing efforts to make Medicaid benefits more accessible. Some states have been more successful than others in developing the internal political support and resources to craft the systems and procedures required to measure performance, to ensure that clients are aware of their eligibility, and to manage the Medicaid application and retention process in a "user friendly" fashion.

Food Stamps:
Take-up Versus "Quality Control"

The continued viability of the food stamp program was important to the enactment of the Personal Responsibility Act. Members of Congress who supported welfare reform often claimed not only that any job was better than welfare but that even low-wage jobs offered families more money than welfare — at least once food stamps, the Earned Income Tax Credit, and other benefits were taken into account. Although the new welfare law cut food stamp spending, the cuts and other restrictions fell hardest on legal immigrants and able-bodied persons without dependents, not on nonimmigrant families with children, the population most central to the new TANF program.

Several aspects of the food stamp program ostensibly make it an excellent work support program. First, families with incomes as high as 130 percent of the poverty level — well above the amount earned by a full-time worker at a minimum wage job — remain eligible for food stamps if they satisfy certain asset limits. Second, food stamp benefits decline only 24 cents for each dollar of earnings, offering greater rewards for families with earnings than nearly all cash assistance programs. Third, the program helps reduce variation across states in overall benefits to AFDC or TANF recipients. By treating cash assistance as income, the food stamp program pays out more to families in low-benefit states than in high-benefit states. Fourth, food stamp benefit levels are adjusted every year for inflation, since the program is designed to permit households to afford a basic meal plan. AFDC cash assistance levels, in contrast, lost value in recent decades, as states infrequently increased them.

The food stamp program was also viewed as vital to the success of welfare reform in recent evaluations of AFDC waiver programs. For example, the New Hope project in Milwaukee and Florida's Family Transition Program were widely interpreted as successful in part because of the boosted earnings. Yet the estimated increase in family income would not have come close to compensating for the loss of welfare benefits if the families had also lost their food stamps (Bos et al. 1999; Bloom, et al. 1998).

In addition to an earnings supplement, some supporters — and many opponents — of welfare reform viewed the food stamp program as a safety net that could cushion the effects of welfare reform on families who "time out" their benefits, who fail to get jobs, or who are unable to comply with the new demands of TANF. The Personal Responsibility Act actually showed some ambivalence regarding this role. Food stamps are available to families who exceed the time limits, and some states, such as New York, even built this feature into their formal programs. However, the act is less forgiving of direct noncompliance. The new law prohibited food stamp assistance from increasing as a result of cuts in cash assistance due to TANF sanctions. The law also required states to eliminate food stamp benefits — for three to six months, depending on the number of violations — for individuals who fail to comply with TANF work requirements, and it gave states authority to extend these sanctions and even to make them permanent. States were also given the authority to eliminate the entire household's food stamp grant, except when the individual violating the TANF rules is caring for a child under six. As of 1998, 12 states have chosen to exercise this option (Dion and Pavetti 2000).

Enrollments Decline

The importance of the food stamp program as a work support and safety net for families with children suggested to many that food stamp caseloads would not decline greatly with the implementation of TANF, at least among nonimmigrant families with children. Yet soon after TANF was implemented, food stamp caseloads fell dramatically. Food stamp enrollments peaked in 1994, when 27.5 million people participated in the program, and declined to 25.5 million in 1996. The decline then became steeper, as enrollments fell to 19.7 million in 1998. Since 1998, declines have slowed. In October 1999, 17.5 million individuals participated in the food stamp program, while in June 2000, 17 million individuals received benefits. Household participation showed the same pattern of change, as it fell from 11.3 million in March 1994 to 7.8 million in September 1998, and more slowly from 7.4 million households in October 1999 to 7.3 million in January 2000. (Enrollments rose slightly to 7.4 million in June 2000.)

Some of the declines in participation have occurred among non-citizens and individuals without children — groups whose eligibility was curtailed in the 1996 Personal Responsibility Act. However, these groups constituted a small part of the food stamp caseload and cannot account for most of the decline in food stamp enrollments. Over 70 percent of the overall decline in food stamp enrollments stemmed from a drop in the participation of families with children, especially single-parent families — groups most affected by state welfare reforms (Wilde et al. 2000).

Some of the decline in enrollments is also attributable to economic growth. Food stamp participation declines during periods of economic growth — such as the middle- and late-1990s — as eligibility depends primarily on family income and assets. In fact, food stamp caseloads have traditionally been more sensitive to economic conditions than AFDC enrollments (Wallace and Blank 1999). Unemployment at the national level has declined since 1992, while poverty rates for individuals dropped from a 1993 high of 15.1 percent to 11.8 percent in 1999. Wallace and Blank (1999) found that unemployment changes accounted for 28 to 44 percent of the decline in food stamp enrollments between 1994 and 1998. A USDA study (Wilde et al. 2000) reported that 35 percent of the participation declines from 1994 to 1998 are attributable to changing employment levels.

However, the evidence suggests that more than economic factors are at work. First, food stamp take-up rates — the percentage of estimated eligible persons actually receiving food stamp benefits — declined at the national level by 9 percentage points between 1994 and 1997, from 71 percent to 62 percent (Schirm 2000), reversing an earlier increase in take-up rates between 1988 to 1994 (U.S. Department of Agriculture 2000b). Second, when USDA analysts tried to estimate the dynamics contributing to the 1994-98 enrollment decline, they found that "26 percent . . . was due to a decline in the share of households with low income, *55 percent was due to decreased use of food stamps among low-income households* [i.e., households whose income is less than 130 of the poverty level; italics added], and 19 percent was due to decreased use of food stamps among medium/high-income households" (Wilde 2000: 15). That is, participation has declined even among persons and households who are most likely to qualify for food stamp benefits.

The Federal Government Signals Concern

The substantial declines in TANF and food stamp caseloads fueled concern among federal officials and program advocates that welfare reform was depressing food stamp participation rates. They focused on three possible barriers to take up. First, they recognized that administrative processes and rules — such as diversion, pre-application requirements, informal messages, and sanctions — might be spilling over into the operations of the food stamp program. In other words, *administrative delinkage from cash assistance may not have gone far enough*, as processes and policies relating to cash assistance programs were also applied to food stamps. Second, they sensed that welfare reform may affect access to the food stamp program by creating *too much institutional and program separation*, especially where TANF programs are administered by private contractors or workforce development systems. This separation may raise the costs to families of enrolling in multiple programs administered through different organizations, information systems, and sites. Third, federal officials, advocates, and others increasingly realized that the administrative operations of the food stamp program *might not fit the new circumstances generated by welfare reform and the growing economy.* Eligibility systems that rely on frequent recertifications and extensive documentation of income and assets may not have created problems for families that relied mostly on cash assistance programs, but they may not be particularly well adapted to families with earnings. Yet one of the clearest trends among poor families is their declining dependence on cash assistance and their growing reliance on earnings (Bavier 1999).

It is still too early to know which of these factors — or something else altogether — accounts for lower food stamp take-up rates among families with children. But these concerns and others prompted federal officials to focus more attention on encouraging greater take-up in the food stamp program. In doing so, they could not easily turn to statutory provisions that called upon states to achieve certain participation rates and provided concrete rewards for meeting these performance targets. Instead, they relied on other tools to elevate the salience of take-up. The Food and Nutrition Service (FNS) of the Department of Agriculture, for example, expended some effort to monitor program operations and voice concern about inappropriate practices. In Milwaukee, New York City, and Portland, Oregon, it uncovered instances where state and local administrators had gone further than the law allowed in closing the door to food stamp enrollment, such as by refusing to accept applications from individuals after 8:30 A.M. in the case of Portland (U.S. General Accounting Office 1999a).

In 1999, the Clinton administration became sufficiently concerned about the possible effects of welfare reform on food stamp participation to launch several initiatives. Secretary of Agriculture Dan Glickman led the way with a letter to governors voicing the administration's concerns that "many poor families have left the [food stamp] program despite their continuing eligibility" (U.S. Department of Agriculture 2000a). Subsequently the Department of Agriculture worked to clarify program requirements in communications to regional officials and others. For instance, a letter to regional administrators in the department in 1999 pointed out that the provision in the Food Stamp Act that gives automatic eligibility for food stamps to TANF enrollees also applies to households receiving non-cash assistance, such as child care benefits, so long as this assistance is funded in part by TANF or state maintenance-of-effort monies.

The Department of Agriculture also attempted to galvanize greater outreach to potential beneficiaries. It established a public education campaign and hotline as well as a new Food Stamp Tool Kit intended to disseminate best practices and explain the program's access requirements. The department also supported the Community Food Security Initiative, which sought to forge alliances with state, municipal, nonprofit, and business groups to encourage best practices aimed at boosting participation in all hunger and nutrition programs. The FNS sought to harness information technology through its Food Stamp Program Education Campaign, designing and placing promotional materials on a Web site and on CD-ROMs for use by local groups.

The Clinton administration also took aim at administrative processes that made it more difficult for food stamp recipients to remain on the rolls. In November 2000, the president used his weekly radio address to announce new food stamp regulations that, among other things, gave states more discretion to eliminate the requirement that enrollees reapply for benefits every three months and report their income as often as monthly. States could instead allow participants to reestablish their eligibility as seldom as twice a year. In the words of Secretary of Agriculture Dan Glickman, a major goal of the regulations was "to make it easier for working families to have a transition period between welfare and work, and to relieve both families and states of the burden of constant recertification" (Morgan 2000).

The Administration on Children and Families of the Department of Health and Human Services has also underscored the importance of take-up. In late August 2000, the department published regulations governing bonuses for high performing states under the TANF program that would take effect in fiscal 2002 (see Boyer and Associates in this volume for a discussion of TANF performance bonuses). Four of these performance measures were to focus on state success in achieving greater take-up of low-income families in food stamps, Medicaid, and CHIP (CLASP Update 2000).

These recent attempts to boost participation rates in the food stamp program build on a number of earlier initiatives. Since the 1985 Food Security Act, Congress has from time to time enacted new legislation that liberalizes food stamp rules (U.S. House Ways and Means Committee 1998: 942-947). The Hunger Prevention Act of 1988 was particularly important, as it created an outreach and education program in which states may receive a 50 percent reimbursement from the federal government to inform low-income households about the availability, application procedures, and benefits of the food stamp program (U.S. House Ways and Means Committee 1998: 946-947). However, few states have responded to this outreach incentive. To receive matching funds, a state must submit an outreach plan to the FNS each year to receive funding, yet only 10 states had submitted such plans by 2000 (Wegener 1999).

A Competing Performance System

Despite these numerous signals from the federal government that food stamp take-up rates are noticed and important, there is little evidence that states have responded vigorously to these signals — and there is reason to be skeptical that they will. The major reason is that the food stamp program is already an example of a successful application of performance management, though this success creates severe problems for improving take-up. Since the early 1970s, the Department of Agriculture has operated a quality-control system designed to minimize eligibility errors in administering food stamps. Under federal oversight, state welfare agencies sample over 90,000 cases each year and perform in-depth investigations of eligibility and benefit decisions. Program managers use the data to identify problems — down to the office and even the worker involved in the error. This database permits the federal government to hold states accountable for their performance in providing benefits: every year, federal officials calculate and impose financial penalties on the states if their error rates are higher than the national average. They estimate a tolerance level — the average national error rate — that is the sum of the percentage of cases where overpayments were made (6.9 percent in 1996) and the percentage of cases where underpayments were made (2.3 percent in 1996). Thus, the tolerance level in 1996 was 9.2 percent. The Department of Agriculture then assesses penalties that become increasingly severe to the extent that the state error rate diverges from the tolerance level. For example, a state with an error rate twice as far from the tolerance level as another state may owe the federal government several times as much in penalties. Although states frequently avoid paying these penalties to the federal government, they often have to fund them by putting more money into their food stamp administrative structures, an investment many states would prefer not to make.

The specificity of the performance measures, the quality and routineness of the data collection, the capacity to disaggregate the data down to local offices and even specific workers, the severity of the sanctions, and the continuous readjustment of performance objectives all suggest that the food stamp quality-control system would be an effective performance management system — and it appears that it has been. Overpayment rates in the food stamp program (expressed as a dollar error rate) were well over 9 percent in the early 1980s, fell below 8 percent in 1987, and dropped below 7 percent for the first time in 1996, when overpayments averaged 6.9 percent (U.S. House Ways and Means Committee 1989; 1991; 1996; 1998).

In 1997, however, error rates began to climb until average overpayments reached 7.6 percent in 1998. Underpayments also increased in 1998 to 3.1 percent, up substantially from 2.3 percent in 1996 (U.S. House Ways and Means Committee 2000; U.S. Department of Agriculture 2000b). One plausible explanation for why error rates have increased is that welfare reform has produced more low-income families with earnings — families who are traditionally more "error prone" than those who rely exclusively on cash assistance. In 1995, before most states implemented work-based welfare reforms, only 21 percent of the households receiving food stamps reported any earnings, while 38 percent relied on AFDC and 69 percent received some combination of AFDC, Supplemental Security Income, or state general assistance (U.S. House Ways and Means Committee 1998: 948). Much of the income information needed to calculate food stamp benefits was somewhere in the welfare office or its information system, simplifying the task of ensuring that food stamp benefit levels were properly adjusted. Only three years later, in 1998, 26 percent of the households receiving food stamps reported earnings, while only 31 percent relied on TANF. As more and more of recipients' income is obtained from sources outside the public assistance system, the administrative challenges of updating earnings and deductions relating to child care, transportation, and other work-related expenses become that much greater.

States seem to act as if they believe that families with earnings are problematic. To get error rates back down, many states have made it more difficult administratively for families — especially those with earnings — to get and keep food stamp benefits. The Center for Budget and Policy Priorities found that between 1994 and 1998, "11 states increased by 50 percentage points or more the proportion of working households with children assigned food stamp certification periods of three months or less" (Greenstein and Guyer 2000: 18). Some states subject households with earnings to "more intensive procedures, such as shorter certification periods (which require households to reapply more frequently) and more intensive verification requirements" (Greenstein and Guyer 2000: 19). Field research in 1997 and early 1998 found that a few states were preoccupied with food stamp error rates all the way down to the local offices, and many states are responding to growing threats of federal penalties by requiring more extensive and frequent documentation of income and deductions (Nathan and Gais 1999).

Other data tend to reinforce these conclusions. In fiscal year 1998, the average certification period for households receiving food stamps without earnings was 10.6 months, while the average period for households with earnings was 7.8 months. Some 31 percent of households with earned income had actual recertification periods of 3 months or less, while only 15 percent of all households had such short recertification periods (Castner and Rosso 2000). These briefer recertification periods increase the transaction costs to families with earnings, and it is plausible to expect that they depress take-up rates. In sum, without steps by Congress to eliminate or modify the quality-control system, it will in all likelihood continue to undercut commitment to take-up in the food stamp program when a growing proportion of families have jobs. The result is a mixed set of signals from the federal government about what constitutes performance.

Performance Management and Greater Take-up

This discussion of health insurance benefits and food stamps suggests that federal reliance on signaling to elevate take-up as a performance measure for states and localities has its limits. Despite the initiatives of the president and other top federal officials, participation rates in food stamps and Medicaid appear to have declined. Of course, in the absence of federal action the take-up problem may well have been worse. Moreover, given the time lag between federal stimulus and state response, it is probably much too soon to assay the impact of current federal initiatives to increase take-up. Allowing for these mitigating factors, however, the experience so far with food stamps, Medicaid, and CHIP suggests that the take-up challenge is formidable. What might be done to enhance participation rates in these safety-net programs? A vast array of possibilities present themselves, and we do not have the space to deal with all of them. But three clusters of issues loom especially large: steps that would encourage states and localities to become more committed to take-up goals, steps that might enhance the administrative capacity of states to foster enrollments, and steps that would fuel prospects for learning and adaptation by improving performance measurement.

The Commitment Challenge

The goal of enhancing participation rates in food stamps, Medicaid, and CHIP must, of course, compete with other objectives for the attention of state and local officials. Proponents of federalism tout its responsiveness to state and local sentiments as one of its virtues. And states do vary greatly in their basic willingness to heed federal exhortations and directions about boosting enrollments. For instance, President Clinton and countless advocacy groups strongly recommended that human service agencies collaborate with the schools to boost enrollments in Medicaid and CHIP. Aware of this initiative, the Arizona legislature passed a law that forbids groups working on behalf of Medicaid and CHIP from trying to enroll children through the public schools (Steinhauer 2000).

Among the many state and local goals that can inhibit a commitment to take-up, a concern with cost control looms large. While the strong economy has increased the flow of revenues to the states and nondisabled women and children are relatively inexpensive to insure, one cannot gainsay the expense to the states (at least over the short term) that success in boosting participation rates would bring. One way to reduce state concern over cost is, of course, to provide more generous federal match rates for these health insurance programs. Success in expanding enrollments would thereby impose less strain on state and local budgets. But while shifting a greater portion of the tab to the federal government may generally galvanize greater commitment to take-up (other things being equal), the case of food stamps also highlights the limits to this incentive. The federal government pays the entire cost of food stamp benefits yet many states have done relatively little to ensure that those qualified for these benefits receive them.

The experience with food stamps points to another dynamic: that commitment to take-up will be more likely to flourish in the absence of conflicting performance management systems. The quality-control system encourages states to emphasize the fight against errors of liberality (putting someone on the rolls who does not meet eligibility criteria) as opposed to errors of stringency (failing to enroll a person who meets eligibility standards). A vigorous quality-control program may not raise many problems for participation in a context where poor families receive a large share of their income from public assistance, but it dovetails less easily with a food stamp program that increasingly serves as a work support.

In addition to providing more attractive federal match rates and to eliminating conflicting performance systems, proponents of greater take-up might seek to etch performance requirements into the statutes that govern Medicaid, CHIP, and food stamps. This would entail establishing performance targets with respect to participation rates, as well as fiscal or other incentives for meeting them (such as bonuses). However, any inclination to follow this path to increased take-up in food stamps, Medicaid, and CHIP should consider possible unintended consequences. Conceivably, for instance, states that adopt more liberal eligibility policies that extend benefits to greater numbers of the uninsured (especially working families) may encounter more difficulties than tightfisted states in achieving higher take-up rates. A performance management system constructed around participation rates (which is, after all, a *ratio* of those on the rolls to those in the state who qualify) might actually make states more conservative about eligibility expansions. Such possibilities need not inevitably distort performance management systems, but they highlight the need for caution in selecting performance indicators.

The Capacity Challenge: Greater Program Delinkage?

Although the barriers to forging greater commitment to take up in a fragmented intergovernmental system loom large, issues of administrative capacity present at least as many difficulties. A state committed to elevating participation rates would typically need to have the capacity to succeed at four tasks, among others. First, it would need to find an effective means of publicizing safety-net benefits, since many potential beneficiaries lack accurate information. Second, it would have to overcome the concerns of potential recipients about stigma, and in the case of Medicaid and CHIP, the propensity of some to ignore the advantages of health insurance when no one in the family is sick. Third, the state would need to modify eligibility processes to reduce the transaction costs to the targeted population of becoming enrolled. Fourth, it would have to make redetermination processes more client friendly so that those who continue to qualify for benefits do not drop off the rolls.

State and local officials face many barriers to accomplishing these tasks — the inertia of existing systems, limited resources, considerable uncertainty (such as concerning the best way to get the word out about program benefits), and more. Existing research has not gone very far in identifying the most cost-effective approaches to yielding higher participation rates. Further complications arise because safety-net programs such as food stamps and Medicaid increasingly target a group that heretofore has received much less attention from welfare bureaucracies — working, low-income families. Achieving high take-up rates for a group that has left welfare or never been on it poses new and special enrollment challenges. It is in this context that dissonant program spillover from TANF to other safety-net programs comes into play.

One frequently voiced recommendation for reducing dependence on welfare while simultaneously maintaining access to Medicaid and food stamps is to separate the programs completely. Traditionally the same workers used common rules and computerized systems to determine eligibility for welfare, Medicaid, and food stamps (Maxwell 1999).

While as a matter of formal policy the welfare reform act significantly decoupled eligibility for Medicaid and food stamps from cash assistance, all three programs in many ways remain administratively linked. Food stamp units are almost universally part of state welfare departments. Although policymakers in some states have transferred Medicaid to health departments (as in New York) or have established a separate Medicaid agency (as in Arizona and Michigan), control over many critical aspects of eligibility determination remains vested in welfare agencies. Even in states that have organizationally decoupled Medicaid from TANF, the welfare agency often maintains control over the computerized systems local workers use to determine eligibility as well as the reporting systems that provide state officials with information about enrollment changes. State human service agencies also typically continue to control official communications with county or other local welfare offices, so that much of the signaling to local actors Medicaid agencies might want to do is through channels controlled by other agencies.

Program integration remains, if anything, even more complete at the grassroots level. Although local welfare offices have in many cases transferred responsibility for dealing with TANF clients to workforce agencies or private contractors, they continue to be responsible for Medicaid and food stamp eligibility. Specialized Medicaid and food stamp units or eligibility workers are rare, and their independent contact with TANF clients is frequently limited. In many states, local welfare workers rely on computerized systems that are still oriented toward determining Medicaid and food stamp eligibility as an adjunct to eligibility for income support. While clients may continue to qualify for both Medicaid and food stamps after they quit receiving TANF funds, the computer systems may not automatically redetermine eligibility thereby cutting off clients who in fact still qualify. It may well be that this problem has led appreciable numbers of Medicaid recipients to be inappropriately terminated after the implementation of welfare reform. In many cases these computer systems also generate "notices" to recipients informing them that they must provide additional information to continue coverage, or telling them that their Medicaid eligibility under one set of rules has been terminated without necessarily disclosing that they may continue to qualify under other rules. While officials in some states have instituted manual fixes, or "work-arounds," to compensate for these systems problems, these are frequently complex and difficult for eligibility workers to use.

These problems of continued program integration, and the potentially adverse effects on enrollment alleged to accompany them, have prompted some advocates to propose greater administrative delinkage of Medicaid and food stamps from the welfare system. Health advocates have long decried the dependence of Medicaid eligibility on welfare, arguing that frequent turnover of eligibles disrupts continuity of care and makes longer-term preventive programs difficult to implement. In some states, intermittent eligibility has also complicated attempts to move Medicaid clients into managed care. Advocates have argued that a complete separation of Medicaid rules, systems, and organizations from welfare might reduce churning and other barriers to enrollment. One prominent advocate has put the case forcefully (Ellwood 1999: 29-30):

> *An obvious direction is to move Medicaid eligibility determination for families away from the welfare-based rules and to use instead a set of simplified rules and procedures. . . . Over time, the creation of a separate infrastructure to deal solely with health insurance eligibility determination might go a long way to reduce confusion among applicants and beneficiaries, as well as reducing the stigma that is associated with Medicaid by virtue of its links to welfare.*

The call for greater delinkage may well make sense for working families who do not qualify for TANF benefits. However, the quest for more delinkage also presents problems. Aside from the added administrative costs of such a move, the fact remains that TANF recipients continue to comprise a significant part of the clientele for both Medicaid and food stamps, and establishing separate infrastructures may well make access to benefits harder for these recipients rather than easier. Some states have used the new flexibility available under TANF to delegate responsibilities to private contractors, workforce development boards, labor departments and other agencies that either do not or, in the case of private contractors, cannot determine eligibility for Medicaid or food stamps. This institutional separation may have made it more, rather than less, difficult for families to enroll and obtain the benefits for which they qualify. Establishing separate offices, workers, and forms for Medicaid and food stamps would require families to contact multiple workers and agencies for applications and recertifications and thereby might have a depressing effect on participation.

Rather than complete delinkage, a reintegration of welfare and other entitlement programs on terms more appropriate to their changed circumstances might do more to bolster take-up. Establishing separate entry points outside welfare offices for food stamps, Medicaid, and CHIP makes sense. Federal regulations have required states to "out-station" Medicaid eligibility workers at some hospitals and clinics, and some have done so. Other states have begun to experiment with mail-in applications without requiring visits to the welfare office. An approach that combines these and other outreach measures with a single point of access for Medicaid and food stamps within welfare offices may do more to foster take up than complete delinkage.

The Measurement Challenge: Transparent Performance Indicators

The efficacy of performance management ultimately depends on the ability of leaders to obtain valid, reliable, and timely data with respect to pertinent goals. Imagine the "ideal" situation for top managers at the federal, state, and local levels in the case of food stamps and health insurance. All of them would have regular, easy access to data on enrollments by category of beneficiary and, even better, take-up rates. Equipped with this feedback, top administrators could (like those who manage political campaigns with the aid of tracking polls) adjust their strategies to achieve better results. In this idealized scenario, performance measurement would also be transparent. Implementing agents would agree on common reporting definitions and procedures so that performance data would allow accurate comparisons from one jurisdiction to the next. Furthermore, data on enrollments and participation rates would be widely available to interested actors, including community groups and the media. Such transparency would pressure officials to assign higher priority to take up in food stamps, Medicaid, and CHIP. A governor, for instance, might wonder why her state ranked 48th in take-up rates for CHIP and demand better results from her subordinates.

A substantial gap (some would say chasm) exists between this ideal and the realities of performance measurement in Medicaid, CHIP, and food stamps. This gap is especially easy to understand in the case of take-up rates. Developing indicators for these rates requires not only knowledge about enrollment (the numerator) but also the number of individuals in an area who meet income, asset, and related eligibility tests such as whether they lack health insurance (the denominator). Not surprisingly, neither the federal government nor the states can generally produce accurate and timely data with respect to this denominator. Of particular importance, the federal government's own statistical agencies have been unable to provide valid estimates of parameters pertinent to gauging participation rates.

Consider, for instance, efforts to determine whether a population has health insurance. Since Medicaid and CHIP target those without insurance, computation of a take-up rate requires understanding the number of uninsured in a given area. In general, federal policymakers rely on estimates produced by the Bureau of the Census through its March Current Population Survey. But experts differ on the degree to which they think this survey presents valid data, with many suggesting that it systematically overestimates the number of uninsured individuals and underreports the number covered by Medicaid (e.g., Lewis et al. 1998; Ullman et al. 1998). Of even greater significance in an era of devolution, the national surveys of the federal government do not as a rule produce highly valid and reliable estimates at the state, let alone local, level. Sample sizes perfectly sensible for providing national estimates of the uninsured or those at various income levels often fail to yield accurate state- and local-level figures.

The inability of officials to obtain high-quality information about participation rates means that data on enrollments become the coin of the realm for measuring program accomplishment. The lack of information on participation rates gives these officials an out in interpreting enrollment data. In the absence of take-up performance measures, officials may look out at a strong economy and find it easy to persuade themselves that they are reaching nearly all of those who need assistance.

Enrollment numbers for nondisabled adults and children therefore comprise a less ideal but a more readily obtainable performance indicator for programs. Yet problems arise even with respect to this indicator, especially at the federal level. Data on food stamp enrollments flow to officials at all levels of government with reasonable accuracy and speed. But federal Medicaid executives to a surprising degree fly blind. Over nearly three decades HCFA has slowly made progress in persuading the states to accept a management information system that adopts uniform definitions and provides reasonably valid, reliable, and comparable data on the number of different types of Medicaid enrollees. But HCFA staff (aided by analysts at the Urban Institute) must toil constantly to uncover and correct errors in the reports that states submit. Analysts who seek to track enrollment trends in the states frequently conclude that they should go through the laborious process of contacting each state rather than rely on HCFA's information system (U.S. General Accounting Office 1999). A lack of timeliness also undermines the ability of federal officials and others to use Medicaid enrollment data to track the performance of states. As of mid-2000, for instance, HCFA had still not released data on Medicaid enrollments for 1998.

State officials may be in a stronger position to monitor enrollment trends than federal executives and to employ them for purposes of performance management. In Indiana, for example, administrators responded to concerns expressed by Governor Frank O'Bannon regarding the state's new Hoosier Healthwise program (a Medicaid expansion under CHIP) by establishing enrollment goals for each of Indiana's 88 counties. As of the end of 1999, only 6 counties had failed to meet these goals and the state had won national recognition for its take-up success (Moore and Sprague 2000).

Progress in developing more valid, timely, and transparent performance measures (both enrollments and participation rates) ultimately depends on two forms of a highly technical politics of numbers (Alonso and Starr 1987). One revolves around the pulling and hauling needed to advance administrative reporting systems for safety-net programs so federal, state, and local officials have ready access to pertinent, comparable enrollment data. The other involves dynamics at the national level that can buttress the capacity of sophisticated statistical agencies, such as the Bureau of the Census, to produce data needed to calculate take-up rates at state and local levels. These federal agencies need additional funding to increase sample sizes and make other methodological refinements in order to yield better state and local-level data on such important indicators as the number of uninsured children and family income. With respect to both technical arenas, some progress has occurred over the last two decades and incremental advances may well be attainable over the next several years (Thompson and Gais 2000).

What Works

Although many have criticized the specific approach mandated by GPRA (e.g., Radin 1998), the allure of performance management and "mission-driven" government remains strong. Proponents of reinvention and the "new public management" have stressed the virtues of forging agreement on goals, developing indicators to measure results, systematically collecting reliable, valid, and timely performance data, and rewarding or penalizing administrative agents based on their performance (e.g., Behn 1991). The institutions of federalism greatly complicate efforts to achieve these imperatives, but this did not deter the Clinton administration and occasionally Congress from endorsing the approach under the banner of "performance partnerships" or statutory provisions directed at particular programs. The Personal Responsibility Act of 1996, for instance, paid some homage to the approach.

The safety-net programs examined in this chapter — food stamps, Medicaid, and CHIP — in no way represent paragons of performance management. Their authorizing statutes do not emphasize this approach. However, the experience of these programs (especially the health insurance initiatives) provides insight into the potential and limits of more informal efforts by top federal officials to elevate the importance of a particular performance goal — greater take-up. In an effort to encourage states to do more to reach out to those targeted for benefits, the president and other top officials:

* Repeatedly endorsed the goal of greater take-up in forums that the mass media covered.

* Rallied federal agencies to examine what they could do to facilitate greater participation.

* Sent directives and missives to state agencies urging greater outreach (and somewhat more formally, made adjustments in the Code of Federal Regulations).

* Conducted studies of state take-up efforts in order to identify best practices.

❀   Provided a stream of advice to states on practices that would foster greater participation.

❀   Secured the support of a broad spectrum of public interest groups (e.g., the National Governors Association), private corporations, and foundations to facilitate greater enrollments.

❀   Conducted reviews of state and local practices critically noting when their procedures deviated from processes conducive to take-up.

As a performance management initiative, this federal effort has much to commend it. A reasonably clear objective has been articulated, there has been significant and sustained public articulation of this objective by the president and senior administration officials, and federal executives have provided substantial and ongoing support and encouragement for states to expand their enrollment efforts. Both the federal government and private foundations have made substantial resources available to assist states with outreach and systems development. As the new decade dawned, it remained hazy whether this initiative would lead to robust enrollments and participation rates in Medicaid, CHIP, and food stamps, but the case clearly represents the creative application of an informal approach to performance management. (One positive note is that CHIP enrollments grew by over 50 percent from 1999 through 2000.)

A key issue with informal approaches to performance management is, of course, their sustainability. It takes persistence and energetic initiative by top leaders to keep efforts focused on the performance target. This focus can be difficult to maintain even if the same high-level executives remain in office. Political leaders often have short attention spans and tire of the quotidian task of sticking with an implementation objective, especially compared with the appeal of new initiatives. Indeed, the American political system, and for that matter many students of public management, tend to place a premium on pursuing innovative policies and practices rather than sustaining an informal approach to performance management over a number of years. This impulse applies not only to government leaders but to those at the helm of private foundations and public interest groups, who as this case illustrates may team with public officials to promote a particular performance objective. Turnover in the leadership ranks of government and its private partners also tends to vitiate efforts to sustain an informal approach to performance management. Thus, with the ascendance of President George W. Bush, federal initiatives on behalf of take-up may well dissipate. Leaving ideological differences aside, few new presidents and cabinet members (especially those from a different political party) want to stake their reputations on management initiatives launched by their predecessors.

The fragility of an informal approach to performance management declines somewhat if information systems routinely produce valid, timely, comparable, and transparent performance data. Such systems can make it harder for top officials to turn their attention elsewhere. High-quality, broadly disseminated performance data serve an agenda-setting (or preserving) function in the political system. Advocates of greater take-up could also attempt to sustain interest in this goal by taking other steps to foster a more formal approach to performance management. Such an effort could revolve around statutory changes that mandate participation goals and incentive systems for safety-net programs. It could entail action to eliminate performance management systems that tend to erode take-up such as the quality-control system for food stamps.

In considering the quandaries of enrollments and participation rates, it is also beneficial to contemplate approaches to intergovernmental implementation other than either formal *or* informal performance management. Consider a possibility that flies in the face of a performance-driven approach to enhancing take-up — overt federal directives to shape inputs, processes, and benefit structures at the state level. Under this approach federal officials would turn away from performance targets, incentive systems, and indicators and pay more attention to shaping specific administrative behavior. For example, a very strong case exists that the adoption of a single step — requiring states to provide continuous eligibility for Medicaid and CHIP enrollees without recertification for one year — would significantly enhance take-up rates in these two programs. Currently, many states and localities impose hefty burdens on Medicaid recipients, who at relatively short time intervals must submit the latest information about their income, assets, and related factors to continue to qualify for benefits. Failure to meet paper-work and other requirements means that many beneficiaries are dropped from the rolls even though they still meet the legal qualifications for benefits. Moreover, the sense among potential applicants that dealing with Medicaid is a hassle even after their initial application is approved may well undercut their motivation to apply for the program in the first place. Under current law, states have the option of providing continuous eligibility for one year to Medicaid and CHIP beneficiaries, but most states have not done so for both programs. At least in theory, the federal government could convert this option into a requirement. Mandating a full year of enrollment before redetermination would not only reduce the transaction costs for program beneficiaries but would simplify implementation for state and local agencies and cut administrative costs.

Of course, this and similar federal mandates focused on inputs, process, and benefit structures can have side effects. Requiring states to provide continuous eligibility for one year would probably increase overall state costs somewhat (Short 2000) and lead some to adopt less-generous eligibility policies or become more stringent in their initial review of applications. Moreover, many students of federalism would object in principle to this form of federal assertive-ness in dealing with the states. Nonetheless, this example of a continuous-eligibility mandate does demonstrate that consideration of approaches other than those embedded in the performance management model could enhance enrollments and participation rates.

In an era when the courts, Congress, and the president all tend to emphasize the importance of devolution and deference to the states with respect to safety-net programs, the prospects are extremely remote that the federal government will impose process mandates on the states as a vehicle to take-up. In this sense, perfor-mance management, with its emphasis on providing states great discretion to pursue different paths to a goal, fits the prevailing po-litical climate much better than alternatives that require states to en-gage in specific administrative behavior.

References

Almeida, R.A., and G. M. Kenney. 2000. "Gaps in Insurance Coverage for Children: A Pre-CHIP Baseline." Washington, D.C.: Urban Institute.

Alonso, W., and P. Starr. 1987. *The Politics of Numbers.* New York: Russell Sage Foundation.

Barnow, B. S. 2000. "Exploring The Relationship Between Performance Management and Program Impact: A Case Study of the Job Training Partnership Act." *Journal of Policy Analysis and Management* 19, 1: 118-141.

Bavier, R. 1999. "An Early Look at the Effects of Welfare Reform." Washington, D.C.: Office of Management and Budget, unpublished.

Behn, R. D. 1991. *Leadership Counts.* Cambridge, MA: Harvard University Press.

Bloom, D., et al. 1998. *The Family Transition Program: Implementation and Interim Impacts of Florida's Initial Time-Limited Welfare Program.* New York: Manpower Demonstration Research Corporation.

Bos, H., et al. 1999. *New Hope for People With Low Incomes: Two-Year Results of a Program to Reduce Poverty and Reform Welfare.* New York: Manpower Demonstration Research Corporation.

Castner, L., and R. Rosso. 2000. *Characteristics of Food Stamp Households: Fiscal Year 1998.* MPR Reference No. 8370-056. Washington, D.C.: Mathematica Policy Research, Inc.

CLASP Update. 2000. "TANF High Performance Bonus: Final Rule Issued." Washington, D.C.: State Policy and Documentation Project, October 2-5.

Dion, M. R., and L. Pavetti. 2000. *Access to and Participation in Medicaid and the Food Stamp Program: A Review of the Recent*

Literature. MPR Reference No. 8661-401. Washington, D.C.: Mathematica Policy Research, Inc.

Ellis, E., and V. Smith. 2000. *Medicaid Enrollment in 21 States: June 1997 to June 1999*. New York: Kaiser Family Foundation.

Ellwood, M. 1999. *The Medicaid Eligibility Maze*. Washington, D.C.: Urban Institute.

Gais, T., R. Nathan, I. Lurie and T. Kaplan. 2000. "The Implementation of the Personal Responsibility Act of 1996: Commonalities, Variations, and the Challenge of Complexity." Paper presented at the New World of Welfare Preliminary Conference, Ann Arbor, Michigan.

Galston, W. A., and G. L. Tibbetts. 1994. "Reinventing Federalism: The Clinton/Gore Program for a New Partnership Among the Federal, State, Local, and Tribal Governments." *Publius* 24, Summer: 23-48.

Gleason, P., et al. 2000. *The Effects of Welfare Reform on the Characteristics of the Food Stamp Population*. Washington, DC: Mathematica Policy Research, Inc.

Greenstein, R., and J. Guyer. 2000. "Medicaid and Food Stamps." Paper presented at the New World of Welfare Preliminary Conference, Ann Arbor, Michigan.

Hernandez, R. 1999. "Inquiry Grows as Rolls Fall for Medicaid." *New York Times*, June 8, p. B1.

Holahan, J., and J. Kim. 2000. "Why Does the Number of Uninsured Americans Continue to Grow?" *Health Affairs* 19 (July/August): 188-196.

Ku, L., and B. Bruen. 1999. *The Continuing Decline in Medicaid Coverage*. Washington, D.C.: Urban Institute, December.

Lewis, K., M. Ellwood, and J. L. Czajka. 1998. *Counting the Uninsured: A Review of the Literature*. Washington, D.C.: Urban Institute.

Maloy, K. et al. 1998. *A Description of the State Approaches to Diversion Programs and Activities.* Washington, D.C.: George Washington University.

Maxwell, T. 1999. *Information Federalism: A History of Welfare Information Systems.* Albany, NY: Rockefeller Institute of Government.

Moore, J. 1999. Personal Correspondence to Thompson, April 8.

Moore, J., and L. Sprague. 2000. *Reinventing Medicaid: Hoosier Healthwise and Children's Health Insurance in Indiana.* Washington, D.C.: National Health Policy Forum, George Washington University.

Morgan, D. 2000. "Food Stamp Rules Aim to Ease Access." *Washington Post,* November 19, p. A-11.

Nathan, R. P., and T. L. Gais. 1999. *Implementing the Personal Responsibility Act of 1996: A First Look.* Albany, NY: Rockefeller Institute.

National Performance Review. 1995. *Common Sense Government: Works Better & Costs Less.* Washington, D.C.: U.S. Government Printing Office.

Pear, R. 1999. "Clinton to Chide States for Failing to Cover Children." *New York Times,* August 8, pp. 1 & 27.

Pulos, V. 1999. *One Step Forward, One Step Back: Children's Health Insurance Coverage After CHIP and Welfare Reform.* Washington, D.C.: Families USA.

Radin, B. 1998. "The Government Performance and Results Act (GPRA): Hydra-Headed Monster or Flexible Management Tool?" *Public Administration Review* 58 (July/August): 307-316.

Schirm, A. L. 2000. "Reducing Those in Need: Food Stamp Participation Rates in the States." *FNS Online.* U.S. Department of Agriculture.

Http://www.fns.usda.gov/OANE/MENU/Published/FSP/ FILES/ FSPart2000sum.htm.

Selden, T. M, J. S. Banthin, and J. W. Cohen. 1999. "Waiting in the Wings: Eligibility and Enrollment in the State Children's Health Insurance Program." *Health Affairs* 18 (March/April): 126-133.

Selden, T. M., J. S. Banthin, and J. W. Cohen. 1998. "Medicaid's Problem Children: Eligible But Not Enrolled." *Health Affairs* 17 (May/June): 192-200.

Short, P. F. 2000. "Hitting a Moving Target: Income-Related Health Insurance Subsidies for the Uninsured." *Journal of Policy Analysis and Management* 19 (Summer): 383-406.

Steinhauer, J. 2000. "States Prove Unpredictable in Aiding Uninsured Children." *New York Times,* September 28, p. A16.

Thompson, F. J. and T. Gais. 2000. "Federalism and the Safety Net: Delinkage and Participation Rates." *Publius* 30 (Winter/Spring): 119-142.

Ullman, F., B. Bruen, and J. Holahan. 1998. *The State Children's Health Insurance Program: A Look at the Numbers.* Washington, D.C.: Urban Institute.

U.S. Department of Agriculture. 2000a. "Food Stamps: Governors Letter." *FNS Online.* Washington, D.C.: Food and Nutrition Service. http://www.fns.usda.gov/fsp.

U.S. Department of Agriculture. 2000b. *National Food Stamp Conversation 2000: Sharing a History of Accomplishment and Targeting Opportunities for Improvement.* Washington, DC: Food, Nutrition, and Consumer Services.

U.S. Department of Health and Human Services. 1998. *Report to the President: Interagency Task Force on Children's Health Insurance Outreach.* Washington, D.C.

U.S. Department of Health and Human Services. 1999. *Supporting Families in Transition: A Guide to Expanding Health Coverage in the Post-Welfare Reform World.* Washington, D.C.

U.S. Department of Health and Human Services. 1999a. "Understanding the Estimates of Uninsured Children: Putting the Difference in Context." Washington, D.C.: Assistant Secretary for Planning and Evaluation, http://www.aspe.os.dhhs.gov/rn/rn21.htm.

U.S. General Accounting Office. 1999. *Medicaid Enrollment: Amid Declines, State Efforts To Ensure Coverage After Welfare Reform Vary.* Washington, D.C.: GAO-HEHS-99-163.

U.S. General Accounting Office. 1999a. *Food Stamp Program: Various Factors Have Led to Declining Participation.* Washington, D.C.: GAO-RCED-99-185.

U.S. Health Care Financing Administration. 2000a. http://www.hcfa.gov, July.

U.S. Health Care Financing Administration. 2000b. Letter to state Medicaid directors, April 7. http:www.hcfa.gov./medicaid/smd40700.htm.

U.S. House of Representatives Committee on Government Reform and Oversight and U.S. Senate Committee on Governmental Affairs. 1996. *Performance-Based Government: Examining the Government Performance and Results Act of 1993.* Washington, D.C.: U.S. Government Printing Office.

U.S. House of Representatives Ways and Means Committee. 1989. *Background Material and Data on Programs Within the Jurisdiction of the Committee on Ways and Means.* Washington, D.C.: U.S. Government Printing Office.

U.S. House of Representatives Ways and Means Committee. 1991. *1991 Green Book: Background Material and Data on Programs Within the Jurisdiction of the Committee on Ways and Means.* Washington, D.C.: U.S. Government Printing Office.

U.S. House of Representatives Ways and Means Committee. 1996. *1996 Green Book: Background Material and Data on Programs Within the Jurisdiction of the Committee on Ways and Means.* Washington, D.C.: U.S. Government Printing Office.

U.S. House of Representatives Ways and Means Committee. 1998. *1998 Green Book: Background Material and Data on Programs Within the Jurisdiction of the Committee on Ways and Means.* Washington, D.C.: U.S. Government Printing Office.

U.S. House of Representatives Ways and Means Committee. 2000. *1998 Green Book: Background Material and Data on Programs Within the Jurisdiction of the Committee on Ways and Means.* Washington, D.C.: U.S. Government Printing Office.

Wallace, G., and Blank, R. M. 1999. "What Goes Up Must Come Down?" In *Economic Conditions and Welfare Reform*, S. H. Danziger , ed. Kalamazoo, MI: W.E. Upjohn Institute.

Wegener, V. 1999. *Food Stamp Education and Outreach Working to Provide Nutrition Benefits to Eligible Households. Welfare Information Network Issue Notes.* Washington, D.C.: Welfare Information Network.

Wilde, P., et al. 2000. "The Decline in Food Stamp Program Participation in the 1990s." *Food Assistance and Nutrition Research Report*, 7. Washington, D.C.: U.S. Department of Agriculture, Economic Research Service.

Zedlewski, S. R., and S. Brauner. 1999."Declines in Food Stamp and Welfare Participation: Is There a Connection?" Discussion Paper DP 99-13. Washington, D.C.: Urban Institute.

10

Empowerment Zones and the Promise of Accountability

David J. Wright

Few governmental programs have had higher aspirations or more ambitious performance measurement plans than the Empowerment Zone and Enterprise Community Initiative, signed into law by President Bill Clinton as part of the Omnibus Budget Reconciliation Act on August 10, 1993. With its mix of block grants, tax credits, and regulatory relief, the Zone program sought to catalyze strong community partnerships and fuel locally tailored investments that would generate sustained economic growth in some of the most distressed communities in America. To contrast the new effort from the perceived failures of federal community revitalization programs of the 1960s, the Clinton administration promised that the Zone program would also meet high standards for accountability, with community goals and programmatic objectives connected via benchmarks to measurable results.[1]

Benchmarking in the EZ/EC Initiative had several purposes, including performance measurement as it is commonly understood (see the Primer Box on page 277). The first was to articulate goals and objectives in a process that involved identifying strategies, prioritizing activities, assigning responsibilities and disseminating plans locally and to federal and state officials. Benchmarking was also the method by which the EZ/EC communities were to connect resources and results: the benchmark system tied the release of funds and evaluation of progress to specific measures of performance. Consistent with the general tenor of the program, those measures were to be selected not by federal officials but by the participating communities themselves. Last, by enabling individual citizens to track the use of EZ/EC resources and the program's progress via the Internet, the Zone program's benchmarking system was supposed to democratize information on performance measurement. Benchmarking, in this respect, was intended to have a direct and positive role in fostering community empowerment and contributing to participatory democracy.

The goals for the Empowerment Zone program's performance-based management system were surely lofty, but the program provided an unlikely setting for success. Like other community building and revitalization strategies, the program was complex, overlapping, and subject to social and economic forces beyond local control — traits that make it all the harder to establish baselines, define the intervention, and measure results. Multiple agencies and layers of government were involved in the EZ/EC Initiative, muddying communication, goal setting, and program control. The federal department most responsible for selecting and overseeing operations of the participating urban sites had little control over the primary funding stream and limited means by which to affect local performance. In the participating sites, non-expert administrators in small governmental or nonprofit organizations were typically charged with implementing the program. They confronted instructions, terminology, and formats for the performance reports that were often unclear, unfamiliar, and subject to frequent change. If performance benchmarking in the Zone program was to work, in short, it would not be because the odds were stacked in its favor.

Results of performance benchmarking in the Empowerment Zone program — very much a work in progress — have been mixed: more positive than a critical observer might expect given the circumstances, though considerably short of what was advertised. Key informants in several cities report that the benchmarks have been useful for setting goals and, in particular, for publicizing information about strategies and projects to a wider range of citizens.

Empowerment Zone Benchmarking: A Primer

Benchmarking as defined by the Zone program does not refer to a comparison between an objective external standard and performance or practice, as the customary use of the term would suggest. Rather, the Zone program has used the term to refer to everything from a specific program document to the whole process of establishing priorities for program spending, from strategic planning onward.

Program documents define benchmarks, meanwhile, as the specific *outputs* that a community must produce to address identified *categories of need*, defined as the community goals or broad problem areas a community's strategic plan identifies and attempts to address. Examples include: "Build or rehabilitate 50 low-cost housing units; provide day care services for 25 children; or provide 15 businesses with micro-loans." Categories of need involve "inadequate supply of affordable housing, insufficient day care services, unavailability of small business loans," and the like.

At a finer grain of specificity, *benchmark activities* are defined as "the actions that must take place in order for a community to achieve the benchmark." Examples offered include: "Develop a housing construction or rehabilitation plan; build a new day care facility; identify local banks willing to participate in funding a micro-loan program." *Tasks/projects*, in turn, are defined as the efforts necessary to complete the benchmark activity, such as: "Conduct a survey of potential housing construction sites or existing housing units in need of rehabilitation; solicit bids for the construction of a day care facility; or form a committee of local bankers interested in jointly funding a micro-loan program."

The definitions of other terms employed in the accountability provisions of the Zone program are more traditional. *Baselines*, for example, "serve as the starting point from which benchmarks are measured." *Outcomes*, in turn, are defined as "the long-term results generated from addressing the categories of need identified in the Strategic Plan." They are also referenced as "the measurable changes that take place in the community over a period of time." *Participating Entities*, meanwhile, are defined as the individual actors/organizations playing a role in achieving a benchmark. Finally, *Costs/Sources* are defined as the financial, human, and other resource commitments needed to achieve benchmarks, as well as the EZ/EC partners (federal, state, and local government agencies, businesses, banks, educational institutions, foundations, utilities, others) providing the resources.

However, as will be discussed, the goal-setting and dissemination function was undercut by the timing of performance reporting, extensive revision in its requirements, an emphasis on quantifiable progress too early in the program, and a reduction in the level and range of stakeholder involvement as activities shifted from planning to implementation. In some sites, the objectives of accountability benchmarking and community empowerment have seemingly been at odds.

Benchmarks and related management reports have been less useful as a gauge of performance. Meaningful baseline information relating to proposed activities has been generally absent, as have solid measures of outcomes. Local reports have typically included extraneous activities as program effects and have had difficulty linking information on funding to individual projects. Connections between the strategic purpose of an activity and what was to be measured as progress have rarely been made.

Taken as a whole, experience with benchmarking in the Zone program serves as something of a cautionary tale. The story — drawn from a review of performance data on all 72 urban program sites and in-depth analysis by indigenous scholars in an 18-city field network study — shows how difficult it can be to implement seemingly straightforward performance measurement systems for complex, multi-level community development efforts; how important it is to try; and how such efforts can improve.

An Atypical Federal Program

The Empowerment Zone/Enterprise Community Initiative occupies hard-won middle ground in a long-standing debate over the direction of targeted community development policy. The program was awarded through a remarkable selection process, was administered by an atypical oversight structure, and offered an unusual combination of assistance. Each of these characteristics bore directly on the program's performance benchmarking efforts.

For more than a decade, as state after state developed its own enterprise zone program, progress on similar initiatives in

Washington was prevented by a protracted debate on whether the federal government could best help distressed communities by "getting out of the way" or by becoming a more active partner. Advocates of the former approach argued that government could help best by removing barriers to development, that is, rewarding private entities for investing in distressed communities through targeted tax and regulatory relief. Supporters of the second approach, in contrast, reasoned that tax and regulatory relief could not compensate for the disadvantages affecting such communities, and argued that the government could and should be a more active catalyst through targeted public investment. A subset of the debate focused on whether such investments and incentives should be "people- or place-based"; targeted to people in need through skills training or wage subsidies, or to the places they inhabit through physical development projects intended to attract new businesses.

The EZ/EC Initiative formed new common ground upon which the sides could agree. The program provided tax credits, including a wage tax credit for new employees who both live and work in a targeted area. Block grants would support a wide range of social development objectives. Both the tax benefits and targeted investment varied in intensity across four categories of site designation: Empowerment Zones on one end of the spectrum, which were few in number and received the deepest and most flexible package of development incentives, followed by Supplemental Empowerment Zones, Enhanced Enterprise Communities, and Enterprise Communities on the opposite end of the range, which were most numerous and received the shallowest subsidy (the latter term was used to refer to all the categories other than EZs). All received equal promises of regulatory relief and program accountability (see Table 1).[2]

The EZ/EC Initiative's application process also broke new ground. The cornerstone of the application for designation as an Empowerment Zone or Enterprise Community was not a predetermined form but rather a *ten-year strategic plan* that was supposed to emerge from a bottom-up process, and meet comprehensive community needs while building on assets.[3] The application process was modeled in part on a series of community-based strategic-planning initiatives under way in many cities, and was designed to

Quicker, Better, Cheaper?
Managing Performance in American Government

Table 1
EZ/EC Benefits to Sites

Site Benefits	Empowerment Zones (n=6)	Enterprise Communities (n=65*)	Supplemental Empowerment Zones (n=2)	Enhanced Enterprise Communities (n=4)
Social Services Block Grant	$100 million	$2.95 million	$2.95 million to Cleveland	$2.95 million
Economic Development Initiative Grants			$125 million to Los Angeles $87 million to Cleveland	$22 million
Section 108 Loan Guarantee Authority			$125 million to Los Angeles $87 million to Cleveland	$22 million
Section 179 Accelerated Depreciation	Yes	No	No	No
Wage Tax Credits	Yes	No	No	No
Eligibility for Tax Exempt Facility Bonds	Yes	Yes	Yes	Yes
Special Consideration for Waiver Requests	Yes	Yes	Yes	Yes
Special Consideration for Various Federal Grants	Yes	Yes	Yes	Yes

* The Cleveland SEZ and the four EECs are also designated as ECs, equaling 65 in total.

capture the spirit and philosophy of the EZ/EC initiative by fostering community building and empowerment. Expecting that some cities would find the process quite different from previous federal grant applications, federal administering agencies prepared a *Guidebook* that drew from the experiences and best practices of many organizations engaged in community-based strategic planning, and held a series of regional workshops to explain the Initiative and the planning process to potential applicants.

Program materials and workshops all stressed a common theme: that applicants must demonstrate that the strategic planning process involved participation from all segments of the community — political and governmental leaders, community groups, nonprofit service providers, religious organizations, medical and educational institutions, the private sector, and most important, residents. Communities did not have to follow a prescribed format in developing their strategic plans. Instead, the application guide listed topics and issues that communities "should consider."

The federal application guidelines were deliberately vague and encouraged communities to be visionary ("what is the overall vision for revitalization of the designated area?"), to be comprehensive ("how will your approaches to different community problems be linked together to make your vision a reality?"), and to leverage public and private resources ("what government resources will be used to support your plan? What private resources are committed to implement your plan?"). Planners were also supposed to be sensitive to the challenge of moving from plan to action ("what are the barriers to the successful implementation of your plan? How will you implement your strategic plan and what benchmarks will you use to measure progress?"[4]). To be selected, each site had to meet detailed criteria establishing relative need, design and adopt a community-based strategic plan that articulated the use of program benefits, and be nominated by state and local governments (see box on eligibility).

The program's administrative structure was also a departure from the norm. A single department or agency administers most federal programs. The Empowerment Zone program, however,

Eligibility for EZ/EC Designation

Designated Empowerment Zone and Enterprise Community sites had to meet the following threshold qualifications involving pervasive poverty, unemployment, and general distress stipulated in the EZ/EC legislation:

- Populations less than 200,000 or greater than either 50,000 or 10 percent of the population of the most populous city in the area;

- Pervasive poverty, unemployment, and general distress;

- A total land area of 20 square miles or less;

- A poverty rate of at least 20 percent in each census tract, 25 percent in 90 percent of the tracts nominated, and 35 percent in 50 percent of the nominated tracts;

- A continuous boundary or not more than three noncontiguous parcels;

- A location entirely within the jurisdiction of the local government(s) making the nomination and within not more than two contiguous states; and

- No portion of a central business district in a census tract unless every such tract has a poverty rate of at least 35 percent for an EZ, or 30 percent for an EC.

Additionally, a community must have submitted a strategic plan that:

- Describes the coordinated economic, human, community, and physical development and related activities proposed for the nominated area;

- Describes the process by which members of the community, local institutions, and organizations are involved in, and have contributed to, the process of developing and implementing the plan;

- Specifies needed waivers or other changes sought in federal, state, and local governmental programming to enable better coordination and delivery; and

- Identifies the state, local, and private resources that will be available to the nominated area.

The area must also have been nominated by the state and relevant local government, ensuring the commitment of these partners to the program's resources and reinvention.

involves three federal cabinet departments in lead roles. The Departments of Agriculture as well as Housing and Urban Development designate and administer the rural and urban portions of the
program, respectively. Meanwhile, the Department of Health and
Human Services provides primary funding for the program
through the Social Services Block Grant. At a broader level, the entire Empowerment Zone Initiative is under the direction of the president's Community Enterprise Board, an entity chaired by the vice
president and which includes the cabinet secretaries and commissioners of nearly every major domestic agency of the U.S. government.

Thus, community development efforts under the Zone program were to run an unusually broad gamut, be selected locally
through an uncommonly broad, open, and iterative process, and be
met by a federal oversight structure where the department most responsible for urban sites controlled neither the funding stream, tax
benefits, nor regulatory relief that the federal government was to
supply. These program characteristics stacked the odds against a
successful performance reporting system.

Strategies, Benchmarks,
and Community Power

Benchmarking in the Zone program began with development of the
strategic plans submitted by local groups in application for designation as an Empowerment Zone or Enterprise Community. The program's *Application Guide* noted that strategic plans should set "real
goals and performance benchmarks for measuring progress" and
suggested that interested applicants identify the specific tasks and
timetables necessary to implement their plans, describe the partnerships involved, explain how the strategic plans would be regularly
revised to reflect new information and circumstances, and identify
the baselines, outputs, and goals that should be used in evaluating
performance in implementing the plan.[5] That these performance
benchmarks were needed was actually more than a suggestion: applicants were informed that selection criteria for designation would
include an assessment of how well the proposed plan incorporates

realistic performance indicators for measuring progress and making needed adjustments.

One of the more important features of these strategic plans and the benchmarks they contained was the involvement of the community in their development. And this aspect of the program produced notable success. In the nearly unanimous opinion of local researchers in a national field network study on the program, citizen participation in the development of local EZ/EC strategic plans was significantly higher than under previous federal urban initiatives, although most citizen participants were reported to be savvy and well-seasoned representatives from community groups, neighborhood-based service providers, and civic associations rather than unaffiliated individuals.[6]

The typical planning process for an EZ application began as a local-government-directed initiative and evolved into a more open process in which community members played an important role. Most communities held a series of town hall style meetings and neighborhood workshops to foster community input. These meetings were often used to recruit citizens to serve on task forces, advisory boards, and steering committees to direct and shape the drafting of the strategic plan.

In some cities — generally those with existing citizen participation structures or neighborhood-based initiatives that could serve as platforms for new strategic planning efforts — citizen control over the process and content of EZ/EC planning was extensive from the outset and without controversy. In Charlotte, for example, neighborhood groups were considered partners by city staff in developing the application. In Minneapolis, the strategic planning process was closely intertwined with the city's Neighborhood Revitalization Program, begun a few years earlier. In San Francisco, the city contracted with a respected community-based organization in each zone neighborhood to facilitate the strategic planning process.

Other cities confronted significant conflict over community involvement in local Zone plans. In Chicago, tensions about what role citizens would play in preparing the application came to a head when a community leader seized the microphone from a startled deputy planning commissioner to ask city officials and their consultants to leave the room so the 200 community representatives attending a town hall meeting could caucus. This session produced a new proposal for a reconstituted planning council to oversee the application process. Unlike the original 30-member coordinating council whose members were appointed by the mayor, half the members of the newly proposed group would be chosen by the community. When presented with the proposal, city officials agreed to take the recommendation to the mayor, who subsequently endorsed and implemented it.[7]

A similar confrontation occurred during the first meeting of a group appointed by the mayor of Atlanta to provide citizen input into that city's EZ planning process. Having endured more than 90 minutes of being told by city officials how behind they were in the EZ application process, one citizen member responded:

> *"I am tired of getting things packaged and handed to us after the fact. This board should have been brought into this process six months ago. We are behind? I have a problem with your definition of the word 'we.' The problem with all this is precisely that you did it, not we. You designed this process, you picked the zone, you chose the consultants, and you control how the money gets spent in the planning process."*[8]

In response, the City Council, at the request of the mayor, rescinded its earlier ordinance designating Atlanta's zone area and called for the expansion of the Community Empowerment Board to include 69 representatives, one from each neighborhood comprised of census tracts with poverty rates of 35 percent or higher. The expanded CEB selected the proposed zone area and played an important role in developing Atlanta's strategic plan.

The result of this broadened participation was a prevailing and unusual sense of community ownership over Zone applications. Hopes were high. Time and vital energy was spent. And community members felt invested in the outcome; a sense felt nowhere more strongly than in those cities where citizen participation was itself seen as a victory that had been won.

Coping with Serial Goal Setting

"Careful, you might get what you wish for," so the saying goes. For cities rewarded with designation through the Zones program — 72 of the 292 that applied — goal setting in the application's ten-year strategic plan was just the beginning. Successful sites had to reconcile their plans with the level of support they received and quickly come to terms with changing benchmark reporting requirements from HUD.

For all but the six Empowerment Zones and a few sites that sought to be Enterprise Communities from the beginning, the success of achieving designation brought a need to fundamentally redesign their strategic plans. The vast majority of participating sites had to translate $100 million Zone plans into $2.95 million Enterprise Community plans. For the sites designated Supplemental Empowerment Zones or Enhanced Enterprise Communities, revisions were needed to accommodate funding that was both lower and from different, less flexible sources than expected. Generally, program sites reconciled plans and available benefits by reducing the number of benchmark activity areas they would undertake, which was far and away the most common approach; by addressing the same range of activities as originally planned but on a considerably reduced scale; or by leaving the benchmarks virtually unchanged while attempting to compensate with private and in-kind investments as well as matching funds from other governmental entities.

Choosing to significantly reduce the range of program activities meant that major changes had to be made in community priorities and strategies reached through a sometimes fractious and only recently concluded planning process. Not surprisingly, advocates of strategies that were to be dropped balked at the prospect of being left out. Conflict and political bargaining typically resulted.

The alternative of maintaining the range but reducing the scale of planned activities carried political as well as programmatic appeal. Across-the-board cuts in the scale of proposed initiatives had the patina of evenhandedness and in theory, would maintain the breadth of the community's vision and avoid intense opposition to more targeted changes. This appeal proved to be largely ephemeral. Reducing the scale of certain activities rendered them all but meaningless and required a complicated redesign process. Making everyone a little unhappy rather than a few people very unhappy did not pan out as a wise political strategy; widespread but shallow changes were still seen as requiring serious alterations to the community's vision.

A third alternative — to leave the plan alone and attempt to fill the resource gap from other sources — had the political appeal of a "fight for" the dreams and program activities enumerated by the stakeholders involved in the planning process. However, it meant that the community agreed to be held accountable for progress on a plan that was originally only partially funded.

Whatever the approach, the rub was finding a way to honor, yet significantly alter, what was produced through the community planning process. This result tended to undercut the very sense of community empowerment that the program sought to support, and contributed to mistrust and political unrest in a number of cities that had a lingering, negative effect on site performance.

It was into this tense, uncertain environment that the U.S. Department of Housing and Urban Development (HUD) introduced a revised benchmarking process for the urban EZ and EC sites. As a rule, in most communities the "visioning" process directed most of its energy into painting the big picture of hopes and aspirations; a sense of what might and should be done over ten years. Planners devoted comparatively little, certainly far less, attention to details like establishing firm measures of current conditions, specific action steps, and item-specific budgets. Soon after the sites were designated, however, HUD moved to require formalized benchmarks containing far greater detail. And the requirement was not subtle: having an approved set of revised benchmarks in place was a prerequisite for funding approval and contract adoption.

To produce the new benchmark reports, participating sites were instructed to begin with their ten-year strategic plan, reexamine its vision and strategies, confirm or adjust them as appropriate, prioritize benchmarks and activities to be implemented during the first two years, and confirm the resulting prioritization/re-ranking with community stakeholders. Program sites were also instructed to organize and report their benchmarks and benchmark activities by category of need, identify the baseline for each category, identify tasks necessary to complete each benchmark activity, identify how each activity would be funded, and input all of this information into a benchmarking template.

Every aspect of these additionally detailed requirements was troublesome for the program sites; a few were minefields. Specific agreements had to be crystallized concerning respective responsibilities and resource commitments, which were technically and politically complicated. Changing from a ten-year to a two-year horizon was the equivalent of reopening the planning process as most if not all local stakeholders wanted their pieces to occur within the program's first two years.

Observers reported that the benchmark process influenced the content of community strategies in other ways as well. Recognizing that urban decline had occurred over decades and would not be turned around overnight, a number of the strategic plans, such as that of the Louisville EC, involved long-term processes. By the time benchmarking rolled around, however, communities faced significant countervailing pressure to show progress. Consequently, the benchmarks tended to emphasize comparatively short-term impact. Close observers in Louisville also reported that the emphasis on quantifiable results made it difficult to gain a meaningful sense of early progress, when intense organizing dominated activities.[9]

The fact that the EZ/EC communities felt themselves to be under considerable time pressure to complete these processes quickly did not make the challenge any easier. Each site was expected to file a complete set of benchmarks in concert with its formal contract with HUD. Otherwise, program resources would be unavailable. Until then, press events to sign such agreements and present oversized checks to local leaders could not be held.

With mounting evidence that the performance management reporting requirements were the cause of inordinate delay in some EZ/EC sites, HUD began to accept some benchmark reports while still at a rather general level, subject to refinement and development. Then, the agency issued what program managers regarded as a substantial refinement in the accountability reporting system: the Performance Review. HUD billed this review as a "simplified benchmark submission," insofar as it "no longer required [Zone or Community sites] to provide the task information requested in the original benchmark submission form."[10]

A revised *Performance Review Template* was distributed to organize and standardize key information from participating cities. The template (Figure 1) asked participating cities to list projected milestones, performance measures, investments, start and completion dates, and participating entities. Progress was to be measured by the degree to which a city accomplished what was projected.

An unintended by-product of this perpetual goal setting was a sense of confusion about what exactly had been identified in the benchmarks/performance review and how it connected to the strategic plan. Nowhere was this disconnect more striking than in the Chicago Empowerment Zone. Chicago's strategic plan described a "tool box" full of possible approaches rather than a detailed plan, undermining the whole premise of the program's benchmark accountability system — that the plan would articulate a community's vision and allow the community to track the results.

Cities achieving mid-level designations as Supplemental Zones or Enhanced Enterprise Communities faced special hardship, as funding for these designations caused their use to be more restricted. The results of the ensuing efforts to redesign the programs tended to be so divergent from the communities' original strategies that in Boston, there was uncertainty and strong differences among stakeholders about what the benchmarks really represented[11] and in Oakland, local observers reported that "not even the people most involved in the EEC know what the benchmarks are or what they mean."[12]

The Louisville Enterprise Community had a different problem. An early programmatic decision to retain the community's $100 million Empowerment Zone strategy despite the area's designation as a $3 million EC had important consequences for benchmarking.

Figure 1
Empowerment Zones/Enterprise Communities
Performance Review

CATEGORY OF NEED:
BASELINE:
ACTIVITY NAME:
ADDRESS:
DESCRIPTION:

PERFORMANCE CATEGORIES	PROJECTED	ACTUAL
PERFORMANCE MILESTONES AND DATES Use this section to report on key interim actions that will result in the completion of the activity. Include projected and actual dates.		
PERFORMANCE MEASURES Use this section to report the final product(s) this activity will produce, e.g. the number of jobs created/retained, housing units built/rehabilitated, business expansions/startups, child care slots created, or other measurable benchmark outcomes of the activity.		
INVESTMENTS Federal State/Local Private		
START DATE		
COMPLETION DATE		
PARTICIPATING ENTITIES		

NARRATIVE Activity ID No.

The city and the stakeholder community determined that they would rather compensate for the gap by finding other funding sources rather than back away from their plan, so benchmarks were designed to track progress on the original strategy. However, local leaders were loath to be held accountable on that basis. The Dallas EC made a similar judgment to pursue the comprehensive EZ-level revitalization effort despite lower designation as an EC, but it chose to fill the gap through other citywide initiatives not enumerated in the benchmarks. Stakeholders in both areas found themselves unsure how to crosswalk from strategic plans to benchmarks.

Atlanta faced much confusion regarding how much of the $100 million block grant award had been "benchmarked." The initial benchmarks applied to roughly $32 million in funding. A later amendment to the benchmarks detailed more than $13 million in projects, but those involved disagreed about whether the set was additive or included in the original total. The Performance Review represented yet a third set of benchmarks, but because it was submitted to HUD without required prior review and approval by the citizen board, there was strong disagreement about whether it or the original benchmarks should be considered the official tally.[13]

A degree of evolution in reporting requirements and methods in the rollout of a new initiative is hardly surprising. Still, the extent and frequency of changes in the Zone program's performance reporting system were notable, and those changes appeared to exert a negative influence on implementation. Revised report requirements, terminology, and instructions contributed to confusion among local sites. Likewise, the process of perpetual goal setting sewed confusion and helped throw hard-won community harmony off-key.

Performance Goals and Governance: Carts, Horses, and Johnny-Come-Latelies

One of the first — and oftentimes testiest — tasks cities faced following their designation as an EZ or EC was the development of a governance structure to guide implementation. Zone governance structures varied across a number of dimensions. Some of the more important included the degree of integration the EZ or EC would have with city government, the extent of decentralization in recognition of neighborhoods or sub-areas within the designated zone, continuity between decisionmakers involved in developing the strategic plan and those in Zone governance, and the level and character of involvement or control by members of community.

At the time they were designated as an EZ or EC, few if any of the sites had a really clear handle on the substance of what they were going to do or on who would be making, executing, and evaluating decisions.[14] Because of the sequencing of steps, sites' benchmarks and performance review reports in many cases were developed and submitted to HUD before organizational structures and staffing were established. As advisory and governing boards were brought online, new leaders were hired and relationships with governmental entities were ironed out, earlier versions of benchmarks — in particular the prioritization of activities and the specification of action steps — were subject to review and revision.

Implementing organizations and staff often possessed rather different views of program activities than planners, and did a fair amount of policy design in fleshing out new projects. As a close observer of the Phoenix Enterprise Community put it: "The people eventually assigned to actually implement the benchmarks are people who had no input into either the benchmark or performance measure development...[and for them, since] they are still working on adequate definition of the problem to be addressed and will start designing a program soon, having benchmarks and performance measures already established is like putting the cart before the horse."[15]

Pushing rather than pulling carts was not the only problem. The horses were changing too. Once the sites achieved designation, the number of parties seeking money tended to expand. This often caused bitter resentments among those who had done the heavier lifting earlier on. In Atlanta, individuals most invested in preparing the strategic plan were plainly irritated by what one of them referred to as all the "johnny come latelies" who lay claim to a share of the EZ resources.[16]

Close observers in San Francisco reported a similar phenomenon, one egged on by the benchmark system itself. With their staff, expertise, and connections, established community organizations were able to respond rapidly and successfully when funding became available in the EC, outcompeting the organizers and neighborhood activists who had been more involved in developing the plan. As described in the field report:

> [T]he old guard leaders of established CBOs [community-based organizations] moved in and essentially took over the neighborhood planning body once the groundwork had been laid by others and the money started flowing. [As a seasoned local leader said:] "when the money comes in everything − benchmarks, funding principles − goes out the window."[17]

Somewhat pushy "new" participants were showing up from above as well, in the form of oversight personnel from state agencies. The states generally had a rather awkward, ambivalent role in the Zone program. At a minimum, their acquiescence was needed in nominating sites to HUD. The practical fact was that the program's primary funding source was a block grant from the U.S. Department of Health and Human Services to states for which a number of states continued to feel fiduciary responsibility, despite admonitions from HUD to simply pass money through.

Soon after Atlanta's designation as an EZ community, for example, Georgia's Commissioner of the Department of Community Affairs (DCA) outlined several issues that needed to be addressed regarding the terms and condition of the award before DCA would release any funds to the city. These issues included clarification of the implementing entity that would carry out Atlanta's strategic plan, the use of EZ block grant funds for local program administration, and detailed description of the mechanisms and procedures by which the city would ensure financial accountability and compliance with laws and regulations. Nearly two years later, the city and state had not reached agreement on all the outstanding issues.[18]

In North Carolina, to draw down the Enterprise Community funds provided by HUD, lengthy negotiations were required to complete a memorandum of understanding between the city of

Charlotte and state Departments of Social Services (DSS) and Community Assistance (DCA), formalizing the responsibilities of each governmental entity. The resulting memorandum granted considerable authority to the state: DSS disburses funds to the City of Charlotte after invoices are approved by DCA.[19] In East St. Louis and the Camden portion of the Philadelphia Empowerment Zone, state oversight committees with the power to review and possibly reverse decisions of the local governmental units were present or imminent because of previous inadequacies of the local governments in both settings.

In a number of places, new governors or mayors had been elected — in New York's case, one of each — since the plans had been composed, and the new officials felt little if any constraint in reevaluating their predecessors' support or insisting that changes be made. They were given much leverage since the states were signatories on program contract documents and because state approval was needed for the benchmarks to be adopted.

While these new participants were arriving on the scene, community participation was declining. As the process evolved from the identification of goals and strategies to the more technical tasks of completing benchmark forms and submitting performance reviews, participation of technicians — government officials, service deliverers, loaned staff and the like — grew significantly and eclipsed that of community stakeholders.[20]

The delegation of technical tasks to technicians should not be unexpected; community members have only limited time and their efforts should be employed where they will make the most valuable contribution. But benchmarking and performance review were not ministerial tasks. Although the process and terminology were highly technical, what was involved was often nothing less than a fundamental reformulation of the vision and strategy expressed by the community. By essentially supplanting the strategic plans without reengaging community members in the process, benchmarking fed a sense in many places that the effort had been "taken over by others" and undermined feelings of trust and partnership between community stakeholders, city leaders, and their state and federal counterparts.

Limits on Accountability Data: Uncertain Responsibilities and Fuzzy Math

Despite these shortcomings and limitations, reports from the field confirmed that the benchmarking and performance review processes were regarded by participants at the local level as generally effective in maintaining a focus on goals and objectives. The primary reason was that, especially in contrast to other programs, the benchmark system provided a mechanism for local Zone stakeholders to hold the process and the institutional actors involved accountable to the "community vision" expressed in the strategic plans. In Atlanta, as well as in Tacoma, Dallas, Minneapolis, East St. Louis, and Louisville, local participants generally agreed that the benchmarks kept them thinking about the programs they had said they were going to work on, provided them with timelines and numbers with which to measure progress, helped them avoid insubstantial "fly-by-night" projects, and provided a means to ensure that local officials implemented the plan.[21]

The benchmarking/performance review system was intended to do more than enable local stakeholders to better define what the sites were doing, however. The accountability provisions were also intended to track *how* the sites would accomplish their intent; specifically, what entities would be responsible for designated activities, and how funding was to be allocated. Unfortunately, these aspects of the Zone program's performance reporting system proved to be more of a struggle. To be effective, performance-reporting systems must be able to provide thorough, unambiguous information about who is to do what by when. But such information was often unavailable from the Zone program's performance benchmarking system at anything beyond the most general level.

In Baltimore, key elements of the plan were to be carried out by six newly created Village Centers. Although the performance reports list the steps in developing the Village Centers, it is unclear from the benchmarks who is accountable for achieving this goal.[22] Atlanta participants cited a similar lack of detail about responsibility for carrying out strategies: the benchmarks identify only broad categories such as "community development corporations," "banks," and the "private sector" rather than specific organizations. One benchmark from Minneapolis consisted entirely of the statement "create one small business incubator," with no responsibility specified. The absence of clearly assigned responsibility makes it difficult to track accountability for program results.

Accountability was also undermined by a lack of clarity in performance review reports bred by confusing instructions from HUD. The agency's description of the performance review template as "an easy way to report progress for each activity the EZ/EC has underway"[23] led some sites to report only on those activities "underway," omitting anything pending, delayed or scheduled to start later. HUD instructed the sites to "complete a template for each activity that has a separate outcome," and told local officials that "if a benchmark establishes a commercial loan program to start 10 small businesses, and if 4 startup businesses received loans during the reporting period, complete a template for each of the 4 businesses."[24] Following the instruction literally, as some sites did, obfuscated actual progress: the difference between reaching an inappropriate conclusion that four separate loan activities are 100 percent complete rather than understanding that 40 percent of loans under a newly created loan activity had been made.

Money was hard to keep track of as well. As a rule, a performance reporting system ought to specify resources for a given set of program activities. This was not the situation in most EZ or EC sites. For many benchmarks, the amount of funding or the source was either unknown or not listed. The benchmarks/performance review often included only broad mention of the resources to be allocated for the respective program or purpose.

Close observers in Dallas reported that the benchmarks captured the receipt and disbursement of the formal EC grant, yet funding obtained from other sources was not described as clearly. Officials in Phoenix reported a problem in accounting for EC activities across departmental lines, given the program's collaborative, multidisciplinary approach.[25] Such questions of attribution and financial accounting go to the heart of program accountability.

An additional complication arose from the fact that in each city, activities were under way or planned that might directly or indirectly affect the target area, but that were not supported with EZ/EC resources. Local governmental efforts that preceded and continued during the Zone program were a common example. HUD instructed the participating sites to include such activities in performance review reports, whether part of the strategy and a cost to program resources or not. The instruction was not without theoretical justification: the EZ/EC initiative, after all, was intended to build upon and catalyze other efforts, not supplant them. However, the leverage and impacts of the program would be artificially inflated to the extent that non-EZ/EC activities are wrongfully included under the definition of "program."

Some test of nexus and causality needs to be imposed to determine whether other activities are, indeed, leveraged by the Zone program. Generally, those tests were not performed, either by the sites individually or by HUD. To some observers, the Department's own Inspector General among them, this problem has made program reports on the extent of EZ/EC leverage suspect if not fatally unreliable.

Limits on Evaluative Data: Absent Baselines, Weak Measures, Overlapping Effects, and Faint Feedback

Effective accountability systems require meaningful baseline information against which to assess progress — not simply data about general conditions in the community but detailed beginning points relating directly to proposed strategies and activities. The lack of appropriate baseline information significantly limited the effectiveness of benchmarks as an evaluation device. It was rare indeed for an EZ or EC site to have developed anything approximating analytic data detailing the conditions that a given strategy and its benchmarking activities were designed to address. It was even more rare for baseline data to relate directly to what was measured as an indicator of progress.

Many of the participating sites called for increasing access to development capital through a micro-loan program, for example. Characteristically, neither the strategic plan nor the benchmark report cited preexisting demand for, or supply of, such capital. Instead, for "baseline," the benchmark would simply state: "There is no existing micro-loan program." The activity would be specified as "create a micro-loan program," and the measure of progress would be whether the program was created rather than whether access to capital had improved.

To the degree that baseline data were used in the benchmarking process, the data were taken directly and without change from the strategic plans. This information was typically out of date, as more than six months elapsed between a site's application and designation, and considerably more time passed as the program was implemented

The absence of analytic starting points for Zone activities became a serious weakness for the program's performance reporting system. It is plainly hard to know where one is headed or how much progress is being made without such information.

The relative quality of performance measures used by local sites posed another important source of weakness for the Zone program's performance reporting system. Early on, program managers at HUD sought to ensure that the sites recognized the distinction between outputs and outcomes, and would stress output data as the measure of activity and progress in the material they submitted for accountability purposes. "The EZ/EC Task Force is asking communities to define their benchmarks in terms of outputs rather than outcomes," HUD staff wrote in a communiqué to participating sites. "The basis for this approach is that the achievement of outcomes is more likely to be hindered by factors outside the scope of the EZ/EC Initiative than is the achievement of benchmarks."[26] This is sound, practical advice from the point of view of a manager who wants to keep his or her head down when the shooting starts. But it sets the accountability bar pretty low.

Information on outputs and milestones can add nuance and detail. To be meaningful, however, such measures need to be compared against standards of expected performance that are objective, rigorous, and clearly articulated. Moreover, such data must be complemented with carefully drawn measures of intermediate or end outcomes: gauges on the extent of change in conditions that program activities are intended to address. On both counts, the experience with benchmarking and performance review in the typical Empowerment Zone or Enterprise Community generally fell short of this ideal.

Even in the best of circumstances, the minority of cases with available and quantifiable baselines and benchmark measures, it is far from evident that performance measures were meaningful. Program managers typically relied to a considerable extent on vendors and service organizations to establish their own benchmark measures, often developed from their own existing activities. Some organizations had direct outcomes that were impact-oriented. Others simply reported programmatic activity as a benchmark (for example, "make presentations to 1300 students"). There is no indication that the sites or HUD examined statements of expected performance to judge their veracity or relevance.

An additional complication arose from the overlapping effects of program activities. It is commonplace for EZ or EC sites to incorporate initiatives that would be measured by similar benchmarks. An evaluation would seek to attribute change to particular activities even though several were occurring in the same place at the same time. However, the capacity of the benchmark information to contribute to such a process is quite limited.

A related issue concerns the attribution of results to one program when they may have been due to a combination of programs, including influences not directly part of the initiative. This problem is inherent in comprehensive community efforts. As our Dallas field associate put it: "In many cases it may be impossible to assign improvements in the neighborhood to a specific component of the program. If property values rise, is it because a new business opened, the crime rate was reduced, or perceptions of the neighborhood changed?"[27] From benchmark/performance review material, it is impossible to tell.

The public safety-related aspects of the Dallas EC plan illustrate the problem. Because other programs were ongoing, and since generating crime statistics for the EC required reporting for a geographic area that did not match existing reporting units, the attribution of reduced crime statistics to the EC Initiative was perceived as somewhat questionable.

A larger problem of measuring the performance of a community-based effort is the inability to hold extraneous factors constant. Macro-level change in the economy, for example, will likely exert far greater influence on neighborhood transformation than EZ or EC activities. The benchmarking/performance review system did not attempt to take such factors into account, preferring to instruct participating sites to focus on activity outputs instead.

Accountability systems should also provide for feedback. A central purpose in gathering and reporting performance information is to put it to practical use in making adjustments and building on what works. Only two sites among the eighteen studied in the Rockefeller Institute's field network achieved this level of functionality in their performance reporting system. In San Francisco, the benchmarking process armed the EC Board and Neighborhood Planning Boards with the means to insist on fulfillment of performance targets in contract compliance reviews and funding decisions. Our field associates reported that local participants in San Francisco became more accomplished in this feedback technique as they underwent training and gained experience.[28]

A similar story unfolded in Tacoma. There, the Board of the Tacoma Empowerment Consortium (an amalgam of nonprofit service providers and other stakeholders that oversees and operates the Zone program) found benchmarking a useful tool for revisiting issues and noting areas of weakness — one that gave them a better chance of success. [29]

For other empowerment zone and enterprise community sites, however, feedback was missing from the benchmarking/performance review processes altogether, or at best was faint. This was particularly the case in using experience to revisit the underlying plans and strategies. As an Atlanta Empowerment Zone board member noted: "The benchmarks must be a living document, capable of adaptation and change. But there seems to be considerable resistance on the part of the citizen board members to deviate at all from what was written in the Strategic Plan. The plan was put together ... years ago and conditions have changed in some areas while new opportunities have opened up in others. Rather than apply strategic planning as a dynamic and evolving process...in Atlanta strategic planning has been carried out as a static, one-shot, exercise."[30] In the Atlanta EZ as in other sites, ironically, this problem of rigidity stemmed in part from the pervasive change in the plans and the process earlier on. A result of plan fatigue or stubbornness borne of political conflict, many if not most Zone program sites were simply not geared to use the performance reporting system as a learning tool.

In Louisville, the Zone program's performance reporting requirements were viewed as an unnecessary and time-consuming burden more important to HUD than to residents or professionals active in the Enterprise Community.[31] City staffs in Phoenix, too, were "clearly disgruntled" with the benchmarking process, which they view as "hoop-jumping."[32] Key informants reported that benchmarks were made purposely easy and vague so a site could meet them with little effort and look good. City departments developed more explicit and appropriate measures of performance for their own internal use instead of those reported in the performance review. One benchmark manager said, "What we actually do and what we report are different — and what we report is vague."[33]

On balance, the view of the Zone program's benchmarking/ performance review from the perspective of local sites was mixed. On the whole, sites deemed the system useful as a mechanism for focusing on and communicating goals. But the process was regarded as burdensome and largely beside the point with respect to gauging performance. Performance reporting was seen as demanding a significant investment of limited commodities like time and comity — a requirement needed to satisfy "the feds" but of little practical use to the Empowerment Zones and Enterprise Communities themselves.

Democratizing Program Information

One of the early ambitions of EZ framers was to use benchmarking/performance review to disseminate program information to residents in participating communities. The idea was to map information on planned activities, resource commitments, and progress against the street grid for each participating city, and to post that information on the Internet. Implementation has not yet achieved that lofty goal — links between program information and geography have not progressed as far as hoped. Nonetheless, the Clinton administration deserves credit for pursuing such an objective and for the progress that has been made.

HUD has established a highly informative and easy-to-use Web site on the Empowerment Zone/Enterprise Community Initiative (see www.hud.gov as well as a joint site with the Department of Agriculture at www.ezec.gov). The site provides links to detailed information about participating sites, including maps of the designated sites illustrating the perimeter and major thoroughfares of these areas as well as neighborhood assets such as key institutions. Extensive summaries of the proposed strategic plans for each designated site are also available, as are the March, 1997 performance review-based Site Management Reports issued by HUD for each of the first round urban sites. A host of background material is also provided, along with "tools" for community development and notices of available funding. What is not available on the Web site are individual benchmark/performance review reports filed by the Empowerment Zones and Enterprise Communities with the federal government.

Also missing is the ability to link programmatic information with geography. One of the more interesting and useful aspects of the site enables the user — a business, say, or a resident — to enter a street address and determine whether it falls within a designated program area. But parallel information on the location of planned activities is not available. Users cannot yet pull up a map showing where investments have been made, where housing units are being built or rehabilitated, and where jobs are being created, as intended.

The problem lies in the reporting of the benchmark/performance review material. The quality of the information on program resources and other investments is so spotty as to be generally unreliable — certainly difficult to map. The performance review template did ask the sites to identify the geographic location of each program activity. With rare exception, however, the sites have filled in the address of their own office, rather than, say, the addresses corresponding to the ten small businesses provided loans through the Zone Initiative.

The benchmarking system has disseminated information locally in much the same way, albeit to sometimes greater effect. In the San Francisco EC, for example, benchmarking empowered neighborhood residents in decisionmaking arenas that have traditionally been the province of insiders: city officials and well-established nonprofit service providers.

"Using the [benchmarking] performance criteria as a wedge, the EC Board and neighborhood planning bodies cracked open the local contract award process to admit new players into what had been an insider's game. [S]everal well-established nonprofit service providers chose not to apply for EC funds because they were discouraged by the explicit performance criteria. Many of those that did apply were forced to open their decision-making process to wider community participation and to demonstrate how their proposed activities and services would respond to the targeted needs of neighborhood residents."[34]

Overall, the Zone program has shared valuable information in an unusually wide circle. However, the central idea of enabling citizens to use the Internet to track the implementation of their local EZ/EC has gone unfulfilled.

Parallel Universe: What About the Feds?

Related but separate from the question of how well the Zone program's performance reporting system has functioned for local participants is the question of how well it has served HUD. As it evolved, HUD's posture toward monitoring progress of the local

Empowerment Zone and Enterprise Community sites indicated a growing degree of ambivalence, and consequently some ambiguity, about its use of the benchmarks and performance review reports in ensuring program performance.

At a minimum, HUD had a statutory responsibility to: "require periodic reports for the Empowerment Zones and Enterprise Communities...that will identify the community, local government and State actions which have been taken in accordance with the strategic plan."[35] Moreover, the regulations said that "HUD will regularly evaluate the progress of the strategic plan in each designated Empowerment Zone and Enterprise Community on the basis of performance reviews to be conducted on site and other information submitted" as well as through impartial third party evaluations commissioned through the Department.[36]

On the basis of these performance reviews, HUD was to reevaluate the designations of sites and promptly report findings to all federal agencies providing assistance to EZs and ECs. Changes in the boundaries of the designated area, having "failed to make progress in achieving the benchmarks set forth in the strategic plan," and having "not complied substantially with the strategic plan" were specified in regulation as grounds for the Secretary of HUD to exercise the discretion to revoke site designation, following a letter of warning and subsequent notice.[37]

Despite these requirements, however, HUD program managers do not appear to have used the benchmarks and performance review reports to closely monitor the performance of participating sites. In a communiqué sent by HUD to all its state and local contacts in the Zone program, the agency clearly signaled its role as one of providing technical assistance rather than monitoring performance by local sites, and advocated that states take a similar stance.[38] If a choice had to be made between the objectives of local control and program accountability, local control was the higher priority. As HUD Secretary Andrew Cuomo maintained: "This is a program where we said to the communities on day one, 'No federal mandates, no federal cookie cutter. Come up with your own goals, your own timetable. If it works for you, God bless you, it works for us."[39]

Had HUD determined that exerting leverage over the EZ/EC sites was a desirable strategy, it would have found few and not particularly strong methods available by which to influence performance by individual Empowerment Zones and Enterprise Communities. HUD could object to strategies as well as individual activities in the benchmarks/performance review reports. But the department had qualms about being heavy-handed and also lacked the staff to analyze individual activities at the site level. As a result, federal review of local performance reports did not go much beyond checking whether proposed activities were consistent with relevant statutory and regulatory restrictions on the use of funds.

Moreover, while the benchmarks and the performance review were supposed to represent a "performance contract" between each EZ or EC and HUD, the local sites were free to add, change, or delete benchmarks essentially at will. Under the program's rules, HUD was to approve such decisions automatically unless it acted within 45 days. And local sites had to notify HUD only of substantial changes. According to the rules, "increasing or decreasing a budget, changing participating entities or changing time-frames for an activity would not constitute a substantial change and would not have to be submitted to HUD, the state or city for approval."[40] Inasmuch as key elements like cost, deadlines, and identification of entities responsible for implementation were subject to local change without notice, HUD was not in a strong position to hold its "contractors" accountable for performance.

The peculiarities of EZ/EC funding also made it very difficult for HUD to use the program's purse strings to maintain tight control over participating sites. General practice was to release block grant funds to participating states soon after the memoranda of agreement was finalized, with the states thereafter responsible for dealing with the local EZ or EC site(s). The Social Services Block Grant — the principal source of funding for the Zone program — emanates from the Department of Health and Human Services, and typically flowed to an HHS-designated entity of the state authorized to disburse it. Similarly, the tax benefits provided to eligible sites and businesses were generally as-of-right, without discretion or allocational judgments required of HUD.

HUD also had little ability to tie the availability of other federal resources to behavior among the EZ/EC sites. Since the Administration had an interest in demonstrating that linkages between EZ/EC and other federal programs were maximized, the threat to withhold support for such linkages proved to be largely empty. Such an approach would also require much more elaborate cooperation among federal agencies than program managers were able to deliver.

As a practical matter, this left HUD with little besides the threat of de-designation to leverage improved performance from among the EZ/EC sites. And that proved to be a very blunt instrument indeed. The regulations are not specific regarding the frequency and use of this "validation." The regulations are also permissive with respect to whether this review will result in sanction or penalty: the Secretary "may" reclassify Zones as Communities or vice versa, depending on performance, and "may" revoke designation altogether in certain circumstances. What's more, because the success of the overall initiative rested on the effectiveness of the individual sites, HUD shared an implicit interest in seeing each site do well. Local participants might well believe that federal program managers would be reluctant to pull the plug on components of their own program.

HUD issued only one public report on the progress of the urban EZ/EC sites, in March of 1997. The department produced an individual "management report" for each characterizing progress on benchmarking through the first round of modified performance review documentation. HUD highlighted two categories of performers based on these reports: thirteen "top performers" and five sites said to be making comparatively little progress (the remaining 54 sites falling somewhere in between). HUD officials said the sites risked loss of program funding if they did not "shape up." "This money is precious," Secretary Cuomo said at the press conference. "If it is not used [in these troubled sites] it should be used in other communities." [41]

Contemporaneous news accounts described the underperforming sites as having been put "on probation" through the performance review process,[42] but their status was uncertain. The Camden portion of the Philadelphia-Camden Empowerment Zone was highlighted as one of the five sites in question, for instance. Yet it was unclear whether the HUD secretary was empowered to de-designate only a portion of a given site. Nor was it clear what such a de-designation might mean for Philadelphia, since the Philadelphia/Camden EZ was designated under a special provision for a bi-state empowerment zone. A HUD spokesperson maintained that: "The [performance review] report is a wake up call, not a signal of impending punishment," and that federal and local program administrators "must pull together to meet the program's performance standards for creating jobs and revitalizing neighborhoods."[43] In response to questions from reporters, agency officials acknowledged that no deadline had been set, nor details established, for Camden to demonstrate sufficiently improved performance to protect its designation. The most that was said was that the parties would meet soon to discuss solutions to implementation problems. In the end, designation and lack of progress both continued.

The March 1997 report was the only public use HUD has made of the benchmark/performance review data. However, HUD's Office of the Inspector General employed these reports and other sources to audit four Empowerment Zones — Atlanta, Chicago, Detroit, and Philadelphia/Camden. The IG concluded that control was not adequate to assure efficient and effective use of EZ funds or accurate reporting of accomplishments. In particular, IG inspectors found that no local sites complied with requirements that program funds be used only for activities that primarily benefit Zone residents. Inspectors also discovered violations of prohibitions on assisting establishments that merely relocate jobs or businesses from outside to inside a Zone area.[44]

A common finding concerned the tendency of sites to report a host of activities as falling within the Empowerment Zone when, in the judgment of the auditors, such activity had little to do with the program. According to the HUD IG, this practice created the impression that the benefits of the program were greater than actually achieved.[45]

HUD might also have been expected to use the performance reporting system to determine how well the overall initiative was meeting its goals. However, the emphasis on tailoring content to individual sites appears to have precluded HUD program managers from seeing the performance reporting system this way. Although the department had earlier established four core goals for the EZ/EC initiative, HUD program managers were loathe to report progress on them as that would have imposed national goals on local prerogatives. What's more, had reports on cross-site performance been an objective, participating sites should have incorporated a few intermediate- or end-outcome measures to enable HUD and congressional oversight committees to evaluate the overall program. Unfortunately, that sort of use was not included in the design of the performance reporting system.

Lessons Learned

Performance reporting in the Empowerment Zone/Enterprise Community initiative served several purposes and audiences. It was supposed to be both a management tool and a communications device for local stakeholders: a mechanism to identify goals, measure progress, learn from experience, and engage community members. Performance reporting was also intended to allow federal program managers to ensure accountability, assist the sites in making improvements, and report on the success of the overall program. The ability of the program's performance reports to accomplish this disparate set of purposes was, perhaps not surprisingly, uneven.

Benchmarking and performance review had its greatest success as a vehicle for establishing and communicating goals. Key informants in most of the participating cities reported that the program's performance reporting requirements were useful for goal setting and, in particular, for publicizing information about strategies and projects to a wider range of citizens.

Benchmarks and related management reports have been less useful as a gauge of performance. Meaningful baseline information relating to proposed activities has generally been absent, as have solid measures on outcomes. Local reports have typically redefined and included extraneous activities as program effects and have had difficulty linking information on funding to individual projects. Connections between what was to be measured and the strategic purpose of the activity were rarely made. The reports provided little information federal program managers could use to analyze or report on the program as a whole.

Given the circumstances, it is remarkable that anything positive came out of benchmarking/performance review. The Zones program provided a notably inhospitable environment for performance reporting. Program activities were unusually broad, involved a host of complex and varied benefits, and were selected locally through an uncommonly open and iterative process that made establishing goals and measures more difficult. Community participation was far more active than in other federal grant programs, itself a program goal that resulted in an unusual sense of community ownership over program strategies and decisionmaking that was valuable but complicated and stressful. Multiple agencies and layers of government were involved, administrators in small governmental or nonprofit organizations were typically charged with implementation, and the federal department most responsible for selecting and overseeing participating urban sites had little control over the primary funding stream and limited means by which to affect local performance. Community development programs as a rule are inherently untidy and notoriously difficult to measure. In this respect, the Zones program ran true to form.

Several of the more important shortcomings of the Zone program's performance reporting system were self-inflicted, arising not from intrinsic characteristics but from execution of well-intended implementation choices. These aspects of the Zone program's experience are especially instructive for designers of other performance reporting efforts.

It is unfortunate, though foreseeable, that the goal setting and dissemination function was undercut by the interplay of performance reporting requirements, governance, and funding. Because sites often developed and submitted the benchmarks and performance review reports before establishing organizational structures and staffing, the former were subject to revision as leaders were hired and relationships with governmental entities ironed out. The resulting iterations of plans generated ample confusion and conflict about what had, in fact, been benchmarked.

Benchmarking also affected how communities undertook to match plans with program resources. In the interest of speed and the seeming ministerial nature of the task, the benchmark performance reporting system essentially supplanted the strategic plans and defined local direction without reengaging stakeholders from the community. The combination of these changes fed a sense that the community planning process had been "taken over by others," instilling a sense of embattlement that made it all the harder for sites to learn from experience.

The extent and frequency of revision in the Zone program's performance reporting requirements also had a negative influence on implementation. Evolution in reporting requirements would be expected in any new initiative. But changes in the Zone program were on a wholesale level and recurrent, signaling to the sites a lack of seriousness or competence. Implementing a performance measurement system for the Zone program may have seemed straightforward to program planners, but was actually a complex undertaking. In retrospect, all involved would have been better served had the process of performance reporting not begun so early, and had the kinks been worked out beforehand.

Like other community building and revitalization strategies, the Zone program is subject to social and economic forces beyond local control — traits that made establishing baselines and measuring outcomes difficult. However, many if not most federal programs address complex systems like the economy or the environment, most share responsibilities with other agencies, and most face similar challenges in establishing baselines, defining program interventions, and measuring results. The Government Performance and Results Act of 1993, in requiring federal agencies to report annually on results in achieving their program goals, encourages agencies to include outcomes. It is unfortunate that HUD instructed EZ/EC sites to concentrate on reporting on outputs rather than outcomes in the benchmarking/performance review reports.

In the end, the elements needed for an effective accountability/performance measurement system are few in number but fundamental. They include direct links between plans, benchmarks, activities, and people with responsibility for fulfilling them; unambiguous connections between measures of preexisting conditions and progress on activities, set against a standard; and a process for adjusting plans and methods based on experience. While the Clinton administration deserves credit for attempting to implement performance reporting in Empowerment Zones, the fact is that in large measure these attributes were missing from the program. HUD's general posture toward benchmarking and the performance review deemphasized the use of these procedures in monitoring performance by the individual sites. Though consistent with a programmatic emphasis on federal flexibility and local "ownership" — even laudable from that point of view — HUD's reluctance to closely monitor the sites has undercut the usefulness of those procedures in performance contracting.

The best news is that ample time remains in the life of the Zones program for HUD to use its interest in innovation and performance to perfect the program's reporting system. The same spirit that led the agency to try to democratize information via the Internet could be applied to establishing and monitoring neighborhood conditions, together with and on behalf of Empowerment Zones and Enterprise Communities. Along with information on investments and programs, such a neighborhood monitoring process would produce measures of impacts on the quality of life and the long-run stability of the community so the impact of project activities could be measured and evaluated. Information would be shared among local, state, and federal stakeholders and have great value to local program partners, significantly improving the utility of benchmarking. Even as the administration and Congress are moving to expand the number of designated Zones, it is not too late to embark on the prudent step of deepening and sharing knowledge about the performance of existing sites.

Endnotes

1   The program's many purposes are well described in *Building Communities To-gether: Empowerment Zones & Enterprise Communities Application Guide*, The President's Community Enterprise Board (Washington, D.C., HUD-1445-CPD, January, 1994).

2   All of the six urban Empowerment Zones, both of the Supplemental Empowerment Zone sites, two of the four Enhanced Enterprise Communities, and eight of the re-maining 60 Enterprise Communities were included in a HUD-commissioned field network implementation assessment of the Zone program conducted by the Nelson A. Rockefeller Institute of Government. The research study combined a detailed review of descriptive as well as performance-related data on all 72 EZ/EC sites with in-depth field work in the 18-city sample performed in partnership with a group of indigenous scholars in each city, and it afforded a special vantage point on the aspirations and performance of the Zone program. The associates in the field included Michael Rich in Atlanta, Robert Stoker in Baltimore, Karl Seidman in Boston, William Rohe in Charlotte, Charles Orlebeke in Chicago, Dennis Keating in Cleveland, Paul Jargowsky and Royce Hanson in Dallas, Robin Boyle in De-troit, George Wendell in East St. Louis, IL, Ali Modares in Los Angeles, Hank Savitch and Ronald Vogel in Louisville, Cecilia Martinez in Minneapolis, Avis Vidal and Elizabeth Mueller in New York City, David Tabb in Oakland, Robert Bailey in Philadelphia/ Camden, John Hall in Phoenix, Rich DeLeon in San Fran-cisco, and Betty Jane Narver in Tacoma.

3   The President's Community Enterprise Board, *Building Communities Together: Empowerment Zones and Enterprise Communities Application Guide* (Washing-ton, D.C.: U.S. Department of Agriculture and U.S. Department of Housing and Urban Development, 1994), p. 22.

4   Ibid, pp. 22-24.

5   The President's Community Enterprise Board, *Building Communities Together: Empowerment Zones & Enterprise Communities Application Guide*, (Washington, HUD-1445-CPD, January, 1994), p. 10.

6   Nelson A. Rockefeller Institute of Government, *Building a Community Plan for Strategic Change: Findings from the First Round Assessment of the Empowerment Zone/Enterprise Community Initiative*. Report prepared for the U.S. Department of Housing and Urban Development. (Albany, NY: State University of New York, March 1997).

7   Chicago Field Report by Associate Charles Orlebeke, Round One, Summer 1996.

8   Atlanta Field Report by Associate Michael Rich, Round One, Summer 1996.

9   Louisville Field Report by Associates Hank Savitch and Ron Vogel, Round Two, Fall 1996.

10 July 16, 1996 HUD Policy Memorandum.

11 Boston Field Report by Associate Karl Seidman, Round Two, Fall 1996.

12 Oakland Field Report by Associates David Tabb and Rich DeLeon, Round Two, Fall 1996.

13 Atlanta Field Report, Round Two, Fall 1996.

14 For a fuller discussion of the governance structures see Rockefeller Institute of Government, *Building a Community Plan.*

15 Phoenix Field Report by Associate John Hall, Round Two, Fall 1996.

16 Atlanta Field Report, Round Two, Fall 1996.

17 San Francisco Field Report by Associates Rich DeLeon and David Tabb, Fall 1996.

18 Atlanta Field Report, Fall 1996.

19 Charlotte Field Report by Associate William Rohe, Round Two, Fall 1996.

20 One exception was the Oakland EEC, where there was a strong desire that design and use of benchmarks be consistent with the level and quality of community engagement that went into the initial strategic planning process. The EEC Policy Board forced revision through a participatory process whereby members of the Board, city staff, Community Building Team participants, and community organizations joined in developing revised draft benchmarks to be discussed at public meetings and then adopted by the EEC Board and City Council. Unlike the earlier version filed in a rush to free grant proceeds, EEC participants expected the Revised Benchmark report to be used as a real tool for monitoring and evaluating EEC funded programs and activities. Oakland Field Report, Fall 1996.

21 Field Reports by Associates Michael Rich in Atlanta, Betty Jane Narver in Tacoma, Paul Jargowsky in Dallas, Cecilia Martinez in Minneapolis, George Wendel in East St. Louis, and Hank Savitch and Ron Vogel in Louisville, Fall 1996.

22 Baltimore Field Report by Associate Bob Stoker, Round Two, Fall 1996.

23 HUD policy memorandum.

24 Ibid.

25 Phoenix Field Report, Round Two, Fall 1996.

26 HUD policy memoranda.

27 Dallas Field Report, Round Two, Fall 1996.

28 San Francisco Field Report, Round Two, Fall 1996.

29 Tacoma Field Report, Round Two, Fall 1996.

30 Atlanta Field Report, Round Two, Fall 1996.

31 Louisville Field Report, Round Two, Fall 1996.

32 Phoenix Field Report, Round Two, Fall 1996.

33 Ibid.

34 San Francisco Field Report, Round Two, Fall 1996.

35 Part 597, Subpart E-Post Designation Requirements, §597.400-Reporting, Federal Register. Vol. 59, No. 11, Tuesday, January 18, 1994, Rules and Regulations, 2709.

36 Ibid, §597.401-Periodic Performance Reviews.

37 Ibid, §597.402-Validation of Designation.

38 July 16, 1996 HUD Policy Memorandum.

39 Quoted in the *San Francisco Examiner*, March 8 1997.

40 July 16, 1996 HUD Policy Memorandum.

41 Press conference, Washington, D.C., March 7, 1997.

42 *San Francisco Chronicle*, March 8 1997.

43 Ibid.

44 The specific provisions can be found at Title 20 of the United States Code, Section 2007(c)(1)(B), and Title 26 of the United States Code, Section 1391(f)(2)(F). HUD Inspector General findings concerning Atlanta are from Audit Case Number 98-CH-259-1005, issued September 28, 1998.

45 HUD Inspector General findings concerning Chicago are from Audit Case Number 99-CH-259-1002, issued October 15, 1998. HUD Inspector General findings concerning Detroit are from Audit Case Number 99-CH-259-1003, issued October 20, 1998. HUD Inspector General findings concerning Philadelphia are from Audit Case Number 98-CH-259-1006, issued September 30, 1998. The HUD IG recommended that the Coordinator of the EZ/EC Initiative, in conjunction with officials from the Department of Health and Human Services, assure that the Empowerment Zone Program was reimbursed by the cities for the inappropriate use of Zone funds. Not surprisingly, city and Empowerment Zone officials took strong exception to those audit findings and recommendations. Atlanta and Chicago officials argued that the actions the IG faulted were taken only after direct prior consultation with HUD's Empowerment Zone Program Office. The City of Philadelphia took especially strong offense: "The [HUD IG]findings can only be characterized as shockingly inaccurate and unfair. The City spent $16 million in Zone communities for economic development, education, housing, public safety, and critically needed infrastructure improvements in these neighborhoods. The OIG findings question less than one percent of all funds spent. The City maintains that all of the Empowerment Zone funds were spent to benefit Zone residents." Ibid, p. 9 and Appendix C, p.136

11

Intergovernmental Relationships and the Federal Performance Movement

Beryl A. Radin

The rhetoric of performance became a leading language of the public sector at the end of the twentieth century. This rhetoric employs a vocabulary that highlights outcomes rather than inputs, processes, or even outputs. It focuses on the benefits derived from the use of public funds and seeks to establish a framework that moves away from traditional incremental decisionmaking in which budgets are created largely on the basis of past allocation patterns. It has been used to counter the public's disillusion with government as well as the government bashing that has been employed by political figures at both ends of the political spectrum. However, while the concern about performance is pervasive, it is not expressed consistently. This concern takes many different forms, and it is attached to efforts by all governments in the federal system.

One expectation of the performance movement has focused on the realities of the intergovernmental system, particularly the tension between those who devise programs as well as fund them (at least in part) and those who actually implement them. For some,

The author wishes to acknowledge the advice of Paul Posner, Sharon Caudle, and several anonymous reviewers in revising this article.
Reprinted with permission from *Publius: The Journal of Federalism* 30:1-2 (Winter/Spring 2000).

performance measurement is viewed as the bridge between the goals of the federal government for accountability and the demands of state or local government for discretion and flexibility. In this sense, the performance movement and performance measurement are seen as ways for avoiding the traditional command and control perspective of the federal government and for substituting performance outcome requirements for input and process requirements.[1] According to some proponents of the performance movement, the traditional forms of accountability that are seen to evoke a compliance mentality will be replaced by performance measures that emphasize results.

The concern about performance is closely linked to the reinvention movement popularized by David Osborne and Ted Gaebler[2] and others who have emphasized reinvention of state and local governments. The reinvention movement accentuates the importance of measuring results. According to Osborne and Gaebler, "Because they don't measure results, bureaucratic governments rarely achieve them. . . . With so little information about results, bureaucratic governments reward their employees based on other things."[3]

Two of the most popular approaches to performance at these levels have been report cards[4] and efforts attached to contracting out and privatization.[5] Report cards have been used often in the education sector where schools, classrooms, and often teachers are evaluated on the basis of students' test scores. The increased use of contracting out and other forms of involvement by the private sector have led to performance contracting where contractees are held accountable for specific outcomes written into contract language. These and other performance efforts have been largely focused on the service-delivery level where government agencies either deliver the services themselves or establish relationships with others for the specific delivery of services.

Although some of these state and local efforts do raise interesting and important intergovernmental issues, the concern about performance by federal government is much more complex and difficult than efforts by states and local governments. Because so many federal programs involve intricate intergovernmental relationships, federal agencies have struggled with ways to structure these relationships. Federal agencies are balancing two competing imperatives. On one hand, they are attempting to hold third parties accountable for the use of federal monies; on the other hand, they are constrained by the political and legal realities that provide significant discretion and leeway to the third parties for the use of these federal dollars. In many ways, the performance movement in federal agencies collides with strategies of devolution and a diminished federal role. What is most interesting about this situation is that few of the individuals in the policymaking world (particularly in the Congress) are aware that they are setting up incompatible strategies. Those who argue for more compliance-oriented federal government accountability are often those who argue for a decreased federal role and increased autonomy for states in the way that they expend federal dollars.

GPRA: The Driving Force of the Federal Performance Effort

The tension between these two imperatives is found in a number of current efforts under way within the federal government. Perhaps the most visible expression of this tension is found in the efforts to implement the Government Performance and Results Act — the legislative requirement passed by Congress in 1993 that requires all federal agencies to develop strategic plans, annual performance plans, and performance reports. These stipulations are implemented within the constraints and realities of the annual budget process. All of these requirements are supposed to elicit a focus on the outcomes that have been achieved in the use of federal resources and to justify requests for dollars in terms of both promised and actual outcomes.

On its face, GPRA seems quite straightforward, indeed, almost innocuous. It clearly follows the tradition of past reform efforts within the federal government. In a report on the historical antecedents of the performance budgeting movement, the U.S. General Accounting Office concluded that GPRA "can be seen as melding the best features of its predecessors.... Nonetheless, many of the challenges which confronted earlier efforts remain unresolved and will likely affect early GPRA implementation efforts."[6]

At the same time, there are differences between GPRA and earlier efforts. Its enactment as legislation (rather than as executive orders) has built in a role for Congress that is relatively unusual in government reform efforts. In addition, GPRA's inclusion of pilot projects and providing a number of years for start up are not the usual way for reform efforts to be conceptualized. Although GPRA was enacted in 1993, its real requirements did not take effect until 1997.[7]

To some degree, the passage of GPRA and the interest in its implementation reflect the public attention to management that was a characteristic of the 1990s. Embraced by President Bill Clinton's administration and viewed as complementary to Vice President Al Gore's reinvention effort, GPRA's focus on the performance of government agencies is an example of the almost ubiquitous interest in this topic. The multiple aspects of the legislation — particularly its emphasis on the relationship between budgeting and performance — can be viewed as an attempt to respond to public concerns about the ways that public monies have been expended. The report from the U.S. Senate Committee on Governmental Affairs attached to the legislation noted: "Public confidence in the institutions of American government is suffering from a perception that those institutions are not working well . . . the public believes that it is not getting the level and quality of government service for which it is paying."[8]

John Mercer, the acknowledged "father" of GPRA, brought his local-management reform experience in Sunnyvale, California, to the legislative development process within the U.S. Congress. Advising the Republican members of the Senate Committee on Governmental Affairs, Mercer's agenda was to craft a piece of legislation that provided the mechanism for performance budgeting. He believed that the efforts in Sunnyvale could inform the federal government, leading to tightly constructed cost accounting systems that would lead to technically driven budget decisions. Although his proposals were modified by some of the Democrats on the committee, the legislation that was enacted did accentuate the belief that "congressional policymaking, spending decisions, and oversight are all seriously handicapped by the lack both of sufficiently precise program goals and of adequate program performance information. . . . The legislation will provide the information necessary to strengthen program management, to make objective evaluations of program performance, and to set realistic, measurable goals for future performance."[9]

The Senate committee made a number of assumptions about the GPRA requirements. First, it argued that past and current attempts at performance measurement and reporting had been successful. Second, the report reflected a belief that GPRA would not impose a major additional cost or paperwork burden on federal programs. Third, it argued that at least some federal agencies were already moving toward the development of performance measure systems for results-oriented decisionmaking. There was no acknowledgement in this congressional report that there was a conceptual conflict between these assumptions and a concern about diminishing what some viewed as the "heavy hand" of the federal government.

Indeed, the only cautionary note that was sounded in the Senate report came from Arkansas Democratic Senator David Prior. He wrote: "My concern is that by mandating yet another very specific layer of internal management controls, performance measures and strategic plans, we are building in even more rigidity. I realize that the legislation seeks to allow flexibility in some pilot programs, but after years of watching these well intended reforms transform into routine reports written by contractors using largely boilerplate language, I am not convinced that this legislation will actually enable federal agencies to improve their performance."[10]

The rigidity that was feared by Senator Prior actually took form within the confines of a highly polarized Congress. GPRA was embraced by the Republican leadership in both the House and the Senate as a means of putting pressure on the Democratic administration. House Majority Leader Richard Armey (R-TX) established a grading system to rate the "progress" of federal agencies as they submitted both their strategic plans and their annual performance plans to the Congress as well as the White House. The Senate Governmental Affairs Committee used the GPRA framework to highlight problems of waste, fraud, and mismanagement in federal agencies.[11] Neither setting focused on the difficulties that federal agencies had in establishing measures of performance for programs designed as block grants or with high levels of discretion provided for third-party implementers, particularly state agencies.

In fact, when one examines the GPRA legislation and its history, little in its background provides real guidance regarding federal agency dependence on state and local governments. The only specification of consultation with "external" parties is found in fairly vague language regarding the development of agency strategic plans. Agencies are not required to deal with these "external" parties as they devise their annual performance plans. Some observers have actually been concerned that state and local governments who act as agents for the federal government are relegated to the category of "external" parties. Similarly, there has been little attention to the form that the program takes (e.g., whether it is a competitive grant program, a block grant, or some other form of formula funding).

During the past several years, at least some federal agencies have been pressured by Congress and some of its agents to take direct responsibility for the performance outcomes achieved through federal programs, whether or not the federal agency actually delivers the services provided through federal funding. In some instances, this has moved the agency away from a focus on performance that values state flexibility and discretion and back to a more traditional compliance-oriented posture. GPRA has tended to highlight the federal role of defining goals nationally rather than leaving it to the states (often termed "the laboratories of democracy") to bargain about specific goals and outcomes for their jurisdictions.[12]

Approaches to Performance in an Intergovernmental Context

Although the implementation of GPRA has provided the framework and a point of focus for the federal performance effort, other efforts have been undertaken within federal agencies to balance the two often conflicting imperatives, namely, to provide states with flexibility and yet maintain a commitment to performance outcomes that acknowledges the expectations of those who fund and authorize programs.

The analysis that follows is presented as an initial foray into this topic, and seeks to develop a conceptual foundation that provides a framework for examining the ways that the federal government has attempted to bridge funders' goals with the demands of those who carry out programs. It suggests that the initial expectations of those who believed that performance measures would be a relatively easy way to address intergovernmental tensions were naïve and quite unrealistic. Hopefully, this framework will lead to future research on the approaches, their impacts, and their limitations. Such research would also build on the extant literature that deals with the more technical questions focusing on development of performance outcomes, particularly the techniques that have been devised to deal with multiple stakeholders and situations where competing values are at play.

The discussion highlights six different approaches that have been taken recently within federal agencies to deal with issues of performance. Some of these efforts predated the GPRA initiative, some are distinct from it, and others have been melded into GPRA's framework. Some have been devised as a result of legislation and others through administrative action. All are struggling with the tension between federal agency accountability and devolution, and the discretion provided to state and local agencies. These include performance partnerships, incentives, negotiated measures, building performance goals into legislation, establishment of standards, and waivers.

Performance Partnerships

During the past decade, a number of federal agencies have adopted, or at least explored, the possibility of moving categorical programs into performance partnerships. These partnerships have become increasingly popular as agencies realize the limitations of their ability to achieve desired changes in complex settings. Although partnerships between various agencies and government have been around in some form for years, the performance orientation of the contemporary effort is new. The image of the partnership is one in which partners discuss how to combine resources from both players to achieve a pre-specified end-state. This end-state is expected to be measurable in order for a partnership to be successful.

The design of a performance partnership addresses what some have viewed as one of the most troubling problems faced by federal managers: lack of control over outcomes. Although managers may have control over inputs, processes, and outputs, they cannot specify end outcomes. Performance partnerships may involve agreements between federal officials and state or local agencies; they may be ad hoc or permanent.

The performance partnerships entered into by the U.S. Environmental Protection Agency (EPA) and states have been among the most visible of these arrangements. However, there have been proposals for the development of performance partnerships involving health programs, programs for children, and the Office of National Drug Control Policy.

The National Environmental Performance Partnership System began in fiscal year 1996 with six pilot states. By the end of fiscal year 1998, 45 states had entered into these arrangements.[13] A number of Indian tribes have also entered into these agreements. According to EPA:

> *Performance Partnerships establish a new working relationship whereby the States and EPA determine on an annual basis what and how work will be performed. Traditionally, the process for funding and addressing environmental and public health priorities has been conducted with a single media focus. States have submitted up to 16 annual workplans and received multiple grants to support air, drinking water, hazardous waste, and other pollution control programs.... [T]his approach has fueled administrative management and oversight activity, diverting resources from on-the-ground improvement efforts.... Performance Partnerships are designed to place much greater*

emphasis on environmental results and to achieve better coordination between Federal and State environmental programs.[14]

Further, according to GAO, "the two-way negotiation process inherent in the program has fostered more frequent and effective communication between regional and state participants and improved their overall working relationship."[15] At the same time, however, GAO noted that the process has problems. GAO highlighted a number of "technical challenges":

❀ an absence of baseline data to use as the basis for measuring improvements,

❀ the difficulty of quantifying certain results,

❀ the difficulty of linking program activities to environmental results, and

❀ the level of resources needed to develop a high quality performance-measurement system.[16]

GAO also noted that states and the EPA disagreed over the degree to which states would be permitted to vary from the national core measures and the composition of the measures. Because each EPA regional office enters into the arrangements with the states in its region, there is some variation between agreements across the country. This was of concern to the GAO analysts.

EPA's experience with performance partnerships illustrates some of the problems that are intrinsic to this performance strategy and agreement form. The individual negotiation between the federal agency, and (in this case) states, is likely to result in variability of agreements across the country. In fact, to some observers, the individual tailoring of agreements is the strength of the mechanism. However, others are concerned that this variation results from differential treatment of jurisdictions.

The problems with data that were identified by GAO are also a predictable problem with any performance-partnership agreement. The strategy is often attractive to federal agencies charged with the implementation of programs, which involve policy sectors that do not have well-established data systems or even data definitions. In such settings, it is difficult to establish and to garner data for the performance measures required for achieving the expectations of the approach.

Incentives

Over the past several decades, as the economics paradigm has increasingly influenced policy, some policy analysts have focused on the use of incentives as a way to change behavior. Incentives seek to induce behavior rather than command it.[17] According to David Weimer and Aidan Vining, bureaucrats and politicians have tended to be less enthusiastic about this approach than those who are trained in economics.[18] This has occurred, they argue, because bureaucrats and politicians tend to be attracted to direct regulation since they believe that incentives also require governmental intervention, and therefore, involve regulation.

To some degree, incentives have previously been at play in a number of federal programs through matching fund requirements. When the federal government offers funds as an incentive to induce states to provide their own funds, the matching requirements do serve an incentive function. In many cases, however, performance expectations are not usually made explicit, particularly in programs carried over from the past.

Probably the most dramatic recent example of performance incentives is found in the High Performance Bonus program attached to the Temporary Assistance for Needy Families (TANF) welfare program. That 1996 legislation called on the secretary of the U.S. Department of Health and Human Services (HHS), in consultation with the National Governors Association (NGA) and the American Public Welfare Association (APWA), to develop a formula measuring state performance relative to block grant goals. Bonuses to an individual state cannot exceed 5 percent of the family assistance grant. In addition, the law established a bonus for states that demonstrate the number of out-of-wedlock births and abortions occurring in the state in the most recent two-year period decreasing compared to the number of such births in the previous period. The top five states will receive a bonus of up to $20 million each, and if fewer than five states qualify, the grant will be increased to $25 million each.

The first high-performance bonus awards were made in December 1999. These awards were made in four categories: job placement, job success (measured by retention and earnings), biggest improvement in job placement, and biggest improvement in job success. The awards, totaling $200 million, were made to 27 states. States were chosen on the basis of their ranking in each of the four categories. The states ranked the highest in each category were Indiana for job placement, Minnesota for job retention and earnings, Washington for the biggest improvement in job placement, and Florida for the biggest improvement in job retention and earnings. Eleven states received bonuses in two categories, and one state (Minnesota) was successful in three.

HHS has proposed that additional criteria be added during the next year to the existing four measures; these are family formation measures, enrollment in Medicaid and the Children's Health Insurance Program, and enrollment in the food stamps program.

The bonus effort within TANF has been a subject of some controversy both during the period when the criteria were established for awarding the funds and following the first awards. At one point, a proposal was made to simply divide the $200 million annually available for these awards equally among the 50 states and others eligible for the funds. Some critics of the bonus requirement argue that the categories established for the allocations are not directly related to the behavior of the state welfare agencies charged with implementing the TANF program. Economic conditions within the state are thought to be more responsible for the increases or decreases than the action of the state agency. Others have argued that the criteria that have been established do not measure the real goal of TANF — the well-being of children. They call for the establishment of performance measures that highlight child welfare, child care, Head Start, and other non-cash programs, rather than focus only on the employment behavior of adults. The availability of data, however, has been viewed as one of the reasons why other criteria have not been used to date.

The TANF experience illustrates the dilemma involved in using an incentive strategy. It is difficult to ascertain the direct relationship between the behavior of the state or local government and specific outcomes. In addition, complex programs such as TANF have an array of program goals and expectations, and it is not easy to achieve agreement on performance standards. Some critics of the incentive strategy argue that state or local jurisdictions will attempt to game the system and develop policies that may meet the performance measures rather than achieve the basic expectations of the legislation. Others argue that this already occurs; hence, the situation is not much different than it was in the past.

Negotiated Performance Measures

One of the most common complaints by state and local officials is that the federal government imposes a set of requirements on its funds that do not meet the needs of the nonfederal jurisdiction. Indeed, this is one of the arguments that has been used to justify the transformation of categorical grants into block grants. Block grants have proven to be one of the most difficult grant forms on which to impose GPRA's requirements. Federal officials have had problems balancing the flexibility of the block grant (allowing states and localities to meet their particular needs) with a desire for greater accountability for the use of those funds.

The Maternal and Child Health (MCH) Services Title V Block Grant to States has operated as a federal-state partnership for most of its 60-year history. Even when the program was converted to a block grant in 1981, the professional relationship between the federal agency charged with implementing the program and the state MCH agencies continued to be relatively close. The Omnibus Budget Reconciliation Act of 1989 did require states to report on progress on key maternal and child health indicators and other program information.

In 1996, the MCH Bureau in the Health Resources and Services Administration of HHS began a process with states that would establish a set of mutually agreed-upon measures with data sources that would be used in the program. In the development phase of this process, the MCH Bureau created an external committee of 30 experts representing various interests in the maternal and child health field that would help set overall direction for the process, provide technical expertise, and endorse the final results. Participants from associations and advocacy groups were expected to engage their own constituencies to ensure accurate representation. Review and comment from the state agency officials was solicited at various points during the process.

In March 1997, draft performance measures and guidance revision principles were presented at the annual meeting of the Association of Maternal and Child Health Programs; this meeting was attended by virtually all the relevant directors in the country. Eight representative states, chosen from 17 volunteers, were selected to pilot test the measures for practicality and data-collection issues. The consultation process that was used was approximately two years in duration; one year was spent on the development of the measures and one on pilot testing the process.

By the end of 1997, the MCH Bureau established 18 national performance measures that were incorporated into the application and reporting guidance for the Title V block grant funds. These measures were drawn from goals related to Healthy People 2000 objectives over which grantees exercised substantial control. The measures were categorized as capacity measures (ability to affect the delivery of services), process measures (related to service delivery), and risk factors (involving health problems). Each state also was required to establish and report on between seven and ten of its own supplemental performance measures to provide a more complete picture of the program within that state. In addition, the MCH Bureau set six national outcome measures — ultimate goals toward which the performance measures are directed and for which ultimate achievement depends on external factors beyond the control of the state grantee.

As a result of this process, MCH block grant applications and annual reports contain a wealth of information concerning state initiatives, state-supported programs, and other state-based responses designed to address their MCH needs. The electronic information system that has been developed in this program, based on the applications and reports, collects both qualitative and quantitative data that is useful to a number of audiences.

The MCH experience indicates that it is possible to achieve agreement on performance measures when certain conditions are met. Programs that are not politically volatile or that do not have a widely disparate set of expert opinions are appropriate for this process. In addition, prior work and data systems (in this case, involving Healthy People 2000) laid the foundation for consensus on many outcome and process objectives. The measures recognized and separated objectives over which grantees exercise influence and control from those that depend on external factors beyond their control. Yet, even when these conditions are present, the negotiation process is time consuming, and requires an investment of staff and resources by federal agencies.

Build Performance Goals into Legislation

Over the past few years, various pieces of legislation have been crafted with attention to performance goals. This approach emphasizes the authorizing role in Congress while the GPRA approach focuses on the appropriations process. Two relatively recent pieces of legislation illustrate this strategy: the modifications to the Vocational Education program and the creation of the Workforce Investment Act as a replacement for the Job Training Partnership Act (JTPA). In both cases, the legislation represented a move from an emphasis on input or process requirements to a focus on performance outcomes.

The Workforce Investment Act, signed into law in August 1998, reforms the federal job-training programs and creates a new comprehensive workforce investment system. The reformed system is intended to be customer focused, to help Americans access the tools they need to manage their careers through information and high-quality services, and to help U.S. companies find skilled workers. Increased accountability is one of the principles embodied in the legislation. The act specifies core indicators of performance that become the structure for state and local reporting. These core indicators include measures of entry into unsubsidized employment, earnings received, and attainment of a credential involving educational skills. Indicators were also specified in the legislation for eligible youth and customer satisfaction measures. States are expected to submit expected levels of performance for these indicators in their state plans. Similar indicators of performance were also established in the Carl D. Perkins Vocational and Applied Technology Education Amendments of 1998. The modifications to the existing program emphasized the importance of establishing a state performance accountability system. The legislation requires states to identify core indicators in their state plans involving student skill achievement, attainment of educational credentials, and placement in education, employment, or military service.

Further refinement of these requirements were established by both federal departments through the regulations development process. It is too early to know how effective the process will be and whether sanctions will be imposed for failure to comply with the requirements. In drafting both of these pieces of legislation, Congress assumed that the core indicators reflect common practices across the country and that data systems are available to report on achievement of the goals.

Establishment of Standards

In some cases, the role of the federal government has been to establish performance standards that are meant to guide the behavior of state and local governments. At least theoretically, these standards are to be voluntary, and the ability of a state or locality to conform to them is not tied to eligibility for specific federal dollars. The federal role in this strategy may involve development of the standards, provision of technical assistance, and, at times, payment for meeting these norms and guidelines.

The Clinton administration's proposal for the development of voluntary national tests in reading and mathematics is an example of this approach. The response to this proposal, particularly by some governors and education leaders, illustrates the types of problems that may emerge from this strategy.

According to Secretary of Education Richard W. Riley, "these proposed voluntary tests are about high standards, improving expectations, and giving our young people the basic skills they need that will prepare them for our knowledge-driven economy in the twenty-first century."[19] The proposal would build on existing educational assessment surveys (the National Assessment of Educational Progress and the Third International Math and Science Study). As such, the new tests that would be given in English at grade 4 and in mathematics at grade 8 would be based on content criteria established through national consensus processes. The information that would be available through these tests would be at the individual student level, providing information on how an individual student stacks up against others in the classroom, the school, and the country.

Although several governors were supporters of this administration proposal in 1997, others expressed concern about the initiative.[20] A number of states already had test systems in place and did not want to replace their existing performance accountability systems with the national approach. Still others were uncomfortable with the content of the tests, particularly their accuracy and validity in measuring achievement and their substantive scope.

The proposal for voluntary tests in mathematics and English also uncovered another problem that is likely to be confronted whenever the standards strategy is employed: fear that the information gathered through these assessments has a life of its own and will be used inappropriately. This is particularly problematic because the information that is collected was meant to illustrate achievement at the individual level. Questions of privacy and information security have been raised and were not answered to the satisfaction of critics.

Waivers

Authority to grant state or local governments waivers for specific programs has been in place for many years. While the waiver authority has been viewed as a way to meet the unique needs of individual states, it has also been closely tied to a research and development strategy, providing latitude to nonfederal jurisdictions for experimenting with new innovations and new ways for delivering services. For example, the secretary of HHS had the authority under Section 115 of the Social Security Act to waive specified provisions of the act in the case of demonstration projects that were likely to promote the objectives of the act. These waivers were expected to be rigorously evaluated. The waiver authorization has usually been defined in the context of specific programs, and the criteria for granting the waivers are established within the authorizing legislation or implementing regulations. Certain requirements (such as civil rights requirements or filing performance information) cannot be waived.

This authority has been employed extensively in the past in several program areas, particularly involving welfare, Medicaid, and the Job Training Partnership Act. Waivers have been used to allow states to establish their own approach and to eliminate or modify input or process requirements. Many of the waivers require the proposed modification to be budget neutral: that is, not incurring new costs for either the waiving jurisdiction or the federal government. For some, the waiver process is a mechanism that can be used to make a case for policy change. The experience with waivers in the old Aid to Families with Dependent Children (AFDC) program and in the JTPA program became an important part of the justification for major changes in each of the programs, leading to the TANF program and the Workforce Investment Act.

In November 1999, the U.S. House Government Management, Information and Technology Subcommittee marked up a bill that addresses waivers of regulatory and statutory requirements. This legislation has three main requirements:

* 🏵 Agencies would have to establish a streamlined 120-day review process for responding to states that request waivers of regulatory or statutory requirements of federal grant programs. (While this is similar to an August 1999 Executive Order, the legislation would be judicially reviewable.)

❀ Agencies would have to develop an expedited review
  process to waive a state's statutory or regulatory requirements if a similar waiver had already been approved for another state.

❀ OMB, HHS, and USDA would have to develop common
  approaches and requirements related to budget neutral-
  ity in consultation with the National Governors Association and the National Conference of State Legislatures.

The hearings that were held on this proposed legislation elic-
ited both support and questions by those who testified. NGA Executive Director Ray Scheppach testified in favor of the legislation,
expressing concern about the current process. He called the current
efforts "a redundant process" whereby states must produce and defend waiver requests, even if other states had already received approval to implement similar waivers.[21] Clinton administration
witnesses, however, emphasized the importance of dealing with
each waiver on its own. HHS Assistant Secretary for Management
and Budget John Callahan likened the process to contract negotiations where both parties need to attain a mutual goal of creating
program innovation and flexibility. Other administration witnesses
reminded the members of Congress that some of what they viewed
as denials of waivers actually came about because the agency had
no authority to waive a particular requirement.

At least one House member, Congressman Major Owens
(D-NY) expressed concern about the process. He queried: "In this
process of rushing to grant waivers and place our faith in the State
governments, do we have some safeguards? And can we have more
safeguards and some stringent penalties for people who violate the
law because the waivers give them a situation where nobody will be
watching, monitoring, holding them accountable?"[22]

As Owens suggested, the proposed legislation did not focus on
questions of performance. Although some of the existing waiver authorities did highlight performance issues when they required evaluation as a condition of the waiver, the proposed legislation
accentuated the streamlining of the process, not the results that
emerged from the changes.

Conclusion: A Repertoire of Program-Performance Efforts

Despite the ubiquitous nature of the performance rhetoric, these examples suggest that there are many pathways that can be taken to join the federal government's concern about performance with sensitivity to the needs of the governmental third parties involved in implementing the programs. In some cases, the two goals are not compatible; in others, it is possible to work out a mutually agreeable scenario.

But this process is not an easy one. The approach taken must be sensitive to differences among policies and programs, differences among the players involved, the complexity of the worlds of both the federal and nonfederal agencies involved, and the level of goal agreement or conflict. As this discussion suggests, however, one of the most vexing problems in the performance area involves the availability of "good" data — data that has been verified and believed to be valid by all parties to the relationship. The data problem cuts across all of the strategies. Few policy sectors have the tradition or past investment in the creation of good data systems that would allow one to know whether performance has actually been achieved. In addition, the experience with all of these efforts indicates how difficult it is to achieve a performance measurement system that focuses on outcomes. Part of the problem relates to the lack of control many agencies have over the achievement of program goals and the difficulty of linking program activities to results, even when those results can be measured.

This repertoire of performance efforts also indicates that governmentwide policies such as GPRA are not particularly effective. The process of defining performance measures seems to work when it is devised in the context of specific programs, sensitive to the unique qualities surrounding those initiatives.

As this process unfolds, a number of questions might be considered by researchers who are attempting to examine the ways in which strategies have been designed to link performance accountability with intergovernmental sensitivity. Future research, thus, might examine the following questions:

❀ Who is responsible for establishing the implementation effort?

❀ Does the current system actually provide implementers the opportunity for redefining goals to meet their own needs?

❀ What type of a policy is involved? (It may be more difficult to deal with redistributive policies than with distributive or regulatory policies.)

❀ What is the policy instrument used to implement the program?

❀ Are the decisionmakers involved general-purpose government officials or program specialists?

❀ What is the extent of the federal role or presence in the program area (e.g., level of funding)?

❀ What is the level of risk for noncompliance as perceived by both parties?

❀ What sanctions are available for nonperformance?

❀ What is the history of past oversight relationships (e.g., collegial or conflictual)?

❀ What is the level of diversity of practices across the country?

These are the questions that various intergovernmental actors are attempting to answer as they try to bridge the two competing imperatives of federal accountability and nonfederal discretion. A continued foray into this subject area by researchers should prove useful to those who are examining the more general question of intergovernmental relationships as well as those who are focusing on these relationships within the context of specific policies and programs.

Endnotes

1   See, for example, Deil S. Wright. *Understanding Intergovernmental Relations*, 3rd
    ed. (Pacific Grove, CA: Brooks/Cole Publishing Company, 1988), pp. 244-248.

2   David Osborne and Ted Gaebler, *Reinventing Government: How the Entrepre-
    neurial Spirit is Transforming the Public Sector* (Reading, MA: Addison-Wesley,
    1992).

3   Ibid., p. 139.

4   See William T. Gormley, Jr. and David L. Weimer, *Organizational Report Cards*
    (Cambridge, MA: Harvard University Press, 1999).

5   See Steven Ratahgeb Smith and Michael Lipsky, *Nonprofits for Hire: The Welfare
    State in the Age of Contracting* (Cambridge, MA: Harvard University Press, 1993).

6   U.S. General Accounting Office, *Performance Budgeting: Past Initiatives Offer
    Insight for GPRA Implementation* (Washington, DC: GPO, GAO/AIMD-97-46,
    March 1997), p. 7.

7   Much of this discussion is drawn from Beryl A. Radin, "The Government Perfor-
    mance and Results Act (GPRA) and the Tradition of Federal Management Reform:
    Square Peg in Round Holes?" *Journal of Public Administration Research and The-
    ory* 10 (January 2000): 111-135.

8   U.S. Congress, Senate, Committee on Governmental Affairs, *Report to Accom-
    pany S 20 to Provide for the Establishment, Testing, and Evaluation of Strategic
    Planning and Performance Measurement in the Federal Government, and for
    Other Purposes* (Washington, DC: GPO, June 16, 1993), p. 61.

9   Ibid.

10 Ibid.

11 See Stephen Barr, "Education Initiatives Off to a Slow Start," *The Washington
    Post*, 11 July 1998, p. 18.

12 See, for example, Helen Ingram, "Policy Implementation Through Bargaining:
    The Case of Federal Grants-In-Aid," *Public Policy* 25 (Fall 1977): 499-526.

13 See U.S. General Accounting Office, *Environmental Protection: Collaborative
    EPA-State Effort Needed to Improve New Performance Partnership System*
    (Washington, DC: GPO, GAO/RCED-99-171, June 1999), p. 3. See also Michael
    E. Kraft and Denise Scherberle, "Environmental Federalism at Decade's End: New
    Approaches and Strategies," *Publius: The Journal of Federalism* 28 (Winter
    1998): 131-146.

14 U.S. Environmental Protection Agency, *New Directions: A Report on Regulatory
    Reinvention* (Washington, DC: GPO, 1977): http://www.epa.gov/rein-
    vent/new#Performance.

15 U.S. General Accounting Office, *Environmental Protection*, p. 8.

16 Ibid., pp. 3-4.

17 See discussion in David L. Weimer and Aidan R. Vining, *Policy Analysis: Con-
    cepts and Practices*, 2nd ed. (Englewood Cliffs, NJ: Prentice Hall, 1992), p. 152.

18 Ibid., p. 153.

19 Richard W. Riley, U.S. Secretary of Education, *Statement before the House Sub-
    committee on Early Childhood, Youth and Families, Committee on Education and
    the Workforce*, 29 April 1997.

20 See Rene Sanchez, "Education Initiatives Off to a Slow Start," *The Washington Post*, 11 July 1998, p. 18.

21 National Governors Association, "Ray Scheppach Testimony on the Federal Grant Waiver Process for States Before the House Government Reform Committee. Subcommittee on National Economic Growth, Natural Resources, and Regulatory Affairs, and Subcommittee on Government Management, Information and Technology," September 30, 1999; http://www.nga.org.RegReform/Testimony19990930Waiver.asp.

22 National Governors Association, "John Callahan Testimony on the Federal Grant Waiver Process for States Before the House Government Reform Committee, Subcommittee on National Economic Growth, Natural Resources, and Regulatory Affairs, and Subcommittee on Government Management, Information and Technology," September 30, 1999; http ibid.

IV

Performance Management in States and Local Government

12

Beyond Measurement: Managing for Results in State Government

Patricia W. Ingraham and Donald P. Moynihan

Introduction

In the 1990s all levels of government witnessed many reforms intended to enhance government performance. These reforms included a number of management techniques that focused on improving government's strategic capacity. "Managing for results" (MFR) — the careful setting of public goals and measuring efforts to achieve them — was a central reform effort. MFR has been defined in expansive terms as "managing in pursuit of the policy performance consistent with the mission and aims of the government or agency" (Ingraham, Joyce and Kneedler 2000). MFR is not limited to any single technique but rather implies a planning process that produces a "clarity of task and purpose" (Holmes and Shand 1995) and enables government to understand and communicate how well it is performing. A primary intent of MFR is to improve the ability of government to provide performance information to citizens and others. This definition distinguishes

The authors thank Maja Husar and Kristin Lieser for their research assistance in preparing this chapter.

MFR from previous planning and management reforms such as management by objective (MBO), performance-based budgeting (PBB), and zero-based budgeting (ZBB).

Given the long and somewhat inglorious history of efforts intended to induce rationality into public administration, it should be of little surprise if public officials view reforms with suspicion (Downs and Larkey 1986). However, MFR has yielded significant experiments and new approaches to improving government's strategic abilities. This chapter explores the experiences of state government in creating MFR frameworks. We begin by discussing previous research on strategic planning and performance measurement in state government, showing how these approaches are interconnected in practice.

The data in this chapter come from the Government Performance Project (GPP), a multi-year analysis of government management systems at federal, state, and local levels, funded by The Pew Charitable Trusts. The project is a research initiative of the Alan K. Campbell Public Affairs Institute at the Maxwell School of Citizenship and Public Affairs at Syracuse University and *Governing* magazine. We draw on GPP research to discuss a general model of MFR as it relates to improving the management and strategic capacity of state governments. We also analyze how states are linking decision making to strategic planning and measurement. The analysis proceeds from the following definition and the assumptions it implies: A performance measurement system should produce accurate and meaningful information, be linked to actors (such as managers and elected officials) who will actually use this information to foster better performance, provide information to legislators to improve the quality of budget debates, provide information to decisionmakers on the likely effects of reform on performance, and provide information to citizens about how well their tax dollars are being spent.

What Is MFR in the Public Sector?

The closest antecedents to today's MFR efforts are the approaches to strategic planning traditionally associated with the private sector, and discussed in this section (Ansoff 1965, Mintzberg 1993, Porter 1985, Quinn 1980), and government efforts to measure performance, discussed in the following section (Joyce and Tompkins 2000, Poister and Streib 1999).

Most definitions of strategy recognize the use of purposeful action to direct the behavior of an organization toward a desirable and predetermined set of goals (Quinn 1980, Schick 1999, Skok 1989). However, state governments—like all public entities—need to be aware of the impact of the public-sector environment on the ability to shape and direct these tasks (Wilson 1989). While some practices apply to both the private and public sectors, differences relevant to strategic planning efforts exist (Eldridge 1989,[1] Ring and Perry 1985[2]). There may be a "unique public-sector approach to strategic management" (Miller, 1989, ix).[3] One of the major differences is the lack of competition in the public environment. For many working on strategy in the private sector, the key reference point taps some aspect of the marketplace: either competitive advantage (Porter 1985), growth (Ansoff 1965), or market opportunities (Learned et al. 1969). A reliance on the marketplace as a reference point is clearly not always a feasible or desirable benchmark for public efforts.

Understanding strategic planning in the public sector therefore requires knowledge of key influences on the process and its impacts. One lesson is that an emphasis on planning frequently treats it as a goal in itself rather than as a means to other ends. An active planning process can thus not only substitute for actual action but may contribute to a perception of planning processes and documents as public relations tools that cover up the failings of actual implementation (Mintzberg 1993, Langley 1988). MFR explicitly considers planning as a way of fostering greater accountability and higher performance. For instance, a central criterion of MFR is the communication of actual performance results to citizens and elected decisionmakers to ensure public accountability.

A related lesson is a growing awareness that the success of planning depends on critical contingencies both internal and external to the organization. Strategic management literature came to a similar conclusion in the 1970s, reflected in a change of focus from planning to management (Ansoff, Declerck and Hayes 1976). The shift emphasized that a consideration of the feasibility of management challenges in the setting of goals enhances the likelihood of success. This shift was reflected in the public sector by an appreciation of the complexities of implementation (Pressman and Wildavsky 1973). A focus on implementation—and the ability of organizational stakeholders to block or facilitate it—relegates central technocratic strategic efforts as secondary in importance to political support for program, policies, and activities.

Performance Measurement and Contemporary MFR Reforms

Strong measurement is important to MFR but is only one aspect, and other activities and conditions precede it (see Box I). Understanding MFR begins with the fundamental understanding that performance measurement does not, in itself, necessarily influence performance.

The history of efforts to induce rationality into the governing process is largely one of high hopes dashed. Joyce and Tompkins (2000, 5) offer summary observations on previous PBB efforts that provide a note of caution. The ambitions of PBB reforms have outstripped the analytical and information management capacity of government agencies, lack of political leadership and unclear or conflicting expectations has dogged the reforms, and rational planning systems are incompatible with the inherently political budgetary process characterized by competing interests. Despite this cautionary experience with related reforms, the last decade has seen increased strategic planning and performance measurement in state governments. For example, Melkers and Willoughby (1998) report that 47 of 50 states have PBB requirements. Of these 47, 31 states have performance-based budgeting legislation and 16 more states prescribe PBB through administrative requirements. Melkers and Willoughby define PBB as a system that requires strategic planning at the agency level for missions, goals, and objectives, and requests that quantifiable performance information relate to program outcomes. This definition does not require the use of performance information in budgeting—a standard associated with a narrower and more precise definition of performance budgeting (Fielding

Box I: Core Components of Managing for Results

Managing for results can occur in different ways and overlaps with other management concepts such as strategic planning and performance management. However, MFR does include a number of core components:

* *Government sets goals.*

* *Goals are quantifiable, have identifiable targets, are oriented to outputs and outcomes; and focus on the medium-term perspective.*

* *Goals are informed by consultation and consensus involving the executive and legislative branches and stakeholders.*

* *Goals are communicated to employees.*

* *Goals are communicated to the public.*

* *Goals are specifically linked to a responsible actor.*

* *Goals are broken down to lower-level objectives and action steps.*

* *A performance measurement system tracks the implementation of goals.*

* *Performance is reported on a regular basis.*

* *Performance information is verified.*

* *Performance information is used to hold people accountable, and to improve allocative and operational efficiency.*

Smith 1999). Snell and Grooters (1999) find more specifically that 32 states have overall "governing for results" legislation (including requirements to report performance information). Thirteen require a statewide strategic/long-range planning, 27 states require the use of performance information in the budget, and 18 states require agency planning.

If, as these numbers suggest, state governments are increasingly using the concepts and tools of MFR, what conditions lead states to use the technique? Strategic planning is more likely to occur early in a gubernatorial term as new leaders promote their vision of governance before focusing on reelection. Agencies with slack resources are also more likely to plan. Agencies further tend to adopt strategic planning if similar agencies in nearby states are already doing so, or if they work closely with the private sector (Berry 1994). Other factors prompting state governments to adopt MFR are the devolution of responsibilities from the federal level to the states, a perceived need to involve citizens in decisionmaking, and technological breakthroughs that allow complex performance measurement (Liner and Vinson 1999).

Unfortunately, the exponential use of MFR-related tools in government is not matched by a similar growth in understanding the results of such use (Wechsler 1989). Research on strategic planning in the public sector generally focuses on individual agencies rather than taking a governmentwide approach (Wechsler 1989, Berry 1994, Berry and Wechsler 1995). Even comprehensive descriptive analyses of how states are using information on performance as well as measuring it have been limited.

The Government Performance Project

To fill these gaps, the Government Performance Project (GPP) conceptualizes MFR as a range of associated management processes and actions, and examines MFR as from both the governmentwide and individual agency level. GPP research also examines actual state government experience with MFR. This in-depth approach allows understanding of the extent states use MFR, what aspects of

MFR are in place and used, the performance the process produces, as well as the contextual factors associated with MFR.

The GPP collects data through detailed surveys, content analysis of government documents, and interviews with executive and legislative officials in all 50 states. The survey examines five management systems: financial management, human resource management, information technology management, capital management and managing for results. The project uses clearly specified criteria for each management system to assess and grade the quality of management capacity in each state. Table 1 grades each state in MFR as well as its overall capacity in all five management systems.

Linking Capacity, Measurement, and Performance

The GPP defines management capacity as the "government's intrinsic ability to marshal, develop, direct, and control its human, physical, and information capital to support the discharge of its policy directions" (Ingraham and Kneedler 2000).[4] Management capacity is not a single system, but a wider network of information.

How does management capacity link to performance and its measurement? Recent reform rhetoric has rejected process and pleaded for results, giving the misleading impression that governments must choose between the two. Government reformers also often mistakenly assume that a performance measurement system equates with improved performance or a focus on results. However, performance measurement, by itself, simply produces information; it says nothing about how this information is used. The distinction between measurement and management is important, because it highlights the fundamental point that while having a measurement system in place provides one set of information about performance, it is no guarantee that good performance will occur or has occurred.

Table 1: State Grades on Managing for Results and Overall Management Systems — 1998					
State	*MFR Grade*	*Overall Grade*	*State*	*MFR Grade*	*Overall Grade*
Alabama	F	D	Montana	C	B-
Alaska	C-	C	Nebraska	B-	B
Arizona	B-	C	Nevada	C	C+
Arkansas	D	C-	New Hampshire	D+	C+
California	C-	C-	New Jersey	B-	B-
Colorado	C	C+	New Mexico	D+	C-
Connecticut	D+	C-	New York	D+	C-
Delaware	B	B	North Carolina	B-	B
Florida	B	C+	North Dakota	D	B-
Georgia	C+	C+	Ohio	C+	B
Hawaii	C-	C-	Oklahoma	D+	C
Idaho	C-	C	Oregon	B+	B-
Illinois	C	B-	Pennsylvania	B-	B
Indiana	C	C+	Rhode Island	C	C-
Iowa	B+	B	South Carolina	B-	B
Kansas	C	B-	South Dakota	D	B-
Kentucky	B	B	Tennessee	C	B-
Louisiana	B	B-	Texas	B+	B
Maine	C	C	Utah	B+	A-
Maryland	B-	B	Vermont	B-	B-
Massachusetts	C	B-	Virginia	A-	A-
Michigan	B	B+	Washington	B+	A-
Minnesota	B	B	West Virginia	C	C+
Mississippi	C	C+	Wisconsin	C	B
Missouri	A-	A-	Wyoming	C	C

Box II: GPP Criteria for Evaluating Managing for Results in State Government

1. Government engages in results-oriented strategic planning:

   ● Strategic objectives are identified and provide a clear purpose.

   ● Government leadership effectively communicates strategic objectives to all employees.

   ● Government plans are responsive to input from citizens and other stakeholders, including employees.

   ● Agency plans are coordinated with central government plans.

2. Government develops indicators and evaluative data that can measure progress toward results and accomplishments:

   ● Government can ensure that data are valid and accurate.

3. Leaders and managers use results data for policymaking, management, and evaluation of progress.

4. Government clearly communicates the results of its activities to stakeholders.

In contrast to the approaches of the International City/County Management Association and Urban Institute, the Government Performance Project emphasizes management capacity rather than end performance measures. Good management and strong capacity are significant, in this perspective, because *capacity* is the *platform* for performance. The utility of performance measurement depends on the political environment as well as the government's management capacity. For performance information to be useful, two things need to happen, and both are linked to management capacity. First, performance information needs to be of good quality. This quality depends on the types of measures adopted, how closely measures reflect strategic objectives, and how widely stakeholders accept measures as relevant. Second, governments need to show how performance information feeds decisionmaking[5] and efforts to improve management, allocate resources, and set goals. Such processes underlie an effective MFR system. Such a system has the potential to integrate other management systems in government (GAO 1994, 3):

> *In addition to obtaining stakeholders' agreement on strategic goals and measuring the progress made toward achieving those goals, some of the states were beginning to align their information, human resource, budgeting, and financial management systems to better ensure that the systems support managers in their efforts to achieve statewide and agency goals.*

By identifying, collecting, and using performance information then, leaders have a sound basis for evaluating the efficacy of programs and policies as well as of management systems. MFR also potentially establishes a tool for effective organizational learning – for understanding the reasons for governmental success or failure.

The State of the States in Strategic Management for Results

States rely on a number of MFR systems represented by different types of documents. One approach is to develop an overarching statewide strategic plan. Another is to pursue strategic planning at the agency level. States may also present MFR information through the annual budget.[6] All states have taken some steps towards MFR and 47 have adopted systematic documented MFR processes (see Table 2), while 44 pursue strategic planning (see Figure 1).[7]

Table 2: Types and Nature of Strategic Plans in State Government			
Strategic Planning Elements	*Statewide Plans (17)*	*Budget (31)*	*Agency Plans (34)*
Statewide mission statement	12	3	N/A
Core values	9	1	24
Mission statements for individual agencies	2	11	30
High-level outcome goals	17	9	27
Lower-level objectives	12	14	30
Medium-/long-term goals (3 years or more)	1	2	6
Short-term goals (1-2 years)	0	2	5
Quantified performance targets	3	10	11
Specific performance measures	8	24	20
Implementation strategies	6	2	20
Responsibility for goal linked to agency	4	5	N/A
Responsibility for goal linked to subagency unit	0	14	6
Responsibility for goal linked to program level	0	6	10
Responsibility for goal linked to named manager	1	0	3
Key external factors (the economy, resources, necessary legislation, others)	7	5	15

Seventeen states produce overarching strategic plans to coordinate policy and provide a central vision for the state's future. However, the broad nature of some of these documents allows disconnect between statewide planning and individual agency planning efforts. Statewide plans tend to be somewhat successful at creating a vision for governance and stating core values, high-level outcome goals, and lower-level objectives, but these plans are weakest in explicitly linking broad goals to lower levels of responsibility. Of the 31 state budgets considered as having elements of MFR, 19

Figure 1: States' Different Approaches to Strategic Planning

Statewide plan only	Agency plans only	Budget plan only	Statewide and agency plans	Statewide and budget plans	Budget and agency plans	Statewide, budget and agency plans
4	11	3	7	3	11	2

also qualify as strategic plans. Because most budgets are divided into agency level and program information, budgets are strongest in conveying agency mission statements, lower-level objectives, and performance results. The most popular, and most comprehensive, approach to producing MFR information occurs through strategic planning at the agency level. States employing agency strategic plans are likely to include more of the basic elements of MFR, including setting goal and targets, providing performance data, and linking responsibility for achieving goals to a specific agency, program, or manager. Overall, 24 states choose some combination of statewide planning, presenting goals in the budget or agency strategic planning. Thirteen states plan solely through agency documents, more than any other category.[8]

Types of Performance Measures

Output measures tend to be much more numerous than outcome measures in almost all states; only exceptional states such as Utah, Virginia, and Oregon place primary emphasis on outcomes. Apart from ease of measurement and the ability to more directly link to agency mission, one of the main reasons for focusing on outputs is that these measures are more directly under the control of agencies. North Carolina differentiates intermediate from policy outcomes, clarifying the latter as high-level outcomes that cut across functional responsibilities and cannot be attributed to any single agency. Intermediate outcomes link specific agency efforts with the larger policy outcomes. In fact, states most frequently create outcomes at the agency or program level—intermediate outcomes in North Carolina's terminology.

Efforts to tie policy outcomes to intermediate outcomes carry two main risks. The first is that without careful attention to the logical link between these outcomes and agency activities, outcomes can become irrelevant to day-to-day management. The second risk is that managers setting outcome goals at the program or agency level may not consider the main policy outcomes of state government. If there is no alignment between high-level goals and intermediate outcomes, a disconnect in the government goal-setting process occurs.

Using Performance Information

As we noted earlier, the concepts of capacity and management extend beyond simple performance measurement, and include the integration of MFR with management systems and actively using performance information. Performance measurement can link to management capacity if information is used to:

a) Track the performance of programs and management systems.

b) Promote better decisionmaking in the areas of resource allocation, process improvement, and management systems.

The effective use of information in turn depends on the quality of its distribution, and participants' incentives to use it. At least five clear purposes of performance information contribute to effective use:

❀ *Enhancing accountability through informing the public.*

❀ *Managing for performance improvement.*

❀ *Broadening the understanding of links between management capacity and level of performance.*

❀ *Fostering better resource allocation.*

❀ *Using performance contracting.*

Enhancing Accountability

Strategic planning and performance measurement can produce a clear statement of what government intends to achieve and track how well it succeeds. Providing performance information directly to the public enhances the ability of citizens to be informed about how government works, and shapes public expectations of government's obligation to provide accessible performance information and meet standards of performance. Performance measures are increasingly reported in performance reports and state budgets. Performance measures, particularly outcome measures, may also make a meaningful contribution to the public policy debate and motivate citizen interest. Both Maryland and Hawaii offer examples of lower-than-projected education test scores becoming a matter of public debate, leading the states to invest increased resources in education, and improve their administrative capacity. In its response to the GPP survey, Hawaii noted that performance measures "became the focal point of public demands to change its current governance status and management practices." Hawaii enhanced its capacity by changing its management and personnel policies.

Managing for Performance Improvement

Perhaps the most widespread use of performance information is among managers seeking to improve the operational efficiency of their programs and work processes. The type of performance information useful for understanding and improving work processes are efficiency measures, service quality indicators, workload indicators, and customer satisfaction rates. These measures can be used to set performance targets and develop strategies for achieving these targets, track performance over time, benchmark against other organizations, and establish performance contracts with employees or the private sector. Management and employees are critical users of such information, but elected officials are also important consumers of performance information on which they can base future decisions. These officials can play an important part in demanding improved performance.

States provided a number of examples of the uses of performance information to improve performance. For example, the Connecticut Department of Information Technology benchmarked efficiency measures against public and private organizations. The resulting analysis led the department to adjust its workflow schedules and processes to reduce per unit costs, which in turn led to a drop in the per unit rates charged by the state's data center. Massachusetts's Department of Social Services (DSS) provides another case in which performance measures, coupled with political oversight, heightened pressure to perform. DSS sets annual adoption targets for each area office and closely tracks progress towards achieving these targets throughout the year. The commissioner emphasizes the adoption initiative in meetings with each area office, and senior managers meet frequently with area office managers to discuss adoption activities. Since performance targets were introduced, the number of adoptions has nearly doubled.

Using Information to Strengthen Capacity

State decisionmakers also use performance measures to focus on how work is organized, capacity issues such as management systems and tools, and choices in providing services. Information on capacity is often not performance data per se, but is focused on how present capacity enables or constrains performance, and how capacity changes would improve performance. Government leaders, and especially elected officials, are the critical audience for this information owing to their ability to make decisions that change the way government develops capacity. Linking performance and capacity gives leaders a realistic understanding of how structures, processes, and rules create the parameters of performance, and how purposeful reform of these parameters can improve performance.

North Carolina provides an example of the use of performance information to strengthen capacity. That state benchmarks performance measures to assess not only the competitiveness of costs but also whether to outsource specific services. North Carolina's wider MFR framework identifies strategic missions and client groups of work groups, highlighting duplication of effort and producing structural changes in these programs. For instance, the state has consolidated the Division of Employment and Training in the Department of Commerce and the Workforce Preparedness Office in the Governor's Office.

These examples show that states use performance measures to track the effectiveness of management systems, but the evidence is less clear regarding how states integrate this information into broader reform. A key element in such efforts is changing the allocation of resources.

Fostering Better Resource Allocation

Tying performance measures to resources can yield a number of benefits, including enhancing the quality of the budgetary debate, providing incentives for participants to reach performance targets, investing in effective programs, and tackling areas of poor performance. However, a simple link between performance and budgeting—where high performers gain more resources and low performers receive less—poses a dilemma for decisionmakers: should the rewards go to agencies that perform well, or to those that need help? For example, in Missouri, positive effects on student performance of a program of elementary education prompted the state to allocate more resources to this program. However, such a simple link between performance and reward does not provide a comprehensive recipe for allocating resources. "Survival of the fittest" may be attractive to some, but it is not an appropriate decision rule for government. The ability to measure achievement and perform well may be unevenly distributed across different types of public functions (Wilson, 1989), but that does not mean that more public resources should be diverted to high-performing functions as a result. Given that states rarely eliminate a program or agency, the performance dilemma arises frequently. In responding to questions about how performance measure impacts on resource allocation, most states recognized the complexity of this link. Hawaii noted:

> *When resources are limited or insufficient, the link between per-formance measures and resource allocation becomes blurred. Even if a program "performs well" commensurate funding may not be forthcoming if it is considered a marginal function of gov-ernment. Conversely, less cost-effective, or "poorly-performing" programs may continue to be funded if these are "essential" gov-ernment functions – such as education, welfare or prisons.*

In fact, GPP evidence demonstrating a link between perfor-mance measures and resource allocation shows that legislators al-most always increase or reallocate resources to aid poor performers or meet policy challenges highlighted by performance measures. These experiences suggest that performance measures can highlight issues of capacity for legislators, but that they focus heavily on agencies that need to *build* capacity and performance, not on re-warding those with some success in doing so. For example, Oklahoma's health care agencies used the number of uninsured children as an indicator of efficient health care access. Elected offi-cials determined that this number was unacceptably high and moved to expand Medicaid to target young children and pregnant women. Texas examined the number of cases of preventable child-hood diseases and used this information to boost funding for state immunization.

Joyce and Tompkins (2000) use GPP data to offer another inter-pretation on the link between performance measures and budget-ing. PBB is perhaps the most difficult aspect of MFR to implement, because it is closely linked to the politics of budgeting, and legisla-tors are reluctant to adopt a form of decisionmaking that may limit their discretion. However, once an MFR system is adopted, perfor-mance information may influence budget decisions by actors other than legislators at different levels of the budget process. The budget process ends in legislative decisions but is preceded by budget preparation at the agency level, as well as central budget office re-view and coordination. Use of performance measures at these deci-sion points affects both budget proposals and final resource allocations, but in a way that may not be directly observable. In other words, performance information may shape the kinds of information provided to political decisionmakers, and thus influence their decision indirectly.

Joyce and Tompkins find most states using performance information at the agency level, although it is unclear how much this affects budget proposals. Only four states — Missouri, Texas, Louisiana, and Virginia — use performance information extensively at the central budget office (19 central budget offices report some use). Only in Louisiana is there evidence that legislators actively use performance information in making decisions. Such paucity of use is surprising, given that a large majority of states have some sort of PBB legislation. A legislative underpinning and initial claims of an active PBB process do not, therefore, translate into the use of performance information by state legislators. In responding to the GPP, states explain that legislative officials often view performance measures with skepticism, and are unlikely to use performance information unless it coincides with dominant constituent interests. This skepticism is partly due to the poor quality of the data — a problem that more performance auditing is intended to address — and partly due to lack of legislative involvement in setting goals and measures for performance measurement.

Performance Contracting

One of the relatively unexplored uses of performance information is to manage relations with external partners that provide public services. This is sometimes described as performance contracting (Martin 1999).[9] With the recent shift to a governance perspective (Frederickson 1999) and the growing use of networks (O'Toole 1997) encouraging an agnostic approach in choosing *how* services are delivered, performance information will become increasingly important in judging *how well* these services are delivered. Such use is already occurring. Massachusetts reports that its Department of Mental Health has developed performance indicators for private providers, commenting that "The overall objective is to improve provider's performance through a standardized process that articulates expectations and identifies standards for each service type." The state includes standards and indicators in the request-for-responses it sends to private bidders and negotiates them into contracts, along with specific performance targets. Semi-annual performance reports and review meetings maintain the emphasis on performance standards. Michigan reports that its Department of Education builds performance criteria into grants, and uses them to judge grantee performance. Minnesota's Pollution Control Agency develops performance agreements with regulated industries. By measuring pollution outcomes, the agency can negotiate waivers that enable industries to accelerate pollution reduction by bypassing normal bureaucratic rules. The Minnesota Department of Labor has taken a similar approach with private insurance companies, establishing goals for turnaround times for paying workers compensation and working with companies to reach these goals.

Including performance information in the contracting process has clear potential advantages. The public sector can specify the level of performance it requires and reward contractors accordingly. However, benefits do not automatically accrue from such arrangements. Public managers need to ensure that the targets in contracts accurately reflect program goals. Managers can motivate contractors by formal and specified targets, but if the targets only partially represent program goals, services will be skewed away from their original purposes (Heinrich 1999). In short, public employees need to manage the contract relationship carefully. Unfortunately, despite the growing importance of such contract management skills, traditional public administration curricula do not focus on developing them (Kettl, 1993, 1998).

Managing for Results Gains a Foothold

Embedding performance measures in internal and external contracts shows how performance data, when used well, can improve government. As Hatry (1996, ix) points out: "The ultimate purpose of performance measurement is to use the measurement information to help make improvements—whether to expand, delete or modify programs. This use still appears to be highly limited." Almost all state governments can cite examples where they have used performance data effectively, but they find it much more difficult to demonstrate careful and systematic consideration of performance information—and not simply a happy coincidence. Achieving this objective requires more than a performance measurement system: it also requires a managing for results system. More attention and commitment to the processes and products of MFR are likely to yield more lasting impact on the information the system acquires. As well as measuring performance, states must also plan strategically, create goals that are substantively valuable and linked to measures, have a clear game plan for using performance information, provide the right information to the right people, and create incentives to ensure appropriate results. Increasingly, states are trying to assemble these pieces. Legislative connection and commitment to performance measurement and management is a problem in virtually all states, however, and disconnect between the executive and the legislature in setting goals and sharing information appears to be common.

Despite these failings, the practical contributions of MFR should not be overlooked. State governments are using these tools, and gaining proficiency in their use. While legislative intent and rhetoric may be more ambitious than practice, elements of MFR are common enough in government that they can shed the "novelty" tag. Public service providers have moved beyond the basic questions of: "What is strategic planning?" and "What is benchmarking?" to the questions so important to success: "How do these tools fit with each other?" and "How can I make them work?" Committing to the strategic significance of MFR—and integrating it into the everyday processes of governance—provides one way to answer such questions and ensure improved performance.

Endnotes

1   Eldridge (1989) suggests a number of reasons why strategic management will be applied differently in the public sector: governments confront less competition than businesses, customer influence is likely to be weaker, measuring work performance is more difficult, there are greater restraints on rewards and punishments and a governmental unit is subject to more frequent changes in leadership, more stakeholders and greater outside influence. Governments also normally fulfill far more purposes than private companies.

2 Ring and Perry suggest that the factors that make public strategy unique will also make it more reactive than purposeful *(1985* p. 282). Due to "policy ambiguity, open and intense influence processes and coalition instability, public organizations can be characterized as low on deliberate strategy and high on emergent and unrealized strategy. If this characterization is correct, any manager who is unable, for instance, to relinquish intended strategies in order to pursue emergent strategies is likely to fail."

3 While Miller asserts that there is a unique approach to public strategy, he struggles to identify any uniform approach particular to public management. Rather, he succeeds in identifying the institutional characteristics that are unique to public management and influence public strategy. Among these are goal vagueness, media and interest groups that constrain bold action, a greater emphasis on who gets what rather than the actual quality of goals, conflicting values, and an emphasis on conservative management rather than risk taking.

4 New Zealand, a pioneer in the use of performance to ensure accountability, recently focused on the idea of public management capacity in broadly similar terms. The New Zealand State Services Commission's working definition of capability is: "Having, or being able to access, the appropriate combination of resources, systems and structures necessary to deliver the organization's outputs to customer specified levels of performance on an ongoing basis for the future" (State Services Commission, 1999 p. 5)

5 In addition to relying on data of a high quality, effective use of performance information is dependent upon data that is both timely and easily available.

6 Since all states produced budgets, and all budgets are not MFR documents, budgets had to include some goals or measures to be regarded as an MFR document. Strategic planning is a narrower aspect of MFR. To be regarded as a strategic-planning document, budgets had to have a short or medium term strategic goal or target that is to guide government activities. Nineteen state budgets could be regarded as a strategic planning documents by this criterion, and are included in Figure 1.

7 The analysis of state MFR processes reflect in Table II is based on the documentation of these efforts. The assumption of this research approach is that any systematic effort to manage for results will be reflected in some written format. States that could not provide documentation for an MFR system are not given credit.

8 This is the greatest difference observed between state and city experiences with MFR, which the GPP also studies. The 35 largest cities (on the basis of revenue) showed a strong preference for some form of central coordination of strategic planning through either the budget or a citywide plan. Indeed, no large city relied solely on individual agency plans for strategic planning (Moynihan 2000).

9 Martin offers a definition of performance contracting: "A performance contract is one that focuses on the outputs, quality and outcomes of service provision and may tie at least a portion of a contractor's payment, as well as any contract extension or renewal, to their achievement" (1999 p.1).

References

Ansoff, H. I. 1965. *Corporate Strategy.* New York: McGraw Hill.

Ansoff, H. I., R. P. Declerck and R. L. Hayes, eds. 1976. *From Strategic Planning to Strategic Management.* London: John Wiley

Berry, F. S. 1994. "Innovation in Public Management: The Adoption of Strategic Planning." *Public Administration Review, 54* July/August No. 4: pp. 322-330.

Berry, F. S., & Weschler, B. 1995. "State Agency's Experience with Strategic Planning: Findings from a National Survey." *Public Administration Review, 55* March/April No. 2: 159-68.

Bryson, J.M. 1995. *Strategic Planning for Public and Nonprofit Organizations: A Guide to Strengthening and Sustaining Organizational Achievements.* San Francisco: Jossey-Bass, 1995.

Cook, T.J., Vansvant, J., Stewart, L. & Adrain, J. 1995. "Performance Measurement: Lessons Learned for Development Management." *World Development, 23,* No. 8: 1303-1315.

Downs, G. W. and Larkey, P. 1986. *The Search for Government Efficiency: From Hubris to Helplessness.* New York: Random House.

Eldridge, William H. 1989. "Why Angels Fear to Tread: A Practitioner's Observations and Solutions on Introducing Strategic Management to a Government Culture." In Jack Rabin, Gerald J. Miller, and W. Bartley Hildreth, eds. *The Handbook of Strategic Management.* (pp. 319-336). New York: Marcel Dekker, Inc.

Fielding Smith, J. 1999. "The Benefits and Threats of PBB: An Assessment of Modern Reform." *Public Budgeting and Finance, 19,* No. 3: 3-15.

Frederickson, H. G. 1999. *The John Gaus Lecture.* Presented at the 1999 Annual American Political Science Association Conference, September, 1999.

Hatry, H. 1996. Foreword. In A. Halachmi & G. Bouckaert, eds. *Organizational Performance and Measurement in the Public Sector: Towards Service, Effort and Accomplishment Reporting.* (pp. i-ix). Westport, CT: Quorum Books.

Heinrich, C. J. 1999. "Did Government Bureaucrats Make Effective Use of Performance Management Information?" *Journal of Public Administration and Research Theory,* 9: pp. 363-393.

Holmes, Malcolm and David Shand. 1995. *Management Reform: Some Practitioner Perspectives on the Past Ten Years.* Paper presented at the SOG Ten-Year Reunion.

ICMA and the Urban Institute. 1997. *Comparative Performance Measures: FY 1995 Report.* Washington, D.C.: Urban Institute and the International City/County Management Association.

Ingraham, P. W., Joyce P. J. and Kneedler, A. E. 2000. *Managing for Performance.* Ch. 3, Draft Manuscript prepared for John Hopkins University Press.

Ingraham, P.W. and Kneedler, A. E. 2000. "Dissecting the Black Box Revisited: Characterizing Government Management Capacity." In Laurence E. Lynn, Jr., ed. *Models and Methods for the Empirical Study of Governance,* Georgetown University Press.

Joyce, P. G., and S. Sieg Tompkins. 2000. *Using Performance Information for Budgeting: Clarifying the Framework and Investigating Recent State Experience.* Paper presented at the 2000 Symposium of the Center for Accountability and Performance of the American Society for Public Administration, George Washington University, Washington, D.C.

Kettl, D. 1993. *Sharing Power: Public Governance and Private Markets.* Washington, DC: Brookings Institution Press.

Kettl, D. 1998. *Reinventing Government: A Fifth Year Report Card.* Washington, DC: Brookings Institution Press.

Langley, A. 1988. "The Role of Formal Strategic Planning." *Long Range Planning. 21,* 3: pp. 48.

Learned, E. P., C. R. Christensen, K. R. Andrews and W. D. Guth. 1969. *Business Policy: Text and Cases* (rev. ed.). Homewood, IL: Richard D. Irwin.

Liner, B., and Vinson, E. 1999. *Will States Meet the Challenge?* Washington, D.C.: The Urban Institute.

Martin, L. L. 1999. "Performance contracting: Extending performance measurement to another level." *PA Times* 22, 1: pp. 1, 8.

Melkers, J., & Willoughby, K. 1998. "The State of the States: Performance-Based Budgeting Requirements in 47 out of 50." *Public Administration Review, 58* January/February No. 1: pp. 66-73.

Miller, Gerald L. 1989. "Introduction." In Jack Rabin, Gerald J. Miller, and W. Bartley Hildreth eds. *The Handbook of Strategic Management.* New York: Marcel Dekker, Inc.

Mintzberg, H. 1993. "The Pitfalls of Strategic Planning." *California Management Review 36,* Fall: pp. 32-48.

Mintzberg, H. 1994. "The Fall and Rise of Strategic Planning." *Harvard Business Review,* January-February: pp. 107-114.

Moynihan, D. P. 2000. *Managing for Results in the Cities: Report from a National Survey.* Paper presented at the Western Social Science Association, San Diego, April 26th-29th, 2000.

O'Toole, Laurence. 1997. "Treating Networks Seriously: Practical and Research Based Agendas in Public Administration." *Public Administration Review 57,* January-February No. 1: pp. 45-52.

Poister, T. H. 1983. *Performance Monitoring.* Lexington MA:DC Health and Co.

Poister, T. H., & Streib, G. 1999. "Performance Measurement in Municipal Government: Assessing the State of the Practice." *Public Administration Review, 59* July/August No. 4: pp. 325-335.

Porter, M. E. 1985. *Competitive Strategy.* New York: Free Press.

Pressman, J. L. and Wildavsky, A. 1973. *Implementation: How Great Expectations in Washington Are Dashed in Oakland.* Berkeley, CA: University of California Press.

Quinn, J. B. 1980. *Strategies for Change: Logical Incrementalism.* Homewood, Ill: Richard D. Irwin.

Ring P. S. and Perry, J. L. 1985. "Strategic Management in Public and Private Organizations: Implications of Distinctive Contexts and Constraints." *Academy of Management Review 10*, No. 2: pp. 276-286.

Schick, A. 1999. *Opportunity, Strategy, and Tactics in Reforming Public Management.* Presented at Government of the Future: Getting from Here to There, OECD Symposium held in Paris, 14-15 September 1999.

Skok, James. E. 1989. "Towards a Definition of Strategic Management for the Public Sector." *American Review of Public Administration 19*, June No. 2: pp. 133-148.

Snell, R., and Grooters, J. 1999. *Governing-for-Results: Legislation in the States.* Draft Report to the National Council of State Legislatures.

State Services Commission (Government of New Zealand). 1999. *Assessing Department's Capability to Contribute to Strategic Priorities.* Occasional Paper No. 16. Wellington: State Service Commission.

U.S. General Accounting Office. 1994. *State Experiences Provide Insights for Federal Management Reforms.* Washington. D.C.: US General Accounting Office.

Wechsler, B. 1989. "Strategic Management in State Government." In J. Rabin, G. J. Miller, & W. B. Hildreth, eds. *The Handbook of Strategic Management* (pp. 353-71). New York: Marcel Dekker, Inc.

Wilson, J. Q. 1989. *Bureaucracy.* New York: Basic Books.

13

Performance Budgeting in the States

Katherine G. Willoughby
and Julia E. Melkers

Introduction

Over the past decade, state governments have established legal and/or administrative requirements for performance based budgeting systems that incorporate requirements for measuring and reporting agency and program performance results (Melkers and Willoughby 1998). The adoption of these requirements coincide with the Governmental Accounting Standards Board (GASB) attention to performance measurement development and use in state and local governments. To assist governments in performance measurement reporting, GASB has established the Service Efforts and Accomplishments (SEA) indicators, which involve both financial and nonfinancial performance measures of service efforts and accomplishments information.[1] Their goal is that governmental entities track and report these in their financial documents. In fact, governments have moved beyond the establishment of requirements

We wish to thank the Alfred P. Sloan Foundation for the support that made this research possible. Thank you also to our GASB research team and the hard work of our graduate assistants Brian James, Pratik Mhartre and Kelly Fitzgerald. Most of all, thank you to all the state and local officials who took time from their busy agendas to help us to learn more about performance measurement use.

for results-based systems to the institutionalization of performance measurement and performance budgeting in the routine administration of agency programs and activities. Such systems require stronger roles for planning and goal setting, and stipulate the conduct of performance measurement and reporting about program results. This chapter summarizes the findings of a mail survey focusing on how performance measurement and a results orientation have influenced state budgeting regarding budget actors, budget cycles, relationships, and perceptions of government on the part of the media and citizens. We address state government budget officers' perceptions of the importance of performance measurement and performance based budgeting in particular. We investigate how and when performance measurement information is used in decisions about spending by this select group of budget actors. This research should be helpful to governments as they begin to experiment with methods of presenting indicators externally via financial and program reports in order to provide stakeholders (citizens, other governments, investors, etc.) with reliable information about their performance.

What Do We Mean by Performance, Its Measurement, and Performance Based Budgeting Systems?

Carnevale and Carnevale (1993) point out that the current focus on performance measurement by governments, while reminiscent of the progressive era, is different; there is an enhanced emphasis in public organizations on quality, variety, customization, convenience, and timeliness of services and programs over and above economic efficiency concerns. Similarly, DuPont-Morales and Harris (1994) discuss accountability for purpose (vision/mission), direction (goals/strategies), and impact (output/outcome, results) that is quite distinctive from cost concerns. They clarify the importance of beginning with a clear understanding of mission when considering agency performance and measurement of that performance. For example, they distinguish between possible missions for corrections services as reforming behavior to provide for safer communities versus understanding the mission as one of the safe storage of criminals away from citizens.

The National Center for Public Productivity (1997) recognizes that performance measurement has evolved to consider more than simple efficiency. Rather it points to several components that are important for a complete assessment of government performance regarding any activity or program:

- *Productivity*, which quantifies the outputs and inputs of an organization and expresses the two as a ratio;

- *Effectiveness*, which determines the relationship between an organization's outputs and what an organization is intended to accomplish;

- *Quality*, which examines an output or the process by which an output is produced, indicated by attributes such as accuracy, thoroughness, and complexity; and

- *Timeliness*, which evaluates the time involved to produce an appropriate output (The National Center for Public Productivity 1997).

Hatry (1999), a well-known authority on performance measurement applications, also recognizes that the modern concept is more complicated than that considered adequate for activity based budgeting of the 1950s. He emphasizes that performance measurement incorporates all of the concepts relayed above, in addition to the requirement for *regularity* in the measurement of results. He (1999: Chapter 1) states that, "regular measurement of progress toward specified outcomes is a vital component of any effort at managing-for-results, a customer-oriented process that focuses on maximizing benefits and minimizing negative consequences for customers of services and programs."

In his "how-to" for performance measurement, Hatry (1999) then argues that all agencies that serve the public/citizens/clients can measure performance (some better than others) and such data are useful for:

- budget justification,

- management improvement and monitoring of program success/problems, and

❋ addressing equity concerns.

Regarding equity, he states, "A well-designed measurement system enables agency managers to assess the fairness of a program and make appropriate adjustments. A good performance measurement system will help officials demonstrate to the public and to policymakers that services are delivered fairly and this will build trust." Of the uses for performance data noted by Hatry, we address government officials and staff use of performance data for budget justification and when making spending decisions and trade-offs, for management purposes, and to enhance communication.

In any event, we see that the above considerations of performance measurement require more substantial skills of government employees. Not only must employees hold the basics related to reading, writing, and computing, but they must also be adept at analysis, communication, and presentation. Government officials as well as program staff must be skilled at understanding measurement development (the building components), relativity and benchmarking, and measurement refinement. Essentially, these employees must be able to understand the meaning behind measures, their correct calculation and interpretation, and then when to use them to enhance decision making (Mosso 1999). An understanding of performance based budgeting systems, then, must incorporate an expanded notion of performance measurement and in fact, considers calculation and tabulation of results and communication of those results as important.

Integrating Performance Measurement in the Budget Process in the United States

The history of the development and use of performance measurement by governments in the United States is well documented (Lee 1997; Lee and Johnson 1998). While the focus of this chapter is on the state level, it is clear that the initiatives we are witnessing at that level of government are also evident at the federal and local levels (and are addressed in great detail in other chapters in this volume.) At the federal level, the often-cited Hoover Commission in 1949 provided a very visible push in the direction of performance monitoring by calling for a restructuring of the federal budget into activities rather than line items. The Commission also requested that agencies provide performance reports. Later, the Chief Financial Officers Act (1990) required performance data reporting from a select number of federal agencies. The Government Performance and Results Act of 1993 then extended performance measurement and the generation of performance plans across most federal agencies by establishing a performance reporting schedule to begin by 1997. Finally, the Gore Commission during President Clinton's administration maintained a focus on government reinvention that has sustained interest in performance measurement and monitoring at the federal level.

Specific attention to performance measurement and monitoring has filtered down to local governments as well (Berman and Wang 2000; Poister and Streib 1999). Research results indicate that anywhere from a third to less than one fifth of local governments in the United States (distinguishing between counties and municipalities, respectively) use some form of performance measurement. In a survey where over one half (694 of 1,218) of the cities (of 25,000+ populations) contacted responded, Poister and Streib (1999) find that 15 percent of the cities use performance measurement selectively, not comprehensively throughout their agencies and departments. Larger cities, and those defined as more reformed (council-manager versus mayor-council), tend to use performance data more frequently. The International City/County Managers Association's (ICMA) Center for Performance Measurement, along with the Urban Institute, continue to support efforts to institutionalize the use and effectiveness of performance monitoring, measurement, and reporting by local governments.

Similar to the trends at the local and federal levels, state governments have had deliberate and steady pressure to build performance monitoring and reporting systems in which performance measurement is a chief component. In the early 1990s, both the National Governors Association as well as the National Conference of State Legislators encouraged states to incorporate performance measurement and monitoring into their budgeting systems. During this time, most states complied either by passing legislation, issuing executive orders, or establishing administrative guidelines requiring some type of performance based budgeting system (Melkers and Willoughby 1998). By the late 1990s, all but three states had performance-based budgeting requirements, with most establishing these requirements after 1990. More specifically, as shown in Figure 1, of 47 states with some performance related requirement, 31 have legislated performance budgeting to be conducted, while 16 have initiated the reform through budget guidelines or instructions. By the end of the last decade, only three states, Arkansas, Massachusetts, and New York, did not have either type of mandate to conduct PBB (Melkers and Willoughby, 1998).

The Governmental Accounting Standards Board (GASB) provides financial reporting standards for state and local governments. Their focus on performance measurement via the requirements of Service Efforts and Accomplishments (SEA) Reporting (Concepts Statement No. 2, 1994) further pushed states to continue developing performance monitoring systems, as well as to continue measurement refinement and report generation. More recently, GASB's Statement 34 will phase in application of even more advanced financial reporting on the part of state and local governments, some of which is performance related. This statement outlines new and different information that must be provided by state and local

Figure 1:
Performance Budgeting in the States: Administrative & Legislative Requirements

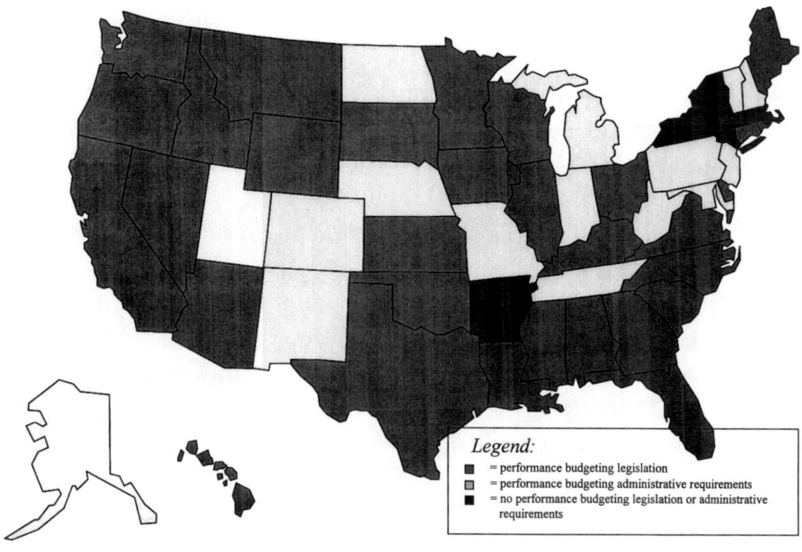

Legend:
■ = performance budgeting legislation
▨ = performance budgeting administrative requirements
■ = no performance budgeting legislation or administrative requirements

governments in their financial reports, requirements for reporting of all capital assets and depreciation expense, as well as the use of full accrual accounting.

Research shows that performance based budgeting initiatives in the states have had some, albeit limited, success over the last few years (Willoughby and Melkers 2000). Such success has been found to relate primarily to the management of programs and not to appropriations that support such programs or regarding the actual costs of the activities entailed therein (Broome and McGuire 1995). We know that state government applications of performance based budgeting systems are complicated, incomplete, and still evolving; each system is different, and implementation strategies and successes are varied. In fact, Lee and Burns (2000) promote a concept of budget system maturation to explain why some states have been "backsliding" regarding performance measurement's relevance to budget decisions. They explain that "institutional memory" may hinder governments from widespread application and acceptance of a performance based budgeting system. Practitioners are cautious based on past experiences with reform and are unwilling or unable to move to immediate and widespread adoption. Rather, "a more realistic perception may exist in the states about the effort required in revising budget systems and the likely outcome of the reforms" (Lee and Burns 2000, 53). In other words, practitioners recognize the existence of a "learning curve" associated with the implementation of performance measures in budgetary decisionmaking.

Jordan and Hackbart (1999) emphasize that performance measurement application to budgeting may have its greatest impact as an important component of the governor's executive budget recommendation. And "advancement of performance in the budget process requires an organizational focus directed at the state budget offices" (Jordan and Hackbart 1999, 85). There is certainly no disagreement here. State budget offices are at the vortex of policy and budgeting; budget examiners who communicate data back and forth between the chief executive and agencies are in a powerful role of garnering, deliberating about, and exposing information about performance to the chief executive, which the governor then can interpret vis-à-vis policy objectives (Thurmaier and Willoughby 2001). Legislative budget offices operate similarly, although more filtered, given their many bosses. In any event, to be considered fiscally relevant, performance data and information on program results must be important to those officials (executive and legislative) responsible for recommending and then passing appropriations bills.

Exploring the Use of Performance Measures in State Budget Processes: Research Questions

Performance budgeting is defined as a process that requests quantifiable data that provide meaningful information about program outputs and outcomes in the budget process. The widespread adoption of performance budgeting requirements at all levels of government in the United States reflects the support for and emphasis on changing the way that budget decisions are made. It does not reflect, however, actual use of performance data in the budget decision processes.

In order to accurately assess the implementation of performance budgeting requirements and activities in the states, we must understand the way that performance measures and data are actually being used in state budget processes. We are particularly interested in the actual use of performance measurement and a results orientation *during* steps in the budget cycle and regarding budget decisions. Specifically, these steps include:

- ❋ budget development,
- ❋ preparation of the chief executive's budget recommendation,
- ❋ appropriation of funds, and
- ❋ budget execution.

The first step in the budget cycle involves budget development — that period during the budget cycle prior to submission of a recommended budget by the executive and passage of the appropriation bill(s) or bills by the legislature. This period encompasses consideration and packaging of budget needs on the part of agencies and departments. The next step involves assessment of agency budget requests by the executive budget office in order to prepare the budget recommendation for the chief executive to present to the legislative body. Legislative branch members then consider the executive budget recommendation when deliberating about final appropriations. Following appropriation of funds, budget execution begins. The cycle is completed with the audit of expenditures. The complexity of the budget process therefore provides several points at which the use of performance data is possible and/or desirable.

The research reported in this chapter is focused on questions developed around the following three themes within the context of state budgetary decision processes:

- ❀ Identification and usefulness of particular measures;

- ❀ Actual use and reasons for the use of performance data in the budget process;

- ❀ The extent to which integration of performance measures in budgetary processes affects communication between budget and policy actors.

First, to what extent are state budget officers accessing reported performance measurement and results data and what is their perception of the use of such data by those in the agencies in their state? For example, we address the extent to which output and outcome performance measures have appeared in documentation throughout the budget process in their state. Second, what role do performance measures play in the budgetary process? What type of information about agency performance is most helpful to budget officers and for what sorts of decisions? For example, we explore budget officers' perceptions of how important output and outcome performance measures have been in the various steps of the budget cycle, beginning with agency budget development, during the chief executive's preparation of the budget recommendation, throughout legislative deliberation of the budget, during budget execution, and in the final audit phase. We also address budget officers' perceptions of what types of performance data (input, output, and/or outcome measures, cost/efficiency measures, effectiveness/quality measures, and/or explanatory measures) are used for various decisions within agencies. Types of decisions considered include: program planning, operational management, budgeting and resource allocation and reallocation, evaluation and assessment. Finally, what are the issues in communicating measures of performance and results? Has performance measurement changed communication patterns in the states? A previous survey of executive and legislative budget office staff in state governments regarding the usefulness of performance based budgeting systems (PBB) found such systems to be *at least* somewhat effective "in improving agency program results, decision making in government, and coordination between agencies and the legislature" (Willoughby and Melkers 2000, 113). Is this assessment of performance data consistent over time for these budget actors?

Methodology

The data reported in this research represents one component of a major study of performance measurement use in state and local governments. The study is part of a multi-year effort by GASB to extend the SEA Research. Funded by the Sloan Foundation, twenty-six case studies (1999) and a major mail survey (2000) were conducted by the GASB Performance Measurement Research Team. The team was comprised of GASB researchers, faculty from the Andrew Young School of Policy Studies at Georgia State University, a government agency consultant, and two graduate students. Overall, the project focused on the depth and breadth of the actual use of performance measures by governments for budgeting, management, and reporting. This chapter presents research about the assessments of executive and legislative budget officers regarding the usefulness of performance measurement and a performance based approach to the budget cycle and budgeting decisions in their state government. GASB's work cited thus far in this area is to support enhanced financial reporting requirements of state and local governments that have been initiated with Statement 34.

For the mail survey, 121 questionnaires were mailed to budget offices and 434 were sent to heads of selected agencies in all 50 states. In addition, more than 700 questionnaires were sent to budget officers and department heads in local governments across the country. Overall, 1,311 survey instruments were mailed out and 491 received, for a response rate of 37 percent. This chapter is limited to questions related to budgetary decisionmaking by state budget officers. Thus, our findings are based on a subset of subjects of the mailed survey; we concentrate our research on 62 responses from executive and legislative budget offices in the fifty states, representing a 51 percent response rate for that group. This subset includes response from 37 states, with 15 states providing response from both the executive and legislative branch budget offices. Admittedly this is a small sample. However, the subjects represent a very specialized budget actor (the executive or legislative budget officer) who retains a global view of budget process and the use of performance indicators across many agencies and programs during such process.

Using a mail survey, we sought to confirm the extent of performance measurement use in state governments, to understand measurement verification/validation activities as implemented, to check subjects' understanding of the purposes of generating and using performance data, to find out where performance data appears in budget and financial reports and when during the budget cycle performance information is most helpful. We also explored governments' ability to reward agencies for reaching performance goals, or alternatively to sanction agencies for missing such targets. And, regarding trends, we sought confirmation about how successful the performance measurement application has been to affect cost savings, efficiency, effectiveness and program results, enhanced communication, and better understanding among government officials and with citizens. We present here our findings from the mailed survey of budget officers. Additional qualitative findings from the GASB (2000) case studies are also integrated with these results to further elucidate uses of performance data in state budgetary decisions.

Research Findings

Our research shows that the application of performance measurement to decision-making is far from comprehensive throughout states and varies depending upon the program or activity of interest. We found that performance measurement is used with the greatest success as a decision aid for budget staff, and that linking results to spending is best accommodated (most helpful) for those activities in which measurement of performance is simple and easily carried out. The usefulness of performance measurement to budget decisions, specifically, depends upon the period in the budget cycle and budget players involved. We hope these results will provide academics and practitioners with information about how to enhance the usefulness of performance measurement to budget decisions, as well as how this one component can be used to strengthen a comprehensive performance budgeting initiative.

Results based on the subset of survey responses (budget officers only) and case studies are presented below. First, we describe the types of performance measures in use in state budget offices and explore perceptions of their utility by budget officers. Second, we explore the details of the use of performance measurement as part of the budgetary process. Finally, we address the "spillover" effects of using performance measurement, focusing on how performance measures affect communication between budgetary actors.

Using Performance Measures in the States

Budget officers in executive and legislative budget offices are likely to have a broad perspective on performance measurement use in their state and are among the most knowledgeable individuals in state government to report on performance measurement activities within their state. Budget officers are likely users of performance data for their own evaluative work, yet they frequently interact with agencies and therefore develop a high level of knowledge about agency processes and procedures including use of performance data. Where performance reporting is incorporated into budget development, budget officers play an important role in examining performance data from agencies for budget justification purposes. Given this, they provide a useful external or global view to agency activities.

Our results show that budget officers reported a high level of performance measurement use in agencies in their states. More than half of the respondents indicated that performance measures were being used by agencies in their state, with one-quarter noting that at least 50 percent of the agencies in their state were using performance measures. Further, more than half of the budget officers responding indicated that program evaluations have also been used in their state to determine why programs or departments are performing at the level they are. While performance measurement involves an ongoing effort, organizations may conduct a program evaluation to gather a "snap shot" view of program activities that provides greater detail for a single point in time. In other words, states have broadly adopted performance measurement and also program evaluation to assess program outcomes in the state.

There was variation, as may be expected, in the organizations involved in the actual performance measure development process. Most respondents indicated that the executive budget office staff were involved in not only measure development, but also in setting performance targets. Respondents were split in the extent to which executive leadership decided which performance measures are adopted — in many states the governor's office plays an active role in measure selection. While some states, like Iowa, have formalized citizen participation in the assessment of government performance (Melkers and Willoughby 1998), most respondents indicated that citizens were not actively involved in the selection of measures. However, subjects were split in their consideration of the importance of citizen opinion to measures and measurement.

We asked budget officers to report the use of performance measures in agencies in their state according to several categories. For example, we asked them to indicate their use of:

- Input measures
- Activity/Process measures
- Output measures
- Outcome measures
- Cost/Efficiency measures
- Quality/Customer Satisfaction measures
- Explanatory measures

❋   Benchmarks

Respondents were provided with a definition for each of these terms so that there was a consistent understanding of the meaning of each. For example, respondents were given the following definition to assist them with distinguishing between outputs and outcomes:

Outputs – Measures of the quantity of services provided or the quantity of service that meets a certain quality requirement. (For example, the number of lane miles of road repaired or the number of serious crimes reported);

Outcomes – Measures of the results that occur, at least in part, because of services provided. This may include initial, intermediate, or long-term outcomes. (For example, the percentage of lane miles of road maintained in excellent, good, or fair condition, or the clearance rate for serious crimes, or the percentage of residents rating their neighborhood as safe or very safe).

The goal of most governments where performance budgeting has been adopted is to move from an activity-level or output-oriented reporting to one with a greater emphasis on quality and especially results. Another important goal is to move from identifying measures and collecting data on those measures to actually using that information in decision processes. Based on the observations of state budgeters responding to our survey, two-thirds indicated that outcome measures were in use in agencies in their state, with one-quarter indicating that more than 50 percent of agencies in their state were using outcome measures. However, respondents were divided when asked whether performance measurement in their state is more focused on program results, rather than straight workload measures. They are also split in terms of reporting the range and coordination of measures. For example, about half of our respondents strongly agreed or agreed that agencies in their state "have developed multiple levels of measures, from output, to outcome, to societal benchmarks." When asked about the specific types of measures that have been useful in budgeting, including for resource allocation or discussion about resource changes, most budget officers (70 percent) indicated that input measures and output measures had been most often used in their state. Cost and efficiency measures were more common than outcome measures; measures of quality and explanatory measures were cited less frequently.

Practitioners are often quick to admit that determining useful and measurable outcomes is an ongoing challenge that they feel poorly equipped to do well. Therefore, these findings are encouraging because they reflect a shift (although a slow one) from the reliance on the easier-to-measure output measures to the more meaningful measures of impact. Results also emphasize the long-term process required to move from a focus on activity measures or outputs to more meaningful measures of outcomes.

Performance Measures and Budgeting Decisions

While budget officers have a unique vantage point from which to view state activities, their report of performance measurement use in their own offices reflects the statewide commitment to integrating performance data in the budgeting process. We asked these officers to indicate the extent to which performance measures appeared and were reported in various phases of the budget process. Almost one-third of our respondents indicate that output or outcome measures have appeared in agency budget requests for more than 50 percent of agencies in their state while almost half of the respondents indicated that this was true for all agencies in their state. Similarly, the vast majority of officers indicated that output or outcome measures appeared in more than 50 percent of agencies in their state's 1999/2000 executive budget report.

That performance measures are evident in budget documents reflects a consistency of performance reporting and also shows a commitment to including this information in the budget process, yet we were unsure of when in the budget cycle performance data are most useful to budget practitioners. We asked respondents their opinion of how important output or outcome performance measures have been in the following stages of the budget process: budget development, appropriations, execution, and audit or assessment. We were interested in budget practitioner views of the use of performance measures at these stages both at the agency level as well as from a statewide budget process perspective. Overall, respondents did not place a great deal of emphasis on the value of output and outcome measures at any of these stages of the budget process at either the agency or statewide levels. For each of these categories, somewhere between two-thirds and three-quarters of respondents called these measures "not important" or "somewhat important." As shown in Table 1, however, there was a difference of opinion about the importance of these measures in the budget process when we compared responses of officers from different branches and from states with different performance based system requirements.

	Stage of Budget Process	Executive Branch	Legislative Branch	Administrative PBB Requirement	Legislative PBB Requirement
	Table 1 **Importance of Performance Data** **in Select Stages of Budget Process**				
	Respondent Mean Responses *How important have output or outcome performance measures been in the following steps in the budget process?* (1=not important...4=very important)				
Agency-wide	Agency budget development	2.54	2.29	2.38	2.37
	Agency appropriations	2.31	1.96	1.94	2.26
	Agency budget execution	2.31	1.92	1.88	2.29
	Agency audit/ assessment of results	2.24	1.96	1.75	2.31
Statewide	Statewide budget development	2.44	2.09	2.06	2.27
	Chief executive budget deliberations	2.50	1.96	2.00	2.24
	Legislative appropriation deliberations	2.23	1.83	1.69	2.21
	Final appropriation determination	2.08	1.58	1.50	1.97
	Statewide budget execution	2.12	1.71	1.62	2.06
	Statewide audit/ assessment of results	2.04	1.92	1.53	2.24

Based on prior research (Melkers and Willoughby 1998), we know that states differ in their approach to performance measurement depending upon whether their performance based budgeting system has been legislated versus administratively required. In this case, respondents from states where performance budgeting is legislated placed a greater importance on measurement use to budgeting, overall. Officers in the two groups more closely agreed regarding use of performance measures early in the budget process during budget development. Next, we compared responses of individuals from executive budget offices to those employed in legislative budget offices. Again, these groups were most alike in their responses to the value of output and outcome performance measures in the budget development phase. However, individuals from executive budget offices consistently placed more emphasis on the importance of output and outcome measures in later phases of the budget process. This was true when asked about agency-level or statewide budget processes.

Practitioners frequently acknowledge that the process of developing measures can be useful from a management and decisionmaking perspective. We asked budget officers to indicate how effective the development and use of performance measures has been in effecting certain changes in their state across a range of items, from resource allocation issues, to programmatic changes, to cultural factors such as changing communication patterns among key players. These categories and individual items are shown in Table 2. Many respondents were willing to describe performance measurement as "somewhat effective," but few were more enthusiastic. Across the board, no more than one-third of respondents described the development and use of performance measures as "very effective" or "effective" for any of these items. Most markedly, few were willing to attach performance measures to changes in appropriation levels. This is not, however, surprising, as the intent behind most performance budgeting requirements is much broader than simply affecting changed appropriations.

Again, we compared respondents from executive budget offices to their counterparts in legislative budget offices; and officers from states where performance budgeting was legislated versus those from states where it was administratively required. Looking

Quicker, Better, Cheaper?
Managing Performance in American Government

Table 2
Budget Officers' Perceptions of the Effectiveness of Performance Measures

Respondent Mean Responses

How effective has the development and use of performance measures been in the agencies in your state regarding the following?
(1=not effective.....4=effective)

	Executive Branch Budget Officers	Legislative Branch Budget Officers	Officers in States with Administrative PBB Requirement	Officers in States with Legislative PBB Requirement
Making Cuts				
Affecting cost savings?	2.00	1.35	1.62	1.76
Reducing duplicative services?	2.00	1.55	1.42	1.94
Reducing/eliminating ineffective services/programs?	1.81	1.45	1.38	1.74
Improving Programs				
Improving responsiveness to customers?	2.37	1.80	2.08	2.18
Improving programs/service quality?	2.42	1.90	2.00	2.26
Improving effectiveness of agency programs?	2.27	1.85	2.00	2.06
Focusing on Results				
Increasing awareness of, and focus on, results?	2.63	2.09	2.29	2.46
Increasing awareness of factors that affect performance results?	2.48	2.14	2.21	2.37
Changing strategies to achieve desired results?	2.50	1.95	1.92	2.32

Performance Budgeting in the States

Table 2 (Continued)
Budget Officers' Perceptions of the Effectiveness of Performance Measures

	Executive Branch Budget Officers	Legislative Branch Budget Officers	Officers in States with Administrative PBB Requirement	Officers in States with Legislative PBB Requirement
Improving Communication and Coordination				
Improving communication between departments and programs?	2.48	2.00	1.92	2.31
Improving cross-agency cooperation/coordination?	2.00	1.67	1.69	1.81
Improving communication with the executive budget office?	2.67	2.00	2.38	2.37
Improving communication with the legislature and legislative staff?	2.50	2.05	1.83	2.43
Communicating with the public about performance?	2.16	1.71	1.85	2.09
Improving external government cooperation/coordination?	1.88	1.43	1.46	1.71
Changing the Substance of Discussions				
Changing the substance or tone of discussion among legislators about agency budgets?	2.12	1.76	1.67	2.09
Changing the substance or tone of discussion among legislators about oversight of agencies?	2.04	1.77	2.08	1.88
Changing the questions legislators or their staff ask government managers or executives?	2.08	1.95	1.85	2.17
Changing State Spending				
Changing appropriation levels?	1.74	1.41	1.50	1.54

at mean responses, it is apparent that budget officers from the executive branch were more willing to attribute change to measurement development and use, including changes in appropriation levels, than were the legislative budgeters. Legislative budget officers ranked the use of performance measures especially low in affecting cost savings and reducing duplicative services. There were fewer differences between officers when type of PBB requirement is considered, with respondents from legislated states appearing slightly more likely to attribute noted changes to the development and use of performance measurement.

One important component of some state performance measurement guidelines involves the use of sanctions or rewards when performance targets are missed, met, or even exceeded. From earlier work (Melkers and Willoughby 1998), we know that a handful of states have formally defined these rewards or sanctions, although few had implemented these sanctions at that time. From this survey, we know that this has not changed dramatically. However, as shown in Table 3, budget officers are aware of the range of options available for reacting to agencies that meet or miss performance targets. Since 1998, more states appear to have defined sanctions and rewards. Further, more of the rewards and sanctions are monetary in nature. However, in these cases, few rewards or sanctions are actually administered by the central budget office.

In general, it seems that budget officers are *somewhat* encouraged about the *use* of performance measures, but are less positive about their *overall experience* with performance measures. More specifically, they are willing to acknowledge the usefulness of performance measures, but at the same time indicate problems in their identification and implementation. The majority of budgeters (70 percent) responded "poor" or "fair" when asked "overall, how would you rate your experience using performance measures to support the budget decisions required of your office?" Finally, we asked budget officers whether they agreed with the statement "performance measures are a vital decision aid regarding budget issues in this state." More than half of our respondents either strongly disagreed or disagreed with this statement. This may suggest that while performance measurement can be useful and even informative to budgeting decisions, it is not critical.

Table 3 Types of Rewards Used for Meeting Performance Targets, by State	
Type of Reward	*States Using Reward*
To the Agency	
Flexibility	Kentucky, Minnesota, Texas, Utah, Vermont
Lump sum budgets	Florida, Idaho, Kentucky, Minnesota, Montana, Texas
Relaxation of budget rules (e.g., transfers between programs, position controls)	Idaho, Kentucky, Minnesota, Montana, New York, Texas, Utah
Additional/supplemental allocations	Florida, Kentucky, Montana, New York, Texas
Discretionary use of surplus resources	Idaho, Kentucky, Maryland, Montana, New York, Texas, Utah
Access to special pools of funding	Florida, Kentucky, Montana, New York
Recognition	Florida, Maryland, Montana, New York, Texas, Utah, Vermont, West Virginia
To Individuals in the Agency	
Additional pay	Connecticut, Idaho, Kentucky, Maryland, Montana, Texas, Utah
Gain sharing	Kentucky, Texas
Individual pay for performance	Connecticut, Idaho, Kentucky, Maryland, Montana, New Jersey, New York, Texas, Utah, West Virginia
Other special recognition (award ceremonies, etc.)	Connecticut, Florida, Idaho, Kentucky, Maryland, Montana, New York, Texas, Vermont, West Virginia

Although budgeters may have mixed experiences with the actual use of performance measures in decisionmaking processes, they are willing to admit the spillover effects that performance measurement can have on communication during budgeting. We asked budget officers a series of opinion questions about the value of performance measurement in changing cultural aspects of the budget process. As shown in Table 4, there is general agreement among

Quicker, Better, Cheaper?
Managing Performance in American Government

Table 4
Budget Officers' Rating the Effects of Performance Measures

Respondent Mean Responses
Extent of budget officers' agreement with the following statements.
(1=strongly disagree.....4=strongly agree)

	Executive Branch Officers	Legislative Branch Officer	Officers in States with Administrative PBB Requirement	Officers in States with Legislative PBB Requirement
Communication effects				
Communication between agency personnel and our budget office has improved with the implementation of performance measures.	2.63	2.67	2.43	2.79
Communication between agency personnel and legislators has improved with the implementation of performance measures.	2.45	2.60	2.31	2.67
Overall, agency program staff is aware of desired program/service results.	2.87	2.94	3.00	2.89
The substance or tone of budget discussions among legislators has changed to focus more on results with the implementation of performance measures.	2.46	2.58	2.36	2.63
Lasting effects				
Overall, using performance measures has enhanced *program efficiency* in this state.	2.50	2.33	2.50	2.57
Overall, using performance measures has enhanced *program effectiveness* in this state.	2.50	2.10	2.30	2.54
Overall, our state is better off since we began using performance measures.	2.80	2.71	2.53	2.96
In the future, our state is likely to increase the use of performance measures for decisionmaking.	3.39	3.14	3.27	3.20

budget officers about effects on communication and understanding about program activities as a result of performance measurement implementation. Overall, budgeters willingly admit that communication has improved between agency personnel and budget officers through the implementation of a performance based system. Slightly more than half the respondents "strongly agreed" or "agreed" when asked whether the implementation of performance measures had improved communication between agency personnel and the budget office and between agency personnel and legislators. Budget officers from states where performance budgeting is legislated tended to feel more strongly about improvements in communication efficacy. Importantly, they also note the change in substance or tone of budget discussions among legislators to a stronger focus on results.

Conclusion: Is It Better Than Nothing?

Earlier research (Willoughby and Melkers 2000) indicates that while a strong majority of executive and legislative budget staff (61 percent) believe that their budget reform system did not directly change appropriations, 85 percent believe that implementing the budget reform is "better than doing nothing." Similarly, most (81 percent) believe that a lack of legislative interest in the initiative is somewhat of a significant problem.

The government officials interviewed for the GASB (2000) research illustrate similar concern yet sustained optimism regarding the usefulness of performance measurement. For example, the following excerpt from the cases illustrate problems with the full integration of performance measurement for resource allocation decisions:

> In **Texas**, a program director stated, "sometimes information is not adequate to reflect efforts, and [the measures] create artificial pictures of success and failure. They can become consuming and [the measures] become the focus rather than an indicator of progress or circumstances. The tendency is to expect more from performance measures than we should and has resulted in

measuring more than using information that is available"
(GASB 2000; Texas Case, p. 19).

Yet budget officers and other practitioners believe in the effectiveness of their performance measurement systems as instituted:

> In **Iowa**, budgeting for results seems well instituted. Legislative committee chairs are beginning to request performance information from agencies, and in one case worked extensively with an agency to streamline its budget format (Department of Public Health). In some cases, it was stated that consideration of performance has resulted in a reallocation of funding (examples provided were in areas of economic development and human services). Agencies have seen a change in focus for decision making, developing and justifying budgets, and seeing budgeting for results as a useful tool for demonstrating need and impact (examples provided included the departments of Corrections, Education and Transportation). (GASB 2000; Iowa Case, pp. 13-15).

> In **Arizona**, the administrators in the Child Support Division of the Department of Economic Security reviewed the processes for tracking child support collections related to the collection of child support to determine what actions or resources were needed to improve performance for this measure. Management and staff identified the establishment of paternity rights and court ordered child support as two key factors that influence child support collections. The Division then re-focused its attention on these two key factors. The result was a substantial increase in child support collections with Arizona being identified as the most improved state for child support collections the following year (GASB 2000; Arizona Case, p. 12).

> In **Texas**, staff of the Office of Budget and Planning acknowledge improved accountability because of legislative and executive involvement in the process. Many agencies have used performance measures to be responsive to external stakeholders. It has "opened the process, allowed benchmarking" and served as a way "to involve stakeholders." For example, the "

Department of Parks and Wildlife held hearings" to involve their stakeholders (GASB 2000; Texas Case, p. 19).

*From **Louisiana**, one subject noted, "I do think that it has had more of an impact internally. People are becoming more cognizant of the fact that we are going to be measured" (GASB 2000; Louisiana Case, p. 20).*

In a discussion of performance measurement and the future of public management Bouckaert (1993) discusses challenges related to performance measurement application and performance based budgeting systems, including:

❁ Establishing valid, legitimate, and functional management systems;

❁ Focusing on performance of individual managers and their effect on the performance of the organization; and,

❁ Institutionalizing performance measurement by linking it to the budget procedure.

We have tried to illustrate how performance based budgeting systems and specifically performance measurement influence budget decisions by assessing how budget officials use performance data when making spending decisions. We have witnessed fairly different application environments, yet there are certain **consistent themes** borne out by our research in the field. That is, considering processes of budgeting across the states leads to conclusions about budgeting, budget reform, and budget changes, and in this case as they relate to performance measurement and performance measurement systems.

Understanding whether a reform is successful must start with determining the purposes for which the reform was instituted in the first place. Earlier, we (Willoughby and Melkers 2000) surveyed central budget office staff in both the executive and legislative branches of state governments and found that 86 percent of these budgeters believe that *improving decisionmaking* was an important or very important intent of instituting the PBB system in their state. On the other hand, just under a quarter (23.4 percent) believe that *changing appropriations* was of similar import to the instigators of such budget reform. Regarding their thoughts on their budget reform effectiveness, survey results show that 32.8 percent consider that their performance based budgeting system has been effective or very effective in improving decisionmaking, while just 6.6 percent believe the same regarding changing appropriations. Clearly, most see the predominant intent of their budget reform to improve decisionmaking generally, and *not* to change spending rates or "budget slices" specifically. From the onset, these budgeters seem to have expected budget reform to *inform* budget decisions rather than dramatically change them.

Culling through the GASB (2000) case studies of performance measurement in government yields concurring findings. That is, other budget actors have similar opinions regarding the intent behind implementation of their performance measurement system. For example, several familiar themes surface when surveying reasons government officials, administrators, and staff give for developing and using performance measures in their government, including, for financial and budgetary decision making, for management purposes, and to promote better communication among budget actors (GASB 2000). Those interviewed claimed that the intentions behind their performance measurement systems are to improve budgetary decisionmaking in general, to support budget justification, to promote efficiency, to promote fiscal prudence, and to foster better-informed legislators. Such intentions are in agreement with earlier cited research (Willoughby and Melkers 2000) in which changing resource allocation is not seen as the chief reason to institute results oriented budgeting systems. Rather, using performance measures for justification, clarification, reporting, and for improved decisionmaking is important. For example, in Arizona, "most believed that resource allocation was a secondary reason for using performance measures. There was a general feeling that if performance measurement improved productivity and accountability, then growth in government expenditures could be controlled" (GASB 2000; Arizona Case, p. 7-8).

More specifically, our study illustrated variations in budgeters' responses on the importance of performance data in select stages of the budget process across branches and depending on the type of performance budgeting requirement. For example, executive branch budgeters find performance measures almost equally important across the various stages of the budget process when compared to their legislative counterparts. And, in states where performance budgeting requirement is legislatively initiated, budgeters consider performance measures equally important throughout the cycle when compared to administratively required states.

Regarding budget officers' perceptions of the effectiveness of performance measures, focusing on results and improving communication and coordination ranks highest for all categories of budgeters. Here, we find no real differences in budgeters' views between branches or across states with different performance budgeting requirements. Finally, some of the highest ratings of the budget officers regarding performance measurement effectiveness specify improving communication with the executive budget office. Given this office's vital role in budget development, this is an encouraging point.

Confirming the work of Jordan and Hackbart (1999), we find performance measurement's greatest applicability at present to be in the budget development phase. Further, performance measures do not seem to receive the same level of appreciation at other points in the budget process and by other actors, such as legislators. This may speak to the conclusions drawn by Lee and Burns (2000) regarding backsliding of performance based initiatives. However, we do not believe that this should be cause for concern, at least just yet. True and lasting reform, like performance budgeting, requires flexibility and time for organizations to become accustomed to changing the type and use of information for decisionmaking.

Endnotes

1   Visit the GASB homepage at http://www.rutgers.edu/Accounting/raw/gasb/ for a more complete description of GASB's performance measurement study initiatives.

References

Berman, Evan and XiaoHu Wang. 2000. "Performance Measurement in U.S. Counties," *Public Administration Review* (September/October) 60, 5: 409-420.

Bouckaert, Geert, 1993. "Performance Measurement and Public Management," *Public Productivity and Management Review* (Fall) 17, 1: 29-30

_____. 1993. "Measurement and Meaningful Management," *Public Productivity and Management Review* (Fall) 17 1: 31-43.

Broom, Cheryle A., and Lynne A. McGuire. 1995. "Performance-Based Government Models: Building a Track Record," *Public Budgeting and Finance* 15 4: 3-17.

Carnevale, Anthony P. and David G. Carnevale, 1993. "Public Administration and the Evolving World of Work" *Public Productivity and Management Review* (Fall) 17, 1: 1-14.

Coe, Charles. 1999. "Local Government Benchmarking: Lessons from Two Major Multigovernment Efforts," *Public Administration Review* (March/April) 59, 2: 110-123.

DuPont-Morales, M. A., and Jean E. Harris. 1994. "Strengthening Accountability: Incorporating Strategic Planning and Performance Measurement into Budgeting," *Public Productivity and Management Review* (Spring) 17, 3: 231-340.

Government Accounting Standards Board 2000. *State and Local Government Case Studies: The Use and the Effects of Using Performance Measures for Budgeting, Management, and Reporting.* (April). Washington, D.C.: author.

Hatry, Harry. 1999. *Performance Measurement: Getting Results.* Washington, D.C.: The Urban Institute Press.

Jordan, Meagan M. and Merl Hackbart. 1999. "Performance Budgeting and Performance Funding in the States: A Status Assessment," *Public Budgeting and Finance* (Spring) 19, 1: 68-88.

Kopczynski, Mary, and Michael Lombardo. 1999. "Comparative Performance Measurement: Insights and Lessons Learned from a Consortium Effort," *Public Administration Review* (March/April) 59, 2: 124-134.

Lee, Robert D. 1997. "A Quarter Century of State Budgeting Practices," *Public Administration Review* 57 2: 133-140.

Lee, Robert D., and Robert C. Burns. 2000. "Performance Measurement in State Budgeting: Advancement and Backsliding from 1990 to 1995," *Public Budgeting and Finance* (Spring) 20, 1: 38-54.

Lee, Robert D., Jr., and Ronald W. Johnson. 1998. *Public Budgeting Systems.* 6th edition (Gaithersburg, MD: Aspen Publishers, Inc.).

Melkers, Julia E., and Katherine G. Willoughby. 1998. "The State of the States: Performance-Based Budgeting Requirements in 47 Out of 50," *Public Administration Review* (January/February) 58, 1: 66-73.

Melkers, Julia E., and Katherine G. Willoughby 2001. "Budgeters' Views of State Performance Budgeting Systems: Distinctions Across Branches," *Public Administration Review* (January/February) 61, 1:54-64.

Mosso, David, 1999. "Accounting for the Business of Government – New Goals, Old Myths," *Public Budgeting and Finance* (Winter) 19, 4: 65-74.

National Center for Public Productivity. 1997. *A Brief Guide for Performance Measurement in Local Government.* Rutgers University.

Newman, Isadore, and Keith McNeil. 1998. *Conducting Survey Research in the Social Sciences.* Lanham, Maryland: University Press of American, Inc.

Poister, Theodore H., and Gregory Streib. 1999. "Performance Measurement in Municipal Government: Assessing the State of the Practice," *Public Administration Review* (July/August) 59, 4: 325-335.

Sorber, Bram. 1993. "Performance Measurement in the Central Government Departments of the Netherlands," *Public Productivity and Management Review* (Fall) 17, 1: 59-68.

Stiefel, Leanna, Ross Rubenstein, and Amy Ellen Schwartz. 1999. "Using Adjusted Performance Measures for Evaluating Resource Use," *Public Budgeting and Finance* (Fall) 19, 3: 67-87.

Thurmaier, Kurt and Katherine G. Willoughby. 2001. *Policy and Politics in State Budgeting.* New York: M. E. Sharpe Publishers.

Willoughby, Katherine G. and Julia E. Melkers, 2000. "Implementing PBB: Conflicting Views of Success," *Public Budgeting and Finance* (Spring) 20, 1: 105-120.

14

Getting to Results in Florida

Robert B. Bradley and Geraldo Flowers

In 1994, the Florida Legislature enacted and Governor Chiles signed into law the Government Performance and Accountability Act (Chapter 94-249 Laws of Florida, Chapter 216, Florida Statutes). This legislation provided for a substantial reform in the state's planning and budgeting processes (Barrett & Greene, 1995). It aimed to shift the emphasis from legal and financial controls towards more management and performance responsibility. The legislation emerged only with the commitment and concern of senior leaders in the Executive and Legislature.

Months of collaboration went into shaping the legislation. With the support of Governor Chiles, Speaker of the House of Representatives Bo Johnson, and President of the Senate Pat Thomas, the act emerged from work begun in the summer of 1993, which focused on improving agency accountability and providing greater flexibility to agency managers in the operation of programs. Then Representative and now Congressman Allen Boyd worked as chair of the House Governmental Affairs Committee along with his subcommittee chair Representative Joe Tedder and staff director Barry Kling to shape the House product. In the upper chamber, Senator Charles Williams led the committee effort in concert with Nelson Easterling working out of President Pat Thomas's Office. David

Coburn, Budget Director for Governor Chiles, directed efforts for the Administration.

Surprisingly, the legislation did not draw upon the federal Government Performance and Results Act, which took form at about the same time. Instead, it grew out of developments in Florida. In many respects, it is tailored to the particular institutions and practices in the state. But it is no less true that the Florida experience offers more general lessons. Several agencies in Florida have used the legislation to improve both the performance and accountability of their programs to the public. To a lesser degree, they have benefited from the operational flexibility granted by the legislation. Florida has formulated mechanisms such as the performance ledger and the Office of Program Policy Analysis and Governmental Accountability that merit wider consideration. The state has proceeded deliberately, facing with mixed success the challenges that accompany efforts to budget for results throughout the country.

Florida is still refining its approach to program performance. Much has been learned over the last six years. But there are still problems. They are worth noting both for what they portend for the future in Florida and for the challenges they suggest for agencies' efforts in getting to results.

Features of the Act

The 1994 Act mandated the implementation of Performance-Based Program Budgeting (commonly referred to as PB^2 in Florida and pronounced as "PB-squared") by all of Florida's state agencies. It was intended to:

- ❀ provide state agencies with the flexibility needed to deploy their resources in the best possible way;

- ❀ establish incentives to deliver services and products in the most efficient and effective manner;

- ❀ hold agencies accountable for the services and products they deliver; and

❀ help keep citizens informed of both the benefits derived from agency programs and their progress in improving performance. (Chapter 94-249, Laws of Florida)

The legislation directed agencies to develop descriptions of their key programs and evaluate each program's suitability for PB². Under the law, each agency's proposed programs are subject to review and approval by the Office of Planning and Budgeting (OPB) in the Executive Office of the Governor working in consultation with the Legislature. OPB also approves the performance measures and standards developed for each program advanced by the agencies. Agency programs subjected to PB² are included in the annual Legislative Budget Request (LBR) submitted jointly to the OPB and both houses of the Legislature. The LBR is developed in conformance with budget instructions promulgated by the OPB and the Legislative Appropriations Committees (the Senate Committees on Budget and Fiscal Policy, and the House Fiscal Responsibility Council). The LBR is submitted to both the Legislature and the Governor for review at the same time. It must include needs of the agency for operating expenditures, approved performance measures, outputs, outcomes, baseline data, performance standards, and evaluation of the agency's previous program performance.

On the basis of agency submittals, the Governor makes recommendations to the Legislature for the inclusion of each program as part of the Governor's Annual Budget Recommendations. Programs recommended under the PB² law are incorporated into the budget as lump sums (or as performance-based program categories) in contrast to line items employing more detailed appropriation categories. Lump sums provide greater flexibility to agency managers than the appropriation categories under conventional line items. The Executive Office of the Governor may recommend incentives or disincentives for agency performance. Incentives include increased budget and personnel flexibility, retention of unencumbered appropriations, employee bonuses, and various improvements in agency resources. Disincentives range from quarterly reports and appearance before the Governor and elected Cabinet to program elimination or transfer and a variety of personnel and management restrictions.

The Legislature must approve all programs and measures used in PB^2. The approval of programs, along with a small number of measures and standards, is incorporated in the annual General Appropriations Act. Most measures and standards are enacted as part of the annual appropriations Implementing Bill, a companion to the General Appropriations Act. The final decisions of the Legislature are incorporated into a performance ledger, an analog to the appropriations ledger, maintained by the OPB. Agencies have an opportunity to appeal and modify entries to the ledger based on feasibility estimates using the state budget amendment process in the 45 days following the end of the Governor's veto process. The OPB is responsible for recording approved adjustments on the performance ledger. Agencies must break out program lump sums into traditional appropriation categories before the beginning of the fiscal year. This breakout is subject to review and approval by the OPB as well as to veto by leadership within the Legislature. Agencies have flexibility to move budget authority across categories and funds within a program appropriated under PB^2 without legislative approval.

The Act assigns responsibility for the review of program performance to the agencies, the OPB, and the Legislature. It also establishes the Office of Program Policy Analysis and Government Accountability (OPPAGA) as the major body set up to conduct program evaluations, deploying a staff of slightly less than 100 in this mission. The OPPAGA was formed from resources previously devoted to the state's Auditor General. It is a part of the Legislative Branch and reports findings and recommendations to the OPB and Legislature annually in time for preparation of budget decisions.

Florida's 1994 Government Performance and Accountability Act (Chapter 94-249, Laws of Florida) calls for PB^2 to be phased in incrementally over a number of years based on a statutory submission schedule, with all state agencies expected to be in compliance by 2002 (State Agency Schedule For Implementing PB^2). Under the act, the schedule may be amended by the Joint Legislative Auditing Committee, the General Appropriations Act, or upon recommendation of the Governor under the consultation processes developed for the budget amendment process (s. 216.177, Florida Statutes).

Tracing the Origins of PB[2]

The contemporary structure of budgeting in Florida can be traced back to the first decades of the twentieth century. Its evolution has mirrored developments nationally in only the most general way (General Accounting Office, 1993). The state's first executive budget was developed in 1921 when the Legislature bestowed responsibility for submitting budget requests upon the executive branch (Easterling, 1999). In this respect, budgeting in Florida followed developments elsewhere. In Florida though, budget requests were made through the Budget Commission, a collegial body comprised of the Governor, the Treasurer, and the Comptroller.

The Commission provided the focus for budgeting in Florida for nearly a half century. According to most observers, it worked well, especially during the years when the Legislature met only every other year. But the process always had its critics — ones who thought it did not encourage efficiency, diffused accountability, and conceded too much authority to the Legislature. The Commission undoubtedly weakened the Governor's hand in budgeting and contributed to his diminished authority in state affairs. For years, Florida did not provide its Governor the powers given Executives in other states.

In the mid-forties and again in the mid-sixties, study commissions were established to evaluate the budgeting process and make recommendations. They tackled issues ranging from the use of trust funds to accounting standards. In the process, they made scores of recommendations that influenced state operations. In response to one such set of recommendations, state planning, for example, was placed under the direct control of the Governor at a time when the budget was still a responsibility of a shared Executive. Overall, changes were minor. The contours of the budgeting process in Florida remained largely untouched until the late sixties.

In 1967, the state enacted the Planning and Programming Act, the beginnings of a PBB initiative. Two years later, working to implement the new Constitution, the Legislature embarked upon an effort to introduce Programming, Planning, and Budgeting Systems (PPBS) (Chapter 69-106, Laws of Florida). The enabling statute required that each state agency compile a comprehensive program budget that reflected all program and fiscal matters related to it and to each of its programs, sub-programs, and activities.

Over the next several years, the state developed an elaborate program structure into which all the activities of the state were recorded and registered in associated information systems. There was a sustained, intensive effort to integrate planning and budgeting. Budgets of that period reflect well on the efforts of those involved. They combine the major elements of the PPBS model: a well-articulated program structure, mission statements, program objectives, and performance measures. The budgets were cross-referenced to state planning documents and provide, in an era when every budget was manually typed, a scope and depth of information regarding goals, objectives, and performance enviable even today.

Unfortunately, the effort failed to achieve what many of the designers had hoped for, largely for the same reasons that PPBS is documented to have failed at the national level during the 1960s (Easterling, 1999; Schick, 1993). The budgets, despite all their sophistication, did not result in major changes in the way the state did business. Instead, the budgeting format was overlaid on and adapted to prevailing custom, especially in the legislative process. There were strong sentiments in many quarters for maintaining line item budgeting of traditional appropriation categories such as salaries, expenses, and capital outlay. It proved difficult to coordinate disparate program elements in the absence of integrated budget tools and even more difficult to collect and deploy the information needed to make the initiative a success. Significantly, the process did not align program categories, appropriation categories and audit controls. Without such an alignment, program information was set adrift and not tied to meaningful feedback.

The effort was not without its successes, however. The Governor, in particular, recognized its possibilities for improving operations and setting priorities. In the late seventies and early eighties, Governor Graham initiated an effort to link planning, performance, and budgeting. A modified program structure was developed. The state embarked on the development of a computerized integrated financial management system. Agency operating plans were tied to the State Comprehensive Plan and Legislative Budget Requests (LBR). The planning and budgeting process was redone and the Governor's Offices of Planning and Budgeting were consolidated.

In 1985, Governor Graham submitted a State Comprehensive Plan to the Legislature that contained quantified performance measures and timeframes for a series of state goals. It included, for example, a goal calling for deinstitutionalizing 50 percent of the mentally ill and disabled to community facilities; keeping health care costs at or below the rate of inflation, and enabling 15 percent more people over the age of 75 to become self-reliant (Chapter 187, Florida Statutes). In addition, the Governor required that individual agency secretaries commit to contracts that held them accountable for their performance. The State Plan, in this model, not only was to guide state priorities, it also was to shape the local and regional planning processes. As subsequently enacted by the Legislature, the plan was integrally tied to the Governor's growth management efforts, ultimately influencing the timing and siting of local infrastructure projects.

The impact of those initiatives remains. Their influence continues to be significant in many ways. However, their impact on the major aspects of state budgeting and management was short-lived and less significant than their impact on local and regional planning. They influenced the character and more especially the extent of agency budget submissions by requiring detailed relationships between agency plans and the budget. Unfortunately, they did not materially affect either management practices in most agencies or the appropriations process within the Legislature. Nor did they influence state budgeting practices significantly. They did not diminish Legislative controls nor shift the state's emphasis to results. By the late eighties, it was clear to most observers that at the state level the reforms had not had the desired effect. The call for change was renewed.

In the mid-1970s Florida experimented briefly with a modified version of zero-based budgeting (ZBB) that relied on a decremented base. It was formally incorporated in the budget structure, but the effort was abandoned along with other modifications to PBBS. Still, the power of the metaphor remained, especially for those who wanted the budget process to engage the full range of funded programs and who were dissatisfied with practices that relied on concepts such as the "cost to continue" and differentiated "new and improved issues" from "continued issues."

In 1989, the House of Representatives briefly resurrected the idea of a modified ZBB. The proposed reform included a periodic evaluation of every program in state government to be conducted by evaluators from the major certified public accounting firms (Easterling, 1999). Under the House proposal, evaluators would have had the power to recommend reduction, elimination, or continuation of each program reviewed; their proposed reduction or elimination would set the new base appropriation for that program.

For better or ill, many balked at the idea of private, unelected, and out-of-state evaluators setting the base budgets for programs in Florida and proposed instead an internal auditing mechanism based on some activities of the federal Government's General Accounting Office (GAO). This initiative, which ultimately took form in Florida Statutes as Program Accountability and Agency Review (PAAR), was placed under the State Auditor General and helped to widen the circle of concern for budgeting reform while also rekindling an interest in agency programs as the fundamental locus of reform. Ultimately, it led to a series of important studies of the budgeting process by the Auditor General and the Joint Legislative Auditing Committee that helped document the foundations of existing budgetary practice and pointed in the direction of useful change.

By the late 1980s, there was a broadening constituency for reform of the state budgetary process and a wealth of experience in implementing a variety of different practices. The constituency, however, was not of one mind, and the lessons drawn from the experiences were not unambiguous. In this climate of uncertainty, the recession of 1989–1991 helped crystallize the urgency of reforms. State government reduced its budget by more than $2 billion dollars over the period. Despite a decade in which taxes and fees were increased each year, revenues could not keep pace with service demands and the state's persistent population growth nor could they provide a buffer against the business cycle. To seasoned observers of state budgeting, including the leadership of both Houses, the state needed a better way to evaluate how it spent its monies and set its priorities.

The most significant and tangible manifestation of this concern was the formation of the Constitutional Commission on Taxation and Budget Reform. The Commission was established in November of 1988 to make recommended changes to the state's constitution and was empowered to place them directly on the ballot for consideration by the citizenry. After two years of deliberations, the Commission recommended establishing clear, well-defined relationships linking plans, budgets, appropriations, and performance. It also made specific recommendations in fourteen areas including program and performance evaluation, performance measurement and productivity improvement, and auditing.

The Taxation and Budget Reform Commission certified a series of constitutional amendments to the statewide ballot. Among them were proposals creating a budget stabilization fund, restructuring of the format used in the annual budget, and requiring the itemization of special projects within the budget. The Commission also advocated constitutional language designating the Governor as chief administrative officer of the state responsible for planning and budgeting (Article IV, section 1a) as well as requiring that general law implement a quality management and accountability program (Article III, section 19h). The amendments were approved in 1992 by 83 percent of the electorate (Florida TaxWatch, 1995).

The Commission's recommendations were supported and promoted by a number of groups in the state. Prominent among these were Florida TaxWatch (a good government watchdog group), the Florida Council of 100 (an association of business executives), Associated Industries of Florida (a business lobbying group), and Partners in Productivity (a public/private initiative under an Executive Order established in 1987 to monitor and reward public sector productivity). These groups, especially TaxWatch, forcefully advocated the introduction of performance budgeting, performance measurement, and incentive-based concepts. As early as December 1986, for example, a Florida TaxWatch publication entitled "Building a Better Florida" argued the merits of the state employing performance budgeting, measurement, and incentives as a means of improving government accountability (Florida TaxWatch, 1986).

The case for a change in the budgeting system was given another boost with the election of Lawton Chiles in 1990. Governor Chiles had previously served in the Florida Legislature and was intimately familiar with the state appropriations process. Perhaps more importantly, he had served 18 years in the U.S. Senate and as Chairman of the Congressional Budget Committee. There he had developed an appreciation for the deficiencies in both the state and national approaches to budgeting.

In his first State of the State address on March 5, 1991, Governor Lawton Chiles called for a budget process that would end so-called "micromanagement" by the Legislature and provide greater flexibility in administration of the budget by the Executive (Easterling, 1999). In response to his proposal, the Legislature authorized a one-year pilot project in the Department of Revenue and the Division of Workers' Compensation, Department of Labor and Employment Security. This project provided for a relaxation of bureaucratic rules on personnel management and budget implementation. An oversight board was created to monitor accomplishments. The project was extended by the 1992 and 1993 Legislatures for both entities. In 1991, Governor Chiles also appointed a Commission designed to make the government more accountable. The Commission made scores of recommendations, many around the theme that government become more results-focused, with funding of public programs based on desired outcomes rather than determined by program inputs.

Early in 1992, Governor Chiles directed his Office of Planning and Budget to develop a prototype performance-based program. During the summer, the OPB worked with the Department of Environmental Regulation to build an initial model. Those efforts were swept away with the demands made on state administration by Hurricane Andrew, which struck South Florida in August of 1992. Work did not begin again on budget reform until after the 1993 General Session of the Legislature.

Following the 1993 General Session, the Governor's Office of Planning and Budgeting (OPB) renewed its examination of the budgeting process. Throughout the summer, the OPB worked with the House Committee on Governmental Operations chaired by Representative Allen Boyd (with the appropriate subcommittee chaired by Representative Joe Tedder) and Senate President Pat Thomas to frame legislation for the 1994 session. At the direction of the state Budget Director David Coburn, the OPB worked with the Department of Revenue (DOR) to construct a working model of a new budget process.

Framework and Design Parameters

The confluence of circumstance that resulted in the enactment of the Government Performance and Accountability Act carried with it a raft of shared understandings and common experiences. The designers of the 1994 Act were determined to not repeat the mistakes of the past and to draw upon hard won lessons (Rubin, 1990; 1993).

The existing emphasis on budgetary controls and projected workloads was generally recognized to have led neither to better results nor controlled costs. Each year, the Governor and Legislature wrestled over the allocation of positions, the need for equipment, and aggregate levels of salary. They contended over the mileage at which old vehicles might be replaced and the amount of allowable salary lapse associated with the replacement of vacant positions. Still, the demand for expenditures grew. Amidst the recession of the early nineties, it seemed clear that the existing budgetary mechanisms had proved to be neither effective tools for building public support and understanding of state programs nor effective means of providing organizational incentives for service quality, responsiveness, efficiency, or innovation.

Among senior executives in the Chiles Administration and the leadership of the Legislature, three principles emerged as key. Government must:

1. Reward performance and not ignore failure,

2. Allow managers to manage and hold them accountable, and

3. Promote accountability for results by focusing concern on both the outcomes of programs and the core processes that produce those results.

These were not new ideas, but they were approached with a new sense of how reform must be implemented. Remembering the massive efforts of the early seventies and the early eighties, there was broad agreement that reform must proceed gradually. (See Appendix A.) The state must, it was widely thought, resist the temptation to do everything at once. Its experience in moving from comprehensive to strategic planning taught that it would take time to perfect performance measurement. It also provided a sense of how difficult it was to emphasize program impact outcomes in the accountability process. Perhaps as important though, it taught that the state had to avoid the tendency to wait until the system was perfect before moving ahead. Instead, it was clear that the reform must allow for periodic and frequent reconsideration and modification.

There was considerable agreement that the focus on performance measurements should be customized to help both managers and policymakers. Also, most of those involved agreed that systems had to be constructed to help assure the validity and reliability of the measures and data. There was even widespread, if grudging, recognition that meaningful reform would require active collaboration between the Executive and Legislature. The reform was to be evolutionary, integrative, and grounded in measurable impacts.

For all the agreement, large, often unspoken differences remained between the Executive and the Legislature over some of the most basic features of the reform among the many actors involved. How much of the current system was to be carried into the future? Who ultimately defined the contours of programs? Some flexibility should and could be extended to managers. How much, though, should be extended and under what conditions? There were to be rewards and sanctions, but what level and extent of performance triggered their use? Should outputs or outcomes be the focus of attention? And perhaps most fundamentally, how were the measures and standards to be used in the budgetary system? Should performance measures be used to allocate appropriations?

In Florida, both the functional and procedural aims of budgetary reform were a matter of continuing contention. The Executive, for example, began with the idea that performance measures would serve as a diagnostic to help improve the business processes of agencies as well as their programs. The clear focus was on improvements to the claiming or justification processes of the budgetary system. In short, it resembled in some ways an initiative to implement performance management, in this case accompanied by the delegation of flexibility. Among many in the Legislature though, the concern was for improved mechanisms of allocation. The hope in such quarters was to implement a means of apportioning scarce dollars that rewarded performance. Still, others in each branch hoped the new emphasis would entice agency managers to concentrate more on the results of their activities and, as a corollary, provide more convincing claims for state resources.

The Executive argued for a decreased emphasis on legislative controls in exchange for greater attention given to performance. In 1994, the primary statute governing appropriations contained 26 major controls on Executive action. (See Appendix B.) These ranged from rather conventional requirements that all appropriations are maximum spending authorizations to less commonly found restrictions on the amount of salary rate[1] an agency might carry and to limitations on the transfer of funds between appropriation categories within a particular budget entity. The Executive argued that such restrictions should be relaxed slightly by bundling the activities under restriction and by allowing more flexible transfers.

Controls linked to categories such as expenses and salaries would be replaced by a focus on the larger set of activities found in a program whose results were to be measured. After a period of acceptable performance, it was argued, the list of 26 controls should be pared back to 15.

For the Legislature, of course, controls lay at the center of what was perceived to be its ability to make fiscal policy. It was concerned about the scope and timing of relaxation. It was especially concerned about the locus of the intersection between process and function — namely, the identification and definition of individual programs. The Governor initially proposed a dramatic approach to this issue in the fall of 1993, substituting lump sum line items that consolidated services and programs for the traditional categories that constituted line items. (See Appendix C.) In response, the Legislature vigorously urged a less comprehensive approach. In a shift from an organizationally based scheme of accountability focused on inputs to one centered on programs, outputs, and outcomes, it was inevitable that the new unit of budgeting would become the center of attention.

Curiously, neither the Executive nor the Legislature gave much thought during the initial design period to conservation processes within the budgetary scheme. Issues of efficiency were neglected, for the most part, in favor of issues of effectiveness. Unit cost performance and notions of return on investment were deferred. Conservation processes, which were to assume greater importance during implementation, took a back seat in the initial deliberations.

During the 1994 Legislative session, the contentious issues of the previous fall were put aside. Budget reform had the support of both the Executive and the Legislative branches. Both were bolstered in their support by the enactment of a constitutional amendment with the approval of 83% of the electorate for a state accountability program. At crucial points in legislative deliberations, reform was given wide media support through the pivotal actions of groups like Florida TaxWatch. Executive and legislative leaders, despite their differing institutional perspectives, were able to frame a compromise.

In the end, reform was embraced in most quarters with almost an air of inevitability. It came to be seen as the next step in an evolutionary process. According to one participant,

> *When you get down to it, as we progressed in the design of this thing [PB^2] we began taking the good ideas of yesterday and massaged them into the better ideas of today. Performance-based budgeting is the massage of program budgeting; performance-based budgeting is the massage of zero-based budgeting; performance-based budgeting is the massage of management by objectives; it is just a progression. What had happened in Florida is that we have evolved to the position that we are at today.* (Berry & Flowers, 1999)

Status and Accomplishments

In FY 1999, Florida passed the midway point in its eight-year phase-in of PB^2. Of 33 state agencies, 22 presented PB^2 budgets for at least some of their programs. In all, 72 programs and 350 measures were in place, a sizeable, but not overwhelming number.

In this regard, it is important here to note that the process of implementing PB^2 takes almost two years from the initial identification of programs to the receipt of funds. It is another two years before those programs subject to PB^2 will be evaluated by OPPAGA. From initial workshops on programs and measures to the completion of the justification and evaluation review performed by OPPAGA, it will be fully 5 years. In Florida, the process is complete for just a few programs. To that extent, it is premature to pass judgment on the reforms.

Still, there are preliminary assessments to share. OPPAGA has conducted dozens of midcourse reviews and scores of program assessments that report on the success of implementation. Three examples will provide a flavor of developments by the agencies since the law was enacted.

Florida Department of Law Enforcement

The Florida Department of Law Enforcement (FDLE) has been very proactive in its implementation of PB², including volunteering to be one of the first agencies to implement PB² and the first agency to implement it in all its organizational divisions. Much of this proactive approach, according to members of the agency, is due to the adroit leadership of Florida Department of Law Enforcement (FDLE) Commissioner Tim Moore, regarded by many as one of the most effective state agency leaders and named as one of *Governing* magazine's Top Public Officials in 1999 (Berry, Brower & Flowers, 2000). As a result of actions that he inspired, FDLE has been asked to appear before legislative committees and has been cited on numerous occasions as a "model" of how to implement PB².

Early on, FDLE reorganized its operations and restructured itself to improve performance. Traditionally, programs involving activities such as forensic sciences had relied upon personnel from various divisions. After enactment of the legislation, the Department merged its operations into three divisions aligned with PB² programs and core business processes. It used the budgetary flexibility allowed under the act to move resources around within the new programs during the course of implementation in order to achieve standards set within the PB² framework. Perhaps most importantly the agency was able to demonstrate meaningful program improvement both to concerned legislators and their own personnel.

In 1997, after their initial successes, FDLE unveiled its own version of an incentive program — the sustained high performance salary model geared toward awarding pay increases to employees whose performance achieves individual, agency, division, or sub-unit mission or goals. The model was refined considerably in discussion with other agencies and public interest groups over the course of a year before FDLE approached the Florida Legislature to seek permission to use funds for a "pilot test." In 1998, the Legislature approved pilot usage of the sustained High Performance Salary Model. Agency officials believe that the model has the potential of becoming an archetype for an incentive-based state agency system.

Florida Department of Revenue

Perhaps no agency in state government has worked harder to change its organizational culture and to improve its performance than the Florida Department of Revenue (DOR). For much of this decade, DOR has been a leader within state government in continuous quality improvement (Berry, Brower & Flowers, 2000). Recently, it won recognition as among the best-managed organizations in the state, private or public, with receipt of the Sterling Award (a detailed management evaluation modeled after the Malcolm Baldrige National Quality Award).

The agency has used PB^2 to help foster innovation, integrating budgetary efforts with its ongoing total quality and process reengineering efforts. The resulting system, in addition to enabling DOR to measure processes, requires substantive outputs and outcomes to be measured, thereby allowing DOR to budget according to results, not just practices, by:

❀ Identifying the agency's customers, its products, and its critical suppliers;

❀ Mapping the business process;

❀ Developing key measures called Performance Ability Measures (PAMS);

❀ Analyzing the measures for deficiencies and problems;

❀ Planning strategically based on the measures; and

❀ Continuously improving the business process using PAMS and team assessments.

PB^2 has been implemented within the context of broader efforts at organizational changes. DOR's integration of total quality management, process reengineering, and private sector learning has enabled it to go beyond less inclusive, more pedestrian applications of performance budgeting. The agency maintains a model performance accountability measurement system that is published widely and updated monthly across a host of indicators. In recognition of its sustained performance improvement, the Department was given the additional responsibility of managing the state's troubled child support enforcement program. The accountability system has helped justify the need for resources before the Legislature and focus the Department's priorities in the resolution of problems of child support.

The Florida Department of Children and Families

For much of the last two decades, Florida incorporated most of its social and welfare services in a single unified department, the Department of Health and Rehabilitative Services, with over 40,000 employees. Beginning early in the Chiles' Administration, the department underwent a pervasive restructuring, resulting in the creation of several new agencies. The former secretary of one of those new agencies, Ed Feaver of the Department of Children and Families (DCF), adopted PB^2 as a way to improve management of a regionally decentralized and recently reorganized department (Berry, Brower & Flowers, 2000). Through a strategic planning process that focuses on mission and major clients, DCF identified fifteen major targeted client groups and developed strategic and key outcome measures for each group suitable for uniform application across the agency's thirteen regions. The agency then used performance standards and outcome measures, as well as best practices from high performing regional programs, to identify problems and foster improved performance. Along the way, the Department uncovered a number of problems in its services. Chief among these was the ability to quantify what it does as "outcomes."

During the fall of 1997, the Department first attempted to describe in a rigorous, quantitative way the client populations it serves. It began estimating the populations of 15 client groups in the areas of family safety, mental health and substance abuse, disability, and economic self-sufficiency. It established a set of strategic objectives of continuing concern to the Department. These objectives were linked to performance measures and served as the basis of annual performance agreements entered into by the Department, district management, and the local Health and Human Services

Boards. These agreements and the emphasis on performance helped renew the Department's credibility with legislators.

PB^2 has given DCF a useful platform from which to defend its performance to the Legislature. As one manager explained, "it keeps us from getting beat up as a welfare agency by putting a human face on what the money does, what the agency should accomplish, and who it should serve" (as quoted in Berry & Flowers, 1999). The agency was able to show how its programs impacted clients, how much various units of service cost, and what the benefits of preventive action were. This was especially important in the aftermath of the budget crisis brought on by recession in the early 1990s. One informant explained that during the early nineties the agency's budget was consistently being reduced, and that, "absent the ability to say what we were doing for whom, and how well and how much," the agency would be told to "take three million from the budget" (Berry, Brower & Flowers, 2000). And policy makers would ask, "what happened from doing that?" The inevitable answer was, "well, we don't know." PB^2 offered the agency the ability to answer such questions.

Long before PB^2's enactment, Secretary Feaver saw performance measurement as a tool for lobbying the Legislature. This recognition led DCF's leaders to a protracted process for educating themselves, agency members, and policymakers about a new way of looking at the agency centered on client target groups. They soon discovered that the Governor's budget office and legislators and their staff did not know how to deal with the new framework. They also learned that policymakers were uncomfortable in the realm of societal outcomes rather than matters such as caseloads processed or vaccinations provided. As one participant explained,

It was safer to have us count widgets, like we always did. Policy makers want easy answers. They don't want to know about the complexity of measurement that those of us trained in measurement know is involved. And so we've had to learn what is politically viable and what kinds of information they, the legislators, need to have in order to make decisions. (Berry, Brower & Flowers, 2000)

This put DCF's central office in a contentious negotiating role between the professional community and legislators whose value systems often clash over the disconnects that occur between the logic of policy and the harsh realities of implementation. The enactment of PB^2 has altered this equation. Among legislators, the learning and participation in the development and use of program measures have been quite uneven, although most observers agree that a core of staffers have become much more sophisticated in their understanding and their questions and expectations. One participant, noting that the agency is now introducing PB^2 into its final program area, economic self-sufficiency, suggested that "it doesn't take nearly as much effort to educate legislators about what we're doing" (as quoted in Berry, Brower & Flowers, 2000). There is a sense that some participants truly found a common language through which to communicate their expectations. For others the new approach is so complex that they may appear to concur about things they just do not understand. Alternatively, it may be that the agency has turned the corner in terms of its image and legitimacy in the minds of policy makers. The answer most likely involves some combination of these possibilities (Berry, Brower & Flowers, 2000).

The PB^2 framework has helped shape conversations within the social welfare community. District representatives historically have had incentives to run to local legislators for line-item "turkeys" (Florida's term for "pork barrel" projects) especially when doing so often reinforced legislators' efforts to please local constituents. Over the years, DCF's central office worked diligently to convince district administrators and Health and Human Service Boards that it is in everyone's interest to present a united front. This effort has been assisted by PB^2 through structuring the message. District officials are more united, figuratively arguing, "look, we know what we're doing; this is the agency's plan." Actions are keyed to a common set of objectives and measures. DCF's central office is aware that various stakeholder groups maintain channels with individual legislators, but they now see the districts' engaging in legislative end runs as the exception rather than the rule.

DCF has worked to incorporate PB^2 into its strategic planning and evaluation processes. Among its more impressive initiatives is amalgamation of three major functions — strategic planning, evaluation, and PB² — into one office, the Division of Standards and Evaluation. As part of the PB² implementation process, this office has been involved in developing a new strategic plan that has enabled DCF to identify client target groups and match broad outcomes with program and district inputs. The real impact of these actions has yet to be evaluated, but there is some evidence that the system has enabled the agency to better focus its work and to better inform the public and the Legislature about what it does. The change has helped the agency identify and reduce some areas of program duplication.

Florida Office of Program Policy Analysis and Government Accountability

The Office of Program Policy Analysis and Government Accountability (OPPAGA) has been central to the continuing implementation and evaluation of PB². It has offered timely assistance and specific commentary on the progress of agencies, including Revenue, Law Enforcement, and Children and Families. Since early 1997, OPPAGA has issued 9 reports on the efforts of the Department of Revenue, 6 on the Department of Law Enforcement, and 7 on the Department of Children and Families. Its reports have helped identified successes, pointed out deficiencies and helped keep agencies on track.

Under the direction of John Turcotte, OPPAGA has not only provided an independent assessment of agency activities, it has also positioned itself as a bridge and coordinator between state government agencies and legislators and their staff with regard to many PB² issues. Its broadened responsibilities under PB² now include:

- ❀ Training agency and legislative staff;
- ❀ Managing information database;
- ❀ Assessing the validity and reliability of performance measures for the Legislature;
- ❀ Assessing agency progress in implementing PB² through agency performance evaluations and justification reviews; and

❀ Making recommendations to the Legislature on whether programs should be modified or terminated.

OPPAGA[2] has developed the Florida Government Accountability Report (FGAR), an on-line Internet encyclopedia of state government programs, as a mechanism for realizing the purposes of the Government Performance and Accountability Act. FGAR allows citizens and policy makers to compare information both across programs and over time, with performance measurement information being updated quarterly instead of yearly. The report offers a single source of information on all aspects of PB[2]. In 1999, it issued 75 reports on program performance (see Appendix D) and maintained 374 program profiles for use by interested officials and the general public. OPPAGA issues periodic and timely reviews of individual programs that are widely read by agency personnel and Legislative staff alike. Through the Florida Monitor it provides weekly information on data and reports dealing with policies of interest to state officials and the citizenry. OPPAGA received over 133,000 visits to its Internet pages featuring FGAR and the Florida Monitor in 1999 alone.

Areas of Concern

Over the last several years, the PB[2] has been subject to several formal assessments. A number of concerns have surfaced (Berry, Chackerian & Wechsler, 1995; Florida OPPAGA, 1997; Berry & Flowers, 1999; Florida TaxWatch, 1999). Some focus on the conceptual foundations and expectations of the reform. Others relate to the character and pace of institutionalization. Still another set focuses on technical deficiencies. Several are of special note:

❀ Conflict between the Executive and Legislature over goals

❀ Problems in the program structure

❀ Poor performance measures and lack of appropriate data

❀ Misalignment of the cost accounting system

❀ Poor links with overall management processes

❀ Absence of a sufficient payoff

The Persistence of Conflict Over Goals and Perspective

Various participants and institutional actors had different convictions about the purpose and use of PB^2 from its inception. Agency officials and executive representatives typically were in pursuit of greater flexibility in the management of their affairs — a relaxation of what was often termed legislative "micromanagement." They sought fewer legislative controls in exchange for greater accountability of program results. Within that common sentiment though, there was a substantial range of commitment and understanding. Several secretaries saw the possibilities for management improvement through use of the system and were committed to a thorough going implementation. Others sought the flexibility, but hoped to avoid disruption of internal procedures and practices.

Within the Legislature similar divisions dwelled amidst the desire for improved program accountability. Substantive committees hoped to wrest a greater role in promoting program priorities from the appropriations committees. Appropriations committees sought to retain their position in the appropriations process. Their concern had real practical as well political bases. Ultimately, the Appropriations Act, shaped in conference negotiations, must be physically assembled and brought to the floor in the closing days of session. The sheer number of last minute decisions and the technical challenge of bringing them together are simplified by the unified decisions process currently in place. The need to square performance standards with appropriations added complexity, in the minds of some, and threatened the mechanics of "end-of-session" decisionmaking.

There were also divisions among those who brought different conceptual expectations to the reform. For many, and especially appropriations staff, the real value of PB^2 lay in its ability to rationalize the budgeting process. PB^2, it was thought, could drive the allocation process for a host of programs through algorithms linking performance and funding as unit costs and thereby narrow the range of arbitrary political choices, the way revenue sharing and educational distribution formulas had helped resolve difficulties in other areas. For others, this sort of streamlining seemed beyond the existing information capacities and, more importantly, contrary to the need for regular, fully considered determination of priorities.

Such differences remain. The perspective of the Executive remains at odds with that of the Legislature on several particulars. Here both the perspectives and the prerogatives of the two branches clash most directly. Agency managers have not embraced the possibilities of PB^2 uniformly. The reform requires consolidating program activities that are often organized in different parts of an agency. The move to programs calls for sustained recasting and reengineering efforts that are of little interest in some quarters. And while the search for allocational uses of PB^2 in the Legislature has diminished somewhat, there are still those who hope to make unit cost measures a central aspect of the appropriations process.

Problems in the Program Structure

Beginning in the 1970s, Florida adopted an elaborate program structure as part of its budgeting and accounting system. The program structure was designed to capture information about the expenditure of state resources on sets of related activities, characterized as programs. It presumed to be a comprehensive inventory of activities with similar activities in separate organizational settings cross-linked through a common coding structure. For the last 25 years, the budget has been built on a foundation of defined components as part of a program structure. The components of the program structure were rolled up and used to build issues in the budget. Notably though, until the advent of PB^2, funds were not appropriated to programs. The Governmental Performance and Accountability Act sought to change this, forcing decisionmaking to grapple with programs as the fundamental concern of budgeting.

The program structure exists alongside an organizational and object classification system. The chart of accounts forms the basis of the accounting system. It in turn is tied to the auditing system through the levels of control established in the general appropriation act each year by the Legislature. The basic unit of control is the budget entity, which traditionally has been an organizational entity with embedded appropriation categories.

Despite the enactment of PB^2, the program structure has not been systematically aligned with the accounting and auditing systems. In fact, programs still exist below the levels at which auditing controls exist. The ramifications of this one feature are many. Agencies do not capture audited information at the program level, compromising the reliability of the available information. Instead program information is often aggregated, ad hoc, from activities not subject to audit checks. Programs exist within and among budget entities, making management difficult. In 1994, as PB^2 began in Florida, about 95% of the state's expenditures were contained in 100 program components — too few components to provide the level of detail that state policymakers felt was needed for effective management and oversight of programs. Programs, like Medicaid for example, can be huge. Lawmakers were unwilling to give managers broad discretion over such activities. Instead, they wanted to ensure control over elements of the program such as nursing homes or drug payments. In this sense, the integration of activities into large programs actually works against the full range of accountability demanded of public organizations. Interest groups are particularly interested in ensuring that the activities they support receive continuing attention and support. They want funds appropriated at something other than the program level. The program structure becomes quite central politically.

The design of a program structure necessarily involves choices about the kinds of activities and level of information for which there is to be accountability. Ideally, a structure will capture accurate information in a consistent way. Similar activities in different agencies will be treated similarly.

In Florida, the program structure is being revised one area at a time. This has lead to inconsistent application across agencies. In some agencies, such as the Department of Environmental Regulation, programs are cast at a relatively low level. In others, such as the Department of Revenue, programs capture large sets of activities. The gradual pace of implementation has contributed to the confusion. The architecture of the program structure has suffered as a result.

The sheer amount of work needed to review all the program activities of state government has proven a substantial obstacle. Florida requires legislative approval of programs. The process proceeds within the legislative committee structure, compounding the difficulties of producing a unified approach. Programs are created to fit the demands and particular concerns of legislative oversight and are not necessarily aligned with core business processes in the agencies. The desire for legislative controls often clashes with concerns for program management. This is especially true when programmatic issues cross organizational boundaries, for example, drug enforcement by separate agencies.

It is useful to remember that legislators usually want to fix accountability clearly. Organizations have been the focus of that effort since individual agencies, divisions, or bureaus can be held to account. Programs, however, often involved many elements of an organization. And this raises problems. Ultimately, legislators want to know both what is being accomplished with public resources and who they can contact to make things happen. Producing this degree of alignment has proven difficult within PB^2.

Poor Performance Measures and Lack of Appropriate Data

State agencies began developing measures for their programs in the early 1970s. These measures have been incorporated in the budget process ever since. Still, problems remain even as PB^2 is implemented. Florida TaxWatch, for example, noted in 1999 that state agencies have not developed adequate performance measures to address their programs' critical functions. Nor were they adequately assessing critical program outcomes. These omissions are attributed generally to unclear standards, insufficient expertise, incomplete conceptualization of critical performance, and lack of data on critical program results.

Part of the problem is technical. Since agencies are held accountable to standards set on the measures, they must have an adequate basis of information to insure the standards can be related to agency activities. That information is often lacking. The systems needed to collect and warehouse a full-blown PB^2 are inadequate. Agencies, lacking adequate resources, have not deployed information technology to address the concerns. In this context, it is significant that agencies under the current legislation do not have to submit the logical models that link their activities to outputs and outcomes. This linkage, of course, lies at the heart of the accountability sought by PB^2. Without it, meaningful assessment is not possible.

Agency administrators are reluctant to advocate outcome measures for functions over which they have, or perceive to have, limited control. As a result, the outcome measures recommended for PB^2 have often focused on peripheral issues or agency outputs. OPPAGA (1997) suggested that the process might be improved by reconceptualizing outcomes to include factors that influence outcomes and that are explicitly linked to program results. For example, a job-training program might report the unemployment rate as an external factor worth considering in evaluating its success or failure in placing participants in high-paying jobs. The difficulty here, of course, is that again the linkages are problematic and such factors may also be well beyond the compass of meaningful state action.

There are other difficulties as well. Agencies officials, no less than legislators, are often conceptually uncertain about the results programs are supposed to achieve. Education, for example, is not concerned solely with achievement. Schools are also supposed to socialize students and ready them for the workplace. The components of successful employee and citizen development are matters of considerable contention, rooted in part in philosophical differences. This sort of problem is an unavoidable difficulty within PB^2 that cannot be resolved but must be addressed within the context of how the measures are to be used in the overall effort to improve accountability. There are no obvious measures. Every measure must be viewed within the overall accountability scheme adopted by the state. The emphasis is likely to differ state by state, and even administration by administration.

The accountability sought by PB[2] demands a rich and varied set of information. But the appropriate data for tracking program outputs and outcomes at the state level over time are often lacking (Berry & Flowers, 1999). Agencies gather the data they need to manage their operations and those data are typically focused on operational issues — how things are working rather than what impact they are having. OPPAGA (1997) asserts that lack of data on programs could be the reason why agencies often propose weak outcome measures. In 1999, OPPAGA found that only a handful of programs have data whose reliability meets expectations. Most need attention. Management needs to improve its quality control and testing. Florida TaxWatch (1999) found that many agencies traditionally have tracked program processes, and in some cases program outputs, but rarely have they measured citizen outcomes or otherwise accounted for them in relationship to how well government is delivering services. While some agencies are collecting new data in order to develop performance measures, they too are often unreliable and suspect. Agency inspectors general have not made data issues a central priority.

A large part of the difficulty lies in the sheer costs of collecting the necessary information. The program measures sought by policy makers and the public alike often center on concerns that have not been examined empirically before and for which ready information is unavailable. Deploying the systems to identify and collect new information is a formidable challenge in its own right. It pales, though, beside the difficulties of having such systems funded. The request for appropriations for new information systems must compete against priorities both within the requesting agency and across all of state government. While in some instances, the funds have been forthcoming, in most others they have not.

Misaligned Cost Accounting System

Several observers have expressed concern about the absence of a state cost accounting system suitable for tracking expenses in achieving desired program outputs and outcomes. The state's primary accounting system (SAMAS) does not readily support the allocation of all direct and indirect costs to programs and services.

With the exception of the reconstruction executed in the federally required Statewide Cost Allocation Plan, neither the Legislature nor the Executive can easily consider the costs and the benefits of agency programs. That plan is driven by federal concerns and is not aligned with PB^2.

In Florida, agencies account for their spending by funding sources, appropriation categories, and organization units rather than by programs or services. They typically do not allocate indirect costs, such as overhead, to individual programs except in an ad hoc fashion. These are long-standing practices, rooted in the concern for accountability over the purchase of inputs and the possibilities of public corruption. They are reinforced by a variety of federal requirements as well as Legislative focus on organizational responsibility. As a consequence, it is not generally possible to get accurate information on the cost for producing the outputs or outcomes specified in an accountability measure.

There are those who argue that, in the age of computerized data systems, there is no justifiable reason for this accounting deficit to persist. Perhaps. And in fact, the state is in the process of redesigning its integrated financial management system (FFMIS). It has spent the last two years examining the business case for a statewide Enterprise Resource Planning system (ERP). It is clear though that implementation will require much more than a few accounting changes. It will take a full-scale reengineering effort to get the most from the integration of contemporary "back office" technology with budget reform. The experience of the private sector in managing such changes suggests the process will be lengthy and expensive.

Difficulties in Awarding
Incentives and Disincentives

There has been considerable criticism in several quarters over the use of incentives and disincentives in PB^2 (Berry, Brower & Flowers, 2000; Berry & Flowers, 1999; Florida TaxWatch, 1999). The concern is especially acute among agency officials for whom the initiative has represented a major commitment of time, energy, and resources. The Legislature has awarded incentives to several agencies. But the awards have not been linked to PB^2 in the ways anticipated in the enabling legislation. Instead, they have involved political considerations not directly associated with performance. There has been, as noted by Berry & Flowers (1999), an ongoing lack of clear processes for awarding incentives or imposing negative sanctions for lack of agency program performance. The commitment of legislative leadership, which created and sustained PB^2, did not include rendering their prerogative to appropriate funds subject to automatic authorization.

In 1996, the only Florida agency to have implemented PB^2 long enough to be eligible for performance awards under the statute's general incentives/disincentives criteria was the Florida Department of Revenue (DOR). Despite the fact that the Department's General Tax Administration Program was eligible for an incentive award of up to 50 percent of its unspent funds, no award was tendered. In subsequent years, the Florida Department of Law Enforcement and the Department of Transportation were awarded greater management flexibility, in part for their efforts as captured by PB^2. While their performance as documented under PB^2 contributed to the Legislature's action, it is not possible to quantify that influence. In any case, interviews by Berry & Flowers (1999) reveal that agency officials remain skeptical about receiving incentive awards should they meet performance goals under PB^2. They continue to worry that they will be punished should they fail to meet them even though the Legislature has not imposed any of the disincentives allowed under the law.

It must be noted that while incentives were awarded, disincentives have not been employed. Agencies have not been asked to appear before the Governor and the elected cabinet to report on their efforts even when standards have not been reached. Nor have managerial salaries or agency positions been reduced. Programs have not been transferred. So, if agencies have not been granted the flexibility they hoped for, neither have they been sanctioned as some thought.

The Governor's Office supported an initiative in 1998 designed to address such concerns about incentives and disincentives. It remains to be seen whether it will be fully executed. And in fact, the real sense of legislative reaction may be registered in ways that are difficult to apprehend or formalize. Agencies with "good" track records typically have smooth sailing before legislative committees, all else being equal. Those perceived to be "off course" have a more difficult time funding their initiatives, getting additional staff, and making their case for increased managerial flexibility. Neither incentives nor disincentives are likely to be employed formulaically.

Absence of an Integrated Management Focus

At the present, the budgeting system does not handle PB^2 information easily. Worse, it does not get the information before decision makers in a format conducive to extensive use. This difficulty lies at the heart of the difficulties in implementing PB^2. The reforms initiated by PB^2 must be complemented and supported by other changes (Flowers, 1999). Part of the challenge in implementing PB^2 is the challenge of changing the fundamental management processes of state government.

State government is a large enterprise — $50 billion a year in expenditures and over $100 billion in its pension fund assets alone. It differs in fundamental ways from similar private concerns, however. It funds literally thousands of product lines. Its affairs are publicly accountable in ways unimaginable to most private managers. So, it is hardly surprising the character and thrust of management in state government has focused on issues quite apart from results or even performance. State managers, perhaps more than their private sector counterparts, are schooled in knowing what counts in the long run. And what counts has often had more to do with managing inputs prudently than producing outputs that influence outcomes.

All state managers, it should not be surprising, are not interested in improved management. Among appointees in particular the mechanics of government are among the least interesting aspects of their jobs. Often, they are managing organizations more complex and larger than anything their experience could anticipate. Policy issues rather than management issues dominate their working agenda and their ever-shortening activity horizon.

Getting such managers to commit the time and energy to embed PB^2 in their agencies' operations has been difficult. The phase-in has helped somewhat, but too often the reform has not been infused throughout organizations. Here, the fact that PB^2 has been implemented largely in isolation from other management initiatives is a matter of concern. The Chiles Administration focused considerable effort on reorganizing agencies and implementing quality management. It did not target reengineering of key business processes with the same vigor. In large measure, it did not attempt to link quality management with PB^2; in part because the efforts were run by different agencies; in part because quality management was never embraced by legislative leadership the way PB^2 was. As a consequence, it was easy for some managers to compartmentalize PB^2.

For all the concerns, however, some Florida agency administrators believe it is just a matter of time before PB^2 becomes more integral to every facet of budgeting. There is widespread belief that the current stage is proof that PB^2 is evolutionary and takes time to be implemented. As one such Florida agency administrator stated:

> If there is nothing else we have learned, it is that you don't spring fully formed into PB^2, particularly in the area of social services where the data and programs are so hard to translate into PB^2. But I think that over the whole system – getting to where there is confidence in the fact that the right goals have been selected, the measurements are the right ones, and we are doing a good job of collecting data – all of that takes time. We have built in that process, but it takes time as a Department to come on board fully. You really have to get to a point of confidence in those first steps before it makes a whole lot of sense to translate it to the budget. But that's the frustration that legislators have since they really want to make that translation, and they understand that until they do, they really have not fully done PB^2. (Berry & Flowers, 1999)

Absence of Sufficient Payoff

According to Berry & Flowers (1999), the general view among Florida state agency administrators is that legislators and the

Governor are not making budget decisions based on PB^2 yet. One agency analyst who has worked for the past three years on PB^2 implementation frankly stated:

> *A handful of legislators have been involved [in PB^2 over the years] but most aren't interested. PB^2 probably hasn't changed decision-making but without a doubt, it drew attention to accountability issues, and I believe it has influenced other pieces of legislation. But I don't think any legislator has made a decision based on PB^2 data.* (Berry & Flowers, 1999)

Asked for an overall assessment of PB^2, another Florida agency administrator took a very negative view:

> *I don't believe PB^2 has accomplished anything, to be honest, except in those agencies that have used it to change their culture. PB^2 has not changed decision-making in this agency or in the Legislature. They are absolutely not equipped to budget by the large units. Legislators want to micro-manage.* (Berry & Flowers, 1999)

There is clearly a sense in which these observations are on target. PB^2 is used to allocate funds in only a few programs. Performance measures, standards, and program justifications do not shape the major features of the appropriation process. For most legislators, the work of putting together meaningful measures and engaging in comprehensive oversight does not have the same appeal as targeted inquiries.

In part though, these observations mistake allocation for use. PB^2 has been fully incorporated into the process whereby appropriations are justified. There is even evidence that it plays a part in the process of conserving resources. Still it is clear, even here, that expectations about how PB^2 might work greatly exceed what its role can be. It is important to remember not only that the reform is in its infancy, but that there is a lack of consensus on what can be reasonably accomplished in the decisionmaking process through such changes. The structure of the appropriations process suggests that PB^2 must necessarily take a back seat to other considerations ranging from the level of revenues to architecture of federal mandates.

State budget making will always be a political process. Decisions can be isolated temporarily at times. Ultimately though, even the most sacrosanct areas get their "turn in the box." PB^2 is not an apolitical, neutral process. It does attempt to rationalize elements of the three major budget processes, but it must surrender before political intentions. Expectations to the contrary distort what PB^2 can be expected to accomplish and misdirect its evaluation.

If some expect too much of PB^2, others underestimate its impact. The drive to measure performance is not without impact, even when it is poorly done. OPPAGA has repeatedly pointed out the problems of using inappropriate or badly designed measures. More recently, it has noted the tendency among agency officials and legislators alike to incorporate too many activities within a program. Both developments are of concern.

Agencies promote what they measure. Measures, in turn, can act as shortcuts around more careful consideration of complex interactions, often with unintended results. The current accountability measures used by the State University System in Florida, for example, are powerful disincentives to public service. The measures hold universities to account for federal grants and contracts, but ignore those from the state. State public service is not included as part of the accountability system. Not being encouraged, state related activities are implicitly discouraged. Similar observations hold for a variety of other activities throughout state government (Herrington, 1999). On such matters, the influence of an increasingly institutionalized PB^2 may work against truly informed public policy. It may actually displace thoughtful deliberation.

Lessons Learned

Performance measurement and budgeting have been at the forefront of management reform for two decades (Schick, 1990). In Florida, PB^2 continues to unfold. Over 53% of the state agency administrators in a recent poll were positive about the implementation of PB^2 (Flowers, 1999). One agency leader remarked that his agency would still go ahead with the implementation and institutionalization of PB^2 even if the Legislature withdrew support.

The actions of other managers indicate they would agree to do so also. In a similar vein, the experience with PB² has helped refocus managers on results. Managers, ever alert to the concerns of the Legislature, are more concerned with agency outputs and outcomes than ever before (Sheffield, 1999).

The orientation of state administrators is important but its significance must be assessed against the difficulties of change management. Much of today's policy implementation and strategic management literatures focuses on the role of agency managers or policy entrepreneurs in transforming public policy (Roberts & King, 1991). Florida's implementation of PB² suggests that the actions of agency administrators (or agency entrepreneurs) affect, and are affected by, agency conditions in fundamental ways (Flowers, Kundin & Brower, 1999). It is no less true for being obvious that the conditions attendant to each agency, such as its structure and culture, influence its ability and willingness to embrace PB². The corollary to this observation is that successful implementation across all agencies is highly unlikely unless accompanied by special steps ranging from the continuing commitment of leadership to an ongoing concern for accurate and timely information linkages. Budgetary reform alone in such cases is not reform enough. For administrators and legislators alike, this is an enduring lesson.

Presently, one of the key questions in budget reform is how can performance-based program budgeting be implemented efficiently and effectively. Flowers (1999) provides some clues, at least in the Florida context. First, Florida's Government Performance and Accountability Act, although clearly designed to create central control and accountability, has proved to be flexible enough to permit very different approaches to implementation. Agencies' efforts to implement performance-based systems can be dramatically influenced by the manner in which agency leadership defines strategic issues facing the agencies and the chronology of other management initiatives under way. Strategic planning, budget cutbacks, and total quality initiatives all influenced the trajectory of the PB² initiative, although in distinctive ways in the three agencies. An agency's core work technology and professional orientation substantially condition the reception of the performance accountability initiative. All other things being equal, organizations with relatively routine technologies will experience an easier and more coherent implementation of performance-based accountability systems. Those agencies whose street-level workers command significant professional discretion will find implementation more difficult. The task of marrying top-down accountability measurement with bottom-up knowledge of work processes is difficult but essential to successful implementation.

The thoroughgoing nature of the reforms that PB^2 demands can tax the capacity of agencies already under pressure to improve the quality of their services. Administrators in such circumstances can be hard pressed to improve the reliability of the data on their programs absent additional resources or special assistance. Coping with improvements, even salutary ones, involving their key operating systems only compounds the challenges.

In this regard, the phased implementation used in Florida has proved beneficial. It has eased the training burdens, softened the cultural adjustments, and eased the financial pressures. It has also provided an opportunity to customize implementation. Different programs in different agencies have, in fact, been treated differently by the OPB and the Legislature. The phased implementation has also mitigated the conflicts among different groups. The Legislature controlled by Republicans was able to find common ground with a Democratic Governor over appropriations issues that lie at the very heart of each branch's authority and power precisely because not everything was at stake. Agencies were given the opportunity to forge new relationships with the administration and deal with internal reticence in a measured manner.

The gradual phase-in has also worked against implementation in some ways. It has diffused the energy behind the initiative and deprived it of continuing champions. While there has been considerable stability among legislative staff, their influence necessarily is mediated through leadership. Legislative leadership in Florida changes every two years. It is legislative leadership that dictates the pace of change even when staff champions are afoot. The Coordinating Board of the Legislative Appropriation System/Program Budgeting Subsystem, for example, was not able to control implementation of PB^2 though it was comprised of the staff directors of

House Appropriations and Senate Appropriations Committees in addition to the Director of the OPB.

In fact, no single group coordinated implementation. OPPAGA has been a locus of PB^2 energy and attention, an invaluable asset to the reform. But OPPAGA does not have the institutional position to drive the implementation alone. Like legislative staff, its influence is mediated.

In the final analysis, the extended implementation has diffused the intellectual coherence of the initiative. It diluted leadership commitment. While helping to avoid many of the inherent conflicts in the reform, the extended implementation has also failed to resolve certain features. The program structure was not revisited in a systematic fashion. The continuing debate over agency flexibility and control was not worked to resolution. The process of rewarding agencies was not formalized. Incentives and disincentives have not been deployed to good effect. Legislative aspirations to make performance central to allocation decisions have been largely deflected in the face of persistent technical problems.

Implementation of PB^2 continues. Its full potential has yet to be realized. In January of 2000, Governor Bush unveiled recommendations to carry the initiative forward. The Legislature enacted an extensive set of further reforms. The results of this initiative will help determine whether PB^2 succeeds or becomes yet another archaeological layer among the earlier reforms to Florida's Budgeting System.

Endnotes

1   Annual salary rate is the salary estimated to be paid or actually paid a position of positions on an annualized basis (216.011(1), Florida Statutes 1999).

2   www.oppaga.state.fl.us

References

Barrett, K. and Greene, R. (September 26, 1995). "State of the States — Tick, tick, tick." *Financial World:* 36-60.

Berry, F. S., Brower, R., and Flowers, G. (March, 2000). "Implementing Performance Accountability in Florida." *Public Productivity and Management Review* 23 (3):338-358.

Berry, F. S. and Chackerian, R. & Wechsler, B. (1995). "Reinventing Government: Lessons from a State Capital." Paper prepared for presentation at the 3rd National Public Management Research Conference, Lawrence, Kansas, October 5-7, 1995.

Berry, F. S. and Flowers, G. (Winter, 1999). "Public Entrepreneurs in the Policy Process: Performance-Based Budgeting in Florida." *Journal of Public Budgeting, Accounting and Financial Management* 11 (4):578-617.

Easterling, N. (Winter, 1999). "Performance-Budgeting in Florida: To Muddle or not to Muddle, That is the Question." *Journal of Public Budgeting, Accounting & Public Finance* 11 (4):559-577.

Florida Constitution. (1998). State Budgeting, Planning, and Appropriation Processes. Article III, Section 19(h).

Florida Office of Program Policy Analysis and Government Accountability (OPPAGA) (April, 1997). "A Report on Performance-Based Program Budgeting in Context: History and Comparison." Tallahassee, FL: Florida Office of Program Policy Analysis and Government Accountability.

Florida Statutes. (1999). Planning and Budgeting. Chapter 216.

Florida Statutes. (1999). Legislative Organization, Procedures, and Staffing. Chapter 11, Sections 11.51 – 11.513. Office of Program Policy Analysis and Governmental Accountability.

Florida TaxWatch. (December, 1986). "Building a Better Florida: A Management Blueprint to Save Taxpayers Over $1 Billion." Tallahassee, FL: Florida TaxWatch Inc.

Florida TaxWatch Research Report. (May 1995). "Taxpayers Win at the Wire." Tallahassee, FL: Florida TaxWatch, Inc.

Florida TaxWatch Research Report. (March, 1999). "Florida's Performance-Based Budgeting (PB²) — A Diamond in the Rough or Just a Zirconium Bauble?" Tallahassee, FL: Florida TaxWatch Research Institute.

Flowers, G. (1999). "An Evaluation of the Effect of Agency Conditions on the Implementation of Florida's Performance-Based Program Budgeting." Ph.D dissertation, Florida State University, Tallahassee, Florida.

Flowers, G., Kundin, D., and Brower, R. S. (Winter, 1999). "How Agency Conditions Facilitate and Constrain Performance-Based Program Systems." *Journal of Public Budgeting, Accounting and Financial Management* 11 (4):618-648.

General Accounting Office. (February, 1993). "Performance Budgeting: State Experiences and Implications for the Federal Government." Washington, D.C.: U.S. General Accounting Office.

Herrington, Carolyn. (1999). "Performance Based Budgeting in Public Schools in Florida." In Margaret Goetz and Allen Odom (Eds.) *School Based Financing*. Thousand Oaks, CA: Corwin Press, pp. 188-214.

Moore, Mark (1995). *Creating Public Value: Strategic Management in Government*. Cambridge, MA: Harvard University Press.

Roberts, N. C. and King, P. J. (1991). "Policy Entrepreneurs: Their Structure and Function in the Policy Process." *Journal of Public Administration Research and Theory* 2:147-175.

Rubin, I. S. (September/October 1993). "Who Invented Budgeting in the United States?" *Public Administration Review* 53 (5):438-444.

Rubin, I. S. (March/April, 1990). "Budget Theory and Budget Practice: How Good the Fit?" *Public Administration Review* 50 (2):179-189.

Schick, A. (March/April, 1993). "A Death in the Bureaucracy: The Demise of Federal PPB." *Public Administration Review* 33 (2):146-156.

Schick, A. (January/February, 1990). "Budgeting for Results: Recent Developments in Five Industrialized Countries." *Public Administration Review* 50 (1):513-519.

Schick, A. (1988). "An Inquiry into the Possibility of a Budgetary Theory." In Irene S. Rubin, (ed.), *New Directions in Budget Theory*. Albany, NY: State University of New York Press, pp. 59-69.

Schick, A. (November/December, 1978). "Contemporary Problems in Financial Control." *Public Administration Review* 38 (4): 513-519.

Schick, A. (December, 1966). "The Road to PBB: The Stages of Budget Reform." *Public Administration Review* 26:243-258.

Sheffield, S. R. (Winter, 1999). "Implementing Florida's Performance and Accountability Act: A Focus on Program Measurement and Evaluation." *Journal of Public Budgeting, Accounting, and Financial Management* 11 (4):649-669.

Appendix A
State Agency Schedule for Implementing PB[2]

Fiscal Year	Agency	Programs (Approved where listed)
1994-95	Revenue	General Tax Administration
1995-96	Revenue	Property Tax Administration
	Management Services	Facilities
1996-97	Community Colleges	AA Degree
		AS Degree
		Vocational Certificate
	Labor and Employment Security	Disability Determination
		Rehabilitation
	Law Enforcement	Criminal Justice Investigations and Protection
		Criminal Justice Information
		Criminal Justice Professionalism
	Management Services	Support
		Technology
		Workforce
	Division of Retirement	Retirement
1997-98	State University System	Instruction
	Game and Fresh Water Fish Commission	Law Enforcement
	Highway Safety and Motor Vehicles	Highway Patrol
	State	Library, Archives and Information

Appendix A

State Agency Schedule for Implementing PB[2] (continued)

Fiscal Year	Agency	Programs (Approved where listed)
	Transportation	Toll Operations
		Support Services
		Motor Carrier Compliance
		Highway Construction and Engineering
		Right-of-Way Acquisition
		Public Transportation
		Routine Highway Maintenance
	Labor and Employment Security	Safety and Workers Compensation
	Children and Families	Alcohol, Drug Abuse and Mental Health Services
1998-99	Agency for Health Care Administration	Health Services Quality Assurance
		Medicaid Health Services
	Game and Fresh Water Fish Commission	Fisheries Management
		Wildlife Management
	Highway Safety and Motor Vehicles	Driver Licenses
		Motor Vehicles
	Management Services	State Employee Group Insurance
	State	Commercial Recording and Registration Licenses
	Labor and Employment Security	Employment Security
	Juvenile Justice	Detention
	Banking and Finance	Financial Accountability for Public Funds

Appendix A
State Agency Schedule for Implementing PB² (continued)

Fiscal Year	Agency	Programs (Approved where listed)
	Corrections	Custody and Control
		Health Services
		Community Corrections
		Offender Work, Training and Restitution
	Education	Public Schools
	Environmental Protection	Recreation and Parks
		Law Enforcement
		Marine Resources
		State Land
	Executive Office of the Governor	Economic Improvement
	Children and Families	Mental Health Institutions
		People with Developmental Disabilities in Communities
		People with Developmental Disabilities in Institutions
		Families in Need of Safety and Preservation Services
		Abuse Hotline
		Aging and Adult Services
	Legal Affairs	Civil Representation and Legal Services
		Statewide Prosecution
		Criminal Justice and Victim Support Services
	Insurance	Fire Marshall

Appendix A
State Agency Schedule for Implementing PB^2 (continued)

Fiscal Year	Agency	Programs (Approved where listed)
1999-2000	Agriculture and Consumer Services	Food and Resource Protection
		Food Safety and Quality
		Consumer Protection
		Agricultural Economic Development
	Children and Families	Families in Need of Child Care
		Economic Self Sufficiency Services
	Elder Affairs	Services to Elders
	Lottery	Sales of Lottery Products
	Military Affairs	Readiness and Response
	State	Historical, Archaeological and Folklife Appreciation
2000-2001	Division of Administrative Hearings	
	Business and Professional Regulation	
	Parole and Probation Commission	
	Public Service Commission	
	Health	
	Education	
2001-2002	Citrus	
	Community Affairs	

Getting to Results in Florida

Appendix A
State Agency Schedule for Implementing PB[2] (continued)

Fiscal Year	Agency	Programs (Approved where listed)
	Insurance	
	Veterans' Affairs	
	State Attorneys	
	Public Defenders	
	Justice Administration Commission and Capital Collateral Council	

409

Quicker, Better, Cheaper?
Managing Performance in American Government

Appendix B: Major Budget and Personnel Controls: 1993

Statutory Controls	Existing Controls	Pilot Agencies FY 1992-94	Proposed Program Budgeting
Budget			
All appropriations are maximum spending authorizations.	X		X
Salary rate may not be transferred between budget entities unless associated positions are also transferred.	X	X	X
Authorized positions are established in the GAA. All additional positions requested require approval. (OPB, Legislative consultation, Administration Commission)	X	X	X
Prohibits transfer of positions between budget entities without approval. (OPB, Legislative consultation)	X		X
Prohibits transfer within categories between budget entities of greater than $25,000 or 5% without approval. (OPB and Legislative consultation)	X		X
Prohibits transfers between categories within a budget entity of greater than $25,000 or 5% without approval. (OPB and Legislative consultation)	X		
Lump-sum salary bonuses may be provided only if specifically appropriated.	X		X
Lump-sum appropriations must be approved for transfer by budget amendment to appropriate spending categories, through OPB and Legislative consultation.	X		X
All increases in an agency's total trust fund spending authority requires approval. (OPB, Legislative consultation)	X	X	X
Requests to exceed salary rate must be approved. (OPB, Legislative consultation)	X	X	X
No new programs may be created without approval. (Administration Commission, OPB, Legislative consultation)	X	X	X
Agencies may not initiate fixed capital outlay projects or change the scope without a specific legislative appropriation.	X	X	X
Prohibits transfer of appropriations between fixed capital outlay projects without approval. (Administration Commission, OPB, Legislative consultation)	X	X	X
All balances of unencumbered operating budget revert as of June 30.	X	X	*1

X = Control Remains in Place
*1 Allows agencies to retain 25% of unobligated balances for each entity that meets its performance measures.

Appendix B: Major Budget and Personnel Controls: 1993

Statutory Controls	Existing Controls	Pilot Agencies FY 1992-94	Proposed Program Budgeting
Personnel			
Each agency must operate within the personnel rules promulgated by DMS pursuant to Chapter 110, Florida Statutes.	X		X
DMS shall establish and maintain a uniform classification plan and be responsible for the overall coordination, review and maintenance of the plan.	X		X
Classification and reclassification actions taken by an agency shall be within the classes established by DMS.	X		X
DMS shall establish and maintain an equitable pay plan.	X		X
The agency must use pay additives within the guidelines established by DMS.	X		X
Agencies may not establish additional divisions without approval of the Legislature.	X	X	X
Agencies may not establish additional bureaus, sections, and subsections without approval. (DMS, EOG)	X	X	X
Other Significant Restrictions			
Purchases of motor vehicles must be specifically appropriated by the Legislature, unless approved by EOG after Legislative consultation.	X	X	
All revenues, licenses, fees shall be deposited in the State Treasury and no money shall be paid except as provided by the annual Appropriations Act.	X	X	X
All contracts for purchases in excess of $10,000 must be competitively bid.	X	X	X
Agencies must purchase commodities and services in excess of $10,000 from state term contracts.	X	X	X
The State Comptroller may require proof of delivery and receipt of purchases before honoring any voucher for payment.	X	X	X

X = Control Remains in Place

Appendix C
Governor's Initial Recommended Change in Budget Format

Current Budget Format: 1994

REVENUE, DEPARTMENT OF

OFFICE OF THE EXECUTIVE DIRECTOR AND DIVISION OF ADMINISTRATION

		POSITIONS	
1540	SALARIES AND BENEFITS	202	
	FROM GENERAL REVENUE FUND		4,614,963
	FROM ADMINISTRATIVE TRUST FUND		
	FROM CORPORATION TAX ADMINISTRATION TRUST FUND		3,215,645
	FROM ADMINISTRATIVE TRUST FUND		15,330
1541	OTHER PERSONAL SERVICES		
	FROM ADMINISTRATIVE TRUST FUND		119,976
1542	EXPENSES		
	FROM GENERAL REVENUE FUND	71,402	
	FROM ADMINISTRATIVE TRUST FUND		1,622,269
1543	OPERATING CAPITAL OUTLAY		
	FROM ADMINISTRATIVE TRUST FUND		39,013
1545	SPECIAL CATEGORIES		
	LITIGATION EXPENSES		
	FROM GENERAL REVENUE FUND	50,000	
1548	DATA PROCESSING SERVICES		
	REVENUE MANAGEMENT INFORMATION CENTER		
	FROM ADMINISTRATIVE TRUST FUND		922,235

AD VALOREM TAX, DIVISION OF

		POSITIONS	
1549	SALARIES AND BENEFITS	158	
	FROM INTANGIBLE TAX TRUST FUND		6,111,196
1550	OTHER PERSONAL SERVICES		
	FROM INTANGIBLE TAX TRUST FUND		262,031
1551	EXPENSES		
	FROM INTANGIBLE TAX TRUST FUND		1,461,240
1552	OPERATING CAPITAL OUTLAY		
	FROM INTANGIBLE TAX TRUST FUND		7,805
1553	DATA PROCESSING SERVICES		
	REVENUE MANAGEMENT INFORMATION CENTER		
	FROM INTANGIBLE TAX TRUST FUND		189,108

AUDITS, DIVISION OF

		POSITIONS	
1554	SALARIES AND BENEFITS	1,218	
	FROM GENERAL REVENUE FUND		32,961,999
	FROM ADMINISTRATIVE TRUST FUND		13,641,188

Proposed Performance-Based Program Budget Format

REVENUE, DEPARTMENT OF

Funds in Specific Appropriations 1548A through 1553G for the Department of Revenue are provided in the context of a performance based budget which holds the department accountable for the delivery of services which include, but are not limited to, the achievement of specific standards described in proviso language contained herein. The department shall remain subject to the maximum approved annual salary rate provisions which are described in s. 216.181. Any budgetary adjustments or major program revisions from the funds provided in these specific appropriations which are proposed for implementation by the department under any budget flexibility provisions which may be granted by the legislature shall be subject to the notice and review procedures set forth in s. 216.177.

ADMINISTRATIVE SUPPORT

		POSITIONS	
1548A	LUMP SUM		
	ADMINISTRATIVE SUPPORT PROGRAM	334	
	FROM GENERAL REVENUE FUND		7,499,696
	FROM ADMINISTRATIVE TRUST FUND		9,304,435
	FROM CORPORATION TAX ADMINISTRATION TRUST FUND		438,505
	FROM WORKING CAPITAL TRUST FUND		5,985,604

From funds provided in Specific Appropriation 1548A, the Administrative Support program shall monitor and manage to ensure that agency program targets are met. It shall also submit to the Governor and Cabinet, and the Legislature, a quarterly progress report on meeting agency program targets, including explanations for any projected deviations, and an expenditures report. Instructions for the quarterly report will be developed by the Executive Office of the Governor in consultation with the legislature. The department shall fill 93 percent of its authorized positions as of the end of the fiscal year.

Appendix C
Governor's Initial Recommended Change in Budget Format (Continued)

Current Budget Format

FROM GRANTS AND DONATIONS TRUST FUND...... 46,806

1555   OTHER PERSONAL SERVICES
FROM ADMINISTRATIVE TRUST FUND.......... 43,800

1556   EXPENSES
FROM GENERAL REVENUE FUND...... 3,998,913
FROM ADMINISTRATIVE TRUST FUND........ 2,659,796
FROM GRANTS AND DONATIONS TRUST FUND.... 10,119

1557   OPERATING CAPITAL OUTLAY
FROM ADMISTRATIVE TRUST FUND........ 27,250

1558   DATA PROCESSING SERVICES
REVENUE MANAGEMENT INFORMATION CENTER
FROM ADMINISTRATIVE TRUST FUND.......... 710,999

COLLECTION AND ENFORCEMENT, DIVISION OF

1559   SALARIES AND BENEFITS   POSITIONS   900
FROM GENERAL REVENUE FUND.......... 19,900,247
FROM ADMINISTRATIVE TRUST FUND........ 6,754,963
FROM GRANTS AND DONATIONS TRUST FUND.... 85,218

1560   PERSONAL SERVICES
FROM ADMINSTRATIVE TRUST FUND.......... 75,000

1561   EXPENSES
FROM GENERAL REVENUE FUND.......... 2,302,909
FROM ADMINISTRATIVE TRUST FUND........ 3,428,402
FROM GRANTS AND DONATIONS TRUST FUND.... 39,970

1562   OPERATING CAPITAL OUTLAY
FROM ADMINSTRATIVE TRUST FUND.......... 30,595

1563   DATA PROCESSING SERVICES
REVENUE MANAGEMENT INFORMATION CENTER
FROM ADMINSTRATIVE TRUST FUND.......... 1,138,995

REVENUE MANAGEMENT INFORMATION CENTER

1564   SALARIES AND BENEFITS   POSITIONS   36
FROM WORKING CAPITAL TRUST FUND........ 1,019,699

1565   OTHER PERSONAL SERVICES
FROM WORKING CAPITAL TRUST FUND........ 17,680

1566   EXPENSES
FROM WORKING CAPITAL TRUST FUND........ 1,938,611

1567   OPERATING CAPITAL OUTLAY
FROM WORKING CAPITAL TRUST FUND........ 2,155,041

1568   DATA PROCESSING SERVICES
ADMINISTRATIVE MANAGEMENT INFORMATION
CENTER – DEPARTMENT OF MANAGEMENT SERVICES
FROM WORKING CAPITAL TRUST FUND........ 854,573

Performance-based Program Format

AD VALOREM TAX, DIVISION OF

1552A   LUMP SUM
AD VALOREM TAX   POSITIONS   158
FROM INTANGIBLE TAX TRUST FUND...... 8,031,380

From funds provided in Specific Appropriation 1552A the Ad Valorem Tax program shall increase by 26 percent the number of subclasses of property studied and increase by 10 percent the number of personnel trained in the statutorily required TRIM assessment. The program shall maintain to no more than 11 property subclassification inequities statewide.

1553A   LUMP SUM
TAXPAYER REGISTRATION AND EDUCATION   POSITIONS   175
FROM GENERAL REVENUE FUND...... 3,934,749
FROM ADMINISTRATIVE TRUST FUND...... 3,520,869
FROM CORPORATION TAX ADMINISTRATION TRUST FUND...... 218,138

From funds provided in Specific Appropriation 1553A the Taxpayer Registration and Education program shall increase by 19 percent the number of returns filed correctly by first time filers. The program shall increase the percentage of dollars collected voluntarily to 97.25 percent compared to total dollars collected.

1553B   LUMP SUM
RETURN AND REMITTANCE PROCESSING   POSITIONS   279
FROM GENERAL REVENUE FUND...... 6,545,985
FROM ADMINISTRATIVE TRUST FUND...... 4,858,748
FROM CORPORATION TAX ADMINISTRATION TRUST FUND...... 752,058

From funds provided in Specific Appropriation 1553B the Return/Remittance Processing program shall maintain at 94 percent the accuracy of initial distribution of revenue to state agencies and local governments.

Appendix C

Governor's Initial Recommended Change in Budget Format (Continued)

Current Budget Format

INFORMATION SYSTEMS AND SERVICES, DIVISION OF

		POSITIONS	
1569	SALARIES AND BENEFITS	114	
	FROM GENERAL REVENUE FUND.		2,745,684
	FORM ADMINISTRATIVE TRUST FUND.		1,299,378
	FROM CORPORATION TAX ADMINISTRATION TRUST FUND.		347,810
1570	OTHER PERSONAL SERVICES		
	FROM ADMINSTRATIVE TRUST FUND.		95,628
1571	EXPENSES		
	FROM GENERAL REVENUE FUND.		315,625
	FORM ADMINISTRATIVE TRUST FUND.		566,233
	FROM CORPORATION TAX ADMINISTRATION TRUST FUND.		47,806
1572	OPERATING CAPITAL OUTLAY		
	FROM ADMINISTRATIVE TRUST FUND.		4,327
1573	DATA PROCESSING SERVICES REVENUE MANAGEMENT INFORMATION CENTER		
	FROM ADMINSTRATIVE TRUST FUND.		2,525,401

TAXPAYER ASSISTANCE, DIVISION OF

		POSITIONS	
1574	SALARIES AND BENEFITS	160	
	FROM GENERAL REVENUE FUND.		3,535,818
	FROM ADMINSTRATIVE TRUST FUND.		2,690,412
	FROM CORPORATION TAX ADMINISTRATION TRUST FUND.		149,293
1575	OTHER PERSONAL SERVICES		
	FROM ADMINSTRATIVE TRUST FUND.		19,380
1576	EXPENSES		
	FROM GENERAL REVENUE FUND.		85,895
	FROM ADMINSTRATIVE TRUST FUND.		1,096,504
	FROM CORPORATION TAX ADMINISTRATION TRUST FUND.		9,003
1577	OPERAITNG CAPITAL OUTLAY		
	FROM ADMINISTRATIVE TRUST FUND.		5,085
1578	DATA PROCESSING SERVICES REVENUE MANAGEMENT INFORMATION CENTER		
	FROM ADMINSTRATIVE TRUST FUND.		59,946

TAX PROCESSING, DIVISION OF

		POSITIONS	
1579	SALARIES AND BENEFITS	360	
	FROM GENERAL REVENUE FUND.		4,927,187
	FROM ADMINSTRATIVE TRUST FUND.		2,623,005
	FROM CORPORATION TAX ADMINISTRATION TRUST FUND.		1,122,847

Performance-based Program Format

		POSITIONS	
1553C	LUMP SUM RETURN AND REMITTANCE RECONCILIATION	135	
	FROM GENERAL REVENUE FUND.		2,570,519
	FROM ADMINISTRATIVE TRUST FUND.		2,151,993
	FROM CORPORATION TAX ADMINISTRATION TRUST FUND.		471,497

From funds provided in Specific Appropriation 1553C the Return/Remittance Reconciliation program shall reduce the number of department and taxpayer induced errors by 8 percent. The program shall increase to 93 percent the billings and delinquencies issued accurately.

		POSITIONS	
1553D	LUMP SUM IDENTIFY LIABILITY - REGISTERED TAXPAYER	1,135	
	FROM GENERAL REVENUE FUND.		34,077,756
	FROM ADMINISTRATIVE TRUST FUND.		15,966,846
	FROM CORPORATION TAX ADMINISTRATION TRUST FUND.		14,003
	FROM GRANTS AND DONATIONS TRUST FUND.		56,925

From funds provided in Specific Appropriation 1553D the Identify Liability – Registered Taxpayer program shall maintain the amount of final recovery at 78 percent of the original taxpayer assessment.

		POSITIONS	
1553E	LUMP SUM IDENTIFY LIABILITY - UNREGISTERED TAXPAYER	163	
	FROM GENERAL REVENUE FUND.		3,992,000
	FROM ADMINISTRATIVE TRUST FUND.		2,277,275
	FROM CORPORATION TAX ADMINISTRATION TRUST FUND.		16,003
	FROM GRANTS AND DONATIONS TRUST FUND.		125,188

From funds provided in Specific Appropriation 1553E the Identify Liability – Unregistered Taxpayers program shall increase by 7.5 percent the number of contacts that end in taxpayer registration and shall increase by 37 percent collections per contact.

		POSITIONS	
1553F	LUMP SUM COLLECTION	453	
	FROM GENERAL REVENUE FUND.		11,115,296
	FROM ADMINISTRATIVE TRUST FUND.		6,052,952
	FROM CORPORATION TAX ADMINISTRATION TRUST FUND.		1,282

From funds provided in Specific Appropriation 1553F the Collections program shall increase the collections of taxpayer liability to 90 percent.

Appendix C

Governor's Initial Recommended Change in Budget Format (Continued)

Current Budget Format

1580 OTHER PERSONAL SERVICES
      FROM GENERAL REVENUE FUND. 30,000
      FROM ADMINISTRATIVE TRUST FUND. 363,084

1581 EXPENSES
      FROM GENERAL REVENUE FUND. 2,090,692
      FORM ADMINISTRATIVE TRUST FUND. 2,574,665
      FROM CORPORATION TAX ADMINISTRATION
          TRUST FUND. 249,945

1582 OPERATING CAPITAL OUTLAY
      FROM GENERAL REVENUE FUND. 330,000
      FROM ADMINISTRATIVE TRUST FUND. 380,747

1583 DATA PROCESSING SERVICES
      REVENUE MANAGEMENT INFORMATION CENTER
      FROM ADMINISTRATIVE TRUST FUND. 102,176

Performance-based Program Format

1553G LUMP SUM
       ADJUDICATION
                                                    POSITIONS   316
       FROM GENERAL REVENUE FUND. 8,225,333
       FROM ADMINISTRATIVE TRUST FUND. 4,702,975
       FROM CORPORATION TAX ADMINISTRATION
           TRUST FUND. 30,548

From funds provided in Specific Appropriation 1553G the Adjudication program shall increase the Notices of Decision by 30 percent. The program shall decrease by 33 percent the average number of days to resolve a case by the end of the fiscal year.

Appendix D
Example: Excerpts From the Office of Program Policy Analysis and Governmental Accountability's Review of the State of Florida's Library, Archives and Information Program, Report 99-05

"Accountability Rating System:…

Accoutability Rating	Meets Expectations	Needs Some Modifications	Needs Major Modifications
Program Purpose and Goals	X		
Performance Measures			X
Data Reliability		X	
Reporting Information and Use by Management		X	

Issues and Evaluative Comments:
The program has taken steps to address the problems with its current PB^2 measures. For example, recognizing that one valuable measure of program impact is consumer satisfaction with library services, the program developed customer satisfaction measures to be implemented in September of 1999. These measures include the following:
- Customer satisfaction with relevancy of research response
- Customer satisfaction with timeliness of research response
- Customer satisfaction with Records Management Technical Assistance
- Customer satisfaction with Records Management training

However, the program's 2000-2001 Legislative Budget Request still includes measures that have reliability and/or validity problems (as outlined in OPPAGA's report PB^2 Performance Report for the State's Library, Archives and Information Program, Report 98-72, March 1999). For example, the program's measurement set still includes the following measures that OPPAGA recommends for deletion:
- Annual cost-avoidance achieved by government agencies through records/disposition/micro graphics
- Annual increase in accessibility by library patrons to materials not owned by their local public library."

15

Paying for Performance in Public Higher Education

Joseph C. Burke

Paying for performance in higher education became a hot topic in state capitals and on public campuses in the 1990s. The *Fiscal Survey of the States* in the late nineties called performance budgeting for government agencies "the most significant trend in state budgeting."[1] In public higher education, this practice emerged as the budgeting phenomenon of the decade. A survey by the Rockefeller Institute of Government in June of 2000 showed that nearly three-quarters of the states considered performance in budgeting for public colleges and universities.[2]

This phenomenon emerged from the movements to reengineer business and reinvent government in the early 1990s.[3] Those movements preached a novel gospel for American business and a new heresy for state government and higher education. Managing constituent politics — not customer services — usually dominated state policymaking, and improving institutional prestige — not client services — often drove campus decisionmaking.

Performance management claimed that organizations not only could — but also must — improve quality while cutting costs and increasing services. It advocated management by results rather than control by regulations. By concentrating on performance rather than compliance, managers combined the goals of accountability and improvement. Organizations could improve performance while decentralizing authority by being tight on setting goals and assessing results but loose on the means of achieving them. The focus on customer needs fostered client- rather than provider-centered enterprises. Managing, measuring, and rewarding results became the new trinity. Like all creeds, this one proved easier to proclaim than to practice. Like all crusades, it inspired both fervent champions and fevered critics.

Although academics developed many of these management theories, a common reaction on campus called them all right for business and maybe for government but anathema for academe. Outsiders could have predicted that the accent on efficiency would arouse opposition on campus, but few would have guessed that the focus on quality would prove a greater obstacle. Colleges had declared "Quality Job One" centuries before Ford. Unfortunately, the academic community never determined nor defined with any precision the objectives of undergraduate education or developed systematic methods for assessing campus performance.

By default and preference, the perception of institutional quality depended largely on resource inputs, such as the quantity of campus resources, the quality of admitted students, and the reputation of faculty research. It neglected institutional outputs and outcomes, such as the quantity and quality of graduates and the range and benefits of research and service to states and their citizens. This "Resource and Reputation" model reflected provider desires rather than customer demands.[4] The move of health care to managed care appeared to leave higher education as the last refuge of a provider-driven enterprise.

By the 1990s, public higher education had become too important and too costly to states to ignore campus results. Once considered a luxury for most citizens and a private benefit to graduates, higher education had become essential to the economic success of states in a competitive national and global economy driven by knowledge and information. The recession in the first half of the decade and the competition for funding from health care, public schools, welfare, and corrections also pushed for restraining the rate of spending for higher education, which constitutes one of the few discretionary items in state budgets.[5] Recognition of the rising importance and increasing cost of higher education produced a shift in the notion of accountability. The "old accountability" asked the accounting question of how public campuses expended state resources. The "new accountability" asked the management question of what were their results.

New Accountability Levers

The Greek mathematician Archimedes believed you could move anything with a long enough lever, put in the right place. Until the late 1980s, state governments and coordinating boards of higher education had largely neglected two powerful levers of accountability: *information* and *budgets*. The adage that what gets measured is what gets valued is only half right. The value comes not so much from measuring as from reporting results to policymakers and the general public. By the late 1990s, about 30 states had performance reports from public colleges and universities of campus results on priority indicators.[6]

Unfortunately, state and campus policymakers often ignored these reports, because they had no fiscal consequences. Money matters in state government and higher education no less than in private industry. If what is measured and publicized is what gets valued, what gets funded is even more prized. Performance reporting set the stage for the move to performance budgeting. It is hard to imagine that state policymakers would have reports on the accomplishments of colleges and universities and then totally ignore them when allocating scarce resources. Progressing from reporting to funding seemed a short step to state officials, but a momentous move to campus leaders.

Traditional Budgeting

States traditionally budgeted public colleges and universities based largely on current costs, student enrollments, and inflationary increases. These input or resource factors ignored the quantity and quality of graduates and the range and benefits of services to states and society. This cost-plus budgeting also promoted inappropriate growth in expenditures, enrollments, and programs, even in states with declining demographics and student demands. Some states had previously provided front-end funding to encourage desired campus activities that encouraged economic development.

Performance funding and budgeting differs from these earlier efforts by allocating resources for achieved rather than promised results. This practice shifts somewhat the budget question from what states should do for their campuses toward what campuses do for their states and their students. The shift is slight in all states, since the sums allocated to performance remain relatively small. The workload measures of current costs, student enrollments, and inflationary increases will — and should — receive the lion's share of state allocations. The real issue is whether performance should count for something in state funding.

Performance Funding and Performance Budgeting

Using performance in state allocations for public colleges and universities takes two forms. The two approaches are sometimes confused, because of common characteristics, despite distinct differences.

- ❀ **Performance funding** ties tightly specific allocations to institutional results on each of the designated indicators. The tie is automatic and formulaic. If a campus achieves a set target on an indicator such as its graduation rate, it receives a specific amount of performance money. Performance funding focuses on budget distribution.

- ❀ **Performance budgeting** allows governors and legislators or state coordinating and university system boards to consider campus performance on the indicators collectively as merely one factor in determining the total allocation for an institution. The link in performance budgeting is loose and discretionary. This approach usually concentrates on budget preparation and presentation, and slights, or even ignores, budget distribution.

The advantages and disadvantages of each of these approaches are the reverse of the other. In performance funding, the tie between results and resources is clear but inflexible. In performance budgeting, the link is flexible but unclear.

The authors of earlier surveys do not clearly distinguish performance funding from performance budgeting.[7] Lack of clear definitions has led policymakers to confuse these two practices. Although those earlier surveys call attention to a generic direction in budgeting, they fail to identify how state governments, coordinating boards, or college and university systems actually use campus achievements on performance indicators in the budgeting process. Is the link between resources and results loose or tight? Does campus performance have a direct impact or only an indirect influence on state allocations? And are the funding decisions based on performance automatic or discretionary?

To clarify the connection between results and resources in performance budgeting, a Rockefeller Institute Survey asked State Higher Education Finance Officers to estimate the actual effect of the program on state funding for public campuses.[8] The responses from states with such programs confirm that performance budgeting has only a limited effect on institutional funding.

The loose link between performance and budgets in performance budgeting offers political advantages to policymakers. State legislators may champion, in theory, altering campus budgets based on performance, but they often oppose, in practice, programs that may result in budget losses to colleges or universities in their home districts. Performance budgeting offers a political resolution of this troublesome dilemma. Policymakers can gain credit for considering performance in budgeting without the controversy of altering campus allocations. This program also protects a prized possession of legislators: retaining control and discretion over state budgets.

Components

Performance funding and performance budgeting do contain some of the same components:

- *Program goals* include demonstrating external account-ability, improving institutional performance, and meeting state needs. Increasing state funding for public higher education constitutes an unannounced goal for coordinating boards and campuses.

- *Performance indicators* identify the areas of anticipated achievement. (Indicators run from as few as 3 in Florida to as many as 37 in South Carolina.)

The remaining components apply mostly to performance funding.

- *Funding weights* assign the same or different values to the indicators, or allow some campus choice.

- *Success standards* for the indicators call for improved performance for each campus, comparisons with the results of state or national peers, or a combination of these criteria. (Some performance budgeting programs also have this component.)

- *Funding levels* comprise a percentage of state support for campus operating budgets. (The levels for current programs range from 0.5 percent to about 6 percent, and average around 2 percent.)

- *Funding sources* involve additional or reallocated resources, or a combination of the two. (Nearly all programs call for additional monies beyond base budgets.)

- *Allocation methods* consist of base budget increases or annual bonuses based on performance. (Most programs increase the budget base.)

- *Funding types* are competitive or noncompetitive among public campuses. (Most programs are noncompetitive, allowing campuses to earn only their assigned level of performance. A few permit high-performing institutions to gain funds beyond their assigned levels from monies not earned by other campuses.)

Performance Funding

Performance funding exhibits the conflicting characteristics of popularity and instability. Over a third of the states now have such programs. While its number grew from 9 to 17 since 1996, Arkansas, Colorado, Kentucky, Minnesota, and Washington abandoned their programs during the same period. Clearly, the desirability of performance funding in theory is matched by its difficulties in practice. It is easier to adopt than to implement and simpler to start than to sustain. Projections suggest some future growth with two states considered highly likely and five likely to adopt the program. But they also reveal the resistance to performance funding in state capitals and on public campuses. Three states seem highly unlikely and fifteen unlikely to have the program in the next five years. State finance officers cannot predict the program's future in eight states.[9]

Table 1: Performance Funding	
Number (Percentage)	*States*
17 states (34%)	California*, Colorado, Connecticut, Florida, Illinois*, Kansas, Louisiana, Missouri, New Jersey, New York**, Ohio, Oklahoma, Pennsylvania, South Carolina, South Dakota, Tennessee, Texas
* 2-year colleges only ** State University of New York System only	

Performance Budgeting

Performance budgeting is even more popular and certainly more stable. Its programs expanded from less than a third of the states in 1997 to more than half in 2000. Twenty-eight states now have the program and eleven more seem likely to adopt it. Nearly half of these performance budgeting programs for public campuses are part of a general plan for all or some state agencies. Twenty-two states currently mandate performance budgeting for their state agencies.[10]

Table 2: Performance Budgeting	
Number (Percentage)	*States*
28 states (56%)	Alabama, California, Connecticut, Florida, Georgia, Hawaii, Idaho, Illinois, Iowa, Kansas, Louisiana, Maine, Maryland, Massachusetts, Michigan, Mississippi, Missouri, Nebraska, Nevada, New Jersey, New Mexico, North Carolina, Oklahoma, Oregon, Texas, Utah, Virginia, Wisconsin

Dual Programs

Ten states have both performance funding and performance budgeting for public colleges and universities. Having both programs allows a state to achieve the benefits and counter the problems of each approach. Performance funding provides the clarity of allocating specific sums on each indicator. Adding performance budgeting gives governors, legislators, and coordinating and system boards the discretion to consider additional allocations based on total campus performance, usually on a longer list of indicators. The first adds certainty; the second offers flexibility.

Common Challenges

Despite their important differences, performance funding and budgeting share some of the same challenges. The inputs of critical stakeholders, methods of initiation, and timing of program implementation affect the stability of performance funding more than performance budgeting. The same is true for the details of program design, the emphases on policy values, and the resolution of major difficulties.

A proper start will not guarantee the longevity of either program, but success is unlikely without it. Three methods exist for initiating performance funding and budgeting in ascending order of effectiveness.

1. *Mandated/Prescribed*: Legislation mandates the program and prescribes the indicators.

2. *Mandated/Not Prescribed*: Legislation mandates the program but allows state coordinating agencies in cooperation with campus leaders to propose the indicators.

3. *Not Mandated*: Coordinating or university system boards in collaboration with campus officials voluntarily adopt the plan without legislation.

Mandates, and especially prescriptions, undermine program stability, because they are imposed and ignore the importance of consultation with coordinating, system, and campus officials. No consultation means no consent. According to the new management theories, government officials should decide policy directions and evaluate performance and leave the details to organizational managers. Many of the early programs in both performance funding and performance budgeting ignored this maxim. Four of the five programs that dropped performance funding mandated the program and three prescribed the indicators.

Legislation mandates performance budgeting in nearly half of the current programs but prescribes the indicators in only two. Statutes started performance funding in slightly over a third of the programs and also prescribed the indicators in two states. The newer initiatives for both programs show a welcome move away from mandates and prescriptions. This change reflects the trend in state government to reduce mandates and regulations.

Most of the non-mandated programs came from state coordinating boards for higher education, but more college and university systems are launching programs on their own. University systems in New York and Pennsylvania, and the community college systems in California and Illinois, have adopted their own plan for allocating some resources based on campus performance.

Whatever the method of initiation, performance funding and performance budgeting require continuing support from state, coordinating, systems, and campus leaders. State officials can mandate and prescribe the programs, but the initiatives cannot succeed without the participation of coordinating and system leaders who monitor the policies, and of faculty and administrators who produce the results. Coordinating and system officials can voluntarily initiate either program, but only governors and legislators can supply the funding.

Both performance funding and performance budgeting in varying degrees must cope with conceptual and practical difficulties. Choosing performance indicators, assessing higher education results, and protecting mission diversity and campus autonomy present special challenges. The many objectives in higher education make selecting a limited number of indicators a perplexing problem. The ambiguity of objectives and the lack of agreement on how to measure their achievement complicate the task of assessing results in higher education. Designing a funding program that not only covers but also fits a wide diversity of campus types and missions presents another difficulty. Finally, both programs must specify and support particular priorities without diminishing the campus autonomy required for institutional diversity and faculty creativity.

Other practical problems plague both programs. They include the timing of program planning and implementation, the costs of data collection and analysis, and the changes in state priorities and leaders. Implementing complex and controversial programs also takes time. Complexity of program design, controversy over critical components, consultation with multiple stakeholders, and collection of required data demand a lengthy period for planning and implementation. Achieving results in higher education also takes time. State priorities and program requirements must continue long enough to allow campuses to produce and evaluate the desired and demanding results. Despite this need for continuity, state priorities fluctuate with changes in governors and legislators and shifts in constituent interests and pressing issues. The costs of data collection and analysis for tracking and assessing institutional results add another burden to strained campus budgets and staffs.

Some State Examples

Some states coped with these challenges better than others. The examples used come from performance funding, because it offers the most striking cases of the challenges entailed in developing programs that relate state resources to campus performance. The samples selected include dropped programs that illustrate potential difficulties, and stable programs that identify successful approaches.

South Carolina initiated the most restrictive program. A joint committee of business and legislative leaders designed a radical plan to reform higher education with almost no consultation with campus leaders or educational experts. Legislation mandated funding based "entirely" on performance and prescribed a lengthy list of 37 indicators. Mark Musik, President of the Southern Regional Education Board, called this program "a Star Trek voyage into uncharted territory."[11] After two years of trying to make this unprecedented plan work, amidst campus complaints of budget instability, the coordinating board finally abandoned full funding for a limited performance pool, which restricted losses or gains to about 5 percent of campus operating budgets.[12]

Colorado is the only state that abandoned performance funding and then readopted it. That state's aborted effort hurriedly implemented legislation mandating a complex program prescribing numerous indicators. Changes in legislative leadership and opposition from campus leaders killed this first attempt.[13] Colorado's new initiative mandated a program with general policy goals and allowed the coordinating board, in consultation with campus officials, to develop the indicators.

Kentucky's abandoned program in performance funding illustrates the problem of changing governors, coupled with campus resistance. A Democratic governor mandated a reform program and promised increased campus funding in return for campus cooperation. He delivered the funding. But passive resistance from campus leaders, and squabbles with the coordinating board over the indicators, undermined this initiative. A new governor, also a Democrat, substituted his own initiative, which allocated money for promised rather than achieved performance from public colleges and universities. This "tale of two governors" demonstrates the reality that few governors, even from the same party, make their name by pushing their predecessor's plans.[14]

The established programs in Tennessee and Missouri represent classic examples of performance funding adopted by coordinating boards without legislation or prescription. They illustrate the importance of careful design, full consultation, phased implementation, and periodic reviews. Most important of all, these programs built upon a long tradition of assessing the outcomes of student learning. Missouri and Tennessee led the nation in developing assessment programs that evaluated the knowledge and skills possessed by students at entry and their growth and development by graduation. Both programs had the goal of demonstrating external accountability, but they focused on institutional improvement and favored quality over efficiency in their indicators. Although the coordinating boards in both states adopted their programs voluntarily, these initiatives also reflected external concerns. Tennessee, without the prospect of enrollment increases, hoped for added state funding by emphasizing quality performance. Missouri's plan represented a preemptive strike to avoid the possibility of a state mandate.[15]

Performance Indicators

Both champions and critics concur that selection of performance indicators constitutes a critical choice in performance funding and budgeting. The indicators picked provide clues to the concerns and values of state policymakers about public higher education and offer insights into their preferred models of excellence for state colleges and universities. Both programs seem to select from a common core of indicators. The indicators obviously respond to external criticism of the performance of public colleges and universities. For example, they stress undergraduate education and include few indicators for research and graduate study.

Nearly all of the programs for funding or budgeting include re-tention/graduation rates. Other indicators used in about half of the states include test scores on professional licensure exams, student transfers from two- to four-year campuses, job placements, and sat-isfaction surveys of students and alumni. Some programs include efficiency measures, such as teaching loads, administrative costs, and time-to-degree. Several plans include indicators on com-puter-assisted instruction and distance learning, reflecting the emerging role of technology in higher education and the increasing demand to reduce instructional costs. Indicators on access and affordability in undergraduate education are found in western states with burgeoning student demand and in eastern states with high tuition and fees.[16]

Table 3: Performance Indicators	
Ranked by Frequency	
1. Retention/Graduation Rates	10. Administration Size/Costs
2. Professional Licensure Test Scores	11. Undergraduate Access
3. Time-to-Degrees	12. Class Size
4. Faculty Work Loads	13. Undergraduate Affordability
5. Alumni Satisfaction Surveys	14. Student/Faculty Ratios
6. Job Placements	15. Test Scores in General Education and Academic Majors
7. Program Accreditation	16. Supporting K-12 Reforms
8. Program Review	17. Teacher Preparation
9. Sponsored Research	

It is understandable that funding programs claiming to move from inputs to results should focus on output and slight input mea-sures. The surprise is the inclusion of process indicators in pro-grams that supposedly stress outcomes as well as outputs. Performance funding and budgeting use few input indicators, such as test scores and high school averages of new students or the fund-ing per student. Both include many output measures, which show the quantity of graduates and services produced, such as the num-ber of degrees granted, and graduation rates of admitted students. Outcome indicators that assess the quality of student learning and the long-term impact on states and society are few. Aside from

Missouri and Tennessee, which rely on standardized test scores for general education and academic majors, most programs assess learning outcomes and societal impact through satisfaction surveys of students, alumni, and — to a lesser extent — employers. Process measures — such as program review, administrative cost, and class size — reflect the difficulty of assessing outcomes and results in higher education. They also replicate the focus on improving processes in total quality management.

The indicators reveal the attitudes of program developers toward the traditional policy values of efficiency, quality, choice, and equity. Although the indicators suggest more emphasis on efficiency than quality, they also show a strong interest in measures that combine both values. This combination of efficiency and quality suggests a new notion in state capitals — not shared on most campuses — that the two values complement each other rather than conflict. Performance funding and budgeting programs contain fewer equity indicators than do the earlier performance reports, reflecting the move away from affirmative action policies in higher education in the late 1990s. The performance indicators also exhibit little interest in the academic model of institutional excellence based on resources and reputation. Instead, they support a combined cost/benefit and client-centered model based on the quality, quantity, and costs of services to students and states.[17]

Characteristics of Stable Programs

A study comparing the survey responses from the mature programs in Missouri and Tennessee with those from the four states that dropped performance funding suggests that stable programs exhibit the following characteristics.[18] Although this study looks only at performance funding, the findings also apply to performance budgeting.

1. *Collaboration between governors and legislators, state coordinating and university system officials, and campus leaders and trustees.*
   Collaboration among all these stakeholders is essential, but leadership by coordinating agencies that

have credibility with all constituencies is critical. With a foot in both camps, coordinating officials can mediate the conflicting interests of government officials and campus constituents.

2. *Goals of institutional improvement, external accountability, meeting state needs, and increased state funding for public higher education.*
   Despite inherent tensions between institutional improvement and external accountability, state-funded programs for public colleges and universities cannot survive for long without satisfying both goals. Campus leaders often prefer institutional improvement and complain about external accountability, because they view the former as stressing quality and the latter as emphasizing efficiency. In addition, they see institutional improvement as moving up the ladder on the resource and reputation model of excellence. Governors and legislators naturally demand evidence that performance funding or budgeting increases accountability, but they also desire institutional improvement of programs and services. Meeting state needs constitutes an essential goal in a competitive global economy driven by knowledge and information. The prospect of more state funding offers a needed incentive for campus cooperation.

3. *Policy values stressing quality more than efficiency.*
   Quality is the hallmark of higher education. All public programs should incorporate both quality and efficiency, but the fundamental purpose of pursuing quality in educational institutions makes it a primary priority. Even state policymakers acknowledge that efficiency, while desirable in its own right, is diminished unless coupled with quality programs and services.

4. *Sufficient time for planning and implementation.*
   Planning and implementation usually take longer than state policymakers think necessary, but seldom

long enough to satisfy campus leaders. Government officials must realize that achieving results in higher education takes time; and campus leaders must recognize that it cannot take forever. Perfection is never possible and progress comes with practice. Pilot projects and phased implementation of indicators and funding is the best approach.

5. *Neither too few nor too many **performance indicators**.*
Too few indicators ignore too many of the multiple objectives of colleges and universities. Too many indicators trivialize major priorities with too little funding. A reasonable number for comprehensive programs might range from 8 to 15. Two- and four-year colleges should have some common and some different indicators to reflect their shared and diverse missions.

6. ***Assessment*** *of the knowledge and skills achieved by graduates.*
Commitment to assessing student learning will not ensure stability, but success is unlikely without it. Missouri and Tennessee built on strong traditions in assessment. In contrast, the legislative and business leaders that developed performance funding in South Carolina largely ignored the experience of that state's extensive and effective assessment network. Satisfaction surveys of alumni can assess good practices and perceptions of quality in student learning, while work continues on more objective ways to measure desired knowledge and skills, especially in general education.

7. ***Success standards*** *emphasizing institutional improvement or quality maintenance, supplemented by peer comparisons.*
The diverse types and multiple missions of public campuses make institutional fairness and funding equity essential elements of performance funding and budgeting. The fairest standard of success looks first

at institutional improvement and then at performance in comparison with similar colleges or universities, both in and out of state. The first consideration supports campus differences; the second ensures comparable standards. Programs should follow the practice in Missouri and Tennessee of avoiding competition among campuses for performance funding. In those states, each institution can earn only its share of performance funding. Campus allocations depend on their own results and not on the performance of other institutions.

8. *Limited but substantial and discretionary funding.*
   Limited funding prevents budget instability. Substantial funding recognizes the difficulty of producing results in higher education. About 3 to 6 percent of state operating support seems a reasonable amount. Discretionary allocations — as opposed to targeted funds — make even small amounts effective, when mandated expenditures absorb most of campus budgets.

9. *Additional rather than reallocated resources as the funding source.*
   Additional money makes performance funding or budgeting a desirable project on campus. It becomes a funded initiative rather than another activity competing for limited resources.

10. *Continuity of state priorities and program requirements.*
    State priorities and program requirements must continue long enough to allow campuses to produce the desired and demanding results. Performance funding and budgeting require a patience and persistence rarely found in state budgeting and policymaking. If governors and legislators want improved performance from state colleges and universities, they must abandon their penchant for swift solutions and instant success.

Arguments For and Against:
Rhetoric and Reality

Arguments about both programs, but especially performance funding, have generated more heat than light. Governors, legislators, and their staffs, along with business leaders, generally champion the advantages. Campus presidents, vice presidents, academic deans, and faculty leaders usually criticize the problems.[19] The arguments focus on different points in the process. Advocates applaud its ends and goals, while adversaries attack its means and implementation. Champions commend the potential benefits, while slighting the practical problems. Critics concentrate on the problems, while dismissing the possible benefits. Although adversaries argue about implementation difficulties, many privately oppose both programs, especially performance funding, since they really favor traditional budgeting. Attacking the problems of design and implementation allows them to avoid the appearance of resisting accountability for their performance.

The proponents have the best media sound bites. They merely assert why the program should be done, without defending how it could be done. Their opponents have the negative position — prized by debaters — of attacking a proposal without offering an alternative. Advocates follow the common fallacy in state government of adopting a new program and neglecting its execution. Adversaries exhibit a common fault on campus of condemning new proposals without examining the flaws in current practices.

As is so often the case in such controversies, performance funding and performance budgeting are neither as good as their champions contend nor as bad as their critics complain. Both sides are partly right and partly wrong. The goals proposed by proponents are worthy, but the problems posed by opponents are weighty. Considered together, they could help build programs that achieve the possibilities of performance funding and budgeting while addressing their problems. These arguments deserve careful consideration by state and campus policymakers when they consider initiating or revising their funding programs.

Arguments For

1. *Adds performance as a factor in state funding and budgeting.*

   This rhetoric about budgeting for results exaggerates the reality of both performance funding and budgeting. In many programs, process measures exceed output and outcomes indicators, which directly reflect institutional results. Moreover, funding for performance remains small in most states. Workload factors of current budgets, student enrollments, and inflationary increases still determine nearly all of the funding. Performance funding and budgeting really represent more of a conceptual than a funding shift.

2. *Links planning and budgeting.*

   Budgeting for inputs disconnects budgets from planning; and plans unconnected to budgets stay on the shelf. Setting goals, determining actions, and funding priorities form the trinity of effective planning. Two factors limit the potential for linking performance funding and budgeting to campus planning. First, the small amounts allocated for the programs diminish their actual impact on planning. Second is the lack of visibility of both programs on campuses below the senior administrations, and the absence of performance in internal campus budgeting for schools and departments.

3. *Pushes state officials to identify their priorities and encourages dialogue with campus leaders.*

   Traditionally, educational leaders had to surmise state priorities from budget documents, random comments from state officials, or periodic reports from special commissions. The absence of stated goals for higher education leaves governors and legislators free to shift their priorities for higher education to satisfy political exigencies and constituent complaints. Performance funding and performance budgeting force state officials to set or accept some priorities for public colleges and universities.[20] Although both programs offer an opportunity for dialogue between public officials and campus administrators, they seldom require it in practice. The initial plan in Colorado did mandate such discussions. It required annual meetings of a committee composed of the governor and legislative leaders and coordinating board and campus representatives to set the policy areas of performance funding. Unfortunately, the requirement for annual meetings encouraged frequent and sudden shifts in state priorities.

4. *Fosters both external accountability and institutional improvement.*
   Although all performance programs claim to pursue both accountability and improvement, in practice, the performance indicators usually stress one purpose over the other. Despite this emphasis on indicators, both programs use institutional improvement as their criterion for success. Campus and state leaders cite both increased accountability and institutional improvement as two of the advantages of performance funding. [21]

5. *Presses campuses to become more client- and less provider-centered.*
   Performance helps transform public campuses from provider-centered enterprises driven by the aspirations of administrators and faculty into client-centered organizations focused on the needs of students and society. Students constitute the most favored clients in these performance programs, but they also respond to the needs of states, businesses, and public schools.

6. *Centers attention on undergraduate education.*
   The objectives of both programs center almost exclusively on undergraduate education. This emphasis responds to external complaints. State officials and business leaders complain about the quality and

quantity of faculty teaching and student learning, the preoccupation with graduate studies and research, and the neglect of undergraduate education. Critics charge that baccalaureate campuses admit too many unqualified undergraduates, devote too many resources to correcting their deficiencies, graduate too few of the students admitted, and permit too many to take too long to obtain degrees. They also claim that too many graduates lack the knowledge and skills required for successful careers in an economy driven by technology and information. The indicators used in performance funding and budgeting clearly address these complaints.

7. *Rewards good and penalizes poor performance.*
   All of the programs purport to reward the good and punish the poor performance of state colleges and universities. In spite of this announced intention, the success standards and rating scales in practice limit large institutional losses or funding shifts among campuses. The compromises and concessions necessary to gain consensus, or at least to diminish dissent, tend to prevent large swings in funding. The performance standards and benchmarks adopted for colleges and universities seem set to encourage, if not ensure, success. The program motto might read: "Reward or punish, but not too much or too quickly."

8. *Decentralizes authority without undermining accountability.*
   Performance programs often trade more operational flexibility for increased attention to institutional results. They focus on the objectives assigned to public colleges and universities and leave the means of achieving these ends to the individual institutions. Critics welcome the greater flexibility, but fear that funding may become a more forceful and insidious form of control than regulations. The precedent of federal funding for faculty research — especially from the Defense Department — demonstrates the

power of funding to determine priorities without the approval of campus officers or governing boards. Critics also complain that, despite the rhetoric of concentrating on results, performance funding and budgeting often attempt to control means. These programs include indicators on faculty teaching loads, administrative size, and the distribution of campus budgets among the major organizational functions. Apparently, governors and legislators concerned about swelling bureaucracies and declining teaching loads could not resist reverting to form by including indicators that attempt to control these practices. Some critics see performance programs as the "old accountability" writ even larger to include means as well as ends.

Arguments Against

1. *Fails because of the difficulty of assessing results in higher education.*

   More than two-thirds of the campus respondents to our nine state survey cite the difficulty of measuring the results of higher education as a major problem of performance funding.[22] This complaint also extends to performance budgeting. Most commentators on higher education concede the difficulty of measuring the results of undergraduate education.[23]

   Performance funding and budgeting clearly struggle with this obvious difficulty. Few performance programs even try to evaluate directly the knowledge and skills possessed by graduates. Only 3 of the 11 states in our study of performance funding include test scores on standardized exams for general education or academic majors as a measure of performance.[24] More of them do use licensure exams, which seem more acceptable because they are limited to professional fields, where external authorities require passage for practice. Despite this opposition to standardized tests as valid measures of educational outcomes, both administrators and faculty complain that few of the indicators in performance programs assessed the quality of undergraduate education.

Many outsiders believe that standardized tests can measure the learning outcomes of undergraduate education as they do for public schools. But critics complain that tests can never assess the complex results or capture the elusive character of quality in undergraduate education. State policymakers may agree that only educators can determine the means for evaluating learning outcomes, but they will never accept the response that it cannot be done.

2. *Diminishes the diversity of campus missions.*
Critics claim that no single program could reflect — much less encourage — campus differences in type and mission. This problem obviously concerned program designers, who often included representatives from a range of campuses. They selected success standards and rating systems to protect institutional differences. Most of the programs use institutional improvement as their standard for success and set targets by comparisons with campuses in the same sectors.[25] Some programs allow campuses to choose several indicators that emphasize their diverse missions. Most plans also allow some different and some common indicators for two- and four-year institutions. These precautions have not silenced complaints that performance funding disadvantages small campuses with low enrollments and two-year colleges that emphasize vocational training rather than baccalaureate transfer. Many graduate and research universities also contend correctly that the indicators slight the importance of their graduate and research missions.

3. *Produces budget instability.*
The small sums allocated for performance in both programs tend in practice to prevent budget instability. In addition, the setting of weights, standards, and

scoring in performance funding reduces the possible swings in budgets. The campus fear of budget instability appears to represent more anxiety than reality.

4. *Punishes the poorest institutions.*

   This argument reflects the reality that the amount of resources often affects the level of performance. Using institutional improvement as a success standard and peer comparisons as an institutional benchmark reduces the possibility of penalizing campuses with the least resources. Critics do charge correctly that removing resources from institutions with poor performance will only make improvement more difficult, if not impossible. Performance programs could avoid this problem by placing funds not earned by poor performing campuses in escrow and releasing them when these institutions submit acceptable improvement plans for remediation.

5. *Combines the incompatible purposes of external accountability and institutional improvement.*

   The claim of incompatibility comes from champions of student outcomes assessment, who believe that accountability and improvement cannot be achieved in a single program.[26] The information needed for external accountability, these critics contend, differs from the evidence required for institutional improvement. External accountability focuses on results, while institutional improvement flows from activities. The former presents campus results, while the latter indicates the changes in activities and programs required to improve performance. In reality, external accountability and institutional improvement are complementary and inseparable, for evidence of anything less than good or improved performance can never satisfy external accountability.

6. *Creates excessive costs for data collection and analysis.*

   A constant complaint is the high cost of data collection required for performance programs. No current analysis of the costs of these activities appears to be available. A report from one national study in 1996 noted campus concerns about the increased costs of data collection on institutions, which already face heavy burdens of reporting to state and federal governments, accreditation agencies, and college guides. On the other hand, the report's authors perceived the concerns as confined primarily to the development phase.[27] The best response to the complaint is to examine carefully whether the information derived from each indicator is worth the cost of data collection, and whether with some revision the databases could satisfy several purposes.[28]

7. *Stresses efficiency over quality.*
   Critics charge that performance funding and budgeting programs stress efficiency over quality. Although indicators implying efficiency do constitute a higher percentage than those reflecting quality, about one-fifth of the indicators combine the policy values of both efficiency and quality.[29]

8. *Subjects higher education to shifting state priorities.*
   Critics insist that politics in an age of term limits and changing issues shift state priorities too frequently for performance programs. The history of performance funding confirms this complaint. Arkansas, Colorado, Kentucky, and Minnesota dropped the program because of both shifting administrations and changing priorities. Such shifts and changes also affect performance budgeting, but in a different way. Few of its programs are dropped. More often, new leaders interested in different issues gradually pay less attention to performance results in state budgeting. Performance funding often ends with dramatic death, while performance budgeting usually withers from debilitating neglect.

   Performance funding and budgeting offer two advantages that help to avoid sudden shifts in state priorities. Governors and legislators have officially set the priorities in performance programs or endorsed them in annual budget documents. Such actions give these priorities an official status that makes them more difficult to change. The second advantage is more meaningful. The priorities expressed in these performance programs are not new, for they have already persisted for over a decade and a half. Governors and legislators have repeatedly challenged public colleges and universities to become more efficient and effective in meeting the needs of their students and their states. Their concerns have also continued: retention and graduation rates; job placements; student transfers between two- and four-year institutions; growth of administrative positions; decline of faculty teaching loads; and the satisfaction of students, alumni, and employers.

9. *Favors traditional over nontraditional campuses.*
The provisions in performance funding programs are often unfair to two-year colleges and baccalaureate campuses with nontraditional programs and students. Many of the indicators seem set for traditional baccalaureate campuses with full-time enrollments rather than the part-time students of community and technical colleges and urban universities. Community colleges and urban universities contend correctly that this emphasis on full-time enrollments penalizes them for meeting the diverse needs of nontraditional students.

Impact on Institutional Improvement

Of course, the bottom line in assessing both performance funding and budgeting is the extent to which each has improved institutional performance. A realistic assessment is still premature, since nearly all of these programs are products of the 1990s, and most have been implemented for only a few years. Still, it is not too early to start a preliminary assessment of their effect on performance. The 2000 Survey asked State Higher Education Finance Officers to assess the effect of performance funding or performance budgeting on improving campus performance.[30] Results confirm that it is still too soon to assess their effect, given the short history of both programs. The results do suggest that performance funding has much more effect than performance budgeting and that the impact of both approaches increases in relation to the clarity and the level of the fiscal consequences.

Nearly half of the finance officers from states with performance funding say it is too early to evaluate the impact of the program on institutional improvement. But 35 percent claim that the program has improved performance to a great or considerable extent. They cite "great extent" in South Carolina and Tennessee and "considerable extent" in Connecticut, Missouri, Ohio, and Oklahoma. Respondents indicate "some extent" in South Dakota and "little extent" in Florida and Texas. Program duration and funding levels clearly affect these estimates. Tennessee, Missouri, South Carolina, and Ohio have had programs for some time and have supported them with considerable funding. Although Florida's effort has existed for five years, its university sector has received scant funding in the last few budgets.

Although performance budgeting has a somewhat longer history, almost a third of the finance officers in states where the program exists consider it too early to assess the impact. No program gets a rating of "great extent." Respondents believe performance budgeting has improved campus performance to a considerable extent in 18 percent, and to some extent in 7 percent of the programs. However, they think performance budgeting has had little effect in 36 percent of the existing programs, and no effect in 29 percent. All of the programs cited as having considerable or some effect also have coordinating or system boards that consider performance in campus allocation.

The effect of both programs on improved performance appears to depend on fiscal consequences, which is the rationale for both performance budgeting and performance funding. The loose link of performance to allocation in performance budgeting, as opposed to the tight tie in performance funding, seems to explain why the former appears to have a lesser impact on performance.

The Higher Education Program at the Rockefeller Institute also surveyed state and campus policymakers' attitudes toward performance funding in late 1996 and early 1997.[31] The responses came from over 900 respondents in nine states with performance funding at that time. A critical question asked the extent to which performance funding had achieved its avowed goals of increasing the accountability and improving the performance of public higher education.

The results reveal the division between state and campus leaders. In general, state policymakers cite a more positive impact on enhancing accountability and improving performance than did campus officers. Over 50 percent of the state officials saw a positive impact on both accountability and improvement, although slightly less on improvement. A majority of campus leaders believed the program had a positive impact on accountability, but most considered it too soon to assess the impact on institutional improvement.[32]

Merging Models

Merging performance funding and budgeting could achieve the advantages and avoid the disadvantages of each program. The key is to clarify the funding connection of performance budgeting, and to increase the flexibility of performance funding. The 2000 Survey of State Higher Education Finance Officers shows that these changes are already occurring.[33] The newer programs in performance budgeting are clarifying the connection of resources to performance. Alabama and California join Oklahoma and Oregon in earmarking funds for performance. In addition, coordinating or system boards in Maryland, Missouri, Utah, and Wisconsin consider campus performance in institutional allocations. Only Nevada, among the new programs, takes neither approach. Overall, nearly 40 percent of the states with performance budgeting now have coordinating or system boards considering performance in institutional allocations.

If the new initiatives in performance budgeting attempt to address its problem of uncertainty, several of those in performance funding try to alleviate its defect of inflexibility. Many early efforts at performance funding suffered from rigid mandates that sought radical reform of public higher education. They imposed lengthy lists of statewide indicators that discouraged campus diversity and tied annual funding to institutional results that take years to improve. The newer programs reduce the rigidities of those earlier efforts.

In the last two years, most of the initiatives have come from coordinating and — especially system — boards rather than from legislative mandates. Community college systems in California and Illinois initiated their own programs, as did university systems in New York and Pennsylvania. Legislative prescription of performance indicators — found in earlier programs — has become rare.

Many of the newer programs, including the renewed effort in Colorado, permit campuses to select two indicators related to their strategic plan. The newer plans also tend to have more limited objectives and use fewer indicators than early performance funding programs. Most of the recent plans also permit lead-time for program development and campus consultation before implementation. This careful approach contrasts with the hurried implementation of many programs in place in 1997.

Several of the newer initiatives also link performance funding to multi-year plans. The Partnership for Excellence between California and its Community College System spreads consideration of performance over seven years. The System for Higher Education in Pennsylvania ties funding to institutional performance over four years. Louisiana's program has a five-year time line, with institutions presenting annual operational plans. A stalled effort in Virginia, which is highly likely to receive future approval, involves Institutional Performance Agreements for six years, which include statewide and campus indicators linked to institutional strategic plans.

These changes certainly blur the differences between performance funding and budgeting. They may foreshadow the emergence of a merged model, which retains the advantages and avoids the disadvantages of both programs. The link of state resources to campus results represents the main distinction between performance budgeting and performance funding. This distinction diminishes when performance budgeting commits more coordinating and system boards to consider performance in campus allocations. It almost disappears when programs earmark state funds for campus results. If these trends continue, they could produce a merged model for linking state resources to campus results that is both certain and flexible, and more effective in practice and acceptable to campuses.

Conclusion

The faults of performance funding and budgeting flow mostly from detailed prescriptions, inadequate consultation, poor design, hurried implementation, and an unclear or inflexible connection to funding. Recent developments in both programs suggest creative ways to address those problems. But the fatal flaw for both approaches is the reluctance of the academic community to identify and assess the knowledge and skills that college graduates should possess. Unfortunately, public debate over these programs has not centered on fixing those faults or that flaw. Champions, mostly from state capitals and the business community, focus on the attractive possibilities of those programs. Critics, mostly from campuses, fixate on what they consider intractable problems. The former tend to ignore the complexity of those programs and view campus complaints as a refusal to accept accountability for performance. The latter often dismiss the possibility of relating resources to results and view any effort as a plot to run campuses like businesses.

It is still too soon to tell whether the present versions of performance funding or budgeting represent fads or trends. But one conclusion is becoming clear. Public higher education is too important to states and their citizens to fund only inputs and ignore results. Taxpayers are unlikely to accept forever the proposition that performance should count in all endeavors except state funding of higher education. Academics are too good at criticizing the performance of outside organizations to plead the impossibility of assessing their own performance.

Results will eventually count in the funding of public colleges and universities. The real questions are whether the link between funding and performance will be loose or tight, how to assess campus results, and whether academics will lead, or leave the action to outsiders. Recent developments in both programs suggest creative ways to use performance in budgeting and funding. Only time will tell whether state and especially campus policymakers will have the will to use them.

Endnotes

1   National Association of State Budget Officers, *The Fiscal Survey of the States* (Washington, DC.: author,1997, 1998).

2   J. Burke, J. Rosen, H. Minassians, and T. Lessard, *Performance Funding and Budgeting: An Emerging Merger: The Fourth Annual Survey* (Albany: Rockefeller Institute of Government, 2000).

3   David Osborne, Ted Gaebler, *Reinventing Government: How the Entrepreneurial Spirit Is Transforming the Public Sector* (Reading, MA: Addison-Wesley 1992); Michael Hammer, and James Champy, *Reengineering the Corporation: A Manifesto For Business Revolution* (New York: Harperbusiness, 1993).

4   Alexander Astin, *Achieving Educational Excellence: A Critical Assessment of Priorities and Practices in Higher Education* (San Francisco: Jossey-Bass, 1985), Chapter 2.

5   Steven Gold, *Fiscal Crisis of the States: Lessons for the Future* (Washington, D.C.:Georgetown Press, 1995), Chapter 5.

6   Burke et al., *Performance Funding and Budgeting*, p. 11.

7   Melodie Christal, *State Survey on Performance Measures: 1996-97* (Denver: SHEEO 1998); Mary McKeown, *State Funding Formulas for Public Four-Year Institutions* (Denver: SHEEO 1996).

8   Burke et. al., *Performance Funding and Budgeting*, pp. 2-4.

9   Burke et. al., *Performance Funding and Budgeting*, pp. 7-10.

10 Ibid, pp. 4-7.

11 Conversation with the author.

12 Joseph Burke, "Performance Funding in South Carolina: From Fringe to Mainstream," *Assessment Update* (November-December), 121, 6: 4-5, 16.

13 Joseph Burke and Andreea Serban, "Performance Funding for Public Higher Education: Fad or Trend?" *New Directions in Institutional Research* No. 97 (Spring). 1998: 28-30.

14 Ibid, 32-35.

15 Ibid, 37-40, 45-47.

16 Joseph Burke, *Performance Funding Indicators: Concerns, Values, and Models for Two- and Four-Year Colleges and Universities* (Albany: Rockefeller Institute of Government, 1997).

17   Ibid, pp. 13-16.

18   Joseph C. Burke and Shahpar Modarresi, "To Keep or Not to Keep Performance Funding: Signals from Stakeholders," *The Journal of Higher Education* (July/August 2000), 71, 4: 432-453.

19   J. Kent Caruthers and Daniel Layzell, "Performance Funding at the State Level: Trends and Prospects." Paper presented at the annual meeting of the Association for the Study of Higher Education, Orlando, 1996; A. M. Serban. "Performance Funding for Public Higher Education: Views of Critical Stakeholders," in Burke, and Serban (eds.), *Current Status and Future Prospects of Performance Funding and Performance Budgeting for Public Higher Education: The Second Survey.* (Albany: Rockefeller Institute of Government, 1997).

20   John Folger and Denis Jones, *Using Fiscal Policy to Achieve State Education* (Denver: Education Commission of States, 1993).

21   Serban, "Views of Critical Stakeholders," pp. 26-29.

22   Ibid, 29.

23   Gerald Gaither et al. *Measuring Up: The Promises and Pitfalls of Performance Indicators in Higher Education. ASHE/ERIC Higher Education Report.* (Washington, D.C.: George Washington Press, 1996)

24   Burke & Serban, "Performance Funding: Fad or Trend?" Chapter 4.

25   Ibid, chapter 5.

26   Peter Ewell, "The Current Patterns of State-Level Assessment: Results of National Inventory," in G. H. Gaither (ed.), *Performance Indicators in Higher Education.* (College Park, MD: Ashe-Eric Higher Education Reports, 1996).

27   M. Gray, *Enhancing The Quality and Use of Student Outcomes Data: The Final Report of the NPEC Working Group on Student Outcomes from a Data Perspective.* Washington, D.C., 1996.

28   Thomas Freeman, "Performance Indicators and Assessment in the State University of New York System," in Gerald Gaither (ed.). "Assessing Performance in an Age of Accountability: Case Studies," *New Directions for Higher Education* 91 (San Francisco, 1995): 25-50.

29   Joseph C. Burke. *Performance Funding Indicators* (Albany, N.Y.: Rockefeller Institute of Government, 1997).

30   Burke et al., *Performance Funding and Budgeting: An Emerging Merger,* pp. 11-12.

31   Serban, "Views of Stakeholders," pp. 7-34.

32   Ibid, 30.

33   Burke et al. *Performance Funding and Budgeting: An Emerging Merger,* pp. 13-14.

References

Astin, A. W. 1985. *Achieving Educational Excellence: A Critical Assessment of Priorities and Practices in Higher Education.* San Francisco: Jossey-Bass Publishers.

Burke, J. C. 1997. "Performance Funding Indicators: Concerns, Values, and Models For Two- and Four-Year Colleges and Universities." Albany, N.Y.: Rockefeller Institute for Government.

Burke, J. C. 1999. "Performance Funding in South Carolina: From Fringe to Mainstream," *Assessment Update* (November-December), 121, 6: 4-5, 16.

Burke, Joseph C. and Shahpar Modarresi. 2000. "To Keep or Not to Keep Performance Funding: Signals from Stakeholders," *The Journal of Higher Education* (July/August), 71, 4.

Burke, J. C., J. Rosen, H. Minassians, and T. Lessard. 2000. *Performance Funding and Budgeting: An Emerging Merger: The Fourth Annual Survey.* Albany, N.Y.: The Rockefeller Institute for Government.

Burke, J. C. and A. M. Serban. 1998. "Performance Funding for Public Higher Education: Fad or Trend?" *New Directions in Institutional Research*, 97 (Spring). San Francisco: Jossey-Bass.

Burke, J. C. and A. M. Serban. 1998. *Current Status and Future Prospects of Performance Funding and Performance Budgeting for Public Higher Education: The Second Survey.* Albany, N.Y.: Rockefeller Institute for Government.

Caruthers, J. K. and D. T. Layzell. 1996. "Performance Funding at the State Level: Trends and Prospects." Paper presented at the annual meeting for the Association for the Study of Higher Education. Orlando, FL.

Christal, M. E. 1998. *State Survey on Performance Measures: 1996-97.* Denver: State Higher Education Executive Officers.

Ewell, P. T. 1996. "The current patterns of state-level assessment: Results of a national inventory." In G. H. Gaither, ed., *Performance Indicators in Higher Education: What Works, What Doesn't, and What's Next?* American Association for Higher Education Fund for the Improvement of Postsecondary-Education.

Folger, J. and D. Jones. 1993. *Using Fiscal Policy to Achieve State Education Goals.* Denver: Educational Commission of the States.

Freeman, T. 1995. "Assessing Performance in an Age of Accountability: Case Studies." *New Directions for Higher Education,* 91, San Francisco, CA: Jossey-Bass.

Gaither, G., B. Nedwek, and J. Neal. 1996. *Measuring Up: The Promises and Pitfalls of Performance Indicators in Higher Education.* ASHE/ERIC Higher Education Report. Washington, D.C.: Georgetown University.

Gold, S. D. 1995. *Fiscal Crisis of the States: Lessons for the Future.* Washington, D.C.: George Washington University Press.

Gray, M. J. 1996. *Enhancing the Quality and Use of Student Outcomes Data: The Final Report of the NPEC Working Group on Student Outcomes from a Data Perspective.* Washington, D.C.: NPEC.

Hammer, M. and J. Champy. 1993. *Reengineering the Corporation: A Manifesto For Business Revolution.* New York, NY: HarperCollins.

McKeown, M. P. 1996. *State Funding Formulas for Public Four-Year Institutions.* Denver: State Higher Education Executive Officers.

National Association of State Budget Officers. 1997/1998. *The Fiscal Survey of the States.* Washington, D.C.: National Association of State Budget Officers.

Osborne, D. and T. Gaebler. 1992. *Reinventing Government: How Entrepreneurial Spirit Is Transforming The Public Sector.* Reading, MA: Addison-Wesley.

Serban, A. M. 1997. "Performance Funding for Public Higher Education: Views of Critical Stakeholders" In J. C. Burke and A. M. Serban, eds. *Current Status and Future Prospects of Performance Funding and Performance Budgeting for Public Higher Education: The Second Survey*. Albany, N.Y.: Rockefeller Institute of Government.

16

Performance Management in New York City: Compstat and the Revolution in Police Management

Dennis C. Smith with William J. Bratton

Scholars may argue about the effectiveness of the "reinvention movement" at the state and federal level. At the local level, the managers of urban police forces have in fact reinvented American police administration, and in doing so have contributed to dramatic reductions in crime all across the nation. The story of this reinvention is complex, but central to it is a radical shift in the way police organizations strategically use *information about performance* to achieve greater managerial accountability. Because these new performance management techniques were pioneered in New York City in the mid-1990s, the development and implementation of Compstat by the New York City Police Department (NYPD) is a valuable case study of this new approach to policing.

Traditional texts in the field of public administration and police administration focused on organizational designs and processes and hardly mentioned performance measurement or program evaluation. If the discussion did mention these goals, it usually explained the enormous obstacles to measuring public goods and services, such as producing public safety.

For example, in the wake of a fiscal crisis in the mid-1970s that revealed that the City had been essentially "flying blind" regarding timely information about money spent and services delivered, New York City government introduced the Mayor's Management Planning and Reporting System (MMPRS).[1] However, a study of the MMPRS at the end of the 1980s found that voluminous agency statistics reported to the public twice a year included almost no measures of outcomes or "results." (Smith 1993)

Yet at the heart of the reinventing government movement that has flourished in the past decade is the idea of "managing for results." In New York City, a leading example of reinvention is the change in police management introduced by Police Commissioner William Bratton at the start of the administration of Mayor Rudolph Giuliani in 1994. In an institution long noted for its resistance to fundamental change, the introduction of a new system of management now known by the acronym for Computerized Statistics (Compstat) was remarkable for its scope, speed of implementation, and its impact on performance. The development of the Compstat system of police management involved not only a focus on measuring outcomes but also on *managing for improved outcomes*. Since the introduction of Compstat, various kinds of crime — the outcomes of policing — have plummeted to 1960s levels.

A 1996 article appearing in *NYPD*, published by the police department, entitled "Managing for Results: Building a Police Organization That Dramatically Reduces Crime, Disorder, and Fear," described Compstat in the following words:

> *For the first time in its history, the NYPD is using crime statistics and regular meetings of key enforcement personnel to direct its enforcement efforts. In the past crime statistics often lagged events by months and so did the sense of whether crime control initiatives had succeeded or failed. Now there is a daily turnaround in the "Compstat" numbers, as crime statistics are called, and NYPD commanders watch weekly crime trends with the same hawk-like attention private corporations paid profits*

and loss. Crime statistics have become the department's bottom
line, the best indicator of how police are doing precinct by pre-
cinct and citywide.

At semi-weekly "Compstat" meetings the department's top ex-
ecutives meet in rotation with precinct commanders and detec-
tive squad commanders from different areas of the city. These are
tough, probing sessions that review current crime trends, plan
tactics, and allocate resources. Commanders are called back to
present their results at the "Compstat" meetings at least every
five weeks, creating a sense of immediate accountability that has
energized the NYPD's widely scattered local commands. The
meetings also provide the department's executive staff with a
way of gauging the performance of precinct commanders, who
have a better opportunity to be recognized for what they have ac-
complished in their commands and how effectively they are ap-
plying the NYPD strategies.

Since the introduction of Compstat in 1994 through fiscal 1999, major declines were reported in all categories of crime in New York
City and *in all 76 precincts*.

In fact, New York City outperformed the nation in all categories, often by a wide margin, and was an early and leading contributor in the crime reductions reported nationally. The FBI's total crime
index in New York City from 1993 to 1999 declined 50 percent compared with a drop of 17 percent in other major U.S. cities. Specifically, from 1993 to 1999 in New York:

- Murder and non-negligent manslaughter declined 66
  percent (this crime rate for major cities in the United
  States, *excluding NYC*, dropped 34 percent);
- Larceny theft declined 40 percent (11 percent in the
  U.S.);
- Motor vehicle theft fell 66 percent (U.S.: 24 percent);
- Burglary dropped 59 percent (U.S.: 26 percent);
- Robbery declined 58 percent (U.S.: 35 percent);
- Grand larceny decreased 37 percent (U.S.: 6 percent);

Quicker, Better, Cheaper?
Managing Performance in American Government

Figure 1
Major Felony Crimes in New York City

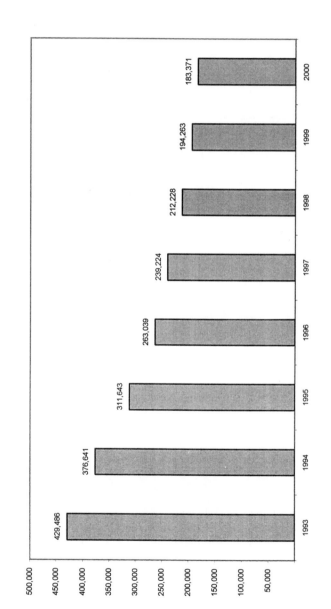

❁ Aggravated assaults dropped 36 percent (U.S.: 19 percent);

❁ Forcible rape declined 40 percent (17 percent in the U.S.).

Moreover, New York City's relative crime rate ranking among the nearly 200 U.S. cities with populations of 100,000 or more also improved, dropping from 88th place to 165th. New York is now the safest large city in the country.

For many years New York City had, with the separate Transit and Housing Police Departments, three of the ten largest police departments in the country. While they were all operating under traditional organizational principles, the idea of creating an even larger bureaucracy was not an appealing prospect to transit riders and housing project residents — or for most police officers. The much more decentralized, information resourceful, and responsive Compstat model finally made possible — and politically saleable — the economies of scale and coordination that combining these departments always promised. Since the departments were consolidated in 1995, crime in the subways has continued to go down. Between 1995 and June 2000, seven major felony crimes have also declined 39 percent in the New York City housing developments (Mayor's Management Report, September 2000).

While several police officials and one scholar have written accounts of recent NYPD history (Bratton and Knobler 1998, Maple 1999, Silverman 1999), no one has published a multivariate empirical study of the impact of Compstat on public safety. Nevertheless, evidence is overwhelming that since Compstat's inauguration, the pace of crime reduction dramatically increased. This chapter describes how Compstat changed thinking about public safety in America.

Police Management Reform:
The Compstat Model

Compstat was introduced in NYPD by the management team assembled by William Bratton when he became police commissioner at the start of of Mayor Rudolf Giuliani's administration in 1994. After reaching a peak in the early 1990s, when homicides exceeded 2000, and after a historic build-up in police personnel under Police Commissioners Lee Brown and Raymond Kelly,[2] funded by the 1991 Safe Streets, Safe City Act passed by the legislature at the insistence of Mayor Dinkins, index crime in New York had begun to decline. Nevertheless, in the 1993 mayoral election the incumbent David Dinkins had trouble winning credit for the success of his "community policing" approach to reduction in crime, and confronted a candidate who ran on the issue that public safety was still a leading problem.

Most analysts and certainly newly elected Mayor Giuliani believed that the voting public's continuing concern about crime and public safety were critical to his victory at the polls. However, Wayne Barrett, in his biography of Giuliani, takes pains to point out that candidate Giuliani had offered no specifics about how he would achieve his goal of reducing crime. Barrett also criticizes Dinkins's second Police Commissioner Raymond Kelly, under whose leadership index crime had declined, for attributing the crime wave to "family values...young people out there on the streets with no supervision...the out-of-wedlock birthrate," but failing to give credit for the decline to changes by the community (Barrett, 2000, p. 352).

By most accounts, Mayor Giuliani selected William Bratton as his police commissioner because Bratton believed the police could reduce crime. Commissioner Bratton had his own reasons to believe in the efficacy of police action. When he served as head of the New York City Transit Police, he had succeeded in dramatically reducing serious crime. The best example of his approach was the strategic enforcement of the laws against the minor criminal offense of "fare beating." The rationale was that persons entering the subways intent on robbery and other crimes were unlikely to pay to ride. By targeting stations where fare beating was most common, by using plainclothes officers to arrest and interrogate fare beaters, by checking for outstanding warrants, by searching those arrested for weapons, and by prosecuting those with weapons, the Transit Police reduced fare beating, but more importantly drove knives and guns out of the system. This kind of strategy-based law enforcement — more akin to "problem-solving policing" than community policing — became a cornerstone of Compstat.[3]

Police Commissioner Bratton's approach to management, which relied on computer-mapped crime statistics, departed from both the traditional model of a highly centralized, reactive bureaucracy and from the newer model of community policing. In fact, Compstat differs in philosophy, structure, and management process from its predecessors. Compstat is based on a complex set of interrelated assumptions about cause and effect in the production of public safety (see Model C). The official police presentation of Compstat focused on only four factors: accurate and timely intelligence, rapid deployment, effective tactics, and relentless follow-up and assessment (Safir n.d.). Increased police personnel (provided by Safe Streets/Safe Cities), leadership (from the commissioner *and* the mayor), and the new role of precinct commanders (decentralization) are also critical inputs. The detailed tracking process cast a net around more than just index crimes. Compstat includes indicators believed to be warning markers, such as shooting incidents, shooting victims, and gun arrests, all displayed in geographically pinpointed detail for regular management review at every level.

The philosophical change entailed in this model rested on the belief that police action can affect crime and public safety. To the consternation of many of his police management colleagues and a chorus of disbelief among academic criminologists, Bratton began his tenure by setting a target of cutting crime by 10 percent the first year. (The actual drop was 12 percent.) The new philosophy was informed by the idea of "broken windows" articulated most clearly by George Kelling and James Q. Wilson who argued that effective crime control starts at the bottom of the scale of seriousness, not the top. However, Bratton emphasized targeting both top (serious felonies) and bottom-ranked (quality-of-life) crimes simultaneously, winning back the city "block by block." Jack Maple, Bratton's deputy commissioner for operations, maintains that the "broken windows" idea actually formed only a limited part of the New York City intervention. He wrote, "While I applaud tactics that reduce disorder and the public's fear of crime, implementing quality-of-life tactics alone is like giving a face-lift to a cancer patient.... For quality-of-life enforcement to make a significant contribution to crime reduction, it has to be supported by a larger strategy" (Maple 1999). The key element of "broken windows" was not the specific focus of

Quicker, Better, Cheaper?
Managing Performance in American Government

Figure 2
Model C: The Compstat Model of Performance Management

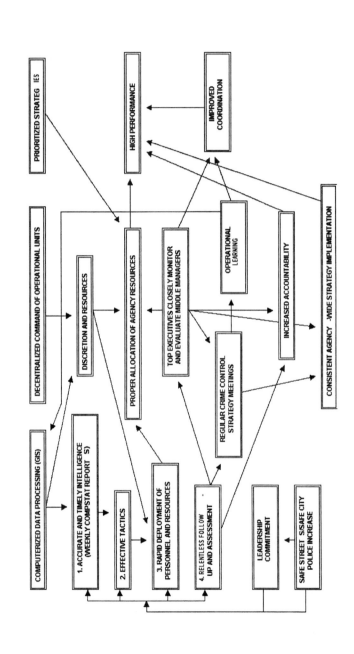

enforcement but the belief that police intervention could have a major impact on crime.

Compstat also includes a significant structural change: the identification of precinct commanders as the locus for operational authority and accountability, and community-oriented problem solving. The traditional NYPD structure centered command, information, and accountability on higher-level officials and specialized units. Community policing could have empowered precinct commanders, but as practiced in New York by Commissioners Ward and Brown it focused more on empowering individual police officers as problem solvers (McElroy, Cosgrove, and Sadd 1993; Ward 1988).

Also under the old system, the job of precinct commander was either the icing on the top of a long career at NYPD or a short stopover on a fast track in the career of upwardly mobile officers. In either case, the performance goal tended to be limited: escape the position before an incident or scandal marred the record.

Under Compstat, precincts became the locus of problem solving and performance management, guided by centrally devised strategies and aided by centrally deployed supplemental resources. Precinct commanders have been given the tools to analyze up-to-date statistics, find patterns of crime and police activity, and devise solutions to problems they identify within the context of priorities and strategies for reducing crime established by the central administration. Precinct commanders know that Compstat staff have the same data they do, and are analyzing it for review.

This change in management process is symbolized by the twice-weekly crime strategy meetings at the Command and Control Center at One Police Plaza. The leaders of one of the City's eight borough commands assemble for a three-hour meeting with the department's top managers to review the performance of precincts — originally one by one, now in adjacent clusters to facilitate awareness of and response to larger patterns. In the early stages these reviews were scheduled well in advance, but precincts now receive only a couple of days notice. The review process is aided by geographic information system (GIS) maps, and trends are presented on computer terminals and projected on large screens. Precinct commanders are questioned about their analyses of patterns and trends, about their actions to solve crime problems, and about their coordination with other police department units. A review session typically covers, in one way or another, all ten central police strategies[4]:

- ❁ Getting guns off the streets.

- ❁ Curbing youth violence in the schools and on the streets.

- ❁ Driving drug dealers out of New York City.

- ❁ Breaking the cycle of domestic violence.

- ❁ Reclaiming public spaces.

- ❁ Reducing auto related crime.

- ❁ Rooting out corruption.

- ❁ Reclaiming the roads.

- ❁ Fostering courtesy, professionalism, and respect.

- ❁ Bringing fugitives to justice.

In addition to sharpening the focus on accountability, Compstat sessions have become major vehicles for organizational learning. In the past, no mechanisms were in place to share lessons learned or advances in crime-fighting tactics. The evidence presented at Compstat meetings is intensely scrutinized for insights into what works — and does not work — in the fight against crime, with the results widely and rapidly disseminated within the department. Since commanders are often grilled in Compstat meetings about their familiarity with successful methods, they have strong incentives to be prepared.[5]

The Unintended Consequences of Compstat

It is hardly news in public administration that policies and programs may have unintended consequences. A management principle underlying Compstat is that what is counted counts in terms of organizational performance.[6] There is a corollary: what is not counted tends to be discounted.

In the first months of Compstat, precinct commanders were not quizzed about civilian complaints or patterns of police misconduct; after several months these data were added to the Precinct Commander Profile, and questions were raised in the Compstat review meetings. This did not receive the same level of attention by the Department — nor certainly by the Mayor — given to crime, but its addition does reflect Bratton's early recognition that performance management is a balancing act.

A focus on police misconduct in the form of overly aggressive policing and discourtesy and lack of respect in police encounters with citizens has gradually been added to the list of strategies. This strategy was introduced not as a result of any systematic evidence of increased misconduct, but in response to several highly publicized police-citizen encounters in which public response suggested poor police community relations. There is little hard evidence of trends in police misconduct in interactions with the community.[7]

Under Commissioner Bratton a special Compstat process for Internal Affairs used the new approach to track and analyze serious offenses such as corruption. The separate Internal Affairs Compstat review process was discontinued by Commissioner Safir, who returned to highly compartmentalized investigations, apparently because of traditional concern about leaks within the Department.

Information Technology and Police Organization

There is a critical technological dimension to the structural reform story engendered by Compstat. At the beginning of the Bratton administration in 1994, precincts typically did not have personal computers. NYPD was one of the last bastions of mainframe computer technology — and the related mentality of excessive central control. Precincts produced most police data, which were sent for analysis to headquarters for processing. It usually took weeks for crime and activity data sent to headquarters to come back to precincts — if they came back at all. There was little if any pressure on precinct commanders to reduce crime, so this lack of timely intelligence was not widely viewed as a problem. Under the old model, 911 dispatchers had more to say about the deployment of patrol officers than commanders.

Information technology played a role in police reform in the United States before Compstat. Before the decentralization afforded by personal computers and the analytic power of GIS maps, there were centralized 911 telephone and radio systems. Following the advice of the Task Force on the Police of the President's Commission on Law Enforcement in the Administration of Justice (1967), police departments aspired to be centrally controlled, highly mechanized, semi-military bureaucratic organizations.[8] The large mainframe computers needed to support enormous 911 systems — which in New York City record 10 million plus calls for service a year — symbolized the centralized structure of this dominant police management model.

Ironically, at the very time the 1967 Task Force was recommending traditional "principles of organization" as the key to improving police management, the academic field of organization theory was producing powerful arguments for a decentralized "contingency" approach to organization design. Prominent works by Lawrence and Lorsch (1967) and James D. Thompson (1967) make a powerful case for the idea that the structure of high-performing organizations varies with the technology used and the environments in which they work. According to that theory, urban police forces, lacking knowledge of cause and effect (James Q. Wilson 1967), and operating in dynamic and complex environments, require decentralized decisionmaking. The survival of the 911 model largely intact well into the 1990s can largely be explained by public and political demand, bureaucratic inertia, and the absence of the "norms of rationality," a constraint that organization theorists assumed to be operating. "Norms of rationality" refers to measures of performance that put pressure on organizations to produce results. Given the view that the police could not have a significant impact on community safety, large police forces focused instead on their internal or "technical rationality," which included concerns such as improving radio dispatch technology and minimizing response time.

But with the shift in focus to community outcomes, crime reduction, and increased public safety, the formula for rational action had to change.

During the last decade of the twentieth century, the level of crime and its seemingly incessant rise was a major public issue in the United States. Criminologists and pundits presented competing explanations for this rise, ranging from sociological to cultural to economic to chemical (drugs), but few placed the blame on the organization and management of police services. Some discussion occurred regarding how many police officers were needed to respond to crime and cope with its consequences, but few analysts looked to the police for solutions.

Scholarly literature on police reinforced lowered expectations. Long before James Q. Wilson articulated the "broken windows" theory of police intervention, he wrote in *Varieties of Police Behavior*, the most widely cited volume on police administration:

> The police share with most other public agencies — the schools, foreign ministries, antipoverty organizations — an inability to assess accurately the effectiveness of their operations.... No police department, however competently led and organized, can know how much crime and disorder a community produces or how much would be produced if the police function differently (or not all).

Wilson went on to argue:

> Even when the police have accurate information, it is often difficult or impossible to devise a strategy that would make the occurrence of a crime less likely. Many serious crimes — murder, forcible rape — are of this character: Though they are often reported with minimum distortion or delay, it may occur, in many cases, in private places among people who know each other and in the heat of an emotional moment.... The rate of certain crimes is determined to a significant but unknown degree by factors over which the police have little control. Street crimes are affected by weather, crimes against property by prevailing economic conditions, crimes against the person by the racial and class composition of the community, delinquency by the nature and strength of

family and peer group controls. The police know these things — or think they know them — but they cannot estimate the magnitude of such factors, or distinguish their effect from that of police tactics, or bring these factors under police control.

Consequently, according to Wilson, "few police administrators show much interest in 'planning' the deployment of their manpower and equipment."

Wilson's "realistic" view was widely shared and reflected in police administration from the 1970s into the 1990s. Police departments in urban America all used the reactive response 911 model of service delivery. Departments deployed officers in random, visible patrol cars in the hope that their presence would not only deter crime, but also distribute response units in a way that minimized response time to unpredictable calls for service. When the City of New York began to present agency performance targets in the Mayor's Management Report, the NYPD prior to Commissioner Bratton refused to set crime reduction targets. The argument made by the Department and accepted by the mayor's office was that the police do not produce crime, they only respond to it, however much there is (Smith 1993). In support of this view, they could cite experts like David Bayley (1994), who wrote: "That the police are not able to prevent crime should not come as a surprise to thoughtful people. It is generally understood that social conditions outside the control of police, as well as outside the control of the criminal justice system as a whole, determine crime levels in the community." [9]

Today, less than a decade later, the long-prevailing belief in the limited and solely reactive role of modern police forces has been dramatically altered. The idea that policing *can* make a difference had its origin in the idea of community policing.

Community Policing and Problem-Solving Policing

Compstat had its roots in the rise of two sometimes-related reforms in managing public safety: community policing and problem-solving policing. As recounted more fully elsewhere (Goldstein 1990,

Sparrow et al. 1990), a series of studies challenged the basic premises on which 911 urban policing strategies were based. The random-patrol model assumed that rapid response gave police their best chance to apprehend criminals and deter crimes, as well as to enhance citizens' feeling of safety. A specialized force of detectives would solve crimes not deterred or where random patrol and rapid response did not result in apprehension (911 Model). Studies in the 1970s — including the now famous Kansas City Preventive Patrol Experiment (Kelling et al. 1974, Greenwood et al. 1977) — called those assumptions into question. Eck and Spellman (1987, p. 35) summarized the policy implications of this research: "In short most serious crimes were unaffected by the standard police actions designed to control them. Further, the public did not notice reductions in patrol, reduced speed responding to non-emergencies, or lack of follow-up investigations."

Research also revealed a growth in the public's fear of crime and perceived physical and social disorder at the neighborhood level. Moreover, these "quality-of-life" conditions were largely ignored by police, who focused on a narrowly defined crime control mission (Wilson and Kelling 1982, more fully explored in Skogan, 1990).

Faced with the need for new approaches to urban public safety, many police departments in the 1980s experimented with new strategies based on two further findings: police contributions to public safety were highly dependent on citizen inputs, and police efforts were oriented to apprehension more than prevention. From the first came "community policing" and a return to the idea of the cop on the beat who knows a neighborhood's people and places. From the second emerged "problem-solving policing," which suggests that police can reduce crime by focusing not just on incidents of crime but also on community problems which lead to those incidents. Some departments combined the two. In New York City a version of problem-solving community policing began in 1984 under Police Commissioner Benjamin Ward and continued into the early 1990s. Since 1994 the city has changed the orientation of problem-solving policing and dropped the rhetoric of community policing almost completely. As will be shown, there has been some distance between rhetoric and reality both during the ascendance of community policing in New York and its apparent eclipse.

As Commissioner Ward was addressing how the department should deploy new officers in the early 1980s, James Q. Wilson and George Kelling (1982) published "Broken Windows." They argued that the neglect of quality-of-life crime enforcement in New York City in the late 1970s might be causally related to the rise in more serious crime in the early 1980s.[10] In 1984, after an extensive study of the needs of the department by the Vera Institute of Justice, the Community Patrol Officer Program (CPOP) was launched to test problem-solving, community-oriented policing in one precinct. CPOP started in Brooklyn with a 10-officer unit, supervised by a sergeant. The officers were assigned to work alone in fixed beat assignments, following a flexible schedule based on the needs of the beat. They were not responding to routine (911) calls for service, but learning neighborhood norms and folkways, identifying patterns of incidents ("problems"), and developing various strategies to address them. While community patrol officers were supposed to act on the information they obtained, they were also expected to serve as a communication link between the neighborhood and the department.

Before much testing of the model could occur, the idea grew wings and took off with a commitment in 1985 to extend it to every precinct in the city. By 1989, when Benjamin Ward left the department, a CPOP unit was operating in all 75 precincts of the City (McElroy, Cosgrove and Sadd 1993). In 1989, mayoral candidate David Dinkins announced his intention to double the number of CPOs if elected.[11]

Mayor Dinkins appointed as police commissioner Lee Brown, a nationally recognized proponent of community policing. He issued a "blueprint for change" in which he made community policing not merely a program but "the dominant philosophy and strategy" of the department. "With community policing, every neighborhood will have one or more police officers assigned to it and responsible for helping residents of the community prevent crime, develop a capacity for order maintenance, and improve the quality of life."

The effects of community policing in New York are not well documented. Testifying before the Public Safety Committee of the New York City Council in 1991, Jack Greene, Jerry McElroy, and Dennis Smith each argued that systematically measuring progress on the near-term, intermediate, and ultimate goals would help guide the department and stabilize public expectations. However, Commissioner Brown testified that the department had very limited resources for evaluation, and that the evaluations it did undertake would be for "managerial" use.

In his campaign for mayor in 1993, challenger Rudolph Giuliani characterized Dinkins's community policing as "social work." A former federal prosecutor, he claimed to be a "real crime fighter." A "student" of George Kelling,[12] he also promised to pay more attention to quality-of-life offenses, symbolized by the "squeegee men" jaywalking city streets at intersections to try to clean the windows of often reluctant and even frightened drivers.[13]

William J. Bratton, who became police commissioner in January of 1994 and directed the departmental reengineering effort, was recognized nationally as a proponent of community policing. A number of his closest advisors while he led the Boston Police, such as George Kelling of Northeastern University and Robert Wasserman,[14] are considered founders of the community policing movement.

But New York in 1994 was a different story. Community policing was associated in the public mind with the Dinkins administration. In his book (1998, pp. 198-9), Bratton explains his view of community policing as practiced in New York City:

> *Beat cops are important in maintaining contact with the public and offering them a sense of security. They can identify the communities' concerns and sometimes prevent crime simply by their visibility. Giving cops more individual power to make decisions is a good idea. But the community-policing plan as it was originally focused was not going to work because there was no focus on crime. The connection between having more cops on the street and the crime rate falling was implicit. There was no plan to deploy these officers in specifically hard-hit areas...and there were no concrete means by which they were supposed to address crime*

when they got there. They were simply supposed to go out on their beats and somehow improve their communities.

But did community policing disappear with the introduction of Compstat? Problem solving, its lesser-known twin, was infused into many parts of the new plan. While the operationalization of problem solving as a street-level police behavior remained problematic, it emerged in Bratton's 1994 *Plan of Action* for NYPD as a key to high performance reviews, favorable assignments, and promotions. However, the new version of problem solving centered on the precinct, and the primary accountable official was the precinct commander, not the individual community police officer.

Precinct commanders could design their own operating strategies and draw on the department's resources in making those strategies work, and were evaluated on their success in "reducing dramatically crime, disorder, and fear." Precinct commanders who had been trained in and believed in the efficacy of community policing almost inevitably relied on a partnership between their police and the community to achieve significant crime reduction. Thus, community policing has played a role in New York City's crime reduction success story.

The Case for Compstat

It was probably inevitable, given the central place of crime-fighting strategies in the campaign that ousted the City's first African-American mayor and brought Rudy Giuliani into office, that the subject of crime and police performance in New York would be highly politicized. Mayor Giuliani did not acknowledge as significant the fact that crime had declined each year under his predecessor, nor credit the Safe Streets/Safe City legislation achieved under Mayor Dinkins for creating a much larger police force with which to pursue the fight against crime. Returning the favor, opponents and critics of the mayor are reluctant to find any merit in the claim that the NYPD under his leadership has played a central role in reducing crime. Most critics are content to offer alternative explanations, but one recent book goes to great if sometimes tortured lengths to challenge even the basic facts of crime reduction.[15]

The case we make here is that, while crime statistics are flawed in well-established ways, there is no evidence that the credibility of crime statistics changed during the Giuliani administration. If anything, crime statistics have been more carefully scrutinized in the last decade than at any time in history. Statisticians recommend the use of multiple measures of almost any complex phenomenon as an antidote to biases. An unprecedented number of police performance indicators are available, and those statistics tell the same story: crime in virtually all categories and in all sub-areas of the City is dramatically down. Not only are homicides now at 1960s levels, but reports of shots fired, gun incidents, and gunshot injuries are also dramatically down. And some of those numbers come from agencies other than the police.

The key point is that there is a remarkably close link between the introduction of the new approach to police management and a dramatic drop in crime, and that other possible explanations do not fit the pattern of crime reduction as closely.

Rival Hypotheses for
Crime Reduction in New York City

Analysts have advanced five alternative explanations to the City's drop in crime: — demographics, drugs, gun control, the economy, and incarceration. Succinctly summarized, here are the arguments:[16]

Demographics: The relative size of the cohort between 15 and 21 years of age has been shown to have enormous influence upon the rate of reported crimes. Criminologists have clearly demonstrated that adolescents commit a disproportionate number and percentage of total crimes, that criminality peaks between the ages of 16 and 20 for the majority of specific offenses, and that the rate of offenses attributable to a particular age cohort declines as it ages (Wolfgang, Figlio, and Sellin 1972; Tracy, Wolfgang, and Figlio 1990). These conclusions are supported by data from the FBI's Uniform Crime Reports, as well as by victimization studies.

Criminology's conclusions about the influence of the age 15-to-19 cohort upon overall crime, however, do not fit the patterns of crime in New York City. The city's youthful population *declined* by almost 22 percent from 1970 to 1990, when index crime rates soared in New York by 23 percent and across the nation. Both homicide and motor vehicle theft hit 20-year peaks in 1990. The proportion of crimes for which the cohort was responsible did increase: per capita arrests for youths between 15 and 19 rose almost 60 percent.

The demographic rationales for crime and their emphasis on criminality among the cohort of males between the ages of 15 and 19 cannot explain the significant crime reductions in New York City over the past several years. In fact, the number of males in that age group has actually increased between 1990 and 1995, when New York City began to realize a notable decrease in crime.[17]

Drugs: A great deal of recent discourse and research in contemporary criminology has focused on the nexus between drug abuse and crime, particularly violent crime. Hypotheses typically establish a causal link between drugs and crime in two ways: a particular drug is said to induce violent crime by removing inhibitions or through some other pharmacological effect, and the prohibitive cost of some drugs is said to cause users to commit crimes (particularly property crimes) to generate income to satisfy their addiction. Although positive correlations between drug use and criminality have been demonstrated, many of the studies are based on convenient samples of prison and jail inmates and therefore present sample bias (Bureau of Justice Statistics 1988, 1991). Another empirical issue is the difficulty of determining what portion of overall crime is committed by drug abusers. As Wilson and Herrnstein (1985, p. 366) point out, it would be impossible to calculate how much crime heroin addicts commit even if we had accurate data about the number of addicts and the monetary cost of their addiction.

Some have argued that the precipitous increases in robbery complaints nationwide during the late 1980s stemmed from the emergence of crack cocaine. Crack exploded onto the drug scene in New York City in 1985 and 1986, a period in which robbery complaints did increase dramatically. Some would argue, in a similar vein, that the reemergence of heroin as the drug of choice among street criminals will translate into an increase in burglary complaints, since burglaries rates have long been associated with heroin addiction. However, neither of these hypotheses is supported by empirical evidence in New York City.

In 1984, just prior to the crack explosion, a Drug Use Forecasting (DUF) urinalysis study at the Manhattan Central Booking facility revealed a 42 percent positive rate for cocaine among all arrestees, regardless of the charge. By 1988 — perhaps the height of the crack epidemic — the prevalence of cocaine use among all arrestees had nearly doubled, to 83 percent, lending credibility to the hypothesized relationship between crack cocaine and crime.

Although cocaine use among all arrestees has since dropped, the decline has been fairly modest. In February 1995, 78 percent of arrestees tested positive for cocaine, and in May 1995, 68 percent did so. Since 1988, the proportion of arrestees testing positive for cocaine in each quarter varied from 59 percent to 83 percent, and since 1993 the proportion varied from 63 percent to 78 percent. Cocaine use among those arrested in New York City has thus not declined substantially, and certainly not to the extent that it could account for the enormous decline in the crime that cocaine supposedly engenders. It should be noted that robberies in New York City peaked in 1981 at about 107,500 — before the advent of crack and seven years before peak cocaine use as measured by DUF. New York City robberies were 49,670 in 1996. [18]

Gun Control: One can intuitively grasp a connection between the availability of funds, particularly handguns, and violent crime. Roughly one-half of the nation's homicides are committed with guns, as are about one-third of all robberies and one-third of all rapes. In New York City at least, the vast majority of those guns are illegally possessed. No significant change in gun control law or any demographic or social variable might have induced street criminals to refrain from carrying or using their guns during the period when gun-related violence in New York City precipitously declined. However, the facts do clearly show a link between the number of guns and a change in police strategy and management.

"Getting guns off the streets" was the first strategic priority of Bratton when he became commissioner of NYPD.[19] The number of firearms (especially handguns) used in criminal activity declined substantially in New York City during the first years of the new administration. The percentage of robberies in which firearms were used, for example, fell from 36 percent in 1993 to 33 percent in 1994 and to 29 percent for the first six months of 1995. The number of shooting incidents declined 40 percent between 1993 and the end of 1994 (and an additional 52 percent between fiscal 1995 and 1999), and the number of shooting victims injured in these incidents dropped 38 percent. The decline in firearms use can also be inferred from the fact that the department received 23 percent fewer "shots-fired" calls during the first nine months of 1995 than during the comparable 1994 period.

The declining number of shooting incidents and victims reflects a general decline in the number of firearms carried and used by criminals, which can reasonably be attributed to the effectiveness of NYPD's strategic gun enforcement efforts. A plausible explanation is that criminals considered the wisdom of leaving their guns at home. Indeed, NYPD gun arrests rose fairly rapidly subsequent to the introduction of the gun strategy, and began to decline only as a function of aggressive enforcement.

The Economy: The question of whether poverty causes crime has been one of the most controversial and enduring issues in criminology as well as politics. Academic research has failed to provide conclusive data to support or reject any of the common economic theories of crime causation.

In any case, none of the common social or economic factors that criminologists typically cite to explain fluctuations in crime seem to be responsible for any appreciable decline in crime. New York City's economic picture was improving only slightly during the first years of the Giuliani administration. Data from the U.S. Department of Labor show New York City's unemployment rate at 10.8 percent in January 1994, at 7.2 percent in September 1994, at 9 percent in February 1995, and at 8 percent in September 1995. The unemployment rate remained over 8 percent for the rest of the decade — well above the national average. The number of city residents receiving public assistance benefits began to decline slightly in 1994 and 1995, and dramatically only after the introduction of national welfare reform in 1996. A comparison of the number of city residents receiving food stamps in August 1994 and August 1995 reveals a very modest decrease of 0.4 percent.

There is more evidence to suggest that *the improvement in the city's economy followed a decline in crime rather than the other way around.* The New York City Convention and Visitors Bureau reported that it serviced 30 percent more visitors in 1996 than in 1993, and that the city attracted 25 million visitors in 1996 — a 14 percent increase over 1995 levels. This translates into 3.5 million more visitors who contributed to the local economy. New York City's hotel occupancy rate rose from 70 percent in 1993 to 82 percent in 1996.

Subway ridership has similarly reflected a decline in subway crime. Daily subway ridership fell 3.5 percent between 1990 and 1991 but increased 0.2 percent between 1991 and 1992, when subway crime fell 15 percent. In 1992 and 1993, when subway crime fell an additional 24 percent, daily ridership rose 5 percent. In 1994, with subway crime falling another 22 percent, ridership rose an additional 5 percent. According to MTA monthly reports, subway ridership rose every year after 1993, after declining steadily in the late 1980s. From these data, we could argue that public fears associated with riding the city's rapid transit system have declined. Investments in subway infrastructure and the new fare policies such as add-a-ride introduced in 1997 are also factors in these upward trends.

Arrests and Incapacitation: Even the best managed and most effective police agency cannot reduce crime solely through arrest and enforcement. Other spheres of the criminal justice system — the courts and corrections, probation and parole — play a salient role in reducing crime and enhancing public safety. Corrections agencies in particular are instrumental in reducing crime through incapacitation and perhaps to some extent through deterrence, although the public rarely acknowledges their importance.

Although it may be difficult to accurately estimate the relative effectiveness of incapacitation strategies, the rationale for incapacitation is fairly simple. We know that some criminals, particularly "career criminals," commit a highly disproportionate number of crimes. Like many other states, New York has significantly increased the number of prisons, the size of the prison population, and the length of incarceration. Some have speculated that this increased incarceration has incapacitated crime.

Aside from the fact that the dramatic increase in prisoners depended on arrests, the key point is that prison population growth occurred during the 1980s and early 1990s and began to reverse when crime trends in New York started downward. The number of new commitments to prisons was 8,649 in 1993, but dropped 33 percent to 5,837 in 1997. With an increase of 32 percent in the mean minimum sentence, one could argue that the two trends canceled each other out. During the same period, however, the number of prisoners released on parole steadily increased from 20,662 in 1993 to 22,329 in 1997 (Citizens Budget Commission 2000).

While NYPD did not deemphasize felony arrests under the management strategy it introduced in 1994, it did attack the problem of serious crime by greatly increasing the emphasis on misdemeanors. In 1993 the department made 127,883 felony arrests and 133,446 misdemeanor arrests. In 1994, the first year of the new regime, all arrests increased, while felony arrests rose 9 percent (to 139,228 arrests) and misdemeanor arrests shot up 31 percent (to 175,128). By 1997 misdemeanor arrests were at 228,080, but felony arrests remained almost level at 135,778.

Reminiscent of the fare beating strategy in the subways, NYPD's quality-of-life enforcement effort did not produce the kinds of arrests that result in incarceration, but these data nevertheless show that dramatic crime reductions can be achieved through sustained and tactical enforcement of quality-of-life misdemeanor offenses, coupled with vigorous enforcement of felony crimes and the concomitant incapacitation of "career criminals." This record offers no support for the view that prisons rather than policing produced more safety from criminal victimization in New York City. Simply put: police can control the main cause of crime — human behavior.

Applying the Model to
Other Public Services

The claim that the new Compstat approach to police management can reduce crime, disorder, and fear is not limited to the experience of NYPD. Compstat received a Ford Foundation Innovations in Government award, and has been replicated in a number of other cities both in the United States and abroad. The extent to which these communities adhere to the New York City model has not been systematically documented, nor have the results. In *Crime Fighter*, former NYPD Deputy Police Commissioner Jack Maple recounts successful use of the Compstat approach in a number of American cities that had not been part of the general downward trend. After introducing a Compstat-like approach, each of these cities saw significant declines in crime.

Two New York City Departments that have attempted to follow the NYPD model in areas other than policing provide additional evidence of the effectiveness of public-sector performance management. At the Department of Correction, the elements of accurate and timely intelligence combined with effective tactics, rapid deployment, relentless follow-up and assessment, and decentralized accountability produced a major turnaround in prisoner safety and drop in overtime expenses. From 1995, when the department introduced its Compstat-like management reform, through 2000, the number of violent incidents dropped from 593 to 54. The Rikers Island Jail, among the more dangerous facilities in the nation, became one of the safest (Smith 1997).

Using the principles of Compstat, the New York City Department of Parks and Recreation created PARKSTAT, which converted a very good systematic method of annually measuring park safety and cleanliness into a system for intensively managing those conditions. The department reported declining performance for two consecutive years after introducing the measurement tool. After using Compstat principles to convert its measurement system into a management system in 1996, the department more than doubled the percentage of park facilities rated as safe and clean, from 39 to 87 percent (Smith 1997).

That these successes occurred immediately after the introduction of Compstat management principles provides additional weight to the argument that a change in police management deserves significant credit for the greater safety of New York City. These experiences suggest that performance management can significantly improve complex urban services.[20]

Endnotes

1   This is in addition, of course, to elaborate new controls on planning and monitoring spending put in place in the wake of the fiscal crisis.

2   Bratton notes in his book *Turnaround* that only a fraction of the more than 6,000 additional officers funded by Safe Streets legislation were on the streets of New York during the critical summer before the fall election of 1993 (1998, p. 198).

3   Maple emphasizes these follow-on actions in what he calls the "quality-of-life-plus" strategy (1999, p. 155).

4   During the first several years, there were only eight strategies; the last two were added by Commissioner Howard Safir.

5   The positive effect of this rapid transmission of "lessons learned" depends on the quality of the learning.

6   Prior to the introduction of the COMPSTAT style focus on measuring "outcomes," such as reduced crime/increased public safety, the measuring of activities and outputs of police was associated with rapid but ineffective radio runs, and arrests that were made to reduce public pressure, and other abuses in the name of "productivity." See Eck and Spellman 1987.

7   Deputy Commissioner for Policy and Planning Michael J. Farrell pointed out in an interview the dependence of Compstat-style performance management on agreed-upon performance measures. Civilian complaints against the police are intrinsically contested data; until they have been investigated and perhaps even adjudicated, they are difficult to use in management. Systematic citizen surveys would provide a general reading on community/police relations, but they are expensive and do not focus on the small percentage of the population that actually interacts with the police. Police Commissioner Bernard Kerrick, Safir's successor, recently announced that the city, using the nonprofit Vera Institute, would survey citizens about police and safety.

8   Thompson (1967), for example, hypothesizes that "under norms of rationality, organizations facing heterogeneous task environments seek to identify homogeneous segments and establish structural units to deal with each." He also maintains that "when the range of task environment variations is large and unpredictable, the response organization component must achieve the necessary adaptation by monitoring that environment and planning responses, and this calls for localized units."

9   Bayley, in *Police for the Future,* was describing the situation under the existing organization of and approaches to urban policing. In his concluding chapters on "Solutions" he articulates many principles that foreshadowed Compstat.

10 This neglect was exacerbated in New York City by NYPD's response to the 25 percent cut in uniform staff that occurred in the wake of the 1975 fiscal crisis. In a

form of triage, NYPD significantly reduced its attention to "lesser crimes" to focus on "real police work"— index crimes (see Smith 1981).

11   What does the CPOP experience show about managing change in complex urban police organizations? That implementing change is very difficult! With the strong support of a knowledgeable police commissioner; with a relatively clear and limited objective in a period of relative munificence, political continuity, and no extraordinary crime crisis; with little need to coordinate implementation with outside agencies; and with facilitation by a leading criminal justice organization, it nevertheless took four years to extend the program to 75 precincts involving 750 officers (less than 3 percent of the force).

12   Both Andrew Kirtzman (2000) and Wayne Barrett's biographies of Mayor Giuliani recount that he met with and was influenced by Professor Kelling during the period between his first unsuccessful and his second successful run for mayor. Both authors of this article participated in the candidate's policy "seminars" organized by Richard Schwartz.

13   The disappearance of "squeegee men" is often cited as an early success of the Giuliani quality-of-life law enforcement. However, William Bratton notes that in the summer of 1993, before the election, Commissioner Raymond Kelly used problem-solving methods to remove the squeegee men from intersections (Bratton and Knobler, 1998). One might concede that candidate Giuliani set this agenda as Mayor Dinkins's compassion for people who were washing car windows on the streets of New York was a matter of public record.

14   Robert Wasserman also played a central role in NYPD as a consultant to former Commissioner Lee Brown, who made community policing "the dominant operational philosophy of the Department."

15   In a chapter entitled "These Statistics Are Crime," Wayne Barrett (1990) argues: 1) that crime statistics clearly show that police efforts under Mayor Dinkins deserve credit for reducing crime, 2) that crime reductions during the Giuliani administration were the result of other factors, such as a changing drug culture, 3) that any reduction in crime that did occur is the work of Police Commissioner Bratton and his management, not the mayor, and 4) that crime statistics supporting the credit claims of Mayor Giuliani are not to be believed. (The same statistics, if issued during the Dinkins administration or other jurisdictions apparently can be believed.)

Even after he conjures every manner of challenge, Barrett's bottom line is not that crime has increased, nor that it has not declined, but rather that it has gone down less than claimed, and that other factors deserve credit besides the police.

16   This section draws heavily on Bratton's presentation at a National Institute of Justice (NIJ) Policing Research Institute conference on "Measuring What Matters," held in Washington DC, November 28, 1995.

17   As crime started to drop in the 1990s, the decline in youth population reversed itself. New York's Department of City Planning estimates that the population of youths between ages 15 and 19 increased by 0.04 percent between 1990 and 1995. Most significant, especially for criminologists who consider race as a variable, the number of male blacks between 15 and 19 rose by nearly 2 percent and the number of male Hispanic youths by 5.7 percent. Asian and Pacific Islander males aged 15 to 19 also increased by an estimated 2.4 percent. Pulling down the average for the entire cohort were male whites, who decreased by 8.4 percent. These data are confirmed by New York State Department of Education figures showing that total

public-school enrollment grew 4.4 percent between 1989/90 and 1994/95. The number of public-school students in grades 9 through 12 — who comprise a significant portion of the high-risk group — grew by 12 percent.

18 Nor was the hypothesized increase in heroin abuse evident in quarterly Drug Use Forecasting data. In 1984, 21 percent of arrestees tested positive for opiates, and positive tests peaked at 27 percent in June 1988 and 25 percent in October 1988. In the most recent DUF testing quarters, February and May 1995, respectively, 22 percent and 20 percent of arrestees tested positive for opiates.

19 NYPD Strategy No. 1, getting guns off the streets of New York City, entailed intensive scrutiny and follow-up of every incident, arrestee, or accomplice involving a gun, and follow-up of every lead on sources of guns. NYPD officer teams that previously focused on narcotics now focus on the link between narcotics and guns. NYPD worked with a joint city-federal task force on illegal gun trafficking that has traveled to other states to make arrests and monitored federal firearms applications that could increase the number of guns coming to New York.

20 The City of Baltimore has introduced CitiStat, a Compstat-inspired approach to performance management, for all city agencies. See Francis X. Cline, "Baltimore Uses Data Bank to Wake Up City Workers," *New York Times*, June 10, 2001, p. 24. See also Christopher Swope, "Restless for Results, " *Governing*, April 2001.

References

Barrett, Wayne. 2000. *Rudy! An Investigative Biography of Rudolph Giuliani*, New York: Basic Books.

Bayley, David. 1994. *Police for the Future*. New York: Oxford University Press.

Bratton, William. 1995. "Measuring What Matters." A presentation at a conference convened by the National Institute of Justice Policing Research Institute. Washington, DC. November 28, 1995.

Bratton, William. 1998. "Crime Is Down in New York City: Blame the Police." In Norman Dennis, ed., *Zero Tolerance: Policing a Free Society*, 2nd ed. London: IEA Health and Welfare Unit.

Bratton, William with Peter Knobler. 1998. *Turnaround: How America's Top Cop Reversed the Crime Epidemic*. New York: Random House.

Brown, Lee P. 1991. "Policing New York City in the 1990s: The Strategy for Community Policing." New York City Police Department, January.

Brown, Lee P. and Elsie L. Scott. 1992. *Executive Session Training Implications of Community Policing*. New York City Police Department.

Citizens Budget Commission. *Making More Effective Use of New York State Prisons: A Report of the Citizens Budget Commission*, May 25, 2000.

Cline, Francis X. 2001. "Baltimore Uses Data Bank to Wake Up City Workers." *New York Times,* June 10, p. 24.

Eck, John. 1982. *Solving Crimes: The Investigation of Burglary and Robbery.* Washington, DC: Police Executive Research Forum.

Eck, John E., and William Spellman. 1987. *Problem Solving: Problem-Oriented Policing in Newport News.* Washington, DC: Police Executive Research Forum.

Goldstein, Herman. 1990. *Problem-Oriented Policing.* Philadelphia: Temple University Press.

Greene, Jack R., and Stephen D. Mastrofski. 1986. *Community Policing: Rhetoric or Reality?* New York: Praeger.

Greenwood, Peter, Joan Petersilia, and Jan Chaiken. 1977. *The Criminal Investigative Process.* Lexington, MA: D.C. Heath.

Kelling, George L. 1974. *The Kansas City Preventive Patrol Experiment: A Summary.* Washington, DC: The Police Foundation.

Kelling, George L., Tony Pate, Duane Dieckman, and Charles E. Brown. 1977. *The Kansas City Preventive Patrol Experiment: A Summary Report.* Washington, DC: The Police Foundation.

Kirtzman, Andrew. 2000. *Rudy Giuliani: Emperor of the City.* New York: William Morrow.

Lawrence, Paul and Jay Lorsch. 1967; 2nd ed. 1986. *Organizations and Their Environments.* Cambridge, MA: Harvard University Press.

Maple, Jack, with Chris Mitchell. 1999.*The Crime Fighter: Putting the Bad Guys Out of Business.* New York: Doubleday.

Mc Elroy, Jerome, et al. 1993. *Community Policing: The CPOP in New York.* Newbury Park, CA: Sage.

New York City Mayor's Office of Operations. 2000. Mayor's Management Report. September.

Safir, Howard. Office of the Commissioner, New York City Police Department, Compstat, n.d.

Silverman, Eli B. 1999. *NYPD Battles Crime: Innovative Strategies in Policing.* Boston: Northeastern University Press.

Skogan, Wesley G. 1990. *Disorder and Decline: Crime and the Spiral of Decay in American Neighborhoods.* New York: Free Press.

Smith, Dennis C., and Robin Barnes. 1998. "Making Management Count: Toward Theory-Based Performance Management." Paper prepared for the annual research conference of the Association of Public Policy and Management. New York, October.

Smith, Dennis C. 1981. "Police." In *Setting Municipal Priorities, 1982.* Charles Brecher and Raymond Horton, eds. New York: Russell Sage Foundation.

Smith, Dennis C. 1993. "Performance Management in New York City: The Mayor's Management Plan and Report System in the Koch Administration." Paper prepared for the annual meeting of the Association of Public Policy and Management. Washington, DC, October.

Smith, Dennis C. 1997. "What Can Public Managers Learn from Police Reform in New York? Compstat and the Promise of Performance Management." Paper prepared for the annual meeting of the Association of Public Policy and Management. Washington, DC, November.

Sparrow, Malcolm K., Mark H. Moore, and David M. Kennedy. 1990. *Beyond 911: A New Era for Policing.* New York: Basis Books.

Swope, Christopher. 2001 "Restless for Results. " *Governing.* April.

Thompson, James D. 1967. *Organizations in Action.* New York: McGraw-Hill.

Tracy, Paul E., Marvin E. Wolfgang, and Robert M. Figlio. 1990. *Delinquency Careers in Two Birth Cohorts.* New York: Plenum.

Ward, Benjamin. 1988. *Community Patrol Officer Program: Problem-Solving Guide.* New York City Police Department City. New York, September.

Wilson, James Q. 1967. *Varieties of Police Behavior.* Cambridge, MA: Harvard University Press.

Wilson, James Q. and Richard J. Herrnstein. 1985. *Crime and Human Nature: The Definitive Study of the Causes of Crime.* New York: Simon & Schuster.

Wilson, James Q., and George Kelling. 1982. "Broken Windows: The Police and Neighborhood Safety." *Atlantic Monthly,* March, pp. 29-38.

Wolfgang, Marvin E., Robert M. Figlio, and Thorsten Sellin. 1972. *Delinquency in a Birth Cohort.* Chicago: University of Chicago Press.

V

Summing Up

17

Is the New Obsession With Performance Management Masking the Truth About Social Programs?

Ann B. Blalock and Burt S. Barnow

Introduction

We have something other than a clandestine purpose in proposing the question "Is the new obsession with 'performance management' masking the truth about social programs?" On the contrary, we intend to grind a particular axe openly. Our major theme is that the "performance management movement" that has swept the post-industrial world in the late 1980s and early 1990s, and has redirected information collection and analysis toward a focus on social program *results* (outcomes), may lead to misinformed judgments of the value of social programs. This potential problem could result in misguided social remedies if those designing and directing performance management systems, and the users of information flowing from such systems, are not careful about distinguishing between 1) results that can be attributed relatively exclusively to the unique interventions of these programs — that is, to net impacts or cause-effect relationships, and 2) results that are due to a variety of influences both within and *outside* these programs, or are occurring simply by *chance*.

If programs are modified or eliminated on the basis of misinformation about the true influence of their interventions on outcomes, we suggest that we are dealing with dysfunctional social policy. Our recommendation is that competent evaluation research, or applied social science research, must be coordinated with or integrated within performance management systems if precise, valid, reliable information about social programs is to be made available to decisionmakers.

In this chapter we are viewing *performance management* and *evaluation research* as "movements." In sociological terms, they may not qualify as movements of the ilk of the civil rights or women's movements. However, movements are characterized by the gradual development and fluorescence of certain patterns of thought and behavior over time, and both *performance management,* as a novel direction in strategic planning and management, and *evaluation research,* as a new direction in applied social research, come close to qualifying as bona fide movements within the life of public and private bureaucracies between the 1960s and the present. This conclusion lends special significance to both phenomena, in terms of the effects each approach has had on planning, managerial, and research approaches.

Our intention is to define the purpose and benefits of both approaches, and to review their disparate histories, as a context for discussing some of the problems we feel need to be addressed, and cautions considered. We are proposing that as performance management has grown in importance and use globally, the critical role of evaluation research has been undervalued. If performance management is viewed as a substitute for the application of scientific research principles and methods, this reflects a lack of sophistication about what constitutes valid and reliable information for improving social policies and programs, and carries the risk of misinforming those making essential policy and program decisions.

Purpose and Nature of the "Movements"

Both the evaluation research and performance management movements· have the general intention of improving the quality and results of social programs and the new coordinated state-level human service systems being developed in the 1990s. However, there are key differences in the two movements. They arise out of different professional disciplines and bureaucratic environments, and have been shaped by different levels of public acceptance. Performance management is a blend of public/private planning and management concepts — particularly strategic planning ideas — that apply to governmental and corporate bureaucracies. Evaluation research is an offshoot of basic social science research supporting economics, sociology, political science, and social psychology, adapted in large part to public social policy bureaucracies. Both movements involve accommodation to bureaucracies in the process of improving the policy process. Both movements seek to increase government *accountability*. As significant elements in an ideal policy process, strategic planning and evaluation are integral and equally important parts. Both yield important benefits and inform one another. But this integration of evaluation and strategic planning concepts has been tentative and often absent in the real world of policymaking.

We are of the firm belief that a more effective coordination or integration of performance management and evaluation research would yield the most useful benefits for social policy development, program and project design, and ongoing program improvement.

Differences Between Performance Management and Evaluation Research

Much of the current tension between the two movements seems to stem from a confusion about each approach's definition and appropriate role in the policy process. Performance measures or indicators are sometimes used to judge program value *in place of* evaluations, and evaluation research is sometimes used *in place of* performance measures. However, performance management is a managerial tool; evaluation research is a research tool. The two movements' different roots and purposes tend to condition the types of activities intended to be conducted — *monitoring* activities for performance management systems; *evaluative* activities for research activities.

Evaluation Research

The ultimate purpose of evaluations is to increase our understanding of key cause and effect relationships in programs. For example, the authors of a major text on evaluation research, Peter Rossi and Howard Freeman, define evaluation research as follows:

> *Evaluation research is the systematic application of social research procedures for assessing the conceptualization, design, implementation, and utility of social intervention programs.* In other words, evaluation researchers use social research methodologies to judge and improve the ways in which human services policies and programs are conducted, from the earliest stages of defining and designing programs through their development and implementation (see Rossi and Freeman 1994).

In this sense, evaluations are conducted to acquire information that will contribute to the development and improvement of social programs. They can be classified within three major categories, based on the questions they seek to answer:

Process Studies. Process or implementation studies answer the question "What happened?" They are undertaken to determine if the program being studied was implemented as intended, and to provide insights about how and why the program may have changed.

Net Impact Studies. Net impact studies address the critical question "What difference did the program make?" These studies seek to determine which program results or outcomes can be attributed exclusively to the program rather than to other influences. Unlike process studies, which are often primarily qualitative in nature, net impact studies depend heavily on quantitative information, relying as they do on experimental research strategies or on nonexperimental approaches that require statistical adjustments in determining the effects of a program on one or more outcome variables of interest. It is important to distinguish net impact studies from studies that simply tell managers what changes may be occurring in outcomes at participants' termination from a program or between the pre-program and post-program periods (see Heckman in Manski and Garfinkel 1993).

Cost-Benefit Studies. Determining that a program has a positive net impact does not mean necessarily that the program is worth continuing. Cost-benefit analyses go beyond net impact studies to answer the question "Is the program's positive net impact sufficient to warrant its costs?" In a cost-benefit analysis, all benefits (positive net impacts) and costs are monetized, and costs and benefits taking place in the future are discounted so that a net present value can be calculated. If the net present value of the program is positive, the program can be judged worthy of continuation.

Without acquiring net impact and cost-benefit information about a program, judgments of its programmatic effectiveness (the extent to which it works as intended) and its cost efficiency cannot be made with any real validity.

Performance Management

Again it is important to point out that performance management stems primarily from management theory and practice rather than from social science research. The federal National Performance Review (NPR 1993) has defined performance management as:

> *The use of performance measurement information to help set agreed-upon performance goals, allocate and prioritize resources, inform managers to either confirm or change current policy or program directions to meet these goals, and report on the success in meeting those goals.*

The NPR states also that performance management is "A process of assessing progress toward achieving predetermined goals, including information on the efficiency with which resources are transformed into goods and services (outputs), the quality of those outputs (how well they are delivered to clients and the extent to which clients are satisfied), outcomes (results of a program activity compared to its intended purpose), and the effectiveness of government operations in terms of their specific contributions to program objectives."

In theory, the minimum components for a performance management system are these: 1) one or more performance measures, which describe the characteristics to be used as proxies for performance, 2) a performance target, standard, and/or benchmark for each measure, which provides the minimum level of acceptable performance, and 3) some type of reward or sanction for deviation from the target, standard, or benchmark.

Performance measures can involve any type of variable of interest to those setting policies for or establishing the system. Measures can include 1) *inputs,* such as the number of individuals enrolled in a program, 2) *processes,* such as implementation of an educational curriculum, 3) *output* variables, such as the number of graduates from a program or the average reading level of participants at completion of a program, 4) measures of *gross change* in a variable, such as the gain in reading scores over the course of a year, and/or 5) measures of *net impact,* such as the change in an outcome (result) that is caused exclusively by the program. However, most operating performance management systems place their primary emphasis on measures of outputs and on gross change in outcomes.

Rewards and sanctions in a performance management system can range, on the positive side, from verbal recognition of a program's standing to monetary rewards for staff or the program as a whole, and, on the negative side, from reduced funding to the loss of the right to operate the program. For example, the Job Training Partnership Act (JTPA) training programs include both carrots — in the form of increased funding with fewer strings attached for good performance — and sticks — in the form of loss of the right to operate the program if poor performance continues for two consecutive years. Interestingly, in its study of "best practices" the NPR concluded that "performance measurement systems should be positive, not punitive."

The fact that performance management is used on a continuous basis while evaluations are typically conducted less frequently has implications for the kinds of measures used in the two approaches. Because the data for a performance management system are collected continuously, the cost of data collection is a more important issue for this system than for evaluations where data are collected less frequently — although many evaluations make some use of monitoring data. Therefore, performance management systems tend to rely more heavily on easier-to-obtain proxy data than do evaluations. Also, to provide meaningful feedback, a performance management system must provide data more rapidly than is the case for evaluations. Consequently, the former tend to rely on existing management information systems, administrative data, and short-term outcomes, compared to the richer data sets and outcome measures involved in evaluations. For example, while an evaluation of the JTPA training programs can look at impacts over one, two, or five years, such a long follow-up period would not be useful in a performance management system.

It should be pointed out also that while the official expectations for performance management systems are strenuous, as in the NPR pronouncements, in practice many such systems fall short of such ideal-type models, as well as inappropriately expanding the purpose of such systems to an evaluative rather than to a more limited monitoring role.

History of the "Movements"

Both movements are older than we may think. The Defense Department in World War II was the source of a beginning focus on *measurable objectives* with its PMRIS (Performance Measurement, Reporting, and Improvement System). And it was an American, W. E. Deming, who conceived "total quality management," an idea adapted first by the Japanese and only much later by selected large-scale American corporations. Many propose that the foundation of performance management lies in Deming's work.

"Management by objectives" was a fashionable concept in the 1960s and 1970s. More recently, Osborne and Gaebler pointed out the failure of the management approach used by most government agencies and suggested how the government could be "reinvented" by applying principles such as competition and mission-driven strategic planning, with an emphasis on customer service and performance management to improve quality and reduce costs (see Osborne and Gaebler 1992).

By 1985, budget deficits in the United States and other post-industrial nations had begun to attract political and media attention. The flexible parts of budgets, including social entitlements and programs, became more vulnerable to scrutiny and emasculation. Determining the public return on taxes spent on social programs was becoming an entrenched requirement.

Meanwhile, in the United States, the evaluation research movement was flourishing during the decades of the sixties through eighties, as the computer revolution took hold, as governments now had the means to collect and analyze large data sets to make judgments about social expenditures, and as taxpayers became more sophisticated about what they wanted for their money. Applied social research came to be viewed as the state-of-the-art strategy for studying the efficiency and effectiveness of social programs and demonstration projects — that is, their efficiency in terms of cost, and their effectiveness in terms of how well they achieved their intended purposes. Evaluation research was distinguished from other approaches by its greater commitment to the study of critical *relationships:* those between 1) implementation policies, practices, and organizational arrangements; 2) program interventions; and 3) program outcomes, net impacts, and costs versus benefits.

For a while, particularly in the 1980s, it seemed that computerization, budget deficits, new taxpayer demands for public accountability, and the utility of competent evaluation research had come together to produce a new, improved climate for defining and judging "government accountability." In the 1980s the Manpower Demonstration Research Corporation undertook a landmark series of evaluations with U.S. Department of Health and Human Services funding to evaluate work/welfare programs, using an experimental design methodology — the least-biased strategy in the evaluation research repertoire for determining the net impact of social programs (see Friedlander and Burtless 1994).

The U.S. Department of Labor (DOL) mounted rigorous evaluations that studied both program implementation and net impact in employment and training programs. Subsequent evaluations were sponsored by U.S. DOL to study homeless and dislocated worker programs, and various demonstration projects. And in 1994, the evaluation research profession developed formal goals and guidelines for evaluators, published in *The Program Evaluation Standards*, that set stringent research standards but at the same time vastly increased the utility of applied research in the policy process, and its potential fit within performance management systems (see Sanders 1994).

In other post-industrial nations in the 1980s, evaluation research was only beginning to evolve as a major strategy for judging the efficiency (in terms of costs) and effectiveness (in terms of goal achievement) of social expenditures. It was not until the 1990s that western European nations began giving serious attention to evaluation research and its potential role in improving government accountability. The recent impetus for evaluation has been spurred by budget deficits and social program decentralization. Evaluation requirements have served as a central government tool for maintaining some level of control over devolved social initiatives. In 1990, the Organization for Economic Cooperation and Development (OECD) produced a monograph on developments in evaluation research across its member nations, to assist members in complying with new evaluation mandates.

In 1994, the European Commission funded panels of research experts to produce an evaluation guide for judging the value of human service and economic development programs funded by the European Union. Recently, professional evaluation research organizations have been formed at the national level in Great Britain and France. But inspectors general, those responsible for government *budgeting*, have remained powerful sources of judgment.

Although some may think of performance management concepts as an American invention, such concepts took hold in New Zealand far ahead of our own use of them, and the model has spread to other countries, particularly Australia, Great Britain, Sweden, and France (see U.S. General Accounting Office, 1993a). The primary goal of these managerial reforms has been to increase accountability through more managerial autonomy and flexibility, and a greater emphasis on the results of government activity rather than its processes. These privatization-oriented reforms have emphasized formal contracts with managers that specify the goals to be achieved and define a set of performance standards for determining goal achievement. New Zealand and the United Kingdom focus on immediate outcomes rather than longer-term net results. Frequently the models have been linked with budgeting, even though cost/benefit studies have not been used to support this linkage. Applied social science only rarely has been an integral part of these approaches.

A cogent illustration of the consequent stereotyping of the performance management and evaluation research movements into two separate camps is the 1997 report of the National Academy of Public Administration on the implementation of the 1993 Government Performance and Results Act (GPRA). Its Panel on Improving Government Performance worked with the American Society of Public Administration and the Office of Management and the Budget (OMB) on studies of the 20 GPRA demonstration projects. The report (NAPA 1997) quotes two of the prime movers on the panel: "Until recently, measuring government performance was an academic exercise with few consequences. The results had little bearing on planning and few lessons and 'best practices' were gleaned for the benefit of others treading in this new area." This was a distortion of the contribution made by evaluation research over the past twenty years in terms of pinning down the results of programs, the influence of their service delivery policies and practices, and their "best practices." And it exaggerated the contribution of performance management to a valid understanding of program efficiency and effectiveness.

So two distinctly different movements have been evolving in the post-industrial nations — one developed mainly in academia and one produced in the crucible of private/public bureaucracies. As these movements were taking shape, the American accounting profession developed a new area of specialization in the 1980s, *performance auditing,* which led budgeting divisions within the federal agencies to conduct their own "evaluative" studies. This event occurred as the American performance management movement gained momentum, increasing the influence of inspector general offices vis-á-vis research offices.

In 1982, the Congress passed the Job Training Partnership Act, which was replaced in August 1998 by the Workforce Investment

Act. JTPA was the first national program to mandate performance measures and standards. This legislation seemed to support the American performance management movement. The legislation involved the decentralization of funds and authority for employment and training programs to states, with accompanying accountability requirements. Performance management, with its emphasis on outcomes, was viewed again as a way for the federal government to compensate for the devolution of resources and authority to the state level. Performance management was also a response to the growing multiplication and fragmentation of the social program network, a response to a renewed emphasis on coordination and human service coordination, echoing the concerns of the 1970s.

During the Clinton administration, states were encouraged to develop human investment councils that would coordinate, monitor, and evaluate an array of related programs. Many states have done so. The State Job Training Coordinating Council Chairs' national organization produced *Bring Down the Barriers,* which supported the creation of investment councils. At the same time, the federal government developed new linkages across agencies with related programs, and has expected new results-oriented accountability internally under the Government Performance and Results Act of 1993. In October 1997, all federal agencies were required to submit an annual results-focused strategic plan to OMB detailing their compliance with this act. Meanwhile, in 1991 the federal Job Training 2000 Performance Standards subgroup recommended a core set of measures for employment and training programs. And the U.S. Department of Health and Human Services produced *Getting Results: A Guide to Government Accountability,* which defined the basic elements of a public accountability system in the performance management mode, borrowing from international models and from home-grown strategic planning concepts. All of these initiatives increased interest in performance management.

At both the federal and state levels, the performance management movement is now taking hold. Performance standards, and incentive/sanction systems to support their use, are now part of Titles II, III, and IV of JTPA, the Jobs Corps under the Department of Labor, and the Food Stamp Employment and Training Program under the Department of Agriculture. And their use was mandated (although never implemented) for the JOBS program under the Department of Health and Human Services. In the early 1990s the Clinton administration sponsored the Core Data Elements and Common Definitions project, which developed a common set of measures that could be used across all employment and training programs in monitoring their results, in most cases against performance standards. In 1994, the National Center for Research in Vocational Education produced *Beyond Performance Standards,* which pinpointed which variables in vocational programs were the most critical to measure in performance standards systems.

Also in 1994, the National Governors Association sponsored the Performance Management Project, involving a dozen states in a demonstration of performance management models. Their report framing this project, *Building State Workforce Development Systems Based on Policy Coordination and Quality Assurance,* focused on strategic planning and performance measurement, including a limited role for evaluation research. The state-level performance management systems being created in the 1990s have typically involved the development of a vision, goals, measurable objectives, performance measures, desired outcomes utilizing these measures, and sometimes performance standards and longer-term benchmarks involving such performance measures. Few have emphasized process issues. Few have incorporated evaluation research.

Problems Related to a Lack of Integration of Performance Management with Evaluation Research

Some performance management systems assume inappropriately that the outcomes measured in these systems are due mainly to the program being monitored, rather than to other causes which may be outside the control of program managers. A major risk is that judgments of program value will be made on the basis of these outcomes, with potential implications for the way programs may be modified and funded.

Conceptualization Issues

Social programs are based on *theories of change*. They hypothesize a particular relationship between *social change agents* (social interventions) and the *net impacts* program designers desire. In proposing such a relationship, the designers make certain *assumptions* about the people, groups, or organizations to be changed, the ability of the change agents to achieve program goals, and the nature of the environment in which the program operates.

To identify problems in implementing programs or systems, or in the results they are having, several key questions need to be answered in collecting information. Otherwise there is insufficient information to pinpoint such problems and make valid judgments about how to resolve them. Continuous program or system improvement is, in this sense, highly dependent on information that goes beyond the collection of measures of outcomes. Focusing as it does primarily on outcomes, performance management systems tend to give too little attention to the whole of program theory. Consequently such systems can be deficient in judging how a program's implementation and/or interventions have contributed to the outcomes reported.

Some major questions to be addressed in contributing information useful to program, system, or policy improvement are these:

- Is the program or system being implemented as intended?

- Are the interventions actually being delivered the intended ones?

- Are those being exposed to the interventions the ones intended to be exposed?

- Are the outcomes for those being exposed to the interventions the results that were intended?

- What are the intermediate, short-term, and longer-term outcomes of those exposed to the interventions?

❀ What outcomes are directly attributable to the implementation mode and/or the interventions (i.e., what are the net impacts)?

❀ What separate influence does the implementation mode appear to have on outcomes?

❀ What separate influence do the interventions appear to have on outcomes?

❀ What is the trade-off between costs and net impacts?

The use of performance measures and standards is appropriate for monitoring compliance with governmental regulations regarding a program (the first four questions), or for comparing program realities against a formal program plan. And they are useful in judging the level of *outcomes* achieved for a program or system's customers. The benefit is in greater managerial control and general accountability. But performance management is of far less use in understanding how the interventions or the implementation process may or may not have caused or influenced these outcomes. Therefore, if bereft of periodic evaluations of implementation and net impact, performance management systems are not capable of testing program theory.

However, if performance management is to improve programs, it must utilize information flowing from a test of program theory. Outcomes can be caused by factors unrelated to a program's proposed relationship between interventions and outcomes — by the nature of those selected to be served, by the environment of the program, by the fact that performance standards and incentives exist, and so on. These potential biases are masked by blind acceptance of outcomes as if they represented net impact information. If performance management data are then tied to budget decisions, such information can lead to flawed social remedies. For example, the National Performance Review requires each federal agency to produce "results-oriented financial statements" based on performance agreements using performance measures, linking policy priorities, results, and funding.

The vocational education community in Washington State, for example, decided to embrace a form of performance management in studying the results of vocational education interventions in the state's community colleges. Managers selected a small set of outcome measures with an emphasis on obtaining employment, and collected employment data from unemployment insurance wage files. The interventions themselves were not measured, nor were there any qualitative measures of the way in which vocational education was delivered to customers. The characteristics of the customers themselves were not well measured. Only outcome data were systematically collected. Reports implied that these outcomes could be attributed to vocational education courses, and concluded that community colleges were highly successful. Later, an independent net impact evaluation of state vocational education and job training programs revealed the complexities of the relationship between vocational education interventions and employment outcomes, suggesting that community colleges were only one influence on the outcomes reported. If legislative budgeting had depended heavily on these performance management reports, colleges might have been given increased funding without any valid evidence of the singular effects of vocational education on employment opportunities.

The Office of Technology Assessment's analysis of the use of educational skills standards as part of performance management points out that a key problem is the lack of information on the complexity of programs and a reliance on the narrow sets of measures in performance standards (see Wirt 1995).

Competent evaluation researchers will recommend that those funding accountability strategies look holistically at all the elements of program theory: at the organizational aspects of a program, at the nature of management, at the steps in the service delivery system, at staffing characteristics, at the nature of the customers eligible to be served, at the way customers are selected for and assigned to service, their experiences in the program, at the mixes and sequences of services they actually received, and at their outcomes at program termination and various points beyond termination.

If funders are alert to the significance of insufficient information, they will underwrite *comprehensive evaluations* that look at process and net impact variables to determine which results can be attributed more exclusively to the program's interventions. By the mid-1980s and into the 1990s, the U.S. Department of Labor has taken this scientific route *along with* an emphasis on performance management.

Measurement Issues

Performance management places great emphasis on the development of measurable objectives and the identification of quantifiable outcomes. These are operational expressions of program or system goals. However, there are a number of measurement issues of concern.

The Emphasis on a Narrow Set of Quantitative Outcome Measures. Two measurement issues limit the utility of performance management information: 1) the development of a restricted set of easily quantifiable and collected outcome measures, and 2) the lack of operational definitions and measures for program and system interventions — measures both of the implementation mode and of the services and/or subsidies provided. Both issues relate back to the need to give attention to the whole of program theory in providing accurate, useful information to those making program and system decisions.

Limiting outcome measures to a small, manageable set, and a set that can be accessed readily in "management information systems" associated with programs, may be efficient in terms of initial cost, but such a set may miss critical variables in explaining what works and does not work within a program or system. In performance management systems involving employment and training programs, most states have confined their outcome measures to job placement and wages at program termination and short-term follow-up, without considering intermediate outcomes such as skill upgrading, short-term outcomes such as job quality, and longer-term outcomes such as job retention.

The heavy dependence on limited quantitative indicators also ignores important qualitative outcomes such as attitude changes or changes in family life that are highly relevant in securing and maintaining satisfactory jobs and income. And measures of taxpaying and job substitution effects frequently are ignored. Evaluation research can complement the performance management system's information repertoire by providing a richer array of outcome measures, as well as of net impacts and costs versus benefits.

Frequency and Length of Measurement. An additional issue is the frequency and length of measurement — that is, at what intervals and over what period of time outcomes are measured in performance management systems. Typically such systems rely on a few measurement points over a relatively short period of time, such as at the end of a program and several months beyond termination. Evaluation research studies have suggested that this limitation can produce misleading information, which a more frequent measurement interval and longer measurement period could correct. Well-designed longitudinal surveys with multiple measurement points can reduce bias in information production, but these are rarely an integral part of performance management.

Validity. The fascination with "indicators" is, of course, not new. But many indicator data sets are secondary data, meaning that users have not developed these measures themselves, based on their own unique information needs, but are utilizing data sets created by others. Frequently the data elements in these sets are adopted without question in management information systems.

"Validity" reflects the extent to which a data element truly represents a more abstract variable. In the performance systems of many employment and training programs, "obtained a job following program termination" stands for "successful employment outcome," even if the job is tenuous, of low quality, and with few benefits and poor working conditions. For example, recent analyses of JTPA data indicated that the short-term measures in JTPA performance standards were only weakly related to JTPA's intended goals of increased employment and earnings. Evaluation researchers have sometimes been naive about measurement issues as well, but the professional commitment to testing the validity of measures has been much stronger.

In some of the states participating in the National Governors Association's project on performance management, certain outcome measures were taken for granted as representing program or system goals. This illustrates the tendency to leap from abstractions to specific measures without first clearly defining the goals, operationalizing objectives under these goals, and then selecting or developing specific measures under these objectives. This leap reduces the validity of the measures. The problem is compounded by selecting measures mainly on the basis of their availability in preexisting information systems. Under cost pressures, this has been the case in some of the NGA states.

Data Reliability and Consistency. In a Washington State evaluation of vocational education and public employment and training impacts, researchers needed to "clean" data sets and compensate for "missing data," a sizable task often encountered in evaluations where studies utilize data from existing administrative data systems. A 1994 Office of Technology Assessment project studied numerous efforts to use administrative data for performance management purposes and identified a number of data reliability problems. The Northeast/Midwest Institute, the National Commission for Employment Policy, and Mathematica Policy Research all found problems with the data collected in management information systems. Yet most states' performance management systems rely exclusively on administrative data.

Also, most states developing statewide human service councils or boards have not integrated the plethora of data systems supporting the programs under these umbrella bureaucracies. The Departments of Labor and Education engaged in unprecedented collaboration in the 1990s to develop a core set of operational definitions and measures for programs under their jurisdiction. (See U.S. Department of Labor 1996.) But states are only beginning to adopt such core sets. Performance management systems that lack crosswalks from one data set to another, or lack a single automated system for all related programs, must use genuine caution in interpreting the program outcomes collected.

The Advisory Panel of the National Academy of Public Administration has, itself, recommended that richer, more valid, more reliable, and more timely measures be used in performance management systems. This is an area in which evaluation research can play an important complementary role (see National Academy 1997).

Various types of performance measures have utility under some circumstances. We have no concern about their use in monitoring the performance of government programs. Our concern is related to the interpretations that are sometimes made of this information. While interpretations of inputs, processes, and improvements from previous years are not likely to be confused with net impacts, there is a danger that information on the level of an outcome variable, or on the change in outcomes between the pre-program and post-program period may be confused with net impacts.

Methodological Issues

Again, the major methodological problem in most performance management systems is the tendency to attribute the outcomes collected in these systems to social programs or entire human investment systems — that is, *to assume that these programs or systems are responsible for the outcomes collected.* They certainly may be, but without conducting a net impact evaluation (and a parallel study of the recruitment, selection, and assignment processes in programs, if a nonexperimental research design is used), there is no way to know whether these outcomes are the program's own product. Therefore it is extremely risky to base management and/or funding decisions on outcomes alone. Furthermore, managers relying exclusively on outcome information do not benefit from cost-benefit information, which is dependent on measuring net impacts. Unfortunately, many performance managers and stakeholders make the assumption that outcomes are, in fact, net impacts, and measure program costs only. Evaluation research therefore serves as an essential check on judgments based only on outcomes and adds information about the trade-off between costs and benefits.

For example, the performance management system for the U.S. Department of Labor's training programs was developed in the late 1970s when the assistant secretary for policy, evaluation, and research was an economist, so the performance management system for JTPA uses proxy measures for net program impacts as its performance measures. Performance by local programs is measured by using management information system data to estimate the relationship between post-program employment and earnings and individual and local area characteristics. Regression analysis is used to estimate this relationship, with performance measured by the deviation of the predicted level of the outcome variable from the actual level. There are two potential problems with such a system. The lack of a control group means that at best the performance management system can measure only the relative performance of local programs. The lack of a control group makes it impossible to determine the net impact of the program. In addition, a limited number of proxy variables are available to control for differences across local areas, making it likely that the performance measures are weak proxies for net impact. One of the authors of this paper, working with data from the JTPA experimental evaluation, demonstrated, in fact, that net impact and performance were only weakly correlated.

None of the points made above are meant to reflect negatively on performance measures if they are properly used. Because a performance management system must provide data quickly and inexpensively, it is not necessary that the interpretation of the data be as accurate, or the assessment of the data hold true for as long a follow-up period, as is the case for an impact evaluation. Clearly, periodic net impact evaluations, process studies, and cost-benefit analyses are needed to determine the program's net impact and efficacy, even though a simpler system can be used for making assessments of day-to-day progress.

Performance Standards

Performance measurement typically involves the development of performance *targets*, *standards*, and *benchmarks* that utilize the limited set of quantitative measures collected in the management information systems of performance management systems. These targets,

standards, and benchmarks have become a key element in performance management systems. The purpose of performance standards
is to increase compliance with the intent of programs, and some studies have suggested this is indeed their benefit.

Going a step further, in federal programs such as JTPA, monetary incentive/sanction systems support compliance with the standards selected. However, where the achievement or surpassing of
standards is rewarded with an increase in funding or poor performance is punished through greater oversight on the part of the
funder, the fear has been that performance standards can act as a
potentially negative influence on programs, such as redirecting
them away from their intent.

A series of studies of the influence of JTPA performance standards and incentives on managerial decisions were conducted in
the 1990s, based on data collected in the National JTPA Experiment,
an experimental net impact evaluation of JTPA. These studies suggested that in some instances performance standards had a strong
influence on program managers and staffs in moving programs
away from their intent, and that the short-term measures used in
setting standards were only weakly, and often negatively, related to
longer-term employment and earnings effects — that is, to the original goals of the program. Program managers were making client
placement, enrollment, and termination decisions consistent with
the need to meet or exceed standards, rather than on the needs of eligible clients.

A National Governors Association report on the use of skills
standards suggested that setting absolute standards of expected
performance had given standards the power to direct behavior, but
often in the wrong direction due to the tendency to use outcomes as
the basis for possibly misleading "go-no go" decisions. A 1988 SRI
International study of JTPA concluded that performance standards
had decreased services to the "hard to serve." A Stanford PhD dissertation suggested that JTPA areas receiving the greatest incentive
payments had enrolled a disproportionate number of clients with
substantial work experience. And some JTPA programs were resisting the enrollment of their expected share of welfare clients in order
to meet performance standards. A Manpower Demonstration

Research Corporation study in the 1990s suggested that the outcomes collected in welfare-to-work programs were only weakly correlated with program goals, and sometimes undercut such goals. A 1991 GAO report suggested that JTPA performance standards and the incentive/sanction system associated with them were resulting in serious inequities, reducing the access of women and minorities to the program, and reducing clients' access to appropriate training options.

Some experts maintain that the risks are most pronounced where gross outcomes are used as a basis for budgeting decisions. The increased power of the accounting profession, in the form of inspector general offices, has been a new concern. The 1990 report of the Government Accounting Standards Board is a case in point (see Hatry and Fountain 1990). The report moves inspectors general into "performance auditing," which emphasizes quick turnaround reviews of outcomes, which are then linked to budget decisions. Auditors performing these reviews tend not to be trained in evaluation research principles and methods, or to be sufficiently concerned about the risk of reporting faulty judgments of programs based on the assumption that they have "caused" the outcomes collected. For example, audits of JTPA have conflicted with information from rigorous evaluations. Where the potential exists for a reduction in funding or the elimination of a program, the results of evaluations need to be a key contribution to decisionmaking.

Improving Performance Management Systems

Clearly there are major benefits to a system that provides a more logical framework for establishing public accountability in the social policy arena. The strategic planning principles and practices that are central to performance management have spawned a new view of how managers must proceed within a commitment to continuously maintain quality, respond more effectively to customers, and improve programs. The General Accounting Office's judgment is that performance management has increased significantly the federal government's efficiency and effectiveness. Also, performance management systems have set a norm for developing improved automated information systems for providing evidence of accountability. However, problems remain to be addressed in all performance management systems, in the United States and elsewhere.

Strategies for Better Performance Management

The following suggestions can increase the capability of performance management systems to provide both ongoing monitoring information and information on program efficiency and effectiveness:

Conceptualization

❀ Include within a performance management system both qualitative and quantitative measures describing all the key variables involved in the theory of a program: its participants; its organizational structure and functions; its service delivery system; its treatments (services) for participants; its gross outcomes for participants; its overall efficiency and effectiveness (its net impact, if feasible, and its costs in the context of that impact — that is, its cost/benefit trade-off).

❀ Utilize evaluation research as a complement to ongoing information collection within the strategic planning emphasis in performance management.

The emphasis in performance management is not only on results but on continuous information production. Evaluation research is frequently viewed only as a periodic activity. In standard studies of implementation and/or net impact, frequently this is true. However, scientifically designed longitudinal surveys provide continuous information. And process, net impact, and cost/benefit evaluations can be conducted at regular intervals, as an integral part of information production. In this sense, evaluation research can be perceived as a tool for increasing the ability of performance management systems to inform public policy through the production of more valid and reliable (less-biased) information about program efficiency and effectiveness.

❀ Provide training on basic research principles and methods to performance management staff, to reduce information bias and to prevent drawing unwarranted inferences from gross outcome information.

Measurement

❀ Encourage evaluation researchers to familiarize themselves more thoroughly with the theory on which a program is based, in order to develop more useful measures of the variables of interest.

❀ Develop a common core set of qualitative and quantitative measures that are valid in representing key aspects of related programs: measures of program implementation, outcomes, longer-term impact, and costs vs. benefits.

❀ Involve evaluation researchers, customers, and stakeholders in the development of a comprehensive set of process, outcome, impact, and cost-benefit measures surrounding the core set.

❀ Move from a simple, timely, easily quantifiable set of rough proxies for program intent to more sophisticated, accurate, and complex approximations of means and goals.

❋ Develop management information systems capable of collecting, storing, extracting, analyzing, and reporting a broad array of program information on individual customers, as well as important information about the organizational aspects of programs.

❋ Collect measures reliably and monitor their ongoing utility and quality.

❋ Build in incentives for managers to actually use the information available to them.

❋ At the same time, avoid reinforcing the development of "performance information bureaucracies."

Methodology

❋ Mesh evaluation research with performance management to reduce the use of biased and misleading information in making judgments of the value of programs, to gain a better knowledge of the critical relationship between program interventions and goal achievement, and to acquire information about the trade-off between program costs and program impact (benefits).

❋ Bring researchers into the strategic planning process throughout, as collaborators in an interdisciplinary team, so that this process is infused with competent advice about the kind of evaluations that will be most feasible and useful to decision makers, and at what decision points.

Performance Standards

❋ Base the development of standards on a comprehensive set of measures describing program participants, service treatments, participant outcomes, and net program impact.

❀ Develop standards only after a broad range of relevant program information has been collected over a reasonable length of time, so that analysts can determine which measures are the most valid, reliable, and useful for incorporation in standards.

❀ Utilize panels of experts to develop outcome measures that can be used initially as targets or benchmarks, rather than as goals circumscribed by incentives and sanctions.

❀ Develop incentive/sanction systems only very gradually, drawing insights from the operation of a program, the use of standards, and the results of evaluations, being aware of the potential negative impact of incentive/sanction systems on decisions affecting a program's direction. Large incentives to exceed performance standards raise issues of feasibility and fairness.

❀ Make available to funders and stakeholders information that will help explain the meaning and significance of the gross outcomes collected in performance management systems and from program evaluations.

❀ Ensure that adjustments to performance standards are fair and create the right incentives. Adjustments can be used to encourage equity as well as to correct for different environments — but determining the appropriate adjustments can be difficult.

❀ Adjust standards to take account of differences in the environment, and in the characteristics of participants.

As a monitoring tool for program managers, performance management can provide important short-term turnaround information for tracking progress against stated goals, focusing on outcome measures. As a research tool, evaluation research can provide the broad range of information needed to make relatively unbiased judgments of program or system efficiency and effectiveness. Each approach has the benefit of increasing the accountability of programs and human service systems to their customers and stakeholders, and enhance policymakers' ability to make choices among a range of program options.

Used as complementary tools, both "movements" can offer vastly more valid and reliable information to decision makers, and more accurately guide improvements in programs. Performance management contributes information for strategic planning, monitoring, and operational efficiency. Evaluation research contributes information about the causal processes involved in programs, and provides a check on the validity of shorter-term performance strategies. Evaluations can be used in selecting performance measures and developing strategic plans, and the strategic planning process can help agencies determine the outcomes against which programs should be evaluated. The U.S. General Accounting Office has recommended this kind of collaboration, suggesting that evaluations constitute one of the six broad components of agency strategic plans (see U.S. GAO 1997d).

Consequently we recommend that the major direction for the future is to coordinate evaluation research with performance management systems more fully, moving toward full integration of evaluations within performance management. Such integration will require that performance management systems treat evaluators not as aliens from outer space, who land only periodically to study and give advice, but as part of an interdisciplinary team. It will require that evaluators become more sensitized to managers' needs to have ongoing information for tracking outcomes, and to express the benefits of their professional roots with greater humility.

References

Baj, J. et al. (1991). *Feasibility Study of the Use of Unemployment Insurance Wage Record Data as an Evaluation Tool for JTPA.* Washington, DC: National Commission for Employment Policy.

Barnow, B. (1992). "The Effect of Performance Standards on State and Local Programs," in *Evaluating Welfare Training Programs,* edited by C. Manski and G. Garfinkel. Cambridge, MA: Harvard University Press.

Bartik, T. J. (1995). *Using Performance Indicators to Improve the Effectiveness of Welfare-to-Work Programs.* Kalamazoo, MI: W.E. Upjohn Institute for Employment Research.

Bishop, J. (1989). *Policy Evaluation and Archived Wage Record Data: Limitations of Existing Data Sets.* Washington, DC: Northeast/Midwest Institute.

Blalock, A. B. (senior author). (1980). *Introduction to Social Research* (2nd Edition). Newbury Park, CA: Sage Publications.

Blalock, A. B. (editor and author). *Evaluation Forum.* A research journal. U.S. Department of Labor: Office of Policy and Research, 1988-1998. In particular, see a series of articles on performance management in issues #11 and #12.

Blalock, A. B. (Ed.) (1990). *Evaluating Social Programs.* Kalamazoo, MI: W.E. Upjohn Institute for Employment Research.

Chelimsky, E. (1985). "Comparing and Contrasting Auditing and Evaluation," *Evaluation Review* 9.

Cook, T. and C. Reichardt. (Eds.) (1979). *Qualitative and Quantitative Methods in Evaluation Research.* Newbury Park, CA: Sage Publications.

Decker, P. (1989). *Systematic Bias in Earnings Data Derived from Unemployment Insurance Wage Records and Implications for Evaluating the Impact of Unemployment Insurance Policy on Earnings.* Princeton, NJ: Mathematica Policy Research.

Deming, W. E. (1982). *Out of the Crisis.* Cambridge, MA: Massachusetts Institute of Technology's Center for Advanced Engineering Study.

Epstein, P. (1992). "Get Ready: The Time for Performance Measurement is Finally Coming," *Public Administration Review,* September/October.

Friedlander, D. and G. Burtless. (1994). *Five Years After: The Long-Term Effects of Welfare-to-Work Programs.* New York, NY: Russell Sage Foundation.

Hatry, H. et al. (1981). *Performance Measurement — A Guide for Local Elected Officials.* Washington, DC: The Urban Institute.

Hatry, H. and D. Fountain. (1990). *Service Efforts and Accomplishments Information: Its Time Has Come.* Norwalk, CT: Governmental Accounting Standards Board.

Hatry, H. and J. Wholey. (1994). *Toward Useful Performance Measurement: Lessons Learned from Initial Pilot Performance Plans Prepared Under the Government Performance and Results Act.* Washington, DC: National Academy of Public Administration.

Heckman, J. (1993). "Randomization and Social Program Evaluation," in *Evaluating Welfare and Training Programs* edited by C. Manski and G. Garfinkel. Cambridge, MA: Harvard University Press.

Herman, J. (1987). *Program Evaluation Kit.* Thousand Oaks, CA: Sage Publications.

Kettl, D. (1993). *Improving Government Performance: An Owner's Manual.* Washington, DC: The Brookings Institution.

_____ (1997). *The Global Revolution in Public Management.* Washington, DC: The Brookings Institution.

Levin, H. (1983). *Cost-Effectiveness: A Primer.* Thousand Oaks, CA: Sage Publications.

Mark, M. and E. Pines. (1995). "Implications of Continuous Quality Improvement for Program Evaluation and Evaluators," *Evaluation Practice,* June.

Meyer, K. and K. O'Shaugnessy. (1993). "Organizational Design and the Performance Paradox," in *Explorations in Economic Sociology,* edited by R. Swedberg. New York, NY: Russell Sage Foundation.

Mohr, L. (1992). *Impact Analysis for Program Evaluation.* Thousand Oaks, CA: Sage Publications.

Moore, M. (1993). *Accounting for Change: Reconciling the Demands for Accountability and Innovation in the Public Sector.* Washington, DC: Council for Excellence in Government.

National Academy of Public Administration (1997). *Improving Performance/Improving Government,* Washington, DC.

National Performance Review (NPR). (1993). *From Red Tape to Results: Creating a Government That Works Better and Costs Less,* Washington, DC. See also *Putting Customers First: Standards for Serving the American People* (1994) and *Common Sense Government* (1995).

Osborne, D. and T. Gaebler. (1992). *Reinventing Government: How the Entrepreneurial Spirit Is Transforming the Public Sector.* Reading, MA: Addison-Wesley Press.

Patton, M. (1990). *Qualitative Evaluation and Research Methods.* Thousand Oaks, CA: Sage Publications.

Pawson, R. and N. Tilley. (1997). *Realistic Evaluation.* London, England: Sage Publications.

Rahn, M. et al. (1992). *State Systems for Accountability in Vocational Education.* Washington, DC: National Center for Research in Vocational Education, U.S. Department of Education.

Rossi, P. and H. Freeman. (1994). *Evaluation: A Systematic Approach.* Thousand Oaks, CA: Sage Publications.

Sanders, J. (1994). *The Program Evaluation Standards.* Thousand Oaks, CA: Sage Publications.

Shadish, W. et al. (1991). *Foundations of Program Evaluation: Theories of Practice.* Newbury Park, CA: Sage Publications.

Smith, P. (1995). "On the Unintended Consequences of Publishing Performance Data in the Public Sector," *International Journal of Public Administration* 18.

Stern, Elliot. (1996). An interview with the European Commission's Financial Controller, *Evaluation.*

Strauss, A. (1987). *Qualitative Analysis for Social Scientists.* New York, NY: Cambridge University Press.

Stevens, D. (1989). *Using State Unemployment Insurance Wage Records to Trace the Subsequent Labor Market Experiences of Vocational Education Program Leavers.* National Assessment of Vocational Education. Washington, DC: U.S. Department of Education.

U.S. Congress. (1994). *Performance Standards for the Food Stamp Employment and Training Program.* Washington, DC: Office of Technology Assessment.

U.S. Department of Labor. (1996). *Core Data Elements and Common Definitions for Employment and Training Programs.*

U.S. Department of the Treasury. (1993). *Performance Measurement: Report on a Survey of Private Sector Performance Measures.* Washington, DC.

U.S. General Accounting Office (1997a). *Measuring Performance: Strengths and Limitations of Research Indicators.* Washington, DC, March.

_____ (1997b). *GPRA – Managerial Accountability and Flexibility Pilot Did Not Work As Intended.* Washington, DC, April.

_____ (1997c). *Managing for Results: Analytic Challenges in Measuring Performance.* Washington, DC, May.

_____ (1997d). *Agencies' Strategic Plans Under GPRA: Key Questions to Facilitate Congressional Review,* Washington, DC, May.

_____ (1995). *Government Reform: Goal-Setting and Performance.* Washington, DC.

_____ (1994). *Managing for Results: State Experiences Provide Insights for Federal Management Reforms.* Washington, DC, December.

_____ (1993a). *Managing for Results: Experience in Four European Countries and How They Might be Applied in the U.S.* Washington, DC, January.

_____ (1993b). *Performance Budgeting.* Washington, DC, February.

_____ (1993c). *Improving Government: Measuring Performance and Acting on Proposals for Change.* Washington, DC, March.

_____ (1993d). *Using Performance Measures in the Federal Budget Process.* Washington, DC.

_____ (1993e). *Measuring Performance and Acting on Proposals for Change.* Washington, DC.

_____ (1992). *Program Performance Measures.* Washington, DC, May.

Volcker, P. (1989). *Leadership for America: Rebuilding the Public Service.* Washington, DC: The Federal Reserve.

Wirt, J. G. (1995). *Performance Assessment Systems: Implications for a National System of Skill Standards.* Washington, DC: National Governors Association.

Wholey, J., K. Newcomber and Associates. (1989). *Improving Government Performance.* San Francisco, CA: Jossey-Bass.

18

Pitfalls in Designing and Implementing Performance Management Systems

Dall W. Forsythe

During the second half of the 1990s, the federal government worked its way through a long, slow, and still incomplete implementation of a governmentwide performance management system, as mandated by the Government Performance and Results Act of 1993 (GPRA). As Richard Nathan's introduction to this volume makes clear, reasonable people can still disagree about whether performance management in the federal government is a glass half full or half empty. Optimists believe that GPRA will help improve management in Washington, make the federal government more accountable, and improve resource allocation decisions. Pessimists worry that incoming officials will succumb to the temptation to pick another three or four letters of the alphabet and start all over again, or that GPRA will end up another in a long list of costly and failed reform initiatives, adding to the federal paperwork burden as did earlier reforms like Performance Planning Budgeting Systems (PPBS), Management by Objective (MBO), and Zero-Based Budgeting (ZBB).

Drawing on the case studies and analytic chapters in the rest of this book, this essay summarizes findings from earlier experience at all levels of government with performance management, and uses those findings to look ahead to the problems GPRA will face in its next phase of implementation. Along the continuum from optimism to skepticism, I sit uncomfortably in the middle. On the one hand, I see performance management (PM) systems as valuable tools for managers and overseers of public agencies. Skeptics often understate the benefits of performance measures linked to strategic plans, and overstate the difficulties of obtaining useful information from PM systems. On the other hand, there are limits to the value of performance data, and many difficulties associated with designing and implementing PM systems. Advocates sometimes commit what Schick calls "the great mistake of the performance measurement industry" — assuming that "an organization can be transformed by measuring its performance" (chapter 3 in this volume). The limits of performance management are especially evident in performance budgeting, which has not transformed governmental budgeting as its most optimistic proponents expected. This chapter focuses more carefully those problems and discusses some successful strategies for overcoming them, so managers and overseers have a better chance to reap the benefits of performance management systems.

A "performance management system" is an interrelated set of performance plans and performance indicators and or measures. Strategic plans or other multi-year business plans are key ingredients of all performance management systems. Without such plans, a government may boast of a set of performance indicators, but does not have a performance management system. Some PM systems provide incentives for high performance or sanctions for shortfalls in results. Some are also linked to budgetary decision processes through one or another variant of what is usually called performance budgeting. In chapter 2, Hatry provides a more extensive introduction to the vocabulary of performance measurement and management.

Any of these elements may be the source of design and implementation problems. Confusion about the goals or audiences of performance information, inattention to measurement challenges, and poor choices of incentives are all sources of difficulties for PM systems. Special problems arise when trying to manage the performance of agents outside the direct control of an agency, including independent contractors and other levels of government. Opposition within the bureaucracy can derail PM systems during implementation, and additional difficulties arise when a government tries to use performance data to allocate resources. Finally, performance management systems sometimes clash with the political needs of elected officials. I discuss each of these problem areas in turn. At the end of the chapter, I return to GPRA to examine the pitfalls and possibilities it faces during the next stages of its implementation.

Designing Performance Management Systems to Fulfill Multiple Goals

Performance management systems seek improvement in three primary areas:[1]

- *Accountability*: Data on government performance can help elected officials as well as citizens and the media judge whether government is performing adequately.

- *Management improvement*: While "performance measurement does not, in itself, produce performance," (Ingraham and Moynihan, chapter 12), PM systems can provide strategic focus, useful metrics, and goals and incentives to help government agencies manage better.

- *Decisionmaking*: Information about the performance of government agencies and programs can be used in budget deliberations and other decisionmaking processes.

Disputes about the proper design of performance management systems often reflect confusion about the relative priority of these three goals. High-level, top-down systems designed for accountability may not link easily to actual agency operations, and may not provide data useful for managers of those operational units. For example, the Oregon Benchmarks system was originally designed to help citizens and government officials gauge the progress of the state on broad social goals such as reducing poverty and improving air quality. But Oregon's top-down social indicators (or "end outcome measures," to use the performance management term) were so sweeping that they were distant from the day-to-day activities of most government managers. Thus, the benchmarks have proved to be of limited value in encouraging management improvement.[2]

Alternatively, bottom-up systems producing data for day-to-day management may not yield information of much value for accountability and oversight. For example, the City of New York has produced a semi-annual Mayor's Management Report for 25 years. Some of the data in that report are useful for tracking real-time agency performance, but provide little information that is useful to the public, the mayor, or the City Council. For example, the Sanitation Commissioner may care about simple output measures such as the number of mechanical broom routes scheduled and the percentage of those routes completed. But for accountability purposes, the Mayor's Office of Operations also publishes trained observers' survey data on street cleanliness — a much better measure of at least one of the outcomes the public wants.[3]

Additional PM design issues arise if a goal is improved budgetary decisionmaking. While agency managers require data about all the activities in their departments, budget offices and the chief executives whom they serve need fewer indicators, focused on strategically important activities in each agency. To be employed in budget making, performance data must be available for the same organizational units as used in budget accounts, and must be delivered on a schedule that meshes with the calendar for preparing the budget. The critical work of budget preparation takes place part way through the fiscal year, but performance management systems may produce data at the end of a fiscal year. Budget officials may also want efficiency or productivity measures based on cost-accounting data that can be expensive and difficult for agencies to collect. The budget office and the chief executive, together with the legislature, may also want performance data about similar programs delivered by agencies in different departments. Data on activities that spill over agency lines — called crosscutting programs in the parlance of federal performance management — have been painfully hard to produce.

Although the chief executive and the legislature may agree on the need for data on crosscutting programs, divergent legislative and executive goals for performance management data can imperil PM systems. In 1981, as part of legislation requiring New York State to use generally accepted accounting principles (GAAP) in its budgeting and financial reporting, the legislature also authorized a performance measurement system called the Key Item Reporting System (KIRS). The executive branch, led by the Division of the Budget, complained bitterly. Opponents argued that that KIRS indicators measured performance in marginal programs of special interest to the legislature, and that those data were not suitable for comprehensive oversight or decisionmaking, much less management improvement. In spite of the statutory basis of KIRS, executive branch compliance was grudging and spotty. After the executive branch was criticized in the press for poor compliance, Governor Cuomo argued that the statute was a failure and eventually won its repeal.

Overall, without careful attention to each goal, managers can easily make mistakes as they design useful performance indicators and PM systems. In chapter 14, Robert Bradley and Geraldo Flowers show how officials in Florida designed Performance-Based Program Budgeting (PB^2) with an eye toward different goals and the needs of different audiences, and thereby reduced the risk that Florida's PM system would malfunction.

Measurement Challenges

A recurring theme in the debate over performance management concerns the usefulness of measures of end outcomes. Legislators and other overseers often argue that the executive's preferred performance indicators are too narrow, and push for broader outcome measures. Agency managers and their bosses respond that output measures are more useful for tracking and evaluating their work, and for improving agency management. In Washington, this is a regular theme in GAO assessments of agency performance plans and reports.

Agency managers are uncomfortable about being accountable for broad outcomes, arguing that their work may have only limited impact on them. For instance, prominent among the 90 Oregon

Benchmarks are infant mortality and teen-age pregnancy rates. Success or failure in meeting those targets depends on many factors, including federal policy and programs, the economy, demographics, and community values. However, the legislature and public may find information about end outcomes more valuable than data on workloads, such as the report from the Adult and Family Services Division that the Oregon Health Plan Branch handled 252,000 applications and reapplications during the last biennium.

Experienced designers of performance management systems conclude that governments should use a combination of input, output and outcome measures to track key programs (Hatry, 1999). Support for that approach can be found in recent work to develop "balanced scorecards" for corporations. These include not just financial data but also information on customer needs, internal business processes and procedures, and personnel skill levels and technology systems. Proponents of balanced scorecards also try to complement outcome data, which are retrospective, with forward-looking indicators and milestones tracking progress toward performance improvements (Kaplan and Norton, 1996).

Designers of effective performance reports in state and local governments also include explanatory data, highlighting the impact on agency performance of forces beyond the direct control of agency managers. For example, reports from the ICMA-Urban Institute consortium of local governments include not only performance information about crime rates but also data on poverty and housing conditions — two factors that show statistically significant relationships to crime rates (Urban Institute and International City/County Management Association, 1998).

Debate over whether to use output or outcome data may reflect differences in interests as well as perspectives. In monitoring activities of the U.S. Forest Service, for example, the lumber industry and its allies focus on traditional output measures such as board feet of timber harvested and associated revenue. Environmentalists, in contrast, downplay timber-cutting goals and are trying to develop broader indicators of ecosystem health to assess the agency's success or failure.

Another source of dispute can occur when designers of PM systems require a comprehensive set of measures tracking every program in every agency, as Congress did with GPRA. This drive to comprehensiveness conflicts with the need of CEOs and top agency managers to focus on smaller numbers of performance targets for programs with strategic importance. Typically, these would include key presidential or gubernatorial initiatives, programs of particular interest to key legislators, and those programs with special budgetary or implementation risks. Behn takes the argument for a smaller subset of strategic measures to its logical extreme by making the case for the "value of a single, simple goal" for an agency or program (1991, pp. 79-80).

These tensions are more apparent than real. In Chapter 3, Schick reminds us that while it may make sense to establish many performance *indicators*, performance *targets* should be few in number. Indeed, he argues, "Targeting everything is equivalent to targeting nothing." A narrower subset of key strategic indicators — called an Executive Information System (EIS) — can be easily drawn from comprehensive data, presented in an accessible format, and revised as chief executives change. Meanwhile, the full set of data is still useful for monitoring agency operations and providing early warning of problems in agencies or programs.

We can imagine a hierarchy of performance measures, with many tracking outputs available to agency managers, and a smaller number more focused on outcomes provided to agency heads and budget examiners. Of these, an even narrower subset would be made available to the chief executive, the legislature, and the general public.

Frequency of reporting is another issue of some technical importance but little policy relevance. Agency managers need data frequently to fine-tune operations. In chapter 16, Smith and Bratton show how top managers convene monthly to use the New York City Police Department's COMPSTAT — a high-stakes performance management technique — to review precinct performance. Budget offices and top executive branch staff, in contrast, may be satisfied with quarterly data, and legislatures and the public with annual indicators. In fact, it may be impractical or too costly to obtain end outcome data, such as student test scores on standardized tests, more frequently than once a year.

After lengthy efforts to develop timely and verifiable measures that link to their strategic plans, the designers and users of performance management systems alike may forget that those data may not support in-depth analysis of program performance. If programs' strategic goals are primarily operational — getting checks to Social Security recipients on time, for example — performance indicators may suffice. But as Blalock and Barnow argue in chapter 17, full-fledged evaluation studies will still be needed to analyze programs with more far-reaching goals. Such costly and time-consuming studies are still the gold standard for understanding the net impacts and limitations of complex programs.

Overseers concerned with tracking crosscutting programs administered by more than one agency may find it difficult to create a common set of indicators for reviewing and managing performance, as those programs are likely to have different goals. GAO has focused considerable attention on this question in its reports on federal strategic plans and performance reports, but each program cluster presents unique problems.

Another measurement problem involves what Fossett, Gais, and Thompson call in chapter 9 "dissonant spillover," which occurs when operating agencies are expected to pursue potentially conflicting objectives, but are held accountable for only a subset of those objectives. Agency managers may produce good performance on the closely watched activities, but not on others. As Schick points out in chapter 3: "[T]argets skew behavior by emphasizing some aims and leaving out others."

As Boyer and Lawrence show in chapter 8, state welfare administrators showed positive results under welfare reform by cutting welfare rolls and increasing work participation rates. "Ending welfare as we know it" was not supposed to reduce access to health insurance and food stamps — important elements in what remained of the social safety net. Yet, as Fossett and his colleagues document in chapter 9, eligible families and individuals have lost these benefits. Indeed, increasing participation in the Child Health

Insurance Program (CHIP) was one of President Clinton's priorities. However, eligibility for Medicaid, CHIP, and food stamps was determined by the same agencies responsible for reducing welfare rolls, and those bureaucrats apparently found it difficult to pursue conflicting objectives. The Clinton administration responded with informal performance management initiatives designed to boost participation rates for health insurance and food stamps, but participation rates continued to fall. The lesson for designers of performance management systems is that performance on the full range of important goals should be measured and rewarded, given potential conflicts among related objectives.

Designing Effective Incentives

Designers of performance management systems often find themselves on the horns of a dilemma. On the one hand, PM systems are much less robust if they are not backed up by incentives for high-performing individuals or organizations. On the other hand, powerful incentives in response to poorly conceived or imperfectly measured performance indicators can produce unexpected and even counterproductive behavior. As Marschke puts it in chapter 4, "Bureaucrats do respond to financially backed performance incentives, but that bureaucratic response is often dysfunctional." For example, the Job Training Partnership Act (JTPA) awarded additional funds to its contractors for high performance. However, the contractors sometimes responded to those incentives by signing up clients who were more likely to get jobs and keep their organizational scorecards high and ignoring clients who were more needy and more difficult to place (Barnow, 2000).

Organizational incentives in some PM systems include waivers of rules and regulations governing purchasing, hiring, salaries, and reallocation of funds across budget categories (Willoughby and Melkers, chapter 13, Table 3). Other incentives include allowing an agency to roll over some or all of its budget surplus, access to special pools of funding, and public recognition. Robert Bradley's discussion of performance budgeting in Florida shows that disincentives — in the form of additional reports and reinstatement of controls — may also be part of a PM scheme (chapter 13).

Marschke relies on principal-agent analysis to show that designers of incentive systems must be cautious when the principal (the governor, for example) decides to use indicators that are not completely under the control of the agent (the agency manager). This "noise" in the indicators diminishes the value of the incentives for controlling the agent's behavior (chapter 4).

Most government agencies find it even more difficult to design effective incentives for individual managers and front-line workers, especially in programs where outcomes and even output are hard to measure. In such programs, Marschke points out, "performance incentives should be used sparingly or not at all." Questions may arise about the contribution of the specific worker to the outcome in question, and whether the baseline condition is measured carefully enough so workers get credit for "value added," not just for high performance. These issues arise even when incentives entail awards and recognition, but they are debated more hotly when the reward is additional pay for performance. A case in point is merit pay for teachers.

An alternative approach provides performance pay for all workers in an organizational unit — a school, for instance. Proponents of this design argue that paying bonuses to everyone reinforces teamwork. But it still makes little sense to provide incentives for workers who operate under narrow bureaucratic rules and procedures and have little room for discretion. According to Marschke, "The general principle here is that incentives should be placed on agents who are able to respond to them." What's more, in most jobs, workers perform several tasks, and failure to provide incentives to some of those tasks may lead to their neglect. For example, teachers and schools that are rewarded solely on the basis of reading and math test scores may neglect arts education or student counseling. Overall, practitioners must remember that high-stakes incentives for organizations and individuals can distort as well as improve performance, and that performance pay for individuals is especially difficult to design and implement successfully.

Managing the Performance
of Independent Agents

While government faces many difficulties in measuring and managing the programs it operates directly, those problems multiply when applying performance management to contractors and local governments. Indeed, programs are often contracted out or devolved precisely because a government is less certain of its goals or how to achieve them. A recent example is the Department of Housing and Urban Development's Empowerment Zone and Enterprise Community (EZ) Initiative. As David Wright points out in chapter 10, the EZ program was "inherently complex, overlapping, and subject to macro-level social and economic forces beyond local control." Without a clear sense of goals, HUD had trouble even defining a process for goal-setting in each community, and those problems were compounded as the agency tried to measure progress and establish sanctions when cities and local organizations fell short of their objectives.

Beryl Radin argues in chapter 11 that Congress and the federal bureaucracy are pursuing conflicting objectives in applying PM to the intergovernmental arena.

> *On the one hand, they are attempting to hold third parties accountable for the use of federal monies; on the other hand, they are constrained by the political and legal realities that provide significant discretion and leeway to the third parties for the use of those federal dollars. In many ways, the performance movement in federal agencies collides with strategies of devolution and a diminished federal role. What is most interesting about this situation is that few of the individuals in the policymaking world (particularly in the Congress) are aware that they are setting up incompatible strategies.*

She makes the case that governmentwide approaches such as GPRA that require measures and targets for direct federal programs simply will not work in the intergovernmental arena. She holds that a careful strategy, based on such tools as performance partnerships, incentives, negotiated performance measures, legislated performance goals, voluntary standards, and waivers, can sometimes bridge the gap between devolution and accountability.

Implementation Challenges

In the absence of support from top management, a makeshift coalition of nervous agency heads, the staff of legislative appropriations committees, cynical budget examiners, and lower-level and less visible agency managers may undermine implementation of PM systems. These actors may wonder why it is necessary to go to the trouble of providing the public and potential political and bureaucratic opponents with performance information for use as ammunition against them. The political staff of chief executives may be sympathetic to such concerns, and join the anti-measurement coalition. Less frequently, implementation of PM systems can be halted when a new elected chief executive takes office and reflexively discards the initiatives of his or her predecessors.

A statute mandating performance management may give firmer footing to implementation than an executive order. Analysts who have studied the implementation of GPRA agree that its standing in permanent law helped it outlive predecessors such as PPBS, MBO, and ZBB, which were based on executive orders (Posner 1997). Similarly, Bradley (chapter 14) points out that disputes between the governor and legislature in Florida might have derailed implementation of that state's PB^2 initiative had it not been enacted into law.

However, while embedding the design of a performance management system in statute encourages all parties to work through transitory disputes, it will not guarantee successful implementation of a system that is poorly designed or lacks fundamental support by key players. In 1981, when the New York State legislature added the Key Item Reporting System (KIRS) to a broader fiscal reform bill, the governor and his budget office saw the initiative as a legislative power-grab, designed without significant input from the executive. The budget office complained about the legislature's choice of agencies, programs, and indicators for monitoring, and simply refused to take the statute seriously. Nearly ten years after its enactment, as

New York State suffered through its worst economic downturn since the 1930s, the executive branch stopped providing the required data. After a brief dust-up in the press over this noncompliance, the governor persuaded the legislature to repeal the KIRS requirement. Twenty years after the initial enactment of KIRS, New York is one of only three states that make no claim to do performance budgeting.[4]

Statutory creation of a PM system was presumably less threatening at the federal level in Washington, D.C., and at the state level in Tallahassee, two jurisdictions where strong legislatures were already a fact of life. Florida's PB[2] and the federal GPRA share several common traits. Both provided for slow and cautious implementation, phasing in agency participation over several years. Both allowed for relief from some regulations and controls as incentives, although this provision has gone essentially unused in Washington. Both are generally deemed limited successes.

In implementing GPRA, Congress and the General Accounting Office reviewed the strategic plans of agencies in detail, and congressional leaders even developed a short-lived grading system for them. GAO's careful and sustained analysis encouraged strategic and performance plans that were comprehensive, well grounded in agency activities, and accompanied by performance indicators that provided overseers and the public a good understanding of results in key programs (Forsythe, 2000). Similarly the PB[2] effort in Florida benefited from consistent and careful follow-up by the Office of Program Policy Analysis and Governmental Accountability, a legislative office created to oversee the new performance management initiative.[5]

Where to lodge responsibility within in the executive branch for PM staff work is an open question. In New York City, a specialized management office collects and publishes the Mayor's Management Report (MMR), a twice-yearly two-volume compendium of performance targets and indicators. While academics and others have demonstrated shortcomings in the MMR (see Smith, 1993 for one such critique), the Office of Operations does use it to monitor agency operations, and the City Council and the media rely on it for performance information about key agencies and programs.

In Albany and in Washington, the executive branch assigned responsibility for implementation of KIRS and GPRA to the Division of the Budget and the Office of Management and Budget. For those budget shops, performance management was clearly a lower priority than preparing and executing the budget, and implementation of performance management systems suffered. In Florida, however, the Governor's Office of Planning and Budgeting, with strong leadership from the state budget director, played a central role in implementing the PB^2 system.

These examples show that where strong support from chief budget officers does not exist, it makes sense to lodge executive branch responsibility for performance management in a stand-alone management office. This location may help keep performance management systems alive during economic downturns, when managing the fiscal effects of business cycles tends to overshadow any other activities in budget offices.

In New York City, the long history of the MMR also illustrates a tension between maintaining a consistent set of indicators to allow comparisons over time, and tinkering with indicators to improve them. In the published material that accompanies the release of MMR data every six months, the Office of Operations does note when indicators are changed or dropped. Whatever the technical value of these changes, critics complain that their true purpose is to hide data that might have been of value to mayoral opponents. Accountability therefore suffers when technicians or politicians tinker with long-standing series of performance data.

Powerful PCs and inexpensive but robust database programs have made the collection and display of performance data much easier. However, the relative ease with which these data can be stored and analyzed does not mean that those data will be "timely, complete, accurate, useful or consistent" (GAO, 1999, p. 7). Managers and overseers of PM systems need to provide specific and credible information about how they will verify and validate performance data if they want overseers and the public to believe them. The series of reports by GAO on federal performance indicators provides a useful tutorial.[6]

The Special Problems
of Performance Budgeting

Those who yearn for performance budgeting seem to share a recurring fantasy: that the availability of performance data will suddenly simplify the process of allocating funds, automatically providing additional funding to high-performing programs while cutting funds from poor performers. However, as Willoughby and Melkers point out in chapter 13, performance budgeting has not produced this kind of change, although it has stimulated some efforts at formula budgeting to allocate funds between similar organizational units. The leading example is in higher education, where 17 states allocate some of their funds to institutions of higher education according to formulae. In general, those formulae reward success in reaching specific targets, such as graduation rates. They are used to allocate relatively limited amounts of dollars, with upper limits of about 6 percent of funding, although South Carolina did briefly experiment with allocating all of its higher education funds by performance formula (Burke, chapter 15). Higher education's experience seems to show that formula allocations may have some limited value in distributing funds among competing institutions within a single program area.

In general, however, performance data have not made it easier to answer V. O. Key's famous question, "On what basis shall it be decided to allocate x dollars to activity A instead of activity B?" (Key, 1940). In battles between programs for funds, advocates of activity A are likely to use poor performance reports as a rationale for additional funding ("we can't fix the public schools without more money") while supporters of activity B argue greater investment in successful programs ("WIC works; let's expand its funding and reach"). State officials who have implemented performance budgeting told researchers that performance information has not radically changed the character of budgetary decisionmaking, and that from the beginning they "expected budget reform to *inform* budget decisions rather than dramatically change them" (Willoughby and Melkers, chapter 13).

Whether or not their governments have adopted performance budgeting formally, most examiners in high-performing budget offices do use performance data to help them understand their programs and their operational problems. They also use both output and outcome data, sometimes informally and sometimes formally, to analyze budget needs. Because they already collect performance data on an ad hoc basis, many budget officers see no special need to build large data systems to collect performance measures, and have little interest in allowing legislators and the public systematic access to all information. Meanwhile, less capable budget examiners may focus on financial data and ignore performance information, fearing that it will saddle them with responsibility for agency performance as well as agency spending.

In chapter 6, Virginia Thomas speaks for many legislative advocates for a smaller government when she argues that performance data can be a critical tool in budget cutting. In theory, legislators may like the idea of responding automatically with budget cuts when agencies cannot meet performance targets. In practice, however, they respond differently when performance data are used to challenge their pet program or spending in their district. When Ingraham and Moynihan looked at managing for results in the states, they found that legislators interpreted performance shortfalls as indicators of inadequate resources in agencies, and responded by increasing funding or reorganizing programs to address a social problem (chapter 12). In sum, in the legislative arena, poor performance is more likely to lead to funding increases than cuts.

Performance budgeting schemes also create organizational tensions between appropriators, who allocate funds, and substantive committees with programmatic expertise. For this reason, legislators and staff on appropriations subcommittees often resist the implied shift in power as substantive committees seek a wider role in performance budgeting (Bradley, 2000). These realities confirm the expectation, based on survey information from state officials, that performance measurement's greatest impact is likely to be during executive branch budget development, not legislative budget review and adoption (Willoughby and Melkers, chapter 13).

Two technical issues also arise when implementing performance budgeting. First, the account structures of budgets — the frameworks within which budget data are reported — have been developed over many years to meet the needs of legislators and chief executives concerned about budgeting for specific programs, not about performance reporting. In many agencies, the program accounts displayed for budgeting purposes are not the organizational units with responsibility for delivering specific results. Meshing performance information with budget data may involve substantial realignment of existing budget accounts — a step that budget office and legislators and their staff often resist. Sometimes the problem can be solved by the use of crosswalks — tables reconciling old and new account structures. But creating those crosswalks may require considerable additional work by agency and budget office staff.

A second problem is that many agencies lack the kind of cost-accounting data that businesses collect as a matter of course. Without those data, however, analysis of unit costs for outputs and outcomes must remain crude and oversimplified, and the use of unit cost data in budgeting will be limited. Schick concludes that governments need to invest the time and money required to build the cost accounting infrastructure:

> *Performance budgeting failed half a century ago for many reasons, but one of the most prominent facts was the inadequacy of government cost-accounting and allocation systems. The lack of data on the costs of particular services made it exceeding difficult to link resources and results....Fifty years later, cost accounting is still underdeveloped in the public sector....[F]ew governments allocate budget resources among cost centers, or distinguish between fixed and variable or average and marginal costs. These cost measures are essential for successfully implementing performance budgeting* (chapter 3).

The Politics of Performance Management

As suggested above, chief executives and their staff sometimes worry — not without reason — that collecting and publishing performance information will provide ammunition to political opponents and legislative critics. However, performance data can also provide early warning of failures in agency management. With adequate notice, chief executives can solve some of those problems before they grow into crises, sending management teams in to fix troubled agencies, and reprimanding or replacing failing agency heads. Even the modest warning time provided by publication of performance data can be enough to elicit a pledge of effective response. When the press reported on shortfalls in several key performance measures in a Mayor's Management Report, Rudolph Giuliani's promise of quick action dominated the coverage, not the failure to meet his management goals.[7]

Forceful governors and mayors should be able to use performance management systems to their advantage by monitoring key initiatives more systematically. Successful implementation of a performance management system also provides evidence of a chief executive's skills as a manager and deflects criticism from management watchdogs like the Government Performance Project, headquartered at Syracuse University's Maxwell School (Ingraham and Moynihan, 12).

Less dramatically, the publication of performance data can sharpen differences over programs and their goals that were blurred when debate focused on funding instead of results. Adding performance goals and data to the budget debate may make timely agreement on the compromises required to get budgets adopted more difficult. In Florida, for example, discussion of performance funding formulae for community colleges provoked a sharp debate over goals for those schools in particular and higher education in general. These disagreements may be useful in principle but are painful in practice.

Next Steps in Implementing GPRA[8]

Since the passage of the Government Performance and Results Act in 1993, executive branch agencies in the federal government have been working their way through many of the problems state and local governments faced as they implemented PM systems. Although varied across agencies, the impact of the Results Act has generally been positive. Like states and local governments, the federal government has seen greater success in developing and using performance measures and targets for services that agencies deliver directly, and where government action is the primary factor in achieving expected outcomes. Among federal agencies that meet those criteria, several have produced serious plans and thoughtful performance measures. A smaller number of program areas have documented real improvements in performance.[9] In chapter 7, Broadnax and Conway describe management improvements in the Social Security Administration, an agency with clear responsibility for the delivery of checks and related eligibility activities.

As governor of Texas, George W. Bush worked with a performance management system that is in many ways better developed than GPRA. His MBA-trained management style seems to mesh well with performance management, and as president he has said that he expects to set targets for his executives and hold them accountable. Thus, the GPRA apparatus could be a useful tool for the new president as he establishes his goals and measures progress toward achieving them.

Over the next few years, however, the federal government must steer carefully around pitfalls to realize its goals of improved accountability, better management, and more informed decision making. The government faces particularly daunting problems in measuring and managing performance in federally funded programs implemented at the state or local level or by independent contractors.

Fostering Accountability

The Results Act requires the federal government to compile detailed performance data, program by program, for each agency. Some interest groups may welcome systematic data tracking the programs of importance to them. Others may find those data threatening. But in either case, interest groups, agency personnel, and congressional staff members responsible for individual programs are likely to pay close attention to performance. As annual performance reports provide more and more complete data and GAO helps digest and display those data, Congress will begin to use this timely information in its oversight activities. On the agency side, many program managers hope that regular reports required by GPRA will obviate the need for other special reports to Congress, especially those that require extraordinary detail on spending and activities. This trade-off — more flexibility in agency reporting and controls in return for high performance by agency managers — has been a valuable incentive in states like Florida where performance management systems are taking root.

From the perspective of the public at large, GPRA performance reports are a jumble of raw data. So far, little effort has been devoted to making those data understandable and meaningful. Given the volume of the performance reports, some staff units somewhere in the federal government will have to provide the public with a sub-set of those data and some sense of their strategic significance. This need could, in fact, present the new administration with an oppor-tunity to design its own report cards, selecting those programs most important to the president. Such report cards could also provide management focus for White House staff and cabinet officials. The problem, of course, will be to keep these new summaries from themselves growing so large as to be unwieldy.

Another challenge for accountability will be measuring results in crosscutting programs, sometimes in different cabinet agencies, that pursue related goals and serve the same or similar constituen-cies. For example, Congress has asked planners in the Forest Ser-vice, the Bureau of Land Management, and the National Park Service to develop common performance indicators for federal land-management agencies. While progress has been slow, cross-cutting programs could become a focus of OMB's mandated gov-ernmentwide performance plan — an annual GPRA report that has drawn little attention to date.

Improving Agency Management

Echoing the rhetoric of the GPRA statute, many program oversight officials, especially but not only in GAO, have pushed hard for agencies to use broad outcome measures to track performance. For example, the Forest Service has adopted ecosystem health — an end outcome — as a strategic goal. It has not, however, developed useful baseline measures of the health of its forest systems. In the field, foresters continue the work they have always done — cutting timber, putting out fires, maintaining roads, and assisting visitors, to name a few activities that are easily measured with output data. But front-line personnel find it difficult to see how those activities affect the strategically desirable but ill-defined outcome of ecosystem health.

Agency managers are the troops in any battle to improve results, and they are understandably concerned about being held accountable for outcomes that are so broad that they can be controlled only partially, if at all, by agency actions. To maintain linkages between their work and strategic goals, agency planners and oversight officials at the GAO and OMB are trying to devise detailed logic models that trace the relationships between higher-level outcomes and day-to-day output and process indicators. Performance plans and reports also need to include explanatory data describing other factors — in the case of the Forest Service, for example, weather and the economy — that affect performance.

To build the capacity of its agencies to improve performance, the federal government also needs to invest money and management talent in the development of new computer systems, in auditable financial statements for key agencies and other financial management initiatives, in human resource systems, and in the management of its capital assets. While such initiatives do not produce "results" in the programmatic sense, they build the "government's intrinsic ability to marshal, develop, direct, and control its human, physical, and information capital, to support the discharge of its policy directions," according to Ingraham and Moynihan (chapter 12). In Schick's words, "Organizations must be transformed to make use of data on results" (chapter 3). An important part of that transformation involves investment in management systems, which lay the groundwork for future improvements. Agency performance reports should track the progress of these initiatives.

For the first GPRA performance reports in 2000, OMB and the agencies were focused primarily on displaying baseline data. With those reports now available annually, overseers and top managers should concentrate on setting performance targets that agencies must reach to achieve them, but not so high as to discourage effort. "Reach targets" are especially important in programs areas where funding is growing. In a fresh look at the value of incrementalism in performance management, Schick suggests that governments establish their own "services baseline" and negotiate performance targets as projected changes from that baseline (chapter 3).

To reinforce the importance of meeting performance objectives, the federal government also needs to develop a wider variety of incentives for high-performing individuals and departments. As detailed above, government faces many problems in designing incentives, but it is important to keep trying. Such incentives might range from higher levels of pay for performance to organizational incentives, such as flexibility and access to agency-generated surpluses for one-time spending needs.

Measurement myopia also looms as a threat to the 1993 Results Act. In New York City, where performance management and measurement has been operational for more than twenty-five years, the Mayor's Management Report has lost its value as a cutting-edge tool and become for many participants a routine technical exercise. Effective management innovation, such as the New York Police Department's COMPSTAT system, detailed by Smith and Bratton in chapter 16, occurs outside of the MMR framework. New York City has tackled important technical issues, validating performance data and developing reliable historical series for baseline comparisons, and those areas still need work at the federal level. However, the New York City experience shows how easy it is for technical concerns over baselines and data to displace the operational goals of performance management systems, bogging down keepers of the systems in shortsighted disputes over measurement. Similarly, in Texas, another jurisdiction where a performance management system has been in place long enough to become mature, one program director complained that performance measures can "become the focus rather than an indicator of progress or circumstances" (Willoughby and Melkers, chapter 13). As GPRA ages, federal managers will need to balance the technical concerns entailed in maintaining and improving the GPRA system itself with more fundamental goals of improving federal programs and services.

Improving Budgetary Decisionmaking

Beyond providing feedback on agency performance, GPRA proponents hope that performance data will be used for budgeting in the executive branch, and for resource allocation in Congress. However, this hope will be difficult to realize, based on experience with performance budgeting at other levels of government.

Budgeting for Results in the Executive Branch

The GPRA legislation calls for OMB to institute performance budgeting pilots, using performance data linked to budgeted resources in a limited number of program areas. OMB has been slow to implement this provision. This caution is neither surprising nor unwarranted. Careful students of performance budgeting in the states — held up as models to the federal government — have found that "state government applications of performance-based budgeting systems are complicated, incomplete and still evolving; each system is different, and implementation strategies and successes are varied" (Willoughby and Melkers, chapter 13). Moreover, even though all but three states report that they use performance budgeting, more pointed inquiries reveal that their use of performance data for budgeting is actually quite limited. Researchers at the Government Performance Project found that "...in only four states—Missouri, Texas, Louisiana, and Virginia—are performance measures used extensively by the budget office (with 19 budget offices reporting some use)" (Ingraham and Moynihan, chapter 12).

Implementation at the federal level will be even more difficult. Federal programs are less likely to provide direct services and more likely to use independent agents — contractors or state and local governments — to deliver services. These characteristics significantly increase the problems with performance management and budgeting. OMB has made progress revising budget account structures so they link to performance measures, but more work needs to be done in the agencies on cost accounting before it will be possible to develop reliable data on the cost of federal services. This is a high priority of GAO Controller David Walker.

Attitudinal changes are also necessary before OMB embraces performance budgeting. OMB budget examiners know their program areas well. They already use performance data to track key programs, and we should not be surprised if they see little advantage in collecting additional data and making them publicly available. While GAO pushes for more use of outcome measures, budget examiners overseeing direct federal programs may agree with Schick that data on activities and outputs are most useful in budgeting. Indeed, Schick contends in chapter 3 that the emphasis on measuring outcomes has undermined progress in performance budgeting:

> [I]n allocating resources, activities are an indispensable yardstick for decisions. I sense that if measurers had emphasized activities, performance budgeting would be more advanced than it is. There would less wrangling over definitions and more attention to allocations.

However, some OMB staff who oversee complex social programs know that measures of outputs and/or even outcomes cannot by themselves provide clear answers to more complex questions of program impacts. The point made in chapter 17 by Blalock and Barnow is essential and inescapable: for all but the simplest federal social programs, costly and time-consuming evaluation research will still be needed to determine the program's net impact, and policymakers and the budget officers who serve them will need that kind of information to determine whether program benefits equal or exceed their costs.

OMB is also the federal agency with the most painful memories of failed budget systems in the past, such as PPBS, MBO, and ZBB.[10] While each of these initiatives had some value, they created huge paperwork burdens, produced data of limited use for presidential and congressional decisionmaking, and did not last.

President Bush's experience with performance budgeting in Texas has undoubtedly taught him that performance data are no substitute for political preferences in allocating funds among program areas. But in his first budget message he has promised wider use of performance budgeting pilots. If Bush sustains his interest, OMB's pride in being responsive to the president will outweigh its haunting memories of budget systems past, and the agency will speed up its progress on performance budgeting. And OMB will respond with real enthusiasm if the new president actually uses performance data in making his own budget choices.

Even with enthusiastic support from the president and new responsiveness from OMB, performance budgeting is not likely to transform executive branch budgeting. State experience shows that performance measures have not been vital decision aids, and state budget officers are still lukewarm about their value, although the vast majority of state respondents agree that moving ahead with performance budgeting is "better than doing nothing" (Willoughby and Melkers, chapter 13). At the federal level, systematic use of performance data will help examiners focus on results at the same time they consider resources, and will make it easier to communicate to the public and to Congress the rationale for executive branch budget decisions.

Performance Budgeting and Oversight in Congress

Experience in the states does not inspire confidence in the willingness or ability of legislatures to use performance data effectively. Willoughby and Melkers conclude that legislators and their staff find performance data much less useful than does the executive branch, and that these data have had very little impact on actual appropriations levels. As outlined earlier, the states have primarily used formula budgeting — or performance funding, as Burke prefers to call it — in higher education, and the funds dispensed by formula have been quite limited. According to Ingraham and Moynihan, "In responding to the GPP, states explain that performance measures are often viewed with skepticism by state officials, and unlikely to be used unless performance information coincides with dominant constituent interests" (chapter 12).

In Washington, the legislative agenda is much busier than in state capitols. Congress often is unable to come to timely agreement on budget bills, and professional staff are understandably concerned about further burdening the budget process. Staff members also worry that changing familiar account structures to clarify links to performance data will disrupt negotiating routines of legislators and interest groups. They also know that clarifying objectives sometimes can sharpen conflict instead of reducing it. In sum, Congressional staff members say that they fear that making decisions about performance in conjunction with spending will delay and overburden the budget process.

On the other hand, members of Congress can reasonably expect higher levels of performance when allocating additional funds to programs, and performance targets can and should be used selectively to highlight areas where programs are being expanded or contracted, or where major quality-improvement initiatives are under way. The use of performance data for basic oversight may spread, beginning with new or priority programs and expanding into other areas.

If the use of performance data takes hold in Congress, members and their staff should — and certainly will — resist asking too much from performance data when reviewing complex programs. By definition, performance measures are relatively simple, collected frequently, and comparatively inexpensive to produce. To make more definitive judgments about the long-term impact of complex initiatives, Congress will still need additional data from evaluation research.

Members of Congress are likely to use performance data in key program areas to focus and inform bargaining and negotiation, not to determine funding levels. With state experience reinforcing the concerns of congressional staff, GPRA proponents should be neither surprised nor discouraged if Congress fails to move quickly to make extensive use of performance data in its budgeting routines.

Performance Management
in the Intergovernmental Arena

Success stories in implementing GPRA stem from federal agencies that deliver services directly. However, in many important domestic program areas, ranging from education and welfare to highways and urban development, the federal government provides the funds but states and local governments deliver the services. Much less progress has occurred in measuring and managing performance in these areas.

In the past, a decision not to require strict and detailed accountability has often allowed Congress to reach agreement in intergovernmental programs. Sometimes that decision took the form of allowing freedom to experiment at the state and local level — in the legislation implementing welfare reform, for example. Sometimes — in education, for example — such an approach has reflected the relatively small share of federal funding in the program area. When the federal government doesn't really pay the piper, it is hard to see how it can call the tune. Sometimes the decision not to try to measure and manage program performance may signify a realistic judgment about the problems likely to be encountered in collecting data from systems and agents not under the federal government's direct control. The chapters on welfare reform by Boyer and Lawrence and by Fossett, Gais, and Thompson highlight these difficulties.

Other intergovernmental programs have encountered similar problems. In chapter 10, David Wright sums up his analysis of HUD's efforts, initiated with some enthusiasm, to manage performance in the Empowerment Zone program:

> *Taken as a whole, this review of benchmarking in the Zone program serves as something of a cautionary tale. The story helps illustrate how difficult it can be to implement seemingly straightforward performance measurement systems for actually quite complex, multi-level community development interventions; how important it is to try; and how such efforts in the future may be can be improved.*

When federal funds are cut back, the government has often consolidated categorical programs into block grants, which allow states and localities greater discretion in the use of federal funds. However, by definition, block grants create "problems balancing the flexibility of the block grant (allowing states and localities to meet their particular needs) with a desire for greater accountability for the use of those funds" (Radin, chapter 11). Incentives for high performance have sometimes exacerbated disagreements about a program's intended objectives. For example, the TANF bonus program for states has drawn fire from critics of welfare reform, who argue that:

> ...the criteria that have been established [to track reductions in the welfare rolls and increases in work participation] do not measure the real goal of TANF — the well-being of children. They call for the establishment of performance measures that highlight child welfare, child care, Head Start, and other non-cash programs, rather than focus only on the employment behavior of adults.

As suggested earlier, a full array of performance indicators in broad social programs such as TANF can help avoid the problem of dissonant spillover — success in some goals, such as reduction of the welfare rolls, accompanied by failure in others, such as boosting participation in the Child Health Insurance Program.

In short, the use of performance data in oversight of intergovernmental programs has proven problematic, and intergovernmental PM initiatives have seen limited success. As Fossett and his colleagues put it in chapter 9:

> Intergovernmental arrangements complicate virtually all aspects of performance management — agreement on key goals, the development of indicators, the timely collection of pertinent and timely performance data, the implementation of an incentive system (e.g., rewards for strong performers), and more.

Nonetheless, the growing emphasis on results in directly operated federal programs has increased pressures to develop workable performance measures and targets in intergovernmental programs.

The problems outlined above will take center stage in debates regarding many new programs, beginning with President Bush's educational initiatives.

As the federal government reduced its staffing during the Clinton administration, it increased its reliance on independent contractors to deliver federal services. As Marschke's analysis of the Job Training Partnership Act (chapter 4) makes clear, it can be painfully difficult to devise measures that create incentives for independent contractors to improve performance without creating unwanted behavior. Like welfare agencies, contractors may find a way to meet one goal — job placements, for JTPA — at the expense of other goals, such as serving the most needy job searchers. However, the decision to contract out a program often reflects the hope that contractors will develop new approaches to solve old problems. This hope argues in favor of giving leeway to contractors and against the level of performance oversight that might be employed with directly provided services. Given the difficulties, federal officials sometimes settle for minimal performance data and easy-to-reach goals.

Pitfalls and Possibilities for GPRA

The overall aim of this volume is to strike a balance between the positive views of performance management advocates, who believe that GPRA will bring deep-seated changes to the federal government, and the negative views of skeptics, who see it as another in a long line of failed federal budgetary and management reforms. If pushed off the fence, I would stand uneasily with the optimists, believing that GPRA will lead to improved accountability and management in many federal programs, and that systematic use of performance data in budget offices can produce a more disciplined focus on results in allocating resources.

However, I also believe that the federal government will have to work hard to get full value from the GPRA initiative, and that victory is not assured. No governmentwide strategy for performance management will magically solve the difficult problems of monitoring the results of federally funded programs administered by state and local governments and by private contractors. Indeed, poorly designed performance measures and incentives can heighten disagreement about intergovernmental programs. Radin's conclusion about intergovernmental programs — that performance measures and approaches need to be carefully tailored for each situation — holds true as well for programs where governments provide complex services directly. For complex social programs, as Blalock and Barnow warn, even the best designed performance measures cannot answer questions about net program impacts.

For many, the use of performance data to transform budgeting is a touchstone for success of the GPRA effort. Schick is pessimistic, based on prior federal effort, concluding that "efforts to budget on the basis of performance almost always fail" (chapter 3). While most of the state budget officials surveyed by Willoughby and Melkers thought that the use of performance data in budgeting was "better than doing nothing," they did not report significant changes in budgeting methods or outcomes based on performance data. Still, my own experience in working with state and local budget offices suggests that they can integrate performance data into decisionmaking without much disruption, and that systematic use of data on activities and outcomes can bring additional discipline and focus on results to the budgeting process.

If we cannot expect executive branch use of performance data in budgeting to bring major transformations, extensive use by Congress of performance data for budgeting is even less likely. If the state experience provides lessons for the federal government, we should expect to see more impact from GPRA in improving management and accountability, and less in transforming budgeting practices and outcomes.

As GPRA implementation proceeds, its proponents must still overcome technical problems, especially those concerning the validity and reliability of data. They must also strive to measure outcomes without losing the connection to GPRA's important management objectives. But if GPRA proponents can steer around these pitfalls, they can continue to refine a tool that can help the federal government achieve several notable goals — helping decision makers consider results while they think about dollars, improving agency management, and helping elected officials and the public understand what the federal government does and how well it does it. Performance management may not bring revolutionary change in the federal government, but it should yield a reasonable return on the investment in money and time required to implement it.

Endnotes

1   Ingraham and Moynihan (chapter 12) argue for four goals, and Behn (2000) offers a much different and more extensive set of goals just for performance measurement.

2   See www.econ.state.or.us/opb/index.htm for the complete Oregon Benchmarks presentation.

3   The New York City Mayor's Management Report can be found on-line at www.ci.nyc/ny/us/html/ops/html/mmr.html.

4   I am grateful to Frank Mauro, one of the designers of KIRS, for his recollections concerning this initiative. Additional discussion of KIRS can be found in Carroll, 1984.

5   OPPAGA's reports monitoring Florida government can be found on the Internet at www.oppaga.state.fl.us/government/.

6   See GAO, 1999 for references to key reports in this series.

7   *New York Times*, February 9, 2001.

8   This section draws heavily on Forsythe and Nathan, 2001.

9   See GAO 1999 for detailed assessment of agency performance plans, and Mihm, chapter 5, for a quick review of performance reports.

10 See Posner, 1997 for a thoughtful review of these initiatives.

References

Barnow, Burt S. 2000. "Exploring the Relationship between Performance Management and Program Impact: A Case Study of the Job Training Partnership Act." *Journal of Policy Analysis and Management* 19,1: 118-141.

Behn, Robert D. 1991. *Leadership Counts: Lessons of Public Managers from the Massachusetts Welfare, Training and Employment Program*. Cambridge, MA: Harvard University Press.

Behn, Robert D. 2000. "Why Measure Performance? Different Purposes Require Different Measures." Paper prepared for the fall conference of the Association of Public Policy and Management.

Bradley, Robert D. 2000. "The Transformation of Performance-Based Budgeting in Florida." Paper prepared for the fall conference of the Association of Public Policy and Management.

Carroll, Thomas W. 1984. "A Legislative Initiative in Budgetary Reform: New York's Key Item Reporting System." New York Case Studies in Public Management, Number 1. Albany, NY: Rockefeller Institute of Government.

Forsythe, Dall W. 2000. *Performance Management Comes to Washington: A Progress Report on the Government Performance and Results Act.* Albany, NY: Rockefeller Institute of Government.

Forsythe, Dall W. and Richard P. Nathan. 2001. "The Next Phase of Performance Management in Washington: What You Can Do," in *Memos to the President: Management Advice from the Nation's Top Public Administrators,* edited by Mark A. Abramson. Washington, DC: PricewaterhouseCoopers Endowment for the Business of Government.

General Accounting Office, U.S. 1999. *Managing for Results: Opportunities for Continued Improvements in Agencies' Performance Plans.* GAO/GGD/AIMD-99-215. Washington, DC: U.S. General Accounting Office.

Hatry, Harry P. 1999. *Performance Measurement: Getting Results.* Washington, DC: Urban Institute Press.

Kaplan, Robert S., and David P. Norton. 1996. *The Balanced Scorecard: Translating Strategy into Action.* Boston: Harvard Business School Press.

Key, V. O. Jr. 1940. "The Lack of a Budgetary Theory." *American Political Science Review* 34: XX.

Posner, Paul. 1997. *Performance Budgeting: Past Initiatives Offer Insights for GPRA Implementation.* GAO/AIMD-97-46. Washington, DC: U. S. General Accounting Office.

Smith, Dennis C. 1993. "Performance Management in New York City: The Mayor's Management Plan and Report System in the Koch Administration." Paper prepared for the annual meeting of the Association of Public Policy and Management.

The Urban Institute and the International City/County Management Association. 1998. *Comparative Performance Measurement: FY 1996 Data Report.* Washington, DC: Urban Institute Press.

Bibliography

Abernethy, Margaret A., and Peter Brownell. "The role of budgets in organizations facing strategic change: An exploratory study." *Accounting, Organizations & Society* 24, no. 3 (1999): 189-204.

Adams, Charles F., and Miriam S. Wilson. "Welfare reform meets the devolution revolution in Ohio." In *Learning from Leaders: Welfare Reform Politics and Policy in Five Midwestern States*, edited by Carol S. Weissert. Albany, NY: Rockefeller Institute Press, 2000.

Ahnell, Leif, Linda Davidson, and Karen McKenzie. "Case note: a first experience with SEA reporting." *International Journal of Public Administration* 18, no. 2,3 (1999): 581-591.

Allen, John R. "The uses of performance measurement in government." *Government Finance Review* 12 (1996): 11-15.

Almeida, Ruth A., and Genevieve M. Kenney. *Gaps in Insurance Coverage for Children: A Pre-CHIP Baseline*. Washington, D.C.: Urban Institute, 2000.

Alonso, William, and Paul Starr. *The Politics of Numbers*. New York: Russell Sage Foundation, 1987.

Ammons, David N. "Overcoming the inadequacies of performance measurement in local government: The case of libraries and leisure services." *Public Administration Review* 55, no. 1 (1995): 37-47.

Ammons, David. "Raising the performance bar . . . locally." *Public Management* 79 (1997): 10-16.

Ammons, David N. "A proper mentality for benchmarking." *Public Administration Review* 59, no. 2 (1999): 105-109.

Anderson, Kathryn H., Richard V. Burkhauser, and Jennie E. Raymond. "The effect of creaming on placement rates under the

Job Training Partnership Act." *Industrial & Labor Relations Review* 46, no. 4 (1993): 613-624.

Anderson, E. D. "Meeting future challenges: Business planning in Grande Prairie, Alberta." *Government Finance Review* 13 (1997): 11-13.

Anonymous. "Good performance through effective budgeting." *Accountants Journal* 72, no. 1 (1993): 34-36.

Anonymous. "Strategic planning and budgeting in the 'new Texas': Putting service efforts and accomplishments to work." *International Journal of Public Administration* 18, no. 2,3 (1995): 409-441.

Anonymous. "Bellevue: Performance measurement, benchmarking, and improvement." *PM. Public Management* 82, no. 4 (2000): A3, A11.

Ansoff, H. Igor. *Corporate Strategy.* New York: McGraw-Hill, 1965.

Ansoff, H. Igor, Roger P. Declerck, and Robert L. Hayes, eds. *From Strategic Planning to Strategic Management.* London: Wiley, 1976.

Armey, Richard. "The Results Act: Setting a New Course." U.S. House of Representatives, 2000.

Ashenfelter, Orley. "Estimating the effect of training programs on earnings." *The Review of Economics and Statistics* 60, no. 1 (1978): 47-57.

Astin, Alexander W. *Achieving Educational Excellence: A Critical Assessment of Priorities and Practices in Higher Education.* 1st ed. San Francisco: Jossey-Bass Publishers, 1985.

Atkinson, Anthony A., and James Q. McCrindell. "Strategic performance measurement in government." *CMA Magazine* 71, no. 3 (1997): 20-23.

Baj, John, Charles E. Trott, and David Stevens. "A feasibility study of the use of unemployment insurance wage-record data as an evaluation tool for JTPA : Report on project's phase activities." Washington, D.C.: National Commission for Employment Policy, 1991.

Bajjaly, Stephen T. "Managing emerging information systems in the public sector." *Public Productivity & Management Review* 23, no. 1 (1999): 40-47.

Baker, George P., Michael C. Jensen, and Kevin J. Murphy. "Compensation and Incentives: Practice vs. Theory." *The Journal of Finance* 43, no. 3 (1988): 593-616.

Baker, George P. "Incentive Contracts and Performance Measurement." *The Journal of Political Economy* 100, no. 3 (1988): 598-614.

Baker, George P. "Distortion and Risk in Optimal Incentive Contracts." Harvard Business School (unpublished), 1999.

Balk, Walter L., Geert Bouckaert, and Kevin M. Bronner. "Notes on the Theory and Practice of Government Productivity Improvement." *Public Productivity & Management Review* 13, no. 2 (1989): 117-131.

Bane, Mary Jo, and David T. Ellwood. *Welfare Realities: From Rhetoric to Reform.* Cambridge: Harvard University Press, 1994.

Barnow, B. "The Effect of Performance Standards on State and Local Programs." In *Evaluating Welfare and Training Programs,* edited by Charles F. Manski and Irwin Garfinkel. Cambridge: Harvard University Press, 1992.

Barnow, Burt S. "Exploring the Relationship between Performance Management and Program Impact: A Case Study of the Job Training Partnership Act." *Journal of Policy Analysis and Management* 19, no. 1 (2000): 118-141.

Barrett, Katherine, and Richard Greene. "Managing for results: Phoenix." *Financial World* 16, no. 3 (1994): 47.

Barrow, Michael, and Adam Wagstaff. "Efficiency Measurement in the Public Sector: An Appraisal." *Fiscal Studies* 10, no. 1 (1989): 72-97.

Bartik, Timothy J. *Using Performance Indicators to Improve the Effectiveness of Welfare-To-Work Programs.* Kalamazoo, MI: W.E. Upjohn Institute for Employment Research, 1995.

Bavier, R. *An Early Look at the Effects of Welfare Reform.* Washington, D.C.: Office of Management and Budget, 1999.

Bavon, Aloysius. "Innovations in performance measurement systems: A comparative perspective." *International Journal of Public Administration* 18, no. 2,3 (1995): 491-519.

Bayley, David H. *Police for the Future.* New York: Oxford University Press, 1994.

Becker, David O., Michael A. George, Adrienne E. Goolsby, and Douglas C. Grissom. "Government: The ultimate service turnaround." *McKinsey Quarterly*, no. 1 (1998): 116-125.

Behn, Robert D. *Leadership Counts: Lessons for Public Managers from the Massachusetts Welfare, Training, and Employment Program.* Cambridge: Harvard University Press, 1991.

Behn, Robert D. "The wrong way to motivate." *Governing* 8 (1994): 70.

Behn, Robert D. "Why Measure Performance? Different Purposes Require Different Measures." Paper presented at the Fall Conference of the Association of Public Policy and Management, November 2000.

Berman, Evan M., and Jonathan P West. "Productivity enhancement efforts in public and nonprofit organizations." *Public Productivity & Management Review* 22, no. 2 (1998): 207-219.

Berman, Evan, and XiaoHu Wang. "Performance measurement in U.S. counties: Capacity for reform." *Public Administration Review* 60, no. 5 (2000): 409-420.

Berry, Frances S. "Innovation in public management: The adoption of strategic planning." *Public Administration Review* 54, no. 4 (1994): 322-330.

Berry, F. S., R. Chackerian, and B. Wechsler. *Reinventing Government: Lessons from a State Capital.* Tuscaloosa, AL: University of Alabama Press, 1995.

Berry, Frances S., and Barton Wechsler. "State agencies' experience with strategic planning: Findings from a national survey." *Public Administration Review* 55, no. 2 (1995): 159-168.

Berry, Frances S., and Geraldo Flowers. "Public Entrepreneurs in the Policy Process: Performance-Based Budgeting Reform in Florida." *Journal of Public Budgeting Accounting & Financial Management* 11, no. 4 (1999): 578-617.

Berry, Frances S., Ralph S. Brower, and Geraldo Flowers. "Implementing performance accountability in Florida: What changed, what mattered, and what resulted?" *Public Productivity & Management Review* 23, no. 3 (2000): 338-358.

Bichard, Michael. "Developing structures, processes and leaders for the future." *Public Administration and Development* 18, no. 4 (1998): 327-333.

Bishop, J. *Policy Evaluation and Archived Wage Record Data: Limitations of Existing Data Sets.* Washington, D.C.: Northeast/Midwest Institute, 1989.

Blalock, Ann B., and Hubert M. Blalock. *Introduction to Social Research.* 2nd ed. Englewood Cliffs, NJ: Prentice-Hall, 1980.

Blalock, Ann B., ed. *Evaluating social programs at the state and local level: The JTPA evaluation design project.* Kalamazoo, MI: W.E. Upjohn Institute for Employment Research, 1990.

4

Blalock, A. B. "Economic Competition, Restructuring and Worker Dislocation." *Evaluation Forum*, no. 11 (1995).

Blalock, A. B. "Youth and the Post-Industrial Future." *Evaluation Forum*, no. 12 (1997).

Blondal, Jon. *Modern Budgeting*. Paris: Organisation for Economic Co-operation and Development, 1997.

Bloom, Dan. *The Family Transition Program: Implementation and Interim Impacts of Florida's Initial Time-Limited Welfare Program*. New York: Manpower Demonstration Research Corp., 1998.

Borgia, Carl R., and Randolph S. Coyner. "The evolution and success of budgeting systems at institutions of higher education." *Public Budgeting & Financial Management* 7, no. 4 (1996): 467-492.

Bos, Johannes M. *New Hope for People with Low Incomes: Two-Year Results of a Program to Reduce Poverty and Reform Welfare*. New York: Manpower Demonstration Research Corp., 1999.

Bouckaert, Geert. "Measurement and meaningful management." *Public Productivity & Management Review* 17, no. 1 (1993): 31-43.

Bouckaert, Geert. "Performance measurement and public management." *Public Productivity & Management Review* 17, no. 1 (1993): 29-30.

Bradley, Robert D. "The Transformation of Performance-Based Budgeting in Florida." Paper presented at the fall conference of the Association of Public Policy and Management, Seattle, WA, 2000.

Bratton, William J. "Crime is Down in New York City: Blame the Police." In *Zero Tolerance: Policing a Free Society*, edited by Norman Dennis. London: IEA Health and Welfare Unit, 1998.

Bratton, William J., and Peter Knobler. *Turnaround: How America's Top Cop Reversed the Crime Epidemic*. New York: Random House, 1998.

Brickley, James A., Clifford W. Smith, and Jerold L. Zimmerman. *Managerial Economics and Organizational Architecture.* Chicago: Irwin, 1997.

Brignall, Stan. "Performance measurement and change in local government: A general case and a childcare application." *Public Money & Management* 13, no. 4 (1993): 23-30.

Brown, Lee P. "Policing New York City in the 1990s: The strategy for community policing." New York: New York City Police Department, 1991.

Brown, Ken W., R. Steve McDuffie, and Karyn L. Molnar. "Impending changes in government financial reporting." *CPA Journal* 64, no. 8 (1994): 42-46.

Brown, Ken W. "Group selection of service efforts and accomplishments indicators for colleges." *International Journal of Public Administration* 18, no. 2,3 (1995): 311-353.

Bryson, John M. *Strategic Planning for Public and Nonprofit Organizations: A Guide to Strengthening and Sustaining Organizational Achievement.* San Francisco, CA: Jossey-Bass Publishers, 1995.

Burgess, Simon, and Paul Metcalfe. *Incentives in Organisations: A Selective Overview of the Literature with Application to the Public Sector.* Bristol: Centre for Market and Public Organisation, 1999.

Burgess, Simon, and Paul Metcalfe. *The Use of Incentive Schemes in the Public and Private Sectors: Evidence from British Establishments.* Bristol: Centre for Market and Public Organisation, 1999.

Burke, Joseph C. *Performance-Funding Indicators: Concerns, Values, and Models for Two- and Four-Year Colleges and Universities.* Albany, NY: Nelson A. Rockefeller Institute of Government, 1997.

Burke, Joseph C., and Andreea M. Serban. *Performance Funding for Public Higher Education: Fad or Trend?* San Francisco: Jossey-Bass Publishers, 1998.

Burke, Joseph C., and Andreea M. Serban. *Current Status and Future Prospects of Performance Funding and Performance Budgeting for Public Higher Education: The Second Survey.* Albany, NY: Nelson A. Rockefeller Institute of Government, 1998.

Burke, Joseph C. "Performance Funding in South Carolina: From Fringe toward Mainstream." *Assessment Update* 11, no. 6 (1999): 4.

Burke, Joseph C., J. Rosen, H. Minassians, and T. Lessard. *Performance Funding and Budgeting: An Emerging Merger: The Fourth Annual Survey.* Albany, NY: Nelson A. Rockefeller Institute of Government, 2000.

Burke, Joseph C., and Shahpar Modarresi. "To Keep or Not to Keep Performance Funding." *Journal of Higher Education* 71, no. 4 (2000): 432-453.

Burnaby, Priscilla A., and James R. Fountain, Jr. "Service efforts and accomplishments: Its time has come." *Government Accountants Journal* 43, no. 3 (1994): 43-53.

Burton, Dan, and C. W. Young. *Joint Letter to Agency Heads.* March 10, 1999. Available from http://www.house.gov/reform/press/99.03.10.a.htm.

Caiden, Gerald E. "Administrative reform — American style." *Public Administration Review* 54, no. 2 (1994): 123-128.

Caiden, Naomi. "Public service professionalism for performance measurement and evaluation." *Public Budgeting & Finance* 18, no. 2 (1998): 35-52.

Carnevale, Anthony P., and David G. Carnevale. "Public administration and the evolving world of work." *Public Productivity & Management Review* 17, no. 1 (1993): 1-14.

Carpenter, Vivian L. "Improving Accountability: Evaluating the Performance of Public Health Agencies." *Government Accountants Journal* 39, no. 3 (1990): 43-54.

Carpinello, Sharon, Chip J. Felton, Elizabeth A. Pease, Mary DeMasi, and Sheila Donahue. "Designing a system for managing the performance of mental health managed care: An example from New York State's prepaid mental health plan." *The Journal of Behavioral Health Services & Research* 25, no. 3 (1998): August.

Carroll, Thomas W. *A Legislative Initiative in Budgetary Reform: New York's Key Item Reporting System* (New York Case Studies in Public Management). Albany, NY: Rockefeller Institute of Government, 1984.

Caruthers, J. Kent, and Daniel T. Layzell. "Performance Funding at the State Level: Trends and Prospects." Paper presented at the Annual Meeting of the Association for the Study of Higher Education, Orlando, FL, November 2-5, 1995.

Castner, Laura, and Randy Rosso. *Characteristics of Food Stamp Households – Fiscal Year 1998*. Washington, D.C.: Mathematica Policy Research, Inc., 2000.

Caudle, Sharon L. "Reengineering strategies and issues." *Public Productivity & Management Review* 18, no. 2 (1994): 149-162.

Caudle, Sharon L. "Managing information and technology for results." *Public Manager* 23, no. 1 (1994): 48-50.

Chalos, Pete , and Joseph Cherian. "An application of data envelopment analysis to public sector performance measurement and accountability." *Journal of Accounting & Public Policy* 14, no. 2 (1995): 143-160.

Chan, Amy, and Dan Rich. "Sunnyvale's outcome management: Taking performance budgeting one step further." *Government Finance Review* 12 (1996): 13.

Chelimsky, Eleanor. "Comparing and contrasting auditing and evaluation." *Evaluation Review* 9, no. 4 (1985): 483-503.

Christal, Melodie E. "State survey on performance measures, 1996-97." Denver, CO: State Higher Education Executive Officers, 1998.

Citizens Against Government Waste. *2000 Congressional Pig Book Summary.* Washington, D.C.: author, 2000.

Clancy, Donald K., and Terry K. Patton. "Service efforts and accomplishments reporting: A study of Texas public schools." *Public Budgeting & Financial Management* 8, no. 2 (1996): 272-302.

Clark, Steven A. "Performance auditing: A public-private partnership." *Public Productivity & Management Review* 16, no. 4 (1993): 431-436.

Coe, Barbara A. "How structural conflicts stymie reinvention." *Public Administration Review* 57 (1997): 168-173.

Coe, Charles. "Local government benchmarking: lessons from two major multigovernment efforts." *Public Administration Review* 59, no. 2 (1999): 110-115.

Cook, Thomas D., and Charles S. Reichardt, eds. *Qualitative and Quantitative Methods in Evaluation Research.* Beverly Hills, CA: Sage Publications, 1979.

Cook, Thomas J., Jerry Vansant, Leslie Stewart, and Jamie Adrian. "Performance measurement: Lessons learned for development management." *World Development* 23, no. 8 (1995): 1303-1315.

Cope, Glen Hahn. "Walking the Fiscal Tightrope: Local Government Budgeting and Fiscal Stress." *International Journal of Public Administration* 15, no. 5 (1992): 1097-1120.

Cothran, Dan A. "Entrepreneurial budgeting: An emerging reform?" *Public Administration Review* 53, no. 5 (1993): 445-454.

Courty, Pascal, and Gerald Marschke. "Measuring government performance: Lessons from a federal job-training program." *American Economic Review* 87, no. 2 (1997): 383-388.

Courty, Pascal, and Gerald Maschke. *An Empirical Investigation of Gaming Responses to Explicit Performance Incentives.* Albany: State University of New York, 2000.

Courty, Pascal, and Gerald Marschke. "The JTPA Incentive System: Program Years 1987-1989." In *Performance Standards in Government Bureaucracy*, edited by James Heckman. Kalamzoo, MI: W.E. Upjohn Institute for Employment and Research, Forthcoming.

Cragg, Michael. "Performance Incentives in the Public Sector: Evidence from the Job Training Partnership Act." *Journal of Law, Economics, and Organization* 13, no. 1 (1997): 147-168.

Crew, Robert E., and Belinda Creel Davis. "Florida welfare reform: Cash assistance as the least desirable resource for poor families." In *Managing Welfare Reform in Five States: The Challenge of Devolution*, edited by Sarah F. Liebschutz. Albany, NY: Rockefeller Institute Press, 2000.

Cunningham, J. Barton. "Tactics for implementing quality improvement programs." *Optimum* 27, no. 1 (1997): 14-20.

Curro, Michael J. "Federal financial management and budgeting: NPR recommendations and GAO views." *Public Budgeting & Finance* 15, no. 1 (1995): 19-26.

Davies, Marlene, and Elaine Shellard. "The value of performance measurement in the United Kingdom." *Government Accountants Journal* 46, no. 3 (1997): 48-51.

DeBaylo, Paul W. "Ten reasons why the Baldrige model works." *Journal for Quality & Participation* 22, no. 1 (1999): 24-28.

Decker, P. "Systematic Bias in Earnings Data Derived from Unemployment Insurance Wage Records and Implications for Evaluating the Impact of Unemployment Insurance Policy on Earnings." Princeton, NJ: Mathematica Policy Research, 1989.

Deming, W. Edwards. *Out of the Crisis.* Cambridge: Massachusetts Institute of Technology, Center for Advanced Engineering Study, 1986.

Dempsey, Gordon J., August F. Geist, Anita J. Everhard, and Diane M. Chamberlin. "Paving the Road to Success at PennDOT." *Journal for Quality & Participation* 14, no. 3 (1991): 90-94.

Dickinson, Katherine P., and et al. "Evaluation of the effects of JTPA performance standards on clients, services, and costs." Washington, D.C.: National Commission for Employment Policy, 1988.

Dion, M. Robin, and LaDonna, Pavetti. *Access to and Participation in Medicaid and the Food Stamp Program: A Review of the Recent Literature.* Washington, D.C.: Mathematica Policy Research, Inc., 2000.

Dixit, A. *Incentives and Organizations in the Public Sector: An Interpretative Review.* Princeton University, 1999.

Doolittle, Fred C., and Linda Traeger. *Implementing the National JTPA Study.* New York: Manpower Demonstration Research Corp., 1990.

Dopuch, Nicholas, and Mahendra Gupta. "Estimation of benchmark performance standards: An application to public school expenditures." *Journal of Accounting & Economics* 23, no. 2 (1997): 141-161.

Douglas, James W. "Redirection in Georgia: A new type of budget reform." *American Review of Public Administration* 29, no. 3 (1999): 269-289.

Downs, George W., and Patrick D. Larkey. *The Search for Government Efficiency: From Hubris to Helplessness.* 1st ed. New York: Random House, 1986.

Drucker, Peter. "Forward." In *The Leader of the Future: New Visions, Strategies, and Practices for the Next Era,* edited by Frances Hesselbein, Marshall Goldsmith and Richard Beckhard. San Francisco: Jossey-Bass Publishers, 1996.

DuPont-Morales, M. A., and Jean E. Harris. "Strengthening accountability: Incorporating strategic planning and performance measurement into budgeting." *Public Productivity & Management Review* 17, no. 3 (1994): 231-239.

Duquette, Dennis J., and Alexis M. Stowe. "A performance measurement model for the Office of Inspector General." *Government Accountants Journal* 42, no. 2 (1993): 27-50.

Easterling, C. Nelson. "Performance Budgeting in Florida: To Muddle or Not to Muddle, That Is the Question." *Journal of Public Budgeting Accounting & Financial Management* 11, no. 4 (1999): 559-577.

Eck, John E., and William Spelman. "Problem-solving: Problem-oriented policing in Newport News." Washington, D.C.: U.S. Department of Justice; National Institute of Justice, 1987.

Ehrenhalt, Alan. "Performance budgeting, thy name is . . ." *Governing* 8 (1994): 9-10.

Eimicke, William B. "Benchmarking for Best Practices in the Public Sector / Achieving Improved Performances in Public Organizations: A Guide for Managers / Organizational Performance and Measurement in the Public Sector: Toward Service, Effort and Accomplishment Reported." *American Review of Public Administration* 28, no. 1 (1998): 90-95.

Eldridge, William H. "Why angels fear to tread: A practitioner's observations and solutions on introducing strategic management to a government culture." In *Handbook of Strategic Management,* edited by Jack Rabin, Gerald Miller and W. Bartley Hildreth, 319-336. New York: Marcel Dekker, Inc., 1989.

Elliot, Stern. "Interview with European Commission's Financial Controller." *Evaluation* 3, no. 1 (1995).

Ellis, Robert L. "QDF: A tool to sharpen measurement." *Public Manager* 27, no. 2 (1998): 33-36+.

Ellis, Eileen, and Vernon Smith. "Medicaid Enrollment in 21 States: June 1997 to June 1999." New York: Kaiser Family Foundation, 2000.

Ellwood, Marilyn R. *Medicaid Eligibility Maze.* Washington, D.C.: Urban Institute, 1999.

Epstein, Jeff, and Raymond T. Olsen. "Lessons learned by state and local governments." *Public Manager* 25, no. 3 (1996): 41-44.

Esser, Jeffrey L. "A new standard of excellence in budgeting." *Government Finance Review* 13 (1997): 5.

Evans, Martin. "A change for the better?" *Accountancy* 115, no. 1218 (1995): 92.

Ewell, P. T. "The Current Patterns of State-level Assessment: Results of a National Inventory." In *Performance Indicators in Higher Education: What Works, What Doesn't, and What's Next?*, edited by Gerald H. Gaither. College Station, TX: Texas A&M University System, 1996.

Fairbanks, Frank. "Managing for results: The path that Phoenix has followed." *Public Management* 78 (1996): 12-15.

Farquhar, Katherine. "Leadership in Limbo: Organization Dynamics During Interim Administrations." *Public Administration Review* 51, no. 3 (1991): 202-210.

Faucett, Allen, and Brian H. Kleiner. "New developments in performance measures of public programmes." *International Journal of Public Sector Management* 7, no. 3 (1994): 63-70.

Few, Paula K., and John A. Vogt. "Measuring the performance of local governments in North Carolina." *Government Finance Review* 13 (1997): 29-34.

Fielding Smith, Jame. "The benefits and threats of PBB: An assessment of modern reform." *Public Budgeting & Finance* 19, no. 3 (1999): 3-15.

Finnimore, Peter. "Measuring police performance." *Management Services* 37, no. 11 (1993): 12-14.

Fisher, Joseph L. "Formal Mechanisms: Helping the Governor to Manage." *Journal of State Government* 62, no. 4 (1989): 131-135.

Florida Office of Program Policy Analysis and Government Accountability. "A report on performance-based program budgeting in context: History and comparison." Tallahassee, FL: Florida Office of Program Policy Analysis and Government Accountability, 1997.

Florida TaxWatch. "Building a better Florida: A management blueprint to save taxpayers over $1 billion." Tallahassee, FL: Florida TaxWatch, Inc., 1986.

Florida TaxWatch. "Taxpayers Win at the Wire." Tallahassee, FL: Florida TaxWatch, Inc., 1995.

Florida TaxWatch Research Institute. "Florida's Performance Based Budgeting (PB2) — A Diamond in the Rough of Just a Zirconium Bauble?" Tallahassee, FL: Florida TaxWatch Research Institute, 1999.

Flowers, Geraldo E. "An evaluation of the effect of agency conditions on the implementation of Florida's performance-based program budgeting." Ph.D., Florida State University, 1999.

Flowers, Geraldo, and Delia Kundin. "How Agency Conditions Facilitate and Constrain Performance-Based Program Systems." *Journal of Public Budgeting Accounting & Financial Management* 11, no. 4 (1999): 618-648.

Folger, John K., and Dennis P. Jones. "Using fiscal policy to achieve state education goals." Denver: Education Commission of the States, 1993.

Forsythe, Dall W. *Performance Management Comes to Washington: A Status Report on the Government Performance and Results Act.* Albany, NY: Nelson A. Rockefeller Institute of Government, 2000.

Forsythe, Dall W., and Richard P. Nathan. "The Next Phase of Performance Management in Washington: What You Can Do." In *Memos to the President: Management Advice from the Nation's Top Public Administrators,* edited by Mark A. Abramson. Washington, DC: PricewaterhouseCoopers Endowment for the Business of Government, 2001.

Fountain, James R., Jr. "Service Efforts and Accomplishments Reporting." *Public Productivity & Management Review* 15, no. 2 (1991): 191-198.

Fountain, James Jr., and Mitchell Roob. "Service efforts and accomplishments measures." *Public Management* 76, no. 3 (1994): 6-12.

Francis, Charles D., and Allan J. Borwick. "The Equivalency Factor: Municipal Budgeting by the Household." *Government Finance Review* 6, no. 4 (1990): 7-11.

Franklin, Aimee. "Managing for results in Arizona: A fifth-year report card." *Public Productivity & Management Review* 23, no. 2 (1999): 194-209.

Frederickson, H. George. "The Repositioning of American Public Administration." Paper presented at the annual conference of the American Political Science Association, September 1999.

Freeman, Thomas. "Performance Indicators and Assessment in the State University of New York System." In *Assessing Performance in an Age of Accountability: Case Studies,* edited by Gerald H. Gaither. San Francisco: Jossey-Bass Publishers, 1995.

Friedlander, Daniel. *Subgroup Impacts and Performance Indicators for Selected Welfare Employment Programs.* New York: Manpower Demonstration Research Corp., 1988.

Friedlander, Daniel, and Gary Burtless. *Five Years After: The Long-Term Effects of Welfare-To-Work Programs.* New York: Russell Sage Foundation, 1995.

Gais, Thomas L. "Concluding comments: Welfare reform and governance." In *Learning from Leaders: Welfare Reform Politics and Policy in Five Midwestern States,* edited by Carol Weissert. Albany, NY: Rockefeller Institute Press, 2000.

Gais, Thomas, Richard Nathan, Irene Lurie, and Thomas Kaplan. *The Implementation of the Personal Responsibility Act of 1996: Commonalities, Variations, and the Challenge of Complexity.* Washington, D.C., 2000.

Gaither, Gerald H., Brian P. Nedwek, and John E. Neal. "Measuring up: The promises and pitfalls of performance indicators in higher education." In *ASHE-ERIC Higher Education Report No. 5.* Washington, D.C.: Graduate School of Education and Human Development, the George Washington University, 1995.

Galston, William A., and Geoffrey L. Tibbetts. "Reinventing Federalism: The Clinton/Gore Program for a New Partnership Among the Federal, State, Local, and Tribal Governments." *Publius* 24, no. 3 (1994): 23-48.

Garrett, Michael R., and Todd MacDonald. "Program/activity-based management at the Regional Municipality of Peel: An organization in transition." *Government Finance Review* 12 (1996): 7-10.

Garsombke, H. Perrin, and Jerry Schrad. "Performance measurement systems: Results from a city and state survey." *Government Finance Review* 15, no. 1 (1999): 9-12.

Garvey, Gerald. "False Promises: The NPR in Historical Perspective." In *Inside the Reinvention Machine: Appraising Governmental*

Reform, edited by Donald F. Kettl and John J. DiIulio. Washington, D.C.: Brookings Institution, 1995.

Gay, Robert S., and Michael E. Borus. "Validating Performance Indicators for Employment and Training Programs." *The Journal of Human Resources* 15, no. 1 (1980): 29-48.

Gearhart, Jon. "Activity based management and performance measurement systems." *Government Finance Review* 15, no. 1 (1999): 13-16.

Geiger, Dale R. "An experiment in federal cost accounting and performance measurement." *Government Accountants Journal* 42, no. 4 (1994): 39-52.

Ghobadian, Abby, and John Ashworth. "Performance measurement in local government: Concept and practice." *International Journal of Operations & Production Management* 14, no. 5 (1994): 35-51.

Gibbons, Robert. "Incentives and Careers in Organizations." National Bureau of Economic Research, 1996.

Glaser, Mark. "Tailoring Performance Measurement to Fit the Organization: From Generic to Germane." *Public Productivity & Management Review* 14, no. 3 (1991): 303-319.

Glaser, Mark. "Reconciliation of total quality management and traditional performance improvement tools." *Public Productivity & Management Review* 16, no. 4 (1993): 379-386.

Gold, Steven D. *The Fiscal Crisis of the States: Lessons for the Future.* Washington, D.C.: Georgetown University Press, 1995.

Goldman, Frances, and Edith Brashares. "Performance and Accountability: Budget Reform in New Zealand." *Public Budgeting & Finance* 11, no. 4 (1991): 75-85.

Goldstein, Herman. *Problem-Oriented Policing.* Philadelphia: Temple University Press, 1990.

Gore, Albert. "From red tape to results: Creating a government that works better & costs less." Washington, D.C.: U.S. Office of the Vice President, 1993.

Gormley, William T., and David L. Weimer. *Organizational Report Cards*. Cambridge: Harvard University Press, 1999.

Government Accounting Standards Board. *GASB's State and Local Government Case Studies: The Use and the Effects of Using Performance Measures for Budgeting, Management, and Reporting*. 2000. Available from http://www.rutgers.edu/accounting/raw/seagov/pmg/index.html.

"Grading the States: A 50-State Report Card on Government Performance." *Governing*, February 1999.

Gray, Maryann D. "Enhancing the quality and use of student outcomes data: Final report of the National Postsecondary Education Cooperative Working Group on Student Outcomes from a Data Perspective." Washington, D.C.: National Center for Education Statistics, Office for Educational Research and Improvement, U.S. Department of Education, 1996.

Greene, Jack R., and Stephen D. Mastrofski. *Community Policing: Rhetoric or Reality*. New York: Praeger, 1988.

Greene, Richard, and Katherine Greene. "Poisoned measures (performance measurement can drive poor government management)." *Governing* 11, no. 8 (1998): 60.

Greenwood, Peter W., Jan M. Chaiken, and Joan Petersilia. *The Criminal Investigation Process*. Lexington, MA: D.C. Heath, 1977.

Griesemer, James R. "The power of performance measurement: A computer performance model and examples from Colorado cities." *Government Finance Review* 9, no. 5 (1993): 17-21.

Grifel, Stuart S. "Performance measurement and budgetary decision making." *Public Productivity & Management Review* 16, no. 4 (1993): 403-407.

Grote, Dick. "Public sector organizations: Today's innovative leaders in performance management." *Public Personnel Management* 29, no. 1 (2000): 1-20.

Hagen, Jan L., and Irene Lurie. *Implementing JOBS: The Participants' Perspective.* Albany, NY: Nelson A. Rockefeller Institute of Government, 1994.

Halachmi, Arie, and Geert Bouckaert. "Performance measurement, organizational technology and organizational design." *Work Study* 43, no. 3 (1994): 19-25.

Halachmi, Arie. "Mandated performance measurement: A help or a hindrance?" *National Productivity Review* 18, no. 2 (1999): 59-67.

Hammer, Michael, and James Champy. *Reengineering the Corporation: A Manifesto for Business Revolution.* London: Nicholas Brealey Publishing, 1993.

Harr, David J. "Productive Unit Resourcing: A Business Perspective in Governmental Financial Management." *Government Accountants Journal* 38, no. 2 (1989): 51-57.

Harr, David J., and James T. Godfrey. "The Total Unit Cost Approach to Government Financial Management." *Government Accountants Journal* 40, no. 4 (1992): 15-24.

Harris, Jean. "Service efforts and accomplishments: A primer of current practice and an agenda for future research." *International Journal of Public Administration* 18, no. 2,3 (1995): 253-276.

Harris, Jean. "Service efforts and accomplishments standards: Fundamental questions of an emerging concept." *Public Budgeting & Finance* 15, no. 4 (1995): 18-37.

Hatry, Harry P. et al. *Service Efforts and Accomplishments: Its Time Has Come.* Norwalk, CT: Government Accounting Standards Board, 1990.

Hatry, Harry P., and Joseph S. Wholey. "Toward useful performance measurement: Lessons learned from initial pilot performance plans prepared under the Government Performance and Results Act." Washington, D.C.: National Academy of Public Administration, 1994.

Hatry, Harry. "Foreward." In *Organizational Performance and Measurement in the Public Sector: Toward Service, Effort, and Accomplishment Reporting*, edited by Arie Halachmi and Geert Bouckaert. Westport, CT: Quorum Books, 1996.

Hatry, Harry P., and Joseph S. Wholey. *Performance Measurement: Getting Results*. Washington, D.C.: Urban Institute Press, 1999.

Hatry, Harry. "Mini-symposium on intergovernmental comparative performance data." *Public Administration Review* 59, no. 2 (1999): 101-104.

Heaton, John D., Linda J. Savage, and Judith K Welch. "Performance auditing in municipal governments." *Government Accountants Journal* 42, no. 2 (1993): 51-60.

Heckman, James, and R. Robb. "Alternative Methods for Evaluating the Impact of Interventions." In *Longitudinal Analysis of Labor Market Data*, edited by James Heckman and Burton Singer. Cambridge: Cambridge University Press, 1985.

Heckman, James. "Randomization and Social Program Evaluation." In *Evaluating Welfare and Training Programs*, edited by Charles Manski and Irwin Garfinkel. Cambridge: Harvard University Press, 1993.

Heckman, James, and J. Smith. *The Performance of Performance Standards: The Effects of JTPA Performance Standards on Efficiency, Equity and Participant Outcomes*. Chicago: University of Chicago, 1995.

Heckman, James, J. Smith, and C. Taber. "What Do Bureaucrats Do? The Effects of Performance Standards and Bureaucratic Preferences on Acceptance in the JTPA Program." In *Advances in the*

Study of Entrepreneurship, Innovation, and Economic Growth, edited by Gary Libecap. Greenwich, CT: JAI Press Inc., 1996.

Heckman, James, R. LaLonde, and J. Smith. "The Economics and Econometrics of Active Labor Market Programs." In *Handbook of Labor Economics*, edited by Orley Ashenfelter and David E. Card. Amsterdam: Elsevier, 1999.

Heckman, James, C. Heinrich, and J. Smith. *Understanding Incentives in Public Organizations*. Chicago: University of Chicago, 1999.

Heclo, Hugh H. "Values Underpinning Poverty Programs for Children." *The Future of Children* 7, no. 2 (1997): 141-148.

Heinrich, Carolyn J. "Do Government Bureaucrats make Effective Use of Performance Management Information?" *Journal of Public Administration Research & Theory* 9, no. 3 (1999): 363-393.

Heinrich, C., G. Marschke, and J. Smith. "The JTPA Program: Basic Information on its Design and Implementation." In *Performance Standards in a Government Bureaucracy*, edited by James Heckman. Kalamazoo, MI: W.E. Upjohn Institute for Employment Research, Forthcoming.

Henderson, Ian. "Does budgeting have to be so troublesome?" *Management Accounting − London* 75, no. 9 (1997): 26-27.

Herman, Joan L. *Program Evaluation Kit*. 2nd ed. Newbury Park, CA: Sage Publications, 1987.

Hernandez, Raymond. "Inquiry Grows As Rolls Fall For Medicaid." *New York Times*, June 8, 1999, B, 1:5.

Herrington, Carolyn. "Performance Based Budgeting in Public Schools in Florida." In *School Based Financing*, edited by Margaret E. Goertz and Allan Odden. Thousand Oaks, CA: Corwin Press, Inc., 1999.

Holahan, John, and Johnny Kim. " Why does the number of uninsured Americans continue to grow?" *Health Affairs* 19, no. 4 (2000): 188-196.

Holmstrom, Bengt , and Paul Milgrom. "Aggregation and Linearity in the Provision of Intertemporal Incentives." *Econometrica* 55, no. 2 (1987): 303-328.

Holmstrom, Bengt, and Paul Milgrom. "Multitask Principal-Agent Analyses: Incentive Contracts, Asset Ownership, and Job Design." *Journal of Law, Economics and Organization* 7 (1991): 24-52.

Holt, Craig L. "Performance based budgeting: Can it really be done?" *Public Manager* 24, no. 4 (1996): 19-21.

Ingraham, P. W., P. J. Joyce, and A. E. Kneedler. *Managing for Performance*. Baltimore, MD: John Hopkins University Press, 2000.

Ingraham, P.W., and A.E. Kneedler. "Dissecting the Black Box Revisited: Characterizing Government Management Capacity." In *Models and Methods for the Empirical Study of Governance*, edited by Laurence E. Lynn, Jr. Washington, D.C.: Georgetown University Press, 2000.

International City/County Management Association — Urban Institute. *Comparative Performance Measurement: FY 1996 Data Report*. Washington, D.C.: International City/County Management Association, 1998.

International City/County Management Association — Urban Institute. *Comparative Performance Measurement: FY 1997 Data Report*. Washington, D.C.: International City/County Management Association, 1999.

Jackson, Peter M. "Public service performance evaluation: A strategic perspective." *Public Money & Management* 13, no. 4 (1993): 9-14.

Jensen, Michael C., and Kevin J. Murphy. "Performance Pay and Top-Management Incentives." *The Journal of Political Economy* 98, no. 2 (1990): 225-264.

Johnsen, Age. "Implementation mode and local government performance measurement: A Norwegian experience." *Financial Accountability & Management* 15, no. 1 (1999): 41-66.

Johnson, Pamela R., and Jordan Stern. "From good enough to the best in business: Benchmarking for public managers." *Public Manager* 24, no. 3 (1995): 21-24.

Jones, Ann. "Winston-Salem's participation in the North Carolina performance measurement project." *Government Finance Review* 13 (1997): 35-36.

Jones, David Seth. "Recent budgetary reforms in Singapore." *Journal of Public Budgeting, Accounting & Financial Management* 10, no. 2 (1998): 279-310.

Jones, L. R. , and Jerry L. McCaffery. "Implementing the Chief Financial Officers Act and the Government Performance and Results Act in the federal government." *Public Budgeting & Finance* 17, no. 1 (1997): 35-55.

Jordan, Meagan M., and Merl M. Hackbart. "Performance budgeting and performance funding in the states: A status assessment." *Public Budgeting & Finance* 19, no. 1 (1999): 68-88.

Joyce, Philip G. "Using performance measures for federal budgeting: Proposals and prospects." *Public Budgeting & Finance* 13, no. 4 (1993): 3-17.

Joyce, Philip G. "Appraising budget appraisal: Can you take politics out of budgeting?" *Public Budgeting & Finance* 16, no. 4 (1996): 21-25.

Joyce, Philip G. "The future of federal budgeting: What will the government do? How will it make its choices?" *Journal of Public*

Budgeting, Accounting & Financial Management 9, no. 1 (1997): 72-89.

Joyce, P. G., and S. Sieg Tompkins. "Using Performance Information for Budgeting: Clarifying the Framework and Investigating Recent State Experience." Paper presented at the Symposium of the Center for Accountability and Performance of the American Society for Public Administration, George Washington University, Washington, D.C., 2000.

Jreisat, Jamil E. "Productivity Measurement and Finance Officers." *Public Productivity & Management Review* 13, no. 4 (1990): 315-329.

Kamensky, John M. "Program performance measures: Designing a system to manage for results." *Public Productivity & Management Review* 16, no. 4 (1993): 395-402.

Kaplan, Robert S., and David P. Norton. *The Balanced Scorecard: Translating Strategy Into Action.* Boston: Harvard Business School Press, 1996.

Kaplan, Robert S., and Robin Cooper. *Cost & Effect: Using Integrated Cost Systems to Drive Profitability and Performance.* Boston: Harvard Business School Press, 1998.

Keehley, Patricia, and Sue A. MacBride. "Can benchmarking for best practices work for government?" *Quality Progress* 30 (1997): 75-80.

Kelling, George L. et al. "The Kansas City preventive patrol experiment: a summary report." Washington, D.C.: The Police Foundation, 1974.

Kerr, Steven. "On the Folly of Rewarding A, While Hoping for B." *Academy of Management Journal* 18, no. 4 (1975): 769-783.

Kerr, Deborah L. "Managing Rosie the Riveter: The work between strategic planning and performance measurement." *Public Productivity & Management Review* 17, no. 3 (1994): 215-221.

Kettl, Donald F., John J. DiIulio, and Gerald Garvey. *Improving Government Performance: An Owner's Manual.* Washington, D.C.: Brookings Institution, 1993.

Kettl, Donald F. *Sharing Power: Public Governance and Private Markets.* Washington, D.C.: The Brookings Institution, 1993.

Kettl, Donald F. *The Global Revolution in Public Management.* Washington, D.C.: Brookings Institution Press, 1997.

Kettl, Donald F. "Reinventing government: A fifth-year report card." *CPM Report – 98-1*, 71. Washington, D.C.: Center for Public Management, The Brookings Institution, 1998.

Key, V.O. Jr. "The Lack of a Budgetary Theory." *American Political Science Review* XX (1940): 34.

King, Laura M. "Operating and capital budget reform in Minnesota: Managing public finances like the future matters." *Government Finance Review* 11, no. 1 (1995): 7-10.

Kinser, Kim. "Colorado is redesigning its pay plan to reward employees for their performance." *State Government News* 40, no. 8 (1997): 27-28.

Kirchhoff, Judith J. "Public services production in context: Toward a multilevel, multistakeholder model." *Public Productivity & Management Review* 21, no. 1 (1997): 70-85.

Knezo, Genevieve J., and Virginia A. McMurtry. "Performance Measure Provisions in the 105th Congress: Analysis of a Selected Compilation." Congressional Research Service, 1998.

Kopcynski, Mary, and Michael Lombardo. "Comparative performance measurement: Insights and lessons learned from a consortium effort." *Public Administration Review* 59, no. 2 (1999): 124-134.

Kravchuk, Robert S., and Ronald W. Schack. "Designing effective performance-measurement systems under the Government Performance and Results Act of 1993." *Public Administration Review* 56, no. 4 (1996): 348-358.

Ku, Leighton, and Brian Bruen. *The Continuing Decline in Medicaid Coverage*. Washington, DC: Urban Institute, 1999.

LaLonde, Robert J. "Evaluating the Econometric Evaluations of Training Programs with Experimental Data." *The American Economic Review* 76, no. 4 (1986): 604-620.

Langley, Ann. "The Roles of Formal Strategic Planning." *Long Range Planning* 21, no. 3 (1988): 40-50.

Laurent, Anne. "Stacking up: The Government Performance Project rates management at 15 federal agencies." *Government Executive* 31, no. 2 (1999): 13-18.

Lauth, Thomas P. "State Budgeting: Current Conditions and Future Trends." *International Journal of Public Administration* 15, no. 5 (1992): 1067-1096.

Lawrence, Carol M. , and James M. Kurtenbach. "Medicare reimbursement, debt financing, and measures of service efforts and accomplishments in the healthcare industry." *International Journal of Public Administration* 18, no. 2,3 (1995): 355-381.

Lazear, Edward P. "Performance Pay and Productivity." *NBER Working Paper* 5672. Cambridge: National Bureau of Economic Research, 1996.

Learned, Edmund P., C. R. Christensen, K. R. Andrews, and W. D. Guth. *Business Policy: Text and Cases*. Homewood, IL: R. D. Irwin, 1965.

Lee, Robert D. Jr., and Robert C. Burns. "Performance measurement in state budgeting: Advancement and backsliding from 1990 to 1995." *Public Budgeting & Finance* 20, no. 1 (2000): 38-54.

Leithe, Joni L. "Managing for results: Advancing the art of performance measurement." *Government Finance Review* 12 (1996): 40-42.

Leithe, Joni. "Guidelines for budget making." *American City & County* 113, no. 9 (1998): 8.

Lemov, Penelope. "Measuring performance, making progress." *Governing* 11, no. 4 (1998): 54-56.

Levin, Henry M. *Cost-Effectiveness: A Primer*. Beverly Hills, CA: Sage Publications, 1983.

Lewis, Kimball, Marilyn Ellwood, and John L. Czajka. "Counting the uninsured: A review of the literature." *Assessing the New Federalism: Occasional Paper No. 8*. Washington, D.C.: Urban Institute, 1998.

Light, Paul C. *The Tides of Reform: Making Government Work, 1945-1995*. New Haven, CT: Yale University Press, 1997.

Light, Paul C. *The True Size of Government*. Washington, D.C.: Brookings Institution Press, 1999.

Liner, Blaine, and Elisa Vinson. "Will States Meet the Challenge?" Washington, DC: The Urban Institute, 1999.

Llewellyn, Wayne D. "A review of budgeting systems." *Assessment Journal* 1, no. 5 (1994): 47-50.

Locke, E. A., D. B. Feren, V. M. McCaleb, and A. T. Denny. "The Relative Effectiveness of Four Methods of Motivating Employee Performance." In *Changes in Working Life: Proceedings of an International Conference on Changes in the Nature and Quality of Working Life*, edited by Keith D. Duncan, Michael M. Gruneberg and D. Wallis. Chichester: Wiley, 1981.

Longmire, Laura. "Dare to ask, 'how do we stack up?'" *American City & County* 112, no. 5 (1997): 6.

Lu, Haoran. "Performance budgeting resuscitated: Why is it still inviable?" *Journal of Public Budgeting, Accounting & Financial Management* 10, no. 2 (1998): 151-172.

Lynch, Thomas D., and Cynthia Lynch. "Twenty-first century budget reform: Performance, entrepreneurial, and competitive budgeting." *Public Administration Quarterly* 20, no. 3 (1996): 255-284.

Madler, Lisa. "Overview of GeorgiaGain and the Performance Management Process." *Journal of Environmental Health* 59 (1997): 6-8.

Mali, Paul. "Differentiating High from Low Productivity Performance in City Governments." *National Productivity Review* 9, no. 3 (1990): 281-299.

Maloy, Kathleen et al. *Description and Assessment of State Approaches to Diversion Programs and Activities Under Welfare Reform.* Washington, D.C.: George Washington University, 1998.

Mandell, Lee M. "Performance measurement and management tools in North Carolina local government — revisited." *Public Administration Quarterly* 21, no. 1 (1997): 96-127.

Maple, Jack, and Chris Mitchell. *The Crime Fighter: Putting the Bad Guys Out of Business.* New York: Doubleday, 1999.

Mark, M., and E. Pines. "Implications of Continuous Quality Improvement for Program Evaluation and Evaluators." *Evaluation Practice* (1995).

Marks, Barry R., and Raman K. K. "The behavior of interperiod equity-related performance measures over time." *Accounting Horizons* 10 (1996): 52-66.

Marschke, Gerald. *Performance Incentives and Bureaucratic Behavior: Evidence from a Federal Bureaucracy.* Albany, NY: Unpublished manuscript, 2000.

Marshall, Martha, Lyle Wray, Paul Epstein, and Stuart Grifel. "21st century community focus: Better results by linking citizens, government, and performance measurement." *Public Management* 81, no. 10 (1999): 12-18.

Martin, Lawrence L. "Outcome budgeting: A new entrepreneural approach to budgeting." *Journal of Public Budgeting, Accounting & Financial Management* 9, no. 1 (1997): 108-126.

Martin, Lawrence L. "Performance contracting: extending performance measurement to another level." *PA Times* 22, no. 1 (1999): 1,8.

Martz, Mary Jeanne Reid. "Helpful practices in implementing GPRA." *Public Manager* 27, no. 4 (1999): 35-39.

Mascarenhas, R. C. "Searching for efficiency in the public sector: Interim evaluation of performance budgeting in New Zealand." *Public Budgeting & Finance* 16, no. 3 (1996): 13-27.

Maxwell, Terrence A. "Information Federalism: History of Welfare Information Systems." *Working Paper.* Albany, NY: Nelson A. Rockefeller Institute of Government, 1999.

McCrindell, James, and Paul-Emile Roy. "Public needs, public purse." *CA Magazine* 131, no. 10 (1998): 37-38+.

McKeown, Mary P. "State funding formulas for public four-year institutions." Denver, CO: State Higher Education Executive Officers, 1996.

McKevitt, David, and Alan Lawton. "The manager, the citizen, the politician and performance measures." *Public Money & Management* 16, no. 3 (1996): 49-54.

Medoff, James L. , and Katharine G. Abraham. "Experience, Performance, and Earnings." *Quarterly Journal of Economics* 95, no. 4 (1980): 703-736.

Meekings, Alan. "Unlocking the potential of performance measurement: A practical implementation guide." *Public Money & Management* 15, no. 4 (1995): 5-12.

Melkers, Julia, and Katherine Willoughby. "The state of the states: Performance-based budgeting requirements in 47 out of 50." *Public Administration Review* 58, no. 1 (1998): 66-73.

Melkers, Julia E., and Katherine G. Willoughby. "Budgeters' Views of State Performance Budgeting Systems: Distinctions across Branches." *Public Administration Review* (2001).

Metzger, Lawrence M. "A pricing model for internal service funds." *Government Finance Review* 10, no. 6 (1994): 17-20.

Meyer, Marshall W., and Kenneth C. O'Shaughnessy. "Organizational design and the performance paradox." In *Explorations in Economic Sociology*, edited by Richard Swedberg. New York: Russell Sage Foundation, 1993.

Mihm, J. Christopher. "Management Reform: Continuing Attention Is Needed to Improve Government Performance." In *Has Government Been 'Reinvented'? — Testimony Before the Senate Subcommittee on Oversight of Government Management, Restructuring, and the District of Columbia*. Washington, D.C.: General Accounting Office, 2000.

Milakovich, Michael E. "How quality-oriented have state and local governments really become?" *National Productivity Review* 14, no. 1 (1995): 73-84.

Milgrom, Paul R., and John Roberts. *Economics, Organization, and Management*. Englewood Cliffs, NJ: Prentice-Hall, 1992.

Miller, Hugh T. "Post-progressive public administration: lessons from policy networks." *Public Administration Review* 54, no. 4 (1994): 378-387.

Mintzberg, Henry. "The pitfalls of strategic planning." *California Management Review* 36, no. 1 (1993): 32-48.

Mintzberg, Henry. "The fall and rise of strategic planning." *Harvard Business Review* 72, no. 1 (1994): 107-114.

Mohr, Lawrence B. *Impact Analysis for Program Evaluation.* Newbury Park, CA: Sage Publications, 1992.

Mol, Nicol P. "Performance indicators in the Dutch Department of Defence." *Financial Accountability & Management* 12, no. 1 (1996): 71-81.

Moore, Mark H. "Accounting for change: Reconciling the demands for accountability and innovation in the public sector." Washington, D.C.: Council for Excellence in Government, 1993.

Moore, George C., and Philip M. Heneghan. "Defining and prioritizing public performance requirements." *Public Productivity & Management Review* 20 (1996): 158-173.

Moore, Mark H. *Creating Public Value.* Bridgewater, NJ: Replica Books, 1997.

Moore, J., and L. Sprague. "Reinventing Medicaid: Hoosier Healthwise and children's health insurance in Indiana." Washington, DC: National Health Policy Forum, George Washington University, 2000.

Morgan, Dan. "Food Stamp Rules Aim to Ease Access." *The Washington Post,* November 19, 2000, A-11.

Morris, Matthew J. "The state of performance measurement in the capital budget development process." *Public Manager* 27, no. 3 (1998): 59-61.

Mosher, Frederick C. *Theory and Practice, with Particular Reference to the U.S. Department of the Army.* Chicago: Public Administration Service, 1954.

Mosso, David. "Accounting for the business of government — new goals, old myths." *Public Budgeting & Finance* 19, no. 4 (1999): 65-74.

Nathan, Richard P. *Empowerment Zone Initiative: Building a Community Plan for Strategic Change. Findings from the First Round of Assessment.* Albany, NY: Nelson A. Rockefeller Institute of Government, 1998.

Nathan, Richard P., and Thomas Gais. *Implementing the Personal Responsibility Act of 1996: A First Look.* Albany, NY: Nelson A. Rockefeller Institute of Government, 1999.

National Center for Public Productivity. *A Brief Guide for Performance Measurement in Local Government.* Newark, NJ: Rutgers University, November 1, 1999. Available from http://www.andromeda.rutgers.edu/~ncpp/cdgp.

Navaratnam, K. K., and Bill Harris. "Customer service in an Australian quality award winning public sector service industry." *International Journal of Public Sector Management* 7, no. 2 (1994): 42-49.

New Zealand State Services Commission. "Assessing Departments' Capability to Contribute to Strategic Priorities." New Zealand State Services Commission, 1999.

Newcomer, Kathryn E., and Roy E. Wright. "Toward effective use of performance measurement in the federal government." *Public Manager* 25, no. 4 (1997): 31-33.

Newcomer, Kathryn E., and Amy Downey. "Performance-based management: What is it and how do we get there?" *Public Manager* 26, no. 4 (1998): 37-40.

Newman, Isadore, and Keith A. McNeil. *Conducting Survey Research in the Social Sciences*. Lanham, MD: University Press of America, 1998.

Nyhan, Ronald C., and Herbert A. Marlowe, Jr. "Performance measurement in the public sector: challenges and opportunities." *Public Productivity & Management Review* 18, no. 4 (1995): 333-348.

Nyhan, Ronald C., and Lawrence L. Martin. "Comparative performance measurement." *Public Productivity & Management Review* 22, no. 3 (1999): 348-364.

O'Reilly-Allen, Margaret. "Government: GASB's performance measures project." *Pennsylvania CPA Journal* 69, no. 4 (1999): 14.

O'Toole, Daniel E., James Marshall, and Timothy Grewe. "Current local government budgeting practices." *Government Finance Review* 12 (1996): 25-29.

O'Toole, Laurence J., Jr. "Treating networks seriously: Practical and research-based agendas in public administration." *Public Administration Review* 57, no. 1 (1997): 45-52.

Orr, Larry L. et al. "The National JTPA Study: Impacts, benefits, and costs of Title II-A." Bethesda, MD: Abt Associates, 1994.

Osborne, David E., and Ted Gaebler. *Reinventing Government: How the Entrepreneurial Spirit is Transforming the Public Sector*. Reading: Addison-Wesley Pub. Co., 1992.

Osborne, David E., and Peter Plastrik. *The Reinventor's Fieldbook: Tools for Transforming Your Government*. San Francisco: Jossy-Bass Publishers, 2000.

Paarsch, H., and B. Shearer. "Fixed Wages, Piece Rates, and Incentive Effects." University of Laval, unpublished manuscript, 1996.

Paddock, Susan C. "Benchmarks in management training." *Public Personnel Management* 26, no. 4 (1997): 441-460.

Palmer, Anna J. "Performance measurement in local government." *Public Money & Management* 13, no. 4 (1993): 31-36.

Parry, Robert W. Jr., Florence Sharp, Wanda A. Wallace, and Janet Vreeland. "The role of service efforts and accomplishments reporting in total quality management: implications for accountants." *Accounting Horizons* 8, no. 2 (1994): 25-43.

Patton, Michael Quinn. *Qualitative Evaluation and Research Methods.* Newbury Park, CA: Sage Publications, 1990.

Pawson, Ray, and Nick Tilley. *Realistic Evaluation.* London: Sage, 1997.

Pear, Robert. "Clinton to Chide States for Failing to Cover Children." *New York Times,* August 8, 1999, 1, 1:6.

Peters, Thomas J., and Robert H. Waterman. *In Search of Excellence: Lessons from America's Best-Run Companies.* Thorndike, ME: G.K. Hall & Co., 1997.

Pew Research Center for the People and the Press. "Deconstructing Distrust: How Americans View Government." Philadelphia: Pew Charitable Trust, 1998.

Poister, Theodore H. *Performance Monitoring.* Lexington, MA: Lexington Books, 1983.

Poister, Theodore H., and Gregory Streib. "Performance measurement in municipal government: Assessing the state of the practice." *Public Administration Review* 59, no. 4 (1999): 325-335.

Poister, Theodore H., and Gregory D. Streib. "Assessing the validity, legitimacy, and functionality of performance measurement systems in municipal governments." *American Review of Public Administration* 29, no. 2 (1999): 107-123.

Porter, Michael E. *Competitive Strategy: Techniques for Analyzing Industries and Competitors.* New York: Free Press, 1980.

Posner, Paul. "Performance Budgeting: Past Initiatives Offer Insights for GPRA Implementation." Washington, D.C.: General Accounting Office, 1997.

Posner, Paul L. "Performance budgeting: A critical process." *Public Manager* 28, no. 3 (1999): 8.

Prendergast, Candice. "The provision of incentives in firms." *Journal of Economic Literature* 37, no. 1 (1999): 7-63.

Pressman, Jeffrey L., and Aaron B. Wildavsky. *Implementation: How Great Expectations in Washington Are Dashed in Oakland.* Berkeley, CA: University of California Press, 1973.

Pulos, Victoria. "One step forward, one step back: Children's health coverage after CHIP and welfare reform." *Families USA Publication No. 99.* Washington, D.C.: Families USA, 1999.

Quinn, James Brian. *Strategies for Change: Logical Incrementalism.* Homewood, Ill: R.D. Irwin, 1980.

Raaum, Ronell B., and Edwin Soniat. "Measurement-based performance audits: A tool for downsizing government." *Government Accountants Journal* 42, no. 2 (1993): 61-70.

Radin, Beryl A. "The Government Performance and Results Act (GPRA): Hydra-headed monster or flexible management tool?" *Public Administration Review* 58, no. 4 (1998): 307-316.

Radin, Beryl A. "Intergovernmental Relationships and the Federal Performance Movement." *Publius* 30, no. 1/2 (2000): 143-158.

Rahn, Mikala L., E. Gareth Hoachlander, and Karen A. Levesque. *State Systems for Accountability in Vocational Education.* Berkeley, CA: Office of Vocational and Adult Education, U.S. Department of Education, 1992.

Raine, John W., and Michael J. Willson. "From performance measurement to performance enhancement: An information system case-study from the Administration of Justice." *Public Money & Management* 17, no. 1 (1997): 19-25.

Rainey, Anthony H. "Benchmarking to become best in class: Guiding principles in Gresham, Oregon." *Government Finance Review* 13 (1997): 5-9.

Ridley, Clarence E., and Herbert A. Simon. *Measuring Municipal Activities: A Survey of Suggested Criteria for Appraising Administration.* Chicago: The International City Managers' Association, 1943.

Ring, Peter Smith, and James L. Perry. "Strategic Management in Public and Private Organizations: Implications of Distinctive Contexts and Constraints." *The Academy of Management Review* 10, no. 2 (1985): 276-286.

Rogers, Dale S., Patricia J. Daugherty, and Theodore P. Stank. "Benchmarking programs: opportunities for enhancing performance." *Journal of Business Logistics* 16, no. 2 (1995): 43-63.

Rogerson, Philip. "Performance measurement and policing: Police service or law enforcement agency?" *Public Money & Management* 15, no. 4 (1995): 25-30.

Rossi, Peter Henry, and Howard E. Freeman. *Evaluation: A Systematic Approach.* 5th ed. Newbury Park, CA: Sage Publications, 1993.

Roth, William V., Jr. "Performance-based budgeting to enhance implementation of the CFO Act." *Public Budgeting & Finance* 12, no. 4 (1992): 102-106.

Rouse, Paul. "Performance measurement." *Chartered Accountants Journal of New Zealand* 74, no. 9 (1995): 18-19.

Rubin, Irene S. "Budget Theory And Budget Practice: How Good The Fit?" *Public Administration Review* 50, no. 2 (1990): 179-198.

Rubin, Irene S. "Who invented budgeting in the United States?" *Public Administration Review* 53, no. 5 (1993): 438-444.

Sanders, James R., and Joint Committee on Standards for Educational Evaluation. *The Program Evaluation Standards: How to Assess Evaluations of Educational Programs.* 2nd ed. Thousand Oaks, CA: Sage Publications, 1994.

Schedler, Kuno. "Performance measurement in a direct democratic environment: local government reforms in Switzerland." *Public Budgeting & Finance* 14, no. 4 (1994): 36-53.

Scheps, Philip B. "Linking performance measures to resource allocation." *Government Finance Review* 16, no. 3 (2000): 11-15.

Schick, Allen. "The Road to PPB: The Stages of Budget Reform." *Public Administration Review* 26 (1966).

Schick, Allen. *Budget Innovation in the States.* Washington, D.C.: Brookings Institution, 1971.

Schick, Allen. "Contemporary Problems in Financial Control." *Public Administration Review* 38, no. 6 (1978): 513-519.

Schick, Allen. "An inquiry into the possibility of a budgetary theory." In *New Directions in Budget Theory,* edited by Irene S. Rubin. Albany, NY: State University of New York Press, 1988.

Schick, Allen. "Budgeting for Results: Recent Developments in Five Industrialized Countries." *Public Administration Review* 50, no. 1 (1990): 26-34.

Schick, Allen. "The spirit of reform: Managing the New Zealand state sector in a time of change." Wellington: State Services Commission, 1996.

Schick, Allen. "Opportunity, Strategy, and Tactics in Reforming Public Management." Paper presented at the OECD Symposium, Paris, France, September 14-15, 1999.

Schirm, Allen L. *Reaching Those in Need: Food Stamp Participation Rates in the States*. U.S. Department of Agriculture, 2000. Available from http://www.fns.usda.gov/oane/MENU/Published/FSP/FILES/Reaching.pdf.

Schrader, Richard W. "An empirical investigation into the decision usefulness of service efforts and accomplishments measurements." *International Journal of Public Administration* 18, no. 2, 3 (1995): 443-466.

Selden, Thomas M., Jessica S. Banthin, and Joel W. Cohen. "Medicaid's problem children: Eligible but not enrolled." *Health Affairs* 17, no. 3 (1998): 192-200.

Selden, Thomas M., Jessica S. Banthin, and Joel W. Cohen. "Waiting in the wings: Eligibility and enrollment in the state children's health insurance program." *Health Affairs* 18, no. 2 (1999): 126-133.

Serban, Andreea. "Performance Funding for Public Higher Education: Views of Critical Stakeholders." In *Current Status and Future Prospects of Performance Funding and Performance Budgeting for Public Higher Education: The Second Survey*, edited by Joseph C. Burke and Andreea M. Serban. Albany, NY: Nelson A. Rockefeller Institute of Government, 1998.

Shadish, William R., Thomas D. Cook, and Laura C. Leviton. *Foundations of Program Evaluation: Theories of Practice*. Newbury Park, CA: Sage Publications, 1991.

Shane, Bryan. "Improved performance measurement: A prerequisite for better service delivery." *Optimum* 27, no. 4 (1997): 1-5.

Shane, Bryan. "Implementing a performance measurement system in a public service informatics function." *Optimum* 28, no. 3 (1998): 36-44.

Sharifi, Sudi, and Tony Bovaird. "The financial management initiative in the U.K. public sector: The symbolic role of performance reporting." *International Journal of Public Administration* 18, no. 2,3 (1995): 467-490.

Sharman, Paul. "Activity/process budgets: A tool for change management." *CMA Magazine* 70, no. 2 (1996): 21-24.

Sheffield, Sheila R. "Implementing Florida's Performance and Accountability Act: A Focus on Program Measurement and Evaluation." *Journal of Public Budgeting Accounting & Financial Management* 11, no. 4 (1999): 649-669.

Short, Pamela F. "Hitting a Moving Target: Income-Related Health Insurance Subsidies for the Uninsured." *Journal of Policy Analysis and Management* 19, no. 3 (2000): 383-406.

Simpson, Wayne K., and Michael J. Williams. "Activity-based: Costing, management and budgeting." *Government Accountants Journal* 45, no. 1 (1996): 26-28.

Skok, James E. "Toward a Definition of Strategic Management for the Public." *American Review of Public Administration* 19, no. 2 (1989): 133-148.

Smith, Dennis C. "Police." In *Setting Municipal Priorities*, edited by Charles Brecher and Raymond D. Horton. New York: Russell Sage Foundation, 1981.

Smith, Dennis C. "Performance Management in New York City: The Mayor's Management Plan and Report System in the Koch Administration." Paper presented at the annual meeting of the Association of Public Policy and Management, 1993.

Smith, J. *A Note on Estimating the Relative Costs of Experimental and Non-Experimental Evaluations Using Cost Data from the National JTPA Study*. University of Chicago, unpublished manuscript, 1995.

Smith, Kimberly J., and Wanda A. Wallace. "Incentive effects of service efforts and accomplishments performance measures: A need for experimentation." *International Journal of Public Administration* 18, no. 2,3 (1995): 383-407.

Smith, Peter. "On the unintended consequences of publishing performance data in the public sector." *International Journal of Public Administration* 18, no. 2,3 (1995): 277-311.

Soglin, Paul R. "Getting returns on tax dollars." *Government Finance Review* 11 (1995): 26-27.

Sonntag, Brian. "Measuring results: performance based government in Washington State." *Government Finance Review* 15, no. 3 (1999): 52-53.

Sorber, Bram. "Performance measurement in the central government departments of the Netherlands." *Public Productivity & Management Review* 17, no. 1 (1993): 59-68.

Steinhauer, Jennifer. "States Prove Unpredictable in Aiding Uninsured Children." *New York Times*, September 28, 2000, A16.

Stevens, D. "Using state unemployment insurance wage-records to trace the subsequent labor market experiences." Washington, D.C.: U.S. Department of Education, Office of Educational Research and Improvement, 1989.

Stevens, Ted. "Implementation of the Results Act." Paper presented at the Joint Hearing of the Senate Appropriations Committee and the Senate Governmental Affairs Committee on *Implementation of the Results Act*, June 24, 1997.

Stiefel, Leanna, Ross Rubenstein, and Amy Ellen Schwartz. "Using adjusted performance measures for evaluating resource use." *Public Budgeting & Finance* 19, no. 3 (1999): 67-87.

Strauss, Anselm L. *Qualitative Analysis for Social Scientists.* Cambridge: Cambridge University Press, 1987.

Talbot, Colin. "Output and performance analysis: Time to open up the debate?" *Public Money & Management* 18, no. 2 (1998): 4-5.

Taylor, Paul J., and Jon L. Pierce. "Effects of introducing a performance management system on employees' subsequent attitudes and effort." *Public Personnel Management* 28, no. 3 (1999): 423-452.

Teasley, C. E. III. "The perpetual pursuit of purpose: PA — state of the discipline II." *Public Administration Quarterly* 23, no. 1 (1999): 65-76.

Texas Governor's Office of Budget and Planning, Legislative Budget Board. "Instructions for preparing and submitting agency strategic plans, fiscal years 1999-2003." Austin, TX, 1998.

The President's Community Enterprise Board — U.S. Dept. of Housing and Urban Development and U.S. Dept. of Agriculture. "Building communities, together: Empowerment zones & enterprise communities application guide." Washington, D.C., 1994.

Thomas, Virginia L., and Ryan Rogers. "Time to Hold the Legal Services Corporation Accountable." Washington, D.C.: The Heritage Foundation, 1999.

Thompson, James D. *Organizations in Action.* New York: McGraw-Hill, 1967.

Thompson, Fred. "Mission-driven, results-oriented budgeting: Fiscal administration and the new public management." *Public Budgeting & Finance* 14, no. 3 (1994): 90-105.

Thompson, Katherine. "Performance audits: A solution to California's budget crisis?" *Government Accountants Journal* 45, no. 1 (1996): 8-9.

Thompson, James R. "The dual potentialities of performance measurement: The case of the Social Security Administration." *Public Productivity & Management Review* 23, no. 3 (2000): 267-281.

Thompson, Frank J. , and Thomas L. Gais. "Federalism and the Safety Net: Delinkage and Participation Rates." *Publius* 30, no. 1-2 (2000).

Thomson, Trish. "The dynamics of introducing performance metrics into an organization." *National Productivity Review* 18, no. 3 (1999): 51-55.

Thurmaier, Kurt M., and Katherine G. Willoughby. *Policy and Politics in State Budgeting*. Armonk, NY: M.E. Sharpe, 2001.

Tigue, Patricia. "Use of performance measures by GFOA members." *Government Finance Review* 10, no. 6 (1994): 42-44.

Tiller, Carl W. *Governmental Cost Accounting*. Chicago: Municipal Finance Officers Association of the United States and Canada, 1940.

Todd, Rebecca, and Kavasseri V. Ramanathan. "Perceived social needs, outcomes measurement, and budgetary responsiveness in a not-for-profit setting: Some empirical evidence." *Accounting Review* 69, no. 1 (1994): 122-137.

Tracy, Richard C., and Ellen P. Jean. "Measuring government performance: Experimenting with service efforts and accomplishments reporting in Portland, Oregon." *Government Finance Review* 9, no. 6 (1993): 11-14.

Tuck, Nancy, and Gary Zaleski. "Criteria for developing performance measurement systems in the pubic sector." *International Journal of Public Administration* 19, no. 11,12 (1996): 1945-1978.

Tyer, Charlie, and Jennifer Willand. "Public budgeting in America: A twentieth century retrospective." *Journal of Public Budgeting, Accounting & Financial Management* 9, no. 2 (1997): 189-219.

U.S. Bureau of the Budget. "Bulletin No. 68-9, April 12, 1968." In *Governmental Budgeting: Theory, Process, Politics*, edited by Albert C. Hyde and Jay M.Shafritz. Oak Park: Moore, 1978.

U.S. Commission on Organization of the Executive Branch of Government. "Budgeting and Accounting." Washington, D.C., 1949.

U.S. Congress — Office of Technology Assessment. "Performance standards for the Food Stamp Employment and Training Program." Washington, D.C., 1994.

U.S. Congressional Budget Office. "Unauthorized Appropriations and Expiring Authorizations." Washington, D.C., 2000.

U.S. Congressional Record. "Senator Voinovich's remarks." Washington, D.C., 2000.

U.S. Department of Agriculture. *Draft USDA Forest Service Strategic Plan (2000 Revision)*. United States Department of Agriculture, 1999. Available from http://www2.srs.fs.fed.us/strategicplan.

U.S. Department of Agriculture. *Food Stamps: Governors' Letter*. U.S. Department of Agriculture, July 12, 2000. Available from http://www.fns.usda.gov/fsp/MENU/ADMIN/WELFARE /SUPPORT/Governors%20on%20FS%20Eligibility.htm.

U.S. Department of Agriculture, Food, Nutrition and Consumer Services. "National Food Stamp Conversation 2000: Sharing a History of Accomplishment and Targeting Opportunities for Improvement." Washington, D.C., 2000.

U.S. Department of Health and Human Services. "Report to Congress on Out-of-Wedlock Childbearing." Washington, D.C., 1995.

U.S. Department of Health and Human Services. "Report to the President: Interagency Task Force on Children's Health Insurance Outreach." Washington, D.C., 1998.

U.S. Department of Health and Human Services. "Supporting families in transition: A guide to expanding health coverage in the post-welfare reform world." Washington, D.C., 1999.

U.S. Department of Health and Human Services, Assistant Secretary for Planning and Evaluation. "Understanding Estimates of Uninsured Children: Putting the Differences in Context." Washington, D.C., 1999.

U.S. Department of Labor, Employment and Training Administration, Office of Policy and Research. "Core data elements and common definitions for employment and training programs." Washington, D.C., 1995.

U.S. Department of the Treasury, Financial Management Service. "Performance measurement: Report on a survey of private sector performance measures." Washington, D.C., 1993.

U.S. General Accounting Office. "Managing for Results: Experience in Four European Countries and How They Might be Applied in the U.S." Washington, D.C., 1993.

U.S. General Accounting Office. "Performance Budgeting." Washington, D.C., 1993.

U.S. General Accounting Office. "Improving Government: Measuring Performance and Acting on Proposals for Change." Washington, D.C., 1993.

U.S. General Accounting Office. "Using Performance Measures in the Federal Budget Process." Washington, D. C., 1993.

U.S. General Accounting Office. "Measuring Performance and Acting on Proposals for Change." Washington, D.C., 1993.

U.S. General Accounting Office. "Program Performance Measures." Washington, D.C., 1993.

U.S. General Accounting Office. "Managing for Results: State Experiences Provide Insights for Federal Management Reforms." Washington, D.C., 1994.

U.S. General Accounting Office. "Government Reorganization: Issues and Principles." Washington, D.C., 1995.

U.S. General Accounting Office. "Government Reform: Goal-Setting and Performance." Washington, D.C., 1995.

U.S. General Accounting Office. "Community Development: Challenges Face Comprehensive Approaches to Address Needs of Distressed Neighborhoods." Washington, D.C., 1995.

U.S. General Accounting Office. "Executive Guide: Effectively Implementing the Government Performance and Results Act." Washington, D.C., 1996.

U.S. General Accounting Office. "Social Security Administration: Effective Leadership Needed to Meet Daunting Challenges." Washington, D.C., 1996.

U.S. General Accounting Office. "Measuring Performance: Strengths and Limitations of Research Indicators." Washington, D.C., 1997.

U.S. General Accounting Office. "GPRA - Managerial Accountability and Flexibility Pilot Did Not Work As Intended." Washington, D.C., 1997.

U.S. General Accounting Office. "Managing for Results: Analytic Challenges in Measuring Performance." Washington, D.C., 1997.

U.S. General Accounting Office. "Agencies' Strategic Plans Under GPRA: Key Questions to Facilitate Congressional Review." Washington, D.C., 1997.

U.S. General Accounting Office. "Social Security Administration: More Cost-Effective Approaches Exist to Further Improve 800-Number Service." Washington, D.C., 1997.

U.S. General Accounting Office. "Social Security Administration: Significant Challenges Await New Commissioner." Washington, D.C., 1997.

U.S. General Accounting Office. "Performance Budgeting: Past Initiatives Offer Insights for GPRA Implementation." Washington, D.C., 1997.

U.S. General Accounting Office. "Head Start: Challenges in Monitoring Program Quality and Demonstrating Results." In *Letter Report*, Washington, D.C., 1998.

U.S. General Accounting Office. "Teen Pregnancy: State and Federal Efforts to Implement Prevention Programs and Measure Their Effectiveness." Washington, D.C., 1998.

U.S. General Accounting Office. "SSA's FY 1999 Performance Plan." Washington, D.C., 1998.

U.S. General Accounting Office. "Homelessness: Coordination and Evaluation of Programs are Essential." Washington, D.C., 1999.

U.S. General Accounting Office. "Potential Candidates for Congressional Oversight." Washington, D.C., 1999.

U.S. General Accounting Office. "High-Risk Series: An Update." Washington, D.C., 1999.

U.S. General Accounting Office. "Major Management Challenges and Program Risks: A Government-wide Perspective." Washington, D.C., 1999.

U.S. General Accounting Office. "Forest Service: A Framework for Improving Accountability." Washington, D.C., 1999.

U.S. General Accounting Office. "Managing for Results: Opportunities for Continued Improvements in Agencies' Performance Plans." Washington, D.C., 1999.

U.S. General Accounting Office. "Performance Budgeting: Initial Agency Experiences Provide a Foundation to Assess Future Directions." Washington, D.C., 1999.

U.S. General Accounting Office. "Performance Budgeting: Initial Experiences Under the Results Act in Linking Plans With Budgets." Washington, D.C., 1999.

U.S. General Accounting Office. "Medicaid Enrollment: Amid Declines, State Efforts to Ensure Coverage After Welfare Reform Vary." Washington, D.C., 1999.

U.S. General Accounting Office. "Food Stamp Program: Various Factors Have Led to Declining Participation." Washington, D.C., 1999.

U.S. General Accounting Office. "NPR's Savings: Claimed Agency Savings Cannot All Be Attributed to NPR." Washington, D.C., 1999.

U.S. General Accounting Office. "Budget Issues: Effective Oversight and Budget Discipline are Essential—Even in a Time of Surplus." Washington, D.C., 2000.

U.S. General Accounting Office. "Managing for Results: Challenges Agencies Face in Producing Credible Performance Information." Washington, D.C., 2000.

U.S. General Accounting Office. "Management Reform: Continuing Attention Is Needed to Improve Government Performance." Washington, D.C., 2000.

U.S. House of Representatives Committee on Government Reform and Oversight and the U.S. Senate Committee on Governmental Affairs. "Performance-based government: Examining the Government Performance and Results Act of 1993." Washington, D.C., 1996.

U.S. House of Representatives Ways and Means Committee. *1989 Green Book: Background Material and Data on Programs Within the Jurisdiction of the Committee on Ways and Means.* Washington, D.C., 1989.

U.S. House of Representatives Ways and Means Committee. *1991 Green Book: Background Material and Data on Programs Within the Jurisdiction of the Committee on Ways and Means.* Washington, D.C., 1991.

U.S. House of Representatives Ways and Means Committee. *1996 Green Book: Background Material and Data on Programs Within the Jurisdiction of the Committee on Ways and Means.* Washington, D.C., 1996.

U.S. House of Representatives Ways and Means Committee. *1998 Green Book: Background Material and Data on Programs Within the Jurisdiction of the Committee on Ways and Means.* Washington, D.C., 1998.

U.S. Joint Financial Management Improvement Program. "Managerial cost accounting system requirements." Washington, D.C., 1998.

U.S. National Performance Review. "From red tape to results, creating a government that works better & costs less." Washington, D.C.: Executive Office of the President,, 1993.

U.S. National Performance Review. "Putting customers first: Standards for serving the American people." Washington, D.C.: Executive Office of the President, 1994.

U.S. National Performance Review. "Common sense government: Works better and costs less." Washington, D.C.: Executive Office of the President, 1995.

U.S. Office of Management and Budget. "Government-wide performance plan: Budget of the United States government, fiscal year 2000." Washington, D.C.: Executive Office of the President, 1999.

U.S. Office of Management and Budget. "Historical tables: Budget of the United States government, fiscal year 2001." Washington, D.C.: Executive Office of the President, 2000.

U.S. Senate Committee on Government Operations, Subcommittee on Intergovernmental Relations. "Compendium of materials on zero-base budgeting in the States." Washington, D.C., 1977.

U.S. Senate Committee on Governmental Affairs. "Senate Report No. 106-12 on S. 92." Washington, D.C., 1999.

U.S. Senate Governmental Affairs Committee. Press release, January 24 2000.

U.S. Social Security Administration. "Keeping the Promise: Strategic Plan 1997-2002." Washington, D.C., 1997.

U.S. Social Security Administration, Office of Financial Policy and Operations. "Accountability Report for Fiscal Year 1998." Washington, D.C., 1998.

U.S. Social Security Administration. "Short-Term Initiatives to Improve National 800-Number and Program Service Center Service to the Public." 1999.

U.S. Social Security Administration. "Annual Performance Plan for Fiscal Year 2000." Washington, D.C., 1999.

U.S. Social Security Administration. "Accountability Report for Fiscal Year 1999." Washington, D.C., 1999.

U.S. Social Security Administration. "Social Security — A Brief History." 2000. Available from www.ssa.gov/history/history6.html.

U.S. Social Security Administration. "Performance Plan for Fiscal Year 2001 and Revised Final Performance Plan for Fiscal Year 2000." Washington, D.C., 2000.

U.S. Social Security Administration — Office of Finance, Assessment and Management; Office of Quality Assurance and Performance Assessment. "800 Number Customer Survey for February 1999." 1999.

Ullman, Frank, Brian K. Bruen, and John Holahan. "The state children's health insurance program: A look at the numbers." In *Assessing the New Federalism Program — Occasional Paper no. 4*, 22. Washington, D.C.: Urban Institute, 1999.

Urban Institute. *Performance Measurement: A Guide for Local Elected Officials*. Washington, D.C., 1980.

Van Wart, Montgomery. "The first step in the reinvention process: assessment." *Public Administration Review* 55, no. 5 (1995): 429-438.

Vinson, Elisa. *Performance Contracting in Six State Human Services Agencies*. Washington, DC: The Urban Institute, 1999.

Volcker, Paul A., and National Commission on the Public Service. *Leadership for America: Rebuilding the Public Service*. Lexington, MA: Lexington Books, 1989.

Wade, Beth. "Performance measures: What's the score?" *American City & County* 113, no. 11 (1998): 36.

Walker, Gary C., and Manpower Development Research Corporation, Grinker, Walker & Associates, and Syracuse Research Corporation. "An Independent Sector Assessment of the Job Training Partnership Act, Phase I: The Initial Transition." Chapel Hill: MDRC, Inc., 1984.

Walker, Gary, Hilary Feldstein, and Katherine Solow. "An Independent Sector Assessment of the Job Training Partnership Act — Phase II: Initial Implementation." New York: Grinker, Walker & Associates, 1985.

Wallace, G., and R.M. Blank. "What Goes Up Must Come Down?" In *Economic Conditions and Welfare Reform*, edited by Sheldon H. Danziger. Kalamazoo, MI: W.E. Upjohn Institute for Employment Research, 1999.

Wallick, Ruth. "GFOA recommended practices promote the professional management of government." *Government Finance Review* 10, no. 4 (1994): 42-43.

Ward, Benjamin, and New York Police Department. "The Community Patrol Officer Program: Problem-Solving Guide." New York: Vera Institute of Justice, 1988.

Ward, Janet. "The changing focus of public works: Federal strategies, local can-do." *American City & County* 111, no. 9 (1996): 70-84+.

Wechsler, B. "Strategic management in state government." In *Handbook of Strategic Management*, edited by Jack Rabin, Gerald Miller and W. Bartley Hildreth. New York: Marcel Dekker, Inc., 1989.

Wegener, Victoria. *Food Stamp Education and Outreach Working to Provide Nutrition Benefits to Eligible Households*. Welfare Information Network, 1999. Available from http://www.welfareinfo.org/foodstampout.htm.

Weiss, Barbara. *Activity-Based Costing and Management: Issues and Practices in Local Government*. Chicago: Government Finance Officers Association, 1997.

Weller, Alfred O., and Lisa Sayeg. "Benchmarking tools for public risk management programs." *Government Finance Review* 14, no. 5 (1998): 41-46.

Welsh, Susan. "Hitting the mark: Communicating outcomes to the citizens." *Government Finance Review* 13, no. 6 (1997): 13-15.

Westat, Inc. "Implementation of the Job Training Partnership Act: Final Report." Rockville, MD: Division of Research and Evaluation, Office of Strategic Planning and Policy Development, Employment and Training Administration, U.S. Department of Labor, 1985.

Wholey, Joseph S., and Kathryn E. Newcomer. *Improving Government Performance: Evaluation Strategies for Strengthening Public Agencies and Programs.* 1st ed. San Francisco: Jossey-Bass, 1989.

Wholey, Joseph S., and Harry P. Hatry. "The Case for Performance Monitoring." *Public Administration Review* 52, no. 6 (1992): 604-610.

Wholey, Joseph. "Evaluation and performance." *Australian Accountant* 63, no. 11 (1993): 28-33.

Wholey, Joseph S. "Assessing the quality and usefulness of performance measurement systems." *Public Manager* 27, no. 3 (1998): 23.

Wildavsky, Aaron. *The Politics of the Budgetary Process.* 2nd ed. Boston: Little, Brown and Company, 1974.

Wildavsky, Aaron. *Budgeting: A Comparative Theory of the Budgetary Process.* Boston: Little Brown, 1975.

Wilde, Parke et al. " The decline in Food Stamp Program participation in the 1990's." In *Food Assistance and Nutrition Research Report* no. 7, 22. Washington, D.C.: U.S. Department of Agriculture, Economic Research Service, 2000.

Williamson, Oliver E. "Transaction-Cost Economics: The Governance of Contractural Relations." *Journal of Law and Economics* 22, no. 2 (1979): 233-261.

Willoughby, Katherine G., and Julia E. Melkers. " Implementing PBB: conflicting views of success." *Public Budgeting & Finance* 20, no. 1 (2000): 105-120.

Wilson, James Q. *Varieties of Police Behavior.* Cambridge: Harvard University Press, 1968.

Wilson, James Q. *Bureaucracy: What Government Agencies Do and Why They Do It.* New York: Basic Books, 1989.

Wipper, Laura R. "Oregon Department of Transportation steers improvement with performance measurement." *National Productivity Review* 13, no. 3 (1994): 359-367.

Wirt, John G. "Performance assessment systems: Implications for a national system of skill standards." Washington, D.C.: Training and Employment Program, Employment and Social Services Policy Studies, Center for Policy Research, National Governors Association, 1994.

Yi, Hyong U. "Benchmarking best practices: lessons from baseball." *Public Manager* 27, no. 2 (1998): 59-62.

Zedlewski, Sheila R., Pamela A. Holcomb, and Amy-Ellen Duke. "Declines in food stamp and welfare participation: Is there a connection?" Washington, D.C.: The Urban Institute, 1999.

Zolt, Stacey. "Going Out with a Bang: Kasich Plans Energetic Final Year as Chairman." *Roll Call*, February 28 2000.

Zornitsky, Jeffrey, Mary Rubin, Stephen H. Bell, and William Martin. "Establishing a performance management system for targeted welfare programs." Washington, D.C.: National Commission for Employment Policy, 1988.

About the Authors

Burt S. Barnow is associate director for research and principal research scientist at the Institute for Policy Studies at the Johns Hopkins University. Barnow has over 25 years of experience as an economist and manager of research projects in the fields of program evaluation, labor economics, welfare programs, child support, and employment and training. Barnow joined the Institute for Policy Studies in 1992 after working for 8 years at the Lewin Group and nearly 9 years of experience in the U.S. Department of Labor. He has a B.S. degree in economics from the Massachusetts Institute of Technology and M.S. and Ph.D. degrees in economics from the University of Wisconsin at Madison. Barnow has published widely in the fields of labor economics, program evaluation, and employment and training. He co-edited two books that were published in 2000: *Improving the Odds: Publicly Funded Training in a Changing Labor Market*, co-edited with Christopher T. King and published by the Urban Institute Press; and *Evaluating Comprehensive State Welfare Reform: The Wisconsin Works Programs*, co-edited with Thomas Kaplan and Robert Moffitt and published by the Rockefeller Institute Press. Barnow is currently serving as vice chairman of the National Academy of Science's Committee on the Information Technology Work Force, chair of the Maryland Governor's Workforce Investment Board Committee on Performance Measurement, and chairman of the Research Committee on the National Association of Schools of Public Affairs and Administration.

Ann Blalock is a sociologist and evaluation research consultant. She has been the editor and principal author of *Evaluation Forum*, a research journal funded by the United States Department of Labor (USDOL) reviewing research on employment, training, work/welfare, and economic development issues. She was co-director of the four-state Flexible Intergovernmental Grant Project funded by the United States Department of Health and Human Services and USDOL testing the feasibility of integrating related social programs and standardizing methods for evaluating them. She was director of the multi-year JTPA Evaluation Design Project funded by the National Commission for Employment Policy, USDOL, The Ford Foundation, and IBM to develop a set of comprehensive evaluation research guides for use by states in evaluating their social programs. She has been a presenter at research seminars sponsored by the Organization for Economic Cooperation and Development in Paris and the European Commission in Brussels, and has contributed to their evaluation guides. Her publications include *Introduction to Social Research, Methodology in Social Research, Evaluating Social Programs,* and a large number of journal articles on social policy and program evaluation.

Kate Boyer is a senior research associate for the Federalism Research Group of the Nelson A. Rockefeller Institute of Government. Dr. Boyer received her Ph.D. from McGill University in May 2001. Her research interests include urban studies, women's participation in the labor force, and managerial and work cultures. Prior to coming to the Institute Dr. Boyer served as a visiting assistant Professor of Geography at the University at Albany, and her work has appeared in *The Journal of Urban Geography,* and *Gender, Place and Culture: A Journal of Feminist Geography.*

Robert B. Bradley is associate vice president for research and director of the Institute of Science and Public Affairs, as well as a professor in the Reubin O'D Askew School of Public Administration and Policy at Florida State University. He directs the Florida Leadership Board for Applied Research and Public Service. He holds a Ph.D. in political science from the University of Florida and served for 8 years in Florida state government as deputy director and director of the Governor's Office of Planning and Budgeting. His research and teaching focus on state and local public finance, state and local relations, and public policy. He served as executive director of the Florida Advisory Council on Intergovernmental Relations and the Constitution Commission on State Taxation and Budget Reform. Bradley has served as consultant to various state, local, and national organizations and chaired the NCSL State-Local Relation Staff Committee Growth, The Florida State Technology Council, the Florida Geographic Information Board, and The Florida Legislative Analysis System/Planning Budgeting System Steering Committee.

William Bratton is president of the New York City-based consulting firm, The Bratton Group LLC. He has led and reengineered five major police agencies, including Police Commissioner for the New

York City and Boston Police Departments. His autobiography, *Turnaround*, was published by Random House. He is widely recognized for his advocacy of problem-oriented community policing, including the New York City "Compstat" system that was created in 1994 during his tenure as New York City Police Commissioner. He is a research fellow at the Harvard University John F. Kennedy School of Government and a member of the Advisory Board of the Center for Excellence in Governance of the Robert Wagner Graduate School of Public Service at New York University. He serves on the Board of Washington, D.C. based advocacy group Fight Crime — Invest in Kids, and is a member of the Board of Directors of The Partnership for a Drug Free America. He is a senior consultant with Kroll Associates.

Walter D. Broadnax is dean, School of Public Affairs, American University in Washington, D.C. Broadnax served as deputy secretary and chief operating officer of the U.S. Department of Health and Human Services; president, Center for Governmental Research, Inc., in Rochester, New York; president, New York State Civil Service Commission; lecturer and director, Innovations in State and Local Government Programs in the Kennedy School of Government at Harvard University; senior staff member, The Brookings Institution; principal deputy assistant secretary for Planning and Evaluation, U.S. Department of Health, Education and Welfare; director, Children, Youth and Adult Services, State of Kansas; and professor, The Federal Executive Institute, Charlottesville, Virginia.

Broadnax received his Ph.D. from the Maxwell School at Syracuse University, his B.A. from Washburn University, and his M.P.A. from the University of Kansas. He is a fellow of the National Academy of Public Administration and a former trustee of the Academy's Board. He was elected president of the National Association of Schools of Public Affairs and Administration and served from 1999-2000.

Joseph C. Burke is director of the Higher Education Program, senior fellow at the Nelson A. Rockefeller Institute of Government, and State University of New York professor of higher education policy and management. He combines the experiences of professor, administrator, and researcher. For twelve years, he served as president of the State University of New York at Plattsburgh, followed by nine years as provost and one year as interim chancellor of the State University of New York System. Burke has written and lectured on a wide array of topics in higher education, including the role of college and university presidents, system governance, accountability and autonomy in higher education, academic outcomes assessment, and performance reporting and funding. The Henry Luce Foundation, The Pew Charitable Trusts, and the Ford Foundation have awarded Burke grants for national studies of the budgeting, accountability, and performance of public university systems and state colleges and universities. He received his Ph.D. from Indiana University.

Kevin J. Conway is a doctoral candidate in political science at American University in Washington, D.C. His fields of concentration include American government, policy analysis, and public administration. Currently, his dissertation examines party defectors — members who vote against their party leader's preferred position on roll call votes — in the U.S. House of Representatives from the 102nd through the 105th Congress.

Geraldo Flowers earned his Doctor of Philosophy in Public Administration from Florida State University with a concentration in performance-based program budgeting and strategic management. He is currently a professor of Public Administration and Finance at Florida Gulf Coast University (FGCU) in Ft. Myers, Florida, where he teaches graduate courses in the Master of Public Administration program, and serves as Interim Director of a Public Policy Institute. Flowers has formulated and managed a number of major community-focused and institutional strategic planning projects. He co-managed the implementation of a Master Degree program in Public Health in Belize with colleagues from the University of Belize and University of South Florida.

Prior to his post at FGCU, Flowers served as an Adjunct Professor of Public Administration at Florida State University and as a Fiscal Policy Analyst for Florida TaxWatch, Flowers has published extensively in the areas of performance budgeting, accountability and strategic management. In addition, he has worked in the public health and nongovernmental sectors in Belize before leaving to extend his education and experience in the U.S. He is currently returning to Belize as Vice President of Finance and Administration at the University of Belize.

Dall Forsythe is a senior fellow at the State University of New York's Nelson A. Rockefeller Institute of Government, and visiting professor in the public administration program at the University at Albany. Forsythe served as budget director for the State of New York and for the New York City Board of Education. In the private sector, he worked as a managing director in Lehman Brother's public finance department. Forsythe spent three years on the faculty of Harvard University's Kennedy School of Government, and has taught political science and finance at Columbia University. He received his bachelor's degree and Ph.D. from Columbia University. Forsythe is the author of two books, including *Memos to the Governor: An Introduction to state Budgeting* (Georgetown University Press), as well as several papers and articles. In 1998, he received the S. Kenneth Howard Award, a career achievement award from the Association for Budgeting and Financial Management (ABFM).

James W. Fossett is associate professor of public administration and health policy and management at the University at Albany of the State University of New York and a senior fellow at the Nelson A. Rockefeller Institute of Government. He is a Phi Beta Kappa graduate of Vanderbilt University, holds a Ph.D. in political science from the University of Michigan, and is a former staff member at the Brookings Institution. He has written extensively on the accessibility of health care for low-income women and children, and budgeting and management issues in public funded health care, particularly the implementation issues associated with Medicaid managed care. He is currently the principal investigator on a large project funded by the Robert Wood Johnson Foundation to examine the relationship between welfare reform and Medicaid in twenty-one states.

Thomas L. Gais is director of the Federalism Research Group of the Nelson A. Rockefeller Institute of Government of the State University of New York. He is director and co-principal investigator of the State Capacity Study, a multi-state field research project on the changing institutions and management systems at the state and local levels in welfare, Medicaid, Food Stamps, and workforce development. He is the author of *Implementing the Personal Responsibility Act of 1996: A First Look* (with Richard P. Nathan; 1999) and many other publications based on data collected for the study. His previous work dealt with issues of institutional change and reform, including campaign finance reform, constitutional change in the states, and interest group mobilization in American politics. His publications on these subjects include *Improper Influence: Political Interest Groups, Campaign Finance Laws, and the Problem of Equality* (University of Michigan Press, 1996) and *The Day After Reform: Sobering Campaign Finance Lessons from the American States* (Rockefeller Institute Press/State University of New York Press, 1998). Gais received his Ph.D. in political science from the University of Michigan-Ann Arbor.

Harry Hatry is a principal research associate at the Urban Institute in Washington, D.C., where he is the director of the Institute's Public Management Program. Since the early 1970s, he has been a leader in developing procedures that allow nonprofit organizations and federal, state, and local government agencies to track how well they are performing their services. Key works in which he has been an author include *How Effective Are Your Community Services? Procedures for Measuring Quality; The Guide to Program Outcome Monitoring for the U.S. Department of Education; Measuring Program Outcomes: A Practical Approach* (for United Way of America); *Service Efforts and Accomplishments Reporting: Its Time Has Come — An Overview* (for the Governmental Accounting Standards Board); *Practical Program Evaluation for State and Local Governments*; and *Program Analysis for State and Local Governments*. He has received awards relating to his work in performance measurement and evaluation from a number of organizations, including the American Society for Public Administration and the National Academy of Public Administration.

Patricia Wallace Ingraham is distinguished professor of public administration at the Maxwell School of Citizenship and Public Affairs, Syracuse University. She was the founding director of the Alan K. Campbell Public Affairs Institute and also served as the first director of the Government Performance Project, a multi-year analysis of management capacity at the state, local, and federal levels. She is author of numerous publications on public management including *Putting Management in the Performance Equation* (forthcoming, John Hopkins University Press). Ingraham recently completed service as an advisor to the Secretary of Defense on the Defense Science Board for Human Resource Management. She was recently named to the Advisory Board for the U.S. Patent and Trademark Office (USPTO), which will advise the PTO as it moves to a performance-based organization under the terms of legislation passed last year; and to the National Research Council Committee to assess Department of Energy Project Management. She is also a member of the U.S. Comptroller General's National Advisory Board. In April, Ingraham received the Herbert Simon Award for Career Contribution to Public Administration and the career award from the American Society for Public Administration for contributions to the study of human resource management.

Catherine Lawrence is a research associate at the Nelson A. Rockefeller Institute of Government. She holds a Masters in social work from the Rockefeller College School of Social Welfare at the State University of New York at Albany, where she is a candidate for a doctoral degree. Her areas of research include U.S. social policy and programs related to poverty and human sexuality, including welfare reform, non-marital and adolescent pregnancy, pregnancy prevention, and sexual abuse trauma. Her publications include reports on state-level policies to reduce non-marital pregnancy and program evaluations of welfare reform.

Gerald Marschke is an assistant professor with appointments in the Graduate School of Public Affairs and in the Department of Economics at the State University of New York at Albany. His research and teaching interests include the economics of labor markets, organizations, the public sector, and technology policy. His recent research has focused on the use of performance incentives for program managers in the federal job training program created under the Job Training Partnership Act. Prior to coming to Albany, he taught at the State University of New York at Buffalo and worked as a research associate for the Center for Social Program Evaluation at the University of Chicago. He holds a Ph.D. in economics from the University of Chicago.

Julia Melkers is an associate professor of public administration and urban studies in the Andrew Young School of Public Studies at Georgia State University. In addition to her research on the use of performance measures in state and local governments, her current research includes a project on the use of economic development incentives in local governments. She has published articles on performance-related topics in *Public Administration Review, Urban Studies Review, Policy Studies Journal, Public Budgeting and Finance, Journal of Technology Transfer, Research Evaluation,* and *Evaluation and Program Planning* and is co-editor of the book *Assessing R & D Impacts: Method and Practice.* In addition to her other funded work, Melkers has conducted performance-related work for the State of Georgia, the City of Atlanta, the State of Alaska, the State of Maine, and the Atlanta Urban League. She has a Ph.D. in Public Administration from the Maxwell School at Syracuse University.

J. Christopher Mihm is director of Strategic Issues at the U.S. General Accounting Office. Since 1993, he has led GAO's efforts on the Government Performance and Results Act and related results-oriented management initiatives. Mihm also is responsible for GAO work on the conduct of the 2000 Decennial Census. Mihm has led the development of many reports, testimonies, and formal briefings that are assisting Congress and federal managers as they seek to instill a more results-oriented approach to federal management. Mihm has appeared as a witness before congressional committees on numerous occasions to discuss federal management reform issues and has been actively involved in working with committees across Congress to show them how GPRA can be used to improve congressional decisionmaking. Prior to assuming his current responsibilities, Mihm managed GAO's reviews of the 1990 decennial census that identified the actions that the Census Bureau needed to take to have a more accurate and less costly census in 2000 and reviews of the effectiveness of the Resolution Trust Corporation, the federal agency responsible for resolving the nation's savings and loan crisis.

Donald P. Moynihan is a Ph.D. candidate in public administration at the Maxwell School of Citizenship and Public Affairs at Syracuse University. As a research associate with the Alan K. Campbell Public Affairs Institute, he works on the Government Performance

Project, an analysis of public management in federal, state, and local government in the United States. His research for the Government Performance Project is focused in the area of managing for results, covering such topics as strategic planning, performance measurement, and performance information use. Moynihan has also performed research for the World Bank in the area of public expenditure, performance measurement, and strategic planning. Other research interests include comparative administration and public sector reform.

Richard P. Nathan directs the Nelson A. Rockefeller Institute of Government, the public policy research arm of the State University of New York, which is located in Albany. Prior to coming to Albany, he was a professor at Princeton and before that a senior fellow at The Brookings Institution. His government service includes directing domestic policy research for the National Commission on Civil Disorders (the Kerner Commission) and the national campaigns of Nelson A. Rockefeller. He was assistant director of the U.S. Office of Management and Budget and deputy undersecretary for welfare reform of the U.S. Department of Health, Education and Welfare. His books include *Implementing the Personal Responsibility Act of 1996: A First Look* (Rockefeller Institute Press, 1999), *Turning Promises Into Performance* (Columbia University Press, 1993), *The Administrative Presidency* (MacMillan, 1983), *Reagan and the States* (Princeton University Press, 1987), and *Social Science in Government* (Rockefeller Institute Press, 2000). Nathan is an advisor to the U.S. General Accounting Office.

Beryl A. Radin is a professor of public administration and policy in the Rockefeller College of the State University of New York at Albany. Her research has focused on a variety of issues dealing with federal management reform as well as intergovernmental issues, highlighting the federal Government Performance and Results Act and intergovernmental issues in a number of policy areas (especially rural development and programs of the U.S. Department of Health and Human Services). In addition, she has written about the policy analysis profession. Her publications have appeared in a range of policy and public management journals and she is the author or co-author of four books. She is currently the managing editor of the *Journal of Public Administration and Theory* and a fellow of the National Academy of Public Administration.

Allen Schick is a professor of public policy at the University of Maryland School of Public Affairs and a visiting fellow at The Brookings Institution. Schick has specialized in reform of budget systems and political institutions in the United States and many other countries. He has worked in 45 states, a large number of countries, and in the federal government. He was one of the authors of the Congressional Budget Act of 1974 and is involved in contemporary efforts to implement performance-based budgeting. His publications include *The Capacity to Budget* (1990), *The Spirit of Reform* (1996), *Modern Budgeting* (1998), *Contemporary Public Expenditure Management* (1998), and *The Federal Budget: Politics, Policy, Process* (2000).

Dennis C. Smith, a political scientist with a Ph.D. from Indiana University, has been on the faculty of the Robert F. Wagner Graduate School of Public Service at the New York University since 1973. He is the author of numerous articles and book chapters on policing. In recent years he has studied and written on the problems of measuring the success of reforms in public sector organizations, especially "problem solving community policing." His article on performance management in UNCIVPOL in a book on the United Nations will be published in Fall 2001. He also studies the non-emergency use of emergency ambulance services in New York City for the Commonwealth Fund. He is a member of the Board of the Institute of Public Administration and has been a consultant to numerous New York City agencies and nonprofit organizations. He is a senior consultant on performance management at SEEDCO in New York City. He now directs the Wagner School Office of International Programs.

Virginia L. Thomas, a former top aide to House Majority Leader Richard K. Armey, serves the Heritage Foundation as a senior fellow in government studies. In this position, Thomas coordinates the Foundation's efforts to monitor both government performance and congressional oversight activities. On Capitol Hill, Thomas helped implement the Government Performance and Results Act, which requires each agency of government to define its mission and set performance goals so Congress can better carry out its oversight responsibilities. Thomas joined Congressman Armey's staff in 1993 as senior policy coordinator for the House Republican Conference (1993-1995). Prior to that she was deputy assistant secretary of Labor (1989-1993) and a labor counsel for the U.S. Chamber of Commerce (1984-1988). Thomas also has served on the legislative staff of former Representative Hal Daub of Nebraska.

Frank J. Thompson is dean of the Nelson A. Rockefeller College of Public Affairs and Policy at the University at Albany, State University of New York. He has published extensively on issues of health policy, policy implementation, personnel policy, and administrative politics. His most recent book, *Medicaid and Devolution: A View From the States* (co-editor and contributor), was published by The Brookings Institution. Thompson is former president of the National Association of Schools of Public Affairs and Administration and has held offices in other professional associations. He has worked for the City of Oakland, California, and was a public administration fellow with the U.S. Public Health Service. He has served as a consultant to various government agencies and universities and as executive director of the National Commission on State and Local Public Service. Thompson is a fellow of the National Academy of Public Administration. He received his B.A. in political science from the University of Chicago and his M.A. and Ph.D. in that discipline from the University of California, Berkeley.

Katherine G. Willoughby is associate professor of public administration and urban studies in the Andrew Young School of Policy Studies at Georgia State University in Atlanta, Georgia. Her areas of expertise are public budgeting and financial management, and policy analysis and evaluation. While her work focuses predominantly on state government processes, she had conducted several studies about local government budgeting and management practices specific to the metropolitan Atlanta region. Willoughby has recently completed a book with Kurt Thurmaier of the University of Kansas in Lawrence, Kansas, about the relationship between budgeting and policy development as seen through the eyes of analysts employed in executive budget offices in 11 state governments in the South and Midwest.

Miriam Wilson is an instructor in Public Administration at Bowling Green State University. Her research interests include welfare reform and development of alternative delivery systems for governmental programs. Her public-sector experience includes managing the Ohio Office of Labor-Management Cooperation and working for the U.S. Senate on the staff of Senator John Glenn. Wilson has a masters degree in human resource management and is a doctoral candidate in public policy and management from Ohio State University

David J. Wright is director of Urban and Metropolitan Studies at the Nelson A. Rockefeller Institute of Government, State University of New York. Responsibility for managing the Institute's program of urban-related research, Wright recently directed national field network assessments of the Empowerment Zone/Enterprise Community Initiative for the U.S. Department of Housing and Urban Development, and of the nine-city Neighborhood Preservation Initiative for The Pew Charitable Trusts. Wright is co-principal investigator and director of a 15-city field network study of social capital in nonpoor predominantly-minority neighborhoods; is co-principal investigator and director of a six-city study on the effects of welfare reform on community development corporations; and serves as an advisor to the New York State Division of Housing and Community Renewal on affordable housing and downtown development policy. Wright's other research interests include neighborhood-based social service delivery, the use of Internet technology to extend and improve public services, workforce development policy, and the role of economic clustering and networking in inner-city development. Prior to joining the Institute, Wright served as deputy secretary to New York Governor Mario M. Cuomo for policy and program design, coordination and budgeting, particularly in the areas of workforce development, targeted economic growth, and technology. Wright first worked for the State of New York as senior examiner in the Office of Management and Productivity, conducting operational audits and program evaluation studies. Before that, he served as a policy analyst with the Setting Municipal Priorities Project/Columbia University's Eisenhower Center for the Conservation of Human Resources and the Trust of Public Land.

Index

Thomas, Pat, 365, 375
Thomas, Virginia L., 8, 534
Thompson, Frank J., 12, 526
Thompson, Fred, 116, 127, 132
Thompson, James D., 464
Tibbetts, G.L., 207
timeliness, 337
toll-free (800) number access,
  used by Social Security Admin-
  istration, 149-53
Tompkins, S. Sieg, 312, 325, 326
tourism, in New York City, 475
Transportation, U.S. Department
  of, 105
transportation vouchers, 188
Truman, Harry S., 5
Turcotte, John, 385

undergraduate education, 436-37
unemployment, 220
unions, 167
United Kingdom, 494
Urban Institute, 339, 524
urban programs, 119

validity (statistical), 501-2
vendor contracting, 197-98
Vera Institute of Justice, 468
Veterans Health Administration
  (VHA), 135
Vining, Aidan, 294
Virginia, 445
vocational education, 499
Voinovich, George, 133

wage subsidies, 188
waivers, 300-302
Walker, David, 117-19, 542
Ward, Benjamin, 467, 468
Washington (state), 295, 499
Washington, D.C., 189
Wasserman, Robert, 469
waste, in federal government,
  121-27

Ways and Means Committee
  (U.S. House of Representatives), 155-59
Weimer, David, 294
welfare reform, 12, 179-80, 526,
  545
  effects of performance goals
    on state behavior, 183-84
  food stamps and, 218, 220-22,
    225
  high performance bonus in,
    187-88
  "illegitimacy bonus" in,
    188-90
  implementation of perfor-
    mance management
    for, 202-3
  non-cash benefits under,
    210
  performance management
    tied to program functioning
    in, 200-201
  performance measures in,
    181-83
  political support for goals of,
    199-200
  state elaboration of perfor-
    mance management in,
    190-98
  unlinking Medicaid and food
    stamps from, 229-32
  work participation and
    caseload reduction in,
    184-86
White House Office of Management and Budget, 130
Wilde, P., 220
Williams, Charles, 365
Willoughby, Katherine G., 8, 9,
  312, 533, 543
Wilson, James Q., 72, 459, 465-66,
  468, 472
Wilson, Miriam, 12-13
Wisconsin, 192, 195, 203